Reflections on International Tourism

Management, Marketing and the Political Economy of Travel and Tourism

edited by

Mike Robinson
Nigel Evans
Philip Long
Richard Sharpley
John Swarbrooke

UNIVERSITY *of*
NORTHUMBRIA *at* NEWCASTLE   *Sheffield Hallam University*

2000

©The Centre for Travel & Tourism, Centre for Tourism and the Authors

ISBN 1 871916 60 7

First published 2000

Cover Design by Tim Murphy Creative Solutions

Published in Great Britain by
the Centre for Travel and Tourism in association with
Business Education Publishers Ltd.,
The Teleport,
Doxford International,
Sunderland   SR3 3XD

Tel: 0191 525 2400
Fax: 0191 520 1815

British Cataloguing-in-Publications Data
A catalogue record for this book is available from the British Library

Printed in Great Britain by Athenaeum Press, Gateshead

Preface

Tourism continues to reach out in to space and time. Implicit within the trite phrase of 'tourism is the world's largest industry', it *appears* that everyone is either a tourist or a potential tourist, everywhere is someone's destination and no human activity is immune from the fleeting glimpses of transient eyes. Appearances, of course, can be deceptive.

Ironically, change, movement, development and growth are the norms that characterise a phenomenon that many still see as an opportunity to slow down, relax and do little. The new millennium will undoubtedly see more tourists, more tourism, more travel, more impacts, more to market, more to manage. Core human traits of creativity and curiosity, desires to consume and commune, along with the need to survive, remain as the fundamental, and often conflicting, drivers for this thing we label tourism. Tourism is an important subject of academic inquiry *precisely* because it is an extension of our humanity and the cultures we inhabit, and because of the rapidity of change and growth that now typifies it.

This series of six volumes arose out of a major international conference held at Sheffield Hallam University, UK, in September 2000. Organised by the Centre for Travel and Tourism, University of Northumbria and the Centre for Tourism Sheffield Hallam University, **Tourism 2000: Time for Celebration?** was designed to reflect on, evaluate and anticipate the growth and development of tourism from its roots in pilgrimage and exploration, to its present and future role as a vast and complex social and cultural activity, a diverse international industry, and a focus for academic discourse. The conference attracted tremendous interest from academics, policy makers and practitioners from across the world and in itself was a touristic experience. These books contain 173 of nearly 200 papers presented at the conference.

The importance of this series lies in its diversity as well as its dimensions. We believe it to be important that authors from differing disciplines, perspectives, nationalities and cultures are able to reflect on the many facets of tourism. With diversity, however, comes problems of categorisation and hard editorial decisions. We trust that in the main we have managed to produce a reasoned and manageable breakdown of papers.

The production of one book can generate a plethora of problems. Not surprisingly the production of six volumes involving so many contributors and from such a diversity of locations has not been without anguish. Differing interpretations of the word 'deadline' is a common source of editorial angst! Technology too, though we are indebted to it, has frequently been the object of derision – the email delivery failure, the server that is down, the lost file, the scrambled text, and the ever popular 'pressing the wrong button.'

Fortunately there are those amongst us that appear to take problems in their stride and who sail on through the waves of worry. Thanks must go to Richard Shipway for his help in chasing the most elusive of authors. Thanks also to Jill Pomfret for her help in the editing process and to Amanda Miller for her assistance. Central to this bout of thanks are the staff at Business Education Publishers Ltd (BEP), who have been down this road with us many times now and continue to deliver a service second to none. Without the professionalism, commitment and good humour of Andrea Murphy, Moira Page and everyone who has worked on this series at BEP, you would not be reading this.

Finally our thanks go, as ever, to all the contributors to the series. Reflections on International Tourism provides a home for over 200 researchers, thinkers, critics and practitioners from nearly forty countries who have been through the processes of contemplation and reflection – those precious intellectual spaces between doing and being.

The important thing that all our authors now offer us through the work contained in these pages, is an invitation for you, the reader, to engage in your own process of reflection.

Mike Robinson
Sheffield, 2000

Introduction

Although the antecedents of 'mass' international tourism can be traced back to Thomas Cook in the 1850's, it can primarily be viewed as a creation of more recent times. Since the early 1950's its growth has been both phenomenal in its scale, and remarkably resilient to periodic economic and political adversity. Although the past trend is not necessarily an accurate predictor of the future, it is clear that in the case of international tourism its ascendancy will continue as we progress through the new millennium. Indeed, in product life cycle terms, tourism might be categorised as having passed through the 'introductory' phase into 'early growth', but since many more countries and new consumers are being drawn into the international tourism net, further growth is to be expected before 'maturity' is reached. Such growth will be uneven both spatially and over time, and will take place against the backdrop of dramatic changes in the business environment thereby creating managerial and marketing opportunities and dilemmas for private sector managers and public sector policy makers alike.

Tourism, and the international travel industry that has grown to support it, has been characterised by: the fragmentation of ownership and control; the diversity of products and destinations; and, largely uncoordinated development that has been divided between public and private sectors. Furthermore tourism as a service sector industry shares many of the defining features of many other services such as: the inseparability of production and consumption; and, the product's perishability, heterogeneity, intangibility and interdependence. Unlike other service sectors though, tourism stands apart in three important respects. Firstly tourism is highly visible in its impact and capable of making profound societal and cultural changes not only to host destinations but also to tourist exporting areas. Secondly, purchasers of tourism products, as the literature has frequently recorded, are purchasing a range of benefits the provision of which are rarely within the control of a single enterprise or government. Thirdly, the level of government involvement in the co-ordination, promotion and development of the industrial sector is rarely replicated in other service sectors, which in turn can be seen as recognition of the industry's economic importance and of its continued fragmentation.

Tourism is at the same time a local or community concern and a burgeoning global phenomenon, the magnitude of which is set to increase. In a world of change then, one constant is that tourism as a phenomenon and as an industry has and will continue to be characterised by sustained growth. This is where the simplicity ends, for tourism's products, markets and impacts are ever changing and becoming more complex. These changes include:

- mass tourism being replaced by mass customisation and ever more discerning tourists;

- increasing industrial polarity as companies make the strategic choice to either become large vertically, horizontally and in some cases diagonally integrated operators or smaller niche players targeting discrete market segments;

- emerging policy and regulatory frameworks such as the move towards deregulated market structures, the privatisation of state companies, and the removal of ownership restrictions, all of which serve to lower entry and exit barriers in the industry;

- competitive and resource pressures necessitating newer ways of working such as the increasing emphasis on collaborative strategy through the formation of strategic alliances, franchising and management contracts in the commercial sector and through the formation of innovative private-public partnerships to facilitate tourism development and regeneration opportunities;

- the threat to the role of intermediaries as new technology empowers consumers to deal directly with principals;

- the need for attractions, destinations, accommodation providers and others in the industry to differentiate and customise their product offerings whilst at the same time meeting international norms for the quality of provision;

- the rise of new destinations and tourism products categories such as cruising and all inclusive resorts; and,

- the rise of international tourism brands in an industry where brand recognition and customer retention has hitherto been weak.

Managers, academics and policy makers are striving to understand both the changes taking place and the managerial responses that are appropriate to the rapidly changing circumstances. The expansion of the academic tourism literature, tourism journals (at least three respected international journals specialise in tourism marketing for instance) and the increasing number of international conferences and industry forums, bear witness to the shift in emphasis towards a more serious consideration of the managerial and policy issues raised by the subject. Whatever the scale or orientation of involvement, it is increasingly being realised that the managerial and marketing lessons drawn from addressing operational and strategic issues are in many cases transferable from one enterprise to another or between geographically distinct locations which may be on either side of the planet. Best-practice, benchmarking, world-class performance, global awareness and sustainable management techniques are amongst the terms that have entered the tourism manger and policy maker's vocabulary providing testimony to the power of shared learning.

The chapters in this book reflect both the breadth and the distinctive nuances of the subject area discussed previously. The papers can be grouped into five major themes, which are not mutually exclusive, with a number of sub-themes and illustrative case studies (drawn from diverse geographical sources) being incorporated within each.

The first, and perhaps most widely discussed theme, is that of managing destinations and products in such a way so as to ensure sustainable economic development or sustainable revenue flows. This is essentially an optimisation as opposed to maximisation debate, in that the appropriate balance must be struck in terms of ensuring financial solvency whilst managing socio-cultural and environmental impacts.

A second theme relates to marketing issues raised in the management of tourism, and in particular papers explore the promotional and branding strategies that are being developed and the images of destinations and products that are being presented. In an industry where image is vital in ensuring commercial success branding and promotion are clearly issues of prime importance.

Thirdly, the changing political and regulatory contexts within which tourism takes place are dealt with by a number of papers. The need for, and the nature of, government and quasi-government involvement in tourism is questioned by a number of papers. Important sub-themes such as the implications of the Euro and the emerging aviation regulatory environment are dealt with elsewhere in the book.

A fourth theme illustrated by this selection of papers relates to the ways in which various sub-sectors of the industry are being managed in response to changing external environmental competitive pressures and examination of the changing industrial structures that are emerging. Thus, changes in the way that products are distributed and sold are discussed by several papers, whilst structural issues such as partnerships and franchising are also addressed.

Finally, the rapid expansion of the phenomenon of tourism and of the industry that supports it has been mirrored in the educational world. The theme manifests itself in this book through an investigation, in several papers, of the development of academic programmes and research oriented towards the field. These educational influences are an important contributory factor in determining the managerial and policy decision-making framework. Managers in the industry now frequently study, or have studied, specialist tourism courses or modules, and developments in doctoral research and research carried out through the use of newer technologies such as the internet help to underpin informed and successful decision making in the industry.

Table of Contents

Wired to go – marketing a tiger in the year of the dragon

L Bauer and E Reid

Nanyang Technological University, Singapore

Introduction

This initial paper shows how Singapore, as a tourism destination, is marketing itself on the Internet. It analyses the Internet marketing approaches used by the tourism organisations and how they are exploiting this revolutionary new tool.

Tourism, the internet and global trends

Internet marketing

Web marketing is "the combination of marketing and modern technology at its peak" (Rohner, 1998) and a tool for conveying a great deal of information, without incurring huge costs. (Bishop, 1998). Offers can be made directly to the consumers and marketing messages can be "instantaneous, interactive and personal" (Murphy, Forrest and Wotring, 1996).

Elston (1997) has developed a "traffic wheel", which graphically displays the sources of 'web traffic' (such as links from other websites and Directories) and analyses how such traffic might be improved. Changes in marketing efforts could then be implemented to obtain better results. Elston's "traffic wheel", illustrated in Figure 1, has been used in this paper as a basis for analysis.

Internet use in the tourism industry

The web's "bi-directional" and interactive nature has enabled electronic visiting and has complemented traditional media such as newspapers, television and radio by introducing animation and virtual tours to potential tourists (Cano and Prentice, 1998).

Online reservation systems like SABRE and ABACUS enable tourists to transact over the Internet conveniently. Lufthansa's "paperless travel" scheme stores all Internet reservations on smart cards (Schertler and Berger-Koch, 1998). Tourism organisations are making use of such advances in IT to their advantage

In a major international study, sponsored by Arthur Anderson and produced by New York University, entitled *Results from Hospitality 2000: The Technology*, findings indicated a trend towards "significant investment in technology applications to be used by consumers". It also revealed that "some 90% of the companies surveyed have a website, and the remaining 10% without a website plan to have one within the next two years" (WebTravelNews, 1999).

There is also an increasing trend for airlines to set up their own websites. Ten of Europe's largest airlines are in negotiations to set up a "jointly-owned Internet travel agency". This may reduce the need for "conventional travel agents", who are being replaced by " new Internet agents" (Straits Times, 20 February 2000).

Several studies have examined the use of web marketing in the tourism industry and the degree of interactivity of the websites. Murphy, Forrest and Wotring (1996) analysed the level of interactiveness of restaurant websites according to ten features, such as 'on-line promotions' or e-mail newsletters, and their findings revealed that the e-mail feature was available in more than two-thirds of websites reviewed.

**Figure 1   Elston's Web Traffic Wheel (methods of generating traffic to a web site)
Source: www.trafficdigest.com**

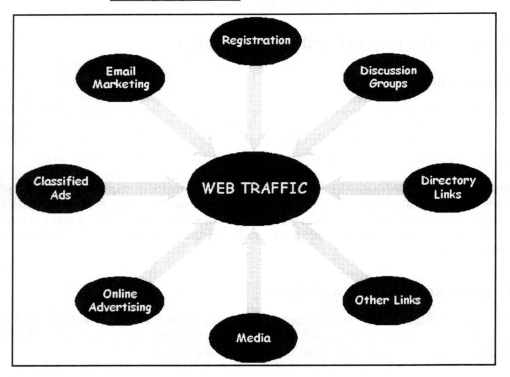

Cano and Prentice's (1998) analysis involved tourism websites in Scotland. They examined the "regional diversity of sites and the extent of the development of a communication concept", which involves facilitating and rewarding interaction between the tourism organisations and the consumer. The findings revealed that the websites were mostly in English and did not cater greatly to the "informational needs of international tourists". The "last updated date" and "free text search" features were also absent from many of the websites.

The important function of website updating involves the correction of hotlinks which have moved, changed or expired, as well as the editing of outdated or incorrect text, graphics, audio, or video. Cano and Prentice (1998) observed: "In the absence of updates, there is little reason for a viewer to return to a site. Thus, the absence of a last updated date, might cast doubt on the accuracy of the information at the site."

Marketing Singapore and the internet

The Singapore Tourism Board (STB) has been an industry leader in using the Internet as a marketing tool. Unpublished research conducted at Nanyang Business School (Chin et al.1996) indicates that in 1996, the Board had already launched the website 'Expressions of New Asia Singapore, in conjunction with *Newsweek* magazine. One of its highlights was the 'Merlion Mysteries' – an innovative, interactive guide, which took surfers on a virtual game through the Lion City.

Since then, the STB has extended its web presence so that by August 1999, it had at least nine tourism websites in operation. This included the award winning 'New Asia – Singapore', which is charged with promoting the nation's brand by expressing the essence of Singapore today: "A youthful city state, where tradition and modernity, East and West, meet in comfortable companionship" (S.T.B. 1998). In line with the STB's wider remit, to develop Singapore into a regional business centre and tourism hub, these websites cater to different market segments, and vary in terms of content and style.

Thus, websites have been created for important overseas markets for example, for the U.S., Canadian, Japanese and Chinese-speaking traveller (www.singapore-usa.com/; www.singapore-ca.com/; int-acc.pr.jp/singapore/; www.singapore.com.tw/ There is a corporate site for information on tourism business (www.stb.com.sg/) and a distinctive one for the travel trade (Singapore Travel Exchange: www.ste.com.sg) For those who seek information on Singapore as a destination, there is New Asia – Singapore (www.newasia-singapore.com/) or the Singapore On-line guide (www.travel.com.sg).

Singapore's tourism 'cyber' presence is considerably enhanced by additional websites which cater to other important markets and which offer further links to the STB. For example, the website Singapore Inc. (www.singapore-inc.com) which focuses on foreign investors and business, or Singapore One (www.s-one.gov.sg/) which is linked to thousands of other Singapore websites many of them tourism/leisure/recreation related. These include Singapore Sightsee (www.sg/sightsee.html), the Sentosa Development Corporation (www.sentosa.com.sg) and the Singapore Science Centre (www.sci-ctr.edu.sg). Cleverly inter-linked, with one website leading on to another, the system ensures that at whatever point of entry, the STB's websites are easily reached.

Successful website are characterised by their professional design, fast display of graphics and text, ease of navigation, frequent updates or current changes and, where appropriate, an element of enjoyment. The STB's websites score highly by these standards. They also convey a consistent destination image by focusing on common themes, such as Singapore's food and spices, religious and cultural diversity and artistic vibrancy. However, a further measure of success is to assess the ways in which Singapore uses the Internet for marketing its destination. The purpose of our pilot study was to find this out.

Methodology

An analysis was conducted of Internet marketing approaches used by tourism organisations in Singapore. Findings will be reported in two stages.

This paper reports on Phase I. The Singapore-based tourism websites were compiled from 1998-1999 bibliographies (reference lists) generated by students studying tourism at the Business School, Nanyang Technological University (NTU), Singapore. A total of 18 local websites were identified as being most frequently accessed for tourism projects. This included eight from the attractions sector, three from the transportation sector, seven from the Singapore Tourism Board and one from the hotel sector. Table 1 provides a list of the websites, the web addresses (URLs), and organisation affiliation. (For Table 1, see next page.)

The research applies the website models, created by Buchanan and Lukaszewski (1998) and Elston (www.trafficdigest.com) to the Singapore context. Buchanan and Lukaszewski's model presents approaches to online marketing from a "problem-driven" and a "promotion-driven" perspective. The "problem-driven" approach is associated with users seeking information to resolve a specific problem. It includes free registration with search engines and reciprocal "hyperlinks" from trade associations or business partners. The "promotion-driven" perspective focuses on fee-based online advertising, which includes paid links for popular websites, (such as 'Yahoo' and 'CNN'), banner advertising and traditional media publicity which makes use of website addresses.

Elston's model of web marketing (see Figure 1) identifies eight major methods to increase Internet traffic. This can be achieved through links with other websites, online advertising, directory links (such as links from search engines) and the inclusion of press releases.

Using a combination of both models, the 18 Singapore tourism websites were analysed in terms of their marketing approaches. This was limited to Internet use only and did not address the wider issue of web marketing integration as part of an overall marketing strategy. This is to be further explored in Phase II.

Table 1 Singapore Tourism Organisations

Accommodation	Website Address	Sponsoring Organisation	Type
Raffles Hotel	www.raffles.com	Raffles International	Commercial
Attractions			
Association of Singapore Attractions	www.asianconnect.com	Association of Singapore Attractions	Commercial
CHIJMES	www.chijmes.com.sg	CHIJMES Investment Pte Ltd	Commercial
National Parks	www.nparks.gov.sg	National Parks Board	Government
Sentosa	www.sentosa.com.sg	Sentosa Development Corporation	Commercial
Singapore Discovery Centre	www.sdc.com.sg	Ministry of Defence	Government
Singapore Museum	www.museum.org.sg	National Heritage Board	Government
Singapore Zoological Gardens	www.zoo.com.sg	Singapore Zoological Gardens	Commercial
Underwaterworld	www.underwaterworld.com.sg	Haw Par Group	Commercial
NTO			
Guide for Canadian Travellers	www.singapore-ca.com	Singapore Tourism Board	Government
Guide for U.S. Travellers	www.singapore-usa.com	Singapore Tourism Board	Government
Millennia Mania	www.millennia-mania.com	Singapore Tourism Board	Government
NewAsia-Singapore	www.newasia-singapore.com	Singapore Tourism Board	Government
Singapore Tourism Cybrary	www.cybrary.com.sg	Singapore Tourism Board	Government
Singapore Tourist Board	www.stb.com.sg	Singapore Tourism Board	Government
Transportation			
Silkair	www.silkair.com.sg	Singapore Airlines	Commercial
Singapore Airlines	www.singaporeair.com	Singapore Airlines	Commercial
Star Cruises	www.starcruises.com	Star Cruises	Commercial

The search procedures for Phase I are outlined in Table 2. Each search procedure is classified according to whether it is providing a local or international perspective on that tourism organisation. For example, a press release is normally generated internally, through public relations representatives. This could be said to provide a local perspective. On the other hand, discussion groups provide comments from individual external to the organisation and therefore an international perspective. Dejanews (www.deja.com, a search engine for news group messages) and links from other websites, are excellent mechanisms for identifying how foreign tourists use Singapore tourism websites.

Table 2   Search Approaches for Web Marketing Data

Web Marketing	Procedure for Searching	Perspective
Directory links such as search engines	Searched name of each web site in the most popular search engine Yahoo (Media Metrix, 1999).	Intl. & Local
Links from other sites (reverse links)	Used reserve linkage option in search engine to identify what organisations linked to the 18 web sites (Reid, 1997; 1999).	Intl. & Local
Press release	Searched for press release at 18 web sites.	Local
	Searched meta-search engine (www.metacrawler.com) for press releases mention any of 18 web sites.	
	Searched for press release at PR Newswire press release database (www.prnewswire.com) (Smith & Catalano; O'Keefe)	
Online advertising	Searched for image files via search engines (image files that mention any of 18 web sites)	Local
Email marketing	Searched for email marketing at 18 web sites	Local
Registration	Searched for registration information at 18 web sites.	Local
Discussion Groups	Searched for discussion groups at 18 web sites.	Local
(DejaNews search - can be classified as Word of Mouth)	Searched DejaNews (www.deja.com) to see if web sites or organisations are mentioned in online newsgroup discussions (Notess, 1998).	Intl & local
Online Transactions	Searched for online transactions at 18 web sites (Dahl & Lesnick, 1999).	Local

Findings

Use of web marketing approaches

An analysis of the 18 Singapore tourism websites indicates that most are using the web marketing approaches described by Elston, Buchanan and Lukaszewski. The results of the analysis are summarised in Table 3.

Table 3   Summary Results

Web Marketing	Summary
Directory links such as search engines	14 mentioned in Yahoo (78%)
Links from other sites (reverse links)	15 had links from other web sites (83%)
Media (Press release)	3 press releases at their web sites (17%)
Online advertising	1 (5.5%)
Email marketing	1 (5.5%)
Registration, Feedback Mechanism	16 (89%)
Discussion Groups (DejaNews search - can be classified as a mechanism for tracing "Word of Mouth")	0 had their own online discussion forum; 16 (89%) were mentioned in other online discussion forums such as rec.travel.asia, rec.travel.cruises, soc.culture.asean.
Online Transactions	4 ((22%)

Links from other websites (reverse links)

Reverse links from other websites provide a free mechanism for increasing web traffic. However, according to Elston, it may be difficult to get other sites to link to your own, unless the relationship is reciprocal. Jackson (1997) describes the process of creating an external hypertext link to someone's website as a strategic decision.

A search engine was used to identify which websites were linked to the 18 in Singapore (reverse link). This provided an effective method of gathering data on their global importance, perception and usage. In addition, it provided raw data for calculating the return on investment (ROI) and identifying potential customers in the e-commerce market

The Singapore websites which generated the greatest number of reverse links were those produced by Singapore Airlines, Singapore's national carrier (2,290), the Singapore Tourism Board's 'New Asia-Singapore' website (840), and the National Museum of Singapore (420) representing three component museums: (the Singapore History Museum, the Singapore Art Museum and the Asian Civilisations Museum).

Figure 2 displays summary of reverse links for the websites. Apart from indicating the total number of reverse links, it also identifies how many links come from North America and Southeast Asia. For example, Time.com-Asia (www.pathfinder.com/time/asia/travel_watch/981221.html) is linked to the 'New Asia-Singapore' website.

Figure 2   Reverse Linkage Data for Singapore Tourism Organisations

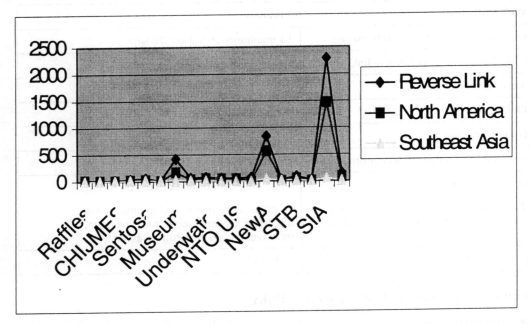

Time.com-Asia, a North-American website, includes an article on 'New Asia-Singapore' that praises its innovative and futuristic features. Given that there are nine other websites that have external links (reverse links) to the Time.com- Asia website, this means Time.com-Asia's recommendation of the 'New Asia- Singapore' website is being linked to by nine other organisations.

This information could be used to identify new tourism markets and to ask fundamental questions. These could include: What is the return on investment (ROI) associated with creating and maintaining the 'New Asia- Singapore' website? Can this be measured? Is it reaching specific North American audiences? If so, how are they using the website's resources? Does this differ from other market segments? Are they planning business or leisure trips to the Asia-Pacific region, (e.g. the Olympic Games in 2000) and if so, would they be interested in e-commerce transactions, such as online scheduling and ticketing for Singapore attractions, en route to Australia?

Use of Press Releases

Results indicate that the tourism organisations were under-utilising this important media link. Only three of them displayed press releases on their websites and those that did were text only versions, and excluded photographs and images as part of the content – the very items that command attention. With the exception of websites offering their own search engines, the press releases were not clearly labelled on the homepage and were difficult to locate. Moreover, the press releases failed to include links to key business partners and other features such as 'Frequently Asked Questions' (FAQs).

Given the vital role such media items have in shaping public perceptions and creating a 'cyber presence', these findings raises issues, which urgently need to be addressed.

One current marketing practice is to submit press releases to a press release database service such as PR newswire (www.prnewswire.com). PR Newswire redistributes the press releases to dozens of online databases, from which it is recopied and retransmitted by others (Smith and Catalano , 1998). The result of a search of the PR Newswire database showed that none of the Singapore tourism organisations had submitted their press releases in this way. In fact, only one of the 18 tourism organisations was mentioned in the PR Newswire database. A press release dated 9th August 1999, describing Singapore Airlines and Pratt-Whitney's business venture was identified. Pratt-Whitney is a member of the PR Newswire service. The service maintains an extensive archive on 2,000 member companies and provides press releases and multi-media resources on member activities.

Other Marketing Functions

Although press releases appeared to be under-utilised, many of the tourism websites provided 'Question and Answer' features (Q & A's), white papers and multi-media resources such as interactive tour guides.

A 'text only' version of the website was often not available. This version is without images and speeds up the display of information on a user's monitor. It is advantageous in situations where Internet connections are slow or congested. Any delay in the downloading of information may deter further exploration of a website and thus a potential marketing opportunity is lost. Any future website development should take account of the users' technological environment and their limitations on the Internet.

Conclusion and recommendations

Although Singapore has emphasised use of the Internet and the 'super highway' in its 'Tourism 21' blueprint, the tourism organisations surveyed did not appear, as yet, to have exploited its diverse services and capabilities. As such, the Internet could become a dynamic global marketing arena for Southeast Asian tourism, if harnessed well.

Many-to-many service

In order for this to be accomplished, more "many-to-many" Internet communication services (many people communicating to many people) could be introduced. Such services include online discussion forums (Usenet), listservs (mailing lists) and Internet Relay Chat services (chat rooms). Table 3 indicates that none of the tourism organisations provided online discussion forums on their websites. But 89% of them were mentioned in newsgroups (Usenet) discussion forums such as rec.travel.asia and soc.culture.asean.

Many-to-many communication services assist in establishing a community of people supporting people. One example could include a Southeast Asian travel discussion forum, which could provide the "global tourist perspective" on Singapore as a destination. For example, this could provide important insights as to which tourism attractions are perceived favourably, as a "must see" experience. A "chat room" service could also identify challenges and issues to which Singapore speedily needs to respond. Another option is to analyse Singapore tourism discussions using Dejanews (www.deja.com.). In this study, the analysis of Dejanews messages identified what tourists consider as "must see" and Singapore tourism issues that should be addressed.

It is vital for tourism organisations to be aware of this excellent, unsolicited source of feedback in order to identify and meet customer expectations. In addition, communication services such as online discussion forums also support the transition of tourism websites into web portals for e-commence. A portal is a web-based supermarket service that provides a set of commonly used sites and services that are linked from a single page (O'Leary, 1999).

Web rings

A web ring is a strategic alliance with other web site owners, in which they agree to link with one another in a ring (Jackson, 1997). The web ring, displayed in bold colours, is considered an online empire building technique and is being used extensively for Year 2000 websites. Such an idea could be applied to Southeast Asia. A reciprocal relationship could be established with other tourism organisations within the region. Thus 'New Asia –Singapore' could be linked to its regional partners (and they to it) supported by smooth navigation from one site to another.

We live in dynamic times and the process of change will continue. Given the speed of technological innovation, it is important for Singapore to maximise opportunities created and to establish an even stronger presence on the net. The task has just begun.

References

Buchanan, R. W. and Lukaszewski, (1998), *Measuring the Impact of you Web Site*, John Wiley & Sons.

Bishop, B. (1998), *Strategic Marketing for the Digital Age,* American Marketing Association: NTC Business Books, pp. 124-132.

Cano, V. and Prentice, R. (1998), Opportunities for endearment to place through electronic visiting: WWW homepages and the tourism promotion of Scotland, *Tourism Management.* 19 (1): 67-73.

Chin, P. (1996), MBA Dissertation, *Tourism Marketspace on the Internet*, Nanyang Technological University, School of Accountancy and Business, Singapore.

Dahl, A. and Lesnick L. (1998), *Internet Commerce*. New Riders.

Elston, B. (1997), *Diversifying your Web traffic: Pros and Cons of the Major Traffic Sources*, http://www.trafficdigest.com/art-diversity.htm,(1997).

Infocomm Development Authority of Singapore (1999) *E-commerce Development*, http://www.ida.gov.sg/.

Jackson M. H. (1997), Assessing the Structure of Communication on the World Wide Web. *JCMC* 3, (1). http://www.ascusc.org/jcmc/vol3/issue1/jackson.html.

MediaMetrix Inc. (1999), Media Metrix Top 25 Sites. (Pioneer and leader in field of Internet and digital media measurement services) http://www.relevantknowledge.com.

Murphy, J., Forrest, E., Wotring C. E. (1998), Restaurant Marketing on the Worldwide Web, *Cornell Hotel and Restaurant Administration Quarterly*. (2): 61-71.

New York University for Hospitality, Tourism and Travel Administration, (1999), *Results from Hospitality 2000*. http://www.webtravelnews.com/225.htm.

Notess, G.R. (1998), On the Net: DejaNews and Other Usenet Search Tools *Online*, (6), http://www.onlineinc.com/onlinemag/OL1998/net7.html.

O'Keele, S. (1997), *Publicity on the Internet*. John Wiley & Sons.

O'Leary, M. Portal Wars, (1999), *Online* (1/2) pp. 77-79.
http://www.onlineinc.com/onlinemag
http://www.onlineinc.com/onlinemag/OL1998/net7.html

Reid, E. (1997), Impact of MSC, *New Straits Times*, 12th November.

Reid, E. (1999), *WHY 2K? A Chronological Study of the Millennium Bug: Why, When and How Did Y2K Become a Critical Issue for Businesses?* Universal Publishers. http://www.upublish.com/books/reid.htm.

Rohner, K. (1998), *Marketing in the Cyber Age: The Why, the What and the How*, John Wiley and Sons, pp. 1-14, pp. 111-138.

Schertler, W., Berger-Kock, C. (1999), Tourism as an Information Business: The Strategic Consequences of E-Commerce for Business Travel, *Information & Communication Technologies in Tourism*.

Singapore Tourism Board (1996), *Tourism 21: Vision of a Tourism Capital*, Singapore Government.

Smith, B. and Catalano, F. (1998), *Marketing Online for Dummies*, IDG Books.

Straits Times, (2000), Ten European Airlines may share website, 20th February.

WebTravel News.com. (1999), *Study finds hospitality companies plan major technology spending*, http://www.webtravelnews.com/225.htm, (June).

Is there a role for visiting friends and relatives in Ghana's tourism development strategy?

Sue Bleasdale and Patience Kwarko

Middlesex University, UK

Introduction

Like several other African countries Ghana is seeking to expand and develop international tourism as a major component in its development strategy. The recent global trend towards long haul tourism and specialized niche tourism (especially culturally and environmentally based tourism) has created an environment within which many new destinations are hoping to grow (Theobald, 1994).

The main question asked in this paper is whether there is significant potential in the Visiting Friends and Relatives (VFR) market? Could VFR tourism contribute positively towards the development of Ghana as an international tourism destination and if the answer is 'YES' should there be specific policies directed at the Ghanaian diaspora to encourage the growth of this market? What steps can be taken to increase the spend of these visitors and how can they be involved more fully in the growth of Ghana's tourism attractions and infrastructure? Before these issues can be addressed it is first necessary to gain some understanding of the nature of VFR tourism and secondly to gain some perspective on the current tourism sector in Ghana.

Visiting friends and relatives tourism and tourism development

Any study of this form of travel is problematic. VFR travellers are difficult to isolate in statistical sources. McKercher refers to VFR travel as 'an invisible tourism activity'. (McKercher, 1996, page 510). There is considerable agreement in the literature that VFR travel is under-researched and under-reported. In addition several writers note that VFR travel is often ignored by National Tourist Boards despite their large numbers whilst others note that VFR travel is difficult to handle within conventional tourism marketing strategies (see Seaton, 1994, Beioley, 1997, Jackson and Richard, 1990, McKercher, 1996, Morrison, 1995). Although they fit the broad definition of a tourist VFR travellers are substantially different in motivation and behaviour from mass tourists and package holiday makers.

Historically visiting friends and relatives pre-dates the era of mass tourism. The motivation for VFR tourism can be broadly defined as 'personal' as opposed to cultural or physical, though it has to be recognised that travel motivations are complex and people may travel for several motives. In general VFR tourists differ from mainstream tourists in that they do not use accommodation that has been specifically built to serve tourists and may not behave like mainstream tourists in other ways being less likely to visit tourist attractions. However VFR tourists are not homogenous. Their motivations vary and this impacts upon their behaviour. Seaton argues that for this reason visiting friends should be distinguished from visiting relatives as those visiting friends are likely to behave more like mainstream tourists (Seaton, 1994). For some the primary motivation for travel is to visit friends and relatives, for others friends and relatives are just a source of cheap or free accommodation. But a widely held perception is that they are not really tourists and market analysts have tended to ignore them as they are believed to spend less and to be difficult to influence. However there is an increasing recognition that they do contribute significantly to the number of international travellers.

For countries which have been, or are characterized by out-migration the VFR market might be expected to have an enhanced significance. Attention to the characteristics and needs of VFR tourists might have benefits for these countries. Migrants and their descendants are more likely to travel to the home country to see family, to reconfirm their cultural roots or to introduce their children to their cultural origins. Migrants, unlike other potential tourists, might also be expected to have a clear and possibly more positive image of the country. In addition it is possible that they will wish to travel regardless of the quality of tourist facilities and attractions. Are migrants and their families to some extent a captive and ready made market for such countries? It could be argued that, in this context, VFR tourists should have a special place in the marketing strategy of a country seeking to develop a larger tourism sector but which has limited capital resources and a limited tourism infrastructure. There is a substantial literature which reinforces these points, although mostly in the context of regions other than Africa (see King and Gamage, 1994; Paci, 1994; Seaton and Palmer, 1996)

Some market advantages are perceived to characterize VFR tourists. They are less likely to show a highly seasonal pattern of travel, more likely to make long stays and more certain to make repeat visits. Because of the strength of personal motivation among VFR tourists they are also believed to be less sensitive to price fluctuations. In addition they are less responsive to the availability of tourist attractions at the destination. For a developing destination therefore the VFR traveller can generate a sizable, stable and recurring demand (McKercher, 1996). In addition the distributional potential of the VFR traveller may be greater than for other tourists for while they may spend less they are more likely to spend directly within the local economy with a lower potential for tourism leakage. Since a high level of tourism leakage is a recognized problem for many developing country destinations a focus on VFR tourists may have very positive benefits.

Market disadvantages of the VFR traveller are believed to be low spend and low usage of tourist facilities. In addition some argue that they are a 'limited life' market as emotional associations with friends and family declining over time will lead to a reduction in the travel motivation. However there is evidence to counter this from many parts of the world as the upsurge in the number of Black African Americans travelling to West Africa illustrates.

But perhaps the most significant factor is the size of the VFR market. Literature based on research from many parts of the world shows the VFR market to be very substantial. Figures of between 30 and 50 % are widely reported (see Kwarko, 1998; Paci, 1994)

Ghana's tourism sector and tourism development

Ghana has a number of significant assets which could provide a basis for the growth of tourism (the Cape Coast with its beaches and slave castles, the rainforest and wildlife reserves, the Ashanti kingdom to name but three). In addition Ghana has an added advantage for travellers from Europe in that the flight time is relatively short (about six hours). However it cannot compete with East Africa or South Africa for wildlife tourism and rugged mountain scenery and the Gambia has a well established reputation for beach tourism. Unlike these countries and regions Ghana does not have an established or well defined image in the tourism industry. In this respect it is in a similar position to several other West African countries. UNESCO has recognized some of the castles as World Heritage features and the treetop (canopy) walkway in Kakum National Park was a winner in the 1999 British Airways Tourism for Tomorrow awards bringing Ghana some much needed positive publicity (Haines, 1999). This will help to establish Ghana as a destination for nature loving tourists.

But in addition to the lack of a clear image with identifiable and well known international attractions several other significant factors also weigh against the rapid development of international tourism in Ghana such as the health hazards of a humid tropical environment (not least the risk of malaria), a lack of capital for investment (both domestic and foreign capital), and a dearth of tourism and general service infrastructure which can meet the standards of international tourism (for a fuller consideration of the factors hindering tourism development in Ghana (see Adu-Febiri, 1994; Teye, 1988).

The government plans to devote some $800 million dollars (75% from overseas) to put the infrastructure in place and increase incoming tourists to one million by 2010. (M Knipe in the Times, April 18 2000, see also Gartner et al, 1995). Clearly sound marketing and investment policies will be crucial if Ghana is to achieve these targets. The current policy framework is provided by the National Tourism Development plan 1996-2010 (NTDP)which is funded by the Government of Ghana and the United Nations Development Fund (UNDP), executed by the World Tourism Organization and implemented by the Ministry of Tourism (Ministry of Tourism, 1996).

The Ministry of Tourism was set up in 1993 to push forward the development of the tourism sector and to co-ordinate, plan and regulate. In addition to providing incentives for investors the government is also addressing those issues of access that are perceived to be problematic such as flight costs, flight availability and visa controls. The Ghana Tourist Board is responsible for marketing and much of the implementation of National policy.

The main policy goals and objectives set out in the NTDP can be summarized as follows:

- Tourism will become a major economic sector catering for the domestic, regional and international market. Tourism planning will ensure a wide distribution of benefits to the Ghanaian people and these benefits will be cultural and educational as well as economic;

- Tourism development will be carefully planned and regulated to ensure integration with the development of other sectors and that tourism in Ghana learns from the mistakes of other destinations. Development will be based on a co-operative blend of public and private initiatives;

- Tourism development will incorporate the principles of sustainable tourism and emphasize community based projects; and,

- Tourism development will focus on projects which will enhance and conserve Ghana's cultural and environmental resources while delivering facilities of an internationally acceptable standard to high spend tourists.

Tourism trends in Ghana in the 1990s

Against the background of this national policy framework what are the current trends in Ghana's tourism sector? The number of incoming tourists has risen steadily throughout the 1990s from 145,780 in 1990 to 256,680 in 1993 and 304,860 in 1996 (the latest year for which confirmed figures exist; source Ministry of Tourism, 1999). Over the same time period the number of hotels rose from 350 to 703 and the number of bedspaces from 8576 to 13791 whilst receipts rose from US$80.83 million to US$248.80. Receipts and tourist expenditure seem to be rising faster than tourist numbers possibly indicating a degree of success in attracting higher spend tourists. By 1995 Government figures showed the tourism industry employed 17000 people directly and 45300 people indirectly. The figures available for the 1990s indicate that in broad terms tourism development in Ghana is achieving the planned targets (all figures are from the Ministry of Tourism, 1999). By 1999 tourism was Ghana's third largest foreign exchange earner (M Knipe in 'the Times', April 18 2000)

Analysis of the origins of those travelling to Ghana can show if there are any significant market patterns. Official figures show that of those arriving in Ghana in 1996 79.7% came from 13 generating countries. 21.5 % were from other West African countries (Nigeria, the Ivory Coast and Togo), 6.6 % from the USA and 8.66 % from the UK. 27.2% were classified as overseas Ghanaians. Of the remainder 9.5% came from Europe and Scandinavia. The figures for other years throughout the 1990s do not show any variation from this pattern. These figures show clearly the importance of returning Ghanaians to the tourism market. 27.2% is probably a substantial underestimate. In 1988 Teye noted that over half of those arriving in Ghana were Ghanaians (Teye, 1988). Many of those travelling with British or USA passports will be people of Ghanaian origin (one only has to queue for a visa to Ghana at the High Commission in London to appreciate this). The same is possibly true of those travelling from Nigeria, Germany and Scandinavia. Certainly countries which have significant Ghanaian communities dominate the current market for visits to Ghana.

VFR tourism to Ghana

It has already been established that VFR tourism is making a large contribution to the total volume of tourism arrivals to Ghana. The Ministry of Tourism has recognized the importance of this market both from the West African region and from the USA. The National Tourism Development plan assumes that VFR arrivals will continue to increase and gives a figure of 109,000 for 1995 rising to 226,000 in 2010. However the plan also assumes that the relative significance of VFR tourism will decline over this period from 38% of total arrivals to 21.2%. The main growth area in the plan is holiday tourism. Nevertheless the Plan does incorporate VFR tourists into other areas of the plan. For example in seeking to increase the economic returns from tourism one stated need is to encourage VFR tourists to undertake more travel within Ghana, to make more visits and to make more use of commercial tourist facilities though the mechanism for achieving this is not defined. Marketing plans also incorporate VFR tourism but the main thrust of the NTDP is to develop Ghana as a new destination for international tourism centring on Ghana as a location for heritage, cultural and environmental tourism (Ministry of Tourism, 1996).

The material in the remainder of this section is based primarily on a survey undertaken among members of the Ghanaian community living in the London region of the UK in 1998. 169 Ghanaians answered questions about their travel behaviour in Ghana. A follow-up survey to pursue some of the issues arising and to clarify some points further and based on in-depth interviewing is planned for summer 2000.

Most of the respondents had been born in Ghana (although 34% of these had become British citizens) and 62% (103) had lived in the UK for more than ten years. The majority (70%) had professional or management positions and most of the remainder were in skilled occupations. 61% had post-school qualifications. These sample characteristics are important in influencing the propensity and the ability to travel. 62.7% of respondents had parents living in Ghana whilst all had some relatives in Ghana. 65% had children living in the UK with less than 6% having children living in Ghana. 96% had visited Ghana within the last three years with 66% having visited more than once in the last five years. 9% had visited every year for the last five years. These figures reflect a very lively pattern of VFR travel. Frequency of visits does fall off with age but one explanation for this could be that many Ghanaians return to live in Ghana when they retire and for those that do not return many will no longer have large families living in Ghana. Indeed for those staying in the UK after retirement it is likely that most of their family will be in the UK - reducing the incentive to travel to Ghana as well as the reduced ability to travel consequent on declining health and income.

VFR tourism is sometimes believed to have the potential to offset the highly seasonal pattern of holiday making tourism. The survey showed that whilst this was true to an extent there were still seasonal peaks coinciding with the main School holiday periods of Easter, July-August and Christmas with a low period from September to November. This probably reflects the fact that most of those travelling were between 26 and 50 and therefore likely to have school age children. This age group is also more likely to be constrained in their travel behaviour by work commitments. VFR travel is also considered to be important for its impact on the demand for flights and thus its potential to affect the economic viability of airlines. 66% of those surveyed used Ghana airways helping to support this airline and to maintain this direct route. The availability of a choice of direct flights can also be important in underpinning and encouraging business travel.

When asked to specify the main reason for their travel the most frequently quoted reasons were visiting friends and relatives (26%) and attending funerals (19%). Only 15% gave holiday as the main reason. In total 43% included VFR as one of the reasons for their journey combining VFR activities with attending funerals, weddings and pursuing business activities. The multi-purpose nature of much travel indicates the potential to develop visits into a broader based activity.

An expected characteristic of VFR travel is a stay of long duration and this survey seems to bear this out. 26% of respondents stayed for 6 weeks and 39% for four weeks. Only 13% stayed for two weeks or less. Funerals seemed to be a major reason for the longer stays as these often involve a great deal of activity around the family. It can be difficult to complete all the required duties in a period of three to four weeks. Many VFR visitors also stayed for longer periods with 12 respondents staying for more than six weeks.

Most of those travelling visited Ghana alone (41%) with 26% travelling accompanied by children. Costs and family size are important factors here. Only 18% travelled with a spouse and this may limit the potential to develop VFR visits into holiday type activities. The main base for VFR travellers in Ghana is Greater Accra (61%) with Kumasi a second important base (26%). Whilst a high proportion were including travel to other regions this was almost exclusively to visit family. There was no awareness of the attraction of the regions other than as the home of family members.

What does the survey reveal about the contribution VFR travellers make to the local economy? Only 6% of those surveyed used hotel accommodation for any part of their stay which is consistent with other surveys and is considered to be one of the main limitations of the VFR traveller. In addition 32% said they had made no visits to bars or restaurants but of those using bars/restaurants a high proportion had made frequent use of them. 27% had used bars/restaurants more than ten times. It is also apparent that VFR travellers were not making much use of the car rental business for their transport needs (under 20%). Most used private cars (37%) thus making very little contribution to the local economy. However extensive use is made of local taxi and bus (tro tro) services (50% used these at some time) thus benefiting local small enterprises. State and public transport were rarely used (only 7%). Another way for VFR tourism to benefit the economy is through purchases made in Ghana. Among the survey respondents food items were the most frequently purchased (with over 100 respondents purchasing food to bring back to the UK) but over half also bought textile goods and carvings - traditional Ghanaian products - thus helping to support local craft industries and maintain skills.

One problem of VFR travel for the tourism industry is that these visitors do not make extensive use of tourist attractions. The survey showed that whilst many were aware of specific features they did not regard them as attractions and often did not know where they were. When shown a list of Ghana's main tourist attractions (as defined by the Ghana Tourist Board [GTB]) 63% had no awareness of any and when asked to name any attractions only 11% could name any and over half of these could only name one. Much of this is related to perceptions of local features which are not always viewed by those familiar with the area as tourist attractions but are simply taken for granted. Awareness of attractions does not seem to be significantly affected by the length of time respondent had lived in the UK or by the frequency of visits to Ghana although there are some slight trends. When asked to name places they had visited only 43% had visited any of the places listed by the GTB and the range of places visited was very narrow, mostly beaches, castles, forests and gardens in the coastal zone and Kumasi area. When asked why they had not visited more attractions 48% said lack of time. However it seems quite likely that, for many, travelling around in Ghana to see 'attractions' would simply not be considered an important activity with other, more family oriented activities or personal business activities, taking precedence. The survey supports the perception which the tourism industry has about the travel behaviour of VFR tourists in this respect. VFR tourists do not behave like sightseers or holiday makers.

Conclusions and recommendations

The survey therefore reinforces many of the expected characteristics of VFR travellers and shows that if this group are to contribute more to the development of tourism in Ghana the tourism authorities will need to develop some very pro-active initiatives targeted on this group. The number and frequency of return visits and the relative affluence of the group indicate that this could be a very worthwhile investment. In addition it is clear that many of the children of Ghanaians are visiting Ghana, even if born in the UK, and these represent, potentially, a continuing market for the GTB.

This paper has shown that there is a substantial flow of VFR travellers visiting Ghana from the UK on a fairly frequent basis. The characteristics of these travellers indicate that here may be value in the development of tourism promotion efforts directed specifically at this group. If these characteristics are applicable to other groups in other countries such as the USA then the value of such policies, if successful, would be considerable. A primary goal is to raise awareness, among Ghanaians both at home and abroad, of the range, quality and accessibility of tourist attractions and facilities. A second goal is to increase the volume of VFR travellers and perhaps increase the frequency of visits. Thirdly attention should be paid to the role that Ghanaians living outside Ghana might play in raising awareness of Ghana as a tourism destination among the travelling population in general.

The following measures should be considered as means to achieving the goals listed above.

- Direct marketing and dissemination of information through the many community based organizations that exist within the Ghanaian community in the UK. This could help to increase VFR activity in the growing tourism areas of Ghana. Perhaps Ghanaian organizations in the UK could be encouraged by the GTB to play a role in promoting travel to Ghana. There may even be a role for children of Ghanaian extraction to promote Ghana through their school work. The Jamaica Tourist board is promoting a scheme whereby UK tourists can visit Jamaican homes - would a similar scheme work for Ghana? Could UK based Ghanaians be encouraged (via discounted flight tickets?) to take a non-Ghanaian on a visit?

- More information on Ghana and more marketing guidance should be provided to tour operators possibly through promotional visits which might include journalists. Students on Tourism courses should be targeted with information - they are the agents and operators of the future.

- Ghanaians returning to Ghana should be encouraged to visit tourist attractions and facilities through the provision of better information and through concessions and discounts. The co-operation of the airlines and the Ministry of Tourism would be needed for this. Bundled discounts offering concessions to a range of attractions might be particularly effective.

- Inflight films could be used to promote places to visit.

- Residents of Ghana should be targeted with promotional material on attractions in their local area. This would help to promote domestic tourism and encourage Ghanaians to make visits with their guests. Again concessions and discounts could be used to encourage this behavioural change. This would also help the government to achieve its target of using tourism to educate Ghanaians about their own culture and heritage. Some School based activities would probably be most effective in this respect. Local radio and TV would also have a role to play in this.

- Discounts and concessions should be targeted to those times of year when it is known that larger numbers of VFR travellers are likely to be visiting Ghana. To be really effective discounts must cover both the VFR travellers and their hosts.

- Within the UK there is a need for Ghanaian tourism to have a more visible presence, probably in the form of a Tourist Board Office. This office could co-ordinate the promotion of information and special offers.

- Reduced flight costs are probably the only way to increase the volume of VFR travellers. Perhaps airlines could be persuaded to reduce prices in the low season - this would have the added advantage of reducing seasonality. Some kind of frequent flier scheme might also be investigated.

This paper has concluded that the VFR market is sufficiently important to merit particular marketing approaches. A many pronged approach is suggested involving activities both in the UK (or other tourist source country) and in Ghana and involving the co-operation of the major airlines, the Ghana Tourist Board and tour operators. Most of these suggestions would, if implemented, also benefit the development of tourism to Ghana in general.

References

Adu-Febiri, F. (1994), Developing a viable tourist industry in Ghana: problems, prospects and propositions. *Tourism Recreation Research*, vol. 19 (1): 5-11.

Beioley, S. (1997), Four weddings, a funeral and a holiday - the visiting friends and relatives market. *Insight*, British Tourist Board, B1-B15.

Durie, A. and Wilkie, E. (1994), Characteristics and trends in North American visitors to Scotland from 1945-1992. Report by Scottish Tourist Board.

Gartner, W. C. et al (1995), An integrated tourism development project: the Central region of Ghana. *Visions in leisure and business*, vol. 14 (2): 13-23.

Haines, M. (1999), No slave to the rhythm. *Geographical*, September 1999, pp.14-16.

Harrison, L. C. and Husbands W. (1996), *Practicing responsible tourism: International case studies in tourism planning, policy and development*. J Wiley and sons, New York.

Hsieh, S. O'Leary, J. and Morrison, A. (1995), Segmenting visiting friends and relations market by holiday activity participation. *Journal of Tourism Studies*, vol. 6 (1): 48-62.

Jackson, R. and Richard, T. (1990), VFR tourism : is it underestimated? *Journal of Tourism Studies*, vol. 1 (2).

King, B. and Gamage, A. M. (1994) Measuring the value of the ethnic connection: expatriate travellers from Australia to Sri Lanka. *Journal of Travel Research* vol. 32 (2): 46-49.

Knipe, M. (2000), A happy people but a tragic history. *The Times* newspaper Focus on Ghana, April 18 2000, London.

Kwarko, P. (1998), *Visiting friends and relatives: a potential market for Ghana's tourism development?* MA Thesis, Middlesex University, Middlesex.

McKercher, B. (1996), Attracting the invisible tourist market: VFR tourism in Albury Wodonga, Australia. in L C Harrison and W Husbands *'Practicing responsible tourism: International case studies in tourism planning, policy and development.'* J. Wiley and sons, New York. pp.509-529.

Meis, S., Joyal, S. and Trites, A. (1995), The US repeat and VFR visitor to Canada: come again, eh! *Journal of Tourism Studies* vol. 6 (1): 27-37.

Ministry of Tourism (1996), *National tourism Development Plan for Ghana 1996-2010*. Accra, Government of Ghana.

Morrison, A. M. (1995), The VFR market: desperately seeking respect. *Journal of Tourism Studies* vol. 6 (1): 2-5.

Paci, E. (1994), Market segments: the major international VFR markets. *EIU Travel and Tourism Analyst*, no. 6, pp. 36-50.

Seaton, A. V. (1994), Are relatives friends? Reassessing the VFR category in segmenting tourism markets, in A V Seaton et al. (eds.) *'Tourism: the state of the art.'* J. Wiley and sons. Chichester, pp. 316-321.

Seaton, A. V. and Palmer, C. (1996), *The structure of domestic VFR tourism in the UK 1989-1993 and what it tells us about the VFR category.* Conference proceedings, VFR tourism issues and implications, Victoria University of Technology, Melbourne, Australia.

Teye, V. B. (1988), Coups d'etat and African tourism: a study of Ghana. *Annals of Tourism Research*, vol. 15, pp. 329-356.

Theobald, W. (1994), *Global Tourism.* Butterworth-Heinemann, Oxford.

A survey of PhD degrees awarded by UK universities for studies of tourism, 1990-1999

David Botterill and Claire Haven

University of Wales Institute, UK

Introduction

The growth in the study of tourism in UK universities through taught course provision at undergraduate and postgraduate levels is well documented (Airey, 1979; Airey and Johnson, 1998; Middleton and Ladkin, 1996; Tribe, 1997). The topic has become the subject of regular surveys. The latest, in progress, survey is sponsored by the British Travel Education Trust. The survey findings are due to be published as an NLG Guideline later in the year. The topic has also inspired work at PhD level, three studies are known to the authors, two completed and one in progress. The overall development of research degree work in the area of tourism is less well documented and this paper seeks to provide evidence of activity in this area through a survey of PhDs awarded in tourism by British universities over a 10 year period. Data are provided at the simple descriptive level in this paper. It is, however, to be received as a contribution to the analytical 'underlabouring' activity in tourism social science that is the primary intellectual project of the lead author of this paper (Botterill, 2000; Botterill, in review). 'Underlabouring', first used by Locke, is a term borrowed from philosophy to mean a process that seeks 'to remove the idols, obstacles or ideologies that stand in the way of, or distort the understanding of, new knowledge to be produced by the sciences' (Collier, 1994: 19). The provision of descriptive data on the nature and extent of PhD work in tourism is a necessary precondition to the 'underlabouring' project. This paper follows a standard format for the reporting of surveys and includes sections on method, results and analysis, and conclusions.

Method

The data reported in this study is drawn from a single source, the *Index to Theses*. Information is sent to the compilers of the index by all universities of the UK and Ireland. Only theses accepted at UK universities have been included in this paper. In general, the main libraries at these institutions have responsibility for sending the information. Index to Theses is available in database form. The database covers theses accepted from 1970 to 1999 covering all of volumes 21 to 48 and part 1 of volume 49 of the equivalent print publication *Index to Theses*. The Index is updated regularly and the final search used to compile the data in this study was conducted on the Index as it stood at the 20th April 2000. We are confident that we have extracted all the relevant data from the Index but it is always possible that some theses have yet to be recorded on the Index and the 1999 data looks incomplete. The Index to Theses provides on-line access to a full abstract of each thesis. The abstract includes title, author, awarding body, level of award, British Library reference where supplied, and a full-script abstract. In order to identify relevant theses the authors undertook multiple searches to trawl the data base utilising the key words and Boolean links for the following: tourism, tourism management, tourist, tourists, visitor, visitor management, visitors.

The information included on the selected abstract pages provided the raw data for the tables shown below. Recording the awarding university and year provided a simple frequency count of accepted theses. The title and abstract were used to produce analyses of both the topics and the methods used in the studies. In order to analyse the topics a simple procedure was adopted. First a suitable category frame was adopted utilising the headings found within the subject index of Cab Abstracts *Leisure, Recreation and Tourism Abstracts*. This created a frame of 35 headings. Second, 2 researchers working independently allocated each thesis to one of the subject headings. The results were corroborated and differences in allocation were resolved through discussion. As a result of these discussions 5 additional categories were created and observations were made in 16 of the original 35 headings. Analysis of the methods involved the authors in categorising the cited methods into quantitative and qualitative categories that were, in tern, sub-divided into a number of techniques. A separate note was kept of the number of techniques cited in the abstract in order to ascertain the extent of multiple-method application.

Results and analysis

Data extracted from the various searches identified 101 theses completed between 1990 and 1999 at 37 British universities.

Table 1   PhD Awards by University and Year of Acceptance

University:	1990	1991	1992	1993	1994	1995	1996	1997	1998	1999	Total
Birmingham							2	1	1		4
Bournemouth	1		1						1		3
Cambridge						2	1	2		1	6
Dundee							1				1
Durham							1				1
East Anglia								1			1
Edinburgh						1					1
Essex							1				1
Exeter		1				2		2	1		6
Hull				1		1					2
Kent						1		1	1		3
Lancaster		1					1	1			3
Leicester								1	1		2
Liverpool								1			1
London Goldsmiths College			1								1
London School of Economics			1		1						2
London University College			1				1	2			4
Manchester			1			1	1	1			4
Manchester Metropolitan							1				1
Newcastle upon Tyne								1			1
New University of Ulster				1							1
Nottingham Trent	1										1
Open University								1	1		2
Oxford				1	1						2
Oxford Brookes				2		1		1			4
Plymouth								1			1
Queens University Belfast							1				1
Reading	1								1		2
Robert Gordon									1		1
School of African & Oriental Studies, London				1							1
Sheffield				1			1				2
Southampton		1						1			2
Strathclyde		2	2	2	3		5				14
Surrey						4	2	5		1	12
Sussex						1					1
Wales, Cardiff		1		1		1					3
York			1		1		1				3
TOTAL	3	6	8	10	6	15	20	23	8	2	101

Of the total, 26 (26%) were completed in roughly equal proportions at two universities, Strathclyde and Surrey. In contrast, 16 universities in the survey recorded just 1 PhD completion of a study of tourism over the decade. In volume of output terms both Exeter and Cambridge accepted 6 followed by Birmingham, Manchester, Oxford Brookes each with 4 and a group comprising Bournemouth, Lancaster, Kent, Wales and York, each with 3 completions. It was not possible to identify the academic departments in which the studies were undertaken.

The analysis of topics is shown in Table 2. Four areas clearly stand out and account for 76 % of theses as follows: Tourism development and impact (33), tourism management in the civic domain i.e. policy and planning (14), tourism management at industry/firm level (14), tourist/visitor behaviour (15). The next largest category was tourism imagery with 6 theses.

Table 2   Frequency of PhD by Year and Modified Cab Abstracts Subject Categories

Subject Categories:	1990	1991	1992	1993	1994	1995	1996	1997	1998	1999	Total
Destinations							1				1
International Tourism				1				1			2
Sustainable Tourism*					1				1		2
Tourism Behaviour	1	1	1			1	3	3	1		11
Tourism Development			3	4	1	1	4	4	1		18
Tourism Education*			1								1
Tourism History*					1	1					2
Tourism Impact			1	2		3	2	5	1	1	15
Tourism Management				1		1					2
Tourism Organisations								1			1
Tourism Planning*			1			2	1	2		1	7
Tourism Policy		3		1	2	1					7
Tourism Theory								1			1
Tourist Attractions							1				1
Tourist Imagery*	1				1		1	1	2		6
Tourist Industry		1	1	1	1	2	3	5			14
Urban Tourism				1			1				2
Visitor Interpretation							1	1			2
Visitors Behaviour	1		1			1	1				4
Visitors Management							1				1
Visitors Motivation									1		1

*Added subject categories

From the abstracts it was possible to identify the location of fieldwork for 65 studies. Of these, UK locations accounted for only 11 % of identifiable locations. Table 3 details the full range of locations by country.

Table 3   Location of Fieldwork Cited in the Abstracts

U.K.			18	Europe		15
East		1		France	1	
London /SE		1		Germany	1	
North East	2			Greece	1	
North West		3		Hungary	1	
Scotland		2		Malta	2	
South/South West		6		Portugal	2	
Yorkshire & Humberside		2		Spain	2	
Wales		1		Turkey	5	
Far East			12	**Asia**		6
Indonesia	2			China	1	
Malaysia		6		India	2	
Papua N.G.		1		Japan	1	
Thailand		3		Pakistan	1	
				South Korea		
Middle East			5	**Africa**		2
Egypt		4		Nigeria	1	
Saudi-Arabia		1		Uganda	1	
Caribbean			2	**Antarctic**		5
Barbados		2				

In analysing the methods used in the studies the researchers initially agreed to two categories: Quantitative and qualitative, and proceeded to build sub-categories using the descriptions of methods found in the abstracts. The frequencies that follow are based on the number of reported observations of each method found in the abstracts. Most abstracts contained a single method but 19 abstracts reported 2 methods and 3 abstracts reported 3 different methods. In a small number of abstracts it was not clear what methods had been adopted. A case study approach was cited in 36 abstracts. Quantitative (47) and qualitative (54) methods were reported in roughly equal proportions with a small number of studies (9) combining the two types of data.

Table 4   Methods Cited in the Abstracts

Quantitative Methods		**47**
Questionnaire survey	32	
Model building and testing	12	
Experimental design	3	
Case Study		**36**
Qualitative Methods		**54**
Interviews	17	
Ethnography	11	
Conceptual model building	6	
Participant observation	4	
Historical document analysis	3	
Observation	2	
Visual surveys	2	
Focus groups	1	
Critical incident analysis	1	
Autobiographical accounts	1	
Diary accounts	1	
Repertory grid	1	
Comparative case study	1	
Semiotics	1	

The full range of methods is displayed in Table 4. The incidences of ethnography were inferred from a set of studies that appeared to be based upon anthropological accounts of fieldwork.

Conclusion

Three conclusions may be drawn from this study.

1. These data indicate a substantial increase in PhDs awarded in tourism across the decade from 3 in 1990 to 23 in 1997. The evidence for continued growth beyond the 1997 peak is unsubstantiated. The major drivers to this growth have been Strathclyde and Surrey universities and the zero scores for Strathclyde and the small return for Surrey in 1998

and 1999 in this study requires further investigation. It should also be remembered that the mean registration period to take a PhD to completion in the Social Sciences is approximately 4 years and these figures therefore suggest considerable investment over time, probably starting around 1991 and perhaps inspired or facilitated by the outcome of RAE 1992. A constraining factor to growth is sometimes the availability of supervisors and this may help to explain a fall away in completions while a further wave of research students work their way through programmes of study. It is interesting to note that in this decade few of the 'newer' universities, where the bulk of expansion in undergraduate tourism studies has occurred, figure at all in Table 1, the exceptions being Oxford Brookes (largely work that would appear to have emerged from the town planning discipline) and Bournemouth. In this study the inclusion of a key word in the thesis title has defined the PhD as a study of tourism. It is very unlikely that for many of the PhD studies they will be so defined by the awarding institutions in reporting research output. The extent of PhD research into tourism in UK universities is likely therefore to be underestimated if 'bald' output measures such as the RAE are used as indicators of activity.

2. The topic categories confirm the influences of economics, geography, sociology and anthropology, business studies and environmental studies upon the study of tourism. Studies of tourism development and planning exhibit interdisciplinary traits. Consumption as a behaviour is a common strand in tourist and visitor studies. Research undertaken in the Antarctic, in Northern Thailand, on the Egyptian Red Sea coast, and in North East England are typical of studies that examine the interactions of tourists and tourism with specific elements of the natural environment. The extent of fieldwork outside of the UK detailed in Table 3 is worthy of comment. While this might be applauded as an indicator of the international scope of the study of tourism the impression given by a quantitative measure of PhDs awarded by might lead to the presumption that a stock of knowledge relating to tourism in the UK is being constructed in its universities. Notwithstanding the conceptual developments afforded by this activity this is obviously far from the case.

3. The analysis of methods confirms the dominance of positivist (questionnaire) and hermeneutic (interview) epistemic traditions in these studies of tourism. The survey identified just 3 abstracts that indicated the influences of critical theory. A Humean empirical truth would seem to be dominant. We would caution, however, against any claim to the emergence of any explicit epistemology for several reasons. The abstracts seldom followed any common pattern and may not be a valid, comparable measure of the theses. By necessity a short abstract can not convey the fullness of the process of study at Ph.D. level. From the very limited accounts of the theses contained in the abstracts there was little evidence of any explicit engagement with epistemic debate as evidenced by the use of the term itself or its principle form of expression in the Social Sciences that is the terms 'Realism' and 'Constructivism'.

References

Airey, D. and Johnson, S., (1998), *The Profile of Tourism Studies Degree Courses in the UK: 1997/98,* London, The National Liaison Group for Higher Education in Tourism.

Airey, D. (1979), Tourism education in the United Kingdom, *The Tourist Review,* 34(3).

Botterill, D. (2000) Social scientific ways of knowing hospitality, in Lashley, C. and Morrison, A. *In Search of Hospitality*, Butterworth-Heinmann.

Botterill, D. (in review) The epistemology of a set of studies of tourism, *Tourism and Hospitality Research*.

Collier, A. (1994), *Critical Realism: An introduction to Roy Bhaskar's Philosophy*, Verso, London.

Middleton, V. T. C. and Ladkin, A. (1996), *The Profile of Tourism Studies Degree Course in the UK: 1995/6*, London, The National Liaison Group for Higher Education in Tourism.

Tribe, J. (1997), The indiscipline of tourism, *Annals of Tourism Research,* 24(3).

Business as usual: Tourism development into the 21st century

Steven L Butts

Buckinghamshire Chilterns University College, UK

Throughout the latter half of this century Western tourism development agencies have made use of the supposedly beneficial underlying notion of economic growth as a platform from which to quell resistance to the development of the industry. As we approach the Millennium most tourism development agencies now put forth policy statements which pronounce the importance of local involvement and suggest that any tourism development should, in some fashion, enhance the quality of life of local people while mitigating any negative impacts. This paper will argue that such policy statements are hollow, and have no empirical support from those who promote them. For example, most tourism development agencies state as fact that the economic benefits of tourism outweigh the costs, yet they are unable to demonstrate how they have arrived at such a conclusion. It is possible, even likely, that in simple economic terms the costs of having tourists may outweigh any revenue generated for a particular destination. Similarly, most tourism development agencies state that public participation is essential to successful development, however, the practice of obtaining and incorporating public views is virtually non-existent. To explain the dichotomous relationship between theory and practice in tourism development policy a hegemonic analysis is provided which concludes that due to the entrenched hegemonic framework within tourism development agencies, the gap between theory and practice will not close in the near future.

Business as usual

Perhaps the most significant consequence in regards to the majority of worldwide tourism development to date is the top down nature in which it has been implemented. Such an approach typically does not allow for community participation, creating a paternalistic situation whereby those communities that resist being "developed" simply cannot understand the benefits of economic growth. Or so the developers would say. Such a model ignores the possibility that a community resists development because it is all too aware of what the effects of that development are likely to be.

Most theories of development are based upon a capitalistic economy that are grounded in notions of equality, continuous growth, and limitless resources. World systems theory tells us that there has been continuous growth in the world market so far, but that the accumulation of wealth is being concentrated in those areas, and indeed individuals that already have it. Environmentalists tell us that the earth's resources are most assuredly not limitless, and that there is a need for curtailing the exploitation of physical resources. Nevertheless, even though the notions of capitalism are contradictory, and quite possibly self-destructive, they continue to be pervasive.

If past development efforts using the capital growth model have failed, and it is accepted that such models do not actively seek out community participation, why then are they still adhered too? To answer this question I must refer to the concept of hegemony and the difficulty of achieving community-wide consensus. Those that use the capital growth model state that the development they are encouraging will somehow benefit the effected community. They are, in effect, manufacturing consensus based upon the notion that capital growth is good for all. Nowhere is this clearer than in Great Britain and the United States where notions of capitalism, continuous growth, and "progress" are seen as both desirable and inevitable. Hegemony is based on the notion that the public believe that those in power have the knowledge and expertise to determine the best course of action. Hence, the job of selling the perceived need for continuous growth is a simple one for developers.

Tourism has been an effective tool for capitalism, and it is already an important source of income for many areas and countries, while an ever increasing number of destinations try to (further) cash in on the tourism dollar (Edgell 1990). However, while the effects of tourism on host communities are well documented, the negative consequences of the industry are rarely mitigated. For most tourism destinations, tourism-related public policy is simple and based on capitalistic growth - bring in as many tourists, and as much revenue, as possible. This paper proposes that such a policy is often harmful to local residents, who are often touted as being the supposed beneficiaries of tourism development.

The approach taken by policy makers has direct bearing on the policies they support, and on the people they represent. Furthermore,

> *A prescriptive-rationalist approach to public policy would see the decisions of government as being part of an inherently rational policy-making process in which goals, values, and objectives can be ranked and identified after the collection and systematic evaluation of the necessary data. However, this approach to policy analysis, though influential, is extremely misleading as it fails to recognise the inherently political nature of public policy* (Hall and Jenkins 1995:65).

Thus the effects of tourism-related public policies cannot be measured as a bottom-line phenomenon because these policies are not based on cost-benefit analysis, but on the political impulses of those in decision making positions.

Because the aim of the tourist industry is to attract visitors, tourism development places a strain on physical resources such as water supplies and transportation infrastructures, and heightens environmental degradation and problems of waste disposal. Increased tourism may also create a demand for increased technology or more elaborate infrastructure than a region may want, or be able to afford. And tourists through sheer numbers can threaten or destroy the attractions they come to see (Murphy 1985).

The development of tourism may also strain a community's cultural resources by causing a change in lifestyle and social structure (Puntenney 1990). Host communities may be forced to adopt cultural traits of the tourists, such as their language, dress, and manner to satisfy visitors. Social problems such as crime and prostitution may also increase (Walmsley et al. 1983). In some instances local populations by their own admission have had their circumstances worsened through tourism development (Robben 1982; Daltabuit and Pi-Sunyer 1990; Bax 1992). Although tourism may not always be detrimental to local populations, case studies presented thus far suggest that in the long term members of local populations only rarely have their circumstances improved as a result of tourism development, and those individuals that do benefit are few in number.

While the body of tourism literature is growing, social sciences' late arrival on the tourism scene has left a time gap in the literature. Nevertheless, because tourism is potentially such an enormous revenue generator greater attention has been given to developing the industry on local, regional, national, and international scales. However, the real and potential effects on a society's social fabric from the tourism industry are rarely considered by policy makers. Even the economic consequences remain unclear for residents and policy makers of most communities because the costs of the industry, such as inflation, tax increases, and the need for maintaining or creating new infrastructure are not weighed against gains from revenue generated by tourists and the industry. I have yet to come across any study that provides a clear cost-benefit analysis in even simple economic terms; much less one that fully considers environmental and social costs and benefits. However, since most tourism development agencies state as fact that the economic benefits of tourism outweigh any costs, then it is only fair that they support their claims and demonstrate how they have arrived at such a conclusion. Yet they do not do so. And the public and the academic community continue to fail to call them to task--an old familiar pattern that is unsustainable and unchanging.

When considering the economics of tourism, proponents of tourism suggest tourism is a way to alleviate poverty and unemployment, and develop areas. Opponents suggest that tourism provides little benefit to local residents, creates poor-paying, servile jobs, and because of economic leakages provides little revenue to the local economy. Due to the complex and integrated nature of the tourism industry it is difficult, but not impossible, to estimate a dollar amount to demonstrate whether tourism is economically advantageous or not.

However, even less clear and seemingly more difficult to measure are the social effects of the industry. Tourists may benefit from their visits to other locales through greater cultural understanding or educating themselves, or even through needed stress relief. But few perceived social benefits are received by the "hosts," or those who live in tourist destinations; these generally refer to personal gains made by being exposed to outsiders (Smith 1989). More commonly, hosts cite their displeasure with increased congestion, crime, and taxes, and having their lifestyle interrupted during the tourist season.

On the surface these may seem to be minor, almost insignificant irritations. However, because they effect their day to day lives, they are not trivial to those who suffer from them. Yet, what is perhaps most surprising of all is that the problems created by tourism for the full-time residents of a tourism destination are not commonly considered to be major causes of alarm for the majority. Why host communities seemingly fail to resist the arrival (or increase in levels) of tourism, even though they are aware of the inevitability of the negative effects, is a topic that I will implicitly attempt to answer in this paper, but one that requires further investigation.

Tourism is often seen by government and development agencies as a quick economic fix. The development of tourism may provide a short term economic boost to an economy, but often falls short of economic expectations and predictions. It also has a tendency to generate inflation by putting pressure on inelastic supplies and creating the need to import goods which tourists require. Most importantly, because of the need for an initial stake, unless provisions such as grants or low interest loans are made available to the community at large, tourism development does not generally allow locals access to the industry, increasing the gap between the haves and the have nots. Tourism does create employment, but the type of jobs created does not provide economic stability or mobility for locals. And often workers from other areas are brought in because of their willingness to work for less, leaving locals the choice to work for little pay, or not work at all.

Tourism development

Ethical considerations

My view of tourism development is that it should be of primary benefit to existing local populations and the communities effected by it, and that the applied tourism researcher's responsibility is to help ensure that this occurs (Butts 1993). This being the case, it is neither practical nor possible for those who share my view to be equally concerned with how our research might effect others, such as tourists, multinational corporations, or a government's GNP. As an applied anthropologist concerned with development, especially tourism development, I find the community approach as suggested by Peter Murphy (1985) to provide an effective starting point for understanding and facilitating change. A community approach considers the implications of an action for the society at large, and to a lesser degree implications for other outsiders, but is primarily concerned with the effected community. My position is that researchers in tourism development have firstly an ethical responsibility to the communities they work in, and that the concerns of groups outside a given community should be considered secondary. This is based on my personal ethics, but it is also rarely contradictory, in principle at least, to the stated goals and mission statements of public tourism agencies.

Development in practice

Black (1991:15) suggests that development as a term lacks a negative connotation simply because it has as many meanings as it has users. Development is often associated with modernisation, which can be defined as the process through which the developed world recreates itself in the developing world through the spread of such devices as urbanisation, mechanised and industrialised agriculture, and a formal capitalistic economy. Nevertheless, definitions of development typically entail notions of progress, growth, or evolution, and this appears to be at the heart of definitions for many "development projects." This type of definition suggests that some sort of inventive or progressive change has to transpire for development to occur. However, such a definition is short-sighted, noninclusive, ethnocentric, and hegemonic. This is because it presupposes a Rostow (1971) perspective that assumes that all "traditional" (those not favourable to a market economy) practices are backward and useless, and that the road toward some sort of modernisation process is the only one that does not end in abandonment in the modern world. In other words this type of definition states that we must give up and blindly follow any strategy that opposes the notions of continuous growth if we are to succeed. Issues such as whether or not a given development is informed by local residents or environmentally sustainable become unimportant when compared to the perceived economic gains.

Development, by its very nature, suggests change, and there exists in the literature a myriad of definitions of "development." It is not the purpose of this work to examine all of them, or to state an all-encompassing definition. A universal definition of development is unwieldy and potentially flawed because: 1) the number of variables involved is too numerous to consider as a whole; and 2) the variables themselves are not static; each potential development project contains its own assortment of unknowns. What constitutes development is dependent upon the measurement used, and there does not currently exist a universal standard for measuring development. Each project has specific goals it strives to achieve, but possible backlashes or the unfeasibility of a project's goals may make a given development scheme flounder.

Much of the development planning that has occurred throughout the world in the twentieth century is a result of "Western growth-theory" which Simonis (1990:79-80) tells us is directed at promoting the modern (formal) sector of the economy by:

> *A process of exponential growth...set in motion in the modern sector by means of a high rate of investment, it being assumed that the transmission of the growth-stimuli to the traditional (informal) sector would bring about improvement of the living conditions to society at large.*

The Western growth model hints at sustainability through continuous growth, but sets no limits on when that growth may cease to be beneficial.

Pearce et al. (1990:1) state that little progress has been made in operationalising "sustainable development," and that attempts at meshing the concept with practical applications have been few and for the most part unsuccessful. They make a distinction between development and economic growth, with development including economic growth as well as factors of quality of life such as education, access to basic freedoms, and nutritional status. However, for development to be sustainable it must consider economic growth and quality of life, but it must also consider the natural capital stock. Natural capital stock is all of the environmental and natural resource assets of a given area. Pearce et al. (1990) argue that for development to be sustainable, natural capital stock must not diminish through time. They go on to point out that:

> *Since 'development' is a value word, implying change that is desirable, there is no consensus as to its meaning. What constitutes development depends on what social goals are being advocated by the development agency, government, analyst or advisor* (Pearce et al. 1990:2).

Pearce et al. (1990) believe that development is a vector of desirable social objectives, and provide a list of elements of this vector that includes: 1) increases in real income per capita; 2) improvements in health and nutritional status; 3) educational achievement; 4) access to resources; 5) a 'fairer' distribution of income; and 6) increases in basic freedoms. Thus, sustainable development occurs when the change wrought by "development" to these vectors is improved during a selected time frame.

However, part of the difficulty with creating a general definition of (sustainable) development is that change does not effect all equally, and communities consist of many different groups. As an example, improvements in health and nutritional status may lower infant mortality in a community. However, a sudden increase in numbers of children may reduce the access of educational resources by other groups, such as those involved in adult education, because educational achievement for children may be given top priority. In a situation of limited resources, not all can benefit equally. Development projects must define their goals, meet with local approval, and design their own criteria for evaluation. Before development takes place standard questions such as: which group(s) are targeted; how are they to benefit; how long are they to benefit for; what are the likely spin-off effects of the proposed development; and what are the implications for the group(s) not targeted, should be answered if evaluation is to be considered. Thus, any definition of development, or what is sustainable, must be operationalised for each development project.

Furthermore, this discussion begs the most troublesome question; how are social and economic impacts measured when people have different needs, aspirations, and standards of living? If the well being of the community were at stake, then I would further suggest that the potential benefits and consequences of an action must be determined by the various groups that make up a given community. Those effected will determine what they believe is best for them. Achieving consensus is rarely a simple task; open discussion by all effected is the first step. The exigency in finding common ground is a far better option than the normal manner in which action is taken, with the majority, or all, of a community having no voice. After all, who is better than those who live in an area to know what is best for them, and how could those who support democratic ideas suggest otherwise?

However, the pervasive belief continues that local communities are unqualified to make "correct" decisions. Even if concerted and majority opposition occurs, there is nothing to stop a handful of officials from pursuing and achieving their own goals in spite of local opposition. It is my view that in spite of talk of such things as local empowerment, environmental economics, and devolved government, in the next century no changes will occur to the tourism development process—that it will be business as usual. The reason for this is that a change would serve no useful purpose to those in power. And without fundamental changes to either the power structure or those who represent it we can expect to see a repeat of the pattern of development witnessed in the latter half of the Twentieth Century where public participation is given lip-service only.

Hegemony

Given the fact that community voices are typically either silenced or ignored in the tourism development process, it is no small wonder that ill feeling towards tourists arises. It is significant that one of the only certain ways a community can keep itself from being inundated with too many tourists, apart from somehow closing physical access to it, is to pose to tourists a threat of violence. This demonstrates that communities who do not wish for tourism development either can not, or will not, take action to curb tourism. If they can not, then we must ask who can? If they will not, then we must ask why not?

Hegemony, as put forth by Antonio Gramsci, is rooted in the notion of "intellectual and moral leadership" (Kurtz 1996:103). Since the time of his writing and subsequent death, Gramsci's original concept of hegemony has been referred to, used, and some would say often misused as a heuristic device. Kurtz (1996), after chiding others for drifting from Gramsci's original ideas in The Prison Notebooks, purports remaining pure to Gramsci and presents a treatise on Gramsci's meaning of hegemony, as well as how others have interpreted Gramsci's work. Kurtz argues that Gramsci's original meaning is as follows.

Kurtz suggests that hegemony, as put forth by Gramsci in The Prison Notebooks, is the basis for his ideas by which the undermining of Western capitalism can take place and the socialist utopia of Marx and Engels brought to light (Kurtz 1996:108). Gramsci believes the leadership of any government engages in two related practices. In the first, domination, force, and coercion are used against those who resist authority. In the second, hegemony, "intellectual devices (are used) to infuse...ideas of morality to gain the support of those who resist or may be neutral, to retain the support of those who consent to its rule, and to establish alliances as widely as possible" (Kurtz 1996:106).

Hegemony refers to the different organisations involved in state formation (Kurtz 1996:107), but it is always a process "aimed at obtaining consent and establishing its legitimacy" (Gramsci 1971:12 in Kurtz 1996). Fundamental to Gramsci's hegemonic practices are political and cultural agents whom Gramsci calls traditional and organic intellectuals (1974:5ff). Gramsci argues that 'All men are intellectuals...but not all men have in society the function of intellectuals' (1971:9), which is to provide direction for hegemonic processes. To overly simplify a complex relationship, traditional intellectuals are agents who tend to represent and direct the interests of those in power. Organic intellectuals are agents who tend to represent and direct the interest of subaltern populations who are being exploited and to provide them with a counter-hegemony to resist their exploitation. It is the intellectuals who contest for the minds and support of the masses and create the alliances necessary either to sustain or establish a hegemonic formation unified under the moral principles of an intellectual leadership (Kurtz 1996:108). These agents may be involved in either cultural or political practices, or both at the same time as for Gramsci, culture is itself a political process (Kurtz 1996:108-9). Thus, what Gramsci is suggesting is that in any complex political formation there exists a balance between domination (coercion and force) and hegemony (intellectual and moral leadership). Intellectuals who oppose the existing hegemonic formation constitute a counter-hegemonic formation (Kurtz 1996:109).

How then is the hegemonic structure subverted and an existing institution ousted? Dependent upon the position of the institution Gramsci offers two avenues for subversion. If an institution is weakly entrenched, that is, recently formed, lacking in public support, or is in some other way weak or threatened, the most effective way to challenge its authority is directly, through what Gramsci (1971:108-10) calls "a war of movement" (Kurtz 1996:109). If however, a government is deeply entrenched and is seen as legitimate by the majority of its population, a direct challenge to its authority, such as revolution, is less effective than "a war of position" or passive revolution (Gramsci 1971:110-11). Kurtz (1996:109) states that a passive revolution "entails a slow and protracted struggle by political and cultural agents for the minds and support of the subaltern population, and is in practice a cultural process."

For Gramsci, culture is part and parcel to the political process. When defining culture he states, "it is the exercise of thought, the acquisition of general ideas, the habit of connecting cause and effect" (Buttigieg 1987:20 in Kurtz 1996:110). Culture is a critical element for Gramsci, and he uses it as a foundation for understanding how people establish relations within, and in spite of, hegemonic organisations.

Culture conceptualised as the product of a process by which human subjects establish relations of cause and effect between themselves and their social, political and economic environments suggests the motivation for why subjects work, fight, think, worship and behave generally in ways that are acceptable to a hegemonic organisation (Kurtz, 1996). A hegemonic organisation of intellectuals attempts to construct a cultural configuration that provides least resistance to practices and ideas an institution deems to be acceptable. It is only when subaltern populations perceive alternatives to their usual cultural business, their practices of cause and effect as determined by those in power, that a counter-hegemonic organisation can marshal that population's energies and culture (Kurtz 1996:110-11).

The strength of an established government, such as those in Western Europe and the United States, is that they are based on "an articulated structure of values, ideologies, symbols...and practices that constitute a unified cultural configuration" (Kurtz 1996:190). Furthermore, in societies like those in Europe (and the United States) Gramsci (1971:349) believed that it was doubly difficult for a counter-hegemonic organisation to marshal its energies against the hegemonic structure because of class differences. Gramsci believed that culture was intrinsic to a society's social classes (Kurtz 1996:111). This being the case, European societies do not represent what Gramsci (1971) calls total cultural configurations. In other words, because these societies are made up of various classes, with each class possessing its own culture, it is unlikely that the classes will perceive alternatives to their usual cultural business in the same way. This, in turn, makes the formation of a unified counter-hegemonic organisation less likely than in a society that has total cultural configurations.

My view of Gramsci's concept of hegemony is that it remains sound as a theoretical perspective and is a useful heuristic device. However, I believe that his conception of how the hegemonic structure can be subverted, and its application to most entrenched complex political formations in the world today, is becoming increasingly limited due to the integration of cultures under the hegemonic structures.

While the relationship between hegemony and culture is an important one for Gramsci, his work fails to adequately address the fact that more than one culture can exist within a society, and that these cultures are not necessarily unified by class. I believe that Gramsci is correct in his statement that culture is intrinsic to the classes within a society. However, in the world of today the movement of different cultural groups increasingly puts them under the same governmental leadership with other cultural groups, with whom they may share very little in the way of culture. These groups do not share a common language, folklore, or worldview. This makes the subversion of the dominant hegemonic structure all the more difficult because the subaltern population is split yet again -- first by class and now by culture, and the classes within each culture -- making it increasingly difficult for a passive revolution, which is a process of cultural change, to occur in a deeply entrenched state.

The 21st century

It is a common plea from public tourism agencies that it is not their fault their community is unaware of their existence or actions; that the community should make more of an effort to find out about them. Such a "blame the victim" mentality only furthers the thesis that the majority of these agencies do not want to be forced to include the public's view in the decision making process. Minimally, the reasons behind public tourism agencies' failure to obtain community participation are: (1) they lack available time and money; and/or (2) they do not have the expertise in obtain it. However, whatever the reason an excuse is always given that it is somehow not the organisation's fault. And here lies the paradox. If a public tourism organisation states that community participation is essential to successful tourism development, which virtually all do, but fail to obtain it, they must then be promoting tourism development that is ineffectual and unsustainable. It should therefore come as no surprise when tourist development projects fail, or are met with strong local resistance. In fact, without public participation it would only be through sheer luck that a project could be conceived, planned, and implemented successfully and without strong local opposition. As it seems luck is what most public tourism development agencies are relying on, and as luck is apparently in short supply, why do they not then hedge their bets and take on the task of public participation? The answer to this question clearly lies in the previous discussion of hegemony. But before this question is fully answered, it is necessary to address the protestations by public tourism agencies that the community is, in fact, involved in the development process.

By far the most common method of obtaining input from the community by public tourism officials is the public meeting. Yet the problems inherent to gaining and making use of information from public meetings, which makes them effectively worthless in obtaining consensus and a representative view, are well documented. Nevertheless, using a series of public meetings to base decisions may mean that the views of a community are no better represented than if they were never "consulted." Clearly public meetings should be prohibited as a means of obtaining community participation. This is because they have the potential to strip the public of its ability to present its views. It is a simple matter for a public organisation, or even a private developer, to ignore the views expressed, or not expressed, at public meetings by stating that those who speak out at public meetings are not representative of the community at large - particularly if the public does not agree with their point of view. On the other hand, if no one bothers to attend or present an opposing viewpoint the organisation can state that there is no opposition to proposed plans.

Another common defensive tactic used by public tourism organisation to avoid criticism is to blame the public for not making its voice heard, even though there may be no recognised channel for doing so. Thus, if people speak out after a policy or development has been approved it is not the public officials' fault they did not know what the community wanted; rather it is the community's fault for not making its voices heard. This is another example of a public organisation blaming the victim, rather than taking responsibility for their actions and their ignorance of public sentiment.

To sum up, smoke and mirrors are being used to give the illusion that community participation has been conducted and incorporated into policy, plans, and development. The term "sustainable tourism development" is incorporated into virtually all public tourism agency's documents and mission statements, with no understanding of what it is or any intention of achieving it - the notions of unlimited growth and sustainability are contradictory. But will public tourism agencies realise the error of their ways, or will they carry on doing what they have always done?

With a few isolated exceptions, the previous discussion of hegemony strongly suggests that the way in which public tourism agencies develop tourism and incorporate community sentiment into their plans will remain business as usual in the foreseeable future. No change will occur until the subaltern population (a community as a united whole) realises that the actions of the existing hegemonic structure (in this case public tourism agencies) are not acceptable and that other effective avenues (such as social impact assessment) for involving the community (not public meetings) exist. The likelihood of this occurring given the large scale of regional public tourism agency networks, and the diversity of classes and cultures present within these areas make the formation of a counter-hegemony unlikely. Thus, communities will continue to be dominated by tourism development policies and decisions that are expeditious to those in power. Whether or not they are good for a given community will, as before, rely to a large degree on chance.

References

Bax, M. (1992), Female Suffering, Local Power Relations and Religious Tourism: A Case Study from Yugoslavia, *Medical Anthropology Quarterly*, 6 (2): 114-27.

Black, J., A. (1991), *Development in Theory and Practice: Bridging the Gap*, Westview Press, London.

Buttigieg, J. (1987), *Antonio Gramsci's Triad: Culture, Politics, Intellectuals,* Centre for Humanistic Studies Occasional Papers, No.10, University of Minnesota.

Butts, S., L. (1993), *Tourism for Whom?...Paying the Fiddler,* Paper presentation for the Society for Applied Anthropology, San Antonio, Texas, March.

Daltabuit, M. and O. Pi-Sunyer (1990), Tourism Development in Quitana Roo, Mexico, *Cultural Survival Quarterly*, 14 (1): 9-13.

Edgell, D. L. (1990), *International Tourism Policy*, Van Nostrand Reinhold, New York.

Gramsci, A. (1971), *Selections from the Prison Notebooks of Antonio Gramsci,* Q. Hoare and G. N. Smith, eds, International Publishers, New York.

Hall, C. M., and J. M. Jenkins (1995), *Tourism and Public Policy*, Routledge, New York.

Kurtz, D. V. (1996), Hegemony and Anthropology: Gramsci, Exegeses, Reinterpretations, *Critique of Anthropology*, 16 (2): 106-135.

Murphy, P. (1985), *A Community Approach*, Methuen Press, New York.

Pearce, D. W., Barbier, E., and Markandya, A. (1990), Sustainable Development: Ecology and Economic Progress, *in Sustainable Development: Economics and Environment in the Third World*, Edward Elgar Publishers, Brookfield, VT, pp.1-22.

Puntenney, P. J. (1990), Defining Solutions: The Annapurna Experience, *Cultural Survival Quarterly*, 14 (2): 9-14.

Rostow, W. (1971), *The Stages of Economic Growth*, Cambridge University Press, Cambridge.

Simonis, U. E. (1990), *Beyond Growth: Elements of Sustainable Development*, Sigma, New York.

Smith, V., L., ed. (1989), *Hosts and Guests: The Anthropology of Tourism*, University of Philadelphia Press, Philadelphia.

Walmsley, J., and R. M. Boskovic, R. M., J. J. Pigim (1983), Tourism and Crime: An Australian Perspective, *Journal of Leisure Research*, (2): 137-155.

What do I want you to think of me? The representationality of tourism brands and implications for future marketing management of tourism products

Jackie Clarke

Oxford Brookes University, UK

Abstract

Using exploratory research, this paper examines the application of the brands box model developed for physical goods by de Chernatony and McWilliam (1989, 1990) to six tourism brands considered 'household names' in the United Kingdom. The brands box model is a four cell matrix based on two dimensions, named 'functionality' and 'representationality'. Representationality addresses the emotional aspects of the brand, or the extent to which it is used by consumers as a non-verbal communications device. It is argued that tourism displays the necessary characteristics to develop a strong representational component to a given brand. Analysis of the data showed that all six brands were located in the high representationality – high functionality cell, although a sub-pattern was discernible within the cell based on the wider range of representationality scores than functionality scores.

Introduction

The World Tourism Organisation's report, 'Tourism 2020 Vision' suggested that

> "the next century will mark the emergence of tourism destinations as a fashion accessory. The choice of holiday destination will help define the identity of the traveller and, in an increasingly homogeneous world, set him apart from the hordes of other tourists" (Luhrman, 1998: 13).

Leisure tourists use props to show their tourist status. Cameras, video-cameras, the dress code from the sunglasses to the casual shoes, display and communicate to others that this person is, for the time being, 'a tourist'. Destinations successfully sell souvenirs stamped with logos, sweatshirts, car and luggage stickers, which form visible statements of tourist consumption. Tourists send postcards to non-participants left behind to underline their position to others. From their behaviour, it would appear that tourists use the tourism experience to communicate to others something about themselves. To what extent are tourism brands also purchased for their ability to communicate meaning to others? And what does such consumer behaviour imply for the marketing of tourism products by industry players? These are the questions that this paper seeks to address.

Brands and the representationality dimension

Brands are too often seen in terms of management input, for example, logos, slogans and advertising campaigns, rather than as output in the form of consumer meaning. Basic definitions regard the brand as a 'name, term, sign, symbol or design or combination intended to identify the seller and to differentiate from the competition' (see, for example, Kotler et al, 1996). Identification and differentiation are just two of the brand roles listed by de Chernatony and McDonald (1992), who believe that *"the most frequent branding error appears to be an undue emphasis on using the brand name purely as a differentiating device"* (de Chernatony and McDonald, 1992: 159). Brands also communicate functional benefits, or the practical performance of the product, and they can be used to communicate emotional benefits. For physical goods, the balance between functional and emotional brand elements can be tested through blind and branded product tests, with brands strong on emotional benefits out-performing functionally superior rivals in branded tests. In short, brands can be developed as non-verbal, symbolic devices that consumers can use to:

- Communicate messages about themselves to other people;

- Ease social situations and facilitate social mixing;

- Decode some initial meaning about a person from their choice of brand usage;

- Help consumers reinforce their own self-concept or develop towards their idealised self-concept; and

- Assist as ritual devices for the celebration of an identified special occasion (de Chernatony and McDonald, 1992).

De Chernatony and McWilliam (1989) proposed the brands box model as a conceptual framework to aid management understanding of the brands with which they worked. The two dimensions of the brands box created a four cell matrix using consumer perceptions of the respective brand. The first dimension, labelled 'functionality', measured the performance capability of the brand based on its physical attributes. The second dimension, labelled 'representationality', measured the expressive nature of the brand, and the beliefs and meanings with which it was associated. In discussing the brands box model, de Chernatony and McWilliam (1989) stressed that brands were not characterised by one dimension alone, but by the *degree* to which they displayed *both* dimensions.

In a later paper (de Chernatony and McWilliam, 1990), the brands box model was applied to ten different brands of physical goods using exploratory research. The results placed the Audi car, J. Walker Black Label whiskey and Sony hi-fi brands in the high representationality – high functionality cell, the Rolex watch and Yves St. Laurent necktie in the high representationality - low functionality cell, the Tippex brand, Formica and Castrol GTX oil in the low representationality-high functionality cell, and the Tate & Lyle brand and Heinz baked beans in the low representationality - low functionality cell. The brands located in the two high representationality cells were purchased and used by consumers to express something about themselves.

Applying the brands box model to tourism brands

The brands best suited as expressive devices are those that are publicly consumed and that include group social acceptance as a motivating factor (Schiffman and Kanuk, 2000), and such brands can be physical goods or services (Palmer, 1999). Typically, leisure tourism is undertaken as a group experience which is visibly consumed in the presence of others, including the employees, community hosts and other tourists as well as the immediate group. It is also a service product consumed over an extended period of time with plenty of scope for individual expression. Indeed, the liberation and freedom from the normal constraints of a working or everyday life is part of its very appeal. The research explored to what extent well-known tourism brands (or household names) are perceived as non-verbal communication devices by applying the brands box methodology to tourism.

Comparison of methodologies

The intention was to replicate as far as possible the exploratory methodology used in the original de Chernatony and McWilliam (1990) study. Table 1 provides an overview of the similarities and adaptations. The interview survey for the tourism brands was carried out in September 1999, and prompted recall was used for each brand through names and logos on show cards. Gender, age category, resident / visitor status, and user or non-user status for each brand were also captured for cross-analysis. The data was analysed using SPSS for Windows, and new variables for the functionality dimension and the representationality dimension were computed for each brand.

The tourism brands chosen by researcher conjecture were considered to be examples of 'household name' brands in the United Kingdom, defined as 'a brand with high awareness or recognition amongst the general public in the United Kingdom so that the brand name might be used in everyday conversation and carry meaning'. The six selected brands were British Airways, Club 18-30, The National Trust, Orient Express, Thomson Holidays and Virgin Atlantic. The status of these brands as 'household names' were tested on a convenience sample of twenty-six non-tourism students by including the six brands in a list of forty-eight real travel and tourism brands that might be household names plus two dummy brands. The respondents were asked to check all the brands they considered to fit the definition of a 'household name' brand. In no case were the dummy variables selected, so it can be reasonably assumed that the respondents completed the task to instruction. The six brands were ranked first, equal fourteenth, equal fourteenth, equal nineteenth, equal nineteenth and equal sixth respectively. For each brand, more than ten students agreed that the brand was a 'household name'. Between them, the six brands represented attractions, tour operating and transport. All were high involvement brands, although it can be argued that the definition is product, situation and segment-dependent (Middleton, 1994).

Table 1.   A comparison of field work methodologies

De Chernatony and McWilliam (1990) study of physical goods brands	Application of study to tourism brands
Exploratory research	Exploratory research
Ten brands	Six brands
Brands chosen by researcher conjecture	Brands chosen by researcher conjecture, plus convenience sample exercise.
Mix of high and low involvement brands	Arguably high involvement brands
Interview survey in Bedford	Interview survey in Oxford
General public	General public
Sample size 48 adults	Sample size 48 adults
Survey instrument 5 point Likert scales of 11 repeated statements for each brand	Survey instrument 5 point Likert scales of 8 repeated statements for each brand
Statements suited to physical goods e.g. buyer, product	Replicated statements 'tweaked' to adjust for the nature of services e.g. user, service

Both methodologies were based on a small sample size drawn from the general public, rather than focusing on product-users. There was a feeling in the Oxford study that people found it harder to relate to tourism as brands than they do physical goods in a street survey situation. The original survey instrument posed problems as the researcher felt that some sentences were overly complex, which would lead to respondent confusion. With ten brands and eleven statements for each, the instrument was too long to hold respondent attention, hence the reduction to six brands and eight statements. Furthermore, some of the statements were expressed in relative form, a characteristic, with hindsight, that should have been adjusted for the tourism survey. Destination brands were excluded from consideration as they are arguably weaker than single organisation brands (Goodall, 1990), and the researcher felt that respondents would not perceive places as brands. This decision was interesting in the light of work by Westwood et al (1999), who indicated that consumers derived status more from the destination visited than from the tour operator used.

Figure 1

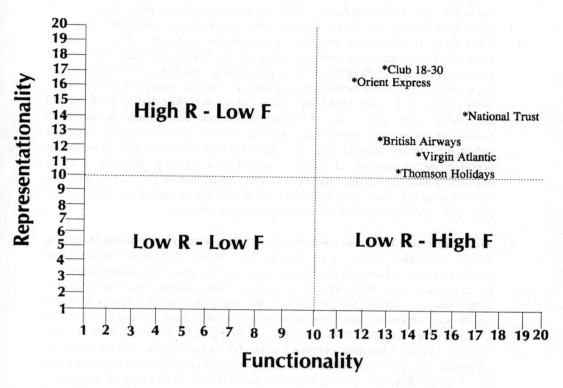

Results and analysis

With prompted recall, brand awareness ranged from 100% of the respondents for British Airways to 52% of the respondents for Orient Express. Non-UK respondents recognised fewer brands, with the two airline brands being the most familiar (a finding matched in the convenience sample exercise). When the computed representationality and functionality scores were mapped onto the brands box (see figure 1), all six brands were placed in the high representationality – high functionality cell, and not spread throughout the matrix as the brands had been in the physical goods study. It appeared that 'household name' tourism brands had developed both dimensions, being used by consumers both for the delivered performance and the expressive value. However, the findings from the exploratory research showed a greater range of values for representationality (10.11 to 16.6) than for functionality (13.16 to 15.82). A tentative pattern emerged in the relative position of the brands within this one cell.

- **More representational than functional – Club 18-30 and Orient Express**. These two brands had higher representational values than functional values; indeed, Club 18-30 had the highest representationality score of any of the researched brands (16.6). Although both are niche brands with a sound knowledge of their target segments, they operate at opposing ends of the luxury – economy spectrum. Club 18-30 is the market leader in the youth sun and sea inclusive tour market, with approximately 100,000 tourists a year (Travel Trade Gazette, 1999), whereas Orient Express, a 'legend' in train travel, has extended the brand into cruise (McArdle, 1989). Of the respondents, none were users of either brand; however, Orient Express drew a positive or associative response, while Club 18-30 drew a negative or dissociative response. This dissociative element with incompatible non-users supports the brand personality and acts to strengthen the attraction of Club 18-30 for its target market as teenagers seek to draw away from adults belonging to different reference groups (Clarke, 1992). With a strong representational brand, whose image is highlighted by controversial advertising campaigns, Club 18-30 can discourage the 'wrong' person from purchasing the product, thereby managing the mix of clients to improve customer satisfaction. From informal comments made by respondents, Orient Express was perceived as an aspirational brand connected to a luxurious lifestyle, a brand enjoyed by reference groups that respondents would wish to join. Of course, one would expect that, had non-adults been included in the sample, Club 18-30 would also draw positive responses from certain younger segments.

- **More functional than representational – British Airways, Thomson Holidays, Virgin Atlantic.** These three brands had higher functional values than representational values. All three might be viewed as mass brands appealing to a broad market. One might speculate whether other airlines and tour operators would show a similar pattern. Indeed, the representationality scores of other brands may be lower. Thomson Holidays is the clear mass market leader in the UK, and other tour operators may own weaker brands (Rogers, 1998; Holiday Which?, 1999a). Mass tour operating in the UK is cost-driven with an emphasis on tactical pricing to re-balance demand with supply capacity, and such measures may frustrate attempts to build representational value. In the case of airlines, it may be that airlines are perceived in terms of the core benefit, with less opportunity for the development of individual expression.

- **More functional than representational – The National Trust.** Although having a functionality score greater than its representationality score, the National Trust was located away from the other brands in this group on account of its relative strength on the representationality dimension. The National Trust was the only brand where the majority of respondents had used the brand over the last two years; as an organisation, it attracts around 11.7 million visits to its properties a year (The National Trust, 1998). There was little difference in opinion between non-users and users of the brand, except on two of the functionality statements, where non-users felt that The National Trust was being used less for its functionality than users did.

Discussion of marketing implications of representationality in tourism

The empirical evidence placed the six tourism brands in the high representationality – high functionality cell. This map represents the current situation for marketing managers, and a directional tool for strategic decisions to build, maintain or reduce either dimension. However, it would seem that to *reduce* the representational value of a brand consumed in a group situation and which lends itself to individual expression might not be the most relevant

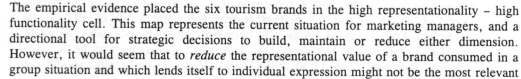

strategy. The representational success of a brand is harder for competitors to emulate than copying improvements to the functional benefits.

De Chernatony and McWilliam (1989, 1990) offered recommendations for marketing managers seeking to develop the representationality dimension of their brands, and these are summarised and developed below.

- Use of market research to monitor user profiles, including qualitative lifestyle research, to better inform tourism marketing decision-making. This should include aspirational reference group profiles, as well as actual users. Market research should also be used to understand the *profile* of the representational element of the brand and how it is used (for example, to develop self-concept, to express messages outwardly to others, to dissociate from others etc).

- Greater reliance in marketing research on branded, rather than blind, product tests.

- Reference group endorsement of the brand in integrated communications campaigns and brochures, either directly by testimonial, or by pictorial and image content.

- Communication to maintain the symbolic meaning to those in contact with brand users. Tourism marketers are comfortable with the importance of word of mouth communication, the value of frequent user programmes in developing relational exchange, and communicating emotional benefits to user segments. However, they may over-look the benefits of strongly promoting the brand's meaning to the reference groups used by their tourists, and to the 'audience' surrounding the product experience.

- Selective media vehicles to reinforce the brand meaning, or matching the message to the medium. This can be extended to printed literature, where brochure paper, colour, texture, thickness and so forth, should mirror the brand image. Distribution pipelines, strategic prices, and on-site physical evidence should also reflect the representational values of the brand.

- Training of intermediaries to strengthen their understanding and ability to communicate the representational profile of the brand. This should be extended to include the employees of the organisation, both front-line and support, and those of third party organisations actively involved in producing the experience. This is particularly important in tourism as a high-contact service, where staff impart brand values with each occurrence of tourist interaction.

Allowing for the exploratory nature of the research, and following the trend of different representationality scores for the six tourism brands, one might expect other 'household name' brands and other brands to show lower representationality scores if tested, probably situated within the low representationality – high functionality cell. Certain common industry practice and characteristics, such as late deal price discounting and high staff turnover, might impede the representational development of a brand and thwart management intentions.

Conclusion

The tourism brands tested exhibited high scores on both the representationality and functionality dimensions, although there was greater variety in the representational values. Given the intrinsic nature of the tourism product, it might be expected that brand strategy would involve either maintaining or building brand representationality; reducing this component appears to be the weaker choice. To develop the exploratory research further, brands might usefully be examined by tourism sub-sector, including destination brands, and by user groups. A study of the representational aspects of the brand profile, as opposed to score generation, could augment further research. An interesting question that integrated marketing with human resource management would be an investigation of whether tourism brands with high representationality scores demonstrated more employee understanding of, and pride in, the brand than tourism brands identified as having low representationality scores.

References

Clarke, J. (1992), A marketing spotlight on the youth 'four S's consumer', *Tourism Management*, 13 (3): pp.321-327.

De Chernatony, L. and McDonald, M. (1992), *Creating powerful brands*, Butterworth-Heinemann, London.

De Chernatony, L. and McWilliam, G. (1989), The strategic implications of clarifying how marketers interpret 'brands', *Journal of Marketing Management*, 5 (2): pp.153-171

De Chernatony, L. and McWilliam, G. (1990), Appreciating brands as assets through using a two-dimensional model, *International Journal of Advertising*, 9, pp.111-119.

Goodall, B. (1990), The dynamics of tourism place marketing, in Ashworth, G. and Goodall, B. (Editors), *Marketing tourism places*, Routledge, London, pp.259-279.

Holiday Which? (1999), Which tour operator?, *Holiday Which?*, winter edition, pp.80-83, The Consumers Association, London.

Kotler, P., Armstrong, G., Saunders, J. and Wong, V. (1996), *Principles of marketing. The European edition*, Prentice Hall, London.

Luhrman, D. (1998), World tourism. Crystal ball gazing, *Tourism, the Journal of the Tourism Society*, issue 96, pp.12-13.

McArdle, J. (1989), Product branding – the way forward, *Tourism Management*, 10 (3): p.201.

Middleton, V.T.C. (1994), *Marketing in travel and tourism*, 2nd edition, Butterworth-Heinemann, Oxford.

Palmer, A. (1999), *Principles of services marketing*, 2nd edition, McGraw Hill, London.

Rogers, D. (1998), Travel: sun, sea and brands, *Marketing*, 26th March, p.17.

Schiffman, L. G. and Kanuk, L. L. (2000), *Consumer behaviour*, 7th edition, Prentice-Hall International, New Jersey.

The National Trust (1998), *Annual report and accounts 1997/98*, The National Trust, London.

Travel Trade Gazette UK and Ireland (1999a), no.2350 Feb 17th, p.45.

Westwood, S., Morgan, N. J., Pritchard, A., and Ineson, E. (1999), Branding the package holiday – the role and significance of brands for UK air tour operators, *Journal of Vacation Marketing*, 5, (3), pp.238-252.

The Scottish Parliament and tourism

Gill Day

The Robert Gordon University, UK

L Rory MacLellan

University of Strathclyde, UK

Introduction

On July 1st 1999, Scotland had its own Parliament for the first time in 300 years. In an atmosphere of anticipation, the tourism industry waits to see the implications of this political change.

When no Minister was given sole responsibility for tourism, the initial industry reaction was anger, disappointment and fear that the new Parliament was not going to place enough importance on supporting an industry that generates £2.5 billion and 177,000 people are in tourism-related employment in Scotland alone (McLeish, 1999). However, it could be argued that responsibility for tourism being placed within the Ministry of Enterprise and Lifelong Learning displays greater importance being attached to this industry than in England where tourism remains in the, arguably, under funded Ministry of Culture, Media and Heritage.

As soon as Henry McLeish was assigned responsibility for tourism within his portfolio, the foundations for a tourism strategy were laid. Detailed consultation with industry members resulted in around 650 responses from both individuals and organisations, with an additional 100 views gathered from focus groups. This is clearly a good basis for development of an appropriate strategy.

In many ways we have come a long way since Labour came to power in May 1997 and set in motion the constitutional reform process which created the Scottish Parliament. However as it has been operating for under two years it may be premature to judge progress made to date, in particular on the subject of tourism, which was not immediately at the top of the political agenda.

This paper sets out to look specifically at two things: first structural changes and shifts in policy direction in tourism; secondly, the direct impact of the Scottish Parliament on visitor numbers and the image of Scotland within the UK and overseas. In order to do this we must first set the background context for tourism in Scotland and in particular review the situation immediately prior to the Scottish Parliament. This includes:

- a review of the tourism industry, support mechanisms, policies and politics;

- the background to, core aims and structure of The Scottish Parliament;

- analysis of direct impacts of the Scottish Parliament on visitors to and the image of Scotland;

- the position of tourism reflected in debates in the Scottish Parliament to date;

- a commentary on The New Strategy for Scottish Tourism (Feb 2000).

Finally, this paper draws conclusions on tourism and the Scottish Parliament and attempts to answer the question: what's new?

Scottish tourism prior to Scottish Parliament

Scottish tourism changed significantly in the last quarter of the twentieth century, in terms of product offering and visitor markets. Whilst trips to Scotland by overseas visitors increased from 620,000 in 1970 to over two million in 1998, trips by UK visitors declined over the same period from 12.3 million in 1970 to 9.8 million in 1998. The domestic market reflects the virtual disappearance of the main holiday market but this has been partially compensated for by the rise in short breaks.

In terms of product, there have been significant shifts in the volume and quality of accommodation stock, with the number of hotels increasing from just over 2,000 in 1970 to 2,500 in 1998. An indication of the upgrading of facilities is shown in the number of hotel bedrooms with en-suite facilities, up from 35% in 1970 to 87% in 1998. The changes in the visitor attraction sector have been almost as dramatic with substantial increases in the number and range over the same period and vast improvements in the quality of visitor facilities and interpretation. Employment in tourism related industries is estimated to have increased from 112,000 in 1970 to 177,000 in 1998.

Therefore the recent history of Scotland's tourism industry has been one of almost steady progress and improvement, with some inconsistent periods in the late 1980s and more recently in the late 1990s. These improvements may be attributed to a variety of factors from the public sector support systems to innovations of individual businesses. A review of the tourism industry in Scotland by Barrie (1999) lists some of the key factors contributing to the improvements in the 1990s as: the renaissance of Glasgow; investment of £120 million in Edinburgh and Glasgow airports; major improvement in the standards of accommodation and cuisine throughout Scotland.

However much the situation has improved; several intractable factors remain as impediments to growth and prosperity through tourism, on a scale witnessed in other countries. The mediocre performance in recent times has been blamed on problems with seasonality; lack of direct air access; service attitudes; price (due to the strength of sterling) and the ineffectiveness of the public agencies, in particular the Scottish Tourist Board. It is worth describing the public sector support mechanisms prior to the Scottish Parliament as it is here that changes in policy would have their most immediate effect.

It might be assumed that the advent of the Scottish Parliament would herald a greater degree of devolution in policy making for tourism, however, by the late 1990s, most power, at government agency level, had already moved north from Westminster, at least as far as Edinburgh and Glasgow. Although some responsibility for tourism promotion of Scotland remains with the British Tourist Authority (as set out in the 1969 Development of Tourism Act) this is a pragmatic arrangement that suited the Scottish Tourist Board. In almost every other respect, the public agencies involved in tourism in Scotland took orders from the Scottish Office in Edinburgh and their head offices were located in Edinburgh, Glasgow or Inverness.

The organisational framework relating to tourism had evolved gradually from the establishment of the first public bodies set up in the late 1960s and early 1970s through a series of policy shifts and administrative restructuring. Although underlying policy objectives for providing government support for tourism broadly reflected Westminster thinking, (from balance of payments priorities, to regional development to employment creation) the structures for implementing these policies evolved to suit the unique political and economic environment of Scotland (for a full discussion of this evolution see Smith, 1998).

By the 1990s the core responsibility for tourism rested with the national tourism organisation, the Scottish Tourist Board, and the economic development agencies, Scottish Enterprise and Highlands and Islands Enterprise, although other important organisations had achieved a greater level of input to tourism policy making (for example: Scottish Natural Heritage, Historic Scotland, Scottish Sports Council, Scottish Museums Council, Convention of Scottish Local Authorities). Tensions still existed regarding the division of responsibility for promoting tourism, although these had been largely resolved through measures taken at national and local levels. The Scottish Tourist Board gained the right to market itself overseas in 1993 in conjunction with the British Tourist Authority. At local level, the rationalisation in 1996 of the Area Tourist Board network, from an unwieldy 32 to a more manageable 14, led to more cohesive and marketable tourist destinations.

Tensions between the Scottish Enterprise Network and the Scottish Tourist Board lay in their overlapping responsibility for supporting the development of tourism businesses and tourism infrastructure. The Scottish Tourist Board were viewed as the lead agency however the Scottish Enterprise Network had the budget to make a difference. The duplication and inefficiencies were real enough however the establishment in 1992 of the Scottish Tourism Co-ordinating Group by the Scottish Office, to oversee tourism policy implementation, went some way to resolve these.

An important achievement of the Scottish Tourism Co-ordinating Group was the development of the Strategic Plan for Scottish Tourism in 1994 which was expected to bring a more integrated approach to tourism support activities of the public agencies (Smith, 1998). In addition to setting measurable targets for the tourism industry up to the year 2000, the plan initiated a more holistic approach to implementing the strategy through the establishment of working groups involving the key players in tourism from both the public and private sector. At local level this involved the Local Enterprise Companies, Area Tourist Boards, local authorities and others, depending on local circumstances. This broadening of involvement, promoted as fostering the spirit of partnership and holistic decision making, achieved a level of success in bringing the key organisations into the fold.

The process of integration takes time, in particular where it is voluntary and several issues remained unresolved by the late 1990s. At national level the organisational separation of responsibility for marketing Scotland (STB) and product development and training for tourism (Scottish Enterprise/Highlands and Islands Enterprise) strained partnership relations. At local level many of the Area Tourist Boards were in crisis over lack of funding. If funding for the Area Tourist Boards is not stabilised, having been falling for a number of years (Aberdeen and Grampian Tourist Board, 1999), their effectiveness as promoters of the areas they represent is likely to diminish with their budgets (Gallagher, 2000).

Many remained unconvinced by the compromises inherent in the 1994 Plan and a downturn in tourism in some parts of Scotland in the late 1990s led to the inevitable industry criticism of public support, directed in particular at the most high profile agency, the Scottish Tourist Board. As this brings us to the period of the Scottish Parliament, it is important to point out that responsibility for addressing the problems of Scottish tourism was largely in the hands of Scottish agencies. Attempting to find unique Scottish tourism solutions to the unique Scottish problems is not new. Will the Scottish Parliament make the critical difference or have the policies initiated in 1994 simply not had time to bed down?

The Scottish Parliament

The establishment of the Scottish Parliament in 1999 followed a lengthy period of debate on constitutional change in Scotland and a whirlwind period of action after the Labour election victory. Some of the milestones were: the Scottish Convention Scheme 1995; Local Government reform 1995/96; Labour victory May 1997; the Scottish Office White Paper July 97; the Referendum Sept 1997; the passing of the Scotland Act 1998; the establishment of the Scottish Parliament July 1999.

Fairley (1999) identifies some key factors in the administrative framework in Scotland prior to the establishment of the Scottish Parliament. Scotland was described as 'one of the most centrally controlled (Scottish Office) polities in Europe' (Fairley, 1999: 17). There was a requirement to redistribute powers in the hands of government agencies by recentralising policy expertise from the quangos to the Scottish Parliament committees. In addition, constitutional change was needed to devolve powers from Edinburgh down to local authorities, placing more policy making in local hands rather than agencies such as the Local Enterprise Companies.

The broad political objectives for devolution and the establishment of the Scottish Parliament were twofold. First to create a new style of politics based on consensus, more representative of Scottish public opinion, more consensual in decision making (exemplified by the first government being a coalition). Secondly, to enhance subsidiarity, devolution and decentralisation within Scotland. Power should flow from Westminster to the Scottish

Parliament, then to local authorities, then to local communities. Again this suggests a reduced role for the quangos and an enhanced role for local authorities.

The structures within the Scottish Parliament, in keeping with the above objectives, are very different from Westminster. The system is based on a Scottish Executive of eleven Ministers, eleven Junior Ministers, six Departments and sixteen Committees. The committee system is intended as a device for holding the Executive to account, building policy expertise and overseeing procedures in parliament. The place of tourism in this structure provides some insight into how policy making for tourism may be directed. Rather than have a separate Department or Committee, with a separate Minister for Tourism (as called for in some quarters, in particular the Scottish National Party) responsibility for tourism is placed within an already packed portfolio in the Department of Enterprise and Lifelong Learning (ELL).

The Minister for ELL, Henry McLeish, has responsibility for many important devolved areas relating to education, training and the economy, such as Further and Higher Education, Lifelong Learning, the 'New Deal', Business and Industry, and Trade and Inward Investment. Direct responsibility for tourism lies with the Deputy Minister, Alasdair Morrison, where he combines tourism policy expertise with responsibility for Highlands and Islands Enterprise (HIE), the University of the Highlands and Islands (UHI) and Gaelic. At committee level, tourism related matters are spread across a range of headings such as Education, Culture and Sport, Local Government, Rural Affairs, Transport and Environment and of course, its official location, Enterprise and Life-long Learning. The effectiveness of policy making in tourism remains to be seen.

Although there are obvious tourism synergies with departmental areas such as training and business development, the northern peripheral focus (HIE, UHI, Gaelic), at junior ministerial level, may concern the tourism sector in the rest of Scotland. Perhaps the greatest concern is fragmentation at committee level, where tourism related policy areas are spread across a range of committees with arguably more relevant matters, such as transport, considered remote from tourism. It seems inevitable that the current system will lead to fragmented consideration of what should be integrated policy areas.

Cross committee communication is one answer to these concerns however the situation of tourism within the administrative structure remains illogical and confusing and is unlikely to lead to a concentration of policy expertise. A separate Minister for tourism may not be necessary; however, the problem of dispersed decision making in tourism is likely to be exacerbated by its position in Scottish Parliament. Rather than a strong, unified voice for tourism emanating from the Scottish Parliament we may see contradictory policy making where, for example, transport policy acts as a barrier to visitors to rural areas, rural policies focus on traditional primary industrial sectors, whilst tourism policies attempt to spread benefits into peripheral locations (MacLellan 1999).

Inclusion of tourism matters in debates in the Scottish Parliament, before the publication of the New Strategy for Scottish Tourism February 2000, broadly reflect concerns of industry documented as part of the consultation exercise in 1999: the funding of ATBs; high cost of fuel; Scotland too expensive (taxation and strong pound); lack of direct links (air and sea) to Scotland; opportunities of e-commerce. These concerns are elaborated on more fully later in this paper. However the subjects raised also give an insight into opposition party views on tourism. Views expressed by opposition parties on support mechanisms for tourism range from moderate calls (conservative) to streamline structures, gain independence from the BTA, fund ATBs direct from the STB, to more radical changes (SNP) such as having one separate Minister for Tourism (presumably with a separate department as in Eire) and taking powers from the STB (abolition) and passing them to the Scottish Enterprise Network (Kerr and Wood 1999).

Direct impacts of the Scottish Parliament

A survey commissioned by the Scottish Executive estimated that over 100,000 bed nights and 200,000 day visits (McLeish, 1999) per year will be the benefits brought to the Scottish tourism industry as a result of devolution. This would give an estimated revenue of £8.5 million with an associated creation of over 300 jobs.

Indeed, the then Secretary of State, now First Minister, Donald Dewar identified the potential benefits of devolution for Scotland's tourism industry in 1997, saying that "the international publicity and higher public profile that devolution will provide for Scotland can be capitalised on and used to help us create or reinforce favourable images of Scottish products and of Scotland as a desirable place to invest" (Griggs, 1999). The new vision that the Scottish Executive has for Scottish Tourism is that of a modern, high quality industry in touch with its customers, which has "embraced the culture of lifelong learning" (Scottish Executive, 2000).

By changing the nature of the industry and the image promoted of it, it is hoped that the image perceived of Scotland by potential visitors will change accordingly, making Scotland an attractive visitor destination. Whilst destination selection is a complicated decision-making process which differs between individuals and amongst individuals themselves over time, one factor which is inter-related to all other factors throughout this decision-making process, suggesting that it is potentially the most significant factor in destination selection, is image (Day, 1999). Therefore, if the image perceived of Scotland by potential visitors' changes in line with the Scottish Executive's vision for the industry, they will be more likely to visit.

In addition to any direct efforts made by the Scottish Executive to change Scotland's tourism industry, there are perhaps two ways that Scotland can increase its tourism potential simply as a result of the devolution process. The first is through an increase in national pride. This may be felt at two levels, that of Scots living in Scotland and that of Scots abroad.

Although Scotland now has a devolved parliament, this does not mean that it is an independent country, with the British Government retaining control of many aspects of Scottish Life. However, Scotland, or the Far North as it is sometimes referred to by the English Press, can now differentiate itself from England and be allowed to relish its own cultural history rather than being part of British history. Recent films, such as Braveheart and Rob Roy, have also helped to nurture this national pride. An increase in national pride may well result in more Scots taking holidays within Scotland. A recent attitudinal survey in Scotland backs this up: 'The Scottish parliamentary Election Survey also found that there had been a significant rise in feelings of Scottishness and a decline in the attachment to a British identity' (Horsburgh, 2000). The most likely destination to suffer as a result of this is

England and the rest of the United Kingdom, since Scotland is in closer competition domestically than with overseas destinations.

There are a high number of Scots living abroad, who often have an even greater sense of national pride than Scots living at home. This is reflected in the higher number of Scottish clubs, such as Burns Clubs, where more exist outside Scotland than inside the nation's geographical boundaries (Butler, 1998). However, Griggs (1999) suggested that the bond with the mother nation is not as strong for Scots as it is for say, the Irish or the Israelis. Devolution may provide a further incentive for Scots living abroad to actively engage in learning about the contemporary side of Scotland.

The 'tartan army' is also an ambassador for Scotland, following the nation's football team abroad. Instantly recognisable with their kilts and painted faces, these sports fans have done much to raise the profile of Scotland, even when the teams themselves have failed to do so.

The second way that tourism potential can be increased for Scotland is through the use of devolution as an external promotional tool. For Scots travelling abroad, the frustration of having to explain to people from other countries that Scotland is not in fact another name for England, may hopefully become a less common phenomenon. The confusion may arise from the number of different names that can be used to describe these areas, Scotland or England, The United Kingdom or Great Britain. On the other hand, the Scottish Tourist Board, in their SWOT analysis of Scotland (Scottish Tourist Board, 1999), describe Scotland's distinctive history, heritage and culture as one of the key strengths of the country, suggesting that Scotland is indeed distinct from England, Wales or Ireland.

Having a higher degree of political autonomy may influence the potential visitor's awareness of Scotland, and therefore may affect their decision to visit. The Scottish Tourist Board is certainly hoping to increase the number of visitors to Scotland through raising awareness. They have already circulated a video news release to 126 TV stations around the world in association with the opening of the new Scottish Parliament, giving a potential audience of over 240 million people. Time will tell if this investment was sound, but since much of Ireland's tourism industry success in recent years has been credited to its government policies and associated press coverage (Lennon and Seaton, 1998), then using such a unique event to promote Scotland can only be to the industry's advantage.

It is hoped that 'Scotland the brand' will also help to raise awareness and promote a quality image of both Scottish products and the country itself. However, the logo that has been selected has been heavily criticised as not really promoting an image at all (Wark, 2000).

To maximise the effectiveness of 'Scotland the Brand', emphasis needs to be placed on different aspects of Scotland's brand image to portray Scotland as an attractive destination to each of its visitor markets. Concentrating on the key markets for Scotland of North America, Germany and France, necessary differences in promotional emphasis can be identified. Focus groups with a cross-section of the North American market revealed that the most motivating images for them encapsulated Scotland's strengths of beauty, history and accessibility of culture; exhibited the potential for a learning experience; implied that civilisation was within reach; generated a slightly mystical feel and contained a human aspect (Scottish Tourist Board, 1998).

Whilst the Germans also considered Scotland's culture to be a key attraction, they were more interested in the solitude that could be found in the great outdoors than the necessity of civilisation nearby. The French are most keen on the mystical aspect of Scotland, perceiving the country as the home of legends, mystery and ghosts. They also value the traditional tartan, as it is considered to be a symbol of heritage, quality and style.

Marketing to potential overseas visitors will continue to be undertaken by the Scottish Tourist Board in conjunction with the British Tourist Authority. However, the expansion of electronic communication between businesses has increased the role played by industry members in the promotion of Scotland as a visitor destination. Co-operation between the public and private sector will therefore maximise the benefits from such developments.

The future promotion of Scotland and its regions may change in the future with the role of the Scottish Tourist Board and Area Tourist Boards currently being reviewed. Therefore, it seems a pertinent time to decide whether the Scottish Tourist Board should be solely responsible for promoting Scotland. Indeed, if the same image is perceived of every area of Scotland, and therefore the image perceived of an area can not be separated from that of Scotland, as research suggests (Finlay, 1998), then this branding may be sufficient. A more appropriate form of branding may be a tiered option. Here, whilst one image is promoted of Scotland, part of that image could be promoted as a sub-brand for an area. This would allow differentiation between areas whilst a unified image was promoted of Scotland.

Industry expectations of the new strategy for Scottish tourism

There are a number of issues facing Scotland's tourism industry today, including reduced visitor numbers due to the strength of the pound, poor weather and increased competition from emerging markets. To address these issues, the consultation process identified the key concerns of industry.

Understand the markets

Existing markets need to be better understood, niches identified and the needs of potential visitors clarified. The provision of more immediate market information would assist the industry to plan their own marketing activities and react quickly to marketing trends.

Effective use of new technology

The time is right for the industry to take advantage of the advent of the Internet and the development of Ossian, the Scottish Tourist Board's on-line booking system, due to be fully operational by June 2000. It is not inconceivable that paper based brochures will become obsolete within a few years, with potential visitors downloading relevant pages from the Internet and booking on-line with increasing frequency. Therefore, if the opportunity is not seized now to use the technology to Scotland's tourism industry's advantage, then it will miss out to other destinations.

Partnerships to raise profile of tourism

Through greater cohesion, a higher degree of confidence and more consistency, the industry hopes to raise the profile of the industry. This would help to attract high quality recruits to the industry.

Improve quality

Standards of quality and service could and should be improved further to ensure that visitors experience the quality that they expect from a destination.

Adequate support for the tourism industry

Although additional public funding would be beneficial, existing resources need to be used more effectively for the industry to realise its potential.

Tackle regionality and seasonality

Whilst the Scottish Tourist Board aims to promote equitable regional spread (Scottish Tourist Board, 1999), the Central Belt of Scotland remains the focus of most promotional campaigns. With visitor numbers skewed heavily in this way (Scottish Executive, 2000) this can be justified from a purely economic viewpoint. However, for those outside this area, this could be considered unacceptable with one in six people in Scotland's rural workforce are in tourism-related employment, compared to one in twelve in Scotland's overall workforce (MacLellan, 1999).

Seasonality continues to be an issue, although promotional campaigns, such as Autumn Gold, have served to increase visitor numbers in the shoulder months. More needs to be done to extend the season to ensure to both increase revenue for the industry and to retain staff throughout the year, making training worthwhile, and therefore raising the quality of the tourism product.

Make Scotland accessible

The development of a direct sea link with Europe is now a strong possibility for the very near future. With 80% of Continental visitors currently arriving in their own cars (Rutherford, 1999), the number of nights these visitors stay in Scotland could be increased by reducing the need for them to travel through England. The site is likely to be Rosyth, chosen because of the shelter it can provide from the wind and sea (McLaughlin, 1999).

The formation of such a link is dependent upon establishing sufficient freight trade to make direct ferry routes to Scotland viable, since visitors alone would not generate enough revenue to make this is a profitable option for the ferry companies. The benefit to rural areas is likely to be linked to how far visitors are then willing to travel from Rosyth and influenced by the promotional activities that are directed at this new market of visitors. However, for Rosyth itself, the benefits would include the building of a terminal and portside facilities, as well as the potential for visitors to stay to explore the surrounding area.

Air access has improved in the Central Belt with Glasgow now a major international airport with 6.7 million passengers in 1998, a 15% improvement on the previous year and Edinburgh a key player in European flights, seeing a 31% growth in 1998 (McMahon, 1999). Although neither airport will become a transfer hub, the continued expansion of scheduled flights gives visitors greater flexibility in their travel arrangements, rendering Scotland a more attractive destination. However, outside the Central Belt airports are not enjoying such fortunes.

In Aberdeen, where the number of passengers flying to or from the airport is inextricably linked to the state of the oil industry, this past year has seen the frequency of flights to many destinations cut and a number of routes stopped altogether. Inverness has also suffered with routes being reduced and has been under the threat of closure for some time. Unfortunately, until business passengers increase in number to these and other regional airports, an increase in scheduled flights or a decrease in fares seems unlikely. This reinforces the perception of areas outside the Central Belt being inaccessible and expensive to get to.

The privatisation of the rail service within the United Kingdom has not enhanced access for visitors. Now faced with different timetables available only from each specific company, the traveller is faced with a reduced service in many rural areas. Government subsidies were withdrawn with privatisation, consequently the frequency of many services has been reduced. The demise of a service as the result of the withdrawal of a subsidy can be exemplified by the failure of Motorail as a privatised company. The cost of taking a car on the train has become prohibitive. With the high number of visitors travelling to Scotland with their own car, this is another access issue that affects particularly those outside the Central Belt where the service has been cut. The Scottish Executive would do well to identify a co-ordination policy for the rail services within Scotland, and consider the further subsidy of some of the routes in outlying areas.

When visitors do visit the rural areas using a car as their mode of transportation, they are faced with higher fuel prices. This is an issue that has been debated extensively by the Scottish Executive. However, at present there remains a significant differential between some areas. If the Scottish Tourist Board can indeed "influence customer choice when car touring" (Scottish Tourist Board, 1999) through their promotional activities, then reducing any disparity in costs between areas in Scotland, provides rural areas with a greater opportunity to attract visitors.

As well as the cost of petrol, availability is also important to visitors. The Rural Petrol Stations Grant Scheme, part of a £4.5 million Rural Transport Funding Package, was set up by the government in 1998 (Scottish Executive, 2000) to maintain the number of rural petrol stations. The eligibility criteria have recently been revised to increase the number of petrol stations eligible for grant funding. Whilst visitor satisfaction will be affected by the number of petrol stations they encounter, the perception of the potential visitor is similarly important. The perception of a visit to rural areas necessitating time spent looking for petrol may send visitors elsewhere. The prioritisation of access to and within Scotland by the Scottish Executive may begin to allay these fears.

The new strategy for Scottish tourism (Feb 2000)

The new strategy, launched on 15th February 2000, has been broadly welcomed, as it seems to address the key concerns of industry. The comprehensive consultation process and speed with which it has been pulled together indicates that the Scottish Executive recognises the urgency of the situation and seems to have moved tourism up the political agenda. The review of the tourism sector performance in the report is informative and comprehensive and identifies some serious concerns but presents an overall picture of an industry that is 'not in crisis' (McLeish, 2000). The core vision for Scottish tourism in the strategy is of a modern tourist industry, a skilled, enterprising industry with a high quality of service for visitors.

The strategy has a long list of 'action areas', with measurable targets and ambitious time frames. The list of indicators and targets presented at the end of the strategy include eleven specific 'industry indicators' and twenty two broader (less specific) 'activity indicators'. Incidentally, the only mention of sustainability in the strategy, conspicuously absent from the vision for Scottish tourism, is here, almost as an afterthought, where 'other social and environmental sustainability indicators' come under the heading 'New research required' (Scottish Executive, 2000: 44).

There is evidence of innovative thinking although many of the headline 'action areas' are repackaging of old initiatives (e.g. Ossian) or restatement of existing policies. For example, specific niche marketing to core overseas markets (USA, Germany and France), part of the STB marketing plan for several years.

On the international marketing of Scotland linking overseas offices of government agencies, the BTA, Locate In Scotland and Scottish Trade International, is a pragmatic solution that should create synergies in promoting all Scottish products. The new promotional campaigns (STB and ATBs), focusing on the niche markets of golf, culture and genealogy create media headlines but there is little market research to support their efficacy. On the other hand the strategy includes several initiatives which give substantial additional funding for tourism, £11 million in total. Five million is allocated to developing e-commerce initiatives, niche marketing initiatives and doubling the number of tourism quality advisers. A further six million is targeted at boosting skills development in tourism: creation of a new body ('Tourism Skills'?) by April 2000-02-24; 1,000 apprenticeships by 2003; 5,000 individual learning accounts by 2002; centres of excellence in tourism and mentoring schemes for industry.

Like many aspects of the strategy, details on implementation of these initiatives are missing. This is hardly surprising as key decisions on the restructuring of support mechanisms await the review of the Local Enterprise Companies network due for completion in May 2000. This review is potentially more important for tourism policy making than the high profile strategy. There are hints in the strategy of a greater role in tourism for Scottish Enterprise national: 'SEn will work with STB, HIE and the private sector to apply the "cluster" methodology to tourism' (Scottish Executive, 2000: 37). The enterprise networks are to '...provide the best possible support for industry and provide the required leadership at national and local level' (Scottish Executive, 2000: 39). Other parts of the strategy hint at an increased involvement of the Scottish Executive and presumably a lower profile role for the STB. For example, the STCG is to be replaced by a new Scottish Parliament Group, chaired by the Minister for ELL, to monitor the implementation of the strategy. The group will have a narrower representation than STCG, reduced to the core tourism and economic development agencies, which is a surprising move for a government committed to widening partnerships.

In addition to a lack of detail on structural changes, the strategy is lacking in commentary on some issues identified by industry as critical. The only response to access and transport issues seems to be the announcement of a national train timetable, which has been expected for some time now. There is no mention of issues such as petrol pricing, taxation or making industry more sustainable. Perhaps these issues are missing from the tourism strategy, as they lie within the domain of other departments in the Scottish Parliament. If this is the case it is hoped that tourism concerns will be adequately represented on the relevant policy making committees.

Conclusions: What's new?

On the surface it seems that there has been a great deal of activity in tourism policy making in the last two years. Devolution seems to hold some advantages for Scotland's tourism industry, with the potential for increased visitor numbers resulting from: the perception of Scotland as a visitor destination, rather than an appendage of England; increased national pride, and development of the Scottish Parliament building itself. However in terms of devolved powers affecting tourism policy making, little has changed. Most changes seem to relate to a redistribution of responsibilities within Scottish public bodies rather than from Westminster to Edinburgh.

The Scottish Executive has shown a keen interest in the future of Scottish tourism through an industry-wide consultation process resulting in development of an industry strategy. However, the recent document (Scottish Executive, 2000) contains nothing extraordinary and it may result simply in minor changes, which do not fundamentally alter the industry or public support mechanisms. One suspects that much of the long term changes affecting tourism policy making may come from outside the department of Enterprise and Life-long Learning, and relate more to underlying objectives of devolving powers from quangos to Scottish Parliament committees and from the centre to local communities.

The extent to which potential visitors will be affected by initiatives in the new tourism strategy, or indeed the higher degree of political autonomy that Scotland now enjoys, remains to be seen.

References

Aberdeen and Grampian Tourist Board (1999), 'Business Plan', Aberdeen.

Barrie, N. (1999), 'Scotland Country Report', Travel and Tourism Analyst, (1): 43-65.

Butler, R. (1998), 'Tartan Mythology, The Traditional Tourist Image of Scotland' in Ringer, G. (Ed.), *Cultural Landscapes of Tourism,* Routledge, London.

Day, G. (1999), 'Trainspotting: data collection from a captive audience', *Tourism Management*, 20, pp. 153-155.

Fairley, J. (1999), 'Scotland's New Democracy - New Opportunities for Rural Scotland?' paper presented at the conference: 'The Scottish Parliament and Rural Policy: What Room for Manoeuvre?' University of Aberdeen, Department of Agriculture, 3rd November, 1999.

Finlay, G. (1998), The Role of Image in the Promotion of a Region as a Visitor Destination, PhD Thesis, The Robert Gordon University, Aberdeen.*

Gallagher, P. (2000), 'Direct Funding Urged for Area Tourist Board, Plea to Remove Local Councils of Burden', Press and Journal, Page 9, Friday 18th February.

Griggs, R. (1999), 'Seeing Scotland in a New Light', The Tourism Society, Stirling.

Horsburgh, F. (2000), 'Research shows rise in feelings of Scottishness' Herald, page 6, Saturday, 26th February.

Kerr, W. and Wood, R. C. (1999), 'Scottish Tourism after devolution?' The Hospitality Review, April: 16-23.

Lennon, J. J. and Seaton, A. V. (1998), 'Pathways to Success: Contrasting Roles in Public Sector Business Development for the Tourism Industry - A Comparison of Glasgow and Dublin', *International Journal of Public Sector Management*, Vol. 11, No 213, pp. 139-153.

McLaughlin, M. (1999), Scottish Enterprise Transport, 'Opportunities for a New Ferry Service Between Scotland and the European Continent', Scottish Tourist Board's Industry Conference, Glasgow.

McLeish, H. (1999), Minister for Enterprise and Lifelong Learning, 'Minister's Address', Scottish Tourist Board's Industry Conference, Glasgow.

McLeish, H. (2000), Speech at the launch of the New Strategy for Scottish Tourism, 15th February.

MacLellan, L. R. (1999), 'The Scottish Parliament and Rural Policy: where tourism fits in?' paper presented at the conference: 'The Scottish Parliament and Rural Policy: What Room for Manoeuvre?' University of Aberdeen, Department of Agriculture, 3rd November 1999.

McMahon, I. (1999), Scottish Airports Ltd., (BAA Plc), 'Getting Here - The Transport Challenge', Scottish Tourist Board's Industry Conference, Glasgow.

Rutherford, K. (1999), Scottish Tourist Board, 'Getting Here - The Transport Challenge', Scottish Tourist Board's Industry Conference, Glasgow.

Scottish Executive, (2000), 'A New Strategy for Scottish Tourism', The Stationary Office, Edinburgh.

Scottish Tourist Board, (1998), 'Motivational Research Study of Visitors from the U.S.A.', Edinburgh.

Scottish Tourist Board, (1999), 'International Marketing Plan', Edinburgh.

Smith, R. (1998), 'Public policy for tourism in Scotland' in MacLellan, L R and Smith, R (eds.) Tourism in Scotland, International Thomson Business Press, London.

Wark, K. (2000), 'Good Morning Scotland', Thursday 27th January, Radio Scotland.

N. B. The author Day, G., was nee Finlay, G.

Air transportation and international tourism: The regulatory and infrastructural constraints of aviation bilaterals and airport landing slots

Keith Debbage

University of North Carolina at Greensboro, USA

The purpose of this paper is to investigate how both the regulatory environment of the international air transport industry and airport-based infrastructural constraints can influence tourist flows, especially between the major gateways of the international tourist system in the North Atlantic market (e.g. London, New York). Particular attention will be paid to the historical evolution of the regulatory framework for international airlines beginning with the restrictive environment of the bilateral approach through the US 'Open Skies' policy to the EU-based liberalisation initiatives of the 1990's and the proposed Transatlantic Common Aviation Area. The role of government policy in shaping and regulating the development of the US-UK market will be examined in detail, and the implications for the tourist product will be discussed.

This paper also argues that the fundamental links between international airport operations and the tourist product have been overlooked in the literature, particularly in terms of the way airport-based infrastructural constraints can profoundly influence the underlying structure of origin-destination tourist flows at the international scale. Particular attention will paid to how the lack of sufficient take-off and landing slots at major international airports can shape and constrain the interaction of tourist demand and supply. The paper concludes by examining the regulatory and infrastructural constraints that have recently impeded the competitive strategies of British Airways in the US-UK market - one of the most important international tourist markets in the world.

Tourism and transportation

The critical role that transportation plays in shaping the tourist product is widely acknowledged in the literature (Britton 1991; Butler 1980; Debbage 1990, 1997; Ioannides and Debbage 1998; Page 1999; Pearce 1995; Prideaux 2000; Vellas and Becherel 1995). Transport is widely viewed as the key element that matches tourist demand (origin) with tourist supply (destination areas). Consequently, much of the tourist transport literature has conceptualised the relationship between tourism and transport in terms of accessibility (Gunn 1994; Inskeep 1991; Lundgren 1982; Miossec 1976). Others have examined the important role that transportation innovations (e.g. the railway, the jet engine, and the automobile) have played in influencing the historical evolution of mass tourism (Gilbert 1939; Holloway 1989; Mill 1992; Prideaux 1993; Robinson 1976).

However, a more thorough understanding of the tourist transport function is critical because the cost of transport is frequently a substantial portion of total travel costs. Additionally, the transport element of a tourist-related trip begins to assume a greater role in influencing destination choice as the distance travelled increases (Martin and Witt 1988, Prideaux 2000). For the individual travelling by air across the North Atlantic, the geography of air fares and airline route networks can significantly impact the overall health of some national tourism markets.

Tourism and air transportation

Some researchers have begun to focus on the central role that air transport has played in the distribution of international tourist arrivals (Hanlon 1995, Raguraman 1995, Vellas and Becheral 1995, Wheatcroft 1994). The development of competitive air fares, the advent of airline deregulation, and the production of wide-bodied jet aircraft have all helped to facilitate the rapid growth of mass intercontinental travel. For example, in 1996, 600 million tourists had visited another country, up from 93 million in 1963 (World Tourism Organization 1997). By some estimates, between 30 and 40 percent of all these international tourist arrivals travelled by air (Mann and Mantel 1992, Page 1999, Vellas and Becheral 1995). Furthermore, in some island destinations (e.g. the Caribbean and the Pacific) the reliance on air transportation is even more acute. It is not uncommon for some destinations to receive over 90 percent of all tourist arrivals by air (e.g. the Bahamas, Bermuda, Fiji). Even in larger and more diversified markets, air transport can play a key role in shaping the development of the tourist product. Prideaux (2000) found that the recent development of the Australian resort city of Cairns was highly correlated to the opening of the Cairns International Airport in 1985. By 1995/6, air travel accounted for 55.5 percent of all travel to Cairns. Table 1 provides a listing of countries hosting more than one million tourists in 1990 where 70 percent or more of all tourists arrived by air (Wheatcroft 1994).

Although the importance of the air transport - tourism interface has been fully acknowledged in the literature, what is less well understood is the manner in which government aviation policy and specific airport-based infrastructural constraints can directly impinge on the supply of tourist transport services. The deregulation of domestic aviation markets in the United States, the creation of 'open skies' continental blocs in the European Union, and the gradual liberalisation of international air transport have all allowed airlines to radically re-configure route networks and thus, dramatically re-shape tourist accessibility levels across the world (Button, Haynes, and Stough 1998, Caves 1997, Debbage 1993, 1994, Doganis 1991, Findlay 1996, Gourdin 1998, Graham 1998, Kasper 1988, de Murias 1989, Oum 1996). Both Wheatcroft (1994) and Raguraman (1995) persuasively argue that more liberal aviation policies will trigger additional tourism growth, but most of the transportation studies literature only indirectly discuss the movement of tourists even though we have seen an explosion of new transportation-related journals in recent years (e.g. the *Journal of Air Transport Management, Journal of Transport Geography, Transportation Research F*).

Table 1   National Tourism Markets and Air Traffic Share (%)

Country	Air Share of International Tourist Arrivals (%)
Australia	99
Bahamas	99
Cyprus	85
Egypt	71
Greece	71
Hong Kong	82
India	83
Indonesia	70
Israel	88
Japan	99
Korea	74
Mexico	70
New Zealand	99
Philippines	99
Singapore	90
Taiwan	99
Thailand	82

Source: Wheatcroft, 1994.

Note: All countries listed hosted more than one million international tourist arrivals in 1990 with 70 percent or more arriving by air.

A better understanding of how government policy and airport capacity issues can constrain tourism is essential given the recent comments of James Goodwin (chief executive of United Airlines). According to Goodwin (*New York Times*, 1999), global aviation is at a crisis point because there is simply not enough runway space, terminals or parking space to accommodate the one billion passengers projected to fly on US airlines by 2012. In Europe, the runway capacity problem may be even more acute. According to Butler and Keller (1994, p.372), "market entry in Europe will necessarily be curtailed by airport capacity constraints and airspace congestion". For tourism policy-makers, these findings are critical because the US-Europe market accounts for approximately 25 percent of all international tourist arrivals worldwide and is the busiest international market in the world.

Although the literature at this interface is scant, both Hobson and Uysal (1992) and Page (1999) are exceptions to the rule. Hobson and Uysal (1992) argued that the inability of tourist transport infrastructure to keep pace with the growth of the tourist product will mean that congestion and infrastructural constraints will be the biggest limitation facing tourism planners in the new millennium. Page (1999, p.217) echoed these sentiments in his analysis of the interaction of supply and demand for tourist travel, when he suggested that "airports are probably the most complex environments and systems in which this interaction occurs and yet they often remain poorly understood in a tourism context". It is part of the agenda of this paper to heed these calls by further investigating the complexities of the tourist transport infrastructure system by analysing how government policy and aviation bilateral agreements influenced air travel and international tourism during the post-world war two era. This will be followed by a discussion of the way in which airport capacity constraints in the US-UK market have contoured tourist demand.

Government aviation policy during the Post-World War Two era

The 1944 Chicago conference

As World War Two drew to a close, world leaders began to focus on establishing an institutional framework capable of nurturing international trade and commerce. To that end, the groundwork was laid for the establishment of the United Nations, the Bretton Woods Agreement, the International Monetary Fund, and the World Bank. In addition, there was a clear understanding that the fledgling aviation industry was directly linked to the facilitation of international trade and tourism. Consequently, pressure emerged to establish a coherent legal framework for the emerging international airline industry (Butler and Keller 1994; Doganis 1994; Kasper 1988; de Murias 1989).

In 1944, the Chicago Conference on International Civil Aviation was convened to develop an acceptable legal framework for the international operation of airlines. The Chicago Conference established the principal 'freedoms of the air' that underpin present-day air travel agreements and fundamentally influence contemporary international tourist flows. The 'Five Freedoms of the Air' established at the Chicago Conference were defined as follows:

- First Freedom: the right of an airline of one country to fly over the territory of another country,

- Second Freedom: the right of an airline to stop in another country for fuel/maintenance reasons but not to pick-up or drop-off passengers or tourists,

- Third Freedom: the right of an airline to carry passengers from its own country to another country,

- Fourth Freedom: the right of an airline to carry back passengers from a foreign country to the country in which the airline is registered,

- Fifth Freedom: the right of an airline to carry passengers between two foreign countries provided the flight originates or terminates in the country in which the airline is registered (e.g. a US airline carrier flying from New York to London and on to Paris)

According to Kasper (1988, p.7), "the drafters of the so-called Five Freedoms Agreement envisioned it as the keystone of a new, multilateral regime for the governance of air services". Although the United States strongly advocated an 'open skies' approach, the United Kingdom and most European countries were more protectionist and pushed for tighter controls on tariffs, capacity and the limitation of fifth freedom rights.

The participants at the Chicago Conference were able to agree on the mutual exchange of the first two freedoms, but these freedoms did not involve the ability to drop-off or pick-up passengers and thus, were relatively innocuous in the context of their implications for the overall international tourism industry. More importantly, no agreement was reached on the crucial third through fifth freedoms which facilitated 'real' commercial traffic rights between countries. The shortcomings of the Chicago Conference subsequently spawned over 2,500 bilateral aviation agreements during the post-world war two era (Butler and Keller, 1994). Rather than regulating the international airline industry on a multilateral basis, each country negotiated generally restrictive nation-to-nation aviation agreements with other countries. The proliferation of the bilateral approach had the effect of fundamentally dictating and constraining international tourist flows in the post-Chicago Convention era. Furthermore, as we enter the new millennium, the international airline industry has remained solidly rooted in a complex web of bilateral agreements (with the recent exception of the European Union).

Ironically, as some airlines continue to develop ambitious global alliance networks (e.g. the Star Alliance which includes United Airlines, Lufthansa, Air Canada, SAS, Singapore Airlines, Thai Airlines and Varig), each individual air carrier remains heavily dependent upon the political and infrastructural support of their respective national governments. Much of this dependency is triggered by a regulatory system where bilaterals are essentially treaties that are negotiated between governments, not air carriers. It is this symbiotic relationship between governmental policy and the airline industry that has been under-appreciated in the tourism literature in terms of its overall impact on international tourism markets.

Bermuda I and II: the critical role of the US-UK bilateral

According to Kasper (1988), the 1946 US-UK bilateral or Bermuda I agreement acted as the intellectual foundation for all subsequent bilaterals. The Bermuda Agreement (so named because the US and UK governments negotiated the bilateral in Bermuda) was signed into law just two years after the Chicago Conference and both delegations agreed that they would use the Bermuda Agreement as a basis for future air transport agreements with other countries (US Department of State, 1946). According to Wheatcroft (1994, p.19), the Bermuda I agreement emerged as the "standard model for air service agreements between many other countries".

Although specific bilateral agreements will vary with regard to content, the essential regulatory issues are generally covered by clauses dealing with the specification of routes, the designation of specific air carriers, ownership and control issues, capacity and tariff regulations and confidential 'memorandum of understandings' between the two nation-states in question. The specification of traffic rights in a bilateral can fundamentally predetermine the configuration of the international tourist system with respect to the specific city-pair markets served by an airline. For example, the Bermuda I route schedule provided a detailed list of points served that, in effect, essentially established the growth parameters for international tourism in the US-UK market.

Most post-world war two bilaterals severely constrained the range of cities served on international routes and controlled the output or production of each airline through various capacity controls. Additionally, the Bermuda I bilateral approved the International Air Transportation Association (IATA) as the primary institution through which international air fares would be mediated. In many regions of the world, the overall effect of all this regulation has been constrained international route networks and air fare price controls that have fundamentally 'distorted' the geography of international tourism in terms of origin-destination tourist flows. In many international markets, tourists have a limited range of destinations and air routes to choose from while in other markets excessively high air fares have substantially constrained propensities to travel by air.

Although many bilateral agreements reflect the protectionist attitudes of the prevailing national governments, the Bermuda I agreement differed from such agreements in two important aspects. First, no *a priori* controls were imposed on either flight frequencies or seat capacities offered on authorised routes (although an *ex post facto* capacity review was allowed). Second, the Bermuda I agreement was the first bilateral to accept the concept of fifth freedom rights or 'beyond rights' enshrined in the 1944 Chicago Conference. The United States obtained the right to operate service beyond London to other fifth freedom points including Amsterdam, Berlin, Budapest, Copenhagen, Frankfurt, Helsinki, Leningrad, Moscow, Munich, Oslo, Stockholm, and Vienna, plus Beirut, Calcutta, Delhi, Karachi, and many other cities.

The generous granting of fifth freedom rights to US-designated carriers was one of the major issues pursued by the UK government in the re-negotiations that led to the 1977 Bermuda II Agreement. The UK government had become increasingly dissatisfied with the share of the transatlantic market achieved by UK-based airlines and wished to limit US-based airlines traffic rights and earnings, particularly between London and points East. The UK achieved important gains in Bermuda II by increasing the number of named gateway points in the US from nine to fourteen with the addition of Atlanta, Dallas-Fort Worth, Houston, San Francisco, and Seattle while the US gave up many of its fifth freedom rights beyond the UK According to Tedesco (1993, p.404), "US negotiators accepted extraordinarily unfavourable proposals" including "onerous capacity control regulations" and "extreme limitations on the number of US carriers permitted to serve the UK".

The Bermuda II agreement marked a watershed in US air transportation policy in the North Atlantic. The 1947-1977 Bermuda era that had been marked by a series of restrictive bilateral negotiations came to a close and was replaced with a radically different 'open skies' approach in late 1977. In a 1978 Annual Report to Congress, the US Civil Aeronautics Board (CAB) stated that:

The renegotiated US-UK bilateral agreement is the last episode in the history of restrictive markets and triggered a major turning point in US international aviation policy. Bermuda 2 symbolises the direction we are moving away from. Rather, the US international policy is now based upon active competitive principles. This procompetitive approach has governed US bilateral aviations since Fall 1977. (US CAB, 1978, p.60-61)

The open skies policy dramatically impacted international tourist flows between the US and Europe by opening-up new, untapped city-pair markets.

'Open skies': a reversal of US aviation policy

In 1978, the US government adopted a strategy formulated to open international air services to greater competition through a process of generalised deregulation. According to Dresner and Tretheway (1992), the US renegotiated a series of liberalised bilateral treaties with over twenty nations between 1978 and 1982. Most of these agreements allowed carriers "the freedom to set capacity without governmental interference, allowed additional routes between (and beyond) two signatories, promoted competitive rather than IATA price-setting, and strictly limited governmental authority over fare-setting" (Dresner and Tretheway, 1992, p.172-173). The introduction of greater pricing freedom through more liberalised bilaterals increased the potential for the diversion of tourist traffic from protectionist markets to more liberalised countries (Pustay, 1993). The US strategy of penetrating the North Atlantic market by establishing 'beachead' agreements with key European countries (e.g. the 1978 Netherlands bilateral) led to other countries later renegotiating agreements with the US to maintain a competitive advantage (e.g. the 1996 German bilateral).

Kasper (1988, p.89) noted that "by using the 'carrot' of access to large, economically attractive markets and the 'stick' of diversion", the US has achieved significant liberalisation in some European markets. A few countries have resisted the trend towards liberalisation (e.g. France) but many countries have embraced the open skies approach (e.g. Austria, Belgium, the Czech Republic, Denmark, Finland, Iceland, Italy, Luxembourg, Norway, Sweden, and Switzerland) although most of these countries have small domestic markets. Because of the geographic disparities in domestic market size (e.g. the US versus Luxembourg), it appeared that additional progress required a multilateral perspective similar to the approach proposed at the 1944 Chicago Conference. From 1987 to 1993, the focus of regulatory reform switched from the largely US-based pro-competitive agenda to the collective multilateral liberalisation initiatives of the European Union (EU).

European-style liberalisation

Up to the mid-1980's, international air service among EU countries was largely governed by a series of restrictive and anti-competitive bilateral agreements (e.g. restrictions on flight frequencies, seat capacity controls, limits on the number of designated airlines allowed, traffic or revenue pools usually on a 50-50 basis, and IATA-based tariff agreements). According to Button (1996, p.279), "the traditional picture of European aviation is one of institutionalised cartelisation and collusion".

In 1986, the EU countries initiated discussion about establishing a more competitive, internal air transport market to complement reform in other economic sectors relating to trade and tariffs, and to stimulate intra-European tourism. EU liberalisation was gradually phased-in through a series of three aviation packages that became effective in 1987, 1990, and 1993. The Third Package removed most of the remaining regulatory constraints acting on intra-EU air transport. The 1993 package widened the range of fares that could be set without requiring government approval, established multiple designation of air carriers by market, removed capacity controls on the number of seats allowed, eliminated all restrictions on fifth freedom rights, and allowed EU airlines to operate between points within an EU country besides the airlines home country (commonly referred to as cabotage). Cabotage within the US is prohibited by law meaning that it is illegal for a foreign carrier to operate on a domestic route within America. By contrast, it was now possible for a EU-based carrier like British Airways to operate solely inside France on, for example, the Paris-Marseilles route.

The theoretical implications of EU liberalisation on tourism were supposed to include cheaper fares and greater choice in terms of destinations served, as competitive forces encouraged the proliferation of new carriers and expanded capacity, exerted downward pressure on tariffs and yields, and encouraged higher passenger load factors. However, empirical evidence now exists which suggests that EU members still continue to significantly control their own domestic air markets and that air carriers are not fully utilising their new cabotage rights (*Aviation Week and Space Technology* 1999a, UK Civil Aviation Authority 1998, US General Accounting Office 1993). According to Caves (1997, p.125), there is also little evidence of lower fares in the EU, probably because "there has been so little new entry on dense routes". An in-depth assessment of EU liberalisation by the UK CAA (1998, p.6) concluded that "no fundamental restructuring of the European airline industry has yet taken place" even though the market has been "freed from the strait-jacket of the Chicago-based bilateral system".

Furthermore, the EU has yet to fully reconcile the conflicting goals of ensuring a competitive industry within Europe *vis-a-vis* the global competitive positions of EU carriers. Some globally-oriented EU carriers (e.g. British Airways) view intra-European traffic as merely hub feed and consider the proliferation of competitors on domestic routes as an impediment to their globalisation strategies particularly across the North Atlantic.

However, a major obstacle in developing a 'post-open skies' accord across the North Atlantic is the lack of geographic parity between the US and the individual EU nation-states. What can a small EU country offer the US in return for access to the enormous US air transport market? Key issues include determining how the EU's Third Package rules apply to air travel between the EU and non-EU markets (e.g. the US). Additionally, it remains unclear how the new EU rules will mesh with existing bilateral air service agreements negotiated independently by individual EU nation-states with other non-EU countries (e.g. the Bermuda II bilateral).

According to Doganis (1991, p.89), "the deregulation of air transport within the European Community will have only limited impact on airline competition if the external dimension is ignored". Resolving the extra-territorial validity of EU liberalisation rules is critical given the fundamental role the North Atlantic plays in determining the overall health of the international tourist industry. The North Atlantic has traditionally been the busiest tourist market in the world accounting for one-quarter of all international tourist arrivals. Ongoing regulatory impediments to the satisfactory operation of air traffic rights across the North Atlantic have the potential to further inhibit international tourist flows and seriously impair the economic performance of the suppliers of tourism services (e.g. hotels, travel agents, tour operators).

The 1999 Chicago Convention and the Transatlantic Common Aviation Area (TCAA): a revolution in the making?

In late 1999, a second Chicago Conference was convened with the declared intent of establishing a Transatlantic Common Aviation Area (TCAA) for the Euro-American air transport market. The summit was sponsored by the European Commission (the executive body of the EU) and the US Department of Transportation. Policy-makers envision that the TCAA will gradually evolve into a post-open skies multilateral scheme involving the abolition of traffic rights and all-new rules for competition, cabotage and foreign ownership of domestic airlines. A reduction of national ownership and control restrictions could facilitate cross-border investments between US and EU airlines and dramatically enhance accessibility levels between regions of tourist demand and supply in the North Atlantic market.

The recent creation of a single aviation market between Australia and New Zealand in 1996 using similar regional arrangements provides some encouragement for TCAA advocates looking to establish a similar aviation accord across the North Atlantic. According to Findlay (1996, p.329), the Trans-Tasman Single Aviation Market "illustrates that ownership and control limits associated with bilateral agreements are significant hurdles to change but are not unsurmountable".

Some of the thorny issues facing TCAA policy-makers include harmonising regulations governing computer reservation systems, code-sharing arrangements, airport slots, state aid, antitrust rulings and cabotage. A particularly contentious problematic is the future status of cabotage in any proposed TCAA. Many American carriers now fly between EU countries by virtue of the numerous fifth freedom rights granted in past bilaterals. However, if the European Commission is granted the authority to negotiate external aviation agreements on behalf of all EU member countries, it is possible that service within the EU (i.e., between EU nations) could be treated as cabotage for non-EU airlines. Cabotage is currently prohibited by US law, but it is possible that the US Congress will use cabotage as a bargaining chip in future TCAA negotiations with the E.U. One possible outcome of TCAA negotiations may be that the US government will extend cabotage rights to permit EU carriers to move passengers between cities in the US in order to retain existing fifth freedom routes for US carriers within the E.U. Gourdin (1998, p.18) argues that such an approach may eventually be acceptable to US carriers because in reality "there are few, if any, foreign airlines that could or would afford the investment needed to offer the domestic frequencies necessary to seriously draw passengers away from American carriers". Furthermore, a dearth of airport gates and landing slots (especially at slot-controlled airports like JFK, La Guardia, Washington National, and O'Hare) make it even more difficult for would-be foreign new entrants to effectively compete in the US market.

Infrastructural constraints: the intractable problem of airport landing slots

Although the EU's Third Package and the proposed TCAA seek to largely remove traffic rights as a regulatory constraint in international air passenger markets, it has become increasingly difficult to exercise these new-found freedoms because of constraints on the ground.

According to a recent report by the Association of European Airlines (1995), severe capacity constraints exist at nearly all the major European airports especially those with the largest international tourist flows. The congested airports identified in the AEA report included: Heathrow, Gatwick, Frankfurt, Charles de Gaulle, Orly, Amsterdam, Brussels, Berlin, Vienna, Dusseldorf, Manchester, Copenhagen, Zurich, Geneva, Barcelona, Madrid, Milan, both Rome airports, and Athens.

As we enter the new millennium, it is increasingly apparent that both US-style deregulation and E.U. liberalisation of the airline-related segment of the air transport industry has not been complemented with equivalent reform in the airport service segment of the industry (Bass 1994, Janda 1993). Most national governments have been unable to formulate an effective and integrated airline-airport policy. Consequently, market distortions in the airport segment are now creating and exacerbating market distortions in the airline segment. According to Graham (1994, p.96), "congestion at the airline-airport interface - slots, gates, and runways - constitutes one primary constraint on efforts to regulate for a more competitive airline industry". The inability of some airports to deploy and expand resources in response to changing tourist demand may eventually inhibit the ability of some tourist destinations in reaching their full potential. Excessive congestion at an airport terminal increases the likelihood that potential visitors may seek alternative destinations as a result.

Since airport capacity is both an increasingly intractable problem and a vital component in the development of many international tourism markets, it is critical that policy-makers develop a clearer understanding of how the distribution of airport slots and gates can colour market behaviour in the airline industry. In the US, some early research suggests that the finite number of available take-off and landing slots at the slot-controlled airports (i.e., JFK, La Guardia, Washington National, and O'Hare) and various restrictive gate-leasing arrangements have restrained competition in some markets, resulting in higher than normal air-fares (US GAO, 1990, 1999). Partly because of these concerns, the European Commission attempted to reduce the protection afforded incumbent carriers by implementing new slot rules through Council Regulation 95/93. The regulation established a process based on neutral, transparent, and non-discriminatory rules to facilitate competition and to encourage new entrant airlines within the EU air transport market (Button, Haynes, and Stough, 1998). However, the guidelines recognised the historical merit of slot usage or 'grandfather rights' whereby an airline inherited the right to a slot if it had already made use of the runway at the same time during the preceding equivalent season. This approach has been criticised by some researchers because of its evident anti-competitive aspects, serving to advantage incumbents over would-be new entrants (Button, Haynes, and Stough 1998; Langner 1996a, 1996b; Starkie 1998; UK CAA 1998).

Finding a plausible and politically acceptable answer to both the problem of allocating scarce airport resources and minimising tourist congestion levels at airport terminals has evaded policy-makers to this point. An expansion of airport capacity (e.g. bigger terminals and more runways) at places like JFK or Heathrow is an obvious first solution, but it can be costly, time-consuming, and subject to intense opposition on environmental grounds. Alternative approaches have tended to focus on developing new capacity allocation methods including the administrative rationing of slots through various scheduling committees, slot lotteries, slot auctions, peak and non-peak landing fee schedules, new gate-leasing arrangements, and various re-regulation initiatives (Bass 1994, Button, Haynes, and Stough 1998; Janda 1993; Kleit and Kobayashi 1996; Langner 1996a, 1996b; Starkie 1992; 1994, 1998; Toms 1994; UK CAA 1995). Particularly controversial have been the proposals to introduce a US-style free-market trading approach to the management of slots whereby the airlines inherit property rights to slots to encourage the free exchange of slots and direct money transfers. Both the IATA and the European Commission have declared free-market slot trading illegal although the UK High Court recently ruled that slots at Heathrow can be freely exchanged for money setting the stage for conflict with the European Commission (*Air Transport World*, 1999)

For the suppliers of tourism services, developing policies that effectively manage airport resources is critical given the profound ways in which regulatory and infrastructural constraints can shape accessibility levels between tourist origins and destinations. The paper now turns to a brief case study of the recent experiences of British Airways at Heathrow Airport - the busiest international airport in the world - in an effort to highlight the complexities of airline-airport relationships with respect to overall government policy.

British Airways and Heathrow Airport: strategic alliances and the regulatory and infrastructural conundrum

To some observers, the recent proliferation of strategic alliance agreements between carriers in the air transport industry resembles an 'end run' around the constraints imposed by the existing regulatory framework (Debbage 1994). Most alliance agreements do not include substantial merger or equity acquisition arrangements because traditional bilateral air service agreements usually prohibit majority ownership and/or impose caps on the extent of equity involvement by foreign airlines in domestic carriers. Instead, most strategic alliances include a mix of joint marketing programs, code-sharing arrangements, joint computer reservation system operations, cross-holding arrangements, and minority ownership clauses.

Although most alliances are fairly modest arrangements, they can provide indirect access to elusive traffic rights and slots that are not directly available to the foreign carrier in any other way. For example, British Airways has successfully developed the OneWorld system (with American Airlines, Canadian Airlines, Cathay Pacific, Quantas, Finnair, Lan Chile, and Iberia) in order to both 'capture' additional traffic demand and to access otherwise restricted foreign markets. In 1998, the OneWorld alliance was the largest in the world accounting for 18% of all international traffic (*The Economist*, 1999). The OneWorld system has also allowed British Airways to solidify its dominant position at Heathrow Airport. In 1999, British Airways controlled 37% of all weekly landing slots at Heathrow but this increases to 45% when factoring in the OneWorld partners at Heathrow (*Air Transport World* 1997a, *Aviation Week and Space Technology* 1999b).

However, recent attempts by British Airways to strengthen its OneWorld partnership with American Airlines have faced significant regulatory hurdles. In 1997, the UK appeared set to approve the BA-AA partnership provided the prospective partners gave up 168 weekly slots at Heathrow so as to facilitate competition from would-be new entrants. BA proceeded to announce its intention to sell-off the 168 slots which immediately triggered a debate over who owns slots at UK airports. The European Commission has claimed jurisdiction over airport slots through Council Regulation 95/93 but the regulations are unclear on the role of money transfers and the UK government has disputed the EU's authority over slots. Additionally, the EU Competition Commissioner argued that in order to avoid stifling competition, the BA-AA partnership would have to relinquish 400 weekly slots (this was later amended to 267 slots in 1998). The Commissioner also indicated that slots must be given away rather than sold. Finally, the inability of the US-UK governments to negotiate a new, innovative Bermuda III bilateral has severely impeded progress in the BA-AA talks. The US government has been unwilling to grant antitrust immunity for the BA-AA alliance until an 'open skies' accord is approved between the two countries. On the other hand, the UK government is unwilling to relinquish additional slots at Heathrow until it is guaranteed additional access to the US market.

It is in this way that regulatory and infrastructural constraints can profoundly impede tourist flows in one of the busiest international tourist markets in the world. "BA and AA combined carry 60% of all US-UK air traffic and 70% of all flights between London and New York, as well as 25% of all traffic between the US and Europe as a whole" (*Air Transport World*, 1997b, p.55). Despite the key role the BA-AA partnership plays in shaping international tourist flows across the North Atlantic, the future status of the partnership remains unclear as we enter the new millennium.

Conclusion: are plurilaterals the answer?

The geography of international tourist flows can be substantially influenced by the regulatory and infrastructural constraints that impinge on the international air transport industry. However, the impact of these constraints on the economic performance of key tourism suppliers (e.g. hotels, tour operators, travel agents, etc.) has traditionally been under-appreciated in the tourism literature. This paper has argued that more attention should be focused on these 'hidden' constraints because they have the potential to fundamentally dictate the essential nature of the tourism playing field. As we enter the new millennium, the economic globalisation of the tourist industry continues apace, but it has not been accompanied by an equivalent political globalisation of aviation's Byzantine regulations. These issues are exacerbated by a critical lack of airport capacity (especially in terms of landing slots) that has collectively 'corrupted' international tourist accessibility levels between key origin-destination markets across the North Atlantic, and elsewhere.

Although the successful resolution of these issues remains elusive, it is possible that a targeted plurilateral or 'phased multilateralism' might provide an interim solution to the problems facing the international air transport industry. Such an approach essentially involves negotiating a multi-national 'open-skies' agreement without regard to geography.

Instead of focusing on a multilateral, regional bloc like the EU, a targeted plurilateral is negotiated with a small group of like-minded liberal airlines and governments consistent with the regulatory structure of the pre-existing 'open-skies' bilaterals already signed into law. Likely candidates for such an approach might include Canada, Germany, the Netherlands, Singapore, the UK and the US Such an approach might mitigate the EU's extraterritoriality issue and provide a useful stepping stone towards the eventual creation of a full-blown, regionally-based 'open-skies' accord on the scale of the TCAA.

Acknowledgement

The author acknowledges the generous support of a UNCG Faculty Research Assignment for the fall of 2000 without which this publication would not have been possible.

References

Association of European Airlines, (1995), *European Airports - Getting to the Hub of the Problem OR the Problem of Getting to the Hub*, AEA: Brussels.

Air Transport World, (1997a), "UK to OK BA/AA" 34(1):7.

Air Transport World, (1997b), "Bilateral Ballistics" 34(2):53-61.

Air Transport World, (1999), "UK High Court Oks Slot Sales" 36(5):11.

Aviation Week and Space Technology, (1999a), "Europe Assesses Deregulation", December 13:44.

Aviation Week and Space Technology, (1999b), "Star Alliance Boosts Presence at Heathrow", November 15:39.

Bass, T. C. (1994), "Infrastructure Constraints and the EC", *Journal of Air Transport Management*, 1(3):145-150.

Britton, S. (1991), "Tourism, Capital, and Place: Towards a Critical Geography of Tourism", *Environment and Planning D: Society and Space* 9:451-478.

Butler, G. F. and M. R. Keller, (1994), "International Aviation Policies: Is It Time For Change?", *Transportation Quarterly*, 48(4): 367-380.

Butler, R. (1980), "The Concept of a Tourist Area Resort Cycle of Evolution: Implications for the Management of Resources", *Canadian Geographer* 14(1):5-12.

Button, K. (1996), "Liberalising European Aviation: Is There An Empty Core Problem?", *Journal of Transport Economics and Policy*, September: 275-291.

Button, K. Haynes, K. and R. Stough, (1998), *Flying Into the Future: Air Transport Policy in the European Union*, Edward Elgar: Cheltenham.

Caves, R. E. (1997), "European Airline Networks and Their Implications for Airport Planning", *Transport Reviews*, 17(2):121-144.

Debbage, K. G. (1990), "Oligopoly and the Resort Cycle in the Bahamas", *Annals of Tourism Research*, 17:513-527.

Debbage, K. G. (1993), "US Airport Market Concentration and Deconcentration", *Transportation Quarterly*, 47(1):115-136.

Debbage, K. G. (1994), "The International Airline Industry: Globalisation, Regulation and Strategic Alliances", *Journal of Transport Geography* 2(3):190-203.

Debbage, K. G. (1997), "Post-Fordism and Flexibility: The Travel Industry Polyglot", *Tourism Management*, 18(4):229-241.

Doganis, R. (1991), *Flying Off Course: The Economics of International Airlines*, Routledge: London.

Dresner, M. and M. W. Tretheway, (1992), "Modelling and Testing the Effects of Market Structure on Price", *Journal of Transport Economics and Policy* 26(2):171-184.

The Economist, (1999), "Flying in Circles" July 17.

Findlay, C. (1996), "The Trans-Tasman Single Aviation Market", *Journal of Transport Economics and Policy*, September:329-334.

Gilbert, E. W. (1939), "The Growth of Inland and Seaside Health Resorts in England", *The Scottish Geographical Magazine, 55(1):16-35*.

Gourdin, K. N. (1998), "US International Aviation Policy Into the New Millennium: Meeting the Global Challenge", *Transportation Journal*, Summer:13-19.

Graham, B. (1994), "Regulation and Liberalisation in the UK Scheduled Airline Industry", *Environment and Planning C: Government and Policy*, 12:87-107.

Graham, B. (1998), "Liberalisation, Regional Economic Development and the Geography of Demand for Air Transport in the European Union", *Journal of Transport Geography*, 6(2):87-104.

Gunn, C. A. (1994), *Tourism Planning*, Taylor and Francis: Washington.

Hanlon, J.P. (1995), "Hub Operations and Airline Competition". In Medlik, S., (Ed.), *Managing Tourism*, Butterworth Heinemann: London, p.147-161.

Hobson, J S. P. and M. Uysal, (1992), "Infrastructure: The Silent Crisis Facing the Future of Tourism", *Hospitality Research Journal* 17(1):209-215.

Holloway, J. C. (1989), *The Business of Tourism*, Pitman: London.

Inskeep, E. (1991), *Tourism Planning: An Integrated and Sustainable Development Approach*, Van Nostrand Reinhold: New York.

Ioannides, D. and K. G. Debbage (Eds.), (1998), *The Economic Geography of the Tourist Industry: A Supply-side Analysis*, Routledge: London.

Janda, R. (1993), "Auctioning Airport Slots: Airline Oligopoly, Hubs and Spokes, and Traffic Congestion", *Annals of Air and Space Law*, 18(1):153-194.

Kasper, D. M. (1988), *Deregulation and Globalisation: Liberalising International Trade in Air Services*, American Enterprise Institute: Cambridge.

Kleit, A. N. and B. H. Koyabashi, (1996), "Market Failure or Market Efficiency? Evidence on Airport Slot Usage". In McMullen, B., (Ed.), *Research in Transportation Economics* 4:1-32, JAI Press: Connecticut.

Langner, S. J. (1996a), "Contractual Aspects of Transacting in Slots in the United States", *Journal of Air Transport Management*, 2(3/4):151-161.

Langner, S. J., (1996b), *The Allocation of Slots in the Airline Industry: A Transaction Cost Economic Analysis*, Nomos Verlagsgesellschaft: Baden Baden.

Lundgren, J. O., (1982), "The Tourist Frontier of Nouveau Quebec: Functions and Regional Linkages", *Tourist Review* 37(2):10-16.

Mann, J. M. and C. F. Mantel, (1992), "Travel and Health: A Global Agenda", *Proceedings of the Second International Conference on Travel Medicine*:1-4, Paris.

Martin, C. A., and S. F. Witt, (1988), "Substitute Prices in Models of Tourism Demand", *Annals of Tourism Research*, 15:255-268.

Miossec, J. M. (1976), *Elements Pour Une Theorie de L'Espace Touristique*, Les Cahiers du Tourisme, C-36, CHET: Aix-en-Provence.

Mill, R. C. (1992), *Tourism: The International Business*, Prentice Hall: New Jersey.

de Murias, R. (1989), *The Economic Regulation of International Air Transport*, McFarland and Company: London.

New York Times, (1999), "Business Travel: An Upbeat Government Report and Some Sour Industry Notes on the Future of Global Aviation" December 15th.

Oum, T. H. (1996), "Some Key Issues in the Increasingly Competitive Airline System", *Journal of Transport Economics and Policy*, September:233-236.

Page, S. J. (1999), *Transport and Tourism*, Addison Wesley Longman: Harlow.

Pearce, D. (1995), *Tourism Today: A Geographical Analysis*, Longman: Harlow.

Prideaux, B. (1993), "Possible Effects of New Transport Technologies on the Tourism Industry in the 21st Century", *Papers of the Australasian Transport Research Forum*, University of Queensland, 18:245-258.

Prideaux, B. (2000), "The Role of the Transport System in Destination Development", *Tourism Management* 21:53-63.

Pustay, M. W. (1993), "Toward a Global Airline Industry: Prospects and Impediments", *Logistics and Transportation Review* 23(1):103-128.

Raguraman, K. (1995), "The Role of Air Transportation in Tourism Development: A Case Study of the Philippines and Thailand", *Transportation Quarterly*, 49(4):113-124.

Robinson, H. (1976), *A Geography of Tourism*, MacDonald and Evans: London.

Starkie, D. (1992), *Slot Trading at United States Airports: A Report for the DG VII*, City Publications: London.

Starkie, D. (1994), "The US Market in Airport Slots", *Journal of Transport Economics and Policy*, September:325-329.

Starkie, D. (1998), "Allocating Airport Slots: A Role for the Market?", *Journal of Air Transport Management*, 4:111-116.

Tedesco, T. (1993), "International Aviation: Not a Level Playing Field", *Transportation Quarterly*, 47(3):397-412.

Toms, M. R. (1994), "Charging For Airports: The New BAA Approach", *Journal of Air Transport Management*, 1(2):77-82.

United Kingdom Civil Aviation Authority, (1995), *Slot Allocation: A Proposal for Europe's Airports*, CAP 644, CAA: London.

United Kingdom Civil Aviation Authority, (1998), *The Single European Aviation Market: The First Five Years*, CAP 685, CAA: London.

United States Civil Aeronautics Board, (1978), *CAB Annual Report to Congress*, Government Printing Office: Washington, D. C.

United States Department of State, (1946), "International Air Transport Policy: Joint Statement by US and British Governments", *Department of State Bulletin*, 15(378):577.

United States General Accounting Office, (1990), *Airline Competition: Industry Operating and Marketing Practices Limit Market Entry"*, GAO: Washington, D.C.

United States General Accounting Office, (1993), *International Aviation: Measures by European Community Could Limit US Airlines' Ability to Compete Abroad*, GAO: Washington, D. C.

United States General Accounting Office, (1999), *"Airline Deregulation: Changes in Airfares, Service Quality, and Barriers to Entry"*, GAO: Washington, D.C.

Vellas, F. and L. Becherel, (1995), *International Tourism: An Economic Perspective*, St. Martin's Press: London.

Wheatcroft, S. (1994), *Aviation and Tourism Policies: Balancing the Benefits*, Routledge: London.

World Tourism Organisation, (1997), *Yearbook of Tourism Statistics*, World Tourism Organisation: Madrid.

Government intervention in tourism: Case study of an English seaside resort

Georgina English

College of St Mark and St John, UK

Abstract

This paper explores the relationship between the British Government and the Tourism Industry, using a case study of Torbay, an English seaside resort and asks if Government intervention in tourism is a necessity. An examination of the importance of tourism to Government, the Industry's expectations of Government and Government's involvement in tourism helps identify the degrees of representation, communication, leadership, co-ordination and partnerships that exist. The stated situation in Government literature is compared with the reality as described by the private sector. The paper argues that both Central and Local Government are very important and influential in terms of tourism and are actively involved, yet from a distance and the relationship is crucial but not close, thus Government intervention is a necessity.

Introduction

This paper focuses on the relationship between the British Government and the tourism industry, first established in the Development of Tourism Act 1969 with the creation of a statutory framework for tourism (Parliamentary Debates 1969) and asks the question, is Government intervention in tourism a necessity? Governments tend to become involved in tourism for a variety of economic, political and social reasons. Any country in which tourism plays a prominent part in national income and employment can expect government to want to take a role. The Government is undoubtedly the central and most influential institution of State (Hall 1994) and it is because of this that the ideology (Henry 1993), paradigms (Guba 1990), policies (DCMS 1999) and roles (Wason 1996) of Government need to be examined to understand the implications for tourism. The possible repercussions of the delegation of some tourism responsibilities from Central Government to Local Authorities and tourist boards must also be considered. Tourism is a highly fragmented industry (ETB 1997), but is of huge value economically (Peat and Mullan 1995), in terms of income and employment. In 1997 tourism expenditure in the UK was estimated at £53 billion; the UK was 5th in the world in terms of visitor receipts and 25.5 million overseas visitors came to the UK (DCMS 1999).

It is because of the importance and significance of both Government and tourism that the relationship between them must be acknowledged and understood. Questions are raised as to whether they work in partnership, why partnerships are important and what the barriers are? The relationship should be mutually beneficial. The purpose of this paper is to explore this relationship and the public and private sector roles, by addressing the following issues: the importance of the Tourism Industry to Government, the Industry's expectations of Government and the current involvement of Central and Local Government in tourism.

Having noted the importance and significance of both Government and tourism, this paper will explore the relationship between them, with the objective of determining whether Government intervention in tourism is necessary. Intervention, being an act of intervening and the adjective, to intervene, meaning to take a decisive or intrusive role in order to determine events (Collins 1995). Thus any interference in the affairs of others can be considered intervention. This idea of intervention immediately raises more questions: what form should this intervention take, should it come from Central Government or Local Authorities, is Government intervention wanted and if so by whom and why? These issues cannot be addressed without first considering the current situation. The paper attempts to discover the current situation in Torbay and ask the aforementioned questions relating to Government intervention.

The relationship being discussed in this paper is that as experienced in Torbay. The English Riviera, one of the Britain's premier resorts, is a stretch of coastline set around Torbay, South Devon, one of the most beautiful bays in Europe and includes the resort towns of Torquay, Paignton and Brixham (ERTB 1998). The partnerships within Torbay are examined and the varying degrees of representation discovered, by analysing lines of communication. The stated situation in Government literature, with reference to partnerships, representation and communication is compared with the reality as described by the private sector. Conclusions are then drawn from the findings of this study and suggestions made as to what action may be needed.

This paper is therefore concerned with the interaction between the British Government and the Tourism Industry. Interaction between persons can be considered to be an exchange of goods, material and nonmaterial. This is one of the oldest theories of social behaviour and one that we still use every day to interpret our own behaviour. Interpreting behaviour in terms of transactions and the idea of social behaviour as exchange has been termed the Social Exchange Theory and it is this basic theory that helps explain the relationship under examination. Homans (1958) discusses an exchange paradigm and believes that in a situation where the exchange is real, the determination is mutual. Thus we must ask if the British Government and the Tourism Industry are engaged in an exchange and if the determination is mutual? In any relationship there are perceived costs and benefits from interaction. For example as Government emits behaviour, both Government and the Tourism Industry may incur costs and each has more than one course of behaviour open to them. How has the interaction affected the relationship? Are they emitting behaviour reinforced to some degree by the behaviour of the other? Perhaps each does find the other's behaviour reinforcing. The 'reinforcers' can be called values. The problem is to state the propositions relating to the variations in the values and costs to each to their frequency distribution of behaviour among alternatives, where the values taken by these variables for one determine in part their values for the other. There seems to be a proportionality between the value to others of the behaviour one gives them and the value to them of the behaviour they give the other (Homans 1958).

Literature review

The Government's paradigms are shaped by the dominant political ideology, which in turn affect policy decisions. However, policies are still difficult to formulate because of externalities and the scale and nature of the economic activity involved. Tourism has benefits and costs but should the government intervene? For both economic and social reasons governments should at least take a direct interest. The system of government, the ideology and paradigms will of course be reflected in the mode and extent of government intervention. The State is called upon to play a co-ordinating role, controlling and supervising as well as helping to facilitate. However to what extent do governments take these issues seriously? Thus the relationship between government and tourism depends on the ideology, paradigms, policies and roles undertaken by government.

Britain is a western state with free market attitudes, therefore limiting direct state involvement and placing emphasis on the private sector. Knowing the ideology of a government helps in understanding the paradigms and policies. Over the years there has been no shortage of British Government involvement in tourism, but the preference has been for private and voluntary bodies to play a predominant role in tourism organisation. There is a reluctance of direct government involvement demonstrating the paradigmatic perspective of a government with a capitalist political ideological leaning. Continuity of a post-Thatcherite ideology is evident in present government policy.

As long ago as 1926 with the 'Come to Britain' Movement the industry has been trying to get Government involved in tourism and by 1929 the Travel Association of Great Britain and Ireland (TAGBI) had managed to get some funding. Funding then fluctuated as the TAGBI reformed in 1932 as the Travel and Industrial Development Association of Great Britain and Ireland (TIDAGBI) but there was an increasing recognition of local government involvement. 1947 saw the creation of the British Tourist and Holidays Board (BTHB) which, although a voluntary initiative, had public support. The amalgamation of BTHB with TIDAGBI resulted in the formation of the British Travel and Holidays Association in 1950 which later (1966) became the British Travel Association. However there was no statutory legislation specifically concerned with tourism until 1969 with the Development of Tourism Act, which created a statutory framework for tourism with domestic national boards for Scotland, Wales and England, plus the British Tourist Authority to promote abroad. Unfortunately there were no clearly defined roles and many areas of overlap. The development of a sub-national structure arose out of the consequences of the Development of Tourism Act of 1969 and was not created by the Act itself. (Jolley 1998) Thus it was not until 1969 that the Government had an 'official' relationship with tourism. Since then there has been no clear or consistent policy for tourism and no serious commitment to tourism. In 1996 the establishment of a Ministerial Tourism Advisory Forum saw the Government's first attempts to unite with the industry. This was followed up in 1997 by the 'Success through Partnership' document, the first tourism strategy to be produced jointly by Government, the industry and the tourist board. Later in 1997 there was a new Labour Government and (14 July 1997) Chris Smith became the first Secretary of State for Culture, Media and Sport (DCMS), following the Prime Minister's decision to rename the former Department of National Heritage (DCMS 1997). Even though the importance of tourism is more fully recognised it still has no Government department of its own. The 1999 DCMS's 'Tomorrow's Tourism' paper is the latest Government tourism strategy. However the usefulness of this document is dependent on the nature of the relationship between the Industry and Government before it was written. So, as this potted history shows, the Government's interest has grown over the years and has been encouraged by the tourism industry but intervention at this stage seems too strong a term to describe the Government's contribution as outlined above.

The policies and actions of the European Union (EU) are affecting governments in Europe by limiting their sovereign powers. In recent years the EU has played an increasingly important role in all aspects of the UK tourism industry. Its influence has increased as the British Government has reduced its direct involvement in the industry leaving the EU to develop specific tourism policies. The EU now represents the only real strategic approach to tourism in the UK (Swarbrooke 1997). The EU's involvement in tourism seems to have facilitated the Government's capitalist political ideology, rather than becoming interventionists the Government seems happy to adopt a laissez-faire approach.

British Government is enthusiastic about improving the quality of the tourism product and about competitiveness (ETB 1997), but less keen to demonstrate any degree of leadership or co-ordination, although working in partnerships is encouraged few appear to be initiated. By reading only Government literature one might assume that the relationship with tourism is very close, it is only after more in-depth research, especially in the field that a more realistic view is gained. Government literature should be the legitimisation of the social exchange that has taken place between people, the social process on the ground. The literature should come after agreement, not before. Central Government appears to prefer keeping a distance between themselves and the industry and having many levels and sectors in-between, possibly to reduce their liability. This is as a consequence of their ideological position.

This reluctance of direct Government involvement demonstrates the paradigmatic perspective of a government with a laissez-faire ideology. Government needs to provide leadership, implement rationalisation to reduce duplication of services and possibly give finance to partnership schemes so as to encourage co-operation and communication. Central Government's Department of Culture, Media and Sport (DCMS) has responsibility for tourism policy in England, for promoting tourism to Great Britain as a whole and sponsoring the industry within Government; so that the industry can make its full contribution to the economy and increase access to our cultural heritage (DCMS 1998). However cross departmental communication within Government can be difficult and working through the statutory tourism boards, who then conduct themselves through non statutory regional tourist boards, the DCMS thus illustrates little direct involvement and a distant relationship between Government and tourism. Thus Government has very little direct involvement, with the exception that it gives direct financial support, in England, in the form of grant-in-aid to the two statutory tourist boards, the English Tourist Board and the British Tourist Authority (DNH 1997). At this juncture it appears that the relationship between Government and tourism is somewhat of a long distance acquaintance more than a close partnership and intervention seems limited but that is not to say it is not required.

If Central Government is to have a major influence on the industry's prospects and performance, it needs to intervene, it needs to provide a framework within which tourism can operate. The 'Tomorrow's Tourism' (DCMS 1999) document suggests such a framework and proposes an action plan. The document attempts to provide a strategy and identifies the responsibilities of government as well as the industry and suggests a new partnership. The document acknowledges that tourism commands the attention of Government and appreciates the need for better co-ordination, co-operation and communication. Central government encourages local authorities in England to play an active role in promoting and developing tourism in their areas, through the support of local partnerships and as members of Regional Tourist Boards, providing strategic direction and focus. Central Government also realises that seaside and other resorts still form a major part of the domestic tourism economy: "We propose to help resorts that have the potential to benefit from regeneration programmes to develop modern and high quality tourism services" (DCMS 1999).

In the past local governments have seldom given tourism the attention which its economic impact merits, but now they are gaining an appreciation of its importance and their wide ranging responsibilities. Local government can provide strategic direction and co-ordinate the industry, they need to play their full part in developing and delivering an effective tourism structure and supporting local businesses (DNH 1997). Central Government has empowered local authorities to develop tourism. No tourism business can survive on its own; they need a framework to work within because most are dependent on the quality of surrounding attractions and infrastructure.

Local governments have a vital role in tourism, providing many facilities and services that are part of the tourist experience. Local authorities, in general, recognise tourism's potential, but are less clear about how to direct and encourage this potential and responsibility is often shared across several committees within each authority. Tourism features as a key expenditure item for many local authorities but they need to have a much closer relationship with tourism because of the localised nature of the Industry. Unfortunately tourism does not have a statutory foundation as a local government function (Bacon and Le Pelley 1994). It is crucial that a close relationship is formed because tourism needs Government support and the economy needs tourism income and employment, this is the exchange. It is impossible to generalise about exactly what sorts of relationship local governments have with tourism, as this will vary from authority to authority, thus Torbay will be used as a case study. Nevertheless, there are some common themes which emerge and which this paper hopes to identify.

Torbay - The English Riviera

Figure 1   Map of Torbay - The English Riviera

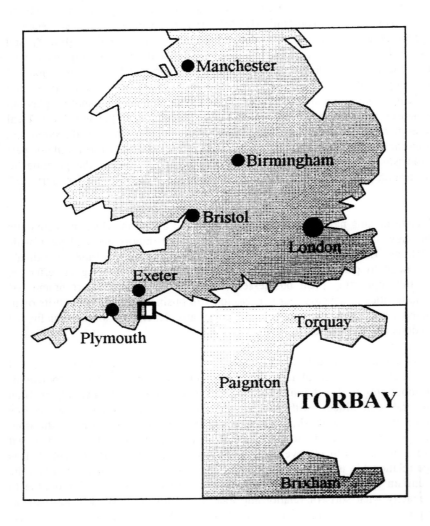

Figure 1 shows a map of Torbay - The English Riviera. The English Riviera on the southern coast of Devon is one of Britain's major seaside resorts and comprises three towns around Torbay along a twenty-two mile stretch of coastline, each location having a very different character. Brixham is the smallest resort, being a working fishing port. Paignton is well known as a family resort with beaches, parks, a pier and several visitor attractions. Torquay is seen as a premier resort of international standing given its scenic backcloth, level of attractions and strong accommodation sector. Having once attracted the gentry in the last century it became more accessible to a mass market with the opening up of the West Country by the Great Western Railway which marketed the area under the banner of the 'English Riviera' (Lumsdon 1992). This case study is crucial to understanding the ontology of the situation, the actual reality of what the relationship between the British Government and the Tourism Industry is and how it works.

For the best part of the twentieth century, Torbay has been a major UK resort catering for the long-stay holidaymaker. However as with so many British resorts, trade began to recede in the late 1970s. The reasons suggested for this downward trend experienced by so many resorts (Walton 1983) can be summarised as the widening of customers' horizons, the increased availability of competitive package holidays abroad (Baum 1995) and the limited marketing activity undertaken by UK resorts (Lumsdon 1992). Torbay has attracted the summer main holiday visitors in recent decades, particularly focused on the family market. The senior citizen market (Hardcastle 1997), conference business and the coaching trade have also featured heavily. Recent trends and social changes have however forced the resort to consider new options. For example the Language School business in Torbay has become extremely important in generating a noticeable income into the tourist economy and is worth in excess of £16m to the resort directly (ERTB 1992). There is a recognition that much has positively occurred in Torbay in recent years to improve and modernise the resort product and the resort is recognised as one of, if not the, premier resort in Great Britain. The English Riviera marketing campaign has been highly successful in creating an image (the palm tree symbol) and awareness in promoting the resort. However, it is also recognised that tourism development and marketing is under-resourced. As Hillary Chambers, Chairman of Strategic Services Committee, explained "We all know the story of Torbay's decline but it's trying to persuade Government that we suffer measurable deprivation that's the big challenge" but she also felt that "At long last ministers are listening and they realise we do suffer problems." This can surely be interpreted as a direct call for Government intervention but also a belief that the Government is not yet taking much action. The Bay is now gearing up for a radical re-think of its holiday industry and tourism leaders are urging local people to pull together (Crowson 1999).

The tourism business in Torbay is projected to earn the resort approaching £300 million per annum and employs both full and part time more than 16,000 people directly. Indirectly there are numerous others who are dependent upon the tourism industry. Its impact is substantial and there is hardly a business in the resort, which does not have some relation to the tourism industry. There are almost 53,000 bedspaces and through the year over 9 million bednights are recorded with an anticipated 1.5 million staying visitors and nearly 3 million day visitors (ERTB 1998). In terms of resorts in Great Britain it is the No. 1 staying resort (DoE figures 1994), with people coming to The English Riviera to relax (ERTB 1997). Research amongst current visitors has been positive, highlighting the value of scenery, climate, accommodation, and many things to do and see (ERTB 1997). To achieve a sustained tourism business in the resort (ILAM 1997) will require an increase in marketing activity, an improvement of the tourism product, new product development and improving standards and service. A focused tourism organisation is needed to co-ordinate all efforts and additional funding is essential. Even in the light of this Torbay has a very positive future if it strives for a resort of excellence, is organised and resourced effectively and develops new, imaginative marketing and development initiatives, including a major national magnet attraction (ERTB 1995). Torbay Borough Council seems to recognise the value of this industry with economic development and support for tourism being seen as major Council activities. Tourism will always remain the core industry in the Borough and as such support for the promotion and marketing of Torbay as a premier holiday resort is, in theory, a cornerstone of the Council's economic development policy.

However, Torbay, in common with other local authorities, is under increasing pressure to maintain services with a decreasing budget. As part of the nation-wide review of local government, by the Local Government Commission, (an independent body established by the Government under the Local Government Act 1992 which has powers to make recommendations for changes to local government structure), (Jolley 1998) Torbay, one of only two councils in Devon, has become a Unitary Authority. This means that the Council has assumed responsibility for all local government services. On the 1st April 1998 Devon County Council transferred its responsibility for providing services in Torbay to Torbay Borough Council (TBC no date). Five directorates replace the original nine borough departments. The Strategic Services Committee takes responsibility for tourism but also for Strategy and Research Co-ordination, Regeneration and European Services, Marketing and Marine Services. There are also two subcommittees, one for Harbours and the other to deal with the Economy, Tourism and Arts Development. The Director of Strategic Services was formerly the Borough's Director of Tourism and Marketing (TBC no date).

Although the Strategic Services Committee has an official obligation to tourism the English Riviera Tourist Board (ERTB), as a division of Torbay Borough Council generally takes responsibility for tourism in Torbay. Therefore the ERTB can be considered as local government. The ERTB has devised a 10-year strategy, which sets a direction for Torbay's tourism and associated organisations to ensure a continued viable and valuable contribution to the Bay's economy and employment. An identified strategy for tourism is needed due to the current dominance of the industry in the local economy. Potential exists for sustaining and perhaps increasing the contribution to the Bay's economy by new initiatives and specific action programmes. This 10-year strategy appears to recognise the importance of tourism, the changes in the market place and the severe competition from overseas holiday destinations. It acknowledges that the aspirations of the British population have changed during this past decade and there is a clear decline in demand for the traditional holiday aspect for which Torbay has been highly successful in the past. The ERTB also produces an in-depth annual marketing plan. Marketing Torbay in the UK centres on the English Riviera Guide, which is backed up by other specific publications. In 1998/99 the ERTB spent £250,000 on advertising (ERTB 1998). Increasingly Government policies are aimed at injecting small amounts of Government money to 'lever out' private sector funding. Partnerships (Briggs 1994) therefore enable the Council to maximise the deployment of its resources. As an example of this, reduced support from Central Government for domestic marketing activities, has resulted in new partnerships being ever more important within the Bay.

Currently there are also strategies for resort renewal being developed both locally, regionally and nationally. Torbay is already playing a lead role in these initiatives, for example hosting the British Resorts Association Conference in December 1998 and helping to draft the South West Regional Development Agency's strategy for the West Country. This new regional strategy for the West Country 'Tourism 2020' is a 20 year vision for tourism in the region and gives long term direction. Torbay in its document 'Putting Resort Regeneration Into Practice', endorses the Tourism 2020 approach and sets out a vision how the Torbay Forum, a private sector organisation, would wish to see tourism 20 years from now. The aim is to achieve an agreed vision for the future and leadership to implement it, to improve partnership activity within the bay and strengthen the private sector organisations and their links with local government (Torbay Forum 1999). This initiative illustrates the private sector both taking a leading role in resort regeneration and calling for Government involvement.

In 1997 maximising the potential of Britain's tourism industry by working in partnership with the industry, local authorities and tourist boards was declared as a high priority for the Government (DNH 1997). In 1999 the Secretary of State for DCMS, Chris Smith said "To maximise tourism's contribution to the economy and to our vision for Britain, we need to work with the industry to an agreed plan, with shared objectives and a common purpose." The Prime Minister, Tony Blair said, "That is what the strategy ['Tomorrow's Tourism'] seeks to achieve through a strong partnership between government and industry." One of the five elements of the new strategy is providing the right framework for tourism to flourish which identifies the responsibilities of government in supporting the development of tourism (DCMS 1999). The strategy was developed in collaboration with the industry via the Ministerial Tourism Advisory Forum which was set up in 1996 to ensure that "the widest possible range of views and expertise is bought into our decision making" (DCMS 1997). Government appears to fully encourage social exchange and seems to want to intervene in a collaborative manner by means of partnerships. Is this approach possible?

In Torbay it is important that the community, the tourist industry and the council join forces. Partnership between the public and private sectors is vital as Laurence Murrell, Torbay Forum's chairman said "Tourism in Torbay will not be successful if we continue to work in isolation" (Crowson 1999). It is crucial that the key individuals and bodies in the public, private and voluntary sectors, with an interest in tourism development, support and become involved in taking forward tourism initiatives, like Torbay's Tourism Development Action Programme, which in 1990 created a unique partnership of public and private sector involvement (ERTB 1990). The private sector also appears to appreciate the value of social exchange, partnerships and Government involvement.

By working closely with South Devon Chamber of Commerce, Torbay Forum, Federation of Small Businesses, Brixham Harbour Advisory Management Board and other bodies both in the public and private sectors the Council is made aware of local needs and concerns. As local and regional economies are so closely inter-linked, the Council is committed, at regional level, to the emerging West Country Development Corporation's strategy for Devon and Cornwall. Torbay Borough Council has been a long standing partner in a series of joint marketing initiatives with Devon County Council, Plymouth City Council and Exeter City Council, aimed at promoting Devon as a business destination, and attracting investment from outside. The Council enjoys a good working relationship with both Teignbridge and South Hams District Councils, and is currently looking at joint schemes with its two neighbours.

The Council is especially keen to work with public and private sector partners to take full advantage of finance available from the European Union e.g. the Initiative PESCA. In 1995, the English Riviera Tourist Board was instrumental in the formation of the Devon and Cornwall Overseas Marketing Consortium (DACOM) (Briggs 1994). By working in partnership DACOM has attracted a major grant from the ERDF Objective 5b Programme, resulting in a budget of £2.2 million over three years. By co-operating with all its partners locally and regionally, Torbay Borough Council is playing its full part in regenerating the economy of the Southwest (ERTB 1996). This example demonstrates the benefits of social exchange. Here we see Government getting involved but moving away from the ideas of intervention and progressing towards notions of partnership. Is this what the tourism industry wants or is intervention necessary?

Methodology

A postpositivist approach has been taken as it is acknowledged that although the reality of the situation exists it may never be fully appreciated and however neutral the researcher attempts to be the epistemological issues may still bias the findings of the research. However the methodological question of how the researcher should go about finding out the knowledge, must still be addressed. A postpositivist paradigm suggests that the findings of an inquiry be based upon as many sources of data, theories and methods as possible (Guba 1990). Thus, having conducted an in-depth literature review, requests for interviews (Briggs 1986) were made to public, private and voluntary organisations, in order to obtain the professional view about the nature of reality, the ontological perspective, of the relationship between Government and tourism. The interviews were semi-structured enquiring about their position within the industry and their views on the relationship under examination. The aim of this form of methodology was to get a holistic view. Comparisons of the opinions help explain the actual relationship between Government and the Tourism Industry in Torbay. These professionals from private, public and voluntary bodies also assisted in the production of a questionnaire (de Vaus 1986) which, after pilot testing and amendments, was used to gauge the views of fifty tourism industry providers, collecting both quantitative and qualitative data (Creswell 1994). The quantitative information was analysed via SPSS and the qualitative material examined separately. The questionnaire provided a framework for the informal interviews. The aim of this research was to determine whether Government intervention in Torbay's tourism industry is a necessity.

Data analysis

A nonprobability purposive sample of professionals from public private and voluntary organisations were approached and interviews were requested; the units were selected subjectively by the researcher who attempted to obtain a sample that appeared to be representative of the population (Nachmias 1981). Unfortunately the request process was of mixed success. No representatives were available for interview from Torbay Borough Council or the English Riviera Tourist Board. As the English Riviera Tourist Board is a division of Torbay Borough Council this meant no one from Local Government was able to discuss the relationship between Government and tourism. However from discussions with public, private and voluntary sector individuals, to be referred to collectively as 'the professionals', there is a general consensus of opinions on many issues. The following section, although not referenced to particular individuals, are the collated views of these professionals on the situation in Torbay.

All appear to encourage the idea of partnership(s), tourism is a whole experience and everyone who provides part of that experience needs to work together and co-operate. Rationalisation is needed to reduce resource wastage. The tourism industry is highly fragmented and it appears that funds are getting tied up in bureaucracy. There is still the need for the number of people involved but they must sort out responsibilities and thus reduce duplication, especially in marketing and promotional work. However, communication is a big problem between agencies, especially between tourism providers and the support groups. In Torbay it is felt that there is a breakdown in communication between local authorities, the industry and support agencies due to a lack of overall co-ordination. There needs to be some form of leadership. The Government could intervene and play a key role in leadership, implement rationalisation to reduce duplication and possible give finance to partnership schemes thus encouraging communication. In Torbay the private sector needs such leadership, guidance and support from the public sector and the local economy needs private sector investment. Determination for social exchange should therefore be mutual.

Government has the power to greatly influence tourism because it can produce legislation that can fundamentally change the way tourism operates, plus it has finance. The Government is thus powerful in setting the environment in which tourism operates. But Tourism is a localised industry and the power to support tourism has got to be generated locally by gaining popular agreement. Tourism is an overall package; the whole community is involved in the experience of the tourist. So the community needs to be educated to understand the benefits of tourism to accept the costs. The localised nature of tourism means Central Government has little direct influence over delivery. Local authority decisions are easier to facilitate as, in theory, they reflect the needs of the locality. This suggests that Government intervention should be performed by Local Authorities which perhaps answers the earlier question of whether implementation should be by Central Government or Local Authorities. However there are often insufficient debates between local authority and the tourism industry. Questions also arise over how truly representative local councils are of the views of the community.

The truly representative nature of support groups needs to be examined. The Hotel and Caterers' Association, for example, professes to support the interests of all hotel and catering establishments, but in actual fact they only represent their members, those who have paid a subscription. To effectively get your views heard you have to go to their meetings. However the majority of the industry is made up of small businesses, who often have little or no time to attend meetings. This leaves the meetings to the bigger establishments who have more staff and time available. So how representative are these organisations of the industry as a whole? To take it a stage further the Torbay Forum, consisting of representatives from all of the more localised and industry related support agencies, must surely be representative of the views of only a select group, probably large establishment providers who are in the minority. So the effectiveness and representativeness is questionable and an increase in power/influence probably undesirable.

Tourism is still low down on the agenda even with the creation of the DCMS. There is still no clear policy or support structure for the Tourism Industry coming from Central Government. Although lines of communication with Central Government have improved with a number of discussion groups set up; the Government still generally works from a distance and often without consultation. The Industry needs to know how decisions were constructed and consensus is needed. Representation is limited even with consultation groups, often only the views of the bigger players are heard, this is even more pronounced in Torbay because of the nature of the industry and the predominance of small businesses.

However, the industry does need help, many tourism providers are trying to be all things to all people and the result is often a lower standard of experience for the tourist. In Torbay the major problem is lack of professionalism and the belief that they do not need help. Many come to the industry with no prior background or training and very little knowledge. There are many organisations providing training but somehow it does not seem to be reaching the industry. Many providers only think short term, few have business plans or tourism development strategies and these are major failings that result in a lack of professionalism. Businesses also feel they are only in competition locally and do not see the broader UK or even European and world-wide perspectives and thus do not work together. On the whole few seem to be investing for long term benefits and standards vary considerably. This research has shown that many supporting the industry would like to see more Government involvement and feel that Government has an important leadership and co-ordination role to play.

Following the interviews (Briggs 1986) with the tourism professionals and informal discussions with tourism providers a questionnaire (de Vaus 1986) was used to semi-structure interviews with fifty tourism providers in the Torbay area. Again a nonprobability purposive sample was used to obtain a sample that appeared to be representative of the population (Nachmias 1981). There was a rich diversity of views, interests and beliefs that highlights the variety of personnel in the industry. The quantitative data was gathered to gain a statistical view of tourism in Torbay and the qualitative information was to provide an understanding of the working of the industry and thus the relationship between Government and Tourism. There was a general lack of awareness concerning both Central and even Local Government implications for tourism implying that the relationship between Government and tourism is a distant one.

The breakdown of the fifty providers questioned confirmed the view that tourism is predominantly a small business industry. The main factors that seemed to effect business varied tremendously but the majority cited climate, the economy and infrastructure. The climate is uncontrollable but the economy can be affected by both Central and Local Government, as can the infrastructure. The industry appears to want increased investment in tourism, a healthier economy generally, improved infrastructure, better marketing of the Bay and more support. So again we hear calls for more Government involvement.

It has been stated that many industry providers lack professionalism and try to be all things to all people. The majority of businesses questioned (72%, n=36) try to cater for all. Of those who did cater for particular market segments there appeared to be no obvious trend. Providing support for an earlier assumption, providers were asked if they had any long-term strategies, even more alarming than the lack of market segmentation, 74% (n=37) of those questioned had no long-term strategy. The lack of professionalism assumption appears to be justified. Especially as even for those who did have long-term strategies the majority were drawn up internally, although some obtained professional advice.

The representative nature of the associations was criticised earlier, so the businesses in Torbay were asked if they belonged/were a member of the Hotel and Caterers' Association and/or the West Country Tourist Board. The results were inconclusive and the division between types of establishment showed no definite trend. Thus the assertion that associations such as the Hotel and Caterers' Association and the West Country Tourist Board, only representing larger establishments is unsubstantiated by this data. The amount of support from the West Country Tourist Board varied, but generally it came mainly in the form of marketing, advice and information and the award/inspection scheme respectively. In connection with harmonisation of standards and issues surrounding, legislation and statutory obligations providers were asked if they were in favour of compulsory registration of accommodation. Encouragingly 72% (n=36) said 'Yes' and many felt it would help raise standards.

With regard to partnerships and the relationship between Government and Tourism, questions were asked about how involved the provider, as an industry representative, was in the decision making of the English Riviera Tourist Board, Torbay Borough Council and Torbay Forum, individually, in matters that affect the Tourism Industry in Torbay. The English Riviera Tourist Board, as the tourism division of Torbay Borough Council, should be in close consultation with the Industry, however, 70% (n=35) were not involved at all and 14% (n=7) only slightly, which suggests an almost non-existent relationship with the majority of the Industry. Involvement with the decision making of Torbay Borough Council, although not solely concerned with tourism, is even less with 80% (n=40) not at all involved and 10% (n=5) only slightly. From this one could conclude that the relationship between Local Government and Tourism in Torbay is very poor, but first one must consider the Industry's involvement with Torbay Forum which is supposed to be the link between the Industry and Government. Unfortunately figures substantiated the previous assumption, as 82% (n=41) are not involved at all with the decision making of the Torbay Forum. The breakdown of involvement by type of establishment does show that the only group that is really very involved in the decision making of the English Riviera Tourist Board, Torbay Borough Council and Torbay Forum is the large hotels. This does confirm the assumption made earlier about representation, which was not substantiated in terms of Hotel and Caterers' Association and West Country Tourist Board membership.

When asked if they considered Government to be involved in tourism 62% (n=31) said 'Yes', but the majority did not know in what ways. Then they were asked if the Government affected their business, 76% (n=38) said 'Yes' but a surprising 26% (n=13) said 'No'. This surely reflects the lack of professionalism in the Industry, as those that said 'No' did not realise that the Government affects the economy, sets business rates, issues legislation and regulations and collects VAT, to name but a few, thus affecting their business in a variety of important ways and to a significant extent. Confusion arose when asked the extent to which Government contributes to tourism in terms of monitoring, guiding, co-ordinating, encouraging and funding tourism. Some who had said Government was not involved in tourism then felt that the Government contributed a lot. Perhaps this is a fault in the questionnaire construction or maybe it reflects the lack of awareness and understanding of the providers interviewed.

The majority questioned believed that the Government was only slightly involved in monitoring, yet had some involvement in guiding. Views were evenly divided on whether the Government was not at all or only slightly involved in co-ordinating tourism. It was felt that the Government was giving some encouragement but only slightly funding the industry. The majority, a staggering 86% (n=43) felt more Government involvement was needed, and when asked in what ways they cited tourism promotion, support and encouragement, more funding and marketing and improved infrastructure.

Conclusion

The case study of Torbay shows that the Local Government and the Tourism Industry have an almost non-existent direct relationship although the Unitary Authority is active in supporting tourism. In terms of Central Government and tourism, providers in Torbay, felt that Government was involved with tourism and affected their businesses, yet only slightly monitored and funded tourism, but gave some encouragement and guidance. Views showed the Government's co-ordinating role as weak. The majority wanted more Government involvement. Research has shown that the Government needs to provide leadership, implement rationalisation to reduce duplication and possibly give finance to partnership schemes so as to encourage co-operation and communication. Government has the power to greatly influence tourism via legislation. Government thus sets the environment in which tourism operates. The majority in Torbay were in favour of compulsory registration of accommodation. Research has confirmed the view that tourism is on the whole made up of many small businesses that are greatly affected by the general economy and infrastructure and in need of investment, improved marketing and support. The relationship between local government and tourism in Torbay is concerning, although Torbay Borough Council and the English Riviera Tourist Board seem to be very active in supporting tourism, writing about it and liasing with various related organisations/bodies, the actual Industry have an almost non existent direct relationship with both Torbay Borough Council and the English Riviera Tourist Board. The Torbay Forum, which is supposed to be the link between Government and the Industry, also has a weak relationship with the actual providers in Torbay.

The overall conclusion to be gleaned from this study into the relationship between the British Government and the Tourism Industry is that both Central and Local Government, public sector roles, are very important and influential in terms of tourism and are actively involved, yet from a distance. There appears to be very little direct contact, partly due to the representative nature of the groups reporting to both Local and central Government. So the relationship is crucial but not close. Government intervention in tourism therefore appears necessary. Those supporting tourism as well as those working in the industry seem to want the Government to intervene, to take a decisions or intrusive role in order to determine events. They seem to positively call for intervention in their affairs and even state what they want. The industry want intervention to take place in the form of leadership, co-ordination, rationalisation and finance. They seem to feel that some general directives should come from Central Government but the majority of local issues should be handled by Local Authorities due to the localised nature of the industry. This raises questions about how the Government can properly support tourism, if it has little or no contact with those actually in the Industry, predominantly the private sector and no real knowledge and understanding on which to base policy decisions. Policy decisions, that have been guided by ideology and paradigms that might be inappropriate to the actual situation. So more direct consultation is needed between the British Government and the Tourism Industry, between public and private sectors. There needs to be more commitment, communication and interaction to encourage the social exchange. If the Government will not initiate this process it is in the best interests of the Industry to do so.

References

Bacon, M. and Le Pelley, B. (1994), 'Should Tourism Be A Statutory Local Authority Function?' *Insights*. London: ETB.

Baum, T. (1995), 'Trends In International Tourism.' *Tourism Intelligence Papers, Insights*. London: ETB.

Briggs, C. L. (1986), *Learning how to ask: A sociolinguistic appraisal of the role of the interview in social science research*. Cambridge University Press.

Briggs, S. (1994), Powerful Partnerships - Setting up and running a marketing consortium.' *Tourism Intelligence Papers: Insights*. London: ETB

Creswell, J. W. (1994), *Research Design - Qualitative and Quantitative Approaches*. London: Sage.

Crowson, T. (1999), Keep Bay Afloat. *Herald Express* Friday June 11th 1999.

de Vaus, D. A. (1986), 'Constructing questionnaires.' *Surveys in Social Research*. London: George Allen and Unwin.

Department for Culture, Media and Sport DCMS, (1998), *Tourism*. [online]. Available from: http://www.culture.gov.uk/TOURISM.HTM [07/06/99].

Department For Culture, Media and Sport DCMS 56/97 Issued on 23 September 1997 *Jennifer Robson is appointed to English Tourist Board*. [online]. Available from: http://www.worldserver.pipex.com/coi/depts/GHE/coi2665d.ok [09/06/99].

Department for Culture, Media and Sport DCMS 71/97 Issued 10 October 1997 *Chris Smith Announces Expanded Role For Tourism Forum*. [online]. Available from: http://www.worldserver.pipex.com/coi/depts/GHE/coi2665d.ok [09/06/99].

Department for Culture, Media and Sport, Tourism Division (1999),*Tomorrow's Tourism*. [online] London: DCMS. Available from: http://www.culture.gov.uk/TOURSTRAT.HTM.

Department of National Heritage DCMS 178/97 Issued on 14 July 1997 *Chris Smith Welcomes New Name for His Department*. [online]. Available from: http://www.worldserver.pipex.com/coi/depts/GHE/coi2665d.ok [10/06/99].

Department of National Heritage DNH 132/97 Issued on 4 June 1997. [online]. Available from: http://www.worldserver.pipex.com/coi/depts/GHE/coi2665d.ok [09/06/99].

Department of National Heritage. (1997), *Success through Partnership - A Strategy for Tourism Competing with the Best*. London: DNH.

English Riviera Tourist Board. (1990), *The Tourism Development Action Programme*. Torbay: English Riviera Tourist Board.

English Riviera Tourist Board. (1992), *The Torbay Language Schools Business Survey*. Torbay: English Riviera Tourist Board.

English Riviera Tourist Board. (1995), *Torbay Tourism Strategy 1995-2005*. Torquay: Torbay Borough Council.

English Riviera Tourist Board. (1996), *The Economic Development Strategy for 1996-7*. Torbay: English Riviera Tourist Board.

English Riviera Tourist Board. (1997), *English Riviera Tourism Talk*. Torquay: Torbay Borough Council.

English Riviera Tourist Board. (1998), *Marketing Plan 1998/99*. Torquay: Torbay Borough Council.

English Riviera Tourist Board. (1998), *Tourism Fact Sheet*. Torquay: Torbay Borough Council.

English Tourist Board. (1997), *Agenda 2000 Brief*. London: ETB.

English Tourist Board. (1997), *Annual Report*. London: ETB.

Guba, E. C. (1990), *The Paradigm Dialog*. Sage.

Hall, M. (1994), *Tourism and Politics: Policy, Power and Place*. Chichester: John Wiley and Sons.

Hardcastle, S. (1997), 'Reaping Benefits From The Over 50s Market.' *Insights*. London: BTA/ETB.

Henry, I. (1993), *The Politics Of Leisure Policy*. London: Macmillan.

Homans, G. C. (1958), 'Social Behaviour as Exchange' *The American Journal of Sociology*, Vol. 63, No. 6, May 1958, pp. 597-600, The University of Chicago Press.

ILAM. (1997), Resort Regeneration - European Conference.

Jolley, S. (1998), *A Chronology of State Involvement in British Tourism*. [online]. Available from: http://apollo4.bournemouth.ac.uk/si/tjolley/teaching_materials/state-inv..._tm_int.htm [11/06/99].

Lumsdon, L. (1992), *Marketing for Tourism*. London: MacMillian.

Peat, J. and Mullen, G. (1995), 'Tourism and the Economy'. *Tourism Intelligence Papers*, Insights, London: ETB.

Swarbrooke, J. (1997) 'The Role of the European Union In UK Tourism.' *Tourism Intelligence Papers*. London: BTA/ETB.

Torbay Borough Council, no date. *New Council is Committed to Providing Better Services*. [online]. Available from: htp://www.torbay.gov.uk/council/your/newcouncil.htm [11/06/99].

Torbay Borough Council, no date. *Strategic Services Committee Function*. [online]. Available from: htp://www.torbay.gov.uk/council/cttee4.htm [14/04/99].

Torbay Borough Council, no date. Torbay Council's Frequently Asked Questions. [online]. Available from: htp://www.torbay.gov.uk/council/faqs.htm [19/04/99].

Torbay Forum (1999), *Putting Resort Regeneration into Practice* Torquay: The Torbay Forum.

Walton, J. K. (1983), English Seaside Resorts. Leicester: Leicester University Press.

Wason, G. (1996), 'Effective Tourism Policy'. *Tourism Intelligence Papers: Insights*. London: BTA/ETB.

Tourism higher education revisited: A business management based framework

Nigel Evans

University of Northumbria, UK

Abstract

The teaching of tourism at a higher education level has become well established in British universities, but in the UK, as elsewhere in the world, the place of tourism studies within the academic curricula remains uncertain. The paper considers the diversity and complexities of tourism studies through a categorisation of journal articles, and through an investigation of the underlying debates that have influenced the design of academic curricula in the UK. The paper concludes that tourism cannot be treated as a discipline but as a field and that the usual approach in the UK, at least at the undergraduate level, has been to emphasise the business studies subjects.

Introduction

Tourism education and training has expanded rapidly over recent years mirroring the growing recognition of tourism (and the travel industry that serves it) as one of the world's most significant economic, social and environmental forces. Education and training has been developed at various levels, ranging from highly vocational courses through to higher research degrees. The growth reflects the widely held belief that one of the major challenges the industry faces is to recruit, develop and retain employees and managers with appropriate educational backgrounds.

Tourism is multi-faceted and inherently multi disciplinary making it difficult to classify and in turn making it difficult to design syllabi which are inclusive, academically rigorous and relevant to the changing needs of the sector's employment market. This paper explores the growth and development of tourism education in general using the UK (where the subject, area is now well developed) as a case study. The paper also considers the diversity and complexities of tourism through an analysis and categorisation of journal articles and through an investigation of the underlying debates that have influenced the design of academic curricula in the UK.

It can be argued that three sometimes-divergent influences have influenced the design of appropriate curricula for tourism degree courses. First, an academic debate has emerged focusing on where tourism studies should fit within the overall framework of knowledge and education. This debate has focused on the inherent difficulties in classification and definition of the tourism phenomena due to its complex nature. Second, a debate has taken place as to the role tourism studies should play in terms of serving the industry Third, the growing body of specialist literature that has developed particularly since the launch of major journals in the 1970's has influenced the tourism curriculum.

The growth of tourism education

The terms 'tourism' and 'tourists' only came into common usage at the beginning of the 19th century Smith, 1989), and higher level studies of the phenomena belong to even more recent times. Formal study of tourism began in North America in the 1940's but the subject area really started to develop in the 1980's (Koh, 1994). In an UK context Airey (1988) argues that it is very difficult to establish exactly when tourism education really commenced in the UK, since practically based courses for hotel managers and ticket agents have long existed. However, the growth in tourism higher education dates back to the early 1970's. Evidence (Airey et al. 1993; Middleton and Ladkin, 1996; Airey and Johnson, 1999) suggests that at the post graduate level the number of courses has risen from two in 1972 to ten in 1991 and 33 in 1997. At the undergraduate level courses have grown from the first two in 1986 (at what have now become the Universities of Northumbria and Bournemouth) to 12 in 1991. The 1990's witnessed an explosion in the provision of under-graduate tourism education in the UK. Figure 1 indicates that there were 46 under-graduate degree courses featuring 'tourism' in the title running in the UK during 1998/99 and that 36 higher education institutions were involved in this provision (CRAC, 1999)

Similar growth in provision has occurred elsewhere in the developed world, Payne (1988) and Koshizucha et al (1988) for instance describe the recent growth in tourism higher education in New Zealand and Japan respectively. In the USA and Canada, tourism studies and hospitality management courses are integrated to a large extent, making it hard to classify all the relevant courses and the range of curricula and modularization make generalisations difficult. However, Cooper et al (1996) estimate that approximately 30 universities, business schools and colleges in the USA offer tourism studies as an option or elective at either under graduate or post graduate levels.

With first year enrolments in the UK on post graduate and undergraduate courses currently standing at about 5,000 (Airey and Johnson, 1999) a debate has been taking place as to the possible over supply of tourism graduates (CNAA, 1993; Evans, 1993; Ryan, 1995;). The concern relates to the perceived inability of the tourism industry to absorb the graduates being produced in turn is a reflection not only on the numbers of graduates, but on the structural characteristics of the industry itself. Employment in the industry is often seasonal, there are comparatively few large companies or public sector organisations with established patterns of graduate recruitment and the nature of many of the jobs in the industry is such that they are perceived to be unsuitable for graduate recruits (Ryan, 1995). A diverse range of tourism courses has thus developed which are difficult to compare across national boundaries leading to calls for international harmonisation of tourism education (Jaspers, 1987; Richards, 1998), but little progress has been evident in this regard. In practice, as

Jenkins points out, the tourism syllabus taught by any institution will reflect its tradition, staff experience and interests (Jenkins, 1980).

Diverse approaches to the study of tourism

Tourism as a field of study has been trying to establish itself for some years as a valid and rigorous subject for higher level academic studies. As Tribe (1997) puts it "conscious of its youthfulness and thus its potential lack of intellectual credibility, tourism studies has sought to define itself in ways which would give it academic weight." In recent years a debate has taken place in the literature as to the most appropriate approaches to tourism studies. The focus of the debate has been upon the conceptualisation of tourism (Faulkner and Ryan, 1999) and specifically on whether or not tourism should be treated as a distinct discipline. It is evident that some authors (Leiper, 1981; Jovicic, 1988; Comic, 1989 and Rogozinski 1985) advocate that tourism should be treated as a distinct discipline. Other, mainly later works, contend that tourism as an area of study fails to meet the necessary criteria in order to be treated as a distinct discipline. (Gunn, 1987; Dann, Nash and Pearce, 1988; Jafari, 1990; Morley, 1990; Pearce, 1993; Pearce and Butler, 1993; Ritchie and Goeldner, 1994; Echtner and Jamal, 1997 and Tribe, 1997).

Jafari (1990) for instance, argues that four platforms of tourism studies have emerged chronologically but that they are not mutually exclusive. The first two platforms Advocacy and Cautionary focus on tourism impacts whilst the third, Adaptancy focuses on forms of development. The Knowledge Based platform, the last of the four identified aims to study tourism holistically and in so-doing strives for the formation of a scientific body of knowledge in tourism, while at the same time "maintaining bridges with other platforms" (Jafari, 1990). Echtner and Jamal (1997) in a wide-ranging review of the 'disciplinary dilemma' argue that the knowledge-based platform is consistent with the move toward the treatment of tourism as a distinctive discipline. However, in order to reach such a position the authors argue that tourism needs to overcome its theoretical fragmentation and research has to move towards an interdisciplinary as opposed to a multidisciplinary approach.

Tribe (1997), building on the work of Hirst (1974), goes further when he maintains that not only is tourism not currently a discipline but also that the search for tourism as a discipline should be abandoned. To continue to advocate that tourism should be viewed as a discipline would involve "casting adrift of important parts of tourism studies in the quest for conceptual coherence and logical consistency". Instead, Tribe (1997), Gunn (1987) and Jafari and Ritchie (1981) argue that tourism should be regarded as a 'field' of study. In this way tourism becomes similar to housing or engineering (Tribe, 1997) in that they concentrate on particular phenomena or practices and call upon a number of disciplines to investigate and explain their areas of interest. In contrasting fields and disciplines Henkel (1988) noted that disciplines "are held together by distinctive constellations of theories, concepts and methods" whereas fields, "draw upon all sorts of knowledge that may illuminate them".

The role of the industry in tourism education

A number of papers have focused attention on the role tourism studies should play with regard to serving the needs of the travel and tourism industry (Collins, Sweeney and Geen, 1994; Middleton and Ladkin, 1996; Cooper and Shepherd, 1997; Busby, Brunt and Baber, 1997; Amoah and Baum, 1997; Leslie and Richardson, 2000). Defining the industry in itself is a complex problem (beyond the scope of this paper) which Cooper and Shepherd (1997) address before going on to produce a valuable summary of the issues regarding the industry's involvement with tourism education. Haywood and Maki (1992) provide a conceptual model for the relationship between employers and the education sector and suggest that there are differing expectations between the two groups in that employers emphasise practical skills and general transferable skills whereas educators are developing more conceptual and tourism-specific materials. This, Haywood and Maki contend has resulted in a communications gap characterised by poor levels of communication between the two groups; a lack of involvement of educators in the industry; and, industry's role in education (through advisory bodies etc), often being poorly defined.

Educators face a dilemma as to whether they develop a curriculum that attempts to meet the needs of the industry as a whole or whether an attempt is made to focus on one particular sub-sector. Covering the industry in its entirety runs the risk of failing to meet the more specific needs of its sub-sectors whilst specialising in one sub-sector inevitably restricts student demand and likely opportunities for graduates.

A further issue faced by educators is that some evidence suggests that knowledge of tourism and of the structure and dynamics of the industry rate lower in tourism employers' requirements than many advocates of specialist tourism education might have expected. In a survey of eight leading UK tourism employers tourism specific knowledge did not rate highly in the desired attributes that graduate recruits should possess (CNAA, 1993). Graduate attributes sought by these employers were cites as:

- General intellect, calibre, personality and academic ability.

- Basic skills such as numeracy and literacy.

- Performance at the same level as non-tourism graduates plus a greater tourism specific knowledge.

- A strong grounding in general business studies.

The same study perhaps implied the need for a core curriculum when it was argued that the travel and tourism industry should be better educated as to what having a travel and tourism qualification actually means. The industry knows what to expect from French or Geography graduates for instance, but it was pointed out that this is not the case for tourism graduates.

The role of the tourism literature in tourism education

The scope and diversity of the growing body of tourism literature have influenced the tourism curricula. One way of considering the diversity inherent in the study of tourism is to consider the papers that have been published in the major journals that are devoted to covering the area of study.

The classification of journal articles – methodology

A sample of key journals was thus selected to consider two periods 1987-1988 and 1997-1998. These periods were chosen in order to provide evidence of any shifts that may have occurred in the focus of tourism studies over the period. All substantive papers presented in the journals were reviewed and categorised by the author into ten categories.

Research conducted by Sheldon (1990,1991) to assess the academic ranking of tourism journals identified the top three rated journals (based on perceived quality) as being Annals of Tourism Research, Journal of Travel Research, and Tourism Management. Although Sheldon's study was carried out prior to the launch of several tourism journals, later research by Howey et al (1999) followed the ranking in selecting three journals to investigate patterns of cross-citations. The Journals chosen for the study are international in their orientation, well established in the field, and generally contain a broad range of material in relation to their subject matter. The journal articles were analysed on the basis of their content and categorised by subject headings into one of ten subject categories. The ten subject categories and the subject headings that were included within each of these categories are shown in Table 1.

Table 1   Subject Categories used in the Classification of Journal Articles

No.	Article Subject Category	Subject Headings Covered by this Category
1.	Management	Marketing, service quality, destination image, strategy and business planning, information technology, visitor management, general management.
2.	Industry sectors	Accommodation owners and operators, cruising, airlines, sea, rail and car travel, travel agents and tour operators, travel and tourism organisations, the 'travel trade'.
3.	Culture and Heritage	Culture and heritage, authenticity, commoditisation, indigenous peoples, identity, interpretation and museums, conferences, exhibitions, festivals and events.
4.	Methodology	Methodologies, models, forecasting, definition issues, data analysis, conceptualisation.
5.	Environment	Geographical and development studies, tourism planning, sustainability, environmental impacts and assessment, tourist flows.
6.	Policy	tourism policy, political economy, legal and regulatory aspects.
7.	Social and Economic	Social and economic impacts and assessment, multiplier analysis, application of economic concepts, finance, pricing.
8.	Cases and trends	Illustrative case studies, emerging tourism trends, regional, area and resort studies.
9.	Education	Tourism education, training and careers.
10.	Tourist behaviour	Tourist behaviour, tourist expenditures, tourist ethics, guest/host relationships.

Source: Author's categorisation of journal articles

The classification of journal articles – research limitations

It is recognized that the methodology has inherent limitations in that a limited number of journals were chosen and that they were analyzed over two discrete periods only, which are not necessarily representative of the intervening period. Furthermore several additional specialist journals have been launched over the intervening period which focus on a particular set of themes. The Journal of Sustainable Tourism for example specializes in the environmental aspects of tourism whilst Tourism Economics concentrates on economic and financial issues. There is clearly a need for further qualitative research in this field using key-word searches and appropriate analytical software in order to provide a more detailed classification. The results are also slightly distorted owing to the publication of several 'Special Editions' of journals covering a particular theme. Notwithstanding these limitations, it is argued here that the research carried out provides a guideline as to the diversity of subject areas that are being considered in tourism studies and identifies any major shifts in focus that have taken place.

The classification of journal articles – research findings

The findings are summarised in Table 2 and Figure 1. Table 2 presents a full breakdown of the articles analysed in the two periods broken down by subject category.

Table 2   Categorisation of Tourism Journal Articles

Article Subject Category	No. of articles 1987-1988			No. of articles 1997-1998		
	Journal of Travel Research	Annals of Tourism Research	Tourism Mgt.	Journal of Travel Research	Annals of Tourism Research	Tourism Mgt.
Management	19	6	12	23	11	18
Business sectors	5	0	6	19	10	6
Culture and Heritage	1	1	3	5	7	8
Methodology	3	19*	9	7	8	15
Environment	0	14*	13	8	6	4
Policy	2	2	4	1	8	3
Social and Economic	10	2	8	5	8	1
Cases and trends	1	2	7	1	10	7
Education	0	2	0	1	5	10
Tourist behaviour	6	1	1	10	10	9
Totals	47	49	63	80	83	81

Source: Author's categorisation

Notes:

1. 1987-88 Journal of Travel Research - 8 issues, Annals of Tourism Research - 8 issues, Tourism Management - 8 issues.

2. 1997-98 Journal of Travel Research - 8 issues, Annals of Tourism Research 8 issues, Tourism Management - 14 issues.

Figure 1 provides an analysis of the percentage of journal articles that have been identified as falling within the subject range of each of the ten chosen categories.

Figure 1.   Analysis of Journal Articles by Subject Category

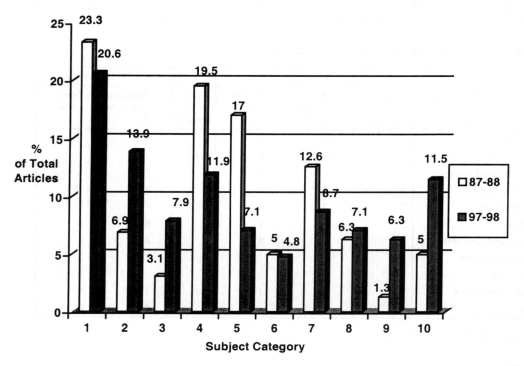

The analysis shows that papers on management issues stand out as the most important category (in both periods). Categories 2, 3, and 10 (Business Sectors, Culture and Heritage and Tourist Behaviour respectively have shown substantial growth in the number of papers presented whilst category 5 (Environment) and 6 (Cases and Trends) have shown significant down turns. Category 9 (Education) has also grown substantially but from a low base. Environmental papers have declined in these journals, possibly as a result of the establishment of more focused tourism journals. The case study approach has perhaps shown a fall because papers have moved from a narrow focus on a particular area or region to a focus that encompasses the wider implications and lessons applicable in different circumstances. Taken together categories 1 and 2 that broadly represent a 'business based' focus represent approximately 30% of all papers presented in both periods. Overall the analysis shows that there has been a marked levelling between the categories indicating a broadening in the scope of tourism studies. The top three categories accounted for 59.8% of all the papers presented in the 1987-89 period, whereas this percentage had fallen to 46.4% in the later period.

The educators' response

In response to the diversity of the subject area (as evidenced by the analysis of journal papers) and the academic and industry debates that have taken place, educators have sought to address the academic curricula issues that arise. (CNAA, (1993); Airey and Middleton, (1994); Koh, (1995); Gunn, (1998); Holloway, (1995); Airey and Johnson, (1999). Demand for the categorisation of the body of tourism knowledge has manifested itself in repeated calls for the establishment of a 'core curriculum' an issue, which as Airey and Johnson (1999) point out, "has been debated for almost as long as tourism has been studied." In the UK at least, the notion has gained increased acceptance as a survey carried out in 1992 showed that 82% of respondents supported the notion of a core curriculum (Cooper, Shepherd and Westlake, 1992).

Various models have been developed of such a core curriculum including one suggested by Burkhart and Medlik (1974). To promote industry-education links the 'Tourism Society' in the UK established the National Liaison Group for Higher Education in tourism (NLG) in 1993. This independent membership organisation provides a focus for development of tourism studies degrees and postgraduate qualifications through collaboration with employers (Busby, Brunt, and Baber, 1997); although ensuring full industry involvement has proved to be problematic. Some agreement was reached by the organisations represented at the NLG on a core curriculum. The following seven areas were put forward:

- The meaning and nature of tourism and its relationship with leisure and recreation;

- The structure of the tourism industry, key sectors in the industry and their principal operating characteristics, linkages within the industry;

- The dimensions of tourism - internationally and domestically - and issues of measurement;

- The significance and impact of tourism - the economic, social and physical environment and issues of sustainable development;

- Marketing - tourism applications;

- Planning and development - tourism applications; and,

- Policy issues, management of tourism, finance and organisation.

The core body of knowledge as it has developed in the UK, is not intended to be prescriptive in that courses do not have to include all these headings or restrictive in that the headings do not preclude the inclusion of other topics (Airey and Johnson, 1999). The notion of such a core body of knowledge has received some support in the literature (CNAA, 1993; Richards, 1993; and Holloway, 1995) whilst some criticism has also been levelled. The CNAA (1993: 3) report in articulating the case in favour of such a body of knowledge cites the following reasons:

- To facilitate the definition of course and teaching objectives;

- To assist in communicating what is offered;

- To facilitate course validation and quality;

- To assist teachers to focus their research and to develop and enhance academic integrity;

- To facilitate the development of understanding and progression between attainment levels;

- To facilitate the transferability of credits; and,

- To facilitate communication, liaison and ease of progression.

Baum (1997) and Amoah and Baum (1997) argue that such a development would weaken the development of tourism as an area of study by reducing variety, hindering flexibility and stifling innovation and would furthermore, lead to a failure to respond to diverse industry requirements. These criticisms may be supplemented by a further criticism relating to the highly competitive environment in which UK universities have to compete for students, resources, industrial placement and graduate opportunities. It can be argued that a core body of knowledge restricts the ability of universities in establishing the unique attributes of the courses they offer. In reality little in the way of co-ordinated action has taken place within British higher education institutions in order to facilitate the introduction of the proposed core curriculum.

Discussion

In the 1980's in particular many persuasive papers, such as Leiper's important work of 1981, argued the case for tourism to be accepted as a distinct discipline. It followed from such a position that tourism could be housed in a university department. Later writers such as Tribe (1997) and Echtner, and Tazim, (1997), have presented contrary arguments suggesting that tourism could not be treated as a discipline and at the same time pressures from the tourism industry have been exerted forcing tourism studies into business orientated approaches.

Here, it is argued that tourism cannot be treated as a discipline and the arguments that have been presented in favour of doing so are not compelling. The concepts which have been utilised in tourism such as life cycle analysis, impact studies, multiplier analysis and yield management are concepts that have been adapted to be used in tourism but are not unique to tourism studies. Thus while economics, sociology, and psychology are all disciplines, since they represent a way of studying; parks and recreation, leisure, education and tourism are not since they represent something to be studied (Tribe, 1997). If tourism is thus a field of study rather than a discipline it can be viewed as having much in common with the business studies subject areas that are themselves multi-disciplinary fields (Faulkner and Ryan, 1999). The techniques and applied knowledge in marketing, strategic management, human resource management and the other functional business areas, are "derivative partly from the disciplines that contribute to them and partly from the world of business practice" (Henkel, 1988).

Business and business schools within universities appear to be exerting a powerful gravitational pull upon the field of tourism studies. "The tourism studies that is developing in higher education tends to be crystallising around the business interdisciplinary approach" (Tribe, 1997). This is because there is some coherence and structure to be observed in the field of tourism business studies (Tribe, 1997) and it is consistent with many employers' views as to the necessary attributes required of tourism graduates. Tourism studied within disciplines, such as sociology, forms a small component of the overall field, and does not appear to have formed in a unified manner. Empirically, the journal analysis represented in Table 3 and Figure 1 appear to confirm that the business based subject areas remain the most popular areas of academic investigation, whilst in the UK most courses have adopted structures which have incorporated a large business based component. Furthermore the tourism business based approach to the subject area represents a way of relating tourism studies to allied fields of study such as hospitality and leisure.

Table 3   Undergraduate Tourism Courses in the UK

Institutions	Course Title
Abertay	Tourism
Birmingham CFT	Adventure Tourism Hospitality and Tourism Management Tourism Business Management Tourism Management
Blackpool and Fylde C.	Hospitality Management with Tourism
Bolton IHI	International Tourism Tourism Management
Bournemouth	Tourism Studies
Brighton	International Tourism Management Tourism Management Travel Management
Canterbury C	Tourism Studies
Central Lancashire	International Tourism
Cheltenham and Gloucester CHE	Tourism Management
Glasgow Caledonian	Tourism Management
Greenwich	Tourism Management
Hertfordshire	Tourism Management
Lincoln	European Tourism International Tourism Tourism
Liverpool John Moores	Tourism and Leisure
London CP and D.	International Travel and Tourism Management
Luton	Sports Tourism Travel and Tourism
Manchester Met.	Hospitality Management with Tourism
Napier	Hospitality (Tourism Management)
Northumbria	Travel and Tourism Management
Norwich City C	Hospitality and Tourism Management
Oxford Brookes	Tourism

Plymouth	Tourism Management
Queen Margaret C.	Hospitality and Tourism Management
	Tourism Management
Robert Gordon	Tourism and Hospitality Management
Sheffield Hallam	Hotel and Tourism Management
South Bank	Tourism Management
Strathclyde	Tourism
Sunderland	Tourism development studies
Surrey	International Hospitality and Tourism Management
Thames Valley	Tourism
UC of Ripon and York	Leisure and Tourism Studies
UC Scarborough	Leisure and Tourism Management
Ulster	Hotel and Tourism Management
Wales (Bangor)	Leisure and Tourism Resource Management
Wales (UWIC)	Tourism
Westminster	Tourism and Planning

Source: Adapted from CRAC Degree Course Guide 1998-1999 (1998), Volume 11, Hobsons Publishing, Cambridge, UK

Figure 2 shows a conceptualisation of tourism taught within a business management framework. In the framework the studies of tourism (and of the travel industry that has grown to support this human activity) are viewed as fields which are linked and interact with other closely related fields such as hospitality. All of these fields can be studied using a business management orientation since they share common features and since the business management field is itself, like tourism, derived from underlying core disciplines.

It can be argued that all these sectors are closely related and their subject matter is, in many cases, complementary and over lapping, with subject borders often blurred. This is explicitly recognised in the Quality Assurance arrangements for courses in UK where hospitality, leisure, sport and tourism have been grouped together as 'Unit 25'. Despite the evident diversity of subject matter, "there are many areas of common knowledge and understanding" (QAA, 2000). These subject fields share a number of unifying factors. All are concerned with:

Enriching the life experiences of people, as consumers, participants and providers (QAA, 2000);

- Delivering efficient services to customers;

- The management of businesses and organisations within "industrial sub sectors characterised by growth, diversity, vitality and volatility" (QAA, 2000); and'

- Having a growing requirement for well-educated managers.

Figure 2   Tourism Management: conceptualisation of related subjects

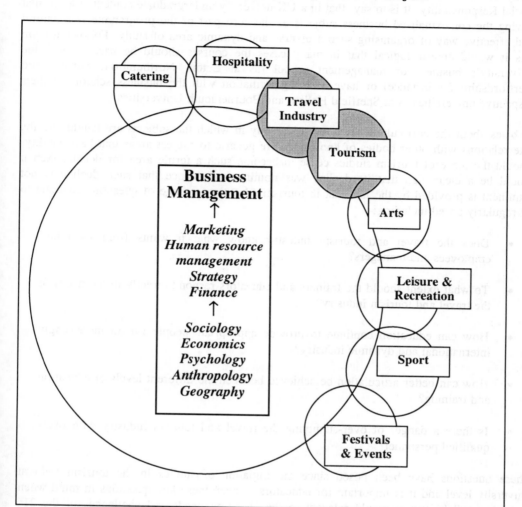

Conclusion

The teaching of tourism at a higher education level in the UK (as elsewhere) has become well established and the subject area, it can be argued, has increasingly crystallised around the business studies field, particularly at the undergraduate level. This represents a response to pressures from business, the arguments surrounding the need for integrated curricula, the focus of the growing tourism literature and, to some extent, student demands to acquire transferable business skills as part of their studies.

That is not to say that other approaches to the field are not possible, and indeed desirable, and that even within such course structures it is necessary to include input from the core disciplines in order to consider the subject area in its fullest sense. At the postgraduate level in particular there is a place for a range of more specialist courses which focus on a detailed study of particular aspects of tourism such as 'Tourism and Sustainability or Tourism and Social Responsibility. It is to say, that in a UK university undergraduate context at least, that having the contextualised business subjects as the core part of the programme is a natural and effective way of organising such a diverse and dynamic area of study. Following from this it would appear logical that in many cases the courses should be based within the university's business or management school (as at Luton, Northumbria, Surrey, and Hertfordshire for instance) or have a strong affiliation with the business schools of their respective universities as at Sheffield Hallam and Bournemouth Universities.

Debates about the curriculum, the appropriate way in which the subjects are taught and the interrelations with other bodies of knowledge are generic to subject areas that have vitality. Should the place of tourism studies cease to become such a fertile area for debate, then it would be a clear sign that its decline was imminent. Evidence that such decline is not imminent is provided by the fact that in tourism education a range of questions continue to be regularly posed including:

- Does the travel and tourism industry know what it wants from its future employees and managers?

- To what extent should the trainers and educators respond directly to the needs of the travel and tourism industry?

- How can education continue to provide appropriate people for an increasingly international and dynamic industry?

- How can better articulation be achieved between the different levels of education and training?

- Is there a danger of over-supplying the travel and tourism industry with over-qualified personnel?

These questions have been posed since the initiation of studies in the tourism field at university level and it is important for educators to keep these key questions in mind when designing syllabi and curricula relevant to the changing needs and challenges of the 21st century.

References

Airey, D. (1988), Cross-cultural approaches to teaching tourism into the 1990's, International Conference for Tourism Educators, University of Surrey. Quoted in Cooper C., Shepherd, R. and Westlake J. *(1996). Educating The Educators: A Manual Of Tourism And Hospitality Education,* World Tourism Organisation, Madrid, 29-30.

Airey, D. Ladkin, A. and Middleton, V. T. C. (1993), *The profile of tourism studies degree courses in the UK 1993.* London: National Liaison Group, for the Tourism Society.

Airey, D. and Middleton, V. T. C. (1994), Tourism education - course syllabi in the UK - a review. *Tourism Management,* 15 (1): 5 7-62.

Airey, D. and Johnson, S. (1999), The content of tourism degree courses in the UK, *Tourism Management,* 20, 229-235.

Amoah, V. A. and Baum, T. (1997), Tourism education: policy versus practice, *International Journal of Contemporary Hospitality Management,* 9 (1): 5-12.

Baum, T. (1997), Tourism education - is it at a crossroads? *Tourism Intelligence Papers,* British Tourist Authority/English Tourist Board, January, A127-Al31.

Busby G., Brunt P. and Baber S. (1997), Tourism sandwich placements: an appraisal, *Tourism Management,* 18 (2): 105-110.

Collins, S., Sweeney, A. E. and Geen, A. G. (1994), Training for the UK Tour Operator industry: advancing current practice, *Tourism Management,* 15 (1): 5-8.

Comic, D. (1989), Tourism as a subject of philosophical reflection, Revue de Tourisme, 44 (2): 6-13.

Cooper, C., Shepherd, R. and Westlake J. (1996), *Educating The Educators: A Manual Of Tourism And Hospitality Education,* World Tourism Organisation, Madrid.

Cooper, C. and Shepherd, R. (1997), The relationship between tourism education and the tourism industry: Implications for tourism education, *Tourism Recreation Research,* Vol. 22 (1): 34-47.

Council for National Academic Awards (1993), *Review of Tourism Studies Degree Courses,* London: CNAA.

CRAC Degree Course Guide 1998-1999 (1998), Volume II, Hobsons Publishing, Cambridge, UK.

Dann, G., Nash, D, and Pearce P. (1988), Methodology in Tourism Research, *Annals of Tourism Research* 15, 1-28.

Echtner, C. M. and Tazim, B. J. (1997), The disciplinary dilemma of tourism studies, *Annals of Tourism Research*, 24 (4): 868-883.

Evans, J. (1 993), Tourism graduates: a case of over production? *Tourism Management*, 14 (4): 243-246.

Faulkner, B. and Ryan, C. (1999), Innovations in tourism management research and conceptualisation, *Tourism Management*, 20, 3 -6.

Gunn, C. A. (1987), A perspective on the purpose and nature of tourism research methods, in (Eds.) J. R. B. Ritchie and C. Goeldner, *Travel, Tourism and hospitality research: A - Handbook for Managers and Researchers*, 3 -1 1, John Wiley, New York.

Gunn, C. A. (1998), Issues in tourism curricula, *Journal of Travel Research,* Spring, 74-77.

Haywood, K. M. and Maki, K. (1992), A conceptual model of the education/employment interface for the tourism industry, in J.R.B. Ritchie and D. Hawkins (Eds.), *World Travel and Tourism Review,* CAB, Oxford.

Henkel, M. (1988), Responsiveness of the subjects in our study: a theoretical perspective, in C. Brennan et al (Eds.), *Higher Education and Preparation for Work*, Chichester UK: John Wiley, 134-195.

Howey, R. M., Savage K. S. Verbeeten, M. J. and Van Hoof H. B. (1999), Tourism and hospitality research journals, *Tourism Management*, 20, 133-139.

Holloway, J. (1995), *Towards a core curriculum for tourism: a discussion paper*, London: National Liaison Group.

Jafari, J. and Ritchie, J. R. B. (1981), Towards a framework for Tourism Education, *Annals of Tourism Research*, 8, 13 -3 3.

Jafari, J. (1989), Structure of tourism, In S. F. Witt and L. Moutinho (Eds.) *Tourism Marketing and Management Handbook*, Prentice Hall, London, 43 7-442.

Jafari, J. (1990), Research and scholarship: the basis of tourism education Journal of *Tourism Studies*, (1): 407-429.

Jaspers, G. (1987), International harmonisation of tourism education, *Annals of Tourism Research,* 14 (4): 580-586.

Jenkins, C. L. (1980), Education for tourism policy makers in developing countries, *International Journal of Tourism Management*, 1 (4): 238-42.

Jovicic, Z. (1988), A plea for tourismological theory and methodology, *Revue de Tourisme,* 43 (3) 2-5.

Koh, Y. K. (1994), Tourism education for the 1990s, *Annals of Tourism Research,* 21 (3): 8 5 3 854

Koh, Y. K. (1995), Designing the four year Tourism Management Curriculum: a Marketing Approach, *Journal of Travel Research,* Summer, 68-72.

Koshizucha, M. Umemura, M. Mori, M. Horiuchi, M., and Shishido, M. (1998), In B Faulkner et al (Eds.) *Progress in tourism and hospitality research]998, Proceedings of the 8th Australian Tourism and Hospitality Research Conference* (p5 79). Canberra: Bureau of Tourism Research.

Leiper, N. (1981), Towards a cohesive curriculum in tourism. the case for a distinct discipline, *Annals of Tourism Research,* 8, 69-83.

Leslie, D. and Richardson, A. (2000), Tourism and co-operative education in UK undergraduate courses: - are the benefits being realised?, *Tourism Management,* 21 (5): 489-498.

Middleton, V. T. C. and Ladkin, A. (1996), *The profile of tourism studies degree courses in the UK 1995/96.* London. National Liaison Group (NLG) for Tourism in Higher Education.

Morley, C. (1990), What is tourism? Definitions, concepts and characteristics, *Journal of Tourism Studies, 1,* 3-8.

Pearce, P. L. (1993), Defining tourism study as a specialism: a justification and implications, *TEOROS International,* 1, 25-32.

Pearce, P. L and Butler, R. (1993), *Tourism Research: Critiques and Challenges,* Routledge, London.

Richards, G. (1993), Survey of tourism teachers, *in Council for National Academic Awards Review of Tourism Degree Courses,* London: CNAA, 56-69.

Richards, G. (1998), A European network for tourism education, *Tourism Management,* 19 (1): 1-4.

Payne, K. (1998), What now for tourism training: Academic adaptation or economic extinction? In B Faulkner et al (Eds.). Progress in tourism and hospitality research 1998, *Proceedings of the 8th Australian Tourism and Hospitality Research Conference* (5-79). Canberra: Bureau of Tourism Research.

Quality Assurance Agency for Higher Education (2000), *Draft benchmark statement for hospitality, leisure, sport and tourism,* QAA: Gloucester UK, January.

Ritchie, J. R. B. and Goeldner C. R. (1994), *Travel, Tourism and Hospitality Research,* John Wiley, New York.

Rogozinski, K. (1985), Tourism as a subject of research and integration of sciences, *Problemy Turystyki,* 4, 7-19.

Ross, G. F. (1992), The anatomy o tourism and hospitality educators in the UK, *Tourism Management,* June, 234-247.

Ryan, C. (1995), Tourism courses: a new concern for new times? *Tourism Management,* 16 (2): 97-100.

Smith, S. (1989), *Tourism Analysis: a Handbook,* New York: Longman, 31.

Sheldon, P. (1990), Journal usage in tourism: perceptions of publishing faculty. *Journal of Tourism Studies,* 1 (1): 42-48.

Sheldon, P. (1991), An authorship analysis of tourism research. *Annals of Tourism Research,* 18, 473-484.

Snaith, T. and Miller, G. (1999), The evolution of the tourism academic: missing links raise questions regarding sustainability and development of the profession, *Tourism Management,* 20, 387-388.

Tribe, J. (1997), The indiscipline of tourism, *Annals of Tourism Research,* 24 (3): 638-657.

New entrants in travel and tourism intermediations and the future of travel agents

W Faché

Ghent University, Belgium

The travel and tourism industry is one that has more intermediaries than other industries. These are the travel agencies and tour operators. Fig. 1 shows the traditional model of distribution. Tourism suppliers such as carriers, hotels, etc., can also sell directly to the consumer, avoiding travel agencies and the tour operator. Tour operators in turn sometimes sell holiday packages direct to the consumer, avoiding the use of travel agencies.

Some suppliers use several communication media in conjunction (mail, telephone, fax, face-to-face contact), catering for differences in consumer needs or product requirements, and a combination of both direct and indirect methods (Cooper et al., 1993; Holloway, 1995; Yale, 1997; Sülberg, 1993; Goeldner, 2000).

So-called experts have been 'predicting' for years that intermediaries would disappear and that with the current level of education, travel experience and communication, consumers could conduct business directly with suppliers, and middlemen would gradually disappear because they were no longer needed (Goeldner et al., 2000).

In the 1990s, the advent of the Internet has brought with it persistent speculations about the impact of the medium on the role of the middle position in business. On the one hand, given that Internet encourages direct and immediate contact between suppliers and customers, together with a simultaneous drop in transaction costs and commission costs, there is a strong case for Internet-driven "disintermediation" - or the elimination of intermediary entirely (Vandermerwe, 1999).

On the other hand we can note the creations of new forms of intermediation. In this article we will analyse these new forms. This paper, based on case studies and interviews with managers of tour operators, travel agents, and new forms of intermediation and literature research, will subsequently develop a strategic framework to guide travel agents on how to take advantage of any potential opportunities and how to minimise potential threats through the use of information technology and co-operation with some of the new intermediaries.

Figure 1   The Traditional Model of Distribution

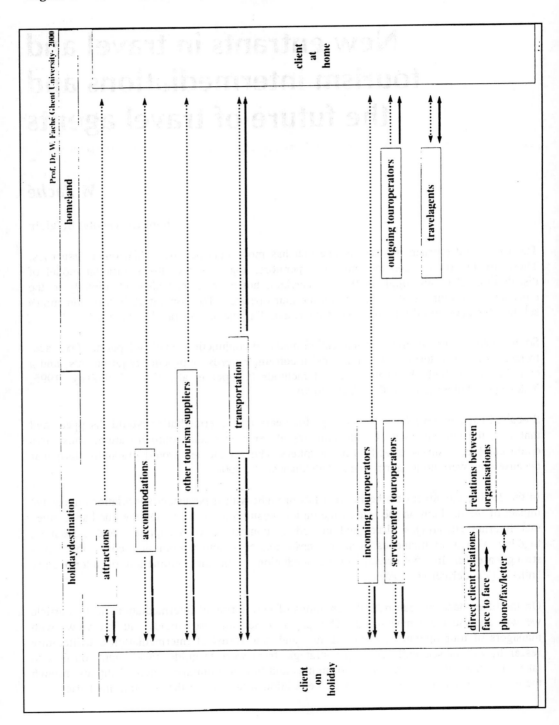

Direct sell through the Internet

Players in the transportation industry, such as airlines, railways and car rental companies, and international hotel chains have been quick to grasp the potential of marketing and selling their products by Internet. They have recognised an opportunity to bypass the intermediaries and sell their basic products directly to the customer through the Internet (Marcussen, 1999).

Increasingly also package holiday tour operators, especially in the Nordic countries and to a lesser degree in the UK, include direct sales via Internet in their sales strategy bypassing the travel agent (Marcussen, 1999).

Some authors have seen this development as the beginning of an internet driven disinternediation. But at the same time new intermediaries are born, mostly internet based.

New intermediaries

Electronic "go between service providers"

Alongside this Internet distribution there is the emergence *of New Net-based forms of intermediation* e.g. *electronic brokers* - whose role is primarily that of aggregating and disseminating data *to* customers, e.g. Preview Travel and Travelocity, who are offering information and reservations for flights, hotels and car hire.

In the present state of flux yet another kind of Net-based form of intermediary is emerging, different to the electronic brokers, referred to by Vandermerwe (1999) as the "electronic go-between service provider".

Go-between service provision involves, according to Vandermerwe, the strategic use of a model distinctly different from the past, to change the way a corporation deals with customers. Under the old, industrial model, so called 'middlemen' were the conduit for getting more discrete goods or services to customers down linear value chains. One or several of these 'middlemen' stood between manufacturers of products and services and end users. The assumption was that through these 'middlemen' - whether book wholesalers or travel agents - 'ownership', and margins, passed down the chain, and that was how corporations produced value (see Figure 2).

Figure 2   Old 'Middle' Role (Vandermerwe, 1999)

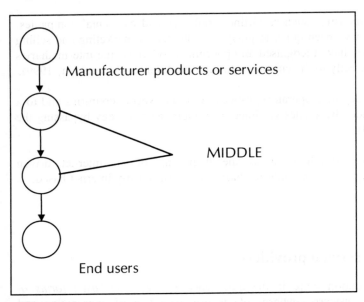

The electronic 'go-between service provider' displays a completely different thinking structure from the old business model of moving core products and services down sequential chains. The electronic brokers and "cybermediaries" serve a valuable purpose in that they are able to collect and aggregate information about markets and disseminate it cost-effectively via the Net. The electronic go-between service provider goes one step further: it recognises and uses the power and potential of advanced interactive technologies in order to link individuals who want products and services with those who can provide them. Then in this new middle role it integrates and delivers these offerings to customers as one superior experience (see Figure 3). (Vandemerwe, 1999, p. 599).

Figure 3   New 'Middle' Role (Vandermerwe, 1999)

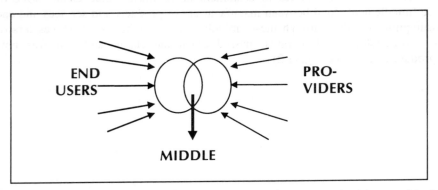

Expedia, for example connects those people wanting to travel with a multitude of players involved in all the various aspects of the total travel experience. Other examples of electronic "go-between service providers" are Amazon (bookbusiness), auto-by-tel (auto), Peapod and Streamline (for retail home shopping).

By enhancing offerings for customers, these "go-between service providers" build the kinds of relationships that bring them back again and again, in the process 'locking' these customers 'on'.

This 'lock-on', which means the corporation becomes the customer's first dominant or sole choice, builds the prospects for huge growth potential.

Lock-on, according to Vandemerwe (1999), is achieved largely because new interactive technologies enable offerings to be more proactive and precise as corporations can obtain more and more knowledge about customers in terms of their needs, likes, dislikes, and habits. In this respect the Internet is as much a relationship revolution as it is an information revolution. And with on-going innovation and adaptation to offerings as the technology and customers move on, the 'lock-on' effect becomes self-reinforcing.

According to Vandemerwe (1999), the following success factors of the new electronic "go-between service provider" are beginning to emerge.

1.   They Link Benefits to Produce a Superior Customer Experience in New 'Market Spaces'.

Expedia gives all the information needed to enable people who travel for business or pleasure in the US and Europe to get a totally integrated experience. This information is available 24 hours a day, with data updated every half-hour. The range of information includes regional weather reports; arrival times; illustrated guide books; best options to get to a particular business or holiday location; different (and exact) prices; and an insider's guide to the lowest published fares. On many flights, customers can pick the seats they want, find out if rental cars are available at any airport in the world, and reserve them; pay for the trip on-line or over the phone with a credit card, with tickets delivered overnight. Regular users can set up a personal profile, which logs them straight into the system, as well as record preferred airlines and hotels. As a result, first time bookings may take 20 minutes of a customer's time, but return visits to the site are much quicker.

2.   They Access and get to Customers the Full Range of Product and Service Brands They Need for This Experience.

Electronic 'go-between service providers' offer the full range of products and services which customers may need. Take that away and they become direct marketing tools or sales outlets, offering only one line of goods - their own, or what they are promoting. These service providers are different in that they give the spectrum, choice, information, and services to customers who have a range of needs depending on events, roles, and circumstances.

3.   They Concentrate on Value-add Service and Service.

Amazon, for example, spends as much time, money and energy on service and building relationships to get to know individuals better as it spends on selling. As in any high-calibre service organisation, staff are dedicated to customer service. In fact, say Amazon managers, they go to greater lengths to exceed expected standards when a customer needs help on, say, a query title, a mistaken address and so on. 'Then the humans take over from the machines in full force'. Twenty per cent of their staff do nothing out answer queries from their e-mail centre.

4.   They Personalise Offerings to Suit the Unique Needs of Individuals.

Ironically, the Internet is not a mass medium. It is a one-to-one medium. It is a powerful tool for customer personalisation because it enables the new enterprise to paradoxically make individual customer relationship management possible, achievable with millions of people simultaneously.

'Go-between service providers' don't just accumulate intelligence on individual customers. They act upon it so that offerings are more highly tuned to their unique needs. Total knowledge of a person - getting to know them increasingly better on an ongoing basis - is what gives them the edge.

Through an ongoing memory bank of information and dialogue, go-between service providers know customer preferences and changes in taste and circumstance. Feedback, which it endeavours to get at the end of each shopping session, is used to make changes.

5.   They Involve and Integrate Relevant Players and Expand Their Electronic Network to Deliver a Total Customer Experience.

This requires a combination of players working as one system to deliver the various bits so that the customer can't tell when one part of their experience begins and the other ends. Amazon for instance deals with several different players, including publishers, wholesalers, retailers, transport companies, Internet media companies, couriers, post offices and so on.

Players who jointly produce the total experience may be complementary. For example, as Expedia began internationalising in 1998 by entering the UK, it immediately cemented relationships with top tier travel vendors and others related to the travel experience, like British Airways and Thomson Holidays, Waterstone's travel book section, and Business Traveller magazine.

When they enter Germany they collaborate with the Austrian destination management system Tiscover.

We agree with Vandemerwe that the electronic "go-between service provider" is a new "middle" concept increasingly endemic to the modern economy. Go-between providers truly take the new "middle" role, dealing different with customers.

Very important for the future of travel agents is the fact that electronic "go-between service providers", can come from anywhere on the linear chain, in this case from tour operators and travel agents.

Destination marketing systems

The services offered on the Internet have focused in the beginning on hotels, to a large extent, because it was only the large international hotel companies who had the technical expertise and could afford to make their information available electronically. However, when we examine how a leisure traveller chooses his holiday, the hotel is not usually the determining factor. Travellers for leisure purposes, travel to a destination for a wide variety of reasons, such as because of something that's happening there, or some attractions near there (O'Connor and Frew, 1999). The leisure segment has very different information needs to those of the business traveller. For example, most business travellers look on hotels as a place to stay: a necessary adjunct to the need to be in a certain place at a certain time. However, when travelling for leisure purposes, the same guest will be far more selective, and often will want to know more about the hotel (its location, its facilities, the local shopping and restaurants, and so on) before making a decision to stay there.

Leisure travellers also tend to purchase a broader range of products when organising a trip. In addition to transportation and accommodation, they also want information about (and to be able to book) entertainment and attractions, restaurants and bars and, increasingly, related products such as insurance, foreign currency, traveller's cheques and credit card services (O'Connor, 1999).

The nature of the leisure segment itself is changing. The number of independent leisure travellers is growing (WTO, 1991). This leisure tourist segment is less likely to make use of a travel agent, preferring instead to organise most element of the trip for themselves (Poon, 1994). As a result, the leisure traveller requires information to help him in his decision-making pre-trip and during his visit.

A new type of intermediary is trying answering this need: *Destination Management Systems*. "There is no precise definition of a DMS and this is reflected in the number of synonyms by which such systems are commonly known: Destination Databases, Destination Marketing Systems, Destination Management Systems, Visitor Information Systems and a variety of other names have been used when referring to the DMS concept over the past number of years. However, despite their differing objectives, the basic theme and common denominator across each of these systems is the distribution of information about, and increasingly, the processing of reservations for, all of the tourism operations and attractions in a given geographical area" (O'Connor and Frew, 1999).

The Austrian TIScover system is one of the leading examples of DMS. Originally established at the beginning of the 1990s as an information system for Tirol the system has now been adopted by the majority of Austria's provinces and also versions are being used in Germany and Switzerland. TIScover 99 is a Web-based system with comprehensive functionality, including information management, distribution, reservations and electronic marketing capabilities in both English and German. It is supported by a comprehensive range of partnership agreements with leading Austrian and international organisations. These agreements include online distribution, information collection and management, technical support and industry training arrangements (WTO, 1999).

Other interesting DMS are: the Finnish Tourist Board System, the Irish Gulliver System, Namibia Wildlife Resorts Central Reservation System, Canadian Travel Exchange, South Pacifis Island Travel Channel (WTO, 1999).

A leisure traveller can find on the website of a DMS easily nearly all the information he needs for planning his holiday. But when the traveller wants to access the information about, e.g. a hotel, then the DMS can not help him.

A new breed of tourist guidebook and tourist journal

At the same time, the explosion in available travel information on the Internet has increased for tourists the need for critical assessment of product and destination information. Tourists need this information before going on a holiday to help them choose between options. This demand for assessment also reflects a more subtle issue: the annual holiday or even the weekend break is increasingly associated with enormous financial and emotional risk. In western society time has become a scarce commodity, particularly for double income families. Therefore, for many consumers their holiday represents a major emotional investment that cannot easily be replaced if something goes wrong. Therefore since travellers cannot pre-test the product, access to accurate, reliable, timely and relevant information is essential to help them to make an appropriate choice.

As consumers became accustomed to the use restaurant and hotel guides, e.g. the Michelin or Gault Millau Guides, they expect to find also these guides for their holidays. Indeed the Michelin and Gault Millau Guides are more focused on city hotels and restaurants.

Different tourist guidebooks became aware of the need for advice and start to give more and more information about which facilities a hotel has to offer, for which travellers a hotel is more appropriate and give quality ratings. Guidebooks, e.g. published by Fodor's or the English Automobile Association, give also detailed information about recommended tours in a country. These guidebooks are intended for multi-destinations holidays.

A new breed of guidebooks are intended for single destination holiday makers. For example the "Relax Guide 2000" (Werner, 1999) gives detailed information about 300 wellness and beauty holiday centres in Austria. The reader is informed about the facilities the centres have to offer and about the quality of their facilities and the service.

Also different tourism journals became aware of this niche and start to supplement their articles about a tourist region or a type of holiday experience, with recommended hotels, restaurants and recreation facilities with their own quality ratings (different from official hotel classifications). The German journal e.g. "Geo Saison" gives this information also about popular sun and beach holiday destinations (e.g. Majorca, Italian lake region).

Some of these guidebooks and journals have a website with updated information and the possibility to book the mentioned hotels and restaurants, via their website.

When a holiday maker has at his disposal a new breed of an up to date travel guidebook or journal, he doesn't need so much a travel agent for assessing the quality of the hotels, restaurants and other tourist services at his holiday destination.

Interactive Digital Television (IDTV)

It is often assumed that the Internet is the domain of the PC, that without a PC, people are not able to access the Internet and the Web. This was certainly true in past years when the Internet was in its infancy but this situation is now changing fast. There is a range of new technologies that are providing access to the Internet and other online channels. These are set to provide mass online access at affordable prices. It will no longer be necessary to purchase an expensive PC to participate online. This means that far more potential tourists will be seeking tourist information online (WTO, 1999).

Two technologies that already have widespread acceptance in the home are the television and the telephone, and the innovation is now to link them into an appropriate medium for electronic commerce. While there are still a number of issues to be worked out before it becomes widespread, interactive digital television is forecast to become an important channel of distribution over the next years (O'Connor, 1999).

The potential of IDTV is that the TV lends itself to the family viewing that is required when purchasing travel, just as a printed holiday brochure will be shared viewing across the family (WTO, 1999).

Strategic alliances

As in other sectors one significant trend in the distribution system is the rapid increase in the adoption of strategic alliance relationship. This organisational arrangement can be defined as: co-operation with firms in order to add to their competencies, improve market and competitive position, and retain independence of ownership. The relationships vary in terms of the degree of commitment, control, co-operation and organisational formality (Morrison and Harrison, 1998).

Many internet based intermediaries establish links from other websites to generate business for their sites. They arranged this often on a reciprocal basis at no cost, although in some circumstances, they have to pay a fee. They also establish partnerships with other organisations that can provide required content cost effectively (WTO, 1999).

For example the German website "Travelchannel" has as partners travel journals (Geo Saison, Der Feinschmecker), guide books (Polyglott), destination marketing systems (Tiscover, KISSswiss), touroperators (TUI, C/N, LTU, ...), airlines (Lufthansa, Condor, British Airways), etc.

Figure 4   The Multi-Channel Model of Distribution

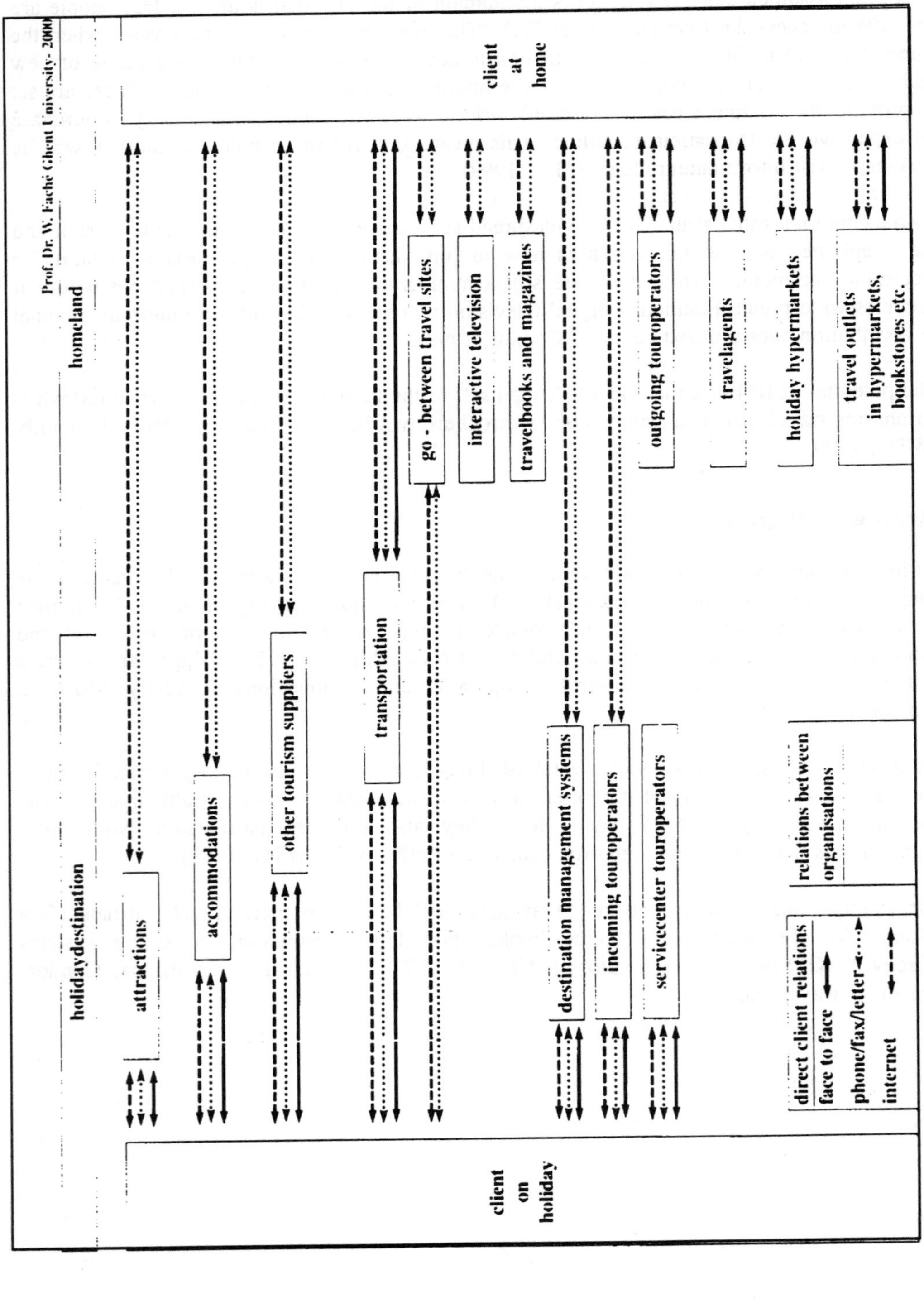

Multi-Channel Model of distribution

Figure 4 shows how the distribution system is developing. It is a Multi-Channel Model of Distribution. Note that the airlines, hotels and other tourism suppliers are connected to the consumer directly and by a whole array of new different intermediaries. The consumer will prefer using the channel who gives him the added value who is the most relevant for him at that moment. The future role of the tour operator and travel agent will depend on the added value they present to the customer in comparison with the other intermediaries. Customer's perception of added value are related to the nature of the transaction. For example, whilst a simple London - New York ticket is more likely to be booked on-line, someone wishing to go on a holiday with small children in Austria or on a once-in-a-life-time trip is likely to be more reassured dealing with a travel agent.

Note also the direct communications between travellers and supplies on the holiday destination. As well as requiring information to help in their decision-making process pre-trip, the leisure traveller also requires information during their visit. This is particularly true as leisure moves away from pre-organised package tours towards more independent travel. Because people are travelling more flexible and spontaneously, many purchase decisions are postponed until after arrival at the destination (O'Connor, 1999).

The WAP technologies facilitate consumer services also during travel. Even more important than developments in a particular technology is the convergence of these technologies and systems in such a manner that the user can flexibly choose where, when, and how to search for information, conduct transactions, and communicate (Järvelä, et al., 1999).

Need to add value

An intermediary will only survive in a distribution system while it continues to add value to the customer in comparison with other intermediaries.

Which activities of travel agents have a high potential for creating differention with other new intermediaries?

Research (O'Brien, 1999; Reinders et al, 1998; Eldering, 1998) has shown that the traditional activities of travel agents - transaction processing and information delivery - are being rapidly devalued by new extrants in the travel intermediation. These new entrants are mostly industry "outsiders", strong in information technology and unhampered by old habits and an expensive high-street infrastructure of retail outlets. They come from respected firms in retail, media and entertainment worlds which capitalise on their reputations and by using their core competencies in distribution, customer databases or teleselling know-how (Reinders and Backer, 1998).

As a result, they can introduce substantial changes without worrying about 'treading on people's toes'. A prime example of such a company is Microsoft, which has entered the travel sector with Expendia and quickly captured a large market share. Intermediaries therefore have every right to be worried because, as their traditional roles are eliminated or absorbed by other members of the distribution system, they will need to find other added values to the customer if they are to remain in business (O'Connor, 1999).

At the same time, the changing travel experience, knowledge and preferences of customers and the explosion in available travel information on the Internet have increased the value of travel agents consulting and information brokering role. A continual shift towards the later two roles will be essential if they are to continue to add value (O'Brien, 1999; Reinders and Baker, 1998; Eldering, 1998).

Innovation can support the increase of the added value. Innovation in retail can be achieved through the products sold (e.g. new and unique holiday concepts) or the process by which they are sold or both. A new retail process is basically a new or different way of serving consumer needs.

Figure 5 proposes a matrix model which combines both types of innovations. Highly differentiated retailers with unique products and process appear in the top right quadrant labelled "total innovators". Process or product innovators appear in the top left or the bottom right quadrants respectively (Davies, 1992).

The objective of innovation is supporting differentiations. In the literature on the disintermediation treats and recommendations for travel agents the focus is on process innovation (O'Brien, 1999; Reinders and Baker, 1998, O'Connor, 1999, Eldering, 1988). But because a travel agent has a position in relation to the product and the process, he is capable of combining the two elements in its repositioning strategy.

Figure 5   Innovators in the travel retail (Davies, 1992)

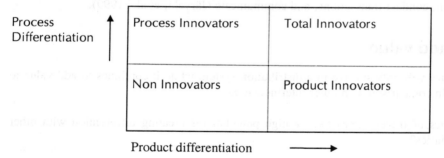

Process
Differentiation

Process Innovators	Total Innovators
Non Innovators	Product Innovators

Product differentiation ⟶

Process innovations

Travel consulting

Building a relationship with a customer and clearly understanding his/her holiday needs and preferences is very important in realising the consulting role. It is not always easy for a customer to make explicit his holiday needs and preferences. And the problem is complicated when the customer is going on holiday with his family or friends, who have also their needs and preferences. A particular problem facing the travel consultant is matching the customer's requirements to available destinations and/or products (O'Brien, 1999).

This is a complex operation that requires a high level of intelligence and ability to understand the desired holiday experience of the customer(s). The consulting role can be supported by a continually updated customers data base.

This personalised consulting advice focuses on the needs of the customer rather than the needs of the travel suppliers (airlines, hotels, tour operators, etc.). The travel agent is working on behalf of the customer.

The travel agent who can find a child friendly hotel, a hotel nearer to the beach for the same money, a better travel connection which saves more time, or a holiday concept that match better with the desired holiday experience, than the d.i.y.netsurfer can, will continue to attract customers (Reinders, 1998).

Essential in the innovative concept of for example the Holiday Hypermarkets in the UK and Havas Planète and Cité des Voyageurs in Paris are travel consulting from experienced advisors.

Travel information broker

While the Web provides information this is not the same as knowledge. A customer can download pages and pages of information about a destination, but he is mostly unable to assess the required information and assemble it into a personalised holiday (O'Brien, 1999).

Most customers will be no more than gifted amateurs in using the new IT-tools (Reinders and Baker, 1998). There are more and more manuals which tell the traveller how to look for the relevant information on the Web (e.g. The Travel Guide Internet from Gohlis and Blittkowsky, 1999). But customers do not always have the time nor the incentive to browse the Web for the relevant information.

Retail Travel Agents who are proficient at using sophisticated intelligent software agents, and their own personal experience and knowledge to critically assess product and destinational information, integrate information from heterogenous sources and assisting the customer to make a suitable choice based on their preferences, are adding value (O'Brian, 1999).

John Naisbitt, in his best selling book, Megatrends, said "High tech requires hightouch". The professional knowledgeable travel agent can provide both high tech and hightouch (Goeldner et al., 2000).

Product innovation

Personalised package developer

The changing preference of customers for more individual, personalised holidays requires the travel agent to develop skills in integrating subproducts from different suppliers into a personalised package targeted to customers' needs and preferences. This is a complex, time-consuming activity that must be highly automated to reduce the cost of sale and make it cost-effective. Intelligent itinerary builders that have access to a wide range of packages, mini packages, and independent operators' products from a wide range of sources including the Internet and CRSs will be required (O'Brien, 1999).

Niche products

The design and service in hotels is more and more standardised. Leisure travellers prefer the experience of a hotel with local characteristics, e.g. an Irish country house. This hotels are mostly small and medium-sized enterprises. This size characteristic makes the use of electronic distribution more difficult (O'Connor, 1999). Some tour operators and travel agents try to select and sell this accommodations.

Other tour operators and hotels develop new holiday concepts. Customers expect to be informed about this.

Travel related products and services

In addition to innovating the retail process, the travel stores Havas Planète and Cité des Voyageurs in Paris have also expanded the travel retail concept to incorporate other related services and products in order to offer a one-stop-shopping possibility. However, they have also remained true to their core concept: travel consultation. Current products and services included are: an outlet of a bank where customers can change money and buy travel cheques, passport and visa service, a possibility to have a passport photo taken, a bookshop specialised in travel guide books, maps and a shop for specialised travel requisites, and a rental car service. In other words they sell and give all the service needed to enable travellers to get a totally integrated experience.

The hypermarket concept appears to be one format, where total innovation can be realised best.

The relevance of the added value to an individual traveller

The relevance of the added value of a travel agent for an individual traveller depends upon the complexity of the product, how travel experienced a customer is and other characteristics of the traveller. Experienced travellers require less information, whereas inexperienced travellers, travellers to unfamiliar destinations or those using unfamiliar or complicated travel arrangements want more information and decision support to find out what they want and how to buy it.

Sometimes the best option would be to book face-to-face, whilst at others to do so by phone or electronic home shopping would be preferred. The similarity between earlier travel purchases and the product the customer now wants to buy is also relevant. There will be limited need for extra travel expertise if the product is highly similar to previous purchases, for example flying with the same airline to a similar destination from the same airport. In contrast, previous summer holidays in Spain are of limited relevance for the choice of a skiing holiday (Reinders and Baker, 1998).

The travel distribution system is continually changing. Convenience and ease of access to service of an type of intermediary can change an entire system. Very few empirical studies have been carried out to identify the effects of intermediaries on each other and the relevance of the added value for travellers.

References

Baker, M., Hayzelde, C., Sussmann, S. (1996), Can destination management systems provide competitive advantage? A discussion of the factors affecting the survival and success of destination management systems, *Progress in Tourism and Hospitality Research,* 2 (1-4): 1-13.

Davies, G. (1992), Innovation in retailing, *Creativity and Innovation Management,* 1 (4): 230-239.

Eldering, P. (1998), Pro Active: boekingsbereidheid Internet-consument groot. *Reisrevue,* March.

Faché, W. (1999), *Innovatie in de distributie van vakanties*. Universiteit Gent, Gent.

Gohlis, T. and Blittkowsky, R. (1999), *Travel Guide Internet*, Dumont, Köln.

Holloway, J.C. (1989), *The Business of Tourism*, Pitman, London.

Järvelä, P., Loikkanen, J., Tinnilä, M., Tuunainen, V.K. (1999), Business models for electronic commerce in the travel services, *Information Technology and Tourism*, 2, pp.185-196.

Laws, E. (1997), *Managing Package Tourism. Relationships, responsibilities and service quality in the inclusive holiday industry*, International Thomson Business Press, London.

Marcussen, C. H. (1999), Internet Distribution of European Travel and Tourism Services. The market, transportation, accommodation and package tours, Bornholms Forskningscenter, Nexø, Denmark.

O'Brien, P.F. (1999), Intelligent assistants for retail travel agents, Information Technology and Tourism, 2, pp. 213-228.

O'Connor, P. (1999), *Electronic information distribution in tourism and hospitality*, CABI Publishing, Oxon.

O'Connor, P., Frew, D. A. (1999), Destination management systems - An overview, *Insights*.

Reinders, J. and Baker, M. (1998), The future for direct retailing of travel and tourism products: the influence of information technology, *Progress in Tourism and Hospitality Research*, 4, pp.1-15.

Romeiß-Stracke, F. (1997), Rund um die weit m im jet order im cyberspace? Herausforderung für reiseveranstalter und reisebüros, *The Tourist Review*, 1, pp.41-49.

Vandermerwe, S. (1999), The electronic 'go-between service provider': a new 'middle' role taking centre stage, *European Management Journal,* 17 (6): 598-608.

Werner, C. (1999), *Relax Guide 2000.* Ibera Verlag, Wien.

WTO Business Council (1999), *Marketing tourism destinations online. Strategies for the information age,* WTO, Madrid.

Image versus identity: Representing and comparing destination images across a tourism system - the case of Wales

Nicola J Foster

University of Salford, UK

Eleri Jones

University of Wales Institute, Cardiff, UK

Introduction

According to Hughes (1992) the tourist-orientation of place occurs when places are 'marketed' as tourist destinations. Much emphasis in tourist destination marketing focuses upon promotion. Since the 1960s there has been growing research interest in destination image promotion and its implications for successful destination management. However, it is observable that there has been little conceptual discussion about the nature of destination image and a lack of recognition that a destination, like any other entity, is open to perception by a range of observers across a tourism system.

Tourism stakeholders

Understanding image as a representational tool is vital to any debate involving destination image promotion. It is important to recognise the potential gap between the intangible, abstract images in the minds of various stakeholders and the implications for the variety of media-based representations or identities of the destination used in its promotion. The need to develop a methodology to capture and compare the images from the various stakeholders is paramount to the design of an effective media-based promotional identity. Leiper's model of the tourism system (1979) highlights the interaction between supply and demand in tourism operations (Figure 1). The supply- and demand sides of the industry are made up of various stakeholder groups (e.g. tourist enterprises, government agencies, intermediaries, tourists). The multiplicity of potential interrelationships between these different groups is however, often overlooked when destination image is discussed and many authors resort to a reductionist approach, focusing solely upon the images held by one particular stakeholder group involved in a tourism system, neglecting the perspective and influence of other groups.

Figure 1   A Tourism System (after Leiper 1979)

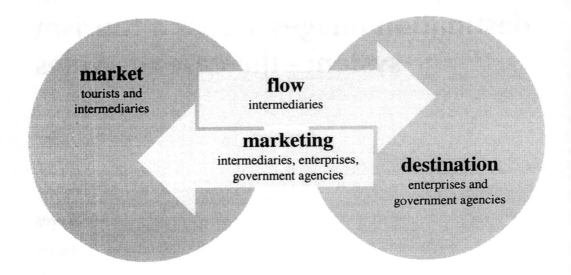

The aim of this paper

This paper adopts a more holistic approach to the study of destination image and considers the extent to which the subjective concept of destination image may be seen to be generic and open to quantification. With the goal of being able to readily compare destination images between tourism stakeholder groups (towards ultimately, being able to design more appropriate and effective destination identities) the main focus surrounds whether destination images can be adequately represented in qualitative or even quantitative terms to enable their comparison.

Defining and conceptualising destination image

Inevitably, the ways in which destination images are defined and conceptualised hold implications for the measurement and subsequent application of destination image content in destination promotion. Closely tied to this issue is the question of whether there exists a most appropriate medium or approach for portraying or representing how people perceive destinations. To date, the literature on destination image illustrates a variety of approaches to the communication of images.

To some, the elicitation of verbalised images has been considered sufficient (e.g. linguistic analyses). Others have studied the perceptions of pictures and symbols (e.g. semiotic analyses). Hughes (1992), for example, argues that the world is perceived and depicted via visual codes of communication whereas Dann (1996) has focused more upon verbal codes, presenting a sociolinguistic analysis of tourist images. Mazanec (1995) recognises a prevalence in tourism destination image literature towards verbalised images and speaks of the need for multi-dimensional rather than uni-dimensional analyses. However, it would appear senseless to advocate a focus on attribute or holistic dimensions of destination image structure prior to investigating destination image representation. In order to measure destination image it is necessary to be able to operationalise the concept.

As part of a wider PhD study, the nature and conceptualisation of destination image was examined. During a comprehensive literature review three key elements integral to understanding destination image were identified: the *context* in which destination images are set; their *structure*; and their *content*. In terms of the former, the destination image of an individual was recognised to be situated within three broad contexts: 'personal-specific'; 'holiday-generic'; and 'destination-specific'. Its structure was recognised to be integral to the measurement of the latter, its content. All too often it would appear that destination image researchers are overly concerned with the content of destination image and fail to take into account the importance of the context and the structure.

Echtner and Ritchie (1991; 1993)

Although existing image-related literature presents 'feature-specific' (i.e. multi-attribute) versus 'gestalt' (i.e. holistic) approaches to image conceptualisation there exists little published material which addresses the structure of destination images and their representation and the work of Echtner and Ritchie (1991; 1993) dominates the literature and thus, the analysis of this paper. Essentially, the authors assert that the highly subjective concept of destination image may be represented using a generic structural framework, applicable across a broad range of destinations (Figure 2).

Figure 2   The Components of Destination Image (Echtner and Ritchie 1991:4)

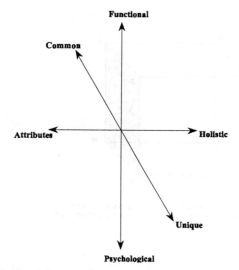

Note: This figure should be envisaged in three dimensions

The underlying premise of Echtner and Ritchie is a belief that the highly subjective concept of image can be accommodated within a generic structure. As Figure 2 illustrates, Echtner and Ritchie identify three continua where six components of destination image are presented as bi-polar extremes: attribute-holistic; functional-psychological; and common-unique.

Referring to a common-unique continuum Echtner and Ritchie (1991:7) suggest that:

> *On one extreme of the continuum, the image of a destination can be composed of the impressions of a core group of traits on which all destinations are commonly rated and compared. For example, a destination's image can include ratings on certain common functional characteristics, such as price levels, transportation infrastructure, types of accommodation, climate, etc. The destination can also be rated on very commonly considered psychological characteristics: level of friendliness, safety, quality of service expected, fame, etc. On the other end of the continuum, images of destinations can include unique features and events (functional characteristics) or special auras (psychological characteristics.*

The notion of a continuum suggests that strength in one area naturally implies weakness in another. Thus, according to the framework individual destination images vary in terms of emphasis of components enabling an individual's image to be distinctly plotted on each of the three continua, i.e. in three dimensions. The framework may be redrawn to clarify this three-dimensional nature (Figure 3).

Figure 3   The three-dimensional nature of the Echtner and Ritchie framework

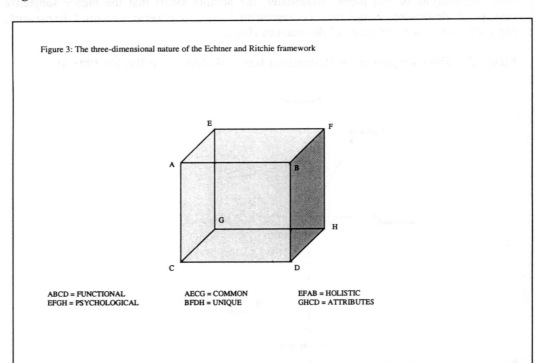

Figure 3: The three-dimensional nature of the Echtner and Ritchie framework

ABCD = FUNCTIONAL   AECG = COMMON   EFAB = HOLISTIC
EFGH = PSYCHOLOGICAL   BFDH = UNIQUE   GHCD = ATTRIBUTES

Whilst the immense potential of such a framework for the advancement of destination image research is acknowledged there is however considerable inherent ambiguity and the extent to which it fully accommodates all possible destination image dimensions is debatable. For example, does the framework allow for the identification of individual idiosyncrasies or inter-dimensional synergism?

Echtner and Ritchie (1993) themselves examined the concept of destination image with the goal of designing more appropriate and rigorous techniques for its measurement, presenting a framework which suggests that several components must be captured to completely measure destination image. Yet the actual framework itself was not drawn into question. It is surely myopic to examine destination image solely via a review and assessment of image research in a number of other disciplines, no matter how extensive such an examination. Although lateral thought based on an extensive review and assessment of image research in other disciplines could assist conceptualisation the need for empirical testing is indisputable. To understand the concept of destination image it is necessary to examine actual destination images. Thus, a study was designed to explore further the concept of destination image via an empirical investigation into the applicability of Echtner and Ritchie's model.

Before an attempt was made to apply the Echtner and Ritchie framework to a tourist destination system it was vitally important that the framework was not accepted uncritically and applied without empirical evidence of its validity. A study was designed to explore further the concept of destination image via an empirical investigation into the applicability of Echtner and Ritchie's model. In particular, the investigation focused upon an assessment of the nature and extent of temporal modification on the representation of destination image from a tourist's viewpoint. The analysis was restricted to tourists' images since the Echtner and Ritchie framework had been designed to capture their images and the first test was to check if it could do what it had been designed for before testing whether its original purpose could be extended.

Gunn (1988)

Gunn (1988) proposes that tourists' images of destinations are in a state of transition throughout the travel experience with images being open to transformation across seven phases of tourism participation, i.e.:

1. accumulation of mental images about vacation experiences;

2. modification of those images by further information;

3. decision to make a vacation trip;

4. travel to the destination;

5. participation at the destination;

6. return travel; and

7. new accumulation of images based on the experience.

These phases may be seen to be reiterative in nature with three broad phases recognisable namely, pre-visit images, on-visit images, and post-visit images.

Gunn is not alone in proposing a temporal aspect to destination image. Other authors such as Pearce (1982) and Gyte (1988) have considered the implications of the effect that images changing over time may have on the design of promotional strategies. Indeed, temporal modification of destination images may be recognised as a potential hazard for destination image representation.

Methodology

The methodology of this paper concerns two key issues:

1. testing the appropriateness of the Echtner and Ritchie (1991; 1993) framework;

2. applying the findings of that exploratory research to the context of evaluating destination images of Wales across a tourism system.

Testing the appropriateness of the Echtner and Ritchie framework

Accepting the likelihood of tourists' images of a destination changing over the travel experience, respondents were sampled to reflect three key states of destination image formation: Phase 1 (Group C); Phase 3 (Group B); and Phase 7 (Group A). A purposive sample comprising eighteen subjects with widely ranging personal characteristics was used to test the general applicability of the framework (see Table 1). It would have been preferable to follow a given sample through all phases however, time and other resources did not permit.

Table 1   The Sample

Respondent #	Profile	Destination	Period of time before/after holiday - days	Length of reported image – minutes (seconds)
Group A (recent holiday-takers):				
1	Female, 28, Research Assistant	Barbados	15	14 (20)
2	Male, 29, Engineer	Barbados	15	4 (5)
3	Male, 29, Research Student	Kalymnos (Greece)	27	9 (17)
4	Female, 59, Secretary	Canada	11	21 (38)
5	Female, 70, retired Headmistress	Brighton (UK)	8	10 (16)
6	Female, 23, Research Student	Malta	10	2 (46)
Group B (prospective holiday-takers):				
7	Male, 28, Research Assistant	Lesbos (Greece)	13	2 (15)
8	Female, 30, Lecturer	Egypt	65	19 (43)
9	Male, 29, Lecturer	Egypt	65	3 (44)
10	Male, 24, Finance Officer	Crete (Greece)	32	2 (19)
11	Female, 40+, Senior Lecturer	Canada	24	3 (47)
12	Female, 24, Administrator	Tunisia	4	4 (40)
Group C (no immediate holiday plans):				
13	Female, 50+, Lecturer	Ideal	n/a	1 (40)
14	Female, 50, Assistant Cook	Ideal	n/a	(36)
15	Male, 51, Retired Engineer	Ideal	n/a	(33)
16	Female, 25, Nanny	Ideal	n/a	(17)
17	Female, 41, Lecturer	Ideal	n/a	1 (38)
18	Male, 24, Lecturer	Ideal	n/a	1 (13)

n/a = not applicable

It was implicit that any attempt to obtain from respondents a verbal description of their mental images of a destination should involve as unstructured a methodology as possible. Hence, subjects were interviewed and simply presented with the following requests:

Group A: *"Tell me about your recent holiday";*

Group B: *"Tell me about your prospective holiday";*

Group C: *"Tell me about your ideal holiday".*

The purpose of the exercise was not disclosed prior to the interview and respondents were left unprompted to respond to the request with as much information as they were willing, and/or, able to provide. Responses were tape-recorded and fully transcribed for analysis.

Analysis

The eighteen unstructured responses were examined using content analysis for any observable patterns which would suggest potential alternative frameworks for destination image representation. Subsequently, Echtner and Ritchie's conceptual framework was applied in the structuring of the data. Although the continua were able to accommodate all image content concern must be expressed over the degree of subjectivity involved in ascertaining what is perceived as 'common' or 'unique' to individuals. It is necessary to be aware that although the respondents in this study automatically expressed the affective nature of their images, an unstructured methodology does not guarantee the clarification of the value of an image to the individual.

Echtner and Ritchie (1993) recognised the difficulty of dealing in three dimensions and separated the components of destination image into a series of two-dimensional diagrams. The same approach was adopted here, entailing the representation of images via quadrants. With each of the eighteen responses the occurrence (frequency) distribution by quadrant was calculated and thus, the dominant structure of each individual's destination image was determined alongside the representative structure for each sample group. In addition, responses were analysed against respondent characteristics.

Vector analysis was used to calculate individual values for the six components, enabling a one-way analysis of variance (SPSS) and the Pearson product-moment correlation coefficient (SPSS) to be applied to the testing for significant differences within and between sample groups and in the relationships between paired components.

Echtner and Ritchie's framework was able to accommodate destination images from all three sample groups on all six components with no redundant items. Figures 4, 5 and 6 present an example for a selected respondent using the same two-dimensional diagram formats as adopted by Echtner and Ritchie (1993) for summarising destination images via the conceptual framework.

Figure 4 **The Attribute/Holistic and Functional/Psychological components of Respondent #6's image of Malta (Group A)**

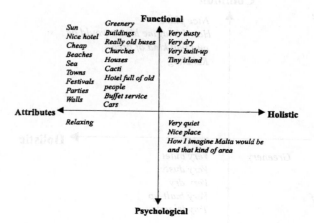

Figure 5 **The Common/Unique and Functional/Psychological components of Respondent#6's image of Malta (Group A)**

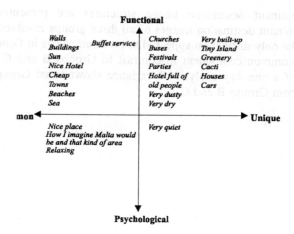

Figure 6   The Attribute/Holistic and Common/Unique components of Respondent #6's image of Malta (Group A)

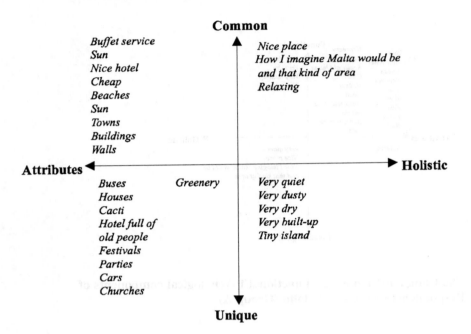

The results of the dominant destination image structures are presented in Table 2. Overwhelmingly the dominant destination images of all three groups involved functional and attribute components. The only distinction appeared to be an emphasis in Group A images on the unique rather than common component in contrast to Groups B and C. However, the subsequent application of a one-way analysis of variance showed that Group A images did not differ significantly from Groups B and C.

Table 2   Dominant Destination Image Structures

Respondent #	Relative weightings of F/P and A/H components				Relative weightings of F/P and C/U components				Relative weightings of C/U and A/H components			
	% F/A	% P/A	% F/H	% P/H	% F/C	% P/C	% F/U	% P/U	% C/A	% U/A	% C/H	% U/H
Group A:												
1	75.0	0.0	12.5	12.5	36.4	9.1	51.5	3.0	33.0	42.0	12.5	12.5
2	50.0	10.0	5.0	35.0	50.0	25.0	15.0	10.0	30.0	20.0	20.0	30.0
3	78.0	3.0	3.0	16.0	47.0	12.5	37.5	3.0	37.5	47.0	12.5	3.0
4	89.1	4.7	1.5	4.7	20.3	3.1	71.9	4.7	20.3	70.3	3.1	6.3
5	91.4	4.3	0.0	4.3	37.0	2.2	54.3	6.5	26.0	70.0	2.0	2.0
6	68.0	4.0	16.0	12.0	36.0	8.0	52.0	4.0	36.0	36.0	8.0	20.0
Group B:												
7	50.0	0.0	0.0	50.0	50.0	50.0	0.0	0.0	50.0	0.0	33.0	17.0
8	40.0	3.0	17.0	40.0	13.0	20.0	33.3	33.3	17.0	33.0	17.0	33.0
9	92.0	0.0	8.0	0.0	54.0	0.0	38.0	8.0	54.0	30.0	0.0	16.0
10	75.0	0.0	0.0	25.0	75.0	17.0	8.0	0.0	67.0	8.0	17.0	8.0
11	100.0	0.0	0.0	0.0	14.0	0.0	86.0	0.0	14.0	86.0	0.0	0.0
12	62.5	12.5	12.5	12.5	69.0	19.0	6.0	6.0	62.5	0.0	25.0	12.5
Group C:												
13	33.3	0.0	33.3	33.3	0.0	25.0	58.0	17.0	8.0	33.3	25.0	33.3
14	80.0	0.0	0.0	20.0	80.0	20.0	0.0	0.0	80.0	0.0	20.0	0.0
15	56.0	0.0	44.0	0.0	56.0	0.0	44.0	0.0	56.0	44.0	0.0	0.0
16	100.0	0.0	0.0	0.0	60.0	0.0	40.0	0.0	60.0	40.0	0.0	0.0
17	70.0	30.0	0.0	0.0	30.0	0.0	40.0	30.0	30.0	70.0	0.0	0.0
18	54.0	8.0	0.0	38.0	46.1	30.8	7.7	15.4	38.5	23.0	30.8	7.7

N. B. Throughout the table 'A' refers to attributes, 'C' refers to common, 'F' refers to functional, 'H' refers to holistic, 'P' refers to psychological and 'U' refers to unique.

Eleven out of the twelve respondents presenting images of specific destinations (i.e., Group A and B respondents) were referring to overseas destinations. Where comparison between domestic and overseas images was possible (Group A) no structural distinctions were observed.

Similarly, neither the destination under consideration, length of visit (Group A respondents), nor the timing of the data collection in terms of length of time before/after a holiday demonstrated any notable effects upon the results. It is, however, acknowledged that, in no case in the present study does the length of time before/after a holiday exceed two months and greater variation is possible the longer the period of time before/after a holiday the data collection is conducted.

The content of destination images has been found in other studies to transform post-vacation (Pearce, 1982; Gyte, 1988). However, there was no distinction in terms of structure between images stemming directly through visitation (termed 'primary images' by Phelps, 1986) and images formed from information received from some external source (termed 'secondary images' by Phelps, 1986). Destination image structures of respondents in Group A (Respondent #5) and Group B (Respondent # 7), who represented repeat visitors, were not distinct from those respondents with first-time images.

Responses varied in length with Group A responses ranging from two minutes and forty-six seconds to twenty-one minutes and thirty-eight seconds, Group B ranging from two minutes and fifteen seconds to nineteen minutes and forty-three seconds, and Group C ranging from seventeen seconds to one minute and forty seconds. However, the actual length of response did not indicate any influence upon overall destination image structure or the sequence in which components were reported: any difference was a matter of degree or detail rather than of kind.

Although images have been argued to be largely person-determined varying considerably from person to person due to differing expectations and manners of processing communications relating to the destination (Crompton, 1979), individual idiosyncrasies in terms of the structure of destination image were not apparent. Rather, any idiosyncratic characteristics of image were displayed within the actual content of a destination image. For example, the significance of flowers and cars in Respondent #4's image of Canada, reflecting a reported personal interest in gardening and driving, formed part of the unique and attribute components of the image. It must however be recognised that the attempt to place unstructured data in a structural framework may simply serve to eliminate any idiosyncrasies.

Relationships between components

The Pearson product moment correlation coefficient indicated very highly significant inverse relationships between 'attributes-holistic' ($r = -1.000$, $p = 0.000$), 'common-unique' ($r = -1.000$, $p = 0.000$) and 'functional-psychological' components ($r = -1.000$, $p = 0.000$). Thus, the validity of the three continua proposed by Echtner and Ritchie may be supported in this study. However, this by no means suggests that the three continua may be viewed as comprehensive and exhaustive and the possibility of further dimensions cannot be overruled.

The three continua that were observed here must, by nature, be recognised to represent three paired rather than six components or 'elements' of destination image. These may be termed 'collectivity' (ranging from attributes to holistic); 'tangibility' (ranging from psychological to functional) and 'familiarity' (ranging from unique to common). The determination of individual component values via vector analysis would enable the destination image of each individual to be rated and compared on each continuum. Table 3 provides an example where the continuum ratings for the destination image of Respondent #1 have been standardised on a scale of -10 to +10. Hence, the image of Barbados has received a 'score' of +7.5, -5.0, -0.9 for its collectivity, tangibility, and familiarity respectively. Repeating the calculation for

Respondent #2's image of Barbados produces a score of +2.0, -1.0, +2.5 and illustrates the potential for comparison between different tourist segments, destination observers and destinations themselves.

Table 3   Standardising the continuum ratings of Respondent #1's image of Barbados

Continuum	% weightings of components within the destination image structure												Component value $\Sigma x^1-\Sigma x^2$	Continuum rating $\frac{y}{20}$
	I/A	P/A	I/H	P/H	I/C	P/C	I/U	P/U	C/A	U/A	C/H	U/H		
Tangibility (I/P)	75.0	0.0	12.5	12.5	16.4	9.1	51.5	1.0	n/a	n/a	n/a	n/a	150.8	7.5
Collectivity (A/U)	75.0	0.0	12.5	12.5	n/a	n/a	n/a	n/a	33.0	42.0	12.5	12.5	-100.0	-5.0
Familiarity (C/U)	n/a	n/a	n/a	n/a	16.4	9.1	51.5	1.0	33.0	42.0	12.5	12.5	-18.0	-0.9

N.B.   Throughout the table 'A' refers to attributes, 'C' refers to common, 'F' refers to functional, 'H' refers to holistic, 'P' refers to psychological and 'U' refers to unique.

n/a = not applicable

x^1 = all quadrant values relating to one element of a continuum

x^2 = all quadrant values relating to the opposite element of that in x^1 (i.e. where x^1 relates to functional, x^2 relates to psychological)

y = component value (i.e. $\Sigma x^1 - \Sigma x^2$)

Significant positive relationships were found between functional-attributes (r = +0.890, p = 0.017), unique-attributes (r = +0.701, p = 0.120), psychological-holistic (r = +0.890, p = 0.017) and common-holistic (r = +0.700, p = 0.121) elements. Correspondingly, significant inverse relationships were found between functional-holistic (r = -0.890, p = 0.017), unique-holistic (r = -0.702, p = 0.120), psychological-attributes (r = -0.890, p = 0.017) and common-attributes (r = -0.700, p = 0.121) elements. However, no significant correlation was found between functional-unique elements (r = +0.486, p = 0.329) or psychological-common elements (r = +0.484, p = 0.331). Table 4 illustrates the proportion of the variability in functional, psychological, common and unique elements which is accountable for by the linear relationships with attributes and holistic elements (r^2). The results suggest that there exists a spurious correlation between the collectivity and familiarity continua whilst the relationship between the collectivity and tangibility continua is synergistic.

Table 4   Variability in the Product Moment Coefficient

Element	% variability accountable by Attributes	% variability accountable by Holistic
Functional	74.0	74.0
Psychological	74.0	74.1
Common	36.3	36.5
Unique	36.4	36.6

The appropriateness of the Echtner and Ritchie framework

Time illustrated no significant effect upon the dominant components involved in the representation of destination image and the way in which they were structured. However, as previously stated, it must be acknowledged that this study was restricted to short-term destination images and appreciation of the long-term impact would require longitudinal research which was beyond the present research limitations.

The identification of inter-dimensional synergism suggests that the tangibility continuum is open to direct influence by the presence and direction of the collectivity continuum. This would explain the overwhelming dominance of functional and attribute elements together throughout respondent images. However, the precise explanation for a dominance of attribute rather than holistic elements in image is open to debate (Navon, 1977).

The subjectivity involved in ascertaining what is perceived 'common' or 'unique' to individuals questions the extent to which a familiarity continuum should be included in a generic destination image structure.

Although the sample was small, the findings suggested that Echtner and Ritchie's framework requires further revision before it could be appropriately applied to the measurement of destination image. In particular, the existence of only two paired component axes, varying in degrees of strength, rather than six individual components must be recognised. Familiarity (relating to common and unique elements of destination image) may be recognised to exist within the *context* of destination image (personal-specific, holiday-generic, destination-specific) rather than being inherent within the *structure* of destination image. Hence a revised version of Echtner and Ritchie's framework may be proposed (Figure 7). The figure may be envisaged in two dimensions:

Figure 7   A Proposed Revised Structure of Destination Image (after Echtner and Ritchie 1991:4)

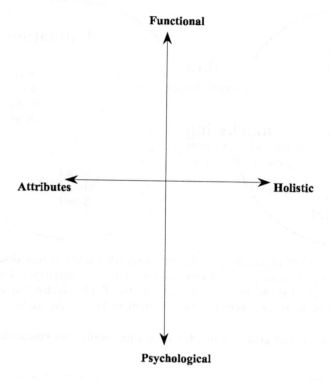

This revision questions the extent to which destination images may truly be quantified, and even 'scored'. Plotting XY co-ordinates on the framework (within two dimensions) can provide an insight into the relative nature of the tangibility and collectivity of stakeholder images and/or the images of competing tourist destinations. Yet if practitioners are to design more appropriate and effective destination identities as a result of comparing images further qualitative information is required. Using the earlier example of Barbados it is impossible to ascertain which of the respondents' 'scores' is 'better'. Further information is required from the respondents in terms of positive or negative connotations of the 'scores' from their images.

Applying the findings to a systems approach to destination image evaluation

As discussed during the introduction to this paper, the examination of the structure of destination image formed part of a wider PhD study. The wider study was concerned with evaluating the image of Wales across a tourism system. Four key stakeholder or 'system component' groups were identified based upon the elements of the tourism system given earlier in Figure 1. These groups were: the Wales Tourist Board (WTB); Welsh tourist attraction operators; existing rather than potential international holiday tourists to Wales; overseas tour operators offering Wales as a holiday destination (Figure 8).

Figure 8   A Tourism Destination Image System for Wales

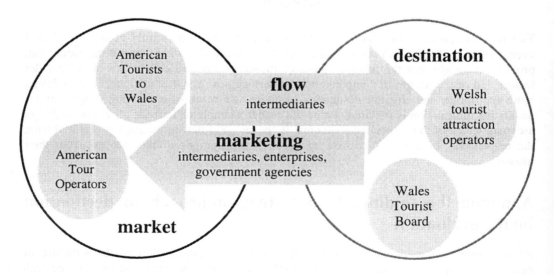

Following a series of further exploratory qualitative research studies it was discovered that image is far too abstract a concept to be discussed in a second language. Thus, the key system component groups for the study were revised: the WTB; Welsh tourist attraction operators; American tour operators; and American tourists to Wales (Figure 9).

Figure 9   System component groups amended following qualitative research studies

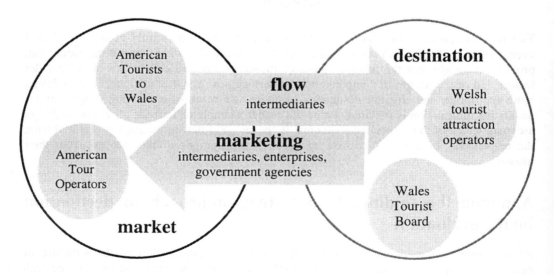

Sampling

Different sampling methods were used for each system component group. Known sample populations exist for the Welsh tourist attraction operators and American tour operators supplying Britain in their programmes via WTB and British Tourist Authority (BTA) database records. However, sampling was conducted mindful of the fact that these databases may not be exhaustive or up-to-date. American tourists are inevitably a less precise sample to identify and resulted in a split sampling method being applied, capturing two distinct American tourist types distinguished by mode of holiday booking - independent tourists (having made separate arrangements for transport and accommodation) and inclusive tourists (having arranged transport and accommodation from tour operators in a single package). The system component groups on which the study was based was thus, revised once more (Figure 10).

Figure 10   System component groups sampled in the questionnaire survey

Measurement

A questionnaire was selected as the most appropriate type of survey instrument for both practical and theoretical reasons. Questionnaires were designed to allow for the collection of destination images incorporating personal-specific, holiday-generic, and destination-specific contexts, and, reflecting the findings of the testing of the Echtner and Ritchie framework (1991; 1993), the two continua involved in the structure of destination image, alongside a number of questions related to the identification of a unique selling proposition (USP) for marketing purposes. The questions facilitated direct comparison between the destination images of system component groups, both in terms of the structure and content of those images. In total, two hundred and ninety-five Welsh tourist attraction operators, sixty-two American tour operators, sixty-three American independent tourists to Wales, and ninety-six American inclusive tourists to Wales were surveyed.

Results

To reiterate, support for the existence of a destination image *structure* enabled the design of a questionnaire to measure destination image *content*, appropriate to the conceptualisation of destination image. During the testing of the Echtner and Ritchie framework the content of unstructured destination images was plotted within two dimensions, enabling the relative weightings of the image to be illustrated (Figures 4, 5 and 6). On an individual-by-individual basis that procedure proved too laborious. However, with respect to examining group-level images in a systems context the two dimensional framework was recognised to hold potential for the visual representation and clarification of congruence and dissonance between destination images. The amendment of the Echtner and Ritchie framework from six individual components to two paired component axes simplified the procedure; the content of the images of a single respondent/system component group could now be accommodated within one diagram rather than three separate diagrams.

The structure of the destination image was controlled by the design of the questionnaire instrument; questions were specifically intended to capture collectivity (i.e., attributes-holistic) and tangibility (i.e., functional-psychological) elements. The actual ratings of the images (via semantic differential and likert scales) did however result in different configurations of the positive ratings for each system component group (Figures 11, 12, 13, 14 and 15).

Figure 11 WTB's Image of Wales

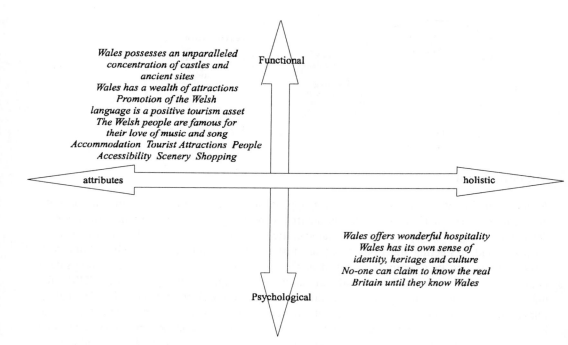

Figure 12 Welsh tourist attraction operator's image of Wales

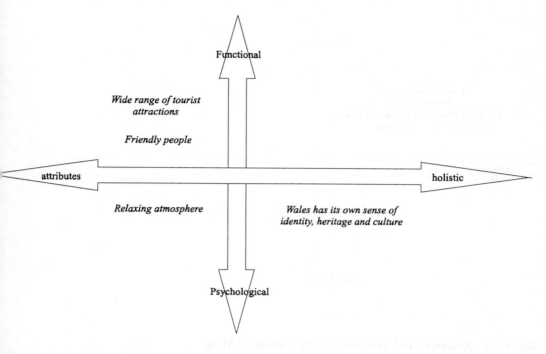

Figure 13 American tour operator's image of Wales

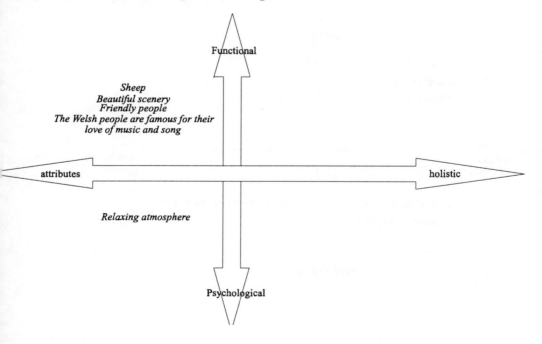

Figure 14 American inclusive tourist's image of Wales

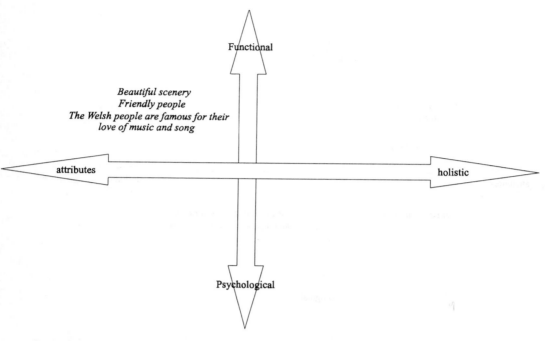

Figure 15 American independent tourist's image of Wales

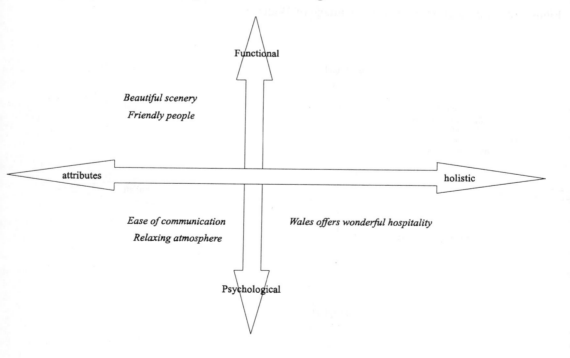

The WTB's image of Wales, (reflected in the identity that it promotes via its marketing literature and measured in this study using content analysis), is the busiest image with, as might be expected, the most positive weightings of Wales. The WTB image falls entirely into the functional-attribute and psychological-holistic quadrants. This suggests that the WTB sees that, in functional-attribute terms, Wales has 'got the lot' but that, as a destination, Wales is distinguished by its psychological-holistic characteristics. Wales' USP, its essential 'Welshness', is based on the very intangibles which are so difficult to 'put across' to its targeted audience.

Of the other four system component group images, they collapse into two pairs of similar images - the American tour operators/American inclusive tourists pair with more restricted views of Wales as a destination and the Welsh tourist attraction operator/American independent tourist pair. In the first pair (American tour operators/American inclusive tourists) both images are strongly oriented to the functional-attribute quadrants with only one other positive rating (that of 'relaxing atmosphere' in the attribute-psychological quadrant for American tour operators). It is very tempting to see a link between these two images and perhaps one fuels the other - certainly the American inclusive tourists are channelled through the destination by the American tour operators and get little opportunity to extend their exposure to Wales. In the second pair (the Welsh tourist attraction operators/American independent tourists) there is a more balanced, holistic perception of the image of Wales with representative positive elements in three of the four quadrants and only the functional-holistic quadrant remaining unpopulated. The American independent tourists arguably have more opportunity to interact with the destination and have the most contact with the Welsh tourist attraction operators as mediators of their experience in Wales, the 'front line' or 'customer interface'.

Discussion

An empirical examination of the Echtner and Ritchie framework (1991; 1993) challenged the appropriateness of the model as a valid conceptualisation of the structure of destination image. Although the research was limited to a small sample of tourists the results suggested that the framework required revision before it could be applied to the understanding and measurement of destination image. Consideration of the revised framework subsequently highlighted an inability to adequately represent destination images in quantitative terms alone. The need for qualitative methodologies was particularly apparent with respect to familiarity (i.e., the distinction between what is perceived to be 'common' or 'unique'), argued to be integral to the context in which destination images are set.

In terms of the application of a revised Echtner and Ritchie framework, the study was limited in its application, focusing upon Wales' relationship with the American geographical market segment. Nevertheless, the scope for extending the original purpose of the Echtner and Ritchie framework from a conceptual model to assist measurement towards a tool to aid the visual representation and hence, comparability, of destination image was illustrated.

With respect to the appropriateness and potential effectiveness of the promotion of Wales, the results indicate that there exists scope for the WTB to pursue more targeted promotional campaigns. Indeed, further comments acquired from the system component group respondents suggest that the WTB is in danger of overemphasising too many aspects and qualities of Wales at once to the extent that 'everything is outstanding so that nothing actually stands out' and differentiates the destination. The application of the modified Echtner and Ritchie framework as a representational tool for the content of destination image (Figures 11, 12, 13, 14 and 15) provides the opportunity to identify promotional tactics to assist the design of more appropriate and effective destination identities. For example, it is apparent that it would appear sensible to focus upon Wales' functional-attribute strengths (e.g., the beauty of the scenery) in promotion aimed at American tour operators/American inclusive tourists whereas American independent tourists may require augmented promotion with an additional focus on psychological-holistic strengths (e.g., Wales' relaxing atmosphere).

Conclusion and recommendations

This paper has highlighted the need for empirical examination of theoretical concepts prior to their implementation for measurement purposes. With respect to the measurement of destination image the value of questioning the validity of conceptual models prior to their utilisation has been demonstrated. However, although the Echtner and Ritchie framework (1991; 1993) was shown to possess a number of weaknesses its value should not be overlooked. The framework was found to possess value beyond its original purpose, providing a representational tool to ease comparison between destination images and identities. The future application of the systems approach adopted in this study, of course, depends upon the application of the approach beyond Wales – focusing on other destinations and other stakeholder or system component groups. The research presented in this paper should not be viewed as definitive nevertheless, it advances the destination image literature one step closer to being able to readily compare destination images against identities and thus, facilitate the design of more appropriate and effective destination image promotion.

References

Crompton, J. (1979), An assessment of the image of Mexico as a vacation destination and the influence of geographical location upon that image, *Journal of Travel Research*, 18 (Fall): 18-23.

Dann, G. M. S. (1996), *Language of Tourism: A Sociolinguistic Perspective*, CAB International, UK.

Echtner, C. M. and Ritchie, J. R. B. (1991), The meaning and measurement of destination image, *Journal of Tourism Studies*, 2 (2): 2-12.

Echtner, C.M. and Ritchie, J.R.B. (1993), The measurement of destination image: an empirical approach, *Journal of Travel Research*, 31 (4): 3-13.

Gunn, C. A. (1988), *Vacationscape: designing tourist regions*, Van Nostrand Reinhold, New York.

Gyte, D. M. (1988), *Repertory grid analysis of images of destinations: British tourists in Mallorca*, Trent Working Papers in Geography, Trent Polytechnic, Nottingham.

Hughes, G.(1992), *Tourism and the geographical imagination,* Leisure Studies, (11), pp.31-42.

Leiper, N. (1979), The framework of tourism: towards definitions of tourism, tourists, and the tourism industry, *Annals of Tourism Research,* 6, pp.390-407.

Mazanec, J. A. (1995), *Consumer Behaviour, Marketing Research and Segmentation.* In Witt, S. and Moutinho, L. (Editors), *Tourism Marketing and Management Handbook,* Prentice Hall, New Jersey, pp.273-285.

Navon, D. (1977*), Forest before trees: the precedence of global features in visual perception,* Cognitive Psychology, (9), pp.353-383.

Pearce, P. L. (1982), Perceived changes in holiday destinations, *Annals of Tourism Research,* 9, (2), pp.145-164.

Phelps, A. (1986), Holiday Destination Image - the problem of assessment. An example developed in Menorca, *Tourism Management,* September, (7), pp.168-180.

Scottish visitor attractions: Issues for the new millennium

Alan Fyall

Bournemouth University, UK

Anna Leask

Napier University, UK

Brian Garrod

University of the West of England, Bristol, UK

Abstract

This paper presents a synthesis of the opinions of a cross-section of experts within the visitor attractions sector in Scotland. The aim of the paper is to identify the issues most likely to have a significant impact on the nature, quality and demand for Scottish visitor attractions over the next two decades. In particular, the paper seeks to pinpoint the key issues that are likely to require a strategic response early in the new millennium. Six thematic areas are identified: political issues, economic issues, socio-cultural issues, ecological issues, technological issues, and issues relating to marketing and the industry itself. In order to meet the demands of a future marketplace that is expected to be more dynamic, volatile, fickle and, as a result, much more demanding, the paper suggests that decisive strategic action will be required on the part of the visitor attractions sector. The principal message is that complacency in a global marketplace that is inherently dynamic and liable to explosive change should be avoided at all costs.

Introduction

Looking to the future has never been something with which academia feels entirely comfortable. Analysis of historical trends and events is a well-established part of most academic disciplines, and the analysis of current issues is widely considered to be essential if an academic discipline is to demonstrate its practical relevance in contemporary society. Analysis of the future, on the other hand, has tended to be perceived as an inexact science at best; a haven for academic charlatans at worst. Yet there are many groups in society for whom looking into the future is an absolute necessity. Governments, non-government organisations and private companies alike must all plan for the future; and to do that effectively they must have some idea of what the world of the future will be like.

This paper sets out to identify some of the key opportunities and challenges for visitor attractions in Scotland as they enter the new millennium. In doing so, the paper attempts to shed light on the issues that are most likely to influence the nature, quality and demand for Scottish visitor attractions, and tries to pinpoint those key issues that are likely to require a strategic response early in the new millennium. This section begins by presenting a broad overview of the economic context in which the Scottish visitor attractions sector presently finds itself. For the purposes of this paper, a visitor attraction is defined as:

> "*A permanently established excursion destination, a primary purpose of which is to allow public access for entertainment, interest or education; rather than being principally a retail outlet or venue for sporting, theatrical or film performances. It must be open to the public, without prior booking, for published periods each year, and should be capable of attracting day visitors or tourists, as well as local residents. In addition the attraction must be a single business, under a single management [...] and must be receiving revenue directly from the visitors*" (ETC, 1999, p.7).

The economic significance of visitor attractions in the Scottish tourism industry should not be underestimated. Evidence from the United Kingdom Tourism Survey indicates that while only a relatively small proportion of visitors come to Scotland specifically to visit attractions, once they have arrived a far greater number visit one or more of the country's castles, churches, historic houses, museums and sites of historical interest during the course of their stay (Smith, 1998). Furthermore, the visitor attractions sector plays an important role in supporting the wider tourism industry of Scotland. In a review conducted by Scottish Enterprise (SE), Scotland's economic development agency, visitor attractions were said to add value to the basic tourism resources of the country by presenting Scotland's environment, history and heritage to the visitor (Scottish Enterprise, 1997). Visitor attractions also provide wet weather facilities for visitors, provide an opportunity for increasing visitor spend, can help to extend the visitor length of stay, and can help tackle the perennial problem of seasonality by spreading the tourist season. Visitor attractions are also important in terms of stimulating destination development, generating revenues and providing employment opportunities (Leask *et al*, 2000).

Yet visitor attractions in Scotland have recently begun to experience a range of market pressures which, taken together, do not appear to augur well for the sector. First, it is evident that Scotland's major competitors have been growing their international tourism receipts more quickly than the Scottish tourism industry has been able to. For an industry that employs one in twelve of the Scottish workforce and contributes almost £2.5 billion to the Scottish economy, it is of concern that after several years of growth between 1994 and 1997, a sudden downturn in both domestic and overseas visitors to Scotland was recorded in 1998 (STB, 1998). A number of factors have been suggested as contributing to this downturn. For domestic visitors the high cost of fuel, the World Cup in 1998, and poor weather arguably kept many potential domestic tourists at home. For overseas visitors, the strength of the pound sterling has contributed to Scotland being regarded as a high cost destination. While offset in part by the growth of 'no frills' airlines and substantial promotional investment by the Scottish Tourist Board (STB), particularly in the form of shoulder-period initiatives such as 'Autumn Gold' and 'Spring into Summer', the overall picture is perhaps an ominous one. In the context of a global tourism industry that is growing by approximately 4% per annum, and with international tourist arrivals forecast to double by the year 2020 (World Tourism Organization, 1998), the Scottish tourism industry as a whole looks set to face troubled times as we enter the new millennium.

A second, and perhaps more significant source of market pressure for the Scottish visitor attractions sector comes from heightened competition in its domestic visitor markets. While international tourist markets are important for the relatively small number of large, nationally recognised, and often well funded attractions such as Edinburgh Castle, domestic day or short-break visitors constitute the major markets for the vast majority of all visitor attractions across the UK as a whole (CBI, 1998). This trend is particularly significant for visitor attractions in Scotland, where approximately 75% of attractions record visitor levels below 50,000 per annum (STB, 1999a). This reliance on day and short-break visitors is important because it implies that visitor attractions are competing directly for consumer leisure spend with highly competitive and professionally managed service sectors such as retailing and hospitality (CBI, 1998).

As a result of these two major development in their markets, it is apparent that visitor attractions in Scotland now find themselves operating in a much more difficult and fast-changing competitive environment. With an overall decrease in visitor attraction attendance of 1%, thirteen of the top twenty paid attractions in Scotland recorded decreases in visitor numbers in 1998 (STB, 1999a). Although this trend is by no means uniform across all categories of attraction, early signs are that conditions for the sector as a whole are unlikely to improve over the next few years. Recent results published for August 1999 show attendance at Scottish visitor attractions down by 3.5% on August 1998, with a year-on-year decrease forecast at 2.8% for the coming year (STB, 1999b). This decrease has been experienced by attractions across the country, with only those in the Western Isles significantly bucking the trend. The presence of particularly harsh trading conditions for visitor attractions was confirmed by a recent report from Deloitte and Touche (1998), which noted an erratic trend in terms of overall visitor numbers to attractions since 1993. The report went on to conclude that further growth is unlikely in any of the main visitor attraction segments in the short term.

Leask *et al* (2000) suggest that in view of these changing market conditions, the visitor attractions sector will be forced, as a survival strategy, to identify new management approaches and new operational techniques. The purpose of this paper is to provide guidance on this process by reporting the outcome of a series of in-depth interviews on the future prospects and challenges for Scottish visitor attractions with leading figures in the sector.

Methodology

In order to identify the issues facing Scottish visitor attractions, the study adopted a qualitative and speculative methodology. This involved exploratory research among a number of expert practitioners in the Scottish visitor attractions sector, who were asked to identify the key issues and trends they perceived as likely to have a significant impact on visitor attractions in Scotland over the next two decades. A key feature of this methodology is that it attempts to tap into the skills and knowledge base of a small group of expert participants, rather than to seek the more-or-less instant responses of a less targeted group to a series of closed questions. The solicitation of expert opinion is an important feature of the research approach given the objective of this study, which is to identify a range of issues and challenges relevant to the Scottish visitor attractions sector in the medium-to-long term. This is not a task to which more conventional forecasting techniques are well suited, the more widely-accepted quantitative forecasting techniques being limited in practice to short-range forecasting only. Speculative approaches, on the other hand, have been identified as highly practical and relevant to strategic decision making, given the inevitable need of strategic planners to look beyond the short term. Indeed Fahey *et al* (1981) consider such approaches to be of 'high utility' in the development of strategic planning scenarios. Uysal and Crompton (1985), meanwhile, argue that by providing subjective assessments, rather than precise statements about the statistical likelihood of occurrence of future trends or events, the speculative approach is more likely to produce outputs that will be useful to the strategic planning process. After all, planning is, almost by definition, carried out under conditions of uncertainty. Helmer (1979), meanwhile, argues that the use of the probabilistic approach, as opposed to one that tries to make precise quantitative predictions, is more suitable because it demonstrates a realistic awareness of the inherent uncertainty of the future.

The issues discussed in this paper were derived from a series of semi-structured, face-to-face interviews, conducted with a broad cross-section of expert participants from the visitor attractions sector in Scotland. Seventeen in-depth interviews were conducted with expert respondents, written correspondence being obtained from another eleven who were unavailable to be interviewed. Six of the interviews were conducted with experts based at the Scottish Tourist Board (STB), Scottish Borders Tourist Board (SBTB), Scottish Enterprise (SE), Lothian and Edinburgh Enterprise Limited (LEEL), and the Association of Scottish Visitor Attractions (ASVA). The remaining eleven interviews were conducted with managers of visitor attractions. A good cross-section of visitor attractions were represented in both the interviews and the written correspondence, with Scotland's premier visitor attraction, Edinburgh Castle, and its newest visitor attraction, 'Our Dynamic Earth', both featuring in the study.

Interviews were normally held at the organisation's premises and recorded on the condition that individual confidentiality be maintained. Throughout the paper, all comments attributed to participants are reported anonymously. A 'non-directive' approach was used to probe the interviewees (Oppenheim, 1992). No parameters were set prior to the interviews. The purpose of the interviews was to elicit the specific and unprompted views of a group of managers in the field, rather than prompt their thoughts with the use of previously published material, as was the case in the work conducted by Moutinho and Witt (1995). As expected, participants held a wide range of views in respect of the issues most likely to have a future impact on Scottish visitor attractions. The approach adopted here is to report those issues where the majority of participants reached broad agreement on issues raised, rather than achieve a Delphi-style consensus of opinion. The authors acknowledge the potential for interviewer and participant bias, but suggest that the recording of the interviews serves to enhance the credibility of the findings reported in the paper.

On completion of all the interviews, the authors identified six thematic areas and grouped the issues identified by the participants accordingly. The six areas are: political issues, economic issues, socio-cultural issues, ecological issues, technological issues, and issues relating to marketing and the industry itself. These thematic areas correspond closely to those outlined by the WTO (1998) in their report *Tourism 2020 Vision: A New Forecast,* in which a number of determinants of, and influences on, international tourism to the year 2020 were identified. While the issues highlighted by the WTO strictly relate to the world tourism industry as a whole, it is interesting to note the close correlation between the global themes identified by the WTO and those identified here at the national and local levels.

It should be emphasised that the remit of this paper is to identify the main factors that are likely to present key opportunities and challenges to the nature, quality and demand for Scottish visitor attractions over the next two decades. Future work by the authors plans to use these issues as a basis for creating a series of potential future scenarios for the Scottish visitor attractions sector. This will enable a range of strategic options for the Scottish visitor attractions sector to be highlighted and, more specifically, it is hoped that this will allow the potential role of collaborative marketing strategies in the sustainable development of visitor attractions in Scotland to be explored.

Issues identified as likely to have a future impact on Scottish visitor attractions

Political issues

While the removal of trade barriers and transport deregulation are posited by the WTO (1998) as being the political events most likely to impact on future tourism developments, the political issue of greatest significance to Scotland would seem to be that of political devolution and possible future independence from the rest of the United Kingdom.

Table 1   Political Issues

POLITICAL	
Devolution/ Independence	Devolution and future independence
	External perception of Scotland and the United Kingdom
	Representation of tourism in the Scottish parliament, the wider British parliament and within the European Union
	Representation for visitor attractions at the industry and parliamentary levels
Industry Structure and Funding	Reorganisation of authorities with a remit for the development of tourism in Scotland
	Decreasing public sector subsidy for visitor attractions with greater influence from the private sector in the future development and funding of visitor attractions in Scotland
	The National Lottery as a source of funds
	Increasing competition from leisure and sport for external 'leisure-related' funds
Other Political Issues	Conflict between local and national authorities as to what is in the 'local' and 'national' interest
	Pressure to adopt 'social inclusion' strategies
	Wider political events across the globe and their impact on visitor behaviour

While the recent move toward political devolution in Scotland was perceived by many participants as being too recent an event to judge whether or not it will be of benefit to Scottish visitor attractions, the possible move to full independence in the longer term was widely regarded by participants as being a threat. Devolution in its current form does not appear to have generated widespread concern, although there is a recognition that Scottish attractions will need to be far more in tune with the future needs and expectations of the English market, Scotland's largest incoming tourist market by far.

Although the external perception of Scotland and the rest of the UK by overseas visitors may be subject to change as a consequence of this constitutional landmark, the question of how the English market will perceive Scotland in the early years of devolution warrants particular scrutiny. This may impact on the interpretation of attractions, especially historic sites, and efforts to re-forge a truly distinct Scottish identity for the attractions concerned. It may also have a bearing on the perceived 'warmth' of welcome by Scottish hosts to their English visitors, and hence impact on future staff training content. These impacts will no doubt vary across Scotland but already various attractions have recorded higher than average number of 'suggestions' from what appears to be a more 'devolution sensitive' English visitor.

The associated threat of dual tax systems would also appear to be an operational threat to many attractions, but it is the fear of Scottish provincialism and a more protectionist stance that appears to raise a greater threat, especially in respect of visitor perceptions. In the longer term this is something that may engender antipathy to Scotland as a tourist destination from the English market. The impact on the branding and promotion of Scotland as a destination to the English market is all too clear. As one participant commented:

> "Devolution can help to sharpen the perception of a different destination. There is the ever-present danger of self-satisfaction or complacency which can diminish the competitiveness of the Scottish experience." (Anonymous Participant)

At a strategic level, devolution provides an opportunity to the Scottish Executive to provide leadership to the nation's tourism industry. As yet, there appears to be much talk but limited action and no obvious strategic change, especially for attractions. In a debate held in the Scottish Parliament on 19th November 1999, David Davidson MSP represented the views of many at the news that there is not to be a designated minister for tourism in the foreseeable future by suggesting that:

> "With 23 ministers – in addition to those in the Scottish Office – surely the Executive could spare someone to give leadership to the tourism industry." ((http//www.scottish.parliament.uk/...1_report/session99-00/or020703.htm)

The failure to appoint a minister for tourism was widely regarded to be a missed opportunity for Scottish tourism by those who participated in this study. The opportunity does exist, however, for the re-organisation of existing authorities with a remit for the development of tourism in Scotland, and the launch of a unified organisation able to offer a co-ordinated 'one-stop-shop' for Scottish tourism. Bruce Crawford MSP raised this point in the recent debate in the Scottish Parliament:

> "On the structure of the public sector, we have inherited a situation in which the lines of responsibility are, to say the least, confused, and in which transparency of policy formation and of delivery mechanisms is severely lacking. That has created an environment in the private arm of the industry where innovation and investment are stifled, and where strategic direction is low or non-existent." (http//www.scottish.parliament.uk/...1_report/session99-00/or020703.htm)

The perceived overlap of authority for tourism in Scotland is viewed as a problem for many attractions, particularly those under private ownership, as are the shortcomings of some local and area tourist boards to attractions looking for more membership-friendly strategies. Although evidently not a cause for concern for all attractions, what the above does seem to demonstrate is a degree of frustration with a public sector unable to keep abreast, both strategically and financially, with developments in the market place. The role of the private sector in the future development and funding of visitor attractions in Scotland, and the introduction of the National Lottery as a source of funds, has already had a significant impact on the visitor attraction market place and is likely to continue to do so in the future.

Many of the disputes over funding relate to disagreements between attractions and financial backers as to what is in the 'local' or 'national' interest, and the extent to which 'social inclusion' policies can be pursued. Historically there has always been a shortfall of visitors to heritage attractions from the lower socio-economic groupings (Fyall and Garrod, 1998). Any future linking of funds to the attraction of groups from the lower social groupings is likely to have widespread implications for the setting of admission charges, access and transportation to attractions, product interpretation and media presentation.

A further political issue is the potential for wider political events across the globe to impact on visitor behaviour. Perceptions of the newly politically devolved Scotland are still probably being formed. Of rather more significance, however, are events that may occur overseas that encourage more domestic visitors to forego trips abroad and vacation at home. Terrorism, wars, political uncertainty and worries over global warming were all suggested as events that can, when they occur, generate enormous benefits for the domestic tourism industry. Given their dependence on domestic tourists, visitor attractions would be a major beneficiary of such political developments in the Scottish context.

Economic issues

The economic issue of greatest concern to Scottish visitor attractions would appear to relate to Scotland being perceived as an expensive market for the English due to fuel prices rising, and for overseas visitors due to the continued strengthening of the pound sterling against other world currencies in recent years. Political lobbying apart, there is little that the tourism industry, and visitor attractions sector, can do about this. Coupled with the lower costs of international travel for domestic visitors taking their holidays abroad, operators can anticipate an uphill battle in drawing visitors to their attractions, especially those located in the more peripheral areas of Scotland.

Table 2   Economic Issues

ECONOMIC	
Macro-economic Policy	• Interest rate and taxation policy • Currency stability and the strength of £ Sterling/Euro
Other Economic Issues	• Minimum wage • High costs of fuel and transportation at the national level • Low cost of global travel • Short-term working contracts • The increasing wealth gap both domestically and internationally

While the WTO report also refers to the growing power of international economic forces, and the reduced power of the individual states and non-global corporations, it would appear to be economic decisions made at the national level that most concern visitor attraction operators. For a country reliant on car-borne visitors, Scotland is likely to be adversely affected by any further 'greening' of the government's transport policies and attempts made to price motorists off the road. Discussion by politicians both nationally and within the European Union about the possible imposition of road and bridge tolls does little to comfort already worried attraction operators, especially those in the more remote parts of the country. As one participant commented:

> "*As a country on the margin of Europe, the cost of access to remote visitor attractions is the main problem. Inter-island services are expensive, and the attractions are below standard in terms of mainland European competition.*"
> (Anonymous Participant)

Virtually all participants in the study believed that the UK would join the Euro in the not too distant future. However there was only limited agreement as to how, if at all, this would impact upon attendance at visitor attractions. While price transparency was heralded as a great benefit, it was anticipated that this would merely reinforce how expensive a trip to Scotland is for overseas visitors. It would also serve to highlight the relative cheapness of foreign holidays for potential domestic visitors. Nevertheless, any means by which currency stability can be achieved was considered as being beneficial to the Scottish visitor attractions sector.

Britain's anticipated entry into the Euro mirrors the prediction of the WTO (1998) that over the next twenty years greater attempts to harmonise currencies around the world will occur. In addition, the WTO identified continued moderate-to-good rates of global economic growth, above average economic performance in the Asian economies, the emerging importance of new 'tiger' economies such as China, India and Brazil, and a widening in the gap between rich and poor countries as those issues most likely to have a future impact on tourism. China is of particular interest as it is forecast to generate 137 million outbound tourists by 2020 (WTO, 1998). However, it is not only between countries that the growing wealth gap is perceived to be a problem. Participants in this study commented on the increasing wealth gap within Britain as a cause for concern in the coming years. In part this relates back to the issue of 'social inclusion' and the anticipated adoption of more rigorous marketing strategies aimed at attracting previously disenfranchised groups to visitor attractions, especially those based in the so-called 'heritage sector'.

Further economic issues raised by the participants were the minimum wage and short-term working contracts. In operational terms, the minimum wage has direct cost implications for visitor attractions. However, the imposition of the minimum wage may also help recruit suitably qualified staff to the sector. To attract a workforce that is genuinely interested in the product, and its visitors, participants in the study believed that visitor attractions will have to pay a more realistic wage in the years to come. The recruitment of suitable staff has always been a problem and will continue to be a problem unless the 'low wage – poor sector perception – low quality staff' cycle is broken and the sector's image as a professional employer takes root. With regard to the trend toward increasing numbers of short-term contracts in the workplace, it is the consequent uncertainty and insecurity over holiday booking that is anticipated to represent both an opportunity and threat in years to come. On the one hand the tendency toward short-term working contracts may inhibit domestic tourists working on those contracts from making plans to travel overseas. Equally there is a good chance that this may also dissuade English visitors from making plans to come to Scotland. On the other hand, there is the chance that short-term working contracts may encourage people to be more conservative in their holiday plans and stay local. This would increase their propensity to visit local attractions. The attraction of the Scottish visitor to Scottish visitor attractions is a perennial problem but one that has become more severe in recent years. Participants in this study noted that not only has there been disinterest in attractions by potential Scottish visitors, but there has been widespread disinterest by many attractions in drawing in local people. Local custom is an important part of the visitor base of many Scottish attractions. For others, local customers are of particular importance in the shoulder periods and the off-season. Strategies to address this problem were seen as crucial to the longer-term survival of many visitor attractions.

Socio-cultural issues

The issues of a socio-cultural nature that dominate this study, as well as that carried out by the WTO (1998), are the ageing of the population, the break-up of the modern family, and the consequent greater diversity of lifestyles in existence.

Table 3   Socio-cultural Issues

SOCIO -CULTURAL	
Demographic Change	• The ageing population • 'Time poor – money rich' visitors • Greater diversity of lifestyles among visitors

One participant commented on new bases of segmentation being adopted around characters in the media which closely reflect their particular market segments. The 'Terry and June' and 'Ross and Rachel' profiles respectively mirror the number of older couples at the 'empty nest' stage of the family life cycle, and the large number of cohabiting younger couples demonstrating no real desire to have children. In tandem with the trend towards 'time poor – money rich visitors', it is clear that socio-cultural issues are likely to have a major impact on the nature, quality and demand for Scottish visitor attractions in the future. Participants in the study generally believed that there will be an increasing need among visitors for instant gratification, that visitors will be more focused with highly 'specific' rather than general 'wandering' interests, and exhibit a decreasing span of attention, thereby encouraging 'maximum thrill - minimum time' products. In turn, the market will be less homogeneous, more educated and more sophisticated, seek new innovations and experiences, be increasingly more active, and generally be seeking a much higher quality of experience. In view of the many small, old and traditional attractions to be found in Scotland, participants anticipated considerable challenges with regard to attraction format, flexibility and management in the need to keep abreast of the fundamental socio-economic changes predicted to be just beyond the horizon.

In addition to the above, the WTO (1998) predict that demand from groups defined on the basis of ethnicity, religion and social structures to grow substantially in their own right. The inclusion of Gaelic-based attractions and interpretation is a particular issue across Scotland; but particularly so in the Highlands where Gaelic is more widely spoken.

Ecological issues

The issue that continues to dominate future ecological trends is the increasing level of ecological and environmental awareness demonstrated by visitors. While accepting recognition of this global trend and the pressure for further outlets for 'green tourism', participants nevertheless felt that while conservation and environmental policies are necessary they should not always be to the detriment of everything else.

Table 4   Ecological Issues

ECOLOGICAL	
Sustainability	• Increasing ecological and environmental awareness • Greater competition for tourism related resources • Compulsory environmental auditing and launch of 'Green Tourism' business schemes
Visitor Management	• Sustaining visitor attractions through general wear and tear and accidental/deliberate visitor damage • Conflict between conservation, preservation and the maintenance of authenticity and visitor management initiatives
Other Issues	• Natural disasters and terrorist threats • Weather factors and global warming • Urban congestion

Of particular concern was the ability to maintain the authenticity of attractions and sensitivity of interpretation while at the same time developing initiatives and facilities to boost income, improve interpretation, facilitate visitor flow, and generally enhance the overall visitor experience. Moreover, it was widely accepted that the likely introduction of compulsory environmental audits, in whatever form, would impact strongly on visitor attractions.

Although natural disasters and terrorist threats are outside the control of operators, participants in the study felt that more could be done to combat the weather through the introduction of more 'all weather' attractions and facilities. Not only would more covered facilities help counter the unpredictable Scottish weather but they would also go some way to redress the problems of a short-season for many attractions. Finally there the issue of urban congestion was raised. While this was not considered a particular problem in Scotland at the present time, participants in the study believed it to be an increasingly important issue in the future; and one that may work in favour of those attractions currently believing themselves to be on the periphery. More generally, the need to escape the crowded cities and seek more natural environment-based attractions would certainly appear to represent a trend very much in Scotland's favour.

Technological issues

Sympathetic inclusion rather than universal adoption was the clear message coming from the study participants with regard to the integration of new technology in attractions. Despite the seemingly irreversible trend towards the adoption of technological gadgets, participants indicated that the particular nature of many Scottish attractions of an environmental and heritage genre was not conducive to the blanket adoption of so-called 'techno-toys'. This said, the creative and imaginative use of technology in newer attractions is testament to the seemingly unstoppable force of this trend.

Table 5   Technological Issues

TECHNOLOGICAL	
	• Increasing demand for technology and technology-oriented interpretation
	• Greater visitor inter-activity at attractions
	• Advances in transportation technology and the demand for integrated transport systems
	• Widespread use of e-commerce and the Internet

Another important technological issue identified by the study participants was the high levels of Internet penetration across the country and the increasing public ownership of mobile phones. With the general population demonstrating apparent greater familiarity with technology, especially among the younger markets, there is the perceived threat that those attractions that fail to adopt new technology will get left behind.

One area where technology is making significant inroads into Scottish tourism is via OSSIAN, the STB's bold attempt to create an electronic destination booking system on the Internet. This massive project is in many ways ahead of its time and represents a significant opportunity for tourism businesses in Scotland, including visitor attractions, to establish a virtual base from which to trade electronically on the World Wide Web. However, while the project is quite revolutionary in its vision, the diffusion of understanding of OSSIAN's full potential among attraction operators remains open to question, as does its ability to meet their high expectations. Participants in the study believed that a combination of 'technophobia' and a degree of scepticism are likely to impact on its future performance. The likely impact on visitors wanting to frequent real rather than virtual destinations, the use of technology in interpretation, and the impact of electronic cash on visitor spending behaviour, were identified as key issues for the future.

Finally, participants argued that probably the issue of most concern to visitor attractions, especially those in remote locations, is the future form and role of an integrated transport system across Scotland. The relative isolation of many attractions ensures that the issue of transportation will be high on the agenda for the future, especially for those attractions seeking to meet 'social inclusion' objectives by targeting visitors from poorer social backgrounds who do not own or have access to a car.

Marketing and industry issues

With approximately 6,100 visitor attractions across the UK, recording 409 million visits in 1998, Scotland is home to about 900 visitor attractions (STB, 1999c). The number of visitor attractions in Scotland represents 20.3 attractions per 100,000 inhabitants as compared to the UK average of 10.5 per 100,000 inhabitants (ETC, 1999). If one were only to include what Scottish Enterprise refer to as 'core' attractions, then these figures would obviously alter; the remaining number of attractions constituting many leisure and recreational facilities which arguably serve the needs of the local resident population. Because of the heavy reliance many smaller to medium-sized attractions have on domestic visitors, there is a widely held perception that Scotland has an oversupply of visitor attractions. Furthermore, one can argue that Scotland lacks that essential 'iconic' attraction capable of drawing international appeal. Arguably this is because Scotland is unable properly to support, due to its size and peripheral geographic location in Europe, a large commercially-driven attraction (Smith, 1998).

Despite the fact that the STB's Strategic Plan of 1995 prioritised the upgrading and renewal of existing sites, rather than the development of new ones, with a particular emphasis on the adoption of new technological and interpretation techniques, new visitor attractions continue to be developed in Scotland. For example, the 'Big Idea' is due to open in 2000, with the Loch Lomond Project and Glasgow Science Centre due to open in 2001. If anything, these projects, by virtue of their location in Scotland's Central Belt, will merely add to the problem of too many tourists in the traditional, clustered, 'honey pot' destinations of Glasgow and Edinburgh, hindering moves to broaden the appeal of Scotland's peripheral areas. Nevertheless, while these new developments are probably very viable projects in their own right, the perception remains that Scotland already has an oversupply of visitor attractions. This situation suggests that too little attention is being paid to policy initiatives coming from the area tourist boards, the STB, and the economic development agencies. Lottery and Millennium funding is unlikely to disappear in the short to mid-term, so it is anticipated that new, well funded visitor attractions will continue to exert a significant influence on the sector as a whole, with considerable displacement effects on existing operators over coming years (STB, 1999a).

In view of the above, participants in the study suggested that greater effort should be made in creating broader destinations, rather than develop yet more purpose-built attractions, so as to create an environment in which existing attractions can flourish. There is also the argument that the market itself will act as a rationalisation mechanism. Rather than to concentrate their efforts in boosting volume, attraction operators might do better to upgrade their facilities and try to increase spend per head. However, this would probably be to the disadvantage of those smaller and medium-sized attractions that are unable to withstand heightened market pressures in the longer-term. There is also the problem of particular attractions working in isolation to the detriment of neighbouring attractions, producing a negative impact on the total number of visitors coming to an area.

Table 6   Marketing and Industry Issues

MARKETING AND INDUSTRY	
Competition	• Increase in local, national and international competition both from within and outside of the attraction and wider tourism sectors • Emergence of new international markets • Oversupply of visitor attractions in Scotland • Visitor attraction operator fragmentation • Maintaining the quality of the wider 'destination'
Visitor Trends	• Visitor expectation and experience • Demand for 'honey pot' destinations rather than peripheral areas and attractions • Changing patterns of tourist trip behaviour • Disabled access and 'visitor' rights • Attraction standards and consistency in the eye of the visitor • Problems in attracting the Scottish, and repeat Scottish, visitor
Attraction Management	• Maintaining attraction viability • Becoming visitor rather than product-driven • Adoption of a more commercial and less 'curatorial' approach to attraction management • Increasing need for greater creativity, innovativeness and entrepreneurship within the attraction sector • Greater collaboration and collective marketing initiatives • Managing seasonality • Flexible attraction formats and wider means of diversification • Improving channel intermediary relationships • Sustaining value for money

The potential for isolationist strategies conducted by individual attractions was also perceived as a significant problem, and one that must be addressed in the future. Hence, the need for greater collaboration among attractions is something that the participants in this study saw as being essential to the long-term future of Scottish visitor attractions. Collaboration, which can take any number of forms, is fundamental to the creation of wider destinations, where the component parts of the tourism product can come together and deliver a cohesive, integrated and distinct tourism product.

One perceived barrier to greater collaboration is the fact that Scotland's current portfolio of visitor attractions is managed by such a diverse range of agencies and organisations. Approximately 33% of all visitor attractions in Scotland are privately owned, 21% are owned by local authorities, and 17% by various trusts, with Historic Scotland and the National Trust for Scotland sharing the remaining sites between them (STB, 1999b). The pattern of ownership of visitor attractions highlights a particular problem with the formulation of a generic strategy, because many attractions in Scotland do not view tourism as their primary objective. For a number of reasons, conservation, education, industry promotion or public relations objectives sometimes supersede tourism as the primary raison d'être (Garrod and Fyall, 2000).

As a consequence of the above, standards can vary quite considerably among sites in terms of facilities, access and management; hence the launch of the STB's Visitor Attraction Quality Assurance Scheme in the early 1990s. Along with initiatives launched by the Association of Scottish Visitor Attractions (ASVA), the Historic Houses Association and the Independent Tourism Consortium, the STB scheme is an attempt to monitor quality and develop best practice (Leask *et al*, 2000). For example, while a small number of high profile attractions such as 'Our Dynamic Earth' and the Royal Yacht Britannia can attract large sums of funding, which may help raise industry standards, many smaller attractions afford little return on investment and therefore offer effectively no opportunity for reinvestment. Reliance upon financial assistance and/or volunteer workers is commonplace, with an increasing number of attractions becoming ever more dependent on levying admission charges and/or the generation of secondary income streams. More than any other issue, it is this search for funds that is responsible for the gradual migration from a 'curatorial' to a 'commercial' mindset among attraction operators (Leask and Goulding, 1996).

Engendering a commercial mindset in a local authority or any public sector environment was, however, perceived as a significant challenge by the participants in the study. To many respondents, the one-dimensional, curatorial mindset of old is not viable in the new millennium. The principal issue is one of organisational change and breaking away from the 'closed loop' cycle of limited creativity, innovation and entrepreneurship. Furthermore the sector's reputation for inattention to research, limited appreciation of 'public benefits', and the use of 'tokenistic' decision-making will have be overcome. It is clear that visitor attractions will have to become more visitor-conscious and less product-driven if they are to survive in the new millennium. Many commentators suggest retraining and possible new recruitment as the answer to this problem. However, as is the case across the entire tourism and hospitality sector, there appears to be no easy solution to the problem of organisational resistance to change. Unfortunately the longer the problem remains, the longer the ability of Scottish visitor attractions to sustain their competitive position in the marketplace will be forestalled.

With regard to the visitor, there was apparently no doubt among participants that visitor expectations are on a continual upward spiral; as is their tendency to have visited other attractions, many on mainland Europe and in North America. Not only does this have an impact on attraction standards, and on the level of service consistency as perceived by visitors, but it also impacts directly on the actual visitation to attractions, especially when up against highly commercial and professionally-run retailing, cinema, catering and sporting attractions. Indeed, as one participants noted:

> *"These problems - competition and poor management - have always been and always will be with us. There is a need for a nationwide strategy to ensure that the service does not become fragmented, that standards are maintained and improved and that we do not become over-supplied with attractions."*
> (Anonymous Participant)

While the above quotation comes across as being somewhat negative, it does reflects a general view among participants in the study. No matter what the plans, policies and strategies of the past, the hour has arrived where Scottish visitor attractions can no longer ignore the growing momentum for change.

Conclusions and recommendations: the need for an industry response

Swarbrooke (1995, p.351) suggests that:

> *"The nature of visitor attractions and their markets will continue to change in the future as they have done in the past. However, there is reason to believe that the pace of change may even increase in the future as a result of a number of powerful factors."*

This would certainly appear to be true for many visitor attractions in Scotland, where the issues outlined in the previous sections of this paper serve as significant opportunities and threats to the nature, quality and demand for Scottish visitor attractions in the future. In terms of their nature, study participants believe that attractions are likely to have to be more sensitive to the future needs of the market place, especially within the context of recent and possibly future political change. In turn, visitor attraction managers will increasingly need to reflect the expectations of all groups within society by developing, interpreting, managing and promoting their attractions in a way that is sensitive to the needs of increasingly disparate visitor groups. Participants to the study also suggested that visitor attractions will need to develop a built-in flexibility that will safeguard the authenticity and novelty of the product and allow them to adapt quickly to market changes, to host events and to organise hospitality, either individually or collaboratively. In addition, operators of attractions will require far greater levels of commercial expertise as the present super-abundance of public sector funds inevitably subsides. They will also need to be more receptive to innovation and change in a fast changing market environment. Furthermore, it is believed that attractions will have to play a more proactive and integral part in the creation, development and maintenance of wider tourist destinations, especially in the more remote and peripheral areas of Scotland. This factor alone should engender a more collaborative orientation among tourism policy makers and, hopefully, create strong destination areas with strong identities which contain visitor attractions of a high standard.

With regard to the individual and collective quality of Scottish visitor attractions, participants suggested the sector will need to address the perception of Scotland being a high price destination, particularly among overseas visitors to Scotland and visitors from elsewhere in the UK. At the same time, the sector will need to demonstrate value for money for an increasingly discerning domestic market. It was also widely believed that the current number of visitor attractions in Scotland is not viable in the medium to long term, and the supply of attractions will require rationalisation if the market is collectively to provide a high quality product in the eyes of the visitor. Furthermore, there is widespread belief that the development of any new attractions should be considered carefully in the light of any 'additionality' and/or possible visitor 'displacement' effects on existing attractions. Above all, the quality of the product must be matched by quality staff and a greater concern for the quality of the entire visitor experience; not just at attractions but throughout visitors' entire trip to Scotland.

Finally, participants to the study generally felt that visitor attractions in Scotland are going to have to meet future demand that is far less homogeneous, better educated and more sophisticated than before. The sector is also likely to encounter visitors in search of new innovations, experiences and thrills. On one hand, many visitors will arrive by public transport rather than by car, and will come from previously disenfranchised groups within society. On the other hand, it is forecast that visitors will also arrive from countries around the world who are relatively new to Scotland and know little of what Scotland has to offer the tourist. Many new overseas visitors will bring with them new customs, new languages, and new expectations. They will also increasingly be driven by Internet-based perceptions. In short, the marketplace of the future will be more dynamic, volatile, fickle and, as a result, much more demanding.

In order to achieve meet this challenge, and to provide a strategy that is both achievable and acceptable to all stakeholder groups, decisive action will be required both on the part of individual visitor attractions and on the part of the sector collectively. Within a political environment wholeheartedly supportive of the tourism industry, and particularly visitor attractions, served by an integrated transport system, and in an environment where attractions, destinations, regions and authoritative bodies all work together for the collective good of tourism, tourism in Scotland has a very bright future indeed. Achieving this, however, requires both a solid platform upon which to build achievement, as well as a desire on the part of the entire industry to think and act strategically. The most important message of this study is that complacency is the enemy. To show complacency in a global marketplace that is inherently dynamic and liable to explosive change must surely be avoided at all costs.

References

CBI (1998), *Attracting Attention: Visitor Attractions in the New Millennium*, Confederation of British Industry, London.

Deloitte and Touche (1998), *A Survey of Continental European Visitor Attractions*, Deloitte and Touche Consulting, St Albans.

ETC, (1999), *Sightseeing in the UK 1998*, English Tourism Council, London.

Fahey, L., King, W. R. and Narayanan, V. K. (1981), Environmental scanning and forecasting in strategic planning: the state of the art, *Long Range Planning*, 14, pp.32-39.

Fyall, A. and Garrod, B. (1998), Heritage tourism: at what price? *Managing Leisure*, 3 (4): 213-228.

Garrod, B. and Fyall, A. (2000), "Managing Heritage Tourism: A Delphi Approach", *Annals of Tourism Research*, Forthcoming.

Helmer, O. (1979), The utility of long-term forecasting, in Makridakis, S and Wheelwright, S. (Editors), *Forecasting Studies in the Management Sciences*, North Holland, Amsterdam, 12, pp. 141-148.

Leask, A., Fyall, A. and Goulding, P. J. (2000), Scottish visitor attractions: revenue, capacity and sustainability, in Ingold, A. and McMahon Beattie, U. (Editors), *Yield Management Strategies for the Service Industries (2nd edition)*, Continuum Publications, London.

Leask, A. and Goulding, P. J. (1996), What price our heritage? A study of the role and contribution of revenue management in Scotland's heritage based visitor attractions, in Robinson, M, Evans, N. and Callaghan, P. (Editors), *Managing Cultural Resources for the Tourist,* Business Education Publishers Ltd, Sunderland, pp. 239-260.

Moutinho, L. and Witt, S. (1995), Forecasting the tourism environment using a consensus approach, *Journal of Travel Research*, Spring, pp.46-50.

Oppenheim, A. N. (1992). *Questionnaire Design, Interviewing and Attitude Measurement*, Pinter, London.

Scottish Enterprise (1997), *Scottish Visitor Attractions Review*, Scottish Enterprise, Glasgow.

Smith, R. (1998), Visitor Attractions in Scotland, in MacLellan, R. and Smith, R. (Editors), *Tourism in Scotland,* International Thomson Business Press, London, pp. 187-208.

STB (1996), *Visitor Attractions Survey 1995*, Scottish Tourist Board, Edinburgh.

STB (1998), *Tourism in Scotland*, Scottish Tourist Board, Edinburgh.

STB (1999a), *1998 Visitor Attraction Monitor*, Scottish Tourist Board, Edinburgh.

STB (1999b), *Scottish Visitor Attraction Barometer (August)*, Scottish Tourist Board, Edinburgh.

STB (1999c), *Visitor Attraction Business Forum*, Scottish Tourist Board, Inverness.

Swarbrooke, J. (1995), *The Development and Management of Visitor Attractions*, Butterworth Heinemann, Oxford.

Uysal, M. and Crompton, J. L. (1985), An overview of approaches used to forecast tourism demand, *Journal of Travel Research*, 23 (Spring), pp.7-15.

WTO (1998), *Tourism 2020 Vision: A New Forecast*, World Tourism Organisation, Madrid.

Travel shows and image making

Monica Hanefors and Lena L Mossberg

Göteborg University, Sweden

Abstract

From a study of package tourists it became clear what kind of information was used before, during and after the trip. For example, the not-yet tourists collected and studied leaflets and brochures, read travel logs and maps, checked travel ads and articles in newspapers and magazines and watched TV travel shows - the latter stood out as essential preparation paraphernalia for these tourists. This paper concentrates on such shows and discusses what is communicated to its viewers through their content. Some selected Swedish and British shows constitute the empirical bases for the discussion and a pre-determined schedule based on a model for visual anthropology is used for the analyses. The concept of image, image making, and travel shows are discussed in the paper. The results show that the film presentations of various destinations, strengthened and accompanied by words, and often sound, are coloured by culture: not necessarily by the culture signified by the destinations presented, more by the culture of the show producers and the prospective viewers. Many of the pictures could easily be used for a number of tourist destinations around the world – showing TV reporters and anonymous tourists taking part in various activities. It is concluded that when a destination is new and different it is worth presenting in a more detailed way with characteristics, attributes and activity, but when it is established activity takes over.

Introduction

This paper concentrates on Swedish and British TV travel shows and discusses how tourist destinations are communicated to the viewers through the content of the shows. The shows help to form images projected to the viewers, irrespective of if they are prospective tourists or just living-room sofa *'dream travellers'*. Often such images are images of something the not-yet-tourists want to be, to have, to experience, or to achieve, says Uzzel (1984, p.84). Later, Fakeye and Crompton (1991) argue that images are of *"paramount importance because they transpose representation of an area into the potential tourist's mind and give him or her a pre-taste of the destination"* (p. 10).

When a desire for travel is recognised by someone, the collection of information soon starts, including, for example, earlier tourism experience, advertising and publicity, word-of-mouth and travel literature. From a study focusing on Swedish package tourists (Hanefors and

Larsson Mossberg, 1999) it became clear what kind of information these tourists use during their decision processes and sometimes also during and after a trip. They think a lot about travel details and make notes, make visits to travel agents (not only for booking, but to socialise with the personnel and to talk about future trips), and gather information from friends, read travel logs and maps, check travel ads and articles in newspapers and magazines, and collect and study leaflets and travel brochures (see also Dann, 1996). Wicks and Schuett (1993) suggest that tourists appear familiar with and accept brochures, and use them to *"help plan travel and as references when travelling"* (p. 88). Pictures in brochures may whet tourists' appetite for vacation products (Hodgson, 1993; Goosens, 1994). In a similar manner, this can be done through pictures transmitted by rented or borrowed video films or through TV travel shows. The latter stand out as particularly important preparation paraphernalia for the investigated tourists, while for others they are merely entertainment or information, even though both groups get the same messages through pictures, accompanying spoken words and music.

Theoretical framework

Destinations trying to attract tourists may be looked at from different perspectives. Some researchers discuss destination image, others prefer tourist attraction systems, and still others departure from theories around tourist behaviour including motivation – three closely inter-linked viewpoints. For example, in 1993 Echtner and Ritchie developed a conceptual framework for destination image. According to them, a destination's image consists of two components. One captures perceptions of separate attributes, such as climate, hotels, service, et cetera. The other includes more holistic impressions (i.e. mental pictures of the destination). Each of the components contains functional and psychological characteristics. On the attribute side can the functional, or tangible, for example, be sport activities and the psychological, for example, relaxation. On the holistic side, the functional impressions consist of mental pictures of physical characteristics of the destination, while the psychological can be described as the destination's atmosphere. Finally, destination image can be based on perceptions about characteristics ranging from common ones to the more unique. Several researchers emphasise the importance of the unique part. Pearce (1988) points at symbols as significant factors for destination image, while MacCannell (1989) discusses the importance of a 'marker'. Milman and Pizam (1995) propose a similar framework and suggest three components in destination image: the product (e.g. level of cost and quality), the behaviour and attitude (e.g. towards the hosts), and the environment (e.g. landscape, weather, scenery).

The components in the conceptual frameworks of destination image are in several ways similar to the ones described in research about tourist attractions. Lew (1987) summarises previous research about tourist attractions in the tourism literature and describes a three-sided framework for categorising these attractions. Three approaches to the topic are identified: the ideographic perspective, the organisational perspective, and the cognitive perspective. The first is the most common one and refers to the general attributes of a place (e.g. any named site, climate, social customs and characteristics, and scenery). The second perspective relates to geographical notions with focus on the spatial capacity and temporal nature of attractions. A spatial attraction can be anything from a small object, such as the Manneken Piis in Brussels, to a very large area such as a country. Finally, the cognitive perspective encompasses a categorisation of attractions based on tourist perceptions and experiences.

This corresponds to some of the research within tourist travel motivation. The so-called 'seeking' motives (see Iso-Ahola, 1982, 1984; Dunn Ross and Iso-Ahola, 1991) allude to what tourists have not got at home, but what they possibly can seek in a destination. Hanefors argues elsewhere (Hanefors and Mossberg, 1999) that a number of preconditions attract tourists: a destination's particular characteristics, possible activities there, and various attributes. The characteristics may be described as a back-drop - what kind of background suits the specific tourist? Some prefer nature - mountains, desert, beach, or jungle; while others prefer urban environment – maybe a quiet small rural town, or the pulse of a big city. Activities relate to what tourists want to do while they are away from home - perhaps swimming, visiting museums, or learning about flowers. Finally, a destination's attributes mean what the tourists prefer, and want to make sure they get, for example, a certain kind of climate, a specific hotel, or level of service.

In a similar manner Hanefors argues that the 'escape' motivation (see also Dann, 1981; Mannel and Iso-Ahola, 1987) – which presents a break from ordinary, everyday life for the tourists - conceals the tourists' individual characteristics, their social and cultural backgrounds. The individual characteristics are age, gender, education, occupation, travel experience, et cetera. The tourists' social context of the ordinary may include family and work situation, a variety of reference groups and the such, while the cultural background may show, for example, whether the individual tourist is an open-minded 'cosmopolitan', or a more culturally encapsulated 'local' (Hannerz, 1993). The argued motivation model leans primarily on the suggestion that every tourist has a situational combination of several interacting 'escape' and 'seeking' motives for each tour, and in its combination they both direct and limit tourists in their travel. The combination is nurtured in the course and change of everyday life.

The discussion, so far, has concentrated on the tourists' perceptions about a particular destination and its attractions, including their motives for travelling. The seeking motives are sometimes also called pull factors due to the possibility for a destination to attract (or pull) tourists. Tourists' perceptions of a destination can be focused on from several view-points, but the different theoretical input presented above appear similar to one another. For example, attributes are discussed both in destination image research, tourist attraction research and research around travel motives. The same can be said about characteristics and activity.

For the purpose of this study – to discuss, analyse, and compare TV travel shows - we have chosen to use the categories characteristics, activity, and attributes, even though the travel shows supposedly try to present pictures of particular destinations. This change of perspective, from not-yet-tourists to destinations, may be explained through a somewhat different image model that comes into mind (Bohlin and Hanefors, 1994). It was developed in connection with a study of a Swedish regional museum, and image then was seen as a two-sided, ever-changing phenomenon created by both the museum itself and the surrounding locals/visitors. The reason for this was, of course, that when the museum gives certain pictures to its surroundings these are simultaneously interpreted by outsiders with individual backgrounds, knowledge, expectations, et cetera. Both parties adding to the image of the museum. So, we can easily borrow part of the model about tourists' travel motives –

the seeking, with the similarities to the frameworks discussed earlier – and instead use it when discussing from a destination's perspective. The figure below visualises the image model from above applied to the present study of TV travel shows.

Figure 1   Travel shows and image

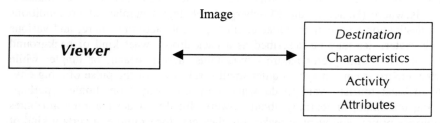

The specific questions we want to address in the study of Swedish and British travel shows are:

1. what does the relation between characteristics, activity and attributes look like at the various destinations presented in TV travel shows, and

2. what patterns are there to be found?

Methodology

Selected Swedish and British travel shows constitute the empirical bases in this study. In all, the number of shows are six Swedish shown during three hours, and nine British during six hours, together including destinations all around the world and also commercial breaks in the British. The six Swedish shows were broadcast via two public TV channels during a period of three weeks in January and February, 2000, while the British shows were shown on cable television (Travel channel) during two evenings in February.

Table 1   Swedish Travel Shows

No	Channel	Show	Destination	Day	Date	Time
1.	4 (public)	När och fjärran	a: Aarlberg, Austria b: Stockholm Archipelago, Sweden c: Australia	Tues	Jan 25	20.30-21.00
2.	2 "	Packat och klart	a: New Orleans, Memphis, US b: Nådendal, Finland c: Thailand	Sun	Jan 30	21.15-21.45
3.	4 "	När och fjärran	a: Switzerland b: Nådendal, Finland c: Australia	Tues	Feb 1	20.30-21.00
4.	2 "	Packat och klart	a: Tenerife, Gran Canaria, Spain b: Hafjell, Norway c: Mississippi, US	Sun	Feb 6	21.15-21.45
5.	4 "	När och fjärran	a: North Italy b: Sälen, Sweden c: Seychelles	Tues	Feb 8	20.30-21.00
6.	2 "	Packat och klart	a: Florida, US b: Gibraltar, UK c: Charmonix, France	Sun	Feb 13	21.15-21.45

Table 2   British Travel Shows

No	Show	Day	Date	Time
1.	Bruce's American Postcards	Wed	Feb 9	19.00-19.30
2.	Planet Holiday			19.30-20. 00
3.	On the Loose in Wildest Africa			20.00-20.30
4.	Holiday Maker			21.00-21.30
5.	The Tourist			21.30-22.00
6.	Planet Holiday	Thur	Feb 10	19.30-20.00
7.	Destinations			20.00-21.00
8.	On Top of the World			21.00-22.00
9.	Going Places			22.00-23.00

The shows were viewed a number of times, following a predetermined schedule based on a model for visual anthropology (Collier and Collier, 1987), also used during an earlier study of video films borrowed or rented by the public from a tour operator (Hanefors and Larsson, 1993). The first step of that model involved a preliminary observation of the material as a whole, listening to its overtones and attempting to discover any patterns that go together and those that contrast with each other. In step two a thorough inventory was made of the content of the show material and categories created which reflected our research questions. A number of key words were generated by the patterns found. The transition from unstructured observation to structured analysis took place when specific questions are asked in step three. These directed our attention towards the most relevant information. Finally, step four was devoted to making a summary collecting together the details into a single entity. It was a clear advantage that the observation was carried out by two persons representing two disciplines, i.e. the authors of this paper.

Findings

The Swedish travel shows

The preliminary observation of the films as a whole gave a preliminary list of aspects – structure of the shows, who can be seen in the pictures, what are they doing – and also knowledge of frequently repeated words. The structure of the shows includes three destinations in every programme, complemented by information about price regarding flights, hotels, and sometimes excursions on the destination – often maps are provided as well. One Swedish reporter always presents the particular destination, and act as a stand-in for the viewing not-yet-tourists, often in a tourist group at the destination or at least together with other tourists. The viewers consume the destinations through the reporter's various experiences. The specific words accompanying the pictures are: *luxury, royalty, untroubled life, solitude, climate, temperature,* and *other tourists.*

The content inventory created categories reflecting our research questions. We found two broad categories, namely one made up by established destinations and another by destinations new to the Swedish viewers. The old destinations are presented as born again, perhaps with a new concept and/or a surprising touch, while the new encompasses a wider description of what is offered at the destination. The key words are 'destination distance' and 'age', which formed the bases for asking specific questions concerning a distance from Sweden (expressed in terms of close-by and far-away), and by how well-known the destination is, i.e. for how long it has been offered the Swedish market.

Activity focussed presentations

Destination characteristics and attributes

The characteristics of the presented destinations in the Swedish shows naturally differ between the various destinations. Two of the films focus on trekking – Switzerland and the Spanish island of Tenerife in the Atlantic, both with breathtaking scenery. In those films there are a lot of back-drop pictures making up the presentation. In Switzerland the reporter experiences the Swiss Alps through a 'cheese-trekking tour'. His eyes catch, for example, Mont Blanc and a couple of glimmering lakes. Beside pictures showing water, green grass and flowers, there are also urban pictures from the town of Gruyere. *"It is as picturesque as a postcard"*, he says and adds, when seeing the black and white cows stroll by *"the most beautiful cows in the world"*.

Likewise, Tenerife is presented through trekking and trekking routes. Lava from volcano Teide makes up the background, and the reporter calls attention to the fact that *"it feels like I'm on planet Mars"*. It is emphasised that she is all by herself – not meeting many tourist – and a comparison is made with the mass tourism on the south coast of the island *"It's hard to imagine that I'm on the charter island Tenerife"*. When the reporter thinks of food she finds only one café open and she makes a remark about *"how lonely Tenerife can be"*.

Surprisingly, some of the destinations almost lack destination characteristics, for example Nådendahl in Finland, Sälen in Sweden and Hafjell in Norway. The pictures can hardly be linked to the specific destination. Is it possible that the closer destination gets to the viewers' own surroundings the less interest for showing scenery or character? In Finland the focus was mostly on the inside of a spa hotel, except for a few second showing the hotel garden and a close-by hotel designed as a cruise ship. Likewise, in the two films about ski destinations only ski-slopes, and the happenings there, are pictured, but not much else, not even many pictures of mountains.

The kind of attributes shown from the various destinations include, for example, words and pictures about climate/weather in Tenerife and high level of service both in Hua Hin and Nådendal. Security is accentuated in the Seychelles, while Thailand and the Seychelles are presented as luxurious paradises. Night-life and after-ski entertainment are pointed out in connection to the presentations of Swedish destination Sälen and of the Norwegian Hafjell. As could be expected, music is the attribute emphasised in New Orleans.

Destination offered activity

Several of the destination films in the Swedish shows totally focus on activity, specific ones like canoeing in the Stockholm archipelago, spa adventures in Finland, or trekking in Switzerland and Spain, and others that in a more general way include activity. We find, for example, in the show about Austria that many different snow-related activities are included – such as new types of downhill skiing and hang-gliding, and more social ones like after-ski.

If we take a closer look at one of the destinations with a sole specific activity, namely Sälen – a ski-resort – the pictures show a female reporter participating in a snowboard school. The spotlight is constantly directed towards the reporter when she tries to master the ski-lift and the various snowboard turns. All her mistakes and hardships are thoroughly described in pictures and words, as is later her participation in a drinking competition in the after-ski bar.

General presentations

Destination characteristics and attributes

The films showing, for example, the Seychelles, New Orleans/Mississippi, North Italy, Florida, and Gibraltar give a more general descriptions of the destination than the others. In the Seychelles hotels are described and shown. Temperature is essential and colour green is put forward, both visiting a national park and through close pictures of coconut trees. In spite of this, no threats – no risk for malaria and no dangerous insects. Likewise, the word paradise is used a number of times during the presentation – *"this is like Robinson Crusoe"*, and *"both the Royal family and Tony Blair have been here"*. The speaker-voice says that moonlight flows abundantly. Pictures give a view of endless, sandy beaches. Two Swedish tourist are interviewed about their impressions and tell the reporter about total relaxation.

Destination offered activities

The reporters in all the destination presentations, whether focussing on characteristics and attributes or activity, always play a leading part. The activities are not only briefly described, but are tried out or conducted by the reporters themselves, and his or her own experiences and feelings are communicated to the viewers. One destination presented through its many activities is south-western Australia. The film covers a holiday by a 4WD car driven by a reporter. Half of it pictures him when he is driving, looking in the car mirrors, and when parking the car. The viewers are also shown when the reporter receives a speeding ticket, and when he, jokingly, pretends to be participating in the Paris-Dakar rally. The other half of the film includes pictures of surfing, fishing and swimming activities. The reporter himself also arranges activity and "pulse" as opposed to the rather calm pictures of the Australian out-back. For example, when he makes an over-night stop we see him dancing by himself in a hotel room accompanied by loud music.

Another example is Hua Hin in Thailand where the female reporter first of all travels by train from Bangkok to Hua Hin, where after she goes shopping, rides a bicycle rickshaw, goes to the beach, and goes trekking to a grotto temple. Also the reporter in the Seychelles rides a bicycle, adds to that a boat trip excursion in which he participates, and a trip with a small plane for visiting another island.

The British travel shows

Originally, one of the purposes of this study was to make comparisons, for example, between the Swedish and British travel shows and their content. However, the shows are far too different to make any thorough and relevant comparison between the two European shows. First of all, the Swedish shows are public and shown among other shows, news and soap-operas. The British, on the other hand, are all shown on a cable channel called 'Travel'. In the Swedish shows there are always three different destinations presented, plus in one of them, a short part about travel related information or discussion, for example about travel insurance, flight safety, or problems related to bringing a wheelchair on an aeroplane. The British shows do not have a common structure like that.

The British travel channel presents a great number of programmes not specially focussing on travel, but are rather documentary in character. There are commercial breaks in the British and not in the Swedish (the British shows are divided into shorter parts due to this), and also a flavour for name-dropping seems to be the case in the British. Generally, their content is more diversified than the Swedish, and short film sequences, for example showing the same belly dancer or attracting waves, come back a number of times in the same destination presentation. In Crete, a rapid and short series of pictures shows: 'tennis, bar, breakfast buffet, swimming-pool, sea, and swimming-pool' and pictures from a car-trip in the Pyrenees show: 'car wheel, car, scenery with car, car, car again from different angle, scenery with car' (same car all the time).

In several Swedish shows the main focus was for the reporter to learn or to take part in a sport activity, and act both as a guide and as a stand-in for the not-yet-tourists. which could not be seen in the British. In these, the reporters only participate a few times, for example, in 'Bruce's American Postcards'. Bruce himself starts in New Orleans drinking wine meanwhile first discussing with a chef, who cooks Cajun food, and then with one preparing blinis at Bruce's table in the Russian Tea room in New York. In South Africa (shown in 'On the Loose in Wildest Africa'), the British reporter participates in a safari – but this does not stop him commenting and explaining to the viewers, despite the fact that the safari was led by three local, competent guides. In general, history, food, and the "exotic" stand out as particularly import in the British shows, which is not the case for the Swedish. However, there are also certain similarities between the two. For example, it is sometimes impossible to understand from the pictures, in either kind of show, which destination is presented. Bruce's show, referred to above, could as well be presented, and rightfully so, in a food channel. Luxury, presented by pictures from, for example, casinos, expensive restaurants and hotels, and both *"royalty"* and *"you may live like a sultan"* reinforce them.

Conclusions

Image making and destination attractiveness through travel shows are discussed in this paper focussing primarily on Swedish travel shows, due to the difficulties to make a comparison between these and British shows. To compare the two would have been a comparison between apples and pears. Therefore, the analysis concentrates on the Swedish shows and the British are left here.

The content of the Swedish travel shows does not always reflect the destinations to any large extent, which seems to be the natural and expected situation, it rather tempts the viewer to travel in a general way. Many of the films are so general in character that they easily could be used for a number of tourist destinations around the world – showing reporters and anonymous tourists taking part in various activities. The activity focus is strengthened by the fact that the reporters are always around and often focussed on, for example, when they try to learn something new like cooking, snow-boarding, canoeing or trekking. This adds to the argument that modern tourism rather is a narcissistic look at one's own culture than at others.

The pictures, strengthened and accompanied by words and sound, are coloured by culture, but not necessarily by the culture signified by the presented destination, rather by the culture of the show producers and of the prospective viewers. When anyone from the destination's population actually appears, he or she is involved in the tourism industry and, if not, seems to acts as a sort of silent marker, as if to lend authenticity. A similar example is that an Austrian ski-instructor is interviewed about the destination and about skiing in Norwegian ski-resort –instead of a local.

The Swedish travel shows can be divided into two categories – one with close-by, established and well-known, but reborn, destinations and another made up by new and/or far-away destinations. What the first group of destinations have in common is the focus on one particular activity per destination, while in the other group there is a mixture of various activities found together with the destinations' respective characteristics and attributes.

Table 3   Categorisation of TV travel shows

Activity focussed presentations	Sälen, Sweden	Established, well-known, close-by, reborn destinations
	Nådendal*, Finland	
	Stockholm Archipelago	
	Hafjell, Norway	
	Charmonix, France	
	Tenerife, Spain	
	Switzerland	
	Austria	
General presentations	Hua Hin, Thailand	New and/or far-away destinations
	New Orleans, US	
	The Seychelles	
	Love path, North Italy	
	Florida, US	
	Australia*	
	Gibraltar, UK	
	Mississippi, US	

* appears twice

What is usually called the ingredients of the tourism experience: activity, accommodation, food, and transportation all are mixed throughout the films. The portions respectively are of different size in the two categories, for example, in Sälen ski-activities are emphasised and the other ingredients play a minor role. Another example is North Italy, where a smorgasbord of tempting accommodation, local transports, romantic restaurants, and various activities are shown.

Opposites are found among the Swedish presentations. Luxury is often shown in the films (e.g. a five-star hotel) and as often we see and hear about discomfort (e.g. camping and annoying insects). Likewise, mass tourism is seen alongside with pictures characterised by solitude. The latter seems to be connected with the rebirth of established destinations. Island Tenerife, for example, has been sold to the Swedish market for several decades as a sun and warmth destination, but is now presenting itself as a trekking destination as well.

The main conclusion from the study is that when a destination is new and different it is worth presenting in a more detailed way with characteristics, attributes and activity, but when it is established activity takes over.

References

Bohlin, M. and Hanefors, M. (1994), *En kulturekonomisk studie av Bohusläns Museum: Image, publik och samhällsekonomi,* ITR-rapport no 1, Högskolan i Falun/Borlänge, Sweden.

Collier, Jr, J. and Collier, M. (1987), *Visual Anthropology: Photography as Research Method,* University of New Mexico Press, Albuquerque.

Dann, G. M. S. (1981), Tourist Motivation: An Appraisal, *Annals of Tourism Research,* 8 (2): 187-219.

Dann, G. M. S. (1996), The People of Tourist Brochures, in T. Selwyn, (Editor), *The Tourist Image: Myths and Myth Making in Tourism,* John Wiley and Sons, Chichester: 61-81.

Dunn Ross, E. L. and Iso-Ahola, S. E. (1991), Sightseeing Tourists: Motivation and Satisfaction, *Annals of Tourism Research,* 18 (2): 226-238.

Echtner, C. and Ritchie, B. (1993), The Measurement of Destination Image: An Empirical Assessment, *Journal of Travel Research,* 31 (4): 3-13.

Fakeye, P. C. and Crompton, J. L. (1991), Image Differences between Prospective, First-Time, and Repeat Visitors to the Lower Rio Grande Valley, *Journal of Travel Research,* 30, (Fall): 10-16.

Goosens, C. (1994), External Information Search: Effects of Tour Brochures with Experimental Information, *Journal of Travel and Tourism Marketing,* 3 (3): 89-107.

Hanefors, M. and Larsson, L. (1993), Video Strategies used by Tour Operators: What is Really Communicated?, *Tourism Management,* 14 (1): 27-33.

Hanefors, M. and Mossberg, L. (1999), Package Tourism and Customer Loyalties, in Pizam, A. and Mansfeld, Y. (Editors), *Consumer Behaviour in Travel and Tourism,* Haworth Press, New York.

Hannerz, U. (1993), Cosmopolitans and Locals in World Culture, in M Featherstone (Editor) *Global Culture. Nationalism, Globalisation and Modernity,* SAGE, London, pp.237-251.

Hodgson, P. (1993), Tour Operator Brochure Design Research Revisited, *Journal of Travel Research,* 32 (1): 50-52.

Iso-Ahola, S. E. (1982), Toward a Social Psychological Theory of Tourism Motivation: A Rejoinder, *Annals of Tourism Research,* 9 (2): 256-262.

Lew, A. (1987), A Framework of Tourist Attraction Research, *Annals of Tourism Research,* 14 (4): 533-575.

MacCannell, D. (1989), The Tourist: A New Theory of the Leisure Class, (2nd ed.), Schocken Books, New York.

Mannel, R. C. and Iso-Ahola, S. E. (1987), Psychological Nature of Leisure and Tourism Experience, *Annals of Tourism Research,* 14 (3): 314-331.

Milman, A. and Pizam, A. (1995), The Role of Awareness and Familiarity with a Destination: The Central Florida Case, *Journal of Travel Research,* 33 (3): 21-27.

Pearce, P. L. (1988), *The Ulysses Factor,* Springer-Verlag, New York.

Uzzel, D. (1984), An Alternative Structuralist Approach to the Psychology of Tourism Marketing, *Annals of Tourism Research,* 11 (1): 79-99.

Wicks, B. and Schuett, M. (1993), Using Travel Brochures to Target Frequent Travellers and "Big-Spenders", *Journal of Travel and Tourism Marketing,* 2 (2/3): 77-90.

Enclave orientalism: The state, tourism, and the politics of post-national development in the Arab world

Waleed Hazbun

Massachusetts Institute of Technology, USA

While European pilgrims and explorers have long travelled to the Arab World in search of the region's past, over the past decade Arab governments have been feverishly promoting tourism as a means to build their own economic futures. The argument posed by tourism's boosters is that the Arab World's tourism resources should be exploited to generate new sources of national wealth providing jobs and economic opportunities to replace those lost after the decline in oil prices in the late 1980s. In Jordan the draw has been especially enhanced by the desire to reap economic rewards from the 1994 peace treaty with Israel. This paper explores why after an influx of foreign visitors in 1994 and 1995, the commission of a tourism plan, and considerable investments in the sector tourism has failed to become an engine of national development and is unlikely to in the future.

This paper argues that the expectation that tourism in the wake of the 1994 peace would be able to rapidly generate broad economic benefits for the national economy led to a widespread misunderstanding and, more critically, a misrepresentation of the dynamics that govern tourism economies. While tourism may offer opportunities for economic development, these gains do not, as Patrick Clawson and others have suggested "come automatically as a more peaceful environment encourages more visitors and stimulates private sector investment." (1994, p. 7). Instead, economic growth through tourism development is difficult to sustain in the context of today's global tourism economy without adequate public and private institutions for its promotion. In Jordan, the creation of such institutions was impeded by state efforts at centralising administrative control over the governance of the tourism sector while lacking the capacities to develop the sector. The state projected a model of the future of tourism development which led most of the private sector to imagine that the gains from tourism would be easily obtainable for even those with limited skills and capital. This occurred, I will suggest, because tourism stands out as an economic sector where there is an ever greater divergence between the nation-state's powerful capacity to represent with maps, pictures, and figures its ability to plan, promote, and regulate the industry while, in fact, having an ever decreasing ability to govern the economic transactions contained within its territorial boundaries.

As a result, most of the local private sector in Jordan has been guided by the tangible objective of transforming available assets (such as property rights over land, traditional dwellings, and cultural artefacts) to conform to the consumptive gaze of international tourists rather than building institutional mechanisms for monitoring and promoting the demand for such products within the global tourism economy. Instead of promoting wide-scale social transformation and economic growth this pattern of tourism development has generated "enclave economies" in a narrow set of highly managed spaces segmented from the national economy where demand and supply can better be regulated, usually with the help of global tourism and hotel corporations. This pattern of economic transformation is leading to a form of "post-national" development where the state and a narrow elite have the ability to reap gains from the global tourism economy while other social sectors become effectively marginalised. If tourism in Jordan is ever to provide a catalyst for national economic development, I conclude, there will have to be a fundamental rethinking of the process of tourism development.

Tourism and the national economy

The core problem with tourism development in Jordan has been not that tourism has been viewed as a potential source of income, but that many in government and the private sector have thought that tourism will or should become the driving engine for the growth and development of the national economy. As recently as the summer of 1999, according to the *Jordan Times*, the Jordanian Prime Minister Adur-Ra'uf Rawabdeh declared that "tourism will constitute the main revenue for the national economy in coming years and that the government is determined to develop and modernise the tourism industry" (July 31, 1991). Such statements are too often made without questioning the foundations on which they depend. Can tourism provide enough jobs and income to sustain the national economy? Does the state have the capacity to develop the sector such that these benefits will be distributed widely across the nation?

The tourism economy in Jordan, I want to suggest, has been represented as a knowable totality similar to the manner in which critic Edward Said (1979) argues that Western scholars of Orientalism have long viewed the cultures of the Middle East. He argues, in short, that the representations of the Middle East these scholars generated were held together by a simplified and ideologically motivated internal logic detached from the complex social reality of the societies under study. Likewise, the plans for tourism development generated by the state and their consultants were representations of the Jordanian tourism economy which, as we will see, carried a misleading and unwarranted certainty about them.

The ability to present tourism as possibly driving national development is anchored in the ability of the state to represent the national economy as both the totality of economic transactions within a territorially bound space and as a self-contained unit subject to state regulation and management. In Jordan the formation of the national economy as a network of economic transactions governed over by the state was shaped by the nexus position of the state in the expansion of transnational flows which developed during the oil boom of the 1970s. Throughout the 1970s and 1980s Jordan's economy was sustained mostly by aid given by Arab states and the remittances sent back by workers in the oil rich Gulf. Jordan's national economy as an object of state policy was formed by the role the state played in disbursing economic resources to support the legitimacy of the regime through networks of patronage (see Brand, 1992, pp. 168-170).

Over theses decades the state accumulated tremendous economic burdens by providing jobs, consumer subsidies supports, and private sector contracts. With the decline of oil prices in the late 1980s the state faced pressures to play a role in promoting economic development. During the Gulf War Jordan was cut off from Iraqi and Gulf sources of aid, remittances, and commerce. This led to added pressures to provide replacements for the incomes, jobs, private sector growth, and state revenues that the oil boom had directly and indirectly provided. While King Hussein's choice to rapidly conclude a peace treaty with Israel was most likely driven by thoughts about the future strategic interests of Jordan, economic incentives must have also factored prominently in the equation (Lynch, 1999, pp. 166-197; Mufti, 1997; Ryan, 1998).

A peace of tourism?

In 1994 as Jordan and Israel were about to sign a document ending their state of war, the U.S. Secretary of State Warren Christopher declared that "This is a situation where the economics of it may be driving the politics of it" (Sciolino, 1994). Playing a central role in the economics of peace is tourism. Patrick Clawson notes the widely held view in the international community that "tourism...holds the prospect of demonstrating the material rewards of Arab-Israeli peace" (1994, p. 7). The connection between peace and tourism, though, remains poorly understood. It is more often used as a mantra rather than a research agenda. The case of Jordan gives us a good opportunity to interrogate this relationship.

The argument for the economic gains of the peace in the tourism sector came directly from the head of state. On November 23, 1993 in a speech to the parliament concerning the peace process and broadcast on Jordanian TV, King Hussein stated, after noting his pride in the national treasures of the archaeological sites and historical buildings of the nation, that the government would support the development of tourism facilities and "This should increase economic returns in a manner that would support the balance of payments, replenish the treasury's hard currency reserves, augment the economic growth rate and expand the gross national product." He made particular reference to the private sector which "would have a major role to play in tourist development" and would be encouraged "though incentive expanding investment, streamlined procedures and tourist development legislation."

In the following years the state came through with a series of tax incentives for foreign and local investors in the sector. The Jordanian government pledged a massive tourism infrastructure plan and aid agencies such as the United States Agency for International Development (USAID) had in the works multi-million dollar tourism development plans. This was all soon to be topped off by plans prepared by the Ministry of Planning to be presented under the eyes of the world media at the Middle East and North Africa (MENA) summits as well as through numerous press conferences relating to the peace process.

In addition to the announcement of the opening of border crossings with Israel and plans for a new Aqaba "Peace" airport, numerous fantastic Jordanian-Israeli projects were officially announced at this time such as a $500 million Holy Land Disney World-like amusement park, a Las Vegas-style Sun City, and a Peace City that would eventually cost one billion dollars and include an artificial lake surrounded by 10,000 hotel rooms. Driven by Israeli investment, it would seem that the Israeli-Jordanian borders across the Wadi Araba and the Jordan Valley were soon to be dotted with deluxe hotels, amusement parks, casinos, and a multifunctional John the Baptist baptism pool and conference centre. They were all to be connected by super highways across the desert and concrete promenades along the shores.[1]

These new opportunities stirred the Jordanian private sector at all levels. They seemed to present opportunities for almost anyone regardless of skill, profession, or even capital endowment while avoiding the question of the limits or distribution of these gains. Everyone interested, it seemed, could imagine a way to profit from the new influx of tourists. The wealthy merchant and banking families could exploit these new opportunities just as in their own way could the Bedouin tribes near ancient ruins, the former workers in the Gulf driving cabs in the wealthy sections of Western Amman, and the souvenir hawkers in the poorer areas of downtown. It was thought that the benefits of tourism could potentially be spread widely both regionally and down the class ladder across the whole imagined national economic community of Jordan. Finding a broad new conduit for disbursing economic incentives the promotion of tourism can be viewed as a mechanism used to sustain the legitimacy of the state.

The flood

Soon after the peace was in place and the border crossings with Israel were opened there was a massive flood of Israeli as well as North American and European tourists. Driven by curiosity and the almost mythic aura that Petra had built up in their minds, Israeli tourism expanded from officially zero before 1994 to over 100,000 in 1995.[2] European and American tourist arrivals grew by 75% from 204,000 over the whole of 1993 to 359,000 over the course of 1995. Most notably, package tourism shot up from 440,000 to 1,141,000 over the same period.

This explosion led to previously unheard of levels of overbooking at hotels while all aspects of the industry, such as bus lines and rental car agencies faced acute shortages. As one index of this, the occupancy rate of hotels classified as 5 star deluxe went from an average of 42% in 1993 to 66% over the course of 1995. This meant that well established hotels like the Inter-Continental in Amman were often experiencing occupancy rates of over 90%.

This in turn led to a frenzy of tourism sector developments not limited to a narrow elite of experienced tourism developers but reaching far and wide. From 1993 to 1996 the number of hotel beds in Jordan expanded 68% from 13,500 to 22,700. Over the same period the number of rental car offices expanded from only 75 in 1993 to 237 in 1996, while the number of rental cars tripled as nearly did the number of tourist guides in the country.

This, though, was not to last. As has now become clear, there was great misjudgment in the general public about the prospects of peace on the tourism economy. Even without the turn to the right in Israel and the continued siege of Iraq, the tourism explosion was unlikely to keep at this radical pace for very long. In 1995 and 1996 tourism receipts grew by over 14%

(in nominal terms), while in 1997 they grew only 4%. Hotel occupancy rates for all hotels went from 46% in 1995 back down to 38% in 1997. In Petra, combining a drop in tourism with an expansion of capacity the highs and lows are more extreme going from almost 62% in 1994 then dropping to 31% in 1997. As one Jordanian economist put it "Hotels, tourist buses and travel agencies are real and sad examples of how parts of the economy went on an investment binge in 1995, only to come down to earth with a thud a year later and then start to wallow in a depression which continues" (Khouri, 1998).

The role of the state in tourism development

The expectation that this tourism explosion could have propelled national economic development in Jordan demonstrates a fundamental misreading and, more critically, a misrepresentation of the dynamics of tourism development. To rethink the possibilities for tourism promotion we need to first understand the dynamics of tourism development and the role the state can play in it.

At a minimum, international tourism requires the co-ordination of tasks deemed prerogatives of national sovereignty such as control over border crossings and the use of national airspace. States have also generally taken responsibility to protect and develop tourist sites such as historic buildings, national parks, and museums. These generate revenues for the state but they also indirectly create other economic opportunities, what economists call positive external economies, for nearby businesses.

More generally tourism development is recognised to rely heavily on a wide number of state provided public goods such as infrastructure, security, and overseas marketing. These generate external economies for firms and foster tourism flows and tourism development by reducing transportation costs and lowering "the cost of specifying, negotiating, and enforcing" (North, 1981, p. 24) various market transactions related to tourism. In other words, these help tourists and tourism firms know what products are available (and which ones are not but should) and make access to them easier and more predictable. The reduction of the costs of transportation, transactions, and information is especially critical for tourism in developing economies as the markets in this sector are often highly fragmented, periodic, and incomplete. These external economies are also subject to the "multiplier effect" where a portion of each additional amount of tourism expenditure leads to a series of other expenditure transactions in the economy.

Such public goods, though, are often costly large-scale projects which resource poor developing states with other needs will not undertake unless there is enough tourism demand to warrant them. Thus states in developing economies seeking to promote tourism often face a dilemma which can be viewed as the struggle to escape from a low tourism equilibrium trap. By this we mean that the tourism economy is at a static point with both a low level of tourism demand and a low (in quantity and quality) level of tourism supply. This is because there are too few tourists to sustain significant external economies to justify the costs of the development of additional tourism services and products by the state or the private sector which would be required to foster and sustain larger tourism flows.

This picture roughly describes the Jordanian tourism economy for most periods between 1967 and the Gulf War. It received only a limited number of tourists interested enough and wealthy enough to go out of their way to a destination with limited tourist attractions or facilities while there was too little tourist expenditure to warrant on the part of the state costly large-scale investments to develop public goods and services and make tourist sites more accessible and attractive.

How can any such economy develop its tourism sector to escape from this low level trap? This problem looks very similar to the issues faced by post-war development economics considering the challenge of traditional economies trying to escape from low productivity, low income equilibrium traps.[3] In this framework the main obstacle preventing the building of modern factories in the setting of a traditional economy is the lack of sufficient demand for the modern products the factories produce as most of the potential consumers in the economy are still working in the low productivity, low wage traditional sector.

As a response advocates of what was called the balanced growth development strategy formulated the idea of the "big-push" (Nurkse, 1953; Rosenstein-Rodan, 1943). This strategy calls for rapid, large-scale investments simultaneously in a number of complementary modern industrial sectors. In this way all at once each factory would initially be ensured an adequate supply of inputs as well as a steady demand for its products from other modern factories and the workers employed in them. This strategy requires extensive state financing and co-ordination of national industrial firms as well as managing flows of capital, labour, and intermediate goods replacing the role of market signals.

This model might well describe a path for a national tourism economy to escape from the low equilibrium trap, but there is one connection missing when we transpose the model onto the tourism economy. Since tourism facilities do not generate demand for other tourism sites (as tourism workers are generally not also tourists), to get out of the low equilibrium trap requires an exogenous element: an expectation of an initial large influx of tourists. With the coming of the peace Jordan, finally, seemed to be approaching such a opportune period.

Envisioning national tourism development

With the onset of the peace process Jordan entered into a phase of extensive tourism development planning. Even as the dreams of joint Israeli-Jordanian megaprojects failed to initialise and then quickly evaporated with a swing to right in Israel and with the domestic opposition to the "normalisation" of ties to Israel, the idea that Jordan needed to promote a state-led "big push" in tourism development remained. Jordan, though, was a country ill prepared for comprehensive centralised tourism development planning (see Jreisat, 1989; Kelly, 1998), but most fundamentally, the problem with tourism development in Jordan is the view on the part of the state, the private sector, and many tourism consultants that tourism must be launched via a balanced growth strategy.

The balanced growth model accorded with state interests in expanding regulatory powers, gaining revenues, and promoting national development. Key to the adoption of this point of view was the need to generate enough external economies that could distribute income and job opportunities broadly for the national economy. Likewise, this model was also reflective of the private sector's interest in short term, risk averse investment opportunities.

The ability of the model of balanced growth to seemingly fulfil these interests hinged, I suggest, on the ability of this model of tourism development to literally be envisioned. Even as the expansion of multinational corporations and the "more fluid circulation and value of money" (Mitchell, 1998, p. 422) have made national economies more elusive to define, measure, and represent as objects of state policy, tourism, I suggest, stands out as an economic sector where national objects - be they tourist sites, maps, air carriers, or development plans - remain prominent identifiable features over which states retain considerable power to manipulate. Balanced growth planning models could seemingly measure and represent the tourism economy as well as unambiguously depict how it should be developed or redrawn. At the same time, the private sector and state planners could easily envision how to produce tourism commodities to fulfil the model since this was also guided by essentially a visual paradigm.

As James C. Scott (1998) shows, the manipulation of representations should be viewed as equivalent to other forms of state capacities because states must rely on representations of society, the economy, territory, and even nature in order to fashion and implement its policies. Furthermore, the structure of both firms and the national economy need to be representable for them to be centrally altered and redrawn. Organisation charts, balance sheets, and gross national product flows all help nation-states monitor and govern the firms and the national economy (Buck-Morss, 1995).

The balanced growth model suggested that the whole tourism sector should be drawn out in a comprehensive manner and then the private sector and the tourism landscape should be made to conform to this picture. As state agencies controlled much of the geographic and cultural resources of tourism as well as the channels of tourist flows, they seemed well positioned to guide the promotion and regulation of the tourism sector. The landscape of tourism - its representability and readability - suggested to policy makers that centralised states had the capacity to promote national tourism development.

The plans published in the 1996 Japan International Co-operation Agency (JICA) study which formulated the most extensive national tourism development plan for Jordan clearly represent the balanced growth model. From December 1994 to January 1996 a team of Japanese experts came to Jordan to draw up a National Tourism Development Plan in co-operation with the Jordan Ministry of Tourism and Antiquities. The result was a massive four volume study setting out parameters for the promotion of tourism in Jordan as well as detailing a number of specific infrastructure and tourism sites projects. The study is framed by an assessment of projected total national tourism demand and existing tourism supply. It begins by clearly recognising "the importance of tourism as the prime mover of the Jordanian economy (tourism is the oil of Jordan)" (JICA, 1996, Abstract page). The plan then maps out future stages of development of the tourism economy throughout the national territory for the next ten to twenty years based on projections of steady tourism growth. It creates, for example, tables of bed requirements for each region of the country to match up with the tourism projections and development plans. It then gives time tables for the various tasks which have to be accomplished by public agencies to see that these supply targets are met.

The "big push" model is even more evident in the Jordan Valley Authority's (JVA) *Dead Sea Master Plan* (revised 1996) which envisioned building about 10,000 bed units by the year 2000 and then another 20,000 or so over the following decade with the plan committing the state to building all the needed infrastructure works in the area. This is how the plan explains its model for tourism development based on future projected tourism flows (JVA, 1996, p. 22):

> *This set of potentialities places the development planning approach in the position of [a] 'supply strategy'; in other words, the essential parameters [for planning tourism development growth] stem rather from the Study Area bearing capacity within, naturally, 'a sustainable development concept', than from any potential market appraisal!*

In the plan this statement is found printed in boldface with the exclamation point (!). This study prepared by a French consultant presents extensive market research analysing numerous market segments, but nevertheless it suggests that the goal of JVA tourism development policy should be to promote a rush of investment in the Dead Sea region so as to absorb as great a share of the expected inflow of tourists to Jordan as possible. This discounts completely the role of market forces from the perspective of the firms which will invest in the zone. In other words, this plan effectively attempts to function as a replacement or at least an informed representation of market information for the direction of the private sector. What does this mean for the private sector?

Between the market and the tourist gaze

In the context of the big push for industrialisation each modern factory is encouraged to organise its production assuming that there will be an adequate market for its products. What firms worry about is not the total volume of short term market demand but following the logic of the division of labour so they can produce as efficiently as possible capturing the maximum economies of scale given their allotment of capital.

Tourism development in Jordan, conforming to "the tourist gaze" (Urry, 1992), is governed as a similar sort of the basic principle for the creation of tourism commodities. Tourism development in the wake of the peace process became a competition to reshape the domestic landscape to conform to the consumptive gaze of the international tourist. This allowed would-be entrepreneurs to envision that they were seemingly conforming to the proscriptions of the balanced growth model. The result was the unsustainable over-commodification of the tourism landscape where creating tourist products (such as hotel rooms, handicrafts, cultural experiences) proved easier and more accessible than attempting to coordinate and ensure the demand for such products. As the landscape of hotel, handicraft, and tourism development in Amman and the World Heritage site of Petra show, the outcome was the over-production of substandard tourism products and a tremendous waste of private resources (see Hazbun 1998).

This was made possible by the promotion of a balanced growth type strategy of national tourism development - beginning with the negotiation of the peace deal and represented in tourism development plans - where firms were encouraged to imagine potentially unlimited markets for tourism products and to invest considerably to meet those markets. In granting licenses for hotel developments and announcing infrastructure projects, they were presenting the private sector with a certain type of "market" information. At the same time, the state was producing tourism figures and projections which touted tourism as the new "oil" for the national economy. State agencies and state plans seemed to lacked any accurate vision of what the tourism economy looked like from the vantage point of the individual private firm in the tourism sector. Not only did this invisibility manifest itself in plans and policies but also in the politics which governed attempts to reshape the governance of the tourism sector. This point is most evident in the story of the effort by USAID to set up the Jordan Tourism Board (JTB).

The USAID plan for the JTB envisioned a privately run organisation to market the destination of Jordan in foreign markets. A main task of the board was to be the development of market intelligence capabilities in order to monitor trends and developments in the international tourism market (USAID, 1993). It was suppose to serve as a link between international markets and local tourism firms by assisting in theme promotion, brochure development, and market interruption strategies. The JTB was officially created in 1990 under USAID pressure. Then the USAID, the Ministry of Tourism and Antiquities (MOTA), and various private sector representatives spent years sorting out the funding and governance mechanism. The USAID's conception was that the JTB would have joint private and public funding but should be staffed by experienced private sector professionals and privately managed with a MOTA representative simply on its board. In the end, the Jordanian authorities, fearing that it would become a slush fund for private firms, refused to give it this sort of decentralised autonomy. After a series of unsuccessful meetings USAID abruptly pulled out of this as well as all their other ongoing tourism development efforts. Without the funding, strong private sector leadership, and skilled staff originally envisioned, the JTB has since been unable to provide the sorts of public goods which Jordanian firms critically need.

We should note here that tourism did not die out in Jordan, and in recent years government figures have shown healthy growth in the number of tourist arrivals. But these numbers do not reflect the changing value of the tourism product and the economic costs of tourism development efforts. The over-development of similar products and the high fluctuations in tourism inflows has led in many sectors to destructive competition, downward price spirals and wasted resources, not to mention dashed hopes. For many in the hotel sector the over-capacity of supply and the desperate quest for revenues has made paying back their loans impossible while eroding efforts to improve the quality of tourism products and services.

Unbalanced growth and enclave orientalism

If we return to the question of the low equilibrium trap as it was defined by development economics in the 1950s, we can find an alternate solution to the balanced growth strategy of the "big push" in the work of economist Albert O. Hirschman (1958). He argued that it would be particularly difficult for developing countries to mobilise the volume and type of capital that the big push required. Instead, Hirschman proposed a strategy he called "unbalanced growth" where the state would deliberately target specific sectors for investment which would then create imbalances between the supply and demand in related sectors. This would then drive investment chains by creating imbalances which encourage investment in other targeted sectors, which then encourage investment in yet others sectors. He termed such chains of investment backwards and forward linkages.

Another way to view this model is that such linkages represent means to capture external economies. Most successful tourism firms in Jordan were indeed driven in their investment by locating various imbalances or market externalities. One notable example is Zara Tourism Investments. Zara was spurned into the market by the hype of 1994 and has since become the leading luxury resort and hotel developer in Jordan. The Zara company, with its deep pockets, has been even able to create externalities and then exploit them through backwards and forwards linkages by establishing their own hotel supply company, engineering consulting firm, a Dead Seas product company, and a travel agency. These firms can provide high quality services to Zara's own hotels, but also in the skills and economies of scale they gain from doing Zara projects they can then outperform competing firms and provide goods and service to other hotel developers as well. Such strategies, of course, can only be pursued by developers with tremendous financial resources unavailable to most other developers in Jordan.

With limited public institutions and private associations for tourism promotion most firms in Jordan have lacked the information and ability to capture external economies via these linkages because tourism flows occur in particular patterns and through networks which are often shaped by changing patterns and tastes of tourism consumption as well as the existing organisation of the tourist sector. I have suggested that this mismatch of public policy to market context was in large measure shaped by the understanding that Jordan was in the process of gaining a big push out of a low equilibrium trap with an expectation of a large influx of tourists which would generate substantial external economies throughout the national tourism economy. This, indeed, is what occurred for many developing countries in the 1960s and 1970s with the initial global expansion of mass tourism products (such as high volume, mid-market sun and sea beach tourism) where tourism development was easily standardised. Standardisation allowed tourism to rapidly expand to new destinations while the state provision of public goods and services could maximise its capture of economies of scale. It made the capture of externalities easier as the type of products demanded where easier to predict and simpler to provide. In many cases the state defined the networks of linkages or often directed developers to them. This, though, was the not the market Jordan faced in the 1990s.

After the oil shocks of the 1970s the global tourism market became more sensitive to everything from floating currency exchange rates and perceptions of political instability to seasonal cultural trends and fashions. By the 1980s the market for mass standardised tourism was highly saturated. Global tourism markets were rapidly expanding but they were also becoming more diversified and segmented. These trends shaped the Middle East market along with the volatility caused by political turmoil (and the public perception of it) in the region. The rise of ecotourism and adventure travel, the expansion of cultural and heritage tourism markets, and the development of integrated multidimensional tourism resorts (such as Disney World theme parks) all called for more sophisticated product development and marketing as each global destination effectively began competing in terms of quality and price with every other. While the larger global tour operators and multisector entertainment corporations have dominated these markets, the use of new forms of information technology, such as computer reservation systems and marketing via the web, can help even smaller firms pick out their market niches from a wide range of markets (Poon, 1993). It was the goal, at least on paper, of the original USAID vision of the JTB to help Jordanian firms develop such capacities.

The problem in seeking to promote tourism development in Jordan is that with high transaction costs and limited public goods, linkages in the tourism economy have become structurally confined to inside enclave space and few positive externalities were extended outside. Meanwhile, these enclaves generated significant negative externalities for the outside firms, local communities, and the natural environment. As a consequence, instead of promoting wide-scale social transformation and economic growth, this sort of "development" has led to the containment of the locations of investment and sources of state revenue and foreign exchange in highly localised and manageable spaces. At the same time this process has displaced local populations, limited their circulation, and radically altered their physical environments in unfamiliar ways while providing limited alternatives means of income generation.

A pronounced feature of this trend has been the development of integrated tourism enclaves where a large number of hotels and other tourism facilities (such as restaurants, bars, shopping arcades, golf courses, car rental agencies, and gift shops) are built in a confined territory. Built or planned to be built on plots of land dotting the Dead Sea and Gulf of Aqaba as well at or near tourist sites such as Petra, these enclaves create extra-territorial zones of tourism consumption which are made to be spatially, culturally, and economically isolated (or de-linked) from their national surroundings (on Luxor, Egypt, see Mitchell, 1995). This spatial geography allows them to contain and capture the external economies generated by tourism. These self-contained complexes not only create tourism spaces cut out of the local geography they often segment space into the areas where the local residents may and may not circulate freely (not at all or at a high cost).

Zones of highly managed tourist space are being created not only in these discrete, isolated tourist complexes, but with attempts to promote various forms of cultural, heritage, and nature tourism similar processes of tourism development are spreading throughout the domestic landscape. In these cases, there is no attempt at the social and economic transformations promoted by classic development projects, but instead spaces, landscapes, and monuments are the objects of transformation. Where local populations are affected it is usually in the form of marginal, low wage seasonal jobs or as performers of cultural displays and markers of authenticity. The transformation of urban spaces for international tourist consumption–such as the JICA plans for downtown Amman–often require the forced or compelled removal of existing small scale businesses which lack the capital to exist in areas of increasing rents and land values. Generally it is only the large experienced corporations and moneyed families who have the means to acquire the property rights and to create establishments to reach the quality, standards, and volume required for the upscale tourist market. This leaves the small-scale entrepreneurs only the budget market which is itself increasingly marginalised and unwanted by tourism planners and developers.

This brings into question the future possible paths of tourism development in the Arab World. As tourism further seeks to segregate itself into enclaves, and as tourist monuments, such as the Egyptians tombs, continue to deteriorate (from the humidity the tourists bring inside) some are arguing that we need to create adjacent to them theme parks of replicas. The ultimate conclusion of this might someday look like the Luxor gambling casino in Las Vegas, Nevada which is a grand hotel in the shape of a pyramid, with an obelisk and sphinx out front. Inside it contains tacky recreations of ancient Egyptian artefacts and brings to life much of Hollywood's images of the country in a "sanitised version of Egypt" such that a tourist from Kansas interviewed on TV can conclude that she does not need to travel to Egypt anymore now that she has seen the Luxor, USA (Gottschalk, 1995, pp. 216-7). As an intermediary step, Fox Television in the USA broadcast "live" the opening of a tomb near Giza in a program that intercut facts from Egyptian archaeology with new age myths about aliens and the Pyramids. The concerns over the environmental and social impacts of tourism have even those debating the future of Israeli/Palestinian tourism speaking positively of the possible "Disneyfication" of tourism there (See discussion in Twite and Baskin, 1994).

The onset of post-national development

While not an exhaustive analysis of the methods of unbalanced growth in Jordan, what these examples hope to bring out is how tourism planning as practiced in Jordan has led to limiting the scope of the economic benefits gained from tourism and shutting out those who lack the capital and skills to conduct such strategies. This result is the reverse image of what the peace process was supposed to produce. It points not to an engine of national economic growth with widely disbursed economic benefits but to a means for the promotion of tourism enclaves managed by a narrow, capital rich tourism elite. The irony is that this "tourism bourgeoisie" is often thought to be simply a parasitic rentier class while in fact they often benefit precisely because they have the skills and capital to generate and capture external economies which the small and medium size investors lack.

One of the culprits of this development pattern is that tourism development in the Arab world was viewed as not requiring integrated national markets (on national markets and industrialisation, see Chaudhry, 1993; and Sabel, 1986) but nevertheless it was thought it would be able to broadly benefit the national economy. Tourism promotion did not seem to require the burdensome bureaucratic techniques used in the public sector industries which were once the heart of their national economies and development strategies. The possibility of such a "post-national" strategy of economic development in tourism opened the way for a new sort of state governed development strategy that was no longer burdened by the need to forge and maintain national markets and support Keynesian economic growth with high local demand and protected markets. Instead, tourism development may be able to shift the burdens of development to within a narrow enclave segment of society that has the tools and skills and capital and technology to benefit from the new global economy. This pattern of economic transformation may then lead to the development of regime and elite allies connected by their ability to reap gains from the global tourism economy while other social sectors become marginalised from it. The state gains access to foreign exchange, locational rents, and new private sector allies, easing the transition from the broad based distributive coalitions supported by the rentier state towards more narrow, elite ones.

Notes:

Research for this project was supported by a grant from the American Centre for Oriental Research (ACOR) in Amman, Jordan. My survey of the landscape of tourism in Jordan was conducted with my photographer partner Michelle Woodward whose intrepid, inquisitive vision gave me a new lens through which to view the geography of Jordan as well as the rest of the world.

1. The following documents are revised versions of the official government schemes presented at the 1994 MENA summit in Casablanca: Government of Israel (1995) and Ministry of Planning (1995). For a sampling of international news reports, see: "Peace City to Be Built," *Jerusalem Post* October 19, 1994; "Profits beckon in the Holy Land," *The Independent* July 17, 1994; and "The Peace Dividend for Israel and Jordan," *Business Week* August 8, 1994.

2. All tourism statistics were gathered from the Ministry of Tourism and Antiquities, Statistical Section.

3. On the notion of low equilibrium traps in development economics, see: Hirschman (1981) and Sabel (1986).

References

Brand, L. A. (1992), Economic and Political Liberalization in a Rentier Economy: The Case of the Hashemite Kingdom of Jordan, in Harik, I. and Sullivan, D. J. (Editors), *Privatization and Liberalization in the Middle East,* Bloomington, Indiana University Press, pp. 210-232.

Buck-Morss, S. (1995), Envisioning Capital: Political Economy on Display, *Critical Inquiry, 21* (Winter), pp. 435-467.

Chaudhry, K. A. (1993), The Myths of the Market and the Common History of Late Developers, *Politics and Society, 21,* 3 (September), pp. 245-274.

Clawson, P. (1994), *Tourism Cooperation in the Levant,* The Washington Institute Policy Focus, Research Memorandum No. 26.

Gottschalk, S. (1995), Ethnographic Fragments in Postmodern Spaces, *Journal of Contemporary Ethnography,* 24, 2 (July), pp. 195-228.

Government of Israel. (1995), *Development Options for Cooperation: The Middle East/East Mediterranean Region: 1996 Version IV,* Chapter 7: Tourism Development Options, Ministry of Foreign Affairs and Ministry of Finance, August 1995.

Hazbun, W. (1998), Landscape of Facades: The Tourist Commodification of Petra, paper presented at the American Center for Oriental Research (ACOR), Amman, Jordan. April 18, 1998.

Hirschman, A. O. (1958), *The Strategy of Economic Development,* New Haven, Yale University Press.

Hirschman, A. O. (1981), The rise and decline of development economics, in *Essays in Tresspassing,* Cambridge, Cambridge University Press, pp. 1-24.

JICA. (1996), *The Study on the Tourism Development in the Hashimite Kingdom of Jordan: Executive Summary,* (Final Report) Ministry of Tourism and Antiquities (MOTA), The HashimiteKingdom of Jordan and the Japan International Cooperation Agency (JICA).

Jreisat, J. E. (1989), Bureaucracy and Development in Jordan, *Journal of Asian and African Studies,* 24, 1-2, pp. 95-105.

JVA. (1996), *Tourism Development Project of the East Coast of the Dead Sea (SPA), Part Four: Market Evaluation and Assessment, Suweimeh and Zara Development Areas,* Jordan Valley Authority, Amman.

Kelly, M. (1998), Jordan's Potential Tourism Development, *Annals of Tourism Research,* 25, 4, pp. 904-918.

Khouri, R. (1998), Bandwagon economics lead nowhere, *Jordan Times.* July 23-4.

Lynch, M. (1999), *State Interests and Public Spheres: The International Politics of Jordan's Identity,* New York, Columbia University Press.

Ministry of Planning, The Hashimite Kingdom of Jordan. (1995), *Jordan: A Winning Business Destination, Tourism Sector,* Amman.

Mitchell, T. (1995), Worlds Apart: An Egyptian Village and the International Tourism Industry, *Middle East Report,* No. 196 (September-October), pp. 8-11.

Mitchell, T. (1998), Nationalism, Imperialism, Economism: A Comment on Habermas, *Public Culture,* 10, 2, pp. 417-424.

Mufti, M. (1997) Jordanian Foreign Policy: State Interests and Dynastic Ambitions. Paper presented at the *Politique et Etat en Jordanie, 1946-1996* conference, held at the Insitute du Monde Arabe, Paris, 24-5 juin 1997.

North, D. C. (1981), *Structure and Change in Economic History,* New York, Norton.

Nurkse, R. (1953), *Problems of Capital Formation in Underdevelopment Countries,* Oxford, Oxford University Press.

Poon, A. (1993), *Tourism, Technology and Competitive Strategies,* Wallingford, C.A.B. International.

Rosenstein-Rodan, P. N. (1943), Problems of Industrialization of Eastern and South-Eastern Europe, *Economic Journal,* 53 (June-September), pp. 202-211.

Ryan, C. R. (1998), Jordan in the Middle East Peace Process: From War to Peace with Israel, in Peleg, I. (Editor) *The Middle East Peace Process: Interdisciplinary Perspectives,* Albany, State University of New York Press, pp. 161-177.

Sabel, C. F. (1986), Changing Models of Economic Efficiency and Their Implications for Industrialization in the Third World, in Foxley, A., McPherson, M. S., and O'Donnell, G. (Editors), *Development, Democracy, and the Art of Trespassing,* Notre Dame, University of Notre Dame Press, pp. 27-55.

Said, E. (1979), *Orientalism*, New York, Vintage.

Sciolino, E. (1994), The Mideast Accord: The Impact, *New York Times*, July 26, 1994.

Scott, J. C. (1998), *Seeing Like a State*, New Haven, Yale University Press.

Twite, R. and Baskin, G. (Editors), (1994), *The Conversion of Dreams: The Development of Tourism in the Middle East*, Jerusalem, Israel/Palestine Center for Research and Information.

Urry, J. (1992), The Tourist Gaze 'Revisited', *American Behavioral Scientist,* 36, 2 (November), pp. 172-196.

USAID. (1993), *Technical Feasibility Studies V Project: Tourism Marketing Strategy,* (September 28, 1993) prepared by Chemonics International.

Selling places: The New Asia-Singapore brand

Joan C Henderson

Nanyang Technological University, Singapore

Abstract

The study is concerned with the challenges of branding tourist destinations. These places are often living and working communities with a unique history and character which serve various groups of visitors. Such users have different motivations, expectations and experiences and the place can acquire several meanings as a consequence. It becomes difficult to capture this complexity in a brand name, especially when applied to a country. The research explores attempts by the tourism authorities to define and implement the particular brand of New Asia-Singapore, and the responses of tourists and locals to it. Results suggest a lack of awareness by both parties, and the dilemmas facing marketers in their efforts to brand places and ensure an appropriate fit between image and reality. The paper also identifies concerns associated with commodification and the wider social and political implications of the branding process.

Introduction

The paper considers the topic of selling places through the use of branding within the context of Singapore which introduced its New Asia-Singapore brand in 1996. It examines the nature of the brand, its effectiveness and attempts to promote it. Resident and visitor responses are assessed and there is a discussion about the appropriateness of branding tourist destinations both commercially and with regard to socio-cultural ramifications. Additional questions arise about efforts to operationalise the brand concept, leading to the physical nature of the destination being shaped to fit and local inhabitants encouraged to act in conformity with it. While emphasis is on the case of Singapore, the subject has a more general relevance as greater numbers of National Tourist Organisations and other bodies at a regional and local level incorporate branding into their promotional campaigns.

The branding strategy employed by the Singapore Tourism Board and progress towards its implementation has been generally well documented, but the outcome of such activity is more difficult to determine. Visitor arrival data since the start of the campaign provides a picture of general trends, although clearly other influences are at work. In order to explore the impact of the branding efforts, a survey to test public knowledge was carried out in

Singapore on a sample of 133 local residents and 120 international tourists. Local residents were selected on a random basis at a variety of sites across the island in order to secure a broad view from diverse areas. Tourists were interviewed in the city centre, again at random, although only Caucasian visitors were invited to participate because of initial problems encountered amongst Asians in completing the English language questionnaire. This limitation and others relating to the sample size and bias introduced by the choice of interview sites and respondents is acknowledged, and the findings represent only a guide to levels of awareness. Nevertheless, the results do permit some tentative conclusions to be derived on the subject and form the basis for a wider debate about the benefits and pitfalls of the branding process for all the parties involved.

Selling places through branding

Destination marketing has become increasingly necessary in the modern travel and tourism industry as places seek to be distinctive and attractive, aiming to establish a favourable position and sell themselves in a highly competitive environment. As Ward (1998, p. 1) states, 'All places, even those least endowed with attractions, vie to ensure that the tourist gaze falls, however fleetingly, on them'. The subject has drawn the attention of academics from a variety of disciplines with a number of texts devoted to it (Ashworth and Goodall, 1990; Heath and Wall, 1992; Kotler, Haider and Rein, 1993), many analysing urban experiences. Place images emerge as an important factor and their characteristics and construction have been the focus of several articles (Ahmed, 1994; Chon, 1992; Walmsley and Young, 1998). Image remains a difficult concept which has been defined as a combination of knowledge, feelings and opinions or a total of all the beliefs, ideas, expectations and impressions a person has of a destination (Crompton, 1979). From a marketing perspective, Hunt (1975, p. 7) claims that 'all places have images - good, bad and indifferent - that must be identified and either changed or exploited'.

In terms of image creation, Gunn (1988) writes of images at the two levels of organic and induced. Organic images are derived from popular culture, the media, literature and education while induced are based upon advertising and promotional material and guidebooks. Gartner (1993) proposes a continuum made up of separate sources including Overt Induced I which represents conventional types of advertising and Overt Induced II comprising material requested from organisations with a vested interest in the travel decision. Other commentators (Selby and Morgan, 1996) identify projected images which correspond to the induced of Gunn's model, and naïve which is a pre-visit combination of organic and projected leading to expectation or the basis of the destination choice. Re-evaluated or modified images are formed as a consequence of actual experience.

Image formation thus emerges as complex and somewhat unpredictable with numerous determinants at work. It is this process which marketers, and especially National Tourist Organisations, become involved as they seek to influence destination preferences and purchase decisions, concentrating particularly on projected and induced forms of image. Effective measurement of image remains a problem, however, given the internal and external dynamics at work (Seyhmus and Brinberg, 1996; Echtner and Brent Ritchie, 1991) and the subjective and often subconscious nature of the image which the holder may not be able to articulate easily (Hollinshead, 1993). Exercising any authority over such a situation and developing strong and positive images is a formidable task.

Images can be conveyed through a brand, defined as 'a name, term, sign, symbol, design or combination of these elements ... intended to identify the goods or services of a seller and differentiate them from those of competitors' (Kotler et al, 1996, p. 283). Branding seeks to encourage awareness and establish perceptions of quality and favourable associations. The brand name allows customers to easily recognise what is being provided, creates a suitable image, offers familiarity and reduces risk. Brands are traditionally associated with consumer goods, but promoters of destinations are increasingly adopting the technique.

Gartner (1993, p. 206) describes 'I Love New York' as an example of 'brand identification statements' which 'create a point of reference and develop a perception based on the images evoked'. He also supports the view that brand images of larger regions will tend to overshadow any existing at a sub-regional level. Waitt (1996, p. 120) explains North Korea's difficulty in establishing itself as an international tourist destination being partly because of its absence of 'visual symbols'. Branding is thus a potentially valuable tool for marketing places.

However, such activities have generated some debate about the consequences (Gnoth, 1998) and criticisms of the marketing industry's apparent objectives of redefining place identities. Morgan and Pritchard (1998) emphasise the ideological role of branding, arguing that is important to acknowledge cultural, political, social and economic issues and agendas. They highlight the need to go beyond the marketing approach and context to explore the politics of branding and appreciate what 'recreations of destination identities reveal about power and tourism discourses' (p. 139). Commodification is a related issue and Tyler, Guerrier and Robertson (1998, p. 233) in their discussion of urban tourism note, 'the imaging and reimaging turns the city into a commodity; a product competing with other products in the marketplace ... a place to be consumed ... with the tourist as consumer'. In this process, 'multiple social and cultural meanings are selectively appropriated and repackaged to create a more attractive place image in which any problems are played down' (Ward, 1998, p. 1).

Promotional literature which is used to communicate images, sometimes linked to a brand, has also attracted attention from researchers and particularly the tourism brochure, with studies based on content analysis and semiotic interpretation. Dann (1993; 1995; 1996a,b) has made a major contribution to the literature about the language and imagery of tourism advertising, and Selwyn (1996), Wicks and Schutt (1991) and Pritchard and Morgan (1995; 1996) have also explored the significance of the brochure. The writers suggest that brochures not only function as a sales vehicle, but reflect the psychological needs of the traveller, the economic power of the commercial sector and inequalities amongst the various parties. Distorted and inauthentic images are presented, shaped to suit tourists and the tourism industry which imposes its demands and exploits places and people. Tourism thus becomes another form of imperialism and neo-colonisation, especially evident in representations of the East for consumption by the West.

These considerations reveal both the commercial difficulties and ethical dilemmas of applying the branding concept to tourist destinations which are multi-faceted entities serving various groups of users who each have their own sets of motivations, expectations and experiences. Places are also societies which are constantly evolving and possess a history with several layers of meaning; capturing this depth in any promotion and distilling it in a brand name represents a serious challenge, compounded when it is a country being sold. The complete tourism product is determined by agencies other than those responsible for its marketing and development, and the communication of a clear and consistent message to all market segments may not be possible. In addition, the distribution of power and exercise of control involved in the processes of defining and implementing brands and the impacts of these decisions on destinations and their residents represent possible causes for concern. These questions are now discussed with regard to the case of Singapore and efforts by the Tourism Board there to brand the country.

The New Asia-Singapore brand

The brand of New Asia-Singapore was introduced as a possible positioning statement in the Singapore Tourist Promotion Board's strategy document entitled Tourism 21: Vision of a Tourism Capital (STPB, 1996) which still directs official policy. The strategy was partly a response to the declining rate of growth in Singapore's international arrivals and its relative maturity as a tourist destination. Six strategic thrusts were presented including that of redefining tourism which was to be partly achieved through telling a new story of a modern and unique Asian destination. In the words of the strategy document,

'Singapore is a vibrant, multi-cultural and progressive Asian city, located in the heart of one of the world's most exciting and fast-growing tourism and economic regions. In other words, it embodies the essence of "New Asia" ... After all, Singapore, with its progressiveness, sophistication and unique multi-cultural Asian identity, can be said to be an expression of the modern Asian dynamism that marks the entire region - the island is a place where tradition and modernity, East and West meet and intermingle comfortably ... "New Asia-Singapore, is thus a possible destination positioning, which suggests a Singapore that has managed to preserve and nurture its Asian heritage, even as it embraces and harnesses the marvels of high technology. It successfully conveys the innovative, enterprising and confident city-state that is the Singapore of today, as well as of the coming new millennium' (p. 25).

The phrase and associated logo, originally accompanied by the tag-line 'So easy to enjoy, so hard to forget', were subsequently adopted by the Singapore Tourist Promotion Board (which changed its name to the Singapore Tourism Board in 1998) and started to appear on its promotional material. Tour guides, who are strictly regulated by the Board and required to undergo formal training and testing, are expected to be familiar with the concept and give examples of the New Asian spirit when conducting tours. Suggested illustrations include Western fast food adapted to suit local tastes, the application of *fengshui* in modern building design to ensure harmony and good fortune and the replacement of traditional merchants along the river bank with business executives enjoying the new leisure facilities there. Despite the efforts of the Board, however, there was some doubts by the end of the decade about the knowledge and acceptance of the brand amongst both the resident population and overseas markets.

The Tourism Board set up a series of task forces in response to the Asian financial crisis which commenced in 1997 and had an adverse effect on international arrivals thereafter. One of these was charged with examining how to promote the brand further in order to realise its full potential. Reporting at a conference the following year (STB, 1998), the group described the brand concept and personality in similar terms to those already noted and added the following,

'New Asia-Singapore tells a story of how a young nation emerged from an uncertain future to become what it is today. It speaks of a bold, visionary approach in revolutionising traditional ways of doing things, and applying them successfully to the situations we face. In essence, the New Asia-Singapore brand is not a product one consciously creates. It presents a total picture of the way we live, work and think' (p. 3).

The brand personality comprises the five characteristics of cosmopolitan, youthful and vibrant, modern Asia, reliability and comfort. Together, these are intended to create an image of a young and exciting place where the people are distinctly Asian yet contemporary and sophisticated. It also aims to offer a sense of safety, security and efficiency to the visitor.

The task force emphasised that it was vital that all Singaporeans understand, identify with and live the brand's New Asian values so that they would become its 'living representations' and 'ambassadors' (p. 5) while the local trade had a collaborative role to play in its dissemination. The members called for greater awareness of the brand and a wider appreciation of it to be achieved through building brand association and a programme of public education, recognising that many of the local population knew little of the term. Action was essential to establish a connection between local residents and the brand, this goal demanding the metamorphosis of the former.

They recommended a series of key steps to be taken in pursuit of these objectives:

- Simplification of the branding

- Identification of New Asia-Singapore products

- Media collaboration

- Artistic entertainment

- Reinforcement through events marketing

- Collaboration with the Ministry of Education

- Sampling of New Asia-Singapore products

- Other channels of promotion

- Recognition through awards

The group called for a certain amount of commercialisation of the brand and the building of partnerships with private industry, as well as the stimulation of popular interest in and support for it. The brand needed to be humanised so that Singaporeans could 'share and live out' its common values (p. 2). Some moves have been made to realise these aims since the conference and the brand continues to feature prominently in Tourism Board material.

Measuring effectiveness

Considering visitor arrivals since the start of the campaign, inbound tourism to Singapore did increase in 1996 to 7.3 million from 7.14 million in 1995. This was followed by a decline to 7.2 million in 1997 and a further drop to 6.24 million in 1998 (STB, 1999a), largely due to the extraordinary events of the Asian financial crisis which depressed travel throughout the region. Recovery was evident by 1999 with forecasts of a return to 7 million visitors as conditions improved. The growth rate in arrivals was already slowing down over the period, however, with 3.5% recorded in 1995, compared to over 7% in 1993 and 10% in 1992. The trends indicate that Singapore is reaching the stage of maturity in its evolution as a tourist destination while the economic problems and their repercussions illustrate the sensitivity of international tourist flows to external developments; these included environmental problems in 1997/98 of air pollution across the region caused by uncontrolled land clearance through forest burning in Indonesia. The introduction of the brand and promotional activity in general may have had a comparatively minor impact in the face of such difficult circumstances, and it is not easy to isolate its effect.

Another guide to success might be visitor satisfaction. Regular research conducted by the Singapore Tourism Board confirms a consistently high level of satisfaction (STB, 1999b), but published results contain no references to feelings about the New Asia-Singapore brand. A series of basic questions to establish brand recognition and reaction to it were thus formulated and the answers provided by survey respondents are summarised below.

Residents and awareness

Of those residents interviewed, 59% claimed never to have seen or heard of the phrase New Asia-Singapore. They also said that it meant nothing to them and they had no response to make to it.

An additional 29% had no knowledge of the phrase, but did offer their interpretation of its meaning and responses to it. In terms of meaning, it was mainly described in positive ways although there was no clear consensus of opinion. Individuals spoke variously of Singapore trying to establish a new look or image as the most advanced country in Asia, conveying a sense of it being a newer part of Asia, a focus for the future and distinct from the rest of the region. Reference was also made to the millennium and Singapore entering a new age, taking the lead in rising above the Asian financial crisis and being forward looking. Only four specific allusions were made to tourism including the promotion of Singapore as an Asian and global tourism hub and a fascinating place to visit.

Responses were more mixed and 18% had nothing further to add. Six respondents found it to be a 'good' phrase. More detailed answers made reference to a positive feeling of a new beginning, change being heralded, the introduction of something new and a vibrant city that never sleeps. It made the future seem bright for Singapore. One individual perceived it as a reminder of the need to upgrade himself in order to keep up with changing surroundings. Over 20% were negative and objectors used words such as strange and complicated. A respondent thought that it was arrogant and might be offensive to Singapore's neighbours.

The remaining 12% agreed that they were familiar with the phrase. About a third could not recall the source of this information; others mentioned a Minister's speech, travel brochures and the Tourism Board website, magazines, newspapers, pamphlets and television. However, it became evident that there was some confusion as 40% connected the phrase with television channel News Asia which broadcasts in Singapore. Apart from this, the meaning was perceived as a message that Singapore was becoming a stronger economic power in the region, was an Asian country, a general hub and about to enter the next millennium. One person identified it as a brand name for Singapore and two others spoke of it as a promotional campaign by the Tourism Board with a reference made to repackaging.

Reactions to the phrase amongst this group varied from 'great' and a feeling of pride as it showed Singapore moving ahead and growing, to 'silly' with five respondents failing to offer any response. Otherwise, it was seen as a good idea which marked a new beginning although it would need a lot of effort to make it come true. One person referred to a Tourism Board campaign and two mentioned news about Asia.

These results indicate a lack of awareness amongst Singaporeans about the brand of New Asia-Singapore and the values invested in it by the marketing industry. Almost 90% of those interviewed had not heard the phrase before and there was a tendency to confuse it with a television station by a significant proportion of those who expressed a familiarity with it. A high proportion of nearly 60% claimed that the phrase meant nothing to them and they had no response to it. Those who had no prior knowledge, and were prepared to ascribe meanings to the phrase, were largely positive and their responses favourable on the whole. Mention was made of the brand personality attributes of vibrancy and modernity, but reactions did not always correspond to the characteristics and values of the brand as outlined by its creators. It would thus appear that the stated goal of ensuring Singaporeans fully appreciate, identify with and enact the brand's New Asian values has still to be met.

Tourists and awareness

Amongst the tourists questioned, 60% had not seen or heard the phrase before and were unable to give any response to it. An additional 18% had never come across the phrase, but were prepared to describe what it meant to them. It was perceived as conveying an impression of a new outlook and modernity, representing a fresh image of Asia. Responses from this group were positive as it was considered to signify something novel and beneficial. Few respondents, however, were prepared or able to elaborate.

The remaining 22% claimed to recognise the phrase. Travel brochures were cited as the most common source of this information by half the group, and individuals listed maps, airport signs and a Singapore International Airlines flight. Three people could not recall where they had seen or heard the brand name. The phrase was interpreted to mean a different image and form of presentation, communicating a modern Asian perspective. Individuals mentioned food, a new economy and greater freedom. It was viewed by one visitor as an attempt by Singapore to be recognised as somewhere more than a holiday destination suitable only for shopping. Responses were approving, as tourists spoke about a better future. One criticised it as a marketing ploy designed to make visitors stay longer while another was worried that Singapore might become just like cities in the United States.

Again, the results suggest limited awareness of the brand and its personality as envisaged by the creators. More than three quarters of the participants failed to recognise the phrase and over half could not respond to it. Actual responses were favourable, associating it with a new image, outlook and opportunities; little mention was made, however, of several important brand characteristics and values. Those familiar with the brand tended to be positive, but many overlooked certain key features the brand aims to embody. In addition, there was a tendency to apply the words to Asia as a whole rather than Singapore alone.

New Asia-Singapore: fact or fiction?

Although the findings indicate that the brand has not been entirely successful in communicating the intended image, it could be argued that it does portray something of Singapore's qualities which were recognised by respondents. Singapore is in Asia and is a highly developed and modernised society. While the country has adopted Western practices, many of these have been adapted to local circumstances with certain traditions related to the three principal cultures of Chinese, Malay and Indian still followed. A taste of the exotic Asian vibrancy promised in the literature can still be found in the historic ethnic enclaves of Chinatown, Little India and Kampong Glam as well as in aspects of everyday life such as food hawker centres and religious festivals.

Nevertheless, the visitor may leave with the over-riding impression of a densely populated, highly urbanised and developed nation; one that is more Western than Oriental in appearance. For some, it seems unclear what exactly New Asia is, how it differs from old Asia or Old Asia and the position Singapore occupies within the region. In many ways, Singapore's history, economy, political system and culture are markedly different from its Asian neighbours and set it apart as a very untypical Asian city-state. It remains a complex society of great richness and diversity, but it is doubtful whether any brand name can effectively convey to outsiders its characteristics and values.

The inability of those questioned to identify essential traits of the brand could indicate insufficient exposure and the need for a more intensive advertising campaign. Yet it may also suggest the image of the tourist destination which marketers are seeking to promote does not correspond with people's experiences. A gap might have emerged between evoked image and perceptions of reality, or the former lack clarity and definition.

There are also doubts which arise under these circumstances regarding operationalising the brand concept and efforts to modify the nature of the place so that there is a better match between the desired image and objective identity. The resulting tension may find expression in conflicts and disputed space. Some evidence of this can be seen in Singapore's Chinatown where changes are occurring which critics have argued are driven more by the interests of the international tourism industry than the needs of local residents.

Following an active conservation policy since the mid-1980s, an ambitious tourism development and promotion programme was announced in 1998. Officials maintain the purpose is to present a new and revitalised Chinatown while preserving the fabric and recalling the atmosphere of the old. In some ways, it is to become a physical manifestation of the New Asia-Singapore spirit. These proposals have generated considerable controversy and attracted opposition from some inhabitants and the Singapore Heritage Society who are concerned about a lack of authenticity and the emergence of a theme park which is no longer a proper home for residents and workers (Henderson, 2000). A feeling persists that the opinions of the people who belong there and Singaporeans as a whole have been neglected. There are already signs of the exclusion of residents from other heritage sites in Singapore (Teo and Yeoh, 1997; Teo and Hung, 1995; Teo, 1994) which have become principally tourist venues with little local identification.

The appropriateness of the brand can therefore be challenged on both the conceptual and operational level. Conceptually, it may appear unconvincing and confusing as an embodiment of contemporary Singapore while attempts to translate it into reality could result in an artificial environment from which locals are alienated and excluded. The matter of implementation provokes questions also about tourism promotion becoming politicised, as governments use it to deliver particular messages to both residents and international tourists in pursuit of other policy objectives. This is an interesting theme, but can only be acknowledged here and is the subject for another paper.

Conclusion

This paper has considered the use of branding by those responsible for tourism promotion in their efforts to establish a clearly defined image of a tourist destination which will appeal to visitors. It has examined some of the dilemmas resulting from such an exercise with reference to the New Asia-Singapore brand. The study reveals a gap between the intentions of the marketers regarding the brand and understanding on the part of both visitors and locals surveyed, as well as concerns about place commodification.

The topic of branding has relevance for commercial practitioners, tourism administrators and planners. Effective communication with target audiences is essential for successful place marketing, but a destination must employ images which reflect reality and capture a genuine sense of the place and its people in order to be sustainable; such diversity and depth cannot easily be captured in a brand and perhaps resources might be better invested elsewhere. Residents should also be consulted about the form the picture presented to tourists takes and about physical changes which aim to make the destinations more attractive for visitors. When residents are called on to live the values of the brand in pursuit of tourism goals, it would seem that marketers are in danger of assuming too much influence and a sense of balance needs to be restored. Societies cannot be engineered or places manufactured for tourist consumption without a loss of authenticity which is ultimately recognised by the visitor who will move on to seek it elsewhere.

Devising and implementing meaningful brands thus remains a challenge for destination marketers and the subject is one that should provide a rich research agenda for the future, encompassing discussion of images held in the minds of tourists and the attempts of the tourism industry to direct their formation. Additional areas for exploration include the relationship between image and reality in the tourist experience and contested notions of authenticity. These are matters for further attention in the 21st century as the competition for tourists becomes even more intense amongst destinations world-wide.

References

Ahmed, Z.U. (1994), Determinants of the Components of a State's Tourist Image and their Marketing Implications, *Journal of Hospitality and Leisure Marketing*, 2 (1): 55-68.

Ashworth, G. and Goodall, B. (Editors), (1990), *Marketing Tourism Places*, Routledge Kegan Paul, London.

Chon, K. S. (1992), The Role of Destination Image in Tourism: An Extension, *The Tourist Review*, 47 (1): 2-8.

Crompton, J. L. (1979), An Assessment of the Image of Mexico as a Vacation Destination and the Influence of Geographical Location upon that Image, *Journal of Travel Research*, 17 (1): 18-23.

Dann, G. (1996a), The People of Tourist Brochures, in Selwyn, T. (Editors), The Tourist Image: Myths and Myth Making in Tourism, John Wiley and Sons, Chichester, pp.61-81.

Dann, G. (1996b), The Language of Tourism: A Sociolinguist Perspective, CAB International, Wallingford.

Dann, G. (1995), A Socio-Linguist Approach to Changing Tourist Imagery, in Butler, R. and Pearce, D. (Editors), Change in Tourism: People, Places, Processes, Routledge, London, pp.114-136.

Dann, G. (1993), Advertising in Tourism and Travel: Tourist Brochures, in Khan, M., Olsen, M. and Var, T. (Editors), VNR's Encyclopaedia of Hospitality and Tourism, Van Nostrand Rheinhold, New York, pp. 893-901.

Echtner, C. M. and Brent Ritchie, J. R. (1991), Meaning and Measurement of Destination Image, *Journal of Tourism Studies*, 2 (2): 2-12.

Gartner, W. C. (1993), Image Formation Process, *Journal of Travel and Tourism Marketing*, 2 (3): 191-215.

Gnoth, J. (1998), Branding Tourism Destinations, *Annals of Tourism Research*, 25 (3): 758-760.

Gunn, C. (1988), *Vacationscape: Designing Tourist Regions,* Van Nostrand Reinhold, New York.

Heath, E. and Wall, G. (1992), *Marketing Tourism Destinations,* John Wiley and Sons, New York.

Henderson, J. C. (2000), Attracting Tourists to Singapore's Chinatown: A Case Study in Conservation and Promotion, *Tourism Management,* 21 (5): 525-535.

Hollinshead, K. (1993), Ethnocentrism in Tourism, in Khan, M., Olsen, M. and Var, T. (Editors), VNR's *Encyclopaedia of Hospitality and Tourism*, Van Nostrand Rheinhold, New York, pp.652-662.

Hunt, J. D. (1975), Image as a Factor in Tourism Development, *Journal of Travel Research*, 13 (3): 1-7.

Kotler, P., Bowen, J. and Makens, J. (1996), *Marketing for Hospitality and Tourism*, Prentice-Hall International, New Jersey.

Kotler, P., Haider, D. H. and Rein, H. (1993), *Marketing Places: Attracting Investment, Industry and Tourism to Cities, States and Nations*, Free Press, New York.

Morgan, N. and Pritchard, A. (1998), *Tourism Promotion and Power: Creating Images, Creating Identities*, John Wiley and Sons, Chichester.

Pritchard, A. and Morgan, N. (1996), Selling the Celtic Arc to the USA: A Comparative Analysis of the Destination Brochure Images Used in the Marketing of Ireland, Scotland and Wales, *Journal of Vacation Marketing*, 2 (4): 346-365.

Pritchard, A. and Morgan, N. (1995), Evaluating Vacation Destination Brochure Images: The Case of Local Authorities in Wales, *Journal of Vacation Marketing*, 2(1), pp.23-28.

Selby, M. and Morgan, N.J. (1996), Reconstructing Place Image: A Case Study of its Role in Destination Marketing, *Tourism Management*, 17 (4): 287-294.

Seyhmus, B. and Brinberg, D. (1996), The Affective Images of Tourist Destinations. *Journal of Travel Research*, 35 (4): 11-15.

Selwyn, T. (Editor), (1996), *The Tourist Image: Myths and Myth Making in Tourism*, John Wiley and Sons, Chichester.

STB, Singapore Tourism Board, (1999a), *Singapore Annual Report on Tourism Statistics 1998*, Singapore Tourism Board, Singapore.

STB, Singapore Tourism Board, (1999b), *Survey of Overseas Visitors to Singapore 1998*, Singapore Tourism Board, Singapore.

STB, Singapore Tourism Board, (1998), *Riding the Asian Tidal Wave*, Conference Papers, Singapore Tourism Conference '98, Singapore Tourism Board, Singapore.

STPB, Singapore Tourist Promotion Board, (1996), *Tourism 21: Vision of a Tourism Capital*, Singapore Tourist Promotion Board, Singapore

Teo, P. (1994), Assessing Socio-Cultural Impacts: The Case of Singapore, *Tourism Management*, 15 (2): 126-136.

Teo, P. and Yeoh, B. (1997), Remaking Local Heritage for Tourism, *Annals of Tourism Research,* 2 (1): 192-213.

Teo, P. and Huang, S. (1995), Tourism and Heritage Conservation in Singapore, *Annals of Tourism Research*, 22 (3): 589-615.

Tyler, D., Guerrier, Y. and Robertson, M. (Editors) (1998), *Managing Tourism in Cities,* John Wiley and Sons, Chichester

Waitt, G. (1996), Marketing Korea as an International Tourist Destination, *Tourism Management,* 17 (2): 113-121.

Walmsley, D. J. and Young, M. (1998), Evaluative Images and Tourism: The Use of Personal Constructs to Describe the Structure of Destination Images, *Journal of Travel Research,* 36 (3): 65-69.

Ward, S.V. (1998), Selling Places: The Marketing and Promotion of Towns and Cities 1850-2000, Routledge, London.

Wicks, B.E. and Schutt, M. A. (1991), Examining the Role of Tourism Promotion through Use of Brochures, *Tourism Management*, December, pp.301-312.

From lakes, poets, and mountains, to rum, slaves, and tobacco: A critical review of the evolution and development of tourism in Cumbria

David W G Hind

University of Northumbria, UK

Introduction

The purpose of this paper is to explore the evolution and development of tourism in the county of Cumbria, England. Cumbria is situated in the north west of England, and stretches from the Scottish Border in the north, to Morecambe Bay in the south, and from the Pennine Hills in the east, to the Irish Sea in the west.

A great variety of landscapes can be found in Cumbria, but perhaps Cumbria is best known for the Lake District, which is an area of outstanding natural beauty right at the geographic heart of the county. The Lake District has been attracting tourists for over 200 years, but at the start of the 21st Century strategies are in place to disperse, and attract tourists to some of the lesser-known sub-regions of Cumbria.

Lakes, mountains, and poets

"The modern 'discovery' of the English Lake District began in the mid-18th century", Wilson (1996, p450). Prior to the 1750s, travel on the Lake District roads by horse drawn coaches was difficult. From the mid C18th (with the Enclosure Acts and Turnpike Acts), but before the Industrial Revolution, improvements in road transport and safety in rural areas encouraged the wealthy classes to travel and explore the United Kingdom. These tours were similar in concept to the European Grand Tour, but were on a smaller scale, with the tourists being members of England's social and intellectual elite.

It was not until the second half of the C18th when changing trends in art and literature influenced the way in which the landscape was looked at, that tourism really started in the Lake District. Wilson (1996, p450) says that a small pamphlet written by J Brown (a physician) in 1767 really encouraged the first tourists to visit the Lake District, describing the "mountain scenery around Keswick as 'horrible grandeur', 'dreadful heights', and 'terrible magnificence'". This style of language became associated with the Picturesque period which saw two artistic themes emerging and being developed in the C19th - the Sublime and the Beautiful. The main tourists to the Lake District at this time were artists, such as Constable, or writers who made sketches of what they saw, or wealthy tourists who brought draughtsman with them to draw the landscapes.

Influential contemporary poets were drawn to the Lake District in the C19th, for example Coleridge and Southey who lived close to William Wordsworth. Wilson (1996, p454) asserts that it was Wordsworth who "..is responsible for the present day image of the Lake District." This view is supported by Newby (1981, p130) who says that "his poetry paved the way for the development of a new tourist style because of its emphasis upon nature and man's response to, and feeling for, the natural world". Newby continues by stating that Wordsworth not only encouraged "the intellectual climate for tourism" but that he also identified locations the tourists should visit in his guides to the Lake District.

As the early years of the C19th passed, the tourists became more interested in exploring the fells and mountains, hiring local guides initially, and then venturing off by themselves as they became more experienced, King (1992, p4). Towards the middle of the C19th, the number of tourists exploring the mountains increased, and a wider range of outdoor activities were being pursued.

The railway age

The Windermere railway line opened in 1847, despite Wordsworth's objections to it, Wilson (1996, p455). Wordsworth was probably the first person to encourage the protection and conservation of the natural landscape in the Lake District, and he feared that the railway would bring increasing numbers of tourists who would have an adverse effect on the landscape. Wordsworth was unable to prevent the opening of the railway, but as a gesture to his efforts the railhead stopped a mile short of Lake Windermere.

The railway age in the mid C19th enabled a wider range of people in the United Kingdom to travel for leisure and tourism purposes, in effect creating a form of mass tourism. The Lake District was an increasingly popular tourist destination during Victorian times as it was seen as a suitable family destination, "....away from the urban squalor, and commercial entertainments that were becoming associated with some of the larger seaside resorts" King (1992, p6). The working classes were seen as an important market segment by the railway companies who organised excursion trains from the large urban centres of the north. Bowness and Windermere were the prime destinations for these day excursionists because poor transport within the Lake District restricted their travels away from the railway station. In the 1860s a rail link was established to Keswick, and trains arriving here were mainly from the North East.

William Wordsworth maintained his influence over tourism in the Lake District throughout his life, helping to attract the middle classes who had read his literary works. He helped to popularise tourism to the Lakes, by offering a new way of looking at the countryside and nature, and encouraging tourists to see for themselves the landscapes and places featured in his writings. Indeed, such was his popularity, that his house became a tourist attraction in its own right, "...not just for the elite who could expect a personal audience with the poet...", but also for the middle classes, and less well-off members of society, King (1992, p6). Wordsworth died in 1850, and after his death tourists were keen to visit any place with a connection to Wordsworth, and by 1896 Dove Cottage in Grasmere was open to the public.

As the C19th progressed the great outdoors became increasingly popular for leisure activities. Fell walking became popular in the 1860s and 1870s as guide books were published describing the ascents of major peaks (see Linton 1864). Mountain climbing became a serious pursuit for the middle classes in the 1880s, with Wasdale Head developing as a centre for the elite.

Tourism in the early - mid twentieth century

The C20th saw greater mobility for the population of the United Kingdom, both at home and overseas. But the appeal of the Lake District for domestic tourism was still strong. Cycling was very popular at the beginning of the C20th with urban based cycling clubs organising trips for their members to the countryside.

By the 1930s "...there was a massive increase in the outdoor movement, with rambling and hiking becoming a pastime for many.." King (1992, p13). As the number of people benefiting from paid holidays increased, and as leisure time increased, less expensive types of accommodation were developed in the Lake District, for example Youth Hostels and farm accommodation. Mountaineering became accessible to the working classes in the early C20th as motor transport in the Lake District improved, and climbing routes were publicised more widely. Thus, the early and mid C20th emphasis in the Lake District was on sport and healthy tourism activities, rather than the literary associations of the C19th. The 'small-scale' nature of the lakes was now emphasised, instead of the Wordsworthian romantic vision of nature, Wilson (1996, p459).

1950s and 1960s

The tourism industry developed very rapidly in Cumbria in the 1950s and 1960s. This is the period when UK domestic tourism grew quickly - more people were able to afford annual holidays and day trips, and the overseas travel explosion had not yet commenced. The development of the tourism industry in Cumbria, though, was primarily in the valleys of the Lake District, where tourists were attracted because of the natural beauty and the opportunity to participate in outdoor pursuits. Tourists arrived by train and coach, as well as an increasing number by private car. The number of guesthouses and hotels increased to cater for the long stay tourists on their annual holidays. Although the summer months were the most popular for tourist visits to the Lake District, an increasing number of tourists did start to visit the area in the shoulder months.

1970s and 1980s

Tourism to Cumbria in the 1970s and 1980s was mirroring some of the national tourism trends that were emerging. Domestic tourism suffered as a result of the overseas travel boom; as the UK population became more elderly and more affluent there was an increase in the number of short break holidays being taken, particularly in the shoulder and off-peak periods; and the 1980s domestic tourist in particular was motivated to take a holiday at home for reasons other than good weather.

However, Cumbria's tourism industry was "...still concentrated in the central part of the Lake District, with relatively little tourism development in most other areas", Cumbria Tourist Board (1990, p16), with the central Lakeland area being the "...backbone of tourism in the region...".

Cumbria's economy

In the 1980s, employment patterns within Cumbria were relatively stable. The Thorp reprocessing plant at British Nuclear Fuels (BNFL), Sellafield in West Cumbria employed 7,500 construction workers, while Sellafield itself employed 9,000 workers; employment in the shipbuilding industry in Barrow-in-Furness increased from 8,000 employees in the mid-1980s to 14,000 by the end of the decade; the food processing industries in Carlisle fared well, and a number of companies producing craft products for sale through factory shops, or by export tended to prosper Peck et al (1997, p49). It could be argued, therefore, that in the 1980s Cumbria had a relatively successful economy, with rates of unemployment below the national average.

The successful 1980s, though, were followed by the turbulence of the early 1990s. The Trident nuclear submarine project at VSEL in Barrow came to an end, and by 1992 the shipyard's workforce stood at 9,500 which reduced to 5,000 by 1993; construction at Thorp had been completed and only 1,500 construction workers were employed at Sellafield in 1993, Peck et al (1997, p52). Other employers experienced a period of re-structuring as the recession of the early 1990s bit hard, for example: the Lillyhall Leyland Bus factory in West Cumbria closed in 1992 with the loss of some 300 jobs; K-shoes rationalised production facilities across Cumbria; Scotts (owned by Kimberley Clark) in Barrow announced job losses; the Hartleys Brewery in Ulverston was closed.

When all these job losses are put into context, the employment picture of Cumbria in the late 1980s and early 1990s in the industrial areas of employment was one of decline: employment in the manufacturing sector fell by 11.6% and construction employment fell by 17.1%. However, service sector employment, particularly jobs in 'distribution, hotels, and catering' increased by 20.8% between 1987-'91, Peck et al (1997, p54). The decline in industrial employment continued into the mid-1990s.

It could be argued that the decline of industrial employment in Cumbria from the late 1980s onwards encouraged local authorities to diversify the economic structure of their districts. Attracting industrial inward investment to a region in the early 1990s was very difficult, especially for a region such as Cumbria which had missed out on the inward investment boom of the 1980s. Tourism, however, was seen as one possible sector for further development, not only because of its recent track record of being an area of employment growth, but also because of the changing structure and patterns of domestic tourism. More people were taking short break holidays, and a wider range of destinations were becoming popular for tourism, perhaps as a result of the post-modernist tourist movement. As mentioned previously, the Lake

District and Cumbria have had a 200 year history of tourism, and some of the peripheral areas of the County, felt that they could capitalise on this.

And so it was in the late 1980s and early 1990s that all districts in Cumbria embraced tourism as a significant sector for development, spurred on not only by the reasons outlined above, but also by a national drive to encourage tourism development in some of the more disadvantaged regions of the UK to assist with regional development.

The role of tourism development agencies in Cumbria

It is recognised both at a national and regional level, that the private sector by itself cannot develop a substantial tourism industry in areas of economic decline. Indeed, it could be argued that the private sector might not even see tourism as a possible area for investment. Thus, to encourage the development of the tourism industry in areas where there was not an established tourism base, Tourism Priority Areas were designated. Public sector/ private sector partnerships were established to develop tourism strategies in these tourism priority areas. These tourism partnerships sponsored by the English Tourist Board were initially known as Tourism Development Action Programmes (TDAPs), but were succeeded by Local Area Tourism Initiatives (LATIs).

In Cumbria LATI's were initially established in Carlisle, the North Pennines, Furness and Cartmel, and West Cumbria, followed by a Hadrian's Wall LATI and the establishment of the Settle-Carlisle Development Company. These areas were recognised as priority areas for tourism development, helping to develop tourism in Cumbria outside the Lake District National Park. The strategies implemented by these local initiatives, however, varied according to local tourism development needs, and the resources for tourism within each of the localities. The strategy for Eden and the North Pennines was based on the high quality of the landscape and the need for sensitive tourism development that would lead to sustainable tourism. Carlisle's strategy emphasised the historic city, with its Roman and Border's heritage. The seafaring traditions of West Cumbria lay at the heart of West Cumbria's strategy emphasising also the distinctive, historical towns of West Cumbria and their local traditions. Furness and Cartmel's strategy was partly based on the sub-region's proximity to the southern lakes as well as the history and heritage of the area. The Hadrian's Wall and Settle-Carlisle initiatives clearly had very focused aims.

The common elements of the role of these LATIs, though, was their emphasis on marketing, the encouragement of the training of staff employed in tourism, improvements to the quality and supply of tourism facilities, improving accessibility to the locality, and developing the environment, attractions, and infrastructure for tourism. A key to the success of the LATIs was that they involved the pooling of resources for marketing purposes in what is recognised as a very fragmented industry, Long (1995, p482). The pooling of resources was also essential when tackling infrastructure problems which required community wide collaboration in order to address them. Each LATI was managed by a project manager, and each scheme lasted initially for three years.

Thus, a strategy that was pursued in the 1990s was that of diversifying the tourism product of Cumbria to areas outwith the Lake District National Park. The work of the LATI's was instrumental in this strategy. Clearly, each LATI would have very specific local objectives, and would pursue a very specific local strategy, but the cumulative effect of all LATI's would be to develop new tourism products for Cumbria, and to promote these to appropriate market segments. A review of what has been achieved in West Cumbria is presented below.

West Cumbria Tourism Initiative (WCTI)

The WCTI was set up in 1990 to assist with the development of tourism in an area that had experienced severe industrial decline - West Cumbria was renowned for its heavy industries - iron ore and coal mining. These industries have now disappeared and unemployment is above the national average. The geographic coverage of the WCTI stretches from Silloth in the north to Millom in the south, and as far inland as Keswick.

The initial work of the WCTI centred around:

- co-ordinating and expanding the marketing of tourism in West Cumbria;

- improving business performance through the provision of business advice;

- improving the quality of the tourism product and customer service through training;

- securing greater involvement in, and raising the awareness of the economic importance of the tourism industry with the local community and the private sector;

- encouraging inward investment in major tourism projects and to support development projects which were already underway.

An important part of the WCTI strategy was to encourage new tourist attractions to be developed, such as heritage centres in Whitehaven (The Beacon) and Maryport (the Maritime Museum), a gateway attraction in Cockermouth (the Lakeland Sheep and Wool Centre), and industry tourism attractions such as the Sellafield Visitors Centre. A wide range of publicity and promotional leaflets were published to help raise awareness of the tourism facilities and attractions of West Cumbria, as well as a Travel Trade Information Pack aimed at tour and coach operators The promotional leaflets included:

- Maryport - A Proud Maritime Tradition;

- St Bees - A Thousand Years of History;

- Silloth-on-Solway - A Town of Victorian Charm;

- West Cumbria - Coastal Heritage Trail; and

- Whitehaven - Georgian Town and Harbour.

To assist with the promotional strategy the WCTI area was branded 'Cumbria Western Lakes and Coast', in order to overcome some of the negative images that were held about West Cumbria. Travel and Tourism exhibitions were attended to promote the area, and local television and local commercial radio stations have been used for advertising, Bousfield (1998, p45).

From 1994 - 1996, staff from the WCTI estimated that the visitor attractions in their area of responsibility experienced, on average, an increase of 56% in visitor admissions, which in turn led to an increase of 100 tourism related jobs, Bousfield (1998, p45).

To contribute to the regeneration of Whitehaven in West Cumbria, a major regeneration scheme is currently underway.

Rum, slaves, and tobacco - Whitehaven

Whitehaven, an example of a Georgian planned town, was once England's third largest port renowned for its trade in rum, tobacco, and slaves. The Whitehaven 'Renaissance Project' has secured some £24 million (from the Millennium Commission, English Partnerships, Copeland Borough Council, European Regional Development Fund Monies, and the Whitehaven Development Company Partnership) to transform the harbour area with four new tourist attractions. The Hub will provide a performance area for street theatre and bands, as well as shops, restaurants, and an exhibition area. The Crow's Nest will be a 40 metre mast situated at the end of one of the piers, from which nine cameras will film panoramic views of Whitehaven and further afield, and transmit them to a public gallery and historic exhibition below. More history will be told in Jeffersons - The Rum Story. The Jeffersons were C19th rum traders and the exhibition will be housed in one of their former warehouses. Finally, The Quest will be an interactive heritage trail to study the history of Whitehaven and the harbour.

This major project has been instigated by the Whitehaven Development Company, established in 1992, to promote the economic regeneration of the town and its harbour. But will major publicly funded capital investment schemes such as that discussed here, encourage further private sector tourism investment? What are the factors that encourage, as well as discourage, private sector investment in non-traditional tourism areas?

During the summer of 1999 semi-structured personal interviews were conducted with eleven leading figures from Cumbria's public and private sector tourism organisations to determine their views on the factors that will encourage and discourage further tourism investment in the peripheral areas of Cumbria. The key findings from these interviews are presented below.

Factors likely to encourage private sector investment

The following factors were mentioned by the interviewees as being potential stimulants to further tourism investment in West Cumbria and Furness:

1. The pro-active work of the tourism, and non-tourism development agencies in raising the awareness of West Cumbria and Furness as tourist destinations, and the pro-active work of key individuals and councillors in targeting particular inward investors.

2. The availability of public sector grants and funding to support developments (RSA, SRB, ERDF) in eligible areas.

3. The improved, and improving infrastructure of West Cumbria and Furness, making these sub-regions more accessible, and aesthetically more attractive.

4. The lower costs of developing new tourist facilities in West Cumbria and Furness, when compared to development costs within the Lake District National Park.

5. The availability of a suitable workforce for employment within tourism – the workforces of West Cumbria and Furness were felt to be flexible and have attained, or have the potential of attaining the skills necessary for tourism employment.

6. The success of the tourism developments that have recently ocurred, for example the South Lakes Wildlife Park, Dalton-in-Furness; the Sheep and Wool Centre, Cockermouth; the Whitbread Travel Inn at Whitehaven; and Maryport Aquaria.

7. Relaxed planning and development regulations in certain localities, for example Maryport and Whitehaven.

8. The availability of 'brown-field' sites.

9. The accessibility of the Cumbrian harbour towns to cruise ships and passenger ferries – Barrow-in-Furness, Whitehaven, and Workington have all got the potential to be developed as maritime gateways to Cumbria.

Factors which may Discourage Private Sector Investment

1. The planning policies of the local authorities – some local authorities were adopting stringent planning policies towards tourism developments.

2. Poor tourism infrastructure in some localities. Millom in Furness would benefit greatly from tourism, but the infrastructure and superstructure to attract investors, and to service tourists is still lacking.

3. A lack of knowledge and awareness by national private sector investors of the opportunities for tourism investment in West Cumbria and Furness.

4. An unwillingness by investors to take a financial risk in sub-regions that still have to demonstrate their full potential as tourist destinations.

5. The challenges of applying for public sector funding, and the perceived difficulties of working through the funding bureaucracy, combined with a lack of locally available private sector capital for matching funding.

6. The perceived remoteness of West Cumbria and Furness from major transport routes (the M6 motorway) and from major centres of population.

7. The image of certain localities in West Cumbria and Furness, which may reduce the attractiveness of these localities to potential tourists.

8. The 'conservative' and 'introspective' outlook of some sections of the local communities, combined with a lack of confidence in tourism as a sector that can be developed as a viable economic activity.

Clearly, the above findings are qualitative, but they do indicate some of the challenges to be faced in developing tourism in non-traditional areas. Whilst publicly funded infrastructure projects can be instigated, and publicly funded flagship tourism attractions can be developed, there can be no guarantee that private sector investment will follow, or that visitors will be attracted to the area in increasing numbers year-on-year.

Those responsible for developing tourism in non-traditional areas need to build on those factors that encourage private sector investment, whilst trying to overcome some of the barriers to investment.

Conclusion

For many people the Lake District still represents tourism in Cumbria. As discussed previously in this paper, it was the harsh beauty of the fells and the lakes in the C18th and C19th that drew the first tourists to Cumbria - the artists and the writers. For much of the C20th it still was the Lake District that represented tourism in Cumbria, with the outdoors and the beauty of the landscape being attractants for a wider range of tourists. In terms of the tourist area life cycle concept (TALC – see Butler (1980), if it were to be crudely applied to the Lake District, an assumption that could be made about tourism in the year 2000 is that it is at the 'consolidation' stage of the life cycle. The market attracted to the Lakes is a 'mass market', more 'conservative' activities are being pursued, and there is concern that the number of car borne tourists is leading to congestion and pollution of the environment.

The TALC suggests that if these issues are not addressed then a destination might move into 'decline' as tourists are deterred from visiting the area. More by coincidence than by an understanding of TALC, it would appear that in the late 1980s and early 1990s strategies were instigated in Cumbria to help spread the distribution of tourism to the more peripheral areas of the county, not only to alleviate the honey pots in the Lakes, but to help diversify the declining economies of the peripheral areas. As a result, some of these peripheral areas find themselves at different stages of the TALC. A fair assumption to make might be that West Cumbria, the North Pennines, Carlisle, and the Furness Peninsula are in the 'involvement' stage of the TALC. The number of tourists visiting these areas is increasing, a tourist season and tourist market have emerged, and public sector/private sector partnerships are heavily involved in developing and improving the infrastructure for tourism. Indeed, community tourism initiatives are quite widespread in these areas for the development and promotion of appropriate types of tourism, with all partners interested in tourism working closely together.

Thus, it could be suggested that there is a case of 'textbook' tourism currently in evidence in Cumbria. The aim of the peripheral areas of the county should be to continue developing and promoting tourism (with existing strategies) to move the local tourism industries into the next stage of TALC - the 'development stage'. But the lessons of tourism in the Lake District (and other tourist destinations) should not be ignored. Tourism can take a very long time to develop. Although the infrastructure for tourism, and the tourism superstructure can be developed relatively quickly, and the tourism product offered to the market place in a short space of time, it might take considerable more time to shift tourists' consumer behaviour. Tourism is a very competitive business, and most regions of the UK are now engaged in some form of tourism activity. Thus, attracting tourists to new, non-traditional tourist destinations is going to be very challenging, and it will probably not be a short term return on investment that is seen, unless the destination has a very distinctive selling point.

But Cumbria does have a number of strengths to help off-set these difficulties. The Lake District attracts a relatively stable, mature market, with a high incidence of repeat visits. Tourists visiting Cumbria tend to come from the higher socio-economic groups and are from the more elderly segments of the population (growth markets). Parts of Cumbria are on transit routes to other tourist destinations (adding to the tourist catchment area). The tourism product of Cumbria has diversified considerably since 1990, and although Cumbria cannot be described as a 'multi-opportunity' destination, there is more to attract and entertain visitors in the peripheral parts of the county than there ever has been before. The tourism partnerships are skilled in developing the local tourism industry and in networking together to devise co-ordinated and synergistic tourism strategies.

The strategy that is being pursued to develop tourism in West Cumbria is to build on the maritime heritage of the region, but only time will tell, if once again, a destination's future lies in its past.

References

Bousfield, T. (1998), *What Needs to be Considered to Market Tourism in West Cumbria Successfully?* undergraduate dissertation, University of Northumbria, Carlisle Campus.

Butler, R. W. (1980), *'The concept of the tourist area life cycle of evolution: implication for management of resources'*, Canadian Geographer, 24, 5-12.

Cumbria Tourist Board, (1990), *A Vision for Cumbria* – Regional Tourism Strategy Review.

Newby, P. T. (1981), *'Literature and the Fashioning of Tourist Taste'*, in Pockock D. C. D. (Ed), Humanistic Geography and Literature: Essays on the Experience of Place, Croom Helm.

King, L. (1992), *The History of Tourism in Cumbria*, A Report for the Cumbria Tourist Board.

Linton, E. L. (1864), *The lake Country*, Smith and Elder.

Long, P. (1995), *'Perspectives on Partnership Organisations'*, in Seaton, A. V. (Ed), Tourism the State of the Art Conference Proceedings, Scottish Hotel School, Strathclyde University.

Peck, F. Durnin, J. Stokes, B. (1997), *'Cumbria vs The North: Contrasting Experience of Industrial Restructuring 1978 – 1995'*, Northern Economic Review.

Wilson, D. (1996), *'Travel Guidebooks and the Changing Image of Place in a Lake District Tourist Town'*, in Robinson, M. Evans, N. and Callaghan, P. (Eds), Tourism and Culture – Towards the 21st Century Conference Proceedings, Business Education Publishers.

Directional selling and the distribution of travel products: An investigation into travel agency recommendations

Simon Hudson

University of Calgary, Canada

Tim Snaith

Global Consultancy Network, UK

Graham A Miller

University of Surrey, UK

Paul Hudson

JMC Holidays, UK

Abstract

Recommendations are generally viewed as an important type of information considered by consumers during the decision-making process, and in the travel industry, travel agents represent a key influence in the tourism marketing system. Of increasing concern to the U.K. government is the practice of 'directional selling', the sale or attempted sale by a vertically integrated travel agent of the foreign package holidays of its linked tour operator in preference to the holidays of other operators. The practice is facilitated by the lack of transparency of ownership links. The objectives of this study were to understand the factors that influence travel agency recommendations, and to determine the extent of directional selling. The objectives were achieved using a mixture of focus groups, interviews and Mystery Shoppers. Exploration into the process of choosing a holiday showed that the brochure plays an important role for many consumers. However, for the travel agent the brochure is low priority, and even when the brochure is used, the travel agent often has a considerable amount of influence. Whether or not the agency is vertically integrated has considerable influence on the recommendation process. Based on analysis of the interviews and focus groups, a model was developed, and tested using Mystery Shoppers. Results from investigating 156 travel agents across the U.K. indicate that the practice of directional selling is widespread, but some companies are more guilty than others. Theoretical and practical implications are discussed.

Introduction

Recommendations are generally viewed as an important type of information considered by consumers during the decision-making process (Howard, 1963; Peter and Olson, 1993). Some researchers have discovered that rather than simply consulting with others (opinion leaders) for opinions or recommendations, consumers often relinquish control of all or part of the decision process to external experts, agents, or surrogates (Solomon, 1986). In the travel industry, travel agents represent a key influence in the tourism marketing system (Bitner and Booms, 1982). In addition to helping travellers book reservations and obtain tickets and vouchers, they influence tourism planning decisions and outcomes. Recommendations of which operator to travel with, may be critical to the success of various tourism businesses.

For marketers it is thus critically important to develop an understanding of the factors that might influence travel agent recommendations. However, given the size and the economic impact of the travel intermediary sector of the tourism industry, surprisingly little research has been reported on travel agencies (Kendall and Booms, 1989; Goldsmith, Flynn and Bonn, 1994). Most previous research has focused on travel agents' consumers, dealing with either their search for information and services (Gitelson and Crompton, 1983; Goldsmith et al., 1994; Hsieh and O'Leary, 1993; Snepenger et al., 1990; Gilbert and Houghton, 1991); or with factors which influence their perceptions of and response to travel agency advertising (Kendall and Booms, 1989; Laskey et al., 1994). In contrast to these studies which focus on potential tourists, only a few studies have focused on travel agents themselves. One study contrasted travel agents' perceptions of destination attributes with those of their clients (Michie and Sullivan, 1990), and another (Contant et al., 1988) examined travel agents and the impact of terrorism on destination recommendations.

A more recent study by Klenosky and Gitelson (1998) presented a conceptual model describing the recommendation process of travel agents (see Figure 1). They empirically examined the impact on agents' destination recommendations of two factors from the model: trip type and origin. Although the study focused on destination choice as opposed to brochure/tour operator choice (as in this piece of research), it was acknowledged that the role of travel agent recommendations is a neglected but critically important area for study, especially in the current environment of increasing competition and reduced promotional resources. The authors suggest that additional research is needed to develop new models focusing on the other types of recommendations that tourists rely on when making decisions. In particular they suggest one potentially fruitful direction would be to examine the impact on recommendations of specific marketing tactics that are typically directed at travel agents such as sales incentives and commissions. Although these promotional tools are widely used, little is currently known about their differential effectiveness in generating business. Such recommendations (as highlighted in bold in the model) are the focus of this study.

Figure 1   Conceptual Model of the Process and Factors Influencing Travel Agent's Destination Recommendations (Klenosky and Gitelson, 1998)

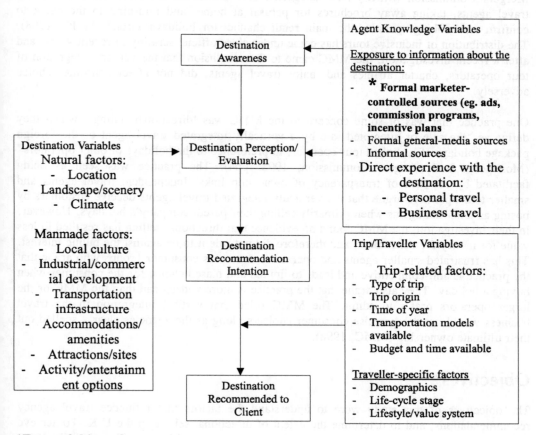

*Focus of this study

Integration in the UK travel industry

Expenditure on holidays by the British came to 22.5 billion pounds in 1998 (Mintel, 1999), representing a four percent share of all consumer spending. In terms of the type of holiday taken by U.K. consumers when they travel abroad, the package holiday or inclusive tour is at the core of the leisure travel industry's business. In 1997, 28 million holidays abroad were taken, of which 15 million were inclusive tours and 13 million were independently organised. The largest three tour operators, Thomson, Airtours, and Thomas Cook, control about 75% of the market, and each has their own chain of travel agencies. Thomson own 791 Lunn Poly agencies, Airtours control 717 Going Places branches and Thomas Cook have over 700 retail outlets under the Thomas Cook and Carlson brand names (Buckingham, 1999).

Travel agents represent a major communication channel for British travellers (Hsieh and O'Leary, 1993). 80-90% of inclusive tours are sold through travel agents, where vertically integrated tour operators are the dominant retailers (Mintel, 1999). The Monopolies and Mergers Commission (MMC) have suggested that the traditional mechanism of visiting travel agents, taking away brochures for perusal at home, and returning to the agent to confirm the booking, remains the main retail channel for holidays abroad (MMC, 1998). The distribution of inclusive tours has come under close official scrutiny in recent years, and after a recent investigation, the MMC came to the conclusion that the vertical integration of tour operators, charter airlines and major travel agents, did not affect consumer choice adversely.

One practice that was of some concern to the MMC was 'directional selling', which they define as "the sale or attempted sale by a vertically integrated travel agent of the foreign package holidays of its linked tour operator, in preference to the holidays of other operators" (Monopolies and Mergers Commission, 1998: pp4). The practice was seen as being facilitated by the lack of transparency of ownership links. Independent travel agents and smaller tour operators argue that the vertically integrated travel agents deceive customers by posing as impartial agents when primarily selling their parent company's holidays. However, in their investigation, the MMC found no evidence that directional selling has resulted in less value for money for consumers, and therefore did not rule it to be against the public interest. This has frustrated smaller agents and operators, as well as consumer groups who argue that the practice is anti-competitive and leads to limited and biased choice for the consumer when buying a holiday. They also argue that the practice is more widespread than the MMC or the larger operators prefer to admit. The MMC ruled that vertical integration in the travel business would not compromise consumer choice so long as the agencies clearly spelled out their ultimate ownership (MMC, 1998).

Objectives

The objectives of this study were to understand the factors that influence travel agency recommendations, and to determine the extent of directional selling in the U.K. To achieve this it was important first to understand the buying process, and in particular, the role of the brochure, for both the trade and consumers.

Methodology

The objectives were achieved using a mixture of focus groups, interviews and 'Mystery Shoppers'. Consumer behaviourists are increasingly embracing qualitative techniques and models in order to deal with relevant topics in meaningful and pragmatic ways (Walle, 1997). Literature suggests that the sensitive use of qualitative (as opposed to quantitative) techniques, can contribute immeasurably to better understanding of consumer motivations in vacation selection (Hodgson, 1993).

The research design had two main stages, and because the results of the first stage determined the structure of the second, the details of each will be discussed in turn.

Figure 2   Model Indicating the Role and Influence of the Travel Agent in the UK

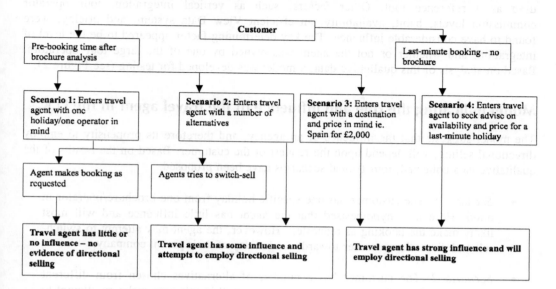

1. Interviews and Focus Groups

Five focus group discussions with consumers, lasting between one and one and half-hours, were conducted in various geographical locations. All consumers had been on holiday with a tour operator in the last 2 years and were considering booking a package holiday through a travel agent in the next year. These were complemented by two focus groups with travel agency counter staff and 6 in-depth interviews with managers. As the research involved two different types of respondent, the focus of the research shifted slightly. For example, travel agents were able to give their perspective on how consumers use brochures and those of other companies, and what influenced their decisions. With consumers, the emphasis was shifted to the use of the brochure and how travel agents might influence their final decision on which tour operator to travel with.

Results

Exploration into the consumer's perspective of the process of choosing a holiday showed that the brochure plays an important role. There appeared to be two distinct routes to booking a holiday using the brochure. One group would have a country or resort in mind and then gather all the relevant brochures. Having looked at the information, they would narrow it down to a few holidays. They would then go into a travel agent with their options to see what is available. The second group - which seemed to be mainly families on a budget - would get all the brochures before consulting the family. They would then look at prices and decide which destinations were possible. They would then either go into the travel agency to book a holiday, or telephone the agent to avoid certain inconveniences such as taking small, children to the shop. For them, the travel agent was a key influence on their final decision, especially in choosing which tour operator to travel with.

For the travel agent however, the brochure was found to be a low priority, and often just used as a reference tool. Other factors, such as vertical integration, tour operator commission levels, habit, availability, an efficient View Data system, and pricing, were found to have considerable influence. The key determining factor appeared to be the level of integration, and whether or not the agent was owned by one of the large tour operators. Based on analysis of this qualitative data, a model was developed for testing (see Figure 2).

Model indicating the role and influence of the travel agent in the U.K.

The model suggests that the influence of an agency, and therefore its propensity to employ directional selling, will depend upon the request of the customer. Based on the results of the qualitative data collected, four typical scenarios have been proposed:

- *Scenario 1*: The customer has one specific holiday from one brochure/operator in mind. Here it is hypothesised that the agent has little influence and will most likely make the booking as requested. However, the agent may attempt to switch-sell and direct the customer towards the holiday of their parent company.

- *Scenario 2:* The customer has a number of alternatives chosen from different brochures. The authors suggest that the agent will in this case make an attempt to push the holiday of their parent company.

- *Scenario 3:* The customer has an amount of money in mind as well as a destination. In this case the agent has strong influence and will recommend the holiday of its parent company.

- *Scenario 4:* The customer is looking for a last-minute holiday and calls the agent to see what is available. Again, the agent has strong influence over the decision the customer makes and is likely to employ directional selling of parent company products.

In the second stage of this research, the above scenarios were tested using mystery shoppers.

2. Mystery Shopping

'Mystery Shoppers' were used to test travel agent recommendations across the country, with the largest three 'linked' travel agency chains coming under investigation. 52 agencies from Lunn Poly (owned by Thomson), Going Places (Airtours) and Thomas Cook or Carlson (Thomas Cook) were sampled. Figure 2 was operationalised and a mixture of actual visits (n=36) and telephone calls (n=120) were used to get an insight into what happens when potential holidaymakers walk into a travel agent to book a holiday.

Mystery shopping is a form of participant observation where the researcher interacts with the subjects being observed, and stems from the field of cultural anthropology. However, it differs from the original anthropological approach to observation in terms of its structured and systematic format. In the services context, mystery shopping is able to provide information on the service experience as it unfolds (Grove and Fisk, 1992), and participant observation helps to develop a richer knowledge of the experiential nature of services. The participant can identify dimensions of the service encounter unlikely to be discerned by a distant or non-participant observer. Concealment of this observation, although raising ethical issues, can ensure that the experience is natural and not contrived for the sake of the observer.

Mystery shopping is used quite extensively by organisations in financial services, leisure services, retailing, motor dealerships, hotels and catering, passenger transportation, public utilities and government departments. The main benefit for these companies is that it gives them a very clear insight into what is happening when their customers meet their staff. In 1998, mystery shopping was worth over 30 million pounds a year to British marketing research companies. However, published academic research on mystery shopping is limited to a small number of papers that have mainly focused on its use in specific sectors (Wilson, 1998). Mystery shopping has been used in banking to find out if the institution is addressing the customer's needs, preferences and priorities (Morrall, 1994), but to the authors' knowledge, has not been used by tourism academics for the same purposes.

For the purposes of methodological comparison, a combination of actual visits and telephone calls were used to achieve the study objectives. Time constraints limited the visits to 36 linked travel agents in the London area. However, this itself translates itself to approximately 18 hours of contact time between mystery shoppers and travel agents sales people. In addition, 120 mystery shopping telephone calls were made to the three largest integrated agencies, randomly sampled from an ABTA list of U.K. travel agents. Agents were not warned in advance about the research project, as this would have reduced the effectiveness of the study considerably. Other researchers have recognised that unconcealed observational methods affect the validity of responses (Grove and Fisk, 1992).

Attempts were made to maximise the reliability of the exercise through the use of objective measurement and the careful selection and training of the shoppers. It was ensured that the shoppers matched a customer profile that was appropriate for the scenario that they were being asked to act out. Shoppers were trained, through role-plays, to adopt a neutral rather than an aggressive or defensive approach in the encounter with agents. The training of data collection skills focused on identifying the elements of the service to be observed as well as the retention and recording of the information. Subjectivity was minimised by using rating scales with labels, supported by verbatim comments from shoppers to justify their rating selection. For example researchers had to record how forcibly the agent tried to 'switch sell' on a five-point scale, and then comment on the tactics employed by the agent.

Researchers were given the four different scenarios and a research report form, and conducted the research over a period of two weeks. Each interview took an average of 30 minutes, whilst the telephone calls averaged out at 15 minutes each. The Market Research Society Code of Conduct specifies that mystery shopping should not involve an unreasonable amount of time or expense on behalf of the organisation being researched. The researchers in this case only made tentative enquiries (asking about availability) rather than positioning themselves as serious buyers. At the end of the encounter the researchers did not reveal themselves to the travel agent, as sometimes is the practice in North America. Such an approach is viewed by those involved in the U.K. marketing research industry as being too confrontational (Wilson, 1998).

Results

The results of the mystery shopping exercise have been summarised in Table 1, and the table indicates the level of directional selling employed as well as the level of transparency (agents indicating that they were owned by a tour operator). Taken as a whole, of the 156 travel agents approached, 95 (60%) clearly employed directional selling tactics. However, only 9 of the Thomson owned agencies, Lunn Poly, attempted to steer the researchers towards the Thomson product. So aside from Thomson, 86 of the other 104 agencies (82%) owned by Airtours and Thomas Cook, gave biased advice. 90% of Going Places agencies pushed the Airtours brand, whilst 75% of agencies owned by Thomas Cook tried to sell their own brands such as JMC Holidays, Thomas Cook (mainly long haul) and Inspirations.

Table 1   Results of Mystery Shopping Exercise

Mystery Shopping Scenarios 156 calls/visits were made to agencies around the UK spread evenly amongst the 3 largest linked agencies (52 each) They were asked the following 4 questions (13 agents per question):	% Of agents that tried to persuade researchers to travel with their parent company/linked operators instead of others			If so, did they make it clear that they were owned by the parent company?		
	Lunn Poly	Going Places	Thomas Cook or Carlson	Lunn Poly	Going Places	Thomas Cook or Carlson
Travel Agent Owned By:	Thomson	Airtours	Thomas Cook	Thomson	Airtours	Thomas Cook
1.Travel agency was asked about the availability of a Cosmos holiday in Majorca. A hotel was chosen where Thomson/Airtours/Thomas Cook go (Cosmos have no travel agencies)	0/13 0%	8/13 61%	4/13 30%	No	No, only when asked, and reluctantly	No, only when asked
2.Travel agency was asked about the availability of two specific holidays from brochures, one a Cosmos holiday and the other a Thomson/Airtours/Thomas Cook holiday	2/13 15%	13/13 100%	10/13 77%	No	Sign on computer in 1 agency	No
3. Travel agency was asked about the availability of a specific hotel and resort chosen from the brochures (where all the major operators go)	5/13 38%	13/13 100%	13/13 100%	No	No	No
4. Travel agency was asked about the general availability in the Canary Islands for the following week	2/13 15%	13/13 100%	12/13 92%	No	No	No
Total % For Each Agent Employing Directional Selling (N = 52)	9/52 17.3%	47/52 90%	39/52 75%			

With the actual visits, for the first scenario none of the agents made an attempt to switch-sell and were happy to check availability as requested. For the second scenario, where the researcher gave the agent 3 options, 7 out of the 9 agents made an attempt to push holidays offered by their parent company. Some of this persuasion was of a subtle nature (the Lunn

Poly agents for example gently convinced the researchers that the Thomson holiday was far better value for money than the rest). Going Places, however, used more force in their attempt to push their Airtours holiday. In the third scenario, where the researcher had a sum of money and a destination in mind, every single one of the 9 agencies visited employed directional selling tactics. Thomas Cook, Going Places, and Lunn Poly all attempted to sell the holidays run by their parent companies. In the fourth scenario, 6 of the 9 agents asked about late availability pushed holidays belonging to their owners. Surprisingly, two Lunn Poly agencies and one Thomas Cook agency were keen to sell an Airtours holiday! This could possibly be explained by the fact that their parent tour operator just did not have any late availability.

The researchers were also asked to look for evidence of ownership links, either through printed material, or through communication with the agents themselves. Only 1 of the 36 researchers saw a sign indicating ownership (one Going Places agency had small signs on the computer indicating links to Airtours). In addition, only 3 of the agencies informed the mystery shoppers of their ownership ties. In these cases, the ownership was used as a selling tactic – "this is why we can offer you such a good deal on insurance" - said one agent.

With the telephone calls, the Lunn Poly agencies, owned by Thomson, the largest tour operator, were unbiased in the information and recommendations they provided. They all gave similar and very helpful answers to all questions asked of them, and at no time made an attempt to push the client towards a Thomson holiday. Their telephone manner was extremely friendly and professional indicating a high and consistent level of customer service training. In fact 93% of Lunn Poly agents offered completely unbiased information. Those few that did recommend a Thomson holiday did so in the last two scenarios, but this was only 3 from 20 agencies, and could have been based on product knowledge and preference rather than internal pressure to sell the Thomson product.

On the other hand the agencies from Going Places (owned by Airtours) and Thomas Cook or Carlson (linked to Thomas Cook), showed strong evidence of directional selling. In fact 95% of Going Places travel agents made an attempt to push the Airtours product, whilst not disclosing the identity of their owner. It was only when asked that they revealed (reluctantly) the name of the operator whose holiday they were recommending. Of those agencies linked to Thomas Cook, 80% employed directional selling tactics. Again, they did not freely admit the connection to the tour operators that they have links with, such as JMC, Thomas Cook Holidays and Inspirations.

Implications

The results from the mystery shopping exercise support the hypothesised model in Figure 2 for two of the vertically integrated companies, but not for the largest operator, Thomson and their travel agency chain, Lunn Poly. Thomson Travel Group have always claimed publicly that they do not have a sales policy of steering customers towards the purchase of Thomson Holidays, and this survey supported their claims. This contradicts results from a previous consumer group survey (Goldsmith, 1997) that suggested Thomson were just as guilty of directional selling as their competitors.

Customers entering a travel agent linked to Airtours and Thomas Cook, however, are likely to receive biased recommendations, and a distinct lack of choice. This means that these travel agents are much more likely to put the interests of large tour operators before the interests of consumers. Ultimately this could mean a consumer ending up on a package holiday unsuited to their needs, as well as being anti-competitive for the industry. Supporters of directional selling (and some have argued that it makes eminent business sense to control the chain of supply) suggest that the real issue is whether the consumer is being left to believe they are getting the best independent advice to suit their holiday needs. The mystery shoppers used for this piece of research did not believe they were receiving such advice except from the Lunn Poly agents.

The results also showed that the vertically integrated companies are not complying with Office of Fair Trading demands to make their ownership links more transparent. Both the vertically integrated companies that employed directional selling failed to disclose their ownership ties, and some were very reluctant to do so when asked. The Monopolies and Mergers Commission suggest that the lack of transparency means that consumers shop around less for holidays, with the result that there is less competitive pressure on travel agents. Consumers are therefore likely to get less value for money (MMC, 1998).

Methodologically, there were a few subtle differences between the mystery shopping visits as opposed to the telephone calls. For the visits in the first scenario, none of the agents attempted to switch-sell, but 12 of the 30 agents called by phone made an attempt to change the caller's plans. Perhaps in person, the travel agent saw more of an opportunity to close a sale and therefore did not want to confuse the customer. When they did attempt to direct the researcher towards their tour operator, the agents visited in person employed much more subtle tactics, often spending considerable time explaining why the customer should chose another product. This was the case even for the Lunn Poly agents who were reported to use less force than the other two chains. However, when called by telephone, the Lunn Poly agents were completely unbiased, and their telephone manner and professionalism indicated a high and consistent level of customer 'tele-sales' service training.

The study has also shown the advantages of direct observational data collection methods in the tourism sector. To date, the distinctive capabilities of observational methodologies for investigating services phenomena have not been widely recognised. Unfortunately, direct observation can be costly, time consuming and sometimes unfeasible. In this study, mystery shopping, whilst being extremely effective, was very time consuming. Concealed observation also raises concerns over the research's ethical nature. Whilst reducing the risk of 'unnatural' subject behaviour, concealed observation represents an unannounced intrusion, and may violate rights to privacy. In this study, the authors were sensitive to the ethical ramifications of mystery shopping, but recognised that to glean the most accurate information, it was necessary to employ a concealed observational approach.

Conclusion

In a mature package holiday market, shareholder demands for constantly-improved profits have left the vertically integrated tour operators with three choices. They can increase prices, but risk losing market share. Alternatively they can cut prices to gain market share, at the risk of also cutting earnings and perhaps sparking a price war. Another option is to ensure those who sell holidays sell their holidays rather than competitors, and that means buying distribution or influencing travel agents. For the time being it is clear that the big tour operators have chosen the latter tactic. This research has shown that two of the three largest vertically integrated travel companies in the U.K. actively employ directional selling tactics. It is not the purpose of this paper to suggest that this has an adverse affect on the consumer, and the travel industry in general, but the issue clearly requires further debate. More importantly, the study, and its use of mystery shopping as a powerful research technique, has highlighted the critical role that travel agents play in the decision process of consumers.

References

Bitner, M. J. and Booms, B. H. (1982), Trends in Travel and Tourism Marketing: The Changing Structure of Distribution Channels, *Journal of Travel Research*, 20 (4): 39-44.

Buckingham, L. (1999), Airtours Goes Back to the Singles Market, *The Guardian*, June 11, pp. 27.

Contant, J. S., Clark, T., Burnett, J. J., and Zank, G. (1988), Terrorism and Travel: Managing the Unmanageable, *Journal of Travel Research*, 26 (4): 16-20.

Gilbert, D. C., and Houghton, P. (1991), An Exploratory Investigation of Format, Design, and Use of U.K. Tour Operators' Brochures, *Journal of Travel Research*, 30 (2): 20-25.

Gitelson, R. J. and Crompton, J. L. (1983), The Planning Horizons and Sources of Information Used by Pleasure Vacationers, *Journal of Travel Research*, 21 (3): 2-7.

Goldsmith, N. (1997), Who's Taking You on Holiday? *Which?* May, pp. 8-10.

Goldsmith, R. E., Flynn, L. R., and Bonn, M. (1994), An Empirical Study of Heavy Users of Travel Agencies, *Journal of Travel Research*, 33 (1): 38-43.

Grove, S. J. and Fisk, R. (1992), Observational Data Collection Methods for Services Marketing: An Overview, *Journal of the Academy of Marketing Science*, 20 (3): 217-224.

Hodgson, P. (1993), Tour Operator Brochure Design Research Revisited, *Journal of Travel Research*, 32 (1): 50-52.

Hsieh, S., and O'Leary, J. T. (1993), Communication Channels to Segment Pleasure Travellers, *Journal of Travel and Tourism Marketing*, 2 (2and3): 57-75.

Howard, J. A. (1963), *Marketing Management* (2nd ed.). Homewood IL: Irwin Publishing.

Kendall, K. W., and Booms, B. H. (1989), Consumer Perceptions of Travel Agencies: Communications, Images, Needs, and Expectations, *Journal of Travel Research*, 27 (4): 29-37.

Klenosky, D. B., and Gitelson, R. E. (1998), Travel Agents' Destination Recommendations, *Annals of Tourism Research*, 25 (3): 661-674.

Laskey, H. A., Seaton, B., and Nicholls, J. A. (1994), Effects of Strategy and Pictures in Travel Agency Advertising, *Journal of Travel Research*, 32 (4): 13-19.

Michie, D. A., and Sullivan, G.L. (1990), The Role(s) of the International Travel Agent in the Travel Decision Process of Client Families, *Journal of Travel Research*, 29 (2): 30-38.

Mintel. (1999), *Inclusive Tours*, Mintel International Group Limited: London.

Monopolies and Mergers Commission. (1998), *Foreign Package Holidays*. HMSO.

Morrall, K. (1994), Mystery Shopping Tests Service and Compliance, *Bank Marketing*, 26 (2): 13-23.

Peter, J. P. P., and Olson, J. C. (1993), *Consumer Behaviour and Marketing Strategy*, Homewood IL: Irwin.

Snepenger, D., Meged, K., Snelling, M., and Worrall, K. (1990), Information Search Strategies by Destination-Naive Tourists, *Journal of Travel Research*, 29 (1): 13-16.

Solomon, M.R. (1986), The Missing Link: Surrogate Consumers in the Marketing Chain, *Journal of Marketing*, 50 (4): 208-218.

Walle, A. H. (1997), Quantitative Versus Qualitative Research, *Annals of Tourism Research*, 24 (3): 524-536.

Wilson, A. M. (1998), The Use of Mystery Shopping in the Measurement of Service Delivery, *The Service Industries Journal*, 18 (3): 148-163.

The incorporation of historically disadvantaged communities into tourism initiatives in the new South Africa: Case studies from KwaZulu-Natal

Heather Hughes

University of Natal, South Africa

Anne Vaughan

University of Durban-Westville, South Africa

Introduction

Since 1994, the South African state has justly accredited many previously neglected black communities with a historical significance they previously held only in very fragmented or stunted ways. There have, for example, been a number of new monuments and sites declared as 'national treasures' in such areas in the six years since the 1994 democratic elections. Moreover, in terms of current national policy, the cultural and historical importance of many of these communities is held to constitute the principal means through which local economic development will occur. Translated into practice, this means the development of tourism potential. There is, of course, no *necessary* connection between history/heritage and tourism, but that is the connection being made strongly in South Africa today - indeed, globally - in terms of policy-making[1]. Tourism in this sense is a political issue, signalling a particular kind of state intervention in order to reach particular kinds of objectives. Thus, we present an account of policy and trends concerning the tourism sector in South Africa by way of introduction to the case studies we present from the province of KwaZulu-Natal.

Our main case studies in this paper are Inanda and Cato Manor, two historically significant localities within the Durban area. We also include comment from two other cases, Wentworth in Durban and Richmond/Ixopo in rural KwaZulu-Natal. Most of these studies arise out of an involvement in planning historical and cultural preservation strategies, as consultants to public local and regional bodies. Our observations therefore stem from the experiences of direct participation in the processes described, and we try to reflect on the processes involved. We outline what each of the areas has to offer in terms of community-based tourism potential and what the plans are for future development. Finally, we draw attention to some of the perceived obstacles and contradictions in the process of launching community-based tourism in these areas.

Community tourism in the new South Africa: The policy framework

In 1996, the South African Government adopted the *White paper on the development and promotion of tourism* as South Africa's official tourism policy. This document identifies tourism as a priority for national economic development and a major stimulus of the government's Growth, Employment and Redistribution (GEAR) strategy.[2] (*White paper*: 1996)

In terms of GEAR, the aim for tourism development has been to increase the market share of tourism from 4.5% (1996 figure) to 8% by the end of 2000. This target is meant to be achieved by attracting a much higher proportion of international visitors from Europe and North/South America (in 1996, these formed only 15% and 12% respectively, the remainder coming from other parts of Africa), as well as stimulating the emerging domestic market.[3]

Three basic principles underpin the implementation of this aim: that 'tourism should be government led', in the sense that the state should articulate efficient policies and allocate appropriate funding to the sector; that tourism will be driven by the private sector, 'primarily directed by the principles of demand and supply'; and that tourism should be community based. ('Tourism in GEAR': 1997)

A definition of what actually constitutes 'community-based tourism' is not clearly defined and has to be derived from information contained in the *White paper*. There would seem to be two basic elements to such a definition:

- Participation of local communities in tourism ventures, particularly where such communities have been economically disadvantaged as a result of apartheid policies. 'Participation' here can cover a wide variety of activities, including jobs in the tourism sector and involvement in SMMEs (Small, Medium and Micro-Enterprises) associated with tourism;

- Local people must have a meaningful ownership of tourism initiatives, and must participate in decision-making about the nature and development of tourism opportunities in their communities – again, with special emphasis on historically neglected communities.

The reason that community-based tourism receives heavy emphasis in the *White paper* is that the tourism sector is considered to be unique in its potential for incorporating previously neglected communities into mainstream economic development. The reasons are that it is labour-intensive, employs a vast range of skills, but not necessarily of a very high order, and creates multiple opportunities for SMME entrepreneurship. The White paper identifies a large number of examples of the kinds of opportunities for community involvement, such as operators of infrastructure (guest houses, taxis, struggle sites); services (guides, bookings); and suppliers (production and sale of craft, construction and maintenance). It also acknowledges the huge difficulties to be overcome in community-based initiatives, such as a lack of awareness, information or training, lack of access to finance, lack of immediate incentive, and so on. (*White paper* 1996: 8-9)

The *White paper* clearly outlines the new public institutional arrangements for tourism development at national and provincial level. Tourism in the new South Africa is a 'dual power' – that is, it is shared by central and provincial government, and funding is allocated accordingly. Thus, there is a national Department of Environmental Affairs and Tourism, which sets the parameters of national policy, and each of the nine provinces has a tourism portfolio, which must be exercised in accordance with national policy. (The province of KwaZulu-Natal has a Department of Economic Affairs and Tourism.) Also in line with this framework, the old national tourism organisation, the South African Tourism Organisation, which had offices abroad as well as in each of the four pre-1994 provinces, has been revitalised as an instrument for marketing South Africa abroad, with added research and development functions. Each of the nine provinces now has its own distinctive tourism body – for example, the KwaZulu-Natal Tourism Authority (KZNTA). Provincial bodies mirror the addition of more proactive functions to the traditional marketing ones.

In line with its development function, KZNTA has elaborated a community-based tourism strategy and has produced a series of 'How to' pamphlets (How to open a tavern, establish a community tourism office, etc), but marketing the province remains the emphasis of its operations (as envisaged by the White Paper). Its current marketing campaign is centred on the slogan 'Wozani [come], our kingdom calls' – playing on the powerful association of the region with the history of the Zulu kingdom. Visually, the campaign uses the actor Henry Cele, who played the role of Shaka, the first Zulu king, in the local and highly popular television drama in the early 1990s. Around this central theme of the Zulu kingdom, the KZNTA has clustered 'the five Bs' of tourism attractions in the province: Beaches, Berg, Battlefields, Bush and Buzz.[4] The KZNTA's own analysis of tourism target markets suggests that while domestic tourism is well-established in terms of 'Beach, Berg and Bush', it is very largely foreign visitors who are interested in the 'Battlefields' – that is, in the unique history and culture of the province. This is key for community-based tourism: relying as it does (as noted in the introduction) on history and culture, it would seem particularly dependent on an increasing volume of foreign visitors.

The different levels of government - provincial, regional and local - have a more direct responsibility in facilitating community tourism development than the Tourism Authority. Assistance from the provincial department is available for: promoting the development of tourism-orientated SMMEs, facilitating 'stakeholder' workshops and training in a variety of tourism-related skills, and facilitating research into the development of new tourism assets. The provincial department has also taken the important step of initiating a legislative framework that would be supportive of community-based tourism. (Rutsch et al 1999)

The local levels, however, are the ones most immediately responsible for community tourism development: regional councils in rural areas and local government structures in towns and cities.[5] These structures assist financially with road signage and brochures, setting up Community Tourism Offices (refurbishment of accommodation, equipment and training) and provide bulk infrastructure to facilitate tourism development (e.g. road upgrading, installation of car parks, street lighting), and promote tourism-related local economic development. An important element in local government's approach to tourism development – in the light of a redefinition of its role as facilitator rather than owner/provider - is to facilitate partnership arrangements with private enterprise. A growing trend in this regard is for local government to set up a dedicated development arm under the aegis of a section 21 (not for profit) company. (MXA 2000: 1)

Our case studies: Cato Manor and Inanda

One of the most common ways in which tour operators have approached the issue of incorporating historically disadvantaged communities into tourism development has been to offer 'the township tour'. Typically, this includes a visit to a shebeen/tavern, a cultural display (such as traditional dancing) and a creche or a similar small-scale educational or welfare facility, where donations can be made. Since Cato Manor and Inanda each possess a unique and historic significance in their own right, it seemed possible, in elaborating strategies for tourism development, to avoid this categorisation of 'township tour'.

Of all the areas within reach of the Durban city centre, Inanda would seem the one to offer most potential for the kind of tourism envisaged in the *White paper*. Located some 30km to the north west of the city centre and now one of the largest urban informal settlements in the country, Inanda has in its past nurtured a number of leaders of both national and international significance, reflected in the different sites that are potential tourist attractions. These are:

Phoenix, where Mahatma Gandhi established his original ashram in 1903, and where he worked out his philosophy of self-restraint and passive resistance. Indian South Africans first used these methods in 1907 and 1913, in campaigns to protest against discrimination. These same methods were later extremely effective in the struggle for independence in India. His original house was razed in the violence which swept Inanda, as so many other black urban areas, in the mid-1980s. Much of the original farm was thereafter occupied by shack dwellers; fierce and protracted violence between followers of different political parties delayed a settlement until very recently. The Phoenix Trust has ceded most of the land to housing development, but the apex of land on which the original buildings stand will be developed as a visitor centre. Gandhi's house, after long and painstaking research, was rebuilt exactly according to the original design in February this year, and re-opened by President Mbeki in the same month. Gandhi's granddaughter, Ela Gandhi (now a Member of Parliament) will move back to the apex, into another renovated property, later in the year.

Ohlange is an educational institution of some note only about 4 kilometres from Phoenix. This was the first African-run and largely African-funded school in southern Africa, founded by John Langalibalele Dube in 1901. Dube also established the newspaper *Ilanga lase Natal* here in 1903, and went on to become the first president of the African National Congress in 1912. As a token of Dube's struggle for justice in South Africa, Nelson Mandela chose Ohlange to cast his vote in the 1994 election.

Inanda Seminary, the first secondary school for African girls in southern Africa was founded in 1869 by missionaries of the American Board. It has produced many women leaders in various fields, including several sitting MPs.

Ebuhleni, the headquarters of the AmaNazaretha, or Shembe, church, founded by the famous prophet Isaiah Shembe (1870-1935), KwaZulu-Natal's best-known prophet. Isaiah Shembe, Shembe founded his original holy place at Ekuphakameni ('Place of Upliftment'), in 1916, very close to both Phoenix and Ohlange. Shembe experienced many visions as a child, and in 1906 when he joined the African Baptist Church, he was already widely known as a healer. He broke away in 1911 to form his own church, the AmaNazaretha. Today it is by far the largest independent church in the region. The doctrines, hymns, dress, rituals and ceremonies of the AmaNazaretha are extremely intricate and elaborate. The prophet died in 1935; he had designated his sons Galilee and Amos to succeed him, but the exact nature of their succession, complicated by legal problems over the status of the church, led to severe divisions and splits within the church. These grew so severe by the 1980s that a majority of followers left to establish a new church centre at Ebuhleni, also in Inanda but about 15 km further to the north west.

The most obvious form of tourism development for this area seemed to be a trail incorporating these sites. In order for local people to become involved in the development of the trail, the establishment of a Community Tourism Office was recommended, employing two local residents, as were the identification of local tour operators and guides who would be available to conduct the tour. It was also suggested that an awareness campaign be mounted among Inanda residents as to the possible benefits of this form of local development, since there would be opportunities for the sale of craft and the provision of other services should the trail take off. Further – since all the sites required some refurbishment – local contractors were suggested for this work.

The Durban metropolitan council was very quick to act on the recommendations, and the Community Tourism Office was opened in November 1998. An Inanda Development Committee was established to move the tourism initiative forwards. However, there was something of a 'chicken and egg' problem: until refurbishment work and a local awareness campaign were complete, little custom could be attracted; until customers were forthcoming, the Community Tourism Office had little to do, and potential tour operators had to find other forms of livelihood. The Tourism Office staff was soon requesting the relocation of the Office to central Durban.

Cato Manor portrays a very different kind of history. Like District Six in Cape Town and Sophiatown in Johannesburg, Cato Manor has come to symbolise the vibrancy and cultural richness that characterised self-made urban black communities until their destruction by the apartheid state in the 1950s and 1960s. Cato Manor is only 3km from the Durban central business district, and was originally alienated as a settler farm in the 1850s. By the early part of this century, the white owners had sub-divided and ex-indentured Indian families, who turned to vegetable production, settled there. Many acquired land of their own before the Second World War, and the many beautiful temples still standing in Cato Manor testify to a flourishing community spirit. The war was a watershed in Cato Manor's history. Due to war conditions, many African people came to live in Durban. Since there was no municipal housing available, they rented shacks in Cato Manor and so began the dense urbanisation of the farm. The pace and nature of urbanisation resulted in many social tensions, and in 1949 Cato Manor was the storm centre of extremely destructive African-Indian race riots. Cato Manor existed for only another decade: the new Nationalist government was determined to 'clear' this prime area for white development, and by the early 1960s, all the African residents had been relocated to townships on Durban's peripheries and most of the buildings destroyed.

The anticipated 'white' development did not, however occur: many Indian land owners clung on tenaciously, and no-one wanted to take the risk of moving into an area so hotly contested. Much of Cato Manor therefore lay fallow, unused, until the early 1980s, when, in its attempts to woo some black support, the apartheid regime ceded a small amount of land back to Indian ownership. Some sub-economic housing was constructed, but events of the early 1990s overtook any planned development: many homeless African families, desperate for a solution to their particular demands, occupied the partially completed houses and many others re-established an informal settlement, currently housing about 40 000 people.

In 1993, all public bodies – the central government, the province, the Durban municipality – handed their interests to an organisation tasked with the re-development of Cato Manor, the Cato Manor Development Association. After the 1994 elections, Cato Manor was declared a 'presidential lead' project, and received huge capital injections from central government and the European Union. The CMDA remains in charge of the planning and development of this area, which, once completed, will have to be reincorporated into the local government structures of the city.

Cato Manor thus represents very much a 'people's history': no great names or famous leaders, but the story of how ordinary people struggled to establish a foothold in or around the city. Because so much of the built environment was destroyed, it seemed that the most useful strategy for tourism would be the construction of a Community Heritage Centre, where the area's history could be portrayed, where local craftspeople could display their skills and sell their wares and where community facilities such as a performance venue could offer a variety of local entertainment. (The European Community has agreed to fund the construction of the heritage centre.) Both because of its geographic centrality and because it encapsulates so many of the themes of 20th century regional history, Cato Manor has the potential to develop as a destination for school tours, and is therefore not as dependent on foreign visitors as many other such areas are.

Taking community-based tourism forward

Having outlined the 'big picture' for tourism development in each of these areas, this section focuses on three key issues: local institutional frameworks to launch and sustain tourism; market analysis and marketing strategies, and the conditions for sustainable tourism development.

Institutional arrangements to orchestrate tourism development

In the cases of both Inanda and Cato Manor, the establishment of a locally based legal entity to drive tourism development was recommended. The recommended formal institution in both cases is a Section 21 Company. The choice of a Section 21 Company for the Inanda tourism project was strongly influenced by existing support for this legal form among local community-based organisations (the Inanda Development Forum and its affiliates, for example). The IDF was in turn, influenced by views emanating from the KwaZulu-Natal Department of Economic Affairs and Tourism favouring Section 21 Companies for community tourism initiatives in urban areas, and Community Trusts for tourism development in rural contexts. In essence, the proposed legal form was simply a ratification of popular opinion, and provincial policy. However, there was a fortunate consonance between local opinion and rational choice. Factors which suggested that a Section 21 Company would be the most appropriate form were private ownership of the major local tourism assets, the need for a spread of representation within the legal entity, and the facilitative role the entity would be required to play - for example, accessing donor funding for projects and events, lobbying local and provincial government for tourism-related development resources, acting as an interface between potential investors and local business partners, and promoting safety and security.

Arriving at a recommendation for a legal entity in the case of Cato Manor was more difficult. There were several reasons for this. First, given the need for the recreation (rather than the rebuilding) of tourism assets, the Business Plan phases tourism development in Cato Manor over a longer period with the existing development agency taking responsibility for an initial set of programmes. The recommended institution would come into being only in the latter phases of the tourism project. Secondly, appropriate institutional arrangements for the management of physical assets incorporating publicly supported elements and private enterprises were required. Thirdly, trends in local government, and the future role of the CMDA had to be considered. Trends in local government and the inevitable winding down of the role of the development agency suggested the need for an autonomous and self-sustaining entity. The ultimate recommendation was for the same legal form as proposed for Inanda, but for vastly different reasons. In Cato Manor, the issue of getting a spread of representation is as important as it is in Inanda, so a Section 21 Company was an appropriate choice for this common reason.

Fragmented, divided or weak community leadership, the absence of civil society or a culture of citizenship, and powerful vested interests in informal settlements can potentially undermine local micro institutions established to manage community assets and promote development. These factors also make it difficult to draw individuals, households and communities into development initiatives. These issues are discussed in the last section of the paper.

Marketing tourism in disadvantaged areas

Analysis of the tourism market was the basis for the marketing strategies recommended for both the case study areas. Key issues which emerged from the analysis in the Inanda case are that:

- it would be a mistake to be over-optimistic about what the area has to offer. A sudden huge influx of tourists, international or domestic, should not be anticipated. A projection of how many tourists will visit Inanda cannot be 'read off' from existing statistics.

- domestic demand for the type of tourism which Inanda has to offer is extremely difficult to assess. There is a big discrepancy between the numbers of domestic tourists who actually visit the sorts of sites and attractions that Inanda would offer, and the number who say they would be interested in doing so. Also, there is a contradiction between what recent survey data suggest, and the on-the-ground experience of tour operators. Poor marketing may be a partial explanation for the discrepancies and contradictions. But other factors are also likely to account for these. The data collected for the KwaZulu-Natal Tourism Authority reveal that a very small proportion of domestic tourists is (as earlier suggested) interested in historical sites - or travels on organised tours. Most travel independently. Many tourists do not feel safe in KwaZulu-Natal. A combination of these factors may explain why so few domestic tourists visit townships. Given perceptions of low levels of safety, many domestic visitors would not consider going to a township or an informal settlement in their own vehicles on an ad hoc and spontaneous basis. Organised tours, which promise a reasonable degree of security are, however, out of the domestic ambit.

- the high volume 'package' market is generally tied up for at least eighteen months in advance. To get a product marketed as part of a 'package' which is booked and paid for in the country of origin will necessarily be a long term process.

- it may be necessary to re-package a tourism product in response to shifts in supply and demand. If the market for a product becomes saturated, it will be necessary to consider how the product can be re-created, perhaps through taking a different angle, perhaps through adding new elements. Although market saturation may have been a problem which some operators have experienced in relation to township tours, it is less likely to be a problem for the Inanda tour. The jewel in the crown of the Inanda tour, the Phoenix Settlement, should, if restored and reconstructed, offer an internationally valued experience.

In promoting and marketing tourism in Inanda, the different perspectives of government and government-linked bodies, and the established industry should be borne in mind. From the point of view of government, the possibility of developing tourism in Inanda seems to be the answer to an unsaid prayer. Criticism has been levelled at government, and perhaps more particularly at tourism bodies, for concentrating on already established tourism assets and attractions, and for failing to develop the unrealised potential in more peripheral areas. Inanda offers an opportunity to make good, and to address the failures. However, from the point of view of the industry, Inanda is an interesting option which may or may not fly in the market place, depending on a host of factors, including the effectiveness of local government support, and the security situation.

In the case of Cato Manor, there is a much stronger emphasis on local and domestic markets. As already noted, because of Cato Manor's central location and easy accessibility, school tours could be encouraged as a basic income-generating activity. Schools do have allocations for pupil outings, and it is felt that this could be a worthwhile niche to develop: no other historically oppressed area has yet done so, and the opportunity would seem to be wide open. (This would be one of the tasks for the Community Tourism Office, once it is set up.) Moreover, if school-goers enjoy their visit, they are the best advertisements to others -

family and friends - to try it out. Again, in the evenings, cultural events could be mounted which would attract a local clientele. For example, jazz is very popular in Durban, and is a key to the cultural history of this area. This approach - establishing and keeping local visitors to various events and sites - is felt to be central to any stable economic development in the heritage/tourism sector. Establishing and keeping local visitors will be crucial for the economic viability of the Community Heritage Centre.

Although local support is critical to the viability of the proposed Community Heritage Centre, the custom of international and domestic tourists is also needed. Standard marketing strategies, for example, marketing through the public bodies responsible for the promotion of tourism in the province and in the city - the KZNTA and Durban Africa, will be fairly effective for both domestic and foreign markets. The wide distribution of promotional literature and reciprocal marketing arrangements with publicity associations and community tourism offices in the City, and in other centres would also be worthwhile.

Significant for tourism development in both Inanda and Cato Manor is the profile of Durban as a tourism destination. What is really significant is that the length of stay in Durban is relatively short - 65% of foreign visitors stay for three nights or less. This suggests that Durban is a stopover rather than a destination, as is asserted by many tour operators. As in the case of domestic tourists, what is also significant is a discrepancy between what people did and what they expressed interest in doing. Sadly, Durban did not rate that highly in the eyes of foreign respondents. Just over half rated it as good, 38% as fair, and more than 8% rated it as poor. The implications of these facts are that the success of tourism in Cato Manor will depend partly on an improved image for Durban as a destination, and that there is a large residual market for Cato Manor's attractions.

Ensuring sustainability

There are a number of pre-conditions for sustainable tourism development in Inanda. These are the development, reconstruction and restoration of the primary sites and attractions; infrastructural improvements and the provision of facilities at these sites and attractions; and ensuring the safety and security of tourists and tourism-related enterprises.

Economic sustainability will derive from a successful, albeit very modest start-up. Political sustainability will depend on the local credibility and legitimacy of the Tourism Project, which, in turn, will hinge on local ownership. Local people must have a real stake in tourism development in terms of economic benefits. The transparent and effective functioning of the Section 21 Company is a fundamental condition for institutional sustainability. Also, Tourism in Inanda must be integrated into the public framework for tourism development. For tourism development to be socially sustainable, it should enhance the quality of life of local people in visible ways. Tourism nodes should be integrated into the social fabric of the area. Many established tour operators are keen to contribute to community development., and should be requested to sponsor social projects. Sustaining the integrity of the environment will involve the provision of adequate services throughout Inanda, and the promotion of environmental awareness.

In the case of Cato Manor, ensuring sustainability poses a somewhat different challenge. The project to develop Cato Manor initiated in the early 1990s has been very controversial.

Established largely middle class communities living on the peripheries of Cato Manor have been alienated. People who have moved into the informal settlements during the 1990s have divergent interests. Some have fled from violence-torn areas, and are desperate for housing and services. Others are living in Cato Manor because they want to be close to town. Some people do not want development because this will mean an end to lucrative informal arrangements, and may imply an increase in living costs. Community-based organisations have been established in Cato Manor. The Development Committees (which were set up by a CMDA Board sub-committee) are supposed to facilitate development, and act as mechanisms for various development agents to interface with communities. Development Committees in the informal settlements are least stable. On the other hand, there seems to be a lack of commitment in the formal areas. Power struggles in some neighbourhoods leads to discontinuity in the leadership and membership of Development Committees. This is the somewhat difficult social, political and institutional context for attempting to ensure project sustainability. Community membership of the Section 21 Company, local employment in tourism enterprises, affordable access to the proposed Community Heritage Centre and the proposed oral history project will play a role in building community ownership of the tourism initiative, and in ensuring sustainability. However, there is a critical relationship between sustainability and micro institutional and community development. An institutional fabric that can sustain broad initiatives and contribute to the maintenance of community assets must be created. In the case of Cato Manor, this is a specially difficult issue which impacts on a range of assets and initiatives. For example, all the public property in the area will not be developed by the time the CMDA has completed its work, so an issue which needs to be confronted is how the property portfolio will be handled. Decisions will also need to be made about long term investment funds. Institutional and management arrangements need to be put in place for the shopping centre, the proposed industrial areas, and the proposed Community Heritage Centre.

Contradictions and obstacles

In this final section, we explore and reiterate the main perceived problems confronting the viability of community tourism.

The first is the question of who takes responsibility for community-based tourism. As suggested above, the *White paper* holds that tourism development must be 'government-led and market-driven'. The incorporation of historically disadvantaged communities into tourism – or any other form of economic development - is essentially a measure of 'social justice', designed to overcome the huge inequalities of the past by stimulating business opportunities and employment in the areas where people live. Measures to ensure social justice do not often obey the laws of supply and demand, and require large-scale commitments of public funding. Yet, as everywhere in the world, the state – at all levels - is simultaneously committed to privatisation and outsourcing (i.e. minimum intervention). Compounding the difficulties in South Africa has been the extensive institutional transformation consequent upon democratisation. We are still in an early phase of this process, which currently is characterised by a high degree of uncertainty over who is responsible for what, and by a sometimes confusing degree of overlap in functions between different institutions in the public and private sectors. Community- based tourism will sink under the contradictions unless some clear policy resolution is forthcoming.

Another difficulty arises from the very real disadvantage at which most neglected communities find themselves. Perry Anderson has recently mounted a criticism of populist thinking that applies to much developmental policy thinking in South Africa today:

> *What populism typically means today is faking an equality of condition – between voters, readers or viewers – that does not exist, the better to pass over actual inequalities of knowledge or literacy: ground on which a cynical right and pious left all too easily meet.* (Anderson 2000: 21)

The fundamental inequalities noted by Anderson are rarely taken fully into account. Rhetoric about participation, consultation and 'stakeholders' masks fundamental questions about whether individuals or communities are able to take up what are proffered as economic opportunities. There are, often, no real 'stakeholders', not because there is a lack of enthusiasm or willingness, but because the basic skills to articulate demands of the state, or to begin the process of entering the market as an SMME, are non-existent.

The creation of sustainable local institutions relates directly to the question of citizenship. This is because a base of citizenship is a pre-condition for the emergence of community leaders who can play a role in sustaining micro institutions. In Cato Manor, for example, a cadre of local people who can take responsibility for public property and community assets does not yet exist. Part of the reason for this is that the population comprised refugees from violence-torn areas for whom relations of patronage have always been a condition of existence. In the Cato Manor context, it has been exceptionally difficult to build civil society. Furthermore, the development agency's own approach to building citizenship has been flawed. The focus has been on building community structures and organisations (which remain weak and divided) instead of concentrating resources on civic education. However, behind these issues which are specific to Cato Manor, lies a basic dilemma: physical planning precedes – indeed, frequently occurs in the absence of - social planning and the development of associations, skills, and training, to ensure the continuation and growth of initiatives beyond the initial phases.

If community tourism development is thought of as solving some of South Africa's most pressing needs, then there are basically two real means for local people to take advantage of it. One is through employment opportunities – in hotels, restaurants, cultural sites, etc. The other is to establish small companies to provide goods and services to the tourism sector. The latter is in many senses more empowering, and has the capacity to spread greater benefits within historically neglected areas. Yet there is much glib discussion about SMMEs. Two case studies, drawn from Cato Manor and Inanda, illustrate the enormous difficulties that individuals confront in trying to break into community tourism development.

Mr Tabete is an emerging tour operator who lives in Wiggins in Cato Manor, who started his business in 1996. He is accredited by the KZNTA, and has a base at the Thekweni Business Development Centre. He does not own a vehicle. Suitable vehicles are hired from taxi owners with whom the tour operator has developed an understanding (rental for a vehicle is in the region of R400 for half a day). The frequency of tours depends on the season. Sometimes a tour will be run once a week, but tours may be run much less frequently. Half-day tours of Cato Manor, or of Cato Manor and the City, cost R160. (The operator regards the fee as on the modest side, but, in fact, the rate is rather more than the average for a half-day City tour.) The operator was assisted by the KZNTA to participate in the recent Tourism Indaba (a fair for the tourism industry) held in Durban, where he was able to arrange a school tour. He is interested in conducting school tours in future, and plans to market his products through writing to school principals. Yet business is, and has been since 1996, very slow: he cannot rely on this form of livelihood alone.

Mr Tabete faces a number of constraints in attempting to establish a tour operating business. He does not have the resources to produce better advertising material, and, in any event, is not permitted to place material at the porters' desks at the major hotels. He lacks the capital to acquire his own vehicle. He misses many business opportunities because reliance on hiring taxis means that he is unable to respond immediately to requests for tours. (Although he has reliable contacts in the taxi industry, it is not always possible to get a suitable vehicle at short notice.) Business may also be lost if the operator does not arrive on time at an appointed place. Inability to respond quickly to market opportunities means few customers, a low level operation, and a negligible market presence. Despite constant enquiry, the operator was not successful in becoming a member of Durban Africa, the body that markets the city of Durban, or in registering with a travel agency. An added difficulty is that the office which he rents at the Thekweni Business Development Centre does not have a telephone, so he is unable to communicate directly with clients. (He said 'Call backs are not a successful way of operating.') Although he could seek employment with one of the larger operators as a step-on guide, he would prefer to establish his own business.

The way in which Thuthuka Tours and Travel in Inanda operates is also instructive in illustrating the real constraints faced by emerging tourism SMMEs. This business was set up in 1998 by two brothers belonging to the Dube family. While they do have their own vehicle, and are better-resourced in terms of communication, the business does not *and cannot depend* on operating the Inanda tour. The tour is just one facet of a business which offers an array of services to a range of clients - transport of workers from the International Convention Centre, and a shuttle service to and from the airport for guests at the Hilton Hotel. The point is that diversification is essential for such operators – and while this can ensure survival, it can also stand in the way of their ability to focus on business opportunities, marketing strategies and so on.

Conclusion

Community-based tourism offers to policy-makers and communities alike a powerful means for the incorporation of economically disempowered people into mainstream economic development in the new South Africa. Yet the many difficulties we have identified in our paper will have to be confronted and addressed before this form of activity can deliver on its many promises.

Endnotes

1. This connection does of course raise questions about the relationship between history and heritage, and about the notion of 'authenticity' in tourist experiences. While these are important issues, they are not addressed directly in this paper, whose focus is somewhat different.

2. GEAR replaced the overall economic development strategy of the 1994 Government of National Unity, the Reconstruction and Development Plan (RDP), which was based on a proactive role for the state and of extensive state spending. GEAR is predicated on a greater private sector involvement, and is accordingly somewhat more conciliatory towards the role of capital in the new South Africa.

3. It is doubtful that this target will be achieved: in the last year, hotel occupancies have declined by 8%, the first time since 1994. The fall is attributable mainly to nervousness over Y2K problems and the unstable situation in Zimbabwe: most tour packages to South Africa include a stop-over at the Victoria Falls. (Sunday Tribune Business Report, 4 June 2000)

4. This is a play on the slogan 'Big Five', meaning the species of big game that tourists most want to see in Africa's game reserves. In this provincial context, 'Berg' refers to the Drakensberg mountains, which rise in places to over 15000 feet; 'Battlefields' to the Anglo-Zulu war of 1879 and the South African War of 1899-1902; and 'Bush' largely to the province's famed game reserves and other wildlife habitats: the Greater St Lucia wetland was declared a World Heritage Site in 1999; and 'Buzz' to urban attractions.

5. At the moment, these structures have not been finalised. A process of urban demarcation is nearly complete, and there is a notable commitment to the development of a 'Unicity' in the Durban area, but elsewhere many are still known as 'transitional local councils'.

References

Anderson, P. (2000), Renewals, *New Left Review*, Jan/Feb.

Futter, M. and L. Wood, (1997), *Tourism Monitor, Indicator* 14, 2

Government of South Africa, (1996), White paper on the development and promotion of tourism.

Government of South Africa, (1996), Tourism white paper implementing strategy and action plan.

Government of South Africa, (1997), Tourism in GEAR.

Hall, C. M. and Jenkins, J. (1995), *Tourism and public policy*, London, Routledge.

Hughes, H. (1989), 'A lighthouse for African womanhood': Inanda Seminary, 1869-1945, Walker, C, (Ed) *Women and gender in southern Africa to 1945, Cape Town, and London*, David Philip and James Currey, 97-220.

Hughes, H. (1987), Violence in Inanda, August 1985, *Journal of Southern African Studies* 13 (3): 331-354.

Hughes, H (1996),The city closes in: the incorporation of Inanda into metropolitan Durban, Maylam, P. and I. Edwards (Eds), *A people's city. African life in twentieth-century Durban*, Pietermaritzburg, University of Natal Press.

Hughes, H. (2000), The Tourism Potential of Indlovu Regional Council Sub-Region 3, Report for the Indlovu Regional Council.

Johnson, P. and Thomas, B. (Eds), (1993), *Perspectives on tourism policy*, London, Mansell.

KwaZulu-Natal Tourism Authority, (2000), *A strategy for tourism in KwaZulu-Natal.*

Laws, E. (1995), *Tourist destination management: issues, analysis and policies*, London, Routledge.

Mackintosh, Xaba and Associates [MXA] (2000), *Best practices newsletter*, May.

Middleton, V. T. C. (1998), *Sustainable tourism: a marketing perspective*, Butterworth, Heinemann.

Pearce, D. (1992), *Tourist organisations*, London, Longman.

Rutsch, P. et al (1999), A review of legislation having an impact on community-based tourism, Prepared for the Department of Economic Affairs and Tourism, KZN.

Smith, S. L. (1989), *Tourism analysis: a handbook*, London, Longman.

Surplus People Project, (1983), *Forced removals in South Africa: Natal*, SPP.

Teo, P. and Yeoh, B.S.A. (1997), Remaking local heritage for tourism, *Annals of Tourism Research*, 24,1.

Timothy, D. J. (1999), Participatory planning: a view of tourism in Indonesia, *Annals of Tourism Research*, 26,2.

Vaughan, A., F. Pupuma, and Hughes, H. (1999), *An historical and cultural preservation strategy for Greater Cato Manor*, Prepared for the Cato Manor Development Association by consultants of MXA.

Vaughan, A., F. Pupuma, McCann, M. and Hughes, H. (1999), Inanda Tourism Development Business Plan, Prepared for Tourism Durban and the Inanda Development Forum by consultants of MXA.

Internationalisation of Norwegian tourism management

Qadeer Hussain and Reidar J Mykletun

Stavanger College, Norway

Abstract

A greater internationalisation has taken place in tourism services, and international tourism corporations are playing a major role in this process. Many of the previous studies have focused on international manufacturing organisations and less research has been directed towards the activities and participation of international tourism corporations both in services in general and tourism services in particular. Changes have taken place in the Norwegian tourism industry as well. Some Norwegian tourism-related studies have been made on tourism in general, and their focus has been mainly the planning of tourism, the inflows and outflows of tourists, and tourism economics. What has not been studied is the role and the importance of the management factor in the process of internationalisation of tourism-related corporations.

This management factor plays a basic and vital role in the direction of the internationalisation issue, since managers are the ultimate decision-makers in internationalisation of tourist organisations and tourism related services. These managers are engaged in industries such as hotel, travel agency business, and transport, including air travel among others. The internationalisation of industry requires an international-oriented overall management (from top to lower-level management). In this respect, it will be interesting to find out the management's internationalisation orientation in various tourism-related industries. The focus of this study is the internationalisation orientation of Norwegian tourism-related management. The research provides some answers to issues such as the trends in management internationalisation, the levels of management international orientation among various tourism-related corporations, and the importance of internationalisation for the Norwegian tourism industry.

For this study, various sources are used for data collection and the most important investigative technique employed is a questionnaire survey. Both qualitative and quantitative approaches are used to analyse the data. Researchers in tourism; the tourism policy makers, like governments and public sector boards; tourism-related international, national and regional organisations; national hospitality promoting organisations; and the management decision-makers themselves may benefit from this research.

The study shows that internationalisation of Norwegian tourism management has already begun. Many of the tourism-related managers tend to become more international-oriented. The study also shows that most of the tourism management has been regional and national-oriented but their focus is becoming more international-oriented.

Introduction

The internationalisation of the tourism industry is expected to continue to grow over the years. The role of the international tourism-related corporations is expected to grow to a greater extent. Due to this greater internationalisation of tourism-related corporations, the role of the management would be changing. For internationalisation of the tourism industry, international-oriented management is required. In fact, senior management's involvement is required for international market decisions. It is the management who makes decisions regarding process and timing of internationalisation and the types of market entries to be used for various markets.

Trends in internationalisation

Some of the internationalisation development issues may be outlined. A greater internationalisation is taking place in the industry of tourism. The tourism industry has become one of the largest industries and has become one of the greater sources of income for many nations. The global earning from international tourism increased by an average of 9 per cent annually for the past 16 years and it reached US$423 billion in 1996 (WTO 1999). The earnings have been predicted to grow to US$621 billion by the year 2000 and US$ 1,550 billion by 2010. Over the period of last 16 years, international arrivals rose by a yearly average of 4.6 per cent and it reached 594 million in 1996. It has been forecasted that international arrivals will top 700 million by the year 2000 and will be about one billion by 2010.

National earnings from tourism are becoming vital for many nations economies. Overall tourism generated 10 % of the global gross domestic product (WTO, 1999). According to a survey (WTO, 1999), international tourism has become the world's largest export earner and an important factor in the balance of payments of many nations. Foreign currency receipts from international tourism reached US$423 billion in 1996, outstripping exports of motor vehicles, telecommunications equipment, textiles, petroleum products or any other product or service. Since it is becoming of the greater earner for the nations, many countries tend to promote their tourism services internationally.

Management internationalisation approach

The role of management in internationalisation

One of most important issues in internationalisation may be the strategic decision-making role of management. Basically, there is a closer link between the "management role and internationalisation". Mostly, it is suggested that internationalisation takes place because of management's conscious efforts to diversify a firm's activities. According to Buckley (1993), management decision-making plays a key role in determining the scope, direction of growth and opportunities for growth of the firm, whereas Aharoni (1966) discusses the role of management's behaviour as a vital factor for international production.

According to Johanson and Vahlne (1977), there are three characteristics of management responsible for stimulating internationalisation behaviour: management aspirations, commitment by the firm to international market development, and management expectations. These factors interact with the other factors of a firm and its resources to produce certain international market behaviour in the firm.

In the literature on the theory of the firm as a determinant of risk-taking behaviour, aspiration levels are widely discussed. The importance the decision-maker places on the achievement of various business goals, such as growth, profits and marketing development, is believed to be a direct determinant of decision-making behaviour. Another important aspect of managerial aspiration relates to the concept of international orientation, which is specific to an individual manager. The difference between individuals in international orientation may explain the differences in their behaviour. It is likely that an individual with a high degree of international orientation will have a higher probability of being exposed to attention-evoking factors and of perceiving them.

A firm's internationalisation depends on its commitment to foreign markets in its efforts for specialised resources and its amount of resources committed. The size of investment may include investment in marketing, organisation and personnel, and other functions. Where managerial expectations are concerned, these expectations reflect the decision-makers present knowledge as well as his perceptions of future events.

Aharoni (1966) examines the "decision-making process" which leads firms to internationalisation. To him, timing of foreign investment depends on chance stimuli and the way the management process converts these stimuli into a decision to invest. He further explains that the propensity to invest depends on the strength and frequency of stimuli to invest. This stimulus may come from two sources: firstly, it may come from within the firm as a self-interested proposal of the management. Secondly, not only from the management itself, but also from external sources such as tariffs of the foreign governments which may change the balance between exports and investments.

According to him, internationalisation occurs as a result of series of sub-decisions. For investment projects, firms first search and collect information, teams are sent out, and at the end, decisions to invest are made by the top management. The behaviour he describes is basically an organised search procedure. For him, profits are an insufficient stimulus, therefore there must be some extra appeal to motivate firms for internationalisation (Buckley 1979).

There are principal inefficiencies, such as lack of routine business scanning for the projects and over-commitment of appraisal managers. According to Buckley and Casson (1976), these inefficiencies may be reduced by firms' greater involvement in international operations.

Patterns of management international-orientation

The trends of management internationalisation may be understood by studying the levels of internationalisation knowledge of the management, by internationalisation environment, and by management mobility (by moving the management in between firm's various locations). These three areas are interrelated and tend to play a vital role in management internationalisation.

The creation on internationalisation knowledge is a fundamental issue and requirement in the process and decision-making of internationalisation. With the knowledge of internationalisation, management becomes able to find out the possibilities and options of internationalisation of the firm. The knowledge of internationalisation includes business knowledge, cultural knowledge, and experience of management.

Figure 1   Patterns of Management Internationalisation

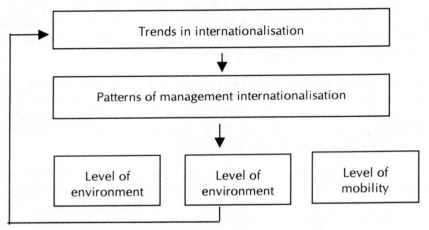

In addition to the internationalisation knowledge, the creation of an internationalisation environment is required. The internationalisation environment inspires management for internationalisation. In-house seminars regarding internationalisation may be arranged to create such an environment. Management communication among the managers in a firm may play an important role in creating an international environment. In such an environment management's interest for internationalisation must be increased by directing their attention toward international competitiveness, international expansions to avail international business opportunities. Incentives for such environmental engagement must be offered to create motivating environment.

The management mobility factor creates internationalisation of the management (Derr and Oddou, 1993). This is also related to knowledge creation of the management. The management must be rotated from time to time in between various locations. With the mobility of management internationally, the management usually gain internationalisation business and cultural knowledge. Both types of knowledge are required for international managers. This issue is related to the environment creating as well.

Research methodology

For this study, various sources are used for data collection and the most important investigative technique employed is a questionnaire survey. The questionnaire was sent to a number of hospitality firms. After various phone calls, 22 of them responded. Those non-participating firms indicated that since their firms are not involved in any types of internationalisation, they were not therefore interested in participating in this survey.

Mainly the quantitative approach has been used to analyse the data. This approach is considered to be important in this type of study. Both descriptive and advance statistical techniques have been used. It has been important to indicate the mean scores and sum of responses to indicate the importance of various variables. Factor analysis has been used to underline major important areas of management internationalisation issues.

Results and discussions

The study indicates that the managers in the hospitality and tourism business tend to be more foreign market culture oriented. Most of them responded that the understanding of the foreign cultures is an important factor toward management internationalisation. The study further indicates that motivated management for internationalisation is another important factor regarding the internationalisation issue. The knowledge of internationalisation and a firm's engagement in internationalisation are some of the other important factors in the direction of management internationalisation. Other issues considered important for internationalisation have been top management's involvement internationalisation, managers international background, management interests in international developments, internationalisation central strategy of the firm, and managers with international education (see Table 1).

Table 1   International Orientation Issues

	Number of responses	Mean Score (a)	Sum (b)	Rank (c)
Internationalisation is a part of your strategy	22	2,3636	52	7
Your management is equipped with internationalisation knowledge	22	2,9091	64	3
Your top management is engaged in internationalisation	22	2,8182	62	5
Your firm is engaged in some internationalisation activity	22	2,8636	63	4
Your management is motivated for internationalisation	22	3,0455	67	2
Your managers have international education	22	2,1364	47	8
Your managers tend to have foreign cultural understanding	22	3,0909	68	1
Your managers have international business background	22	2,6364	58	6
Your managers are international developments' concerned	22	2,6364	58	6

Source: Survey
(a) Mean score of response categories (where 1 = not important and 5 = very important reason). No response considered as not important and recorded in sum of responses and means score; (b) Sum of responses for each factor; (c) Ranking of responses based on their sum.

Most of the firms surveyed tend to consider internationalisation of the their operations and the attitude of their management toward internationalisation very essential and vital for future developments. The managers indicate that building relationships with foreign customers and foreign firms is an important step toward to make their managers more internationalisation oriented. They further mention that international education plays an important role in their internationalisation process. Internationalisation knowledge has been considered vital to create and gain an international management. Both general foreign cultural and business foreign cultural understanding is required in this regard. This issue is concerned with the mobility factor as well. The internationalisation knowledge may be gained by education and by international assignments. Another issue, which is important for managers for internationalisation of management, has been providing more international environment by bringing the management focus toward internationalisation. Other internationalisation issues vital for management internationalisation have included motivating management for internationalisation, hiring managers with international operational experience, working abroad with corporate offices and affiliates, increasing the ability and interest of management to avail foreign market opportunities among others (see Table 2).

Table 2   Management Internationalism Issues

	Number of responses	Mean Score (a)	Sum (b)	Rank (c)
Organising internationalisation campaign by industry/public sector.	22	2,4091	53	11
Providing more international business education	22	3,6818	81	2
Increasing knowledge on internationalisation	22	3,6364	80	3
Arranging seminars on internationalisation in Norway/abroad	22	3,0455	67	8
Introducing internationalisation as firm's central strategy	22	3,1364	69	7
Increasing their ability and interest to avail opportunities abroad	22	3,0000	66	9
Changing their focus from national toward international markets	22	3,3182	73	6
Providing some incentives for internationalisation	22	3,0000	66	9
Providing managers more foreign cultural understanding	22	3,5909	79	4
Providing managers more foreign Business cultural understanding	22	3,4545	76	5
Building relationship with foreign customers and foreign firms	22	4,1818	92	1
Hiring managers with international educational background	22	2,9091	64	10
Understanding management's expectations	22	3,3182	73	6
Getting management more committed for internationalisation	22	3,4545	76	5
Working abroad for corporations' affiliates and foreign offices	22	3,0455	67	8

The issues of internationalisation may be summarised mainly into three areas such as international cultural understanding and mobility, management motivation, and internationalisation knowledge. Factors like providing managers more foreign business cultural understanding, working abroad for corporations' affiliates and foreign offices, arranging seminars on internationalisation in Norway and abroad, understanding management's expectations, building relationship with foreign customers and foreign firms, providing managers more foreign cultural understanding, and hiring managers with international educational background support the area of international cultural understanding and mobility.

Table 3   Factor Analysis of Management Internationalisation Issues

Internationalisation management factors	Principal components			
	1	2	3	Eigen value
Factor 1: International cultural understanding and mobility				4,01
Providing managers more foreign Business cultural understanding	0,886			
Working abroad for corporations' affiliates and foreign offices	0,745			
Arranging seminars on internationalisation in Norway/abroad	0,729			
Understanding management's expectations	0,704			
Building relationship with foreign customers and foreign firms	0,688			
Providing managers more foreign cultural understanding	0,584			
Hiring managers with international educational background	0,560			
Factor 2: Management motivation				3,59
Getting management more committed for internationalisation		0,801		
Introducing internationalisation as firm's central strategy		0,776		
Changing their focus from national toward international markets		0,709		
Increasing their ability and interest to avail opportunities abroad		0,700		
Factor 3: Internationalisation knowledge				1,58
Increasing knowledge on internationalisation			0,809	
Providing more international business education			0,794	
Organising internationalisation campaign by industry/public sector.			0,542	
Providing some incentives for internationalisation			0,537	
N = 22, KMO = 0,457, Total Variance = 68,2%, Barlett Test of Sphericity = 105,1, Significance = 0,000				

The second area of management internationalisation is supported by getting management more committed for internationalisation, introducing internationalisation as firm's central strategy, changing managers focus from national toward international markets, and increasing their ability and interest to avail opportunities abroad. The third area of internationalisation knowledge is supported by factors such as increasing knowledge on internationalisation, providing more international business education, organising internationalisation campaign by industry and public sector, and providing management some incentives for internationalisation.

Conclusion

The study shows that internationalisation of Norwegian tourism management has already begun. Many of the tourism-related managers tend to become more international-oriented. The study also shows that most of the tourism management has been regional and national-oriented but their focus is becoming more international-oriented.

This study indicated that there is greater need for an understanding of internationalisation. Many of the managers indicated that a great number of tourism managers lacked an interest in internationalisation, knowledge of internationalisation, and international focus.

In the process of internationalisation, changes are taking place in the Norwegian Tourism industry as well. Since tourism is a global industry and effects many sectors of the hospitality industry, it tends to influence the Norwegian tourism-related management as well. In order to be keeping up with the global developments, Norwegian management is becoming international and global oriented. Most of the tourism-related firms face competition more from larger foreign firms. Global trends and future developments must become a part of the tourism-related firms.

Most of the Norwegian tourism-related corporations are small in comparison to other European and American international tourism-related corporations. There are a few foreign investors in the tourism-related industry in Norway. But some of the international tourism-related corporations are present with market entries such as business agreements, alliances and networking. The Norwegian tourism-related corporations tend to make alliances throughout the country and tend to join the global networks of the international tourism-related corporations.

In this process of internationalisation, efforts are needed to lead management toward international orientation. Building relationship with foreign clients and firms and foreign cultural understanding must be taken into consideration for tourism related management. The managers must think globally and their global perspective must become a part of their firms' central strategy. By achieving internationalisation, firms may benefit from international existing opportunities and international markets.

References

Aharoni, Y. 66), *The Foreign Investment Decision Process*, Harvard Graduate School of Business Administration, Boston.

Buckley, P. J., and Casson, M. (1976), "*The Future of the Multinational Enterprise*", The Macmillan Press Ltd.

Buckley, P. J. 1979), "The Foreign Investment Decision", in Buckley, P. J., Enderwick, P,. and Davies, H. (Editors) Multinational Corporations, *Management Bibliographies and Reviews*, 5 (3): 171-185.

Buckley, P.J. (1993), "The Role of Management in Internalisation Theory", *Management International Review*, 33: 197-207.

Derr, C. B., and Oddou, G. (1993), Internationalising of managers: speeding up the process, *European Management Journal*, 11 (4): 435-41.

Johanson, J. and Vahlne J. E. (1977), "The Internationalisation process of the firm - A Model of Knowledge Development and Increasing Foreign market Commitments", Journal of International Business Studies, 8: 23-32.

WTO (1999), *Highlights 1999*, Internet Pages of World Tourism Organisation, April 26, 1999.

Virtual tourism

Atanas Kazakov

Sofia St Kilment Ohridski University, Bulgaria

Introduction

This paper attempts to draw parallels between good 'old-fashioned' tourism, and a 'new type' - virtual tourism. The final aim of this article is to show the advantages of the first one, and that we cannot actually speak about virtual tourism, as such.

Let us first look at some definitions of the tourism:

> *"Tourism denotes the temporary, short-term movement of people to destinations outside the places where they normally live and work and their activities during the stay at these destinations."* (Burkart and Medlik, 1974).

They give us five main characteristics of tourism:

1. Tourism arises from a movement of people to, and their stay in, various destinations.

2. There are two elements in all tourism: the journey to the destination and the stay including activities at the destination.

3. The journey and the stay take place outside the normal place of residence and work, so that tourism gives rise to activities, which are distinct from those of the resident and working populations of the places, through which tourists travel and in which they stay.

4. The movement to destinations is of a temporary, short-term character, with intention to return within a few days, weeks or months.

5. Destinations are visited for purposes other than taking up permanent residence or employment remunerated from within the places visited.

As Mill and Morrison describe it:

> *"tourism is a difficult phenomenon to describe... all tourism involves travel, yet all travel is not tourism. All tourism involves recreation, yet all recreation is not*

tourism. All tourism occurs during leisure time, but not all leisure time is given to touristic pursuits... Tourism is an activity taking place when people cross a border for leisure or business and stay at least twenty-four hours..." (Mill and Morrison, 1985*)*.

Virtual tourism does not include any kind of transport (which is essential for any form of tourism), travel outside the normal place of residence and work, stay at a destination. It does not involve anybody in activities connected with these destinations. How then can we speak about tourism without these elements?

Let us now try to identify what virtual tourism is. First of all it requires a computer with colour monitor and access to Internet. Second, the user (who is actually "the traveller") should have skills for work with a computer and the Internet. Third, the software for different tourism destinations should also be available.

The contradiction

If the user (excuse me for not calling this person the virtual tourist) sits in front of the computer and he intends to "travel" to a destination there will be no movement at all. He will be involved in a short (not more than 1-2 hours) retrospection of the particular destination which will give him a feeling of being there much longer. The same feeling we get when we have spent two hours at the cinema. But in both cases we stay at one place during the whole presentation.

Second we do not need any physical destination with its infrastructure, and superstructure. All we use are computers with their software situated at the place of origin of the user. Third there is no transport involved. Fourth there is no stay (no hotels involved), no reservations have to be made, no need for foods and beverages (no restaurants of any type required). It is enough to sit comfortably in a club, and to have electricity. Fifth till the end of the journey we will stay in the so-called "environmental bubble" - we will not actually see, touch, feel the tourist resources. That means we will not have the possibility to ruin them, because we do not actually need them. In our point of view this is the first one positive side of the virtual tourism. It is already possible that we "travel" to destinations like the ancient Rome, ancient Athens, or ancient Jerusalem, at the time of their florescence. The live ancient cultures are around us, although they do not exist anymore. We could not realize any social contact. This is the second, and may be the last one positive side of the virtual tourism. No negative reactions among the local people will be inspired. Till today this type of relations among people were one of the exciting features of each one destination - to meet different people, to see and to understand their way of living and their philosophy. Could the technology destroy all this? Sixth, we do not need people to take care after us. We do not need to be customers of any tourist enterprise. And there is only one activity in which we could be involved - operating with the computer, or it could be even simple, just sit, and watch the presentation. Of course there may be a possibility to make a choice, like if we will "enter" the cathedral, or the museum first.

Is this the better way of "travel"?

A tremendous change of mind will be needed - we are supposed to like this kind of "travel". People should leave their habits of thinking well in advance for the holidays, which in fact is also one of the advantages of the old fashioned tourism. The thrill for the future journey will be forgotten. Something more, there will not be any form of recreation. We will go home after the virtual tourism experience has taken place, more tired than we were at the beginning of it.

During the whole presentation we cannot be sure about the actual destination we will travel to. We must travel "there", where we will be advised, or we will be "supported", which in fact could be very dangerous. We could pay for something, but receive something else, or not exactly what we have imagined. Control over our minds is possible, which could lead to "mind's-wash", and distribution of new ideologies.

New Tour Operators will be created - companies that will form our attitudes towards the world, and that will offer us their images of the destinations. Why should we give to them this new power? We have the traditional Tour Operators now and here - it will not be better. Do we need to pay for something new, revealing a little bit later that it was the same, or even worse? Or let us imagine that we have paid for "travel" to Jamaica, and have been taken to Hawaii, because of software's mistake. Should we allow that? Let us try to keep what we have - natural and man made resources, human attitudes, old cultures, traditions, etc.

These new Tour Operators should be computer specialists first, and after that tourism ones. But still there are not such kinds of specialists. Again the biggest Tour Operators will be able to have separate departments for both activities. And if this happens, if they have specialists with double education, then the prices for this kind of "tourism" will be much more higher then today, and we will not be able to speak for the virtual tourism as an alternative of the mass tourism.

If we look at the target groups of this type of tourism we will see that they are very limited - young people who like to stay in front of computers, instead of travel to a new place, with other young people, and experience something new in their lives. If we lose the adventure of travel we will loose this target group also. Something more, a few months later, tired with the computers the same young people will go out for some fresh air, and a new environment, and they will see the difference.

Change of the environment is a primary need, when we think about tourism today. If we compare it with the situation of the virtual tourism there will not be any actual change and control over the virtual customers may be total.

What kind of outputs, and memories will we be able to keep from this "tourism"? There is no possibility of having pictures in front of any monument, there will be no friendships established during the "journey", no additional money spent for souvenirs or gifts, nothing will be wasted. We cannot taste Bulgarian cuisine, or French wine through the Internet. We cannot smell the air in the Alps through the Internet. We cannot feel the atmosphere of the October Festival through the Internet, which actually will be the biggest lost for us.

Is this the better way of "travel"? Where is the adventure then? Maybe it is in having a headache, or stony legs, or overloaded mind?

In the ancient times there was a desire for travel, but wealth and time were strong limiting factors. The idea of travel has survived through the ages. Now it is already possible - through virtual tourism. We can visit places all over the world, without making a step outside of the room, and – are able to visit these places at certain periods of their development, which we will be able to choose.

And as a final point, we should mention that through virtual reality the largest Tour Operators will lose their incomes, because people will prefer to sit in front of a computer supplied with a virtual simulation, and "travel" without trouble.

At least this is not wholly possible. Tourism is a highly successful industry and it is too early to imagine that this powerful industry will just collapse.

Conclusion

The question is how to use virtual tourism in a less harmful way for those people that have already decided to be virtual tourists. Some suggestions are listed below.

We could use virtual tourism for advertisement of the real destinations. This could be the way of making the places less intangible than in the past. The simulations could be the next media generation.

We could use virtual tourism to construct models of the real areas near to the tourist destinations. These "maps" could be used for the orientation of the tourists, or even better for their enjoyment. They could be even sold as business cards of the destinations. This is possible for real destinations only, and for the real tourism only.

Small countries, like Bulgaria, could really gain popularity through virtual tourism, if appropriate material is shown.

And at the end the contemporary tourism could not use many of the tourist resources. Actually we could not speak of resources, because whether they are underground (remains from ancient cities), or there is no material we could show to the tourists. The other possibility is that the maintenance of these remains is not possible, or very expensive. In both ways virtual models could be constructed providing interesting tourist resources, advertising materials, and souvenirs. Instead of all this we could keep our environment for longer, and experience the reality, and give a possibility to our children to see it, listen to it, feel it, and smell it, taste it, or touch it. Because that is what we have as a gift - six senses.

References

Burns, P. (1995), *Tourism a new perspective*, Prentice Hall Europe.

Burkart, A. and Medlik, S. (1981), *Tourism Past, Present and Future* 2nd ed, Heinemann London.

Virtueller Hammer, (1999), *Berliner Morgenpost*, 20.11.1999.

Antike Reise, (1999), *Frankfurter Allgemeine Zeitung*, 28.11.1999.

Virtuelle Safari, (1999), Die Zeit, 25.12.1999.

Hawkins D., Leventhal, M. and Oden, W. (1995), *The Virtual Tourism Environment*. Utilization of Information Technology to Enhance Strategic Travel Marketing, Tourism Development.

The short waves of the product-cycle of tourism: Cuba's tourism between de-coupling and integration into the world market

Franz Kolland, Jose Ramon Neira Milian,
Martin Scheibenstock and Heinz Schönbauer

University of Vienna, Austria

In Cuba tourism is about to become the engine of the economic development of the country. It is not merely a car among other cars. From 1987 to 1997, a decade during which the expansion of Cuban tourism became the major goal of Cuban economic policy, the arrivals of foreign tourists has just less than quadrupled. During the Nineties the sector of tourism advanced to be the most dynamic of the country, with average growth rates of 17 percent per year (Oficina Nacional de Estadisticas, 1998). In 1998 1.4 million visitors came to the "isle of sugar," which equals 9 percent of all arrivals on the Caribbean islands. The Ministry of Tourism is expecting 2 million visitors for the year 2000 (see Appendix).

However, this development is but new, for Cuba has seen quite some other booms (cycles of tourism) in the 20th century. New and different are the standards of production that are influencing the present development, even if they are not determining them. It is a fact that developing countries have only limited capacities of influencing the tourism-controlling transnational corporations (Lea, 1988). This can be shown by taking a look at the strategies of TNU's. They hardly ever invest large amounts of their own capital in the Third World, but look for private and public resources in the target countries. Investments in the infrastructure (roads, electricity) that are essential in resort development are funded through local resources, or are raised through international credits (foreign loans). The flow of visitors is boosted by world-wide campaigns of marketing and the TNUs participate in the profits of the enterprises in the target countries via the providing of licenses, franchising and contracts of service. To make matters worse more tourists travelling to developing countries have to stay in enclaves, separated from the local population. Moreover the standardisation of the "package" entails that the offer (sun, summer, surfing, sex) is substitutable, which means that the target countries have virtually no control over the tourist flow.

This is a system of division of labour on an international level, in which Cuba specialised (necessarily) in mass tourism, not unlike many other of the developing countries. The reason for this is the interest of the TNU's in industrialised countries to open new markets for standardised goods. A recent development is the implementation of all-inclusive packages. And Cuba relies on all-inclusive tourism. They have their own motives for doing so, too. All-inclusive hotels take care of all their guests needs and make it superfluous to leave the complex of hotels. For reasons of control every guest is provided with his own coloured bracelet that makes him a member of one of the various resorts. Non-members are not welcome – unless a special exchange of armbands of different colours is desired. Wishes on behalf of the guests to make contact with the local population thus cannot be responded to. Contact is limited to the receptionist, the waiter, the animator on the beach. The Cuban government profits from this type of tourism, for the revolutionaries have always despised contact with those rich tourists from capitalist countries, with their status-oriented behaviour and their demonstration of superiority. Even today, Cubans both sexes who are in the company of tourists are stopped and checked closely by the police. Contact with tourists is seen as inappropriate. The differences concerning life in general are much too big for a relation based on symmetry and partnership to be possible.

However, the subject of this paper is not so much the evolution and changing of the present supply side of tourism, but the change in structure of tourism as related to the development of Cuban society.

Cycles of the Cuban evolution of tourism

Past social science studies of tourism lack any historical depth and criticise mass tourism in Cuba as being too non-competitive, too unsegmented, inelastic and heavily dependent on imports (Holan and Phillips, 1997, Mesa-Lago, 1998), or irreversible ecological damages are prophesied (Avella and Mills, 1996). Others argue that Cuba's existence as one of the last bastions of state socialism might itself be a tourist attraction – "perhaps portraying the country as a sub-tropical Brezhnevite theme park" (Hall, 1992). Such studies carry the decisive fault of being primarily pertinent to the paradigm of modernisation and viewing the development of Cuban tourism through the eyes of "old tourism countries". No sooner is the analysis extended into a longer period of time, than it becomes clear that the progress of tourism is not linear, that stagnation and shrinkage is not necessarily correspondent to miscarriage and that tourism cannot be compared to that in the industrialised countries.

A conceptual basis for analysing tourism over a longer period is offered by R. Butler's Tourism Area Life Cycle model (1980). The model of Butler starts from more ancient resort cycle concepts, according to which regions of tourism undergo a cyclic evolution. Up to now there has been one study, using this older procedure (Hinch, 1990). It comes to the conclusion that destinations like the Bahamas, Jamaica or Barbados are positioned at more advanced positions along their cycle of evolution than is Cuba. Do not fail, however, to notice – apart from methodical weaknesses – the huge expansion of international tourism in Cuba during the 1990s.

The conceptual weakness of the older cycle models is the classical method of not making any links to criteria other than tourist arrivals. For this paper the following criteria are therefore considered as a means of assessing change in the Cuban tourism: the economic development of Cuba; the evolution of the destination-areas of tourism; the significance of the labour market; the institutional (legislative) basic conditions; the change in (the social) structure of the guests and social impacts. Behind all this is the thesis that common resort cycle concepts are unfit to describe and explain the evolution of tourism on a national level. The example of Cuba will prove that the cycle of a good's longevity in tourism is not so much determined by the endogene mechanisms of evolution, but rather by the national-societal and international-societal development.

According to this model it can be postulated that we may differentiate three cycles of tourism in Cuba in the 20th century that are in a close connection first of all to the production of sugar, second to the especial evolution of Cuban society and third to the integration (disintegration), into the Socialistic economic system Comecon.

The first subject refers to the close connection of the expansion and concentration of tourism to the evolution of the traditional main economic sector of Cuba: sugar production. Thus it can be revealed that declining sugar harvests, which in turn are related to falling prices of sugar on the World Market, give the emphasis placed on tourism a huge boost. The second point refers to the especial development of the Cuban society that led away from the capitalistic World Market at the beginning of the 60s, bears the signs of de-coupling in tourism during the first decades after the revolution. The third important – external - factor of influence on the evolution of tourism in Cuba was the membership of the socialistic economic system Comecon. The third boom of tourism in Cuba has its roots partly in the early 1980s – still before the fall of Socialism across Europe and Eurasia, as a reaction to dependence on this economic system.

The phases of expansion of tourism before 1959

During the first half of the 20th century the "isle of sugar" was the main destination for American tourists in the Caribbean. After World War I tourism, helped by the Prohibition in the United States and the fact that gambling was legal on Cuba, boomed for the first time. Tourists belonged mainly to the upper class.

For example the Du Ponts, industry tycoons, purchased parts of the Varadero Peninsula and had domiciles established for members of the American economy elite. After the winter season of 1928/29 that ended with yet another record number of visitors, tourism came to an end due to the Great Depression, the fall of the Machado dictatorship 1933 and the end of Prohibition (Hinch, 1990, Bleasdale and Tapsell, 1994).

Cuba's second tourism boom came in the 1950s, spurred by falling sugar prices, the Fulgencio Batista dictatorship's promotion of foreign investment, and the introduction of jet services and package tours. The elite tourism of the 1920s was greatly expanded to include middle- and working-class American vacationers (Honey, 1999).

Between 1951 and 1958 hotel capacity was increased by a third, 80 percent of which took place in Havana. In the year 1957 272.266 tourists (of which 87 percent were US-Americans) spent their vacations on the island. This is a third of all stays in the Caribbean at that time and made tourism, second to the production of sugar, the main source of foreign currency (Hall, 1992). It was not merely the tropical climate that attracted people, but also the fact that Cuba during this second tourism boom was the centre of gambling, nightclubbing and. connected to the latter, prostitution. "Strong US controlling influences in the tourism industry mirrored Cuba's dependency relationship with that country, while the undercurrent of vice and organised crime reflected the close spatial proximity of the two countries and the US perception of Cuba as the nearby underdeveloped sub-tropical playground where anything goes" (Hall, 1992, 110).

De-coupling from the World Market between 1959 and 1982 – Promotion of domestic tourism

After the Cuban Revolution the "People's Department of Beaches" was founded, which prohibited private possession of beaches. With the coming into effect of the *"Ley No. 270"* every Cuban was granted free access to any beach. Immediately after the unsuccessful, CIA-assisted, invasion of the Bay of Pigs the USA imposed an economic blockade on the island, which also made the entry into Cuba illegal for US-Americans and thus practically ended international tourism on Cuba.

The tourism policies of the new government oriented itself at socialistic ideals: emphasis was placed on leisure time as a socialistic right. In addition the *"Instituto Nacional de la Industria Turística"* (INIT) was founded 1960, its duties including the support and execution of development plans for tourism. "Beginning in the late 1960s, the Cuban government developed vacation facilities designed for its own people, much of which was nature oriented: smaller beach resorts, health spas, mountain lodges, fishing clubs, campgrounds, hiking and bicycle trails, and other recreational facilities, all made available to Cubans as part of their employment benefit packages." (Honey, 1999, 186). With hotels being closed down in the capital, humbler habitats in the country were constructed.

The number of foreign visitors fluctuated between three to five thousand in those years. Those visitors came on cultural exchange programs or were health tourists from Comecon countries. Arrivals from other countries were limited to group travel that were organised mainly by unions, solidarity movements as well as clerical and political groups (Bleasdale and Tapsell, 1994).

The revival of international tourism

In the middle of the 1970s the Cuban government began to plan towards international tourism in order to diversify the economic structure and not to be dependent on the sugar sector so much.

Thus the institute of tourism (INTUR) was founded in 1976, whose duty was to establish international tourism on Cuba and to collect data especially on tourism. With the subsidiary firm Cubatur Cubas's only travel agency up to that time was founded. The state enforced tourism in enclaves mainly on Varadero and Guardalavaca. Tourism of that time had the significant advantage of the major profit remaining in Cuba since only a small sum had to be paid to foreign travel agencies and/or airlines.

At the beginning of the 1980s the Cuban government agreed to further enlarge the capacities of tourism. Decree *No. 50* by the Council of State in 1982 legalised joint ventures with foreign companies, whose maximum share of the joint venture (empresa mixta) was limited to 49 percent. Furthermore conditions were created that promised potential investors high chances of capital exploitation in comparison to other islands in the Caribbean. However, joint ventures developed very slowly due to reluctance to realise the *Ley No. 50*. It took falling sugar prices and rising imports to significantly change tourism policy. A huge imbalance of trade, which amounted to a third of all imports and which led to a declining of currency reserves by 21 percent (Burchardt, 1996), marked the beginning of a new wave of international tourism.

In 1987 a program of support for foreign investments was introduced and the exploitation of tourism resources was granted priority. Ambitious aims were set, but the state failed to raise the funds for their realisation. For this reason the enterprise CUBANACAN S.A. was founded in 1987 and in 1989 the group of GAVIOTA, who were supposed to finance new hotels with foreign tourism enterprises in accordance to the joint-venture-law.

The disintegration of the East European economic community, into which Cuba was integrated to a high degree via Comecon since the 1970s, as well as the development of the USSR accelerated the forces of expansion in tourism. The decline in GNP by 34 percent between 1991 and 1994 led to a radical restructuring of national economy. Heavy emphasis was placed on the exploitation of eight centres of tourism (*Havana, Varadero, Jardines del Rey, Santa Lucia, Guardalavaca, Santiago de Cuba, Cienfuegos and Trinidad, Cayo Largo*). The erection of special zones was to be a social layer of protection as concerns possible negative influences of tourism on Cuban society.

The first joint ventures were created with Spanish capital participation: CUBACAN S.A.(Cuba-Canarias) is a joint venture between CUBANACAN S.A. and the Canarian CIHSA. This mixed enterprise opened their first four-star-hotel in 1990 named Sol Palmera, in 1991 the five-star-hotel Melia Varadero and Gran Hotel de Las Americas. Meanwhile this group possesses a super market, discotheques, and the hotel Melia Habana. 95 percent of Cuban tourism was controlled by the national institute of tourism INTUR with its subsidiary firm Cubatur until the early 1990s. Due to a restructuring of the tourism industry INTUR was disbanded in 1994. INTUR's agendas were taken over by a group of agencies under the protection of the newly founded Ministry of Tourism, which is responsible for the planning, policy and co-ordination of tourism. At the same time a diversification of the hotel industry was undertaken. Today there are a large number of tourism enterprises that are under military administration as far as the Cuban side is concerned. The most important are: *Hoteles Cubanacàn S.A., Grupo Hotelero Gran Caribe, Horizontes Hoteles, Islazul, Grupo de Turismo Gaviota S.A.,* (ecologic, health and hunting tourism), *Turismo especializado Cubamar* (ecologic tourism, camping, youth hostels*), Servimed* (health tourism*), Ministerio de educaciòn Superior Mercadù* (study trips of the University of Havana), *Habaguanex* (tourism infrastructure in the ancient down-town of Havana Vieja), *Companìa de Marinas Puerto Sol* (diving and water sports), *Grupo de Recreatiòn y Turismo Rumbos* (restaurants and shops), *Cadena de Tiendas Caracol* (hotels supermarkets), *Empresa de Transporte Turìstico Transtur* (transport of tourists).

A new investment bill (*Ley No. 77 de la Inversiòn Extranjera*) of November 5th 1995 allows foreign investors to purchase majority participation up to direct investments (with a capital share of 100 percent). Direct investments, and investments amounting to more than 10 million $ and some other special cases must be approved by executive committee of the

Council of Ministers. Still conclusions are reached one by one and on the highest political level.

Foreign partners are granted a wide range of rights, in particular the right to choose managers, to determine the number of employees, plans of production and sale, to select the employees, to fix prices, import and export directly, to conclude contracts with Cuban and foreign partners and to chose the way of financial policy. In case of a dissolution of a business foreign participators are granted the tax-free restitution of their net earnings and dividends as well as their shares of business (Lessmann 1996).

In order to demonstrate cost advantages to potential investors the Cuban government places strong emphasis on the fact that there is social stability throughout the country and on the fact that, compared to other countries in the region, the standards of education and qualification are high in regard to the low wages.

However not legalised was the free choice of Cuban employees in the tourism sector. Joint ventures are able to recruit their employees through Cuban loan-employment agencies (*entidad empleadora*) only, with the final decision on the employment in foreign firms still in the hands of the state. Between the joint venture and the loan-employment agency a labour contract is signed according to the Cuban loan regulations. This includes the fact that employees do not receive their wages from the corporation they are work for but from the loan-employment agency. In addition to this the labour market is subject to much higher fluctuations as compared to the remaining situation of employment. Thus the joint venture is able to demand substitution in case of bad work or lack of discipline from the employee. In 1992 47 employees were fired by the manager of the hotel Tuxpan (Lissmann 1996), which leads to the assumption that a mentality of hire-and-fire is present.

The third boom is characterised by a diversification of the guest structure. Half of all guests staying in Cuba in 1997 came from Europe, 30 percent from North America and 13 percent from South America. The lead took Italy with 17 percent of all arrivals, followed by Canada with 15 percent, Spain with 10 percent, France with 8 percent and Germany with 7 percent. As far as South America is concerned Mexico takes the lead with 4.5 percent and Argentina with 3.5 percent. This distribution among Europeans, Canadians and South Americans means the following advantages: the length-of-stays are vast and Cuba remains independent from seasonal and cyclical swaying of single countries as well as regions of economy.

Another aspect of the boom is the increase in gross hard currency receipts, although the increase is not linear according to the specific situation of the tourism sector. Profits from tourism have multiplied by ten in the decade between 1987 and 1997. Tourism apart from the sugar production once again is one the two cores of economy. Tourism's share of GNP was raised from 1.19 percent in the year 1989 to 6 percent in 1994 and in 1995 was at 8.3 percent. Till 1995 profits increased to a larger extend than the arrivals (Haynes, 1996). Since 1996 the relationship between economic usefulness and economic expenditure has shifted in disfavour of income.

A further point in our observation of the production cycle are expectations of the tourists travelling to Cuba. After World War I tourists came to Cuba mainly for the gambling and prostitution – today motives have changed noticeably, although some of the older motives are still present today. Prostitution for example is one of the most severe problems that has arisen in the wake of the tourism boom in the 1990s.

Interviews with 150 German speaking tourists (Kolland, Scheibenstock, Schönbauer et al. 1998) on the beaches of Varadero revealed that 75 percent came to Cuba because of the climate and that every second tourist chose Cuba because of the excellent ratio between price and product and because of the local mentality (originality, hospitality). Two thirds of the questioned visitors claimed to have expected holidays "without masses". Regarding this motive one has to ask himself if there is not a discrepancy to mass tourism.

Another speciality Cuba has to offer is the myth of revolution (see also Hall, 1992). Apart from the sun, the beaches and the mentality 10 percent of all visitors are attracted to Cuba because of the Revolution. They combine their stay with sight-seeing of monuments of the Revolution and rural co-operatives.

How vulnerable tourism is however can be seen in the fact that in the majority of cases the decision for Cuba was a decision against other destinations in the same region (Dominican Republic, Jamaica, Mexico), but there were also destinations which had little to do with the Caribbean (Greece, Sri Lanka, Ghana, Maldives). Tourists choose Cuba the more for its own sake the more they look for individual or alternative tourism. If tourists look for an all-inclusive package not a particular country is chosen but a particular standard, a particular ratio between price and product. In that respect Cuba has serious rivals not only other countries in the region, but other (seemingly) faraway destinations as well.

Social impacts of Cuban mass tourism

The tourism sector is growing against the background of a socialist society and the integration into a world economy at the same time. Tourism today is Cuba's major hope to escape the recession which is taking place since 1989. Tourists seem to be welcome as guests. There is no open protest against this rapidly growing sector of economy, for Cuba concentrates its efforts thoroughly on mass tourism. And still, the distance between locals and visitors is bigger than ever. It is manifested in lifestyle, in habits, in culture. Compared to expenditures during a two-week-stay – soft drinks, excursions and souvenirs – the monthly salary of 20 $ of an employee appears meagre. Foreigners and locals are embarrassed. The distance between the two is immense and doubts are growing if intercultural communication will ever be possible.

Tourism has divided Cuban society. On one hand there are those Cubans who have access to the Dollar, on the other there are those who get only Pesos (Berríos, 1997, Parker, 1998). It is estimated that approximately 50 percent of the population have access to the Dollar (Carlos Lage, in: Die Zeit, No. 30, 1999, p.22). This "tourist apartheid" (Baloyra and Morris, 1993) makes a lot of highly qualified personal abandon their jobs to work as room maids or barkeepers, because their tips amount to far more than what the government pays them. Conditions are in fact much better than in any other branch of the Cuban economy.

The exclusion of Cubans (who have no US currency) from the new joint venture hotels is in violation *Article 43* of the Cuban constitution that grants every Cuban "overnight stays in any hotel" and "to be served in any restaurants".

The government is well aware of this "difficult problem" which undermines one of their essential justifications: the principle of social equality. In the interview cited above Carlos Lage (1999) admits that tourism costs both political and social currency. "There are people who get annoyed or upset when they are confronted with the fact that the government is forced to give priority to tourist services for foreigners. They do not understand, however, the complex reasons that have led the Revolution to this decision."

Another problem is the ecological balance. The Cayeria del Norte, those approximately 400 islands, belonging to the archipelagos of Camagüey and Sabane at the north shore of Cuba, are some of the island's most precious regions. They are part of the World's second biggest coral reefs, and living there are more than 200 different breeds of bird 15 of which are threatened with extinction. According to the will of the government one of the eight projected tourist enclaves of the island will be erected there. Today there are 1500 rooms in three hotels. Five more are already under construction. In the long term more than 30 hotels with 13,000 rooms will be built here, and even golf courses are in the planning stage. It must be feared that this natural reserve will be suffering great damage because of the rapid development on the islands (Honey, 1999).

Another problem is the low degree of actual integration of mass tourism into Cuba's national economy: in order to provide international tourist standards many goods are being imported (Parker, 1998). As long as the demands of the tourists have to be satisfied with imports, two thirds of the seemingly vast gross profits are used up again.

Prospects

Until the mid 1990s the second coupling of Cuba to the international tourism industry only led to moderate growths in numbers of arrivals. Tourism was merely one of the lead sectors in the economic development and Cuba was a comparatively unimportant destination in the region. Side effects known from other countries such as the expansion of an informal sector were unknown. Some of it however has changed over the last years and points to increased needs of problem solving, if the objective of 3 million tourists shall be reached without great frictions i.e. being compatible with the Cuban society and not leading to new forms of social inequality (Hoffmann, 1996). Another factor of uncertainty is the question whether Cuba will achieve further increases out of the expanding international tourism and/or in competition with other destinations (of that region). This competition in particular demands high standards of productivity and quality, if competition shall not to be decided over the best price.

Another question is whether or not the demands– provided a growth that remains stable – can be satisfied simply with the growth of the formal sector or will there be another boost of informalisation of economy due to private and partly illegal and little regulated service offers?

Last, but not least, it remains uncertain how in this third revolution of the cycle of goods' longevity a diversification of offer and structure of guests by political interventions and guiding will be possible. Impossibility would merely entail a shift in the relationship of dependence on the World Market. In place of being dependent on the sugar production there would be a relationship of dependency on tourism, which would further confirm Cuba's status as a peripheral region.

References

Avella, A., Mills, A. (1996), Tourism in Cuba in the 1990s: Back to the future? *Tourism Management*, 17 (1): 55-60.

Baloyra, E. A., Morris, J. A. (1993), *Conflict and Change in Cuba*, The University of New Mexico Press, Albuquerque.

Berríos, R. (1997), Cuba's Economic Restructuring, 1990-1995, *Communist Economies and Economic Transformation*, 9 (1): 117-130.

Bleasdale, S., Tapsell S. (1994), Contemporary efforts to expand the tourist industry in Cuba: the perspective from Britain, in: Seaton, A. V.(Editor), *Tourism. The State of the Art*, John Wiley and Sons, Chinchester, pp.100-109.

Burchard, H. (1996), Kuba. Der lange Abschied von einem Mythos. Lang, Stuttgart.

Burchard, H.; Kuba – Im Herbst des Patriarchen. Stuttgart, 1999.

Butler, R. (1980), The concept of a tourist area cycle of evolution, *Canadian Geographer*, 24 (1): 5-12.

Hall, D. R. (1992), Tourism development in Cuba. In Harrison, D (Editor), *Tourism and the less developed countries*. John Wiley and Sons, London, pp.102-120.

Haynes, L. (1996), Cuba, *International Tourism Reports*, 3, pp.5-23.

Hinch, T. D. (1990), Cuban tourism industry. Its re-emergence and future, *Tourism Management*, 11 (3): 14-226.

Hoffmann, B. (1996), Die Rückkehr der Ungleichheit. Kubas Sozialismus im Schatten der Dollarisierung. in Hoffmann, B. (Editor), Wirtschaftsreformen in *Kuba. Konturen einer Debatte*. Sigma, Frankfurt, pp.101-134.

Holan, P. M., Phillips, N. (1997), Sun, sand and hard currency. Tourism in Cuba, *Annals of Tourism Research*, 24 (4): 77-795.

Honey, M. (1999), Cuba: Growth of tourism and ecotourism during the "Special Period", in Honey, M. (Editor), *Ecotourism and sustainable development*. Who owns paradise, Island Press, Washington D.C., pp.182-219.

Kolland, F., Scheibenstock, M., Schönbauer, H. et al. (1998), Deutsche Gäste in *Kuba. Eine empirische Studie zu Reiseentscheidung und Reisemotivation*. Wien. (Mimeo)

Krohn, F. B., O'Donnell, S. T. (1999), U.S. Tourism Potential in a New Cuba, *Journal of Travel and Tourism Marketing*, 8 (1): 85-99.

Lea, J. (1988), *Tourism and Development in the Third World*, Routledge, London.

Lessmann, R. (1996), *Ausländische Investitionen und wirtschaftliche Strukturreformen in Kuba*, Bonn. (Mimeo.)

Mesa-Lago, C. (1998*), Assessing Economic and Social Performance in the Cuban Transition of the 1990s*, World Development, 26 (5): 857-876.

Oficina Nacional de Estadísticas (1998), *Anuario Estadístico de Cuba*, Havanna.

Parker, D. (1998), The Cuban Crises and the Future of the Revolution. A Latin American Perspective, *Latin American Research Review*, 33 (4): 239-256.

World Tourism Organisation; *Yearbook of Tourism Statistics*. Vol. II, 45-51 ed.

Appendix

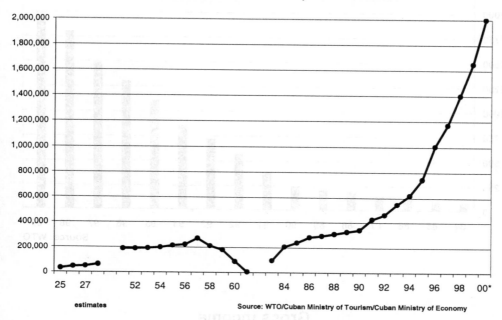

Cuba: Tourist Arrivals, 1925-2000

estimates

Source: WTO/Cuban Ministry of Tourism/Cuban Ministry of Economy

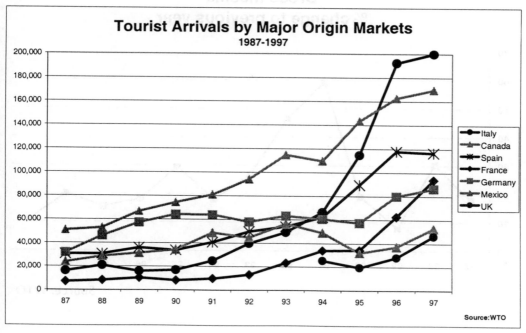

Tourist Arrivals by Major Origin Markets
1987-1997

Italy
Canada
Spain
France
Germany
Mexico
UK

Source:WTO

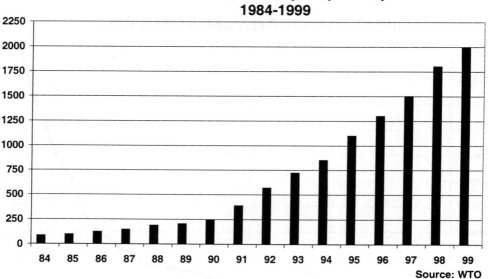

Tourism receipts (Mio $)
1984-1999

Source: WTO

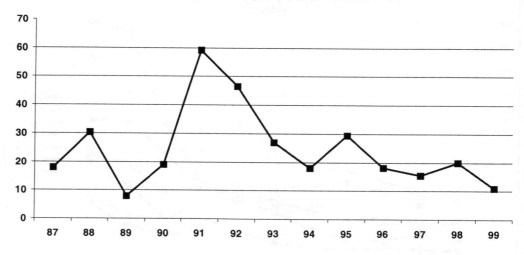

Gross income
% change to previous year

Source: WTO

Tourism policy and politics in a devolved Scotland

Bill Kerr

Malin Court, Turnberry, Ayrshire, UK

Roy C Wood

University of Strathclyde, UK

This paper examines the attitudes, aspirations and perceptions of tourism industry professionals in the context of the 1999 devolution of certain powers from the UK Westminster Parliament to a newly created Parliament and Government in Edinburgh. The present report emanates from a much larger and continuing project on politics, tourism and society that has as its main focus the effects of changes in the Scottish political system on tourism policy making.

The Scottish tourism context

Scotland is a country in which tourism enjoys considerable visibility in public discourse about the country's social and economic future, despite the fact that Scotland is neither a major tourist destination nor a major tourism employer (for the last decade, employment in tourism-related industries in Scotland has averaged approximately 8% of the total) (Kerr and Wood, 1999, 2000, 2000a; Wood, 1993).

Government provision for tourism administration in Scotland is extensive and arguably out of all proportion to the economic significance of the sector. In addition to the national tourism organisation, the Scottish Tourist Board (STB), both national enterprise agencies (Scottish Enterprise [SE] and Highlands and Islands Enterprise [HIE]) have certain tourism administration responsibilities, as do local government authorities. In addition, the STB supervises a network of Area Tourist Boards (ATBs) and SE and HIE a similar network of local enterprise companies (LECs). It is worth pausing to consider how such extensive public sector involvement in tourism has come about.

Until the late 1960s, tourism's role in the Scottish economy was treated as of little importance. The Highlands and Islands Development Board (HIDB) was created in 1965 charged with supporting the social and economic development of the region, including elements of tourism. In 1969 came the UK-wide Development of Tourism Act. This created the Scottish Tourist Board with prime responsibility for all aspects of tourism in Scotland save overseas marketing and promotion. Responsibility for the latter rested with the supra national British Tourist Authority (BTA) (a somewhat ironic situation as the HIDB was able to market their area overseas, at least until 1993 - see Smith, 1998). In 1975, the Scottish Development Agency (SDA) was established with a purely economic remit committed to supporting and stimulating business infrastructure and development. The strength of the STB's role at this time meant that the SDA's involvement in encouraging tourism businesses was minimal and tourism continued to be treated as being outwith the main sphere of industrial policy. In 1991, the SDA was merged with the Training Agency to create Scottish Enterprise. The HIDB became Highlands and Island Enterprise (HIE) in a similar arrangement.

A government review of tourism in Scotland in 1993 saw Highlands and Islands Enterprise yield both its tourism marketing role and co-ordination of Area Tourist Boards (the organisations which deliver tourism services and strategy at local level) roles to the STB. In turn, the STB lost responsibility for providing financial assistance to tourism projects, powers that were ceded to the Scottish Enterprise Network (i.e. Scottish Enterprise, Highlands and Islands Enterprise and the local enterprise companies). A further and longer-term outcome of this review was that a reduction in the number of Area Tourist Boards (ATBs) was mooted. From 1996, the number of ATBs was reduced from 32 to 14.

The tourism sector and the Scottish political context

In 1997, the then new UK Labour government fulfilled a promise to hold a referendum on whether Scotland should have its own parliament and government. The Scottish electorate endorsed the idea and elections to the new 129 single-chamber in Edinburgh were set for May 1999. The referendum also established that the new Parliament would have limited tax-varying powers of up to three pence in the pound, and responsibility over a wide range of policy areas, including tourism.

Before Scottish devolution and at the UK level, tourism was invariably part of a junior ministerial portfolio of responsibilities although the post holder was usually identified as the 'minister for tourism'. In addition, throughout the 1980's, the tourism portfolio was fairly mobile, located in various departments of state, finally coming to rest in a new Department of National Heritage in 1992. A short time after Labour's 1997 election victory, this department was renamed Culture, Media and Sport, where a designated minister for tourism has remained, first at Minister of State level, and latterly, after the government reshuffle of Summer 1998 at the lesser under-secretary of state level. In Scotland, different arrangements existed for the political administration of tourism. Like many other matters of domestic government, tourism was part of the remit of the Scottish Office under the Secretary of State for Scotland who designated a junior minister to take responsibility for the industry, usually as part of a wider portfolio of duties.

The eighteen months before the Scottish parliamentary elections saw considerable public debate about the future of tourism, much of it fed by various sectors of the industry. A substantial proportion of tourism income and employment is attributable to private sector enterprises, mainly in the hotels and catering 'hospitality' sector. Most sponsorship of tourism activity is by public sector organisations including everything from supporting small business start-up, to financial aid to industry and marketing of Scotland at home and abroad. The concerns of the hospitality industry included:

- the absence of a government minister solely concerned with tourism;

- the possibility of a new tourism or 'bed tax': in some quarters of both public and private sectors, a hypothecated bed tax was mooted, revenue from which it was suggested, could be used to support development of the Scottish tourism industry, an idea that received a lukewarm reception from all Scotland's political parties;

- the licensing of tourism operators and registration of tourism businesses; and

- reform (i.e. relaxation of) liquor licensing regulations.

Perhaps the most pressing industry issue in the run-up to the elections concerned the 14 Area Tourist Boards who provide many vital local services, including operation of over 160 Tourist Information Centres (TICs) (a principal function of which is the booking of accommodation) and local marketing of their areas. ATBs are statutory bodies under the supervision of the STB, but without statutory funding. Instead, they are funded by a mixture of STB grant, discretionary payments from local government authorities and other sources, including their own revenue-raising activities.

Relationships between Scotland's ATBs, local enterprise companies and local government councils have rarely been easy. By 1998, several ATBs were in fact, in deep financial trouble, some facing bankruptcy because of a fall in local authority monies and the failure of many such authorities to schedule payments in a manner that allowed ATBs to effectively plan and implement their strategies. Matters were complicated because the ATBs lack geographical fit with the boundaries of local councils. Simply, this means that ATBs must negotiate with several local authority districts for funding for their activities. In 1998, the Ayrshire and Arran Tourist Board faced a financial crisis and almost collapsed. It was rescued in December of that year by a £200,000 package put together by the Local Enterprise Company and the three Ayrshire local councils. By October 1998, Dumfries and Galloway, was also experiencing problems, being £1.2 million in the red. It was saved by a cash injection from the local council. In January 1999, the debts of Angus and Dundee's ATB rose to £45,000, leading to employee redundancies.

The Scottish Tourist Board (STB), encouraged by the conclusions of yet another Scottish Office review conducted in 1998 proposed that the solution to ATB funding difficulties was for government to channel all monies for ATBs through the STB. Several local government authorities and their representative national bodies raised immediate objections. This scheme would most likely involve government putting a value on the monies such authorities should give to ATBs and deducting it from the grant aid government gives each year to local government. Local government would have no discretion over funding given to local ATBs and there would be no local accountability. At the same time, the STB, whose importance in recent years had arguably diminished, would become a powerful broker with the ability to steer national tourism policy (indeed, in July 1999, as the new Scottish Parliament met for the first time, the Chairman of the STB reportedly threatened to make awards of the current monies STB disburses to ATBs dependent on a satisfactory audit of ATB activities by STB officials).

Despite clear lobbying and campaigning on the aforementioned (and other) issues by several sectors of the tourism industry, tourism did not have a high profile in party election manifestos. The SNP committed themselves to a Minister responsible for tourism as part of a broader portfolio embracing industry and enterprise. Informed press reports, not denied by the SNP, suggested that a nationalist government would create far more centralised arrangements for sponsoring Scottish industry, integrating tourism into the policy mainstream. This would entail effective abolition of the STB, transferring responsibility for tourism to Scottish Enterprise and the local Enterprise Company network, while integrating both Area Tourist Boards and the economic development functions for tourism of local councils into this new structure.

The Liberal Democrats only substantial tourism pledge was to require ATBs to establish three-year rolling plans for promoting tourism in their area. The Scottish Labour Party's policies for tourism envisaged no significant change from that established by the UK Labour government when it took office in May 1997. These policies in turn were inherited from the previous Conservative government. Labour made no commitment to specific policy change. The Scottish Conservatives were more forthcoming, promising core funding, through the Scottish Tourist Board, to the Area Tourist Boards. The Conservatives also undertook to review mechanisms for the marketing of tourism in Scotland and initiate a review of alcohol licensing in public places, as well as offering tax-breaks to encourage training. As such, the Conservatives were arguably the only party in the elections to the Scottish Parliament who linked their policy promises to (some of) the issues facing the tourism industry.

The Scottish electoral and post-electoral context

In the May 1999 elections to the Scottish Parliament, no single party obtained an overall majority, although Labour, in power in the UK was the largest grouping, and formed a coalition administration in Scotland with the Liberal Democrats. The Scottish National Party (SNP) is the main opposition and Scottish Conservatives are the smallest 'large' party. There is one Green Member of the Scottish Parliament (MSP) and two independents. The Labour and Liberal Parties subsequently formed an Executive (Government) consisting of 11 cabinet ministers, 11 non-cabinet, junior ministers and formed six new ministries or departments in addition to three 'central services' departments. The six main ministries/departments are the:

- Scottish Executive Justice Department (SEJD);

- Scottish Executive Health Department (SEHD);

- Scottish Executive Rural Affairs Department (SERAD);

- Scottish Executive Development Department (SEDD);

- Scottish Executive Education Department (SEED); and

- Scottish Executive Enterprise and Lifelong Learning Department (SEELLD).

The new government determined not to have a specific Minister for Tourism, in the sense of a person whose responsibilities were concerned exclusively with tourism. The tourism portfolio was allocated to the Department of Enterprise and Lifelong Learning, with responsibility for tourism specifically delegated to the Deputy Minister for the Highlands, Islands and Gaelic.

With some irony, tourism became one of the earliest policy issues facing the Labour-Liberal Democrat coalition upon its election. A report by the Scottish Affairs Committee of the UK House of Commons published in July 1999 contained damning condemnation of the management of Scottish tourism and the Scottish tourism product. In respect of the latter the Report drew attention to poor quality accommodation in many areas; unwelcoming hosts; uncompetitive and inaccurate prices; poor standard of visitor attractions; and lack of accessibility. The Report also included rejection of a bed tax as a way of funding public support for tourism, and support for the central funding of the Area Tourist Boards (ATBs) by the Scottish Tourist Board (STB).

The investigation on which the Report was based commenced before devolution took effect, and the Scottish Executive could have treated its conclusions as purely advisory. In fact, the Report received wide exposure in the Scottish media and a swift response from the Scottish Executive. Within days, the Minister for Enterprise and Lifelong Learning, Henry McLeish announced that he was initiating a review of tourism. Within two weeks, a consultation document for Scottish tourism was launched, inviting responses by the end of August 1999. The purpose of the consultation document was to support the development of a national strategy by the Scottish Tourist Board for the whole of the tourism industry, to be presented early in 2000.

Tourism professionals and policy debates

This paper reports the results of a survey of Scottish hospitality and tourism industry professionals. The research was informed by a number of concerns. The elections to the Scottish Parliament offered a unique opportunity to explore the political values of tourism and hospitality industry professionals. These have traditionally been depicted as intensely conservative in the hospitality sector and more left of centre in those public sector organisations involved in tourism (Aslan and Wood, 1993; Wood, 1996). By establishing voting intentions, it was hoped to further effect a detailed comparison of this section of the electorate with the wider population (Brown, McCrone and Paterson, 1998; Brown, McCrone, Paterson and Surridge, 1999) as well as exploring relationships between electoral preferences and views on tourism policy futures in Scotland in the light of the manifesto promises of the main parties.

This is a somewhat simplistic rendering of the research process. In the period from the election of the UK Labour government in 1997, careful monitoring of media and organisational pronouncements took place relative to government initiatives on tourism. In 1998, key opinion formers in all tourism sectors, including party spokespersons on tourism, were interviewed in-depth. These activities generated the subject matter of the survey instrument, a questionnaire, which consisted of 30, mainly closed, items.

A unique opportunity arose to administer the survey in the form of the Scottish Hospitality Industry Congress (SHIC). This meets every two years for a day conference and attracts delegates from all sectors of the industry, public and private sector and from large and small organisations, including those in the voluntary and education sectors. In 1999 the SHIC meeting took place on March 1 and was attended by some 702 delegates. The 1999 SHIC had as its theme the policy of Scotland's political parties towards the tourism and hospitality industries. Three Scottish party leaders (not their tourism spokespersons) attended (from the SNP, Liberal Democrats and Conservatives) together with the then Scottish Office Minister for Industry. The organisers of the SHIC event, co-operated in supplying their registration database for the conference and the questionnaire was posted to all attendees one week later, requesting completion and return by 31 March. Some 205 (29%) responded, an encouraging level of interest that can partly be accounted for by the proximity of the issue of the questionnaire to the conference event.

Voting behaviour and intentions

Elections to the new Scottish Parliament involved a dual voting system previously untried in the UK. Each elector had two votes, one for a constituency Member of the Scottish Parliament (MSP) administered on the first-past-the-post model, and a second vote for a party list. Here, electors were required to vote for a regional party list. Some 73 of the seats in the 129 member Parliament were reserved for constituency MSPs, the rest for list members. The rationale for this approach was to ensure some degree of proportionality in the elections.

The questionnaire sought information on the voting behaviour of respondents in the 1997 Westminster General Election, and their intentions in the two votes for the Scottish Parliament. Table 1 places these figures in the context of the results of the May 1999 election. The Labour party was less popular among respondents to this study, a fact reflected in the Scottish Parliament election results compared to voting intentions; respondents' voting in the 1997 UK election; and the proportion of votes cast in Scotland for each of the parties. Nevertheless, the first-past-the-post voting intentions of respondents in the Scottish elections did show a close approximation to the final result in that category.

Table 1   Election Results and Voting Intentions of Tourism Professionals

	May 6th Election Results %		Questionnaire results % Intentions for 1999 election		Questionnaire results % how voted in 1997 General Election (first past the post)	National poll in Scotland, May 1997.***
	First past the post	Party list	First past the post	Party list	First past the post	
Labour	39.0	33.0	36.5	24.5	31.0	45.6
Conservative	16.0	15.0	13.0	16.5	23.0	17.5
Liberal Democrat	14.0	12.0	17.5	23.0	14.0	13.0
Scottish National Party	29.0	28.0	20.5	22.5	11.0	22.1
Others*			1.0	2.0	2.0	1.9
Don't know**			11.5	11.5		
Did not vote					19.0	

* Others/Don't know less than 1%   ** Others/Don't know less than 2%
***Source: Brown,   McCrone, Paterson and   Surridge (1999:38)

The relatively high vote for the Conservatives in 1997 among our respondents (23% against 17.5% in Scotland overall) lends minor support to previously aired views concerning the supposed conservatism of many of those in the tourism industry. However, since 1997 the Conservative position in Scotland has weakened further. This was also true of our respondents, whose voting intentions in both the first and second ballots nevertheless expressed a reasonable fit with the final results, the Conservative presence in the new Parliament of 18 members being derived entirely from the second proportional top-up vote.

Intentions to vote Liberal Democrat remained comparatively high in the sample, 14% having voted Liberal Democrat in 1997 but 17.5% intending to select them on their first past the post ballot, rising to 23% on the second 'party list' ballot. In fact, second voting intentions among our respondents were much higher for the Liberal Democrats than was the case for the election result generally, although again, on first voting intentions, those proposing to support the Liberal Democrats were within 3.5% of the outcome.

The Scottish National Party (SNP) position in our results is the most complex. Attaining 22% of the Scottish vote in 1997, they achieved 29% and 28% in the Scottish elections on the first and second ballots respectively. Among our respondents, they fared least well of all the parties in 1997 attracting only 11% of the poll. However, in keeping with national trends, they added ten percentage points to their tally, nevertheless remaining far less popular than with the electorate at large.

Tourism concerns

Earlier in the paper we identified those issues relating to tourism that dominated public debate in the pre-election period. In this section we discuss the results of the survey in respect of the most important of these.

A Minister of Tourism

That the UK has never had a separately defined Minister of Tourism has been a recurrent concern among, in particular, the private sector of the tourism industry. The absence of a separate tourism minister has been seen as an indication of the lack of importance government attaches to the tourism industry (see Hall, 1994, for a general discussion of this point and Wood, 1996, for an account in the UK context). In Scotland, where there have been long-standing rumblings about the effectiveness of arms-length bodies such as the national tourism organisation, the Scottish Tourist Board (STB), the creation of a Scottish Parliament and government threw the issue of a tourism ministry/minister into sharp relief.

Our survey reflects this with 65% of respondents answering 'yes' to the question 'Should there be a minister with exclusive responsibility for tourism in the new parliament?' and 33.5% answering 'no'. The case for a 'dedicated' minister of tourism was most attractive to SNP voters (although the Party's manifesto ultimately envisaged that tourism would be part of a broader portfolio) and operators in the hotel sector (over 70% responding positively to the question). Of those answering 'No' to the question, when asked to what portfolio tourism should belong, 58% responded that it should be the responsibility of a Minister for Industry with only 3% and 1.5% thinking it should be attached to a Minister of Culture or Heritage. The figure of 58% rises to 69% if also taken into account are the 11% of respondents who, in the 'other' category nominated the portfolio of a Minister of Enterprise. These findings give some superficial support to a long-aired view of industry professionals in the UK that tourism has for too long been viewed as a 'soft' industry in the culture/heritage mode as opposed to a major economic sector and chimes well with earlier research into this area (Wood, 1996).

Tourism tax

Unsurprisingly, the private sector and its representative organisations are generally in favour of low taxes on businesses. In Scotland in recent years, the possible introduction of a 'tourism tax', specifically a 'bed tax', has been a recurring theme and is known to be favoured by a number in the public sector, including the current CEO of the Glasgow area Tourism and Convention Bureau. In its briefing document, the BHA (1999: 3) describe the situation thus:

> The introduction of a tourist/bed tax has been suggested in some quarters. Unless the revenue raised is directly ploughed back into the industry or into the tourism infrastructure, such a tax would simply increase costs without improving the value of the visitor experience or the tourism product.

Our questionnaire sought to verify this type of assertion with some emphatic success, 93% of respondents expressing a 'no' to the question 'Would you be supportive of a tourism tax being introduced in the new parliament?'. However, of these, 35% indicated that it would make a positive difference to their view if all of the monies raised by a tourism tax were devoted wholly to the industry, with intending SNP voters most likely to incline this way. The idea of a hypothecated tourism tax thus has some appeal and the results of this survey are at best suggestive of the possibility that some members of the tourism industry are open to possible persuasion.

A 'licence to practice' and business registration issues

An emergent feature of public debates about tourism in Scotland is the view that tourism operators should have a 'licence to practice'. This derives from debates about how best to develop and sustain the quality of the tourism and hospitality product and the management thereof. Scotland's 'official' tourism organisations or representative bodies have yet to express public support for licensing. Discussion has originated at the industry's 'grassroots' and filtered upwards to the public domain (for example, figuring in the 1999 SHIC conference referred to earlier).

The possible future significance of this issue meant it seemed apposite to explore such questions in the survey. In so doing, we linked the issue of licensing to both the professional qualifications <u>and</u> experience of operators of the order 'Would you be supportive of the professional licensing of all tourism businesses (including hospitality businesses) whereby all operators would be required to have appropriate qualifications and experience?'. This allowed five potential responses which, with results, are shown in Table 2.

Table 2   Respondents' attitudes towards the licensing of tourism business operators

Yes - qualifications and experience	58.0%
Yes - qualifications only	9.5%
Yes- experience only	3.5%
Other	15.0%
No	9.0%

Taken as a raw expression of views, that some 71% of respondents felt some regulation of this kind was desirable is significant, given that private sector enterprises, at least as represented by their industry bodies, tend to be broadly hostile to excessive regulation.

It is perhaps at least mildly surprising to find that in addition to the licensed operators issue, a firm majority of respondents to the survey were also in favour of compulsory registration of businesses (66.5%), the idea being most popular among those intending to vote Conservative. Of those in favour of the registration of tourism businesses, 64.5% believed that all such businesses should be included within the Scottish Tourism Board's current classification and grading scheme. Where support for regulation diminishes drastically is unsurprisingly, where it has an impact on 'bottom line' economics. Current regulation of liquor licensing is, within boundaries set by Act of Parliament, at the discretion of local licensing authorities with the result that there is considerable local variation in the times at which establishments are allowed to sell liquor. Here, the resounding response was a clear 79% in favour of more liberal regulations.

Area tourist boards

We considered the issues attendant on the operation of Area Tourist Boards (ATBs) at some length earlier in this paper. Interestingly, there was considerable variation in responses to questions about the future of the ATBs. Only some 54% of respondents were dissatisfied with the existing structure and indeed just over a quarter of respondents rated the number of ATBs as the least important of nine issues facing Scottish tourism in a self-ranking question. Of the 54% dissatisfied with current arrangements, 15% wished to revert to the prior circumstances of 32 ATBs while 43% hoped to see a further reduction in the number of ATBs. Some 37% proposed other options. Likely SNP voters were most dissatisfied with current arrangements while those intending to vote Conservative were most satisfied. Much higher measures of agreement were secured for geographical alignment of the ATB network with that of the LECs, 86% of respondents agreeing with such a proposition.

Party policy bundles

In an effort to go beyond the crude mechanics of assessing voting behaviour, an attempt was made to elicit the party-political policy preferences of respondents without alerting those completing the questionnaire to specific associations between parties and policies. A single question parcelled the stated policies of the four main parties (Labour, SNP, Conservative, Liberal Democrat) into individual 'summary boxes'. To these were added two further 'bundles', one including the published policies of the Scottish Green Party and the second an 'idealised' set of policies constructed by the principal researcher (Kerr). The content of this last was based on analysis of interviews with key players in the Scottish tourism industry, the earlier noted stage of the larger research project. The order in which these boxes were presented on the questionnaire was determined randomly (Table 3). Respondents were asked to mark the box that contained the set of statements with which they most agreed. This exercise produced much less pronounced results than the more direct question elements of the instrument, for example as compared to voting intentions (Table 4).

Table 3   Policy bundles of Scotland's political parties as presented to respondents

The table shows, in descending order, the idealised policy bundle constructed by the Researcher followed by the announced policies of the Green, SNP, Labour, Liberal Democrat and Conservative Parties

- Total restructure in order that one overall body is responsible for tourism and hospitality
- Extension of classification and grading to all accommodation and food premises
- Registration of all tourism businesses
- Central funding of ATBs combined with sectoral revision of ATB Board composition
- Relationship with BTA to cease
- A Minister for Tourism as part of the Enterprise and Industry portfolio

---

- Establish a Countryside Commission for Scotland
- Minister for Tourism who will also have other ministerial responsibilities
- Scottish Tourist Board will remain as at present, but more organic in nature
- Introduce a land value tax
- More emphasis on public transport
- Sustainable tourism and care of the environment would be a high priority

---

- Minister for Tourism who will also have other ministerial responsibilities
- STB incorporated into the Enterprise Network as Come to Scotland both at home and abroad with the whole Enterprise Network being integrated both locally and nationally
- Commercial embassies in various countries world-wide, with tourism an effective part of these embassies, and also share offices around the world with Locate in Scotland
- ATBs integrated into the Enterprise Network/economic development arm locally.
- Relationship with BTA would continue, while fighting for better representation

---

- Retention of the STB, ATB and Enterprise Network structure as at present
- Funding of ATBs from a central body such as STB rather than councils and LECs, after discussion with COSLA
- Continuation of relationship between STB and BTA
- Scottish Tourism Forum to be encouraged to become the voice of the industry – already on the Scottish Tourism Co-ordinating Group
- A review of all aspects of transport links

- Tourism Minister as part of an Enterprise and Education Ministry
- Tourism Commission, with government, industry, consumer and environmental representation.
- Restructuring of the ATB network, reflecting more local needs
- Funding for tourism centralised
- Relationship with BTA, as it stands, would be reviewed
- Introduce a statutory national registration for all accommodation providers providing five or more bedrooms and would review the classification / grading system
- Minister for Tourism as part of a portfolio embracing other responsibilities – probably industry

- Commission into the future of Scottish Tourism
- Sever all links with BTA, with STB taking over that marketing function
- Review licensing
- Introduce a system of tax-breaks for employers to support skills development
- Revise the ATB structure in order that it fitted with local aspirations
- Lobby Westminster to reduce the VAT level on tourists

Table 4   Party policy preferences of respondents compared to voting intention

	Preferred policy bundle of respondents %	Respondent voting intention, 1st vote %	Respondent voting intention, 2nd vote %
Labour	25.12	36.5	24.5
Conservative	13.31	13.0	16.5
Liberal Democrat	14.39	17.5	23.0
Scottish National Party	10.29	20.5	22.5
Green	4.63		
Idealised policies	22.82		
Others	9.44	1.0	2.0
Don't know		11.5	11.5
Did not vote			

The most interesting aspects of these results are that:

- With the exception of the Conservatives, support for individual policy bundles trails first vote intentions in every case perhaps suggesting a substantial diversity of opinion among tourism professionals responding to this survey;

- There was a very high measure of support for the 'idealised' bundle of policies amongst respondents, irrespective of their voting intentions;

- There was a very low measure of support for the SNPs tourism policy as against the first and second voting intentions of the respondents - double the number of respondents intended to vote SNP in each ballot as preferred the SNPs policy for Scottish tourism. In fact, overall some 68% of SNP voters preferred one of the other policy bundles to their own party's;

- Similarly, for the Labour party, around 60% of would-be Labour voters preferred alternative policy bundles (13% selecting the Conservative policy bundle) and more intending Liberal Democrat voters preferred the Conservative policy bundle than intending Conservative voters; and

- Interesting variations according to age, gender and operator category and preferred policy bundles were noted: older respondents tended to prefer Labour's policies over those of other parties; women respondents were always less likely to select their party's policy bundles than men; and, curiously perhaps, all sectors represented by the sample save one (education) selected Labour policies for preference – this included business operators. Those recording themselves as being in 'education' preferred the Liberal Democrat policy bundle.

Conclusions

The preliminary results from the questionnaire reported in this paper cannot be described as high science but they offer small insights into a current issue of some interest. Scotland is a small country where tourism supports 8-10% of all full-time equivalent jobs. More importantly, the interplay between the public and private sectors is highly visible: the role of tourism in society and economy is part of everyday discourse and has been thrown into relief in the run-up to the election of the Scottish Parliament. This makes the study of policy development and policy rhetoric especially interesting. As a focus for such study, the values of those involved at all levels of the tourism industry are an important and under-researched topic for investigation. The present study reflects a particular and highly significant moment in Scottish history but the question of the relationship between political values and policy development is one germane to most complex democracies. Further stages of the wider project of which this study forms a part will investigate these matters. The implications of the present study can possibly be best characterised in terms of the consequences for policy of social actors' location in a political milieu as mediated by their professional interests. The larger, longitudinal study of which the questionnaire results reported here are one element offers significant opportunities for the exploration of a range of issues relating to tourism development in post-industrial economies. The present findings are indicative of the likely richness of such development in the sphere of politics and public policy.

References

Aslan, A. and Wood, R. C. (1993), 'Trade Unions in the hotel and catering industry: the views of hotel managers', *Employee Relations*, 15 (2): 61-69.

British Hospitality Association (1999), *Hospitality and Government in Scotland: a Briefing Document 1999*, Edinburgh: British Hospitality Association.

Brown, A. McCrone, D. and Paterson, L. (1998), *Politics and Society in Scotland*, London: Macmillan.

Brown, A. McCrone, D. Paterson, L. and Surridge, P. (1999), *The Scottish Electorate: the 1997 General Election and Beyond*, London: Macmillan.

Hall, C. M. (1994), Tourism and Politics: Policy, Power and Place, London: John Wiley.

House of Commons Scottish Affairs Committee (1999), Tourism in Scotland, Volume 1: Report and Proceedings of the Committee, London: The Stationery Office.

Kerr, W R and Wood, R C (1999) 'Scottish Tourism after Devolution', The Hospitality Review, April, 16-23.

Kerr, W. R. and Wood, R. C. (2000), 'Tourism policy in a small state: the case of Scotland', Anatolia, 10 (1): 15-28.

Kerr, W. R. and Wood, R. C. (2000a, in press), 'Political values of tourism and hospitality industry professionals: a Scottish case study', *Tourism Management*, 21.

Smith, R. (1998), 'Public policy for tourism in Scotland', in R MacLellan and R Smith (Eds) *Tourism in Scotland*, London: International Thomson Business Press, 42-69.

Wood, R. C. (1993), 'Hotel and catering services and employment in Scotland', *Scottish Affairs*, (3): 77-88.

Wood, R. C. (1996), 'The last feather-bedded industry? Government, politics and the hospitality industry during and after the 1992 General Election', *Tourism Management*, 17 (8): 583-592.

Frequent flyer programmes in the EU

Jesper Fredborg Larsen and Susanne Storm

University of Southern Denmark, Odense, Denmark

Introduction

World regulation of air transport

International air transport is a highly complex area. It is also of great commercial importance and in its origin closely connected with the nations of the world.. Air transport for commercial purposes first became important after World War II. It was a matter of prestige for each State to have its own national airline - which was significantly called the "flagcarrier" of that State. British Airways, KLM, Lufthansa, Iberia, Air France and SAS are examples. Every State maintained complete sovereignty over the airspace of its own territory. This principle somehow had to be regulated, if commercial air transport were to become feasible. The 1944 Chicago Convention, to which most countries in the world adhere, together with two international agreements adopted that same year, did this. An international, multilateral scheme was established under these agreements but only for the very limited traffic rights of overflight without landing and stops for refuelling purposes. The more commercially significant traffic rights, namely the right to carry passengers and freight to and from another country, not to mention the right to fly domestic routes in another country (cabotage), could not be agreed upon on a multilateral basis. These traffic rights are negotiated on a bilateral basis between two nations and the world is now spanned by a network of such bilateral "Air Service Agreements". They are and always have been highly restrictive and only national carriers from the two contracting States were allowed to operate between the two countries. Thus air transport became characterized by regulatory barriers to entry, market sharing and price fixing.

The US market for air transport has always been different from the European. Since it is a large country it has a market for domestic commercial air transport which has no equal in Europe. Nevertheless this internal market was made subject to tight Federal control from the beginning. It was not till the end of the 1970s - beginning of 1980s that the US market for air transport was liberalized. This deregulation also had its effects on air transport to and from the USA across the Atlantic, as the US adopted "Open Skies" policy. This policy did. not involve a departure from the bilateral agreements between the US and other countries, but it did mean that more liberal bilateral agreements could be negotiated. Links were established between US airlines and European partners. The ultimate goal was and is that US companies would be able to fly domestic routes in Europe and vice versa.

The European Union has been and still is weakened by the fact that in relation to third countries there is shared competencies when completing international agreements. The Commission claims it should have sole powers to negotiate, but Member States do still enter into bilateral agreements notably the "Open Skies" agreements with the US. At present the Commission has initiated proceedings in the European Court of Justice (ECJ) for breach of the Treaty against eight European countries who have concluded "Open Skies" agreements with the US.

This paper focusses on a limited aspect of the effect of deregulation on air transport, namely, the effect of frequent flyer programmes (FFPs) on air transport markets. We will compare two economic models of the effects of FFPs on air transport markets with present EU competition practices under articles 81 and 82. Our hope is that this attempt to analyze FFPs will throw some light on the liberalization of air transport in the Community and its success. In order for us to do so, we will examine briefly the state of the deregulated market in the Community. Do we have an internal market for air transport? Then follows an analysis of the characteristics of FFPs, after which an outline of the results of two economic models is presented. We then examine how the Commission has dealt with the FFPs according to the EU competition rules. The aim of the paper is to answer the question whether or not present EU practice with regard to the FFPs is backed up by economic theory and observations of the functioning of the market for air transport. This discussion is followed by our policy conclusions and a final conclusion.

The EU internal market for air transport

Following the failure of the 1944 Chicago Convention to establish a mulitilateral regime, the European governments set up their own regulatory systems for their fledgeling air transport industries with the basic aim of protecting their national flag carriers - mostly publicly owned - from competition. Over the years, a tight international network of bilateral air transport agreements concerning scheduled air transport was developed in Europe.

When the Treaty of Rome was signed in 1957 air (and sea) transport were excluded from the general transport policy provisions of the Treaty (Articles 74 - 84, now 70 - 80). Instead Article 84(2) provides that air transport policy measures shall be taken as and when the Council decides. The reason for this was that the governments did not feel ready to include air transport in the removal of their national barriers.

The Council was reluctant to use its powers under Article 84(2), which in 1983 resulted in the European Parliament taking the Council to Court under Article 175 (now 232). In 1985 the European Court of Justice held in favour of the European Parliament and a few months after the Court's decision the Council presented its "Master Plan" concerning transport policy. It became an object for the Council to achieve the internal market in the air transport sector in two ways: 1) By requiring the Member States to abolish their national barriers and to move from a bilateral to a multilateral system under Article 84(2); 2) by applying the competition rules of Articles 85 and 86 (now 81 and 82) in order to eliminate the anti-competitive agreements between airline companies. In 1986 in the "Nouvelles Frontières", the ECJ was asked for a preliminary ruling concerning fares below the tariffs agreed upon by IATA and approved by the French Ministry of Transport. The Court ruled that air transport was subject to the Treaty's provisions on competition even in the abscence of implementing regulations. The Commission complied with the Court's ruling by proceeding against ten major European airlines for contravening Article 85 (now 81).

The process of liberalization was carried out in three stages, each stage usually termed the first, the second and third package respectively. The first package was adopted by the Council in 1987, the second in 1990 and the third in June 1992. The third package coincided with the completion of the internal market.

Articles 85 and 86 were made applicable to international air transport between member states as part of the first package in 1987. In April 1989 the ECJ delivered a judgement in the Ahmed Saeed Flugreisen case, which established that the competition rules apply also to domestic air transport and to air transport between Member States and third countries. The third package of 1992 extended the scope of application of the competition rules to domestic air transport within a Member State.

The Commission granted wide block exemptions in the area of air transport related services. These block exemptions have been updated continously throughout the1990s. (Blanco and Houtte 1996, p. 169).

Summing up, the competition rules apply to air transport under three different regimes: 1) Articles 81 and 82 are fully applicable to all air transport within the Community; 2) "the interim regime" referred to in the "Nouvelles Frontières case" provided by Articles 84 and 85 (ex 88 and 89) applies to air transport between Member States and third countries; 3) the competition rules apply only to air transport as such. Any other activity in connection with air transport is governed by the ordinary competition rules.

The third package allowed free tariff-fixing as from 1st January 1993. Two policies can be distinguished on the European market: 1) One is employed by the big, established airlines. They compete for market shares by offering a great variety of discounted fares on selected flights during limited seasons and on a limited number of seats; 2) smaller airlines with fewer routes and less flight frequency make use of the policy of offering discounted fares on all their flights. Virgin Express and Ryan Air make use of this practice.

Since April 1, 1997 there has been an internal market within the market for air transport. In 1996, there were 518 routes within the Community of which 64 per cent were flown by airlines with monopoly, 30 per cent were duopolized and 6 per cent were flown by more than two airlines (in 1993, there were 488 routes, and the corresponding figures were 61 per cent, 37 per cent and 2 per cent). In 1996, 30 routes were served under the fifth freedom in the air compared with 14 in 1993. COM (96). The internal market for air transport is still incomplete between Member States and third countries due to the bilateral agreements.

In connection with the establishment of the internal market many European airlines in the EU followed a policy of total or partial privatization. This was a result of reduced government involvement and liberalization. The first airlines to be privatized were British Airways in the UK and KLM in the Netherlands. British Airways is the largest airline company in Europe and fully privately owned. SAS, Lufthansa and Swissair are partly privately and partly publicly owned. AirFrance, Alitalia, Olympic Airways and Iberia are still fully publicly owned.

As a compliment to privatization, practically all the European airlines have entered into partnership agreements. The Commission has two means of controlling such agreements, either by applying Article 81 or the Merger Control Regulation. The objective of partnership agreements is to create competitive advantages for the partners by complementing each other's services and by achieving economy of scale, while still keeping their independence. Most of the agreements made between the European airlines follow a pattern set by British Airways. The main alliances between airlines in Europe created links to airline companies in the rest of the world. The bigger airlines have several other, smaller alliances with partners both inside and outside Europe. The third package helped to promote this type of agreement. Thus there were 59 alliances in 1990, 138 in 1994 and 171 in 1995. COM (96). These partnership agreements will be dealt with below in connection with the application of the competition rules to FFPs.

Frequent flyer programmes - history and facts

The first frequent flyer programme was devised by American Airlines (AA) in 1981 as an attempt to create consumer loyalty in the newly deregulated US market. AA also sought to facilitate acceptance of the "hub and spoke system" which meant longer flight times as compared to direct flights. AA was so successful that all other major US carriers followed.

European carriers first participated in the schemes of US carriers and then developed their own programmes. In 1991 and 1992, most European carriers launched their own plans, but compared to their American counterparts they remained modest in size. In 1992 the AA scheme had 16 million members worldwide; BA: 186,000; KLM: 120,000; SAS: 70,000; Air France: 95,000; Iberia: 100,000; Swissair: 100,000. (Vechère 1993, p. 16). In 1997, AAdvantage had 28 million members worldwide compared to BA's 1 million members worldwide, SAS' 1 million, Air France's 1,3 million and Iberia's 450,000 members worldwide (figures for the other airlines are not available for 1997). (Vechère 1997, p. 31 - 36). However, 86 per cent of European business travellers belong to an FFP. In each Member State the national airline's scheme is easily the most popular, but there are wide differences as to the degree of popularity. In the UK, 52 per cent preferred BA's FFP compared to 34 per cent for Air France's in France or 47 per cent in Germany for Lufthansa's. (Drabbe 1996, p. 1).

An FFP is one of several marketing tools a carrier can use to develop customer loyalty. FFPs are designed in such a way as to encourage a passenger to choose a particular service even if its schedule is less convenient and/or its fares are less competitive as some US empirical surveys suggest to be the case. Stephenson and Fox (1987) and (1993). FFPs have been extended to travel related companies such as hotels, restaurants and car rental companies - even telephone companies - thus extending the network of loyalty.

The traveller participating in an FFP receives bonus points or miles for each flight. The number of points is either related to the distance travelled or to the destination geographical zone. Some FFPs issue points only for full fare price tickets or for first and business class. In this respect, EuroBonus of SAS is remarkable for also allowing discounted fares to give right to bonus points. In the US, discounted fares also entitle programme members to frequent flyer points. European FFPs are more targeted towards business travellers and quality linked compared with their US counterparts. On the whole, European schemes take more flying to accumulate sufficient points or miles to obtain an equivalent flight in comparison to US schemes.

All programmes are constructed to offer bonus points in a non-linear way. Thus, for the consumer to accumulate points in several programmes is a waste of bonus points as he will be unable to accumulate enough points to obtain a free bonus trip with any one of them. In some cases airlines impose a time limit, before expiry of which a minimum number of bonus points has to be accumulated. Failing this, participation in the programme and the bonus points already credited to the participant will be cancelled. Other airlines may require a minimum number of flights during a certain period. Aditionally, some airlines have introduced expiry dates for bonus points already collected. Expiry dates also serve to limit an airline's liabilities in terms of the accumulated stock of bonus points collected by its passengers.

Economic modelling of FFPs and competition between airlines

Two papers explicitly explore the effect of FFPs on competition between airlines. Both papers see FFPs as increasing consumers' switching cost. Switching costs for the consumer are either "natural" costs or costs created by companies which affect the consumer's choice between different suppliers. Natural switching costs for the consumer are typically: transportation costs and uncertainty when gathering information about different suppliers' goods. Firm created, consumer switching costs correspond to benefits for the firm such as reputation, better quality, more favourable discounts than those offered by competitors as well as brand and firm loyalty.

The FFPs with their incorporation of a payoff system similar to normal quantity discounts aim to create artificial loyalty links between the consumer and the programme holding airline. This is done by creating artificial switching costs for the consumer by promising a discount on travels when becoming a member of the programme, on condition that the member flies more often with the programme holding airline, than with its competitors.

The first paper is an article by Cairns and Galbraith (1990) which focuses almost entirely on the behaviour of business travellers who utilise a principal agent relationship to maximise their own benefits from being members of a programme. The principal agent problem arises because of cost to the principal of monitoring the agent. The principal in this case is the employer and the agent is the travelling employee. Cairns and Galbraith model this relationship by assuming that the agent only pays a fraction of the cost of his purchases and that monitoring costs are sufficiently high for the principal to place no restrictions on the agent's choice of supplier or level of supply. The airlines are modelled as having identical cost functions and allowed to have different networks. Cost are assumed to be separable across markets so that there are no economies of scope. They further assume that there exist no network externalities. Markets are characterised by Bertrand competition.

The second paper is a working paper by Banerjee and Summers (1987), who assume that consumers have homogenous preferences. Thus, they do not distinguish between consumer segments. They model competition between airlines in a game theoretic model with sequential prices setting and simultaneous rebate size setting. They allow airlines to have identical cost functions. Their market is also characterised by Bertrand competition. The model examines the effect of FFPs on airline entry and exit, pricing and market structure.

Cairns and Galbraith find that the programmes increase consumers' valuation of otherwise non-related products, or in the words of the two authors creating "artificial compatibility". Artificial compatibility means that buying from the same producer becomes advantageous where it would not otherwise have been so. This is a result of the offer of frequent flyer points when flying on the programme holder's routes but is different from "bundling" where services or goods are sold jointly. The authors conclude that artificial compatibility effects consumers' choice of carrier. By creating such an artificial relationship between a programme holding airline's own routes, the greater the network size, the better the airline is able to compete. The sheer number of routes possessed by the programme holding airline becomes a comparative advantage in the presence of FFPs compared with carriers with smaller networks. Having a large network increases the on offer to programme members and increases the number of available routes on which the FFP members can earn bonus points. In addition the FFP holding airline's services become incompatible with those of rivals, since bonus points obtained when flying with competitors rarely can be used elsewhere.

If a new entrant airline does not have the same network size as the incumbent, entry will not be possible. The authors' main point is that the possession of a larger network enables the incumbent airline to offer its FFP members a better service than the entrant with a smaller network in terms of number of available destinations. To some extent the model even allows for entrants to be more cost effective than the incumbent airline, but still unable to compete with it. For this aspect see Cairns and Galbraith (1990, pp. 810 - 811).

The authors also find that if a network is small, some travellers may find it advantageous to become members of more than one programme, since different networks have different destinations and a small network size may not fit all the traveller's travel needs. Being a member of more than one programme can then be seen as the consumers' way to maximise their overall travel utility.

They conclude: (1) an incumbent with a large network and a frequent flyer programme gives the airline such a strong position on the market that a small competitor wanting to enter on one of the incumbent's routes is unable to do so; (2) having a programme enables an incumbent to keep prices at a high level, at the same time keep entrants out and earn higher than normal profits; (3) an airline with an equal size network and programme as the incumbent is able to stay on the market. But there is no additional profits for either airline as a result of each having a programme.

The second paper by Banerjee and Summers reach the opposite conclusion compared with Cairns and Galbraith. They do not find that the FFPs constitute a barrier to entry. In contrast to Cairns and Galbraith, Banerjee and Summers assume that all travellers pay full fare. They see FFPs as a form of "contract" between the incumbent and the programme members according to which the incumbent promises to pay out a "rebate" when the members have accumulated enough bonus points. Thus, having an FFP, makes the incumbent less willing to compete with new entrants as it must honour its FFP obligation to pay out the rebate to its "hostage customers", namely programme members.

Entry without an FFP in a market where the incumbent is a monopolist, owning a programme, enables the entrant to capture the entire market, since having a FFP ties down the incumbent. In markets with more than one incumbent all having a programme, entry is likely but timing the entrance till after rebate size is announced by the incumbents will ensure successful entry. If entry takes place before the rebate size is announced then entry will fail. In this model having a programme, signals surrender in that the entrant can enter freely without fear of damaging price wars initiated by the incumbent.

In the situation where two airlines exist on a market and no potential entry, it is advantageous for both airlines to have a programme, as it enables them to fix monopoly prices in periods following the introduction of the programme. Contrary to what one might expect, the authors find that this does not lead to sharp price competition in the programme introduction period, since maintenance of collusion, i.e. both firms charging monopoly prices, requires that both firms have hostage customers both before and after the introduction of the programme.

Conclusions of the two models

With regard to price and welfare effects of FFPs, the two models show that the existence of FFPs increases prices and reduces welfare by: (1) transferring resources from consumers to producers; (2) exacerbating the principal agent relationship. This last happens because travel spending and monitoring costs of the employer increase.

The models suggest that FFPs increase the survival chance for monopolies and oligopoly market structures in the air transport markets. But where the model by Cairns and Galbraith claims that this is due to the FFPs' effect on entry and the network size of airlines, Banerjee and Summers regard the effect of FFPs on entry as unimportant and the suggested market structures follow from the contestable market assumption alone. In the Cairns and Galbraith model one market strategy stands out and that is for the airlines to make alliances or merge with existing carriers to increase network size.

FFPs and the applicability of the EC - Treaty's Competition Rules

Article 81

The Commission has not published its position towards FFPs, but it seems that the Commission conducted an unpublished study concerning new entry in air transport in June 1992, which found that FFPs can act as an anti-competitive method employed by large carriers which cannot be matched by small airlines and impedes them from competing profitably. Drabbe (1996, p. 3). Furthermore the Commission's attitude is evident as it appears in different airline partnership agreements and mergers investigated by the Commission under article 81(1) and 81(3). In these decisions, the Commission imposes a condition for granting an exemption under 81(3) on the merging airlines to offer to smaller competitors access to participate in the merging airlines' FFPs on reasonable and non-discriminatory financial conditions. Both in the BA/TAT and Swissair/Sabena mergers in

1992 and 1995, the Commission limited this obligation to last until a Community regulation concerning FFPs were adopted. This limitation was not mentioned again in the Lufthansa/SAS partnership agreement, and it seems that in the meantime the Commission had given up its plan for regulating FFPs. But the Commission stated in paragraph 53 of that decision that, the "...pooling of frequent - flyer programmes is....an aspect that must be taken into account in assessing the economic power of the undertakings. Most of the customers are businessmen, and they will clearly prefer airlines that have a joint frequent - flyer programme, allowing them to earn points whatever airline used. A common system is thus likely to constitute a not inconsiderable barrier to other airlines that do not have comparable programmes."

Article 82

Under article 82, Community law does not prohibit large airlines from taking advantage of their networks by exploiting size-related advantages when marketing their service. As long as a particular airline's FFP does not constitute an abuse in the sense of article 82, then difficulties arising for the smaller competitors because the larger airline exploits its network size must be accepted.

So far the neither the Commission nor the ECJ has considered cases involving FFPs in relation to article 82. But both have considered fidelity rebates in the Hoffmann - La Roche judgement and target rebates in the Michelin judgement. A fidelity rebate is a rebate in which the purchaser explicitly or implicitly undertakes to obtain all or most of his supplies from the supplier. A target rebate on the other hand is a system whereby the granting of the rebate is conditional upon the attainment of a certain target. The results of the decisions may possibly be transferred to FFPs. The ECJ found that fidelity rebates were different from quantity rebates, which are legal, in that they are designed through the grant of financial advantages, to limit consumer choice between competitors and in that sense abusive. In the Michelin case the ECJ argued that towards the end of the reference period set for the attainment of the target, the purchaser is under pressure to reach the target or lose the rebate, thus discouraging the purchaser from choosing freely between different suppliers. Accordingly it was considered abusive under article 82.

Applying above judgments to FFPs, the following results can be obtained:

1. An FFP can be regarded as a fidelity rebate, as it is based on the explicit or implicit condition that the passenger will obtain all or most of his supplies from the airline operating the FFP. As the programmes grant bonus to the consumer on a non-linear basis, the programme members will find it advantageous to concentrate all their purchases of air transport with one programme holding airline. Thus, membership of a programme will limit the customer's willingness to obtain his supplies of air transport from competing airlines.

2. FFPs may also be considered as a target rebates, as the granting of the rebate is conditional upon the attainment of a certain target, for example a certain number of bonus points within a specific reference period in order to obtain a free flight. Particularly towards the end of the reference period, the passenger is under pressure to reach the target. Many FFPs are designed in this way and

accordingly fall within the scope of Article 82. If, as in many of the schemes, the cut-off dates are rolling, i.e. linked in each case to the date on which the points were awarded, the result is less likely. On the other hand, the fact that many airlines reserve their right to alter the terms of the programme and to introduce new time limits, black-out periods and - indeed - to terminate the scheme practically from day to day, the application of Article 82 seems even more justified.

Do the models agree with the Commission position on the FFPs?

Entry

The Commission attitude is that the pooling of FFPs in connection with an airline alliance is likely to constitute a not inconsiderable barrier to market entry, (article 81(1)). The economic model by Cairns and Galbraith agrees with this. Banerjee and Summers disagree. The Commission's approach by requiring merging airlines to allow smaller airlines with no FFP to participate in theirs, (article 81 (3)), does ensure market entry according to Cairns and Galbraith's model. This is because the entrant acquires access to the artificial network of the airline alliance, which makes the switching costs for programme members between flying with the alliance and the entrant to disappear. Both programme members of the alliance and the entrant's customers get a fair share of the benefit of the alliance as required by article 81 (3). Banerjee and Summers regard the effect of FFPs on entry as unimportant and any effects on entry are due to their contestable market assumption.

Price effects

In its investigation of the partnership agreements of the airlines mentioned above, the Commission seems not to have taken into consideration whether or not the FFPs have any price effects. Both models disagree. Cairns and Galbraith show that in the existence of the FFPs and the resulting better utilization of network size will lead to higher than normal prices. The Commissions position when allowing entrant airlines without FFPs to participate in the programme of the merging airlines involves a permission for the merging airlines and the entrant airline to use their combined networks better. In accordance to Cairns and Galbraith this will lead to even higher prices than otherwise.

Banerjee and Summers regard the effect of FFPs on entry as unimportant since entrant airlines do not have hostage customers when the entrants enter the market. The Commission's permission allows entrants to get their fair share of hostage customers from participating in the programme of the merging airlines. In accordance with Banerjee and Summers the fact that airlines have hostage customers will reduce their willingness to compete which will most certainly lead to higher prices.

Both results above resemble situations where undertakings with dominant positions is allowed to abuse thier position with the Commission's permission!

Market structure

The above results under entry and price effects suggest that airlines will want to enter into bigger and bigger alliances. This is because increasing network size and increasing number of hostage customers, will allow airlines to increase their profits in step with the willingness to compete is reduced. Thus, markets will be morer concentrated.

Welfare effects

The Commission position to the mergers and alliances, their decision to permit them, to have joint programmes and allow entrants to participate, will most likely reduce overall social welfare.

Those who will benefit clearly from the existence of the FFPs and the Commission's decision are the airlines themselves and the business travellers who travel for their companies' money. The losers will be the employers, ordinary travellers.

Policy conclusions

A prohibition?

Since FFPs are a worldwide phenomenon it is unrealistic to prohibit FFPs unilaterally in the EU as this will damage or weaken the European airlines' ability to compete on the world market with foreign airlines who are allowed to use the programmes. A prohibition will only be a realistic option globally through WTO, OECD or one of the worldwide air transport associations, such as IATA.

A grey market for selling and buying of bonus points?

A grey market for selling and buying bonus points existed for some time in the US where for a period bonus points were not registered as belonging to a particular user. The bonus could be exchanged or sold on the grey market by brokers who specialized in this. There were even magazines published that advertized the offer of bonus points for sale.

A grey market for selling and buying of bonus points, is based on the idea that programme members are not getting what they are paying for, because they are unable to accumulate enough bonus points. The traveller who realizes that he will be unable to travel the required number of trips to be able to reach the target for a free bonus trip, can still benefit from being a programme member by selling his bonus savings on the grey market. This will enable more travellers to redeem bonus points and obtain free bonus trips which is contrary to the interest of the airlines.

In practice this solution is not viable at least not in the EU as bonus points are always registered under name and non negotiable.

A code of conduct?

A code of conduct for the use of FFPs by the airlines in the EU should contain the following elements: (1) a standard of good marketing practice ensuring correct and adequate information about the FFP to the customer in order to make the customer able to compare different programmes, their advantages and disadvantages. (2) A code of conduct could also incorporate the Commission's attitude that airlines without a comparable programme should be allowed to join the programmes of existing airlines. (3) It could also require to declare outstanding bonus points on their balance sheets, thus making airlines legally and financial liable in case an airline becomes insolvent.

This "soft law" solution is the most realistic solution of the ones mentioned. It would be a good beginning and not too restrictive for the airlines to cope with. It would also be a good starting point for negotiating the future of the programmes on the world air transport market.

Conclusion

As has been shown there appear to be both entry and price effects in connection with the airlines having the programmes. The Commission appears only to have considered entry effects in connection with article 81 and mergers. We therefore find it peculiar that the Commission did not reach a position according to which the programmes could be regulated. We would suggest that such a position should be reached and should involve the elaboration of a code of conduct with the content indicated above.

References

Books:

Blanco, L. O. and van Houtte, B. (1996), *EC Competition Law in the Transport Sector*, Clarendon Press, Oxford.

Havel, B. F. (1997), *In Search of Open Skies: Law and Policy for a New Era in International Aviation*, Kluwer Law International, The Hague.

Vellas, F. and Bècherel, L. (1995), *International Tourism*, Macmillan Press ltd.

Articles:

Banerjee, A. and L. H. Summers, (1987), "On Frequent Flyer Programs and Other Loyalty-Inducing Economic Arrangements." Discussion Paper No. 1337, Harvard Institute of Economic Research, Cambridge, MA.

Cairns, R. D. and J. W. Galbraith, (1990), "Artificial Compatability, Barriers to Entry, and Frequent-Flyer Programs." *Canadian Journal of Economics*, 23(4): 807-816.

Drabbe, H. (1996),"Frequent Flyer Programmes Competition Aspects." Speech held in Copenhagen for the European Air Law Association, 8 November 1996.

Levine, M. E. (1987), Airline Competition in Deregulated Markets: Theory, Firm Strategy, and Public Policy, *Yale Journal of Regulation*, 4: 393 - 494.

Stephenson, F. H. and Fox R. J. (1987), Corporate Attitudes Toward Frequent Flier Programs, *Transportation Journal*, Fall: 10 - 22.

Stephenson, F. H. and Fox R. J. (1993), Criticism of Frequent Flier Plans by Large and Small Corporations, *The Logistics and Transportation Review*, September: 241 - 258.

Vechère, I. (1993), Frequent Flyer Programmes, *EIU Travel & Tourism Analyst*, No. 3: 5 - 19.

Vechère, I. (1997), Airlines' Frequent Flyer Programmes: Counting the Cost of Loyalty, *Executive Travel*, February: 28 - 36.

EC Legislation: (Regulations, Directives, Decisions)

BA/TAT (O.J. 1992 C 326).

Commission Decision of 20 July 1995, IP/95/805 (Swissair/ Sabena).

Council Regulation EC no. 4064/89 of 21 December 1989, Merger Regulation, as amended by Council Regulation EC no. 1310/97 of 30 June 1997.

Lufthansa/ SAS (O.J. 1996 L 54).

First Package:

Council Decision No. 87/602/EEC (O.J. 1987 L 374/19).

Council Directive No. 87/601/EEC (O.J. 1987 L 374/12).

Council Regulation No. EEC/3975/87 (O.J. 1987 L 374/1).

Council Regulation No. EEC/3976/87 (O.J: 1987 L 374/9).

Council Regulation Nos. EEC/2671-2673/88 (O.J. 1988 L 239/9, 13 and 17).

Second Package:

Council Regulation No. EEC/2342/90 (O.J. 1990 L 217/1).

Council Regulation No. EEC/2343/90 (O.J. 1990 L 217/8).

Third Package:

Council Regulation No. EEC/2407/92 (O.J. 1992 L 240/1).

Council Regulation No. EEC/2408/92 (O.J. 1992 L 240/8).

Council Regulation No. EEC/2409/92 (O.J. 1992 L 240/15).

Other EC Material:

Bulletin of European Commission 11/85 (1985).

Commission Communication IP/98/966, 5 November 1998.

Commission MEMO/95/24, 2 March 1995.

IP/98/640: "Commission Publishes its Conditions for Approving the Lufthansa/SAS/United Airlines Air Alliance."

IP/98/641: "Commission Publishes its Conditions for Approving the British Airways/ American Airlines Air Alliance."

"The Effects of the Third Package for the Liberalisation of Air Transport." Report of 22 October 1996 COM(96) 514 final.

Other Legislation:

Convention on International Civil Aviation of 7 December 1944 (the Chicago Convention), The United Nations Treaty Series, 1948, 296. International Air Transport Agreement. International Air Services Transit Agreement.

ECJ Cases:

Case European Parliament v. Council, case 13/83 [1985] ECR 1513 [1986] 1 CMLR 138.

Case 66/86, *"Ahmed Saeed Flugreisen and Silverline Reisebüro v. Zentrale zur Bekämpfung unlauteren Wettbewerbs* EV." [1989] ECR 803; [1990] 4 CMLR 102.

Case 85/76, *Hoffman - La Roche v. Commission* [1979] ECR 461; [1979] 3 CMLR 211.

Case 322/81, N.V. *Nederlandse Bänder - Industrie Michelin v. Commission*, [1983] 3461; [1982] 1 CMLR 643.

ECJ Opinion 2/92, [1995] ECR I - 521 (OECD).

ECJ Opinion 1/94, [1994] ECR I - 5267 (WTO).

Ministère Public v. Lucas Asjès ("Nouvelles Frontières") (Joined Cases 209-213/84) [1986] ECR 1425.

The locational advantage of tourism destinations - determinants, dimensions and dynamics

Zhenhua Liu

University of Strathclyde, UK

Introduction

"Tourism is a resource industry, one which is dependent on nature's endowment and society's heritage" (Murphy 1985:12). As tourism resources are not evenly or randomly distributed across the world, some places are well endowed with tourism resources while others are not. In particular, different locations have different types of resources that are conducive to different types of tourism development, such as beach resort, ski resort or urban tourism. For the tourists, travel is about an experience of place. Location is important in travel because, in addition to the spatial fixity of tourist attractions in a destination, monetary, physical and temporal resources have to be invested to overcome the friction of distance, which is a major constraint in destination selection decisions.

However, the relationship between destination location and tourism development has been largely neglected in tourism research. In fact, no study on the locational advantage of tourism destinations, to the best knowledge of the present author, has ever been published though some efforts have been made to analyse the site-selection process of tourism organisations (e.g., Moutinho and Paton 1991; Smith 1995). An attempt is made here to fill this gap.

This paper aims to explore the locational advantage of tourism destinations. The first section briefly analyses the interrelation between destination location and tourism development in the light of location theory and trade theory, both of which are largely based on the concept of comparative advantages of a place. This is followed by an evaluation of the determinants of locational advantage of tourism destinations. The characteristics of each of the four dimensions of destination location and their implications for tourism development are discussed in section three. The fourth section explores the dynamics of locational advantage through an examination of the main trends of locational changes and the implications for tourism development. Finally it is concluded with a sketch of the future locational changes in world tourism.

Destination location and tourism development

The concept of tourism destination appears to be loosely used to refer to any place where tourists visit and stay during their holidays. Gunn makes the distinction between three different scales – the site scale, the destination zone scale and the regional scale. He defines destination zone as "a geographic area containing a critical mass of development that satisfies traveller objectives" (Gunn 1994:27). A critical mass of tourism development implies a large enough and diverse enough amount of attractions and services to meet the needs and desires of several travel market segments. However, for different types of tourists the spatial scale of a destination may differ substantially. To a package holiday-taker who spends two-weeks at a seaside resort, the small resort itself is the destination while a circuit traveller who joins a multi-country Europe tour may consider the whole continent as a destination. Thus, Medlik (1993:148) defines tourism destinations simply as "countries, regions, towns or other areas visited by tourists". Destination is here conveniently taken to be a country though with an understanding that the two hundred or so countries in the world are extremely diverse in size, ranging from hundreds to millions of square kilometres and from thousands to hundreds of millions of people.

Tourism development

"Tourism development is a dynamic process of matching tourism resources to the demand and preferences of actual or potential tourists" (Liu 1994:21). As tourism resources are usually spatially fixed and tourists involve travel, tourism development is inevitably related to the locational conditions of a destination. The relationship between the location of a country and its tourism development can be examined through either the locational theory or the trade theory as "trade and location are as two sides of the same coin" (Isard 1956:207). Location theory predicts which location will produce given goods, while trade theory predicts which goods will be produced by given locations. Both theories explain the relationship between production and location, though from different angles, on the basis of comparative advantages among locations (Johnson 1981).

The comparative advantage of tourism, though not so much in cross-nation as in cross-industry research, has been relatively well studied in the form of its potential benefits or positive impacts. The role of tourism as a "path to development" has been advocated from the 1950s, especially for developing countries. The advantage of tourism, compared with many primary and manufacturing industries, is based on its rapid growing market, its labour-intensive nature, the ubiquity of many types of tourism attractions, and the wide spread economic benefits in terms of foreign exchange generation, employment and income creation, and regional development. This can, to certain extent, explain why in many countries (especially island states) tourism, has replaced their traditional exports such as sugar, fishery and agricultural produce as the main export item in international trade.

The question of why international tourism development has mainly been clustered in a few regions and not evenly distributed across the world is largely unanswered, at least in a focused and systematic fashion. The substantial amount of literature on location theory has yet to be introduced to tourism research and the role of destination locational advantage in tourism development remains to be duly understood and appreciated.

Location theory

Smith (1983) recognises "three waves" in the development of locational theory. The first wave came with the transportation cost group and began with von Thünen's study of agricultural land uses around an isolated market centre in 1875. Weber tried to predict the best location for a given industry in 1909. The second wave came from the locational interdependence group. Christaller in 1933 and Lösch in 1944 developed central place theory through the principles of hierarchical locations and connections among places. The third wave was generated by the generalised market group in 1956 when Isard combined and broadened previous locational work to all forms of land use and economic activity. Smith (1983) also explores the implications of these locational theories for recreation firms in site selection decisions. As this is not the place for the current writer to indulge himself in a detailed discussion of location theories, the following short paragraphs are intended primarily to exemplify ways to apply these theories in analysing the spatial patterns of tourism development.

The classical theory of the location of industry is concerned with the optimal location for an individual plant in a given industry. Alfred Weber in *Theory of the Location of Industries*, published in 1909, highlighted three main factors that influenced industrial location. He first identified the point where minimum transport costs with respect to material and market costs would operate. He then added labour costs and "agglomerative" forces – external economies that result from the concentration of industry in a given area – as "distortions" that might cause firms to deviate from the minimum transport cost location in the interest of lower overall costs (Grant 1987:98). These three factors can be readily applied to tourism: transport costs may be determined jointly by the distance travelled and the efficiency of transport systems; labour costs may be broadened to include all costs at a destination to reflect the local price level of tourist services and exchange rates; and agglomeration indicates the level of spatial concentration of tourist services and the conditions of the related and supporting industries which affect the economies of scale, economies of scope and, through "linkages" the multiplier effect of tourism.

Johnson (1981) identified two approaches to location problems. The areal approach emphasises the constraints imposed by intra-areal distance, especially in the form of transport costs, as a force behind location patterns within an area; while the punctual approach stresses the influence of differences among geographic points in their predetermined characteristics such as prices, resources, and technology. Both approaches may be applied to tourism research to explain the uneven pattern of global tourism development. For example, over half of the countries in the world are endowed with some sun-sea-sand resources but international coastal tourism is largely concentrated in the Mediterranean and Caribbean regions which are adjacent to the main tourist generating centres. This is because distance modifies the effects of a country's resource endowments by enhancing the attractions of neighbouring lands and raising obstacles to travel to remoter areas. Destinations in more distant locations would have to differentiate their products (though difficult for beach holidays) or produce much more cheaply in order to attract Western visitors. On the other hand, the Scandinavia countries, with a similar distance to the centre of Western Europe as Spain and Portugal, have not developed much beach resort tourism due to their cool climate.

Dicken and Lloyd (1990) suggested that there are three fundamental bases underlying all spatial interaction between two places: complementarity represents a force that encourages interaction, whereas both transferability and intervening opportunity represents different aspects of the frictional effects of distance. Complementarity refers to a demand-supply relationship between two countries due to differences in factor endowments. In international tourism, however, the most important exchanges are between economies which have similar factors. For example, 81 percent of the overseas visitors travelled to the UK in 1997 are from Western Europe and North America while 89 percent UK travellers abroad visited the above two regions (BTA 1999). Globally speaking, the main tourist flows are between neighbouring countries. This phenomenon is caused by both intervening opportunities, which are the alternative sources of tourism supply; and transferability, which refers to the transport cost between two countries. In other words, the main features of global tourism distribution, such as the centre-periphery pattern and the dominant intra-regional flows, are attributable to the "spread effect" and "distance decay effect" of international tourist movement.

The determinants of locational advantage

The locational advantage of a tourism destination, simply defined, is the favourable conditions that exist in a destination which are comparatively more conducive to tourism development than another destination. A country with locational advantages over all other countries will be the most desirable destination to develop tourism. But what are the conditions for tourism development in a destination? There appears to be no universally accepted answer.

Pearce (1989:25) observes that "much of the tourist development literature is destination-oriented with attention being focused on such sectors as attractions, accommodation, supporting facilities and infrastructure". Gunn (1994) argues that all countries must identify opportunities in and deal with the five components of tourism supply – attractions, services, transportation, information and promotion – if they seek to develop or improve tourism. Burton (1995) highlights seven factors that influence tourist flows to a destination – climate, distance, attractions, communications, relative costs, cultural links, and political factors. Vellas and Bécherel (1995) identify four critical factors of international tourism development in a destination – factor endowments, comparative costs, absolute advantage and technology, and conditions of demand.

In a different context, Michael Porter (1990) researches the competitive advantage of nations. He suggests that the reasons for a nation to achieve international success in a particular industry lie in four broad and interrelated attributes – factor conditions, demand conditions, related and supporting industries, and firm strategy, structure, and rivalry – which are further modified by the role of government and the role of chance. Based on the above studies and a recognition of the fact that tourism is a place product, the location conditions of a destination is here believed to include all that the destination has to offer to its actual and potential tourists. These destination elements may be categorised into the following five broad groups:

Factor endowments

Any developments will require access to, or the possession of particular factors of production. Porter (1990) highlights five categories of factors of production: human resource – the quantity, skills, cost and motivations of the labour force; physical resources – the abundance, quality, accessibility and cost of natural assets including land, water, minerals, climate, and geographical position; knowledge resources – intellectual capital associated with science, technology, marketing, organisation and management expertise; capital resources – the amount and cost of capital available to finance business and industry; and infrastructure – the type, quality, and user cost of transportation, communications and other facilities.

All these factors are important in tourism, as in any other kind of development. Of particular relevance here are tourism attractions and supporting facilities. Attraction is the *raison d'être* of tourism. In essence, tourist attractions consist of all those elements of a non-home place that draw discretionary travellers away from their homes. Tourism attractions may be broadly divided into natural, cultural or purpose-built. Each country is blessed with a unique combination of natural attractions in the forms of, for example, sandy beaches, pleasant climate, attractive landscapes, and wilderness areas. The cultural attractions of a destination, such as archaeological sites, ancient monuments, historic buildings, exotic arts and crafts, and folklore and customs are the result of the successive effort of the past and present generations of the population. The purpose-built attractions, such as theme parks and heritage centres are the direct result of tourism development itself. The quantity, quality and diversity of tourist attractions a destination possesses, usually is positively linked to its size in terms of land area, population and economy (Liu and Jenkins 1996).

The supporting facilities in tourism refer to the infrastructure and superstructure of a destination, which generally determine its accessibility and amenities. All types of development, require infrastructure and facilities which include transport systems, communication networks, water and power sources, health care facilities, and so on. Transport is of critical importance in tourism because without it the attractions of a destination are inaccessible. The amenities involved in servicing tourists in a destination include accommodation, catering, recreation and shopping facilities. Although amenities are usually not a factor that attracts tourists to a destination, the absence or inadequacy of these facilities will deter tourists from travelling there.

Generally speaking, the economic development level of a country largely determines the availability and adequacy of infrastructure, superstructure, capital and technology in that country which have been considered as the "dynamic" determinants of the attractiveness of a country (Meinung 1989) or referred as "comfort attractions" or "conditional elements" (Lew 1987). Poor access and inadequate infrastructure have been considered as the major obstacles to tourism development in developing regions (Heraty 1989). However, the adequacy of tourist amenities in a country, is more directly related to the tourism development effort and the priorities given to the industry. It is also worthwhile to note that underdevelopment itself can often become tourist attractions as it is usually linked to pristine natural environment and traditional ways of life.

Relative costs

Relative (actual or opportunity) costs, are the main reason for international trade through the effects of absolute and comparative advantages. In tourism, the comparative cost of a destination is a critical factor in tourist's holiday decision process. There are four elements to be considered here: the cost of transport, the price level of tourist services in the destination, the exchange rates, and the quality-price ratio.

The cost of transport depends on the efficiency of the transport modes and network, size of travel flows, competition between transport providers, and the distance travelled. Of particular importance in the context of the current research is distance. The further the distance between the destination and the market, the less travel we would expect between the two. Factors accounting for this distance decay include increasing costs in time, money and effort, together with decreasing awareness of travel opportunities available. Clearly destinations adjoining the main tourist originating countries have an advantage over the more remote destinations.

The price level of tourist services in the destination is closely related to the level of economic development a country has achieved. The labour-intensive nature of tourism and the disparity in per capita income between the rich and poor nations mean that price level in developing countries is usually substantially lower than in developed countries. To the price conscious tourists, lower prices compared with those in the country of origin or of rival destinations is a strong attraction. This is especially the case of those undifferentiated or less unique tourist products such as beach holidays.

The monetary cost to an overseas visitor in a destination is jointly determined by the local price level and the exchange rates between the local currency and his or her home currency. A devaluation of the national currency can normally improve a destination's price competitiveness in international markets. The quality-price ratio is important because it decides the value of money to the tourists. Through product differentiation and effective market positioning, expensive destinations like Switzerland can also enjoy (non-price) locational advantage by offering unique and high quality products. Some destinations such as the Seychelles may even charge artificially high price to create an exclusive image and target particular market segments.

Domestic demand conditions

Domestic tourism is the predecessor and precondition of international tourism in most developed nations. A high domestic tourism demand creates an environment and conditions favourable for the development of international tourism as tourist attractions and facilities are developed to satisfy this demand and tourism organisations are experienced in understanding and catering the tourist needs.

The composition of domestic demand in terms of its segment structure and level of sophistication shapes how firms perceive, interpret, and respond to buyer needs. For example sophisticated and demanding buyers pressure local firms to meet high standards of product quality and service. The size of domestic demand and its growth pattern affect the economies of scale, investment behaviour and the timing and motivation of innovations in most industries. The extent to which the needs of home buyers anticipate those of other nations also has significant implications for domestic firms in developing new products or upgrading existing ones to compete in emerging segments (Porter 1990).

As travel is a product of affluence, the size of domestic tourism demand in a country is determined jointly by its income level and population size. After decades of rapid growth and democratisation, travel participation has now been extended from a few affluent individuals to a few affluent nations. Therefore, while travel is still a luxury in the developing world, it has become a mass consumption item in developed countries. The developed countries have an overwhelming advantage in this aspect since they have experienced balanced development of both domestic and international tourism. Indeed, international tourism, in both the inbound and outbound forms, is a natural extension of their domestic tourism. In a developed destination, there is not much difference between the two types of tourism, in terms of travel patterns, attraction preferences, service quality and price levels.

In contrast, in many developing countries, inbound international tourism has been purposefully developed, often through government assistance, well before the emergence of a sizeable domestic tourism market. When the two forms of tourism do coexist in a developing destination, they are often separated both spatially (e.g., enclave resorts for foreign tourists) and economically (by disparate price levels between facilities serving overseas and local visitors). The significant differences between the foreign tourists and domestic travellers in terms of motivations, sophistication and ability to pay means that a developing destination can not rely on the domestic market to gauge the needs and preferences of international visitors. This is one of the key factors attributable to the poor product and service qualities in many developing destinations.

The competitiveness of tourism businesses

Porter (1990) argues that the context in which firms are created, organised and managed and the nature of domestic rivalry have significant implications for the international competitiveness of a country. Domestic competition, for example, creates pressure on firms to improve and innovate, to lower costs, improve quality and create new products. The more competitive an industry within the country, the more competent may that country's industry be to handle competition within a wider international context. This explains the US airline industry's competitiveness in the global air transport market as it initiated the deregulation process in the late 1970s which greatly intensified the rivalry between the major airlines. Whereas the European airline industry did not complete its liberalisation process until the mid-1990s and is practically still fragmented by national borders. The difference in the level of internal competition between the USA and the EU has led to the substantial disparity of airfares between the trans-North-Atlantic routes and the intra-European routes.

Tourism businesses, in addition to the attraction, transport and accommodation operators, includes tour operators, travel agents, car rentals, excursions and sightseeing agents and special events organisers. They are the organisations who perform the packaging, distribution and promotion functions in tourism. The levels of these businesses in institutionalisation (as against family owned and run), professionalism and internationalisation affect the effectiveness and efficiency of their operations and marketing activities.

Among the firms of various sectors in the broad tourism industry, tour operators play a key role in modern mass tourism. The tour operator's main functions are primarily to reduce information and transaction costs for the consumer and to reduce promotional expenditures for suppliers by putting together the separate elements that normally make up a tour or travel package. Through purchasing or reserving the separate components in bulk and packaging them into inclusive tours, the tour operators have greatly facilitated the rapid expansion of mass tourism. Without the low price and convenience provided by inclusive tours, the majority of the working class population in the West might not be able to participate in overseas holidays, at least not from the 1960s.

Although in Western Europe, the bulk of the package holidays produced by tour operators tend to be for outbound tourists rather than for overseas travellers visiting the destination where the tour operator is located, the role of tour operators in destination development is critical. Tour operators perform all the major destination marketing functions, including product packaging, pricing, distribution and promotion. In international tourism, effective overseas promotion are the key to inform the availability of tourist products in, to create a favourable image of and to stimulate travel flows to, a destination. The lack or low level of professionalism and institutionalisation in the organisation of the travel industry is also one factor accountable for the low travel demand in and for many developing destinations.

The role of Government

Governments all over the world are involved in tourism and share many common responsibilities in tourism development, such as the co-ordinating, legislation, planning, and financing functions (WTO 1983). But the extent of the involvement is varied across countries and is conditioned by a host of factors, such as a country's size, its level of development, the political system and philosophy, and the adequacy of tourism supply. Generally speaking, governments in developing countries are more actively involved in tourism and assume a wider range of roles, ranging from mandatory, supportive to managerial and developmental (Jenkins and Henry 1982). This is mainly due to the fact that developing countries are usually characterised by a scarcity of capital and advanced technology, an inadequate infrastructure, a small and weak private sector and limited experience in tourism development.

However, government's more fundamental role in the locational advantage of destinations is in influencing the other four determinants examined above. Government can influence these factors both positively and negatively and in a variety of ways. For instance, factor endowments of a destination can be modified through government investment in infrastructure and superstructure, incentives for capital development in the form of tax breaks and subsides, the control over access to national parks or heritage sites. The relative costs may be altered through exchange rates control and taxation, such as airport tax, duty-free allowance, accommodation tax and value-added-tax. Tourism demand can either be promoted through labour legislation to increase the numbers of holiday-with-pay and provide social-travel opportunities for the under-privileged; or more often be restricted through myriad of barriers to international travel such as travel allowance restrictions, the difficulty of obtaining visa and passport approval, currency restriction imposed on residents, and taxes on foreign travel.

Government can also influence the extent of competition in the tourism industry. The world-wide deregulation, liberalisation and privatisation in the tourism industry during the last few decades have undoubtedly promoted competition in the airline, hotel, attractions and tour operating sectors in many countries. Legislation on product quality and safety, working conditions, minimum wages, and changes on interest rates and corporate tax rates all have significant impacts on the competitiveness of tourism firms. Regulations governing special types of tourism, such as gambling and sex tourism, can also shift the locational advantage of some tourism destinations.

The determinants in perspective

A few observations could be readily made here about the determination mechanism of the locational advantage of destinations. First, locational advantage might be related not so much to single attributes of destination but to combinations of characteristics. It is clear that the locational advantages of a destination are a complicated combination of attributes it cannot control (such as the climate and topography), variables it may be able to determine (such as transportation facilities and domestic demand), and factors it often can decide (such as airport taxes and government subsidies). Related to this, some determinants are spatially fixed like most of the natural attractions; some are footloose like capital, labour and technology which can be employed in many other industries in or even flee from the destination; and some are simply based policy-decisions, like the priorities given to tourism development and fund allocated for overseas promotion.

Secondly, not all locational attributes are equally meaningful to different types of tourism or to different market segments that a destination wishes to attract. For instance, although a destination may have a major attraction (e.g., sunny beach), that attraction does not necessarily constitute a locational advantage. First, it may not be an attribute of any importance to the target market, say business travellers. Second, even if it is, competitors may have the same strength level on that attribute. What become important, then, is for the destination to have greater relative strength on an attribute to a target market (Kotler, Haider and Rein 1993:85).

Thirdly, although tourism can not be developed without tourism resources, the mere possession of tourism attractions itself will not guarantee the development of the industry. This is because tourism is only one path of development and "not all states have equal interests in tourism" (William and Shaw 1991:267), its role and importance must be considered in the national socio-economic context and fitted into the overall development plan. Therefore, a country with substantial tourism resources may not develop it with great enthusiasm if it has high opportunity costs, whereas a state which is not so well endowed in tourist attractions will develop tourism in a greater effort if the industry is the one with comparative advantage or is the only available option for development. The extremely wide availability of tourist attractions and a surplus of world-wide tourism resource supply make the development and marketing effort, as reflected in the role of Government and the competitiveness of tourism businesses, the key determinants of the success of the industry in a destination.

The dimensions of locational advantage

The location of a country, as far as tourism is concerned, has four dimensions. First, the geographical situation on the earth determines the general features, climate pattern and physical accessibility of a destination. Second, the relative distance to main tourist generating countries decides the market accessibility and, due to the spread effect, often also the level of general economic development of a destination. Third, the place in the global transport system influences the monetary and temporal cost of travel. Fourth, the perceptual position in the global tourism market, that is the image of a destination in the tourists' mind, affects the perceived attractiveness of and cognitive distance to a destination.

Physical situation on the earth

The geographic situation of a country on the earth measured in degrees of longitude and latitude largely determines its topography, climate and other natural features. It has been argued that the key to successful tourism is the quality, location and perception of the natural environmental assets that are the very foundation upon which all tourism rests. Pleasant climates, scenic wonders, beautiful coastlines and beaches, majestic mountains and valleys are all part of the natural attractions that cause large movements of people world-wide. Every destination has its own unique combination of natural resource features such as climate, topography and scenery. These physical attributes have a major bearing on the potential and type of tourism that develops and may also facilitate or limit accessibility by different modes of transport.

The natural environment has played a key role in the development of nations in history. It has been suggested that all brilliant and wealthy civilisations of early times occurred in "favourable" natural environments, whereas "unfavourable" climate and inaccessible areas bred backwardness and savagery. Climate is often seen as the "mainspring" factor in the progress or regress of civilisation (Berry; Conkling and Ray 1993:30-31). This may explain, at least partly, why the developed world is located in the temperate zone while most developing countries are situated in tropical and subtropical climate zones. The tropical and subtropical regions, despite being considered to be unfavourable for general economic development, are excellent destinations for the sunlust tourists. Indeed, as the major tourist originating regions of the world are in temperate zone, the passion for sun and sea has turned these areas of the world into the tourist "sunbelt".

When a nation-state has no direct access to an ocean, it is said to be landlocked. Although located at or near the centre of their continents, most of the landlocked states are on the periphery of the world economy. Outside Europe, two-thirds of the landlocked countries are classified by the United Nations as least developed countries (UNCTAD 1998). This is because not only a landlocked state has to bear the high overland transport cost, it is also vulnerable to disruptions of transit routes resulting from technical breakdowns, natural disasters, labour disputes, political upheavals in their coastal neighbours. Another disadvantage confronting landlocked states is their lack of access to the resources of the oceans, in the case of tourism, sea and sand.

In contrast, island states have usually done better in tourism than in many other industries. The island status is always related to sea and beach which are the prime stages for tourism activities. Islands, however, have significant geographical constraints resulting from a small land area and separation from other countries. Small islands tend to have limited agricultural and mining potential, limited water supply, high cost in transportation and communications, and their limited domestic market preventing them from gaining economies of scale in many industries (Srimivasan 1986). They are also prone to natural disasters, such as tropical cyclones, earthquakes and volcanic eruptions. This often leads them to be specialized in a few industries, of which tourism is usually a viable and favoured option.

Distance to the main generating countries

A country's relative location in terms of the distance to other countries usually has a significant effect on both its international (inbound and outbound) and domestic tourism. Since not every country has the same potential in generating international tourists, the distance to the main tourist originating centres are most important though the distance to main tourist destinations and the conditions of the neighbouring countries are also relevant. The "distance decay effect" shows that the volume of tourist traffic decreases with distance away from the tourist generating area. This has led to high levels of movements between adjacent countries in international tourism. For example, 79 percent of international tourist arrivals in Europe were intraregional in 1997 while in Americas and East Asia and the Pacific, the share was 72 percent and 77 percent respectively (WTO 1999).

At the international level, proximity to industrialised and urbanised countries in Western Europe and North America is highly valuable. The tourism booms in countries like Austria, Switzerland and Spain is attributable to advantageous location as most of their neighbours are large tourist generators; while in Africa the widespread poverty virtually precludes travelling within the continent. A great distance from the major tourist-generating areas of the world and the existence of many intervening opportunities in between are among the major causes accountable for South America's failure in attracting more inter-continental tourism.

It is possible to construct a "locational condition model" to measure a country's locational advantage or disadvantage, based on the gravity model, as follows:

$$T_i = \sum_{j=1}^{n} \frac{gA_i}{D_{ii}^a} P_j H_j$$

Where: T_i = the locational advantage (disadvantage) of destination i;

g, a = coefficient to be estimated;
A_i = attracting capacity of destination i;
D_{ij} = distance between destination i and originating country j;
P_j = population of originating country j;
H_j = foreign holiday participation rate of originating country j.

The flow and distribution of international tourism may also be seen as a movement from a few central places (namely, Western Europe and North America) fan out over to other regions. This "spread" process exists and operates in a very uneven geographic manner and constrained by two important factors: the effect of geographic distance and the distribution of tourism resources. The spread of tourist flows tends to fall off very rapidly with distance from their source. In other words, the spread effect exerted by a tourist-generating centre is most effective in areas close to the centre itself. The desire of tour operators and travellers to minimise transportation costs has led to the exploitation of the nearest resources first, whether these are seaside resorts, ski resorts or cultural attractions. The mass tourist movement from the generating centres has been predominately directed toward the edges of such centres rather towards new centres in the periphery.

Certainly, different types of tourism development will demand differing degrees of market access and tourists will be prepared to travel different distances for different types of holiday or attractions. Some remote destinations could well develop its small scale but high per visitor spending tourism by promoting its unique cultural and natural attractions to the carefully selected target markets.

Place in the global transport system

Accessibility and travel cost are not always proportional to physical distance, the condition of transport is often more significant in determining the economic and temporal distance. The relationship between transport and tourism is multi-faceted: the availability, frequency, choice of modes, speed, cost, safety, comfort and convenience of transport all affect the demand of travel and the accessibility of a destination. As the necessary precondition of and vital link in tourism, transport has traditionally underpinned the world-wide development of tourism and it will continue to do so. Indeed, the three epochs in tourism development are usually identified with three transportation revolutions: railway, automobile, and aeroplane.

It is desirable for a destination to have more than one form of transport. The higher a destination's position on the transport network hierarchy the more competitive it is in the tourism market, since a few routes and nodes dominate the system. A destination's level of accessibility is conditioned by the transport technology and hierarchies which have preceded it (Murphy 1985). In modern international tourism, the situation of air service provision is of critical importance to most destinations (Jemiolo and Conway 1991). The availability and cost of flights, closeness to key nodes and major routes, provision of both charter and schedule services, all have significant impacts on the physical, temporal and economic accessibility of a destination.

Sealy (1992) suggests, air travel and the expansion of international tourism is largely a nodal transport system dependent upon the airports (the nodes) and the flights (the flows) serving them. There are continuous changes in the relative position of cities, countries and regions in the global transportation system as it is responding to the demands of different areas. However, because of the nature of incremental change, the present shape of existing transport systems are fully explicable only in terms of historical process, the result of the distribution of demand for transport as it existed in past periods. For example, despite the tremendous advance in transport technology, the major airport nodes in the global network are overwhelmingly still those colonial urban centres established a couple of centuries ago (Graham 1995).

The global transport network and most transport routes, like the location of tourist originating centres, tend to cluster together in certain central places. Therefore, certain routes and links between countries are shrunk more than others are, especially in economic distance. For example, airfares from Britain to the Mediterranean countries are substantially lower than to the Scandinavia and Eastern European states; while those to the Western coast of North America are significantly less than to the Far East or Southern Africa. "The globe, is thus effectively distorted away from its spherical shape in conceptual terms" (Cater 1995:190). Clearly through effectively improving its place in the global transport system, a destination can enhance its location advantage or reduce locational disadvantage in international tourism.

Position in the world tourism market

The locational advantage of a destination can not be realised until the tourists start to appreciate its advantageous offerings. In order to attract the actual visitation of a tourist, a destination has to pass a number of "choice sets" in the tourist's destination selection process (Goodall 1991). A well-defined and favourable position of the destination is of critical importance in this process. A product's market position is the consumers' perception of the product in relation to both the competitive products and the consumers' needs (Kotler 1997). A tourist destination's position is assessed by tourists' perceptions of how the destination compares to other destinations in the market on relevant attributes. Of major importance here are the image of and cognitive distance to the destination.

Image differentiates tourist destinations from each other and is an integral and influential part of travellers' decision process. Image is the sum of beliefs, ideas, and impressions that people have of a place or destination and is an expression of knowledge, prejudice, imaginations, and emotional thoughts an individual has of a specific object or place (Baloglu and Brinberg 1997). The image of a destination consists of two parts: cognitive image and affective image. The former refers to the tourists' familiarity with a destination while the later indicates the favourability of a destination among tourists. Both the cognitive and affective components of a destination image is not entirely determined by the physical properties of that destination but largely based on the historical, cultural, economic, social and political connections between the tourist receiving and generating countries. The level of media exposure, for example, is higher in the UK of countries with past colonial ties (like the Commonwealth members), with similar language and culture (like Canada and the USA), with strong trade relations (like Germany and Japan), and at the same socio-economic development levels (like the other developed countries). In contrast, reports on less developed and especially less democratic countries in the mass media are limited and often unfavourable. Many Western governments regularly caution its citizens not to travel to many "troubled" countries or spots in the world. In its extreme form, a government may prohibit its citizens from travelling to a particular destination (like the USA's travel ban to Cuba and Libya).

It is well accepted that tourists incorporate a distance variable in the destination choice process. In the gravity models, physical, monetary and temporal distances are used.

However, tourists often rely on cognitive distance, rather than actual distance or travel time, in evaluating a destination (Cook and McCleary 1983). Cognitive distance "is the mental representation of actual distance moulded by an individual's social, cultural, and general life experiences" (Ankomah and Crompton 1992:324). This implies that different tourists have differing mental maps of the world that can be distorted according to their experiences and perceptions. For instance, for many British tourists, North America may be perceived as nearer than North Africa while China may be perceived as further away than Australia. Ankomah and Crompton (1992) propose that cognitive distance is likely to be underestimated if the tourism destination is information rich or perceived as being very attractive and overestimated if the destination is information poor or perceived as being less attractive. Clearly, in evaluating the locational advantage, the degree of fit of the gravity model can be improved if cognitive distance is used instead of real distance (Walmsley and Jenkins 1992:25). As the familiarity of and preference for tourism destination is normally associated with the level and nature of media exposure, a destination may improve its image and reduce the cognitive distance through effective marketing. In addition, remoteness or peripherality can also be advantageous since distance has a psychological value in that a destination far away gives a greater sense of escape from home. Peripheral destinations may exploit its peripherality through careful targeted marketing and product differentiation to promote their exoticness and exclusivity.

All the above four dimensions of destination location have significant implications for tourism development, but also display different patterns of change over time. The physical location of a country is difficult to change but changes in tourist tastes and preferences will affect the value of the resources each country endowed with. The relative distance to the tourist generating regions can be altered gradually by the relative economic performance of its neighbouring countries. The situation in the global transport system can be improved to a great extent by the effort of the destination itself. The position in the world tourism market, relative to its competitors and the tourist needs, will largely be determined by the effectiveness of a destination marketing activities.

The dynamics of locational advantage

Although the situation of a country on the earth is fixed, ever-changing economic, social, cultural, political and technological forces constantly modify its location conditions. As far as tourism is concerned, alterations in a country's locational advantage can be caused by changes in tourist preferences, shifts in travel patterns, advances in transport technologies, increasing competition between destinations, and varying economic growth rates of countries across the globe. An indication of the shifting advantage of tourism destinations is their relative performance in tourism development. Table 1 shows the actual and predicted average annual growth rate of international tourist arrivals since 1950. The uneven growth of tourism in the six regions reflects a general and gradual trend towards more balanced locational conditions among tourism destinations (at the regional level).

Table 1   Average annual growth rate of international tourists arrivals by region

	1950-60	1960-70	1970-80	1980-90	1990-98	1995-2020
Africa	3.7	12.4	11.8	7.5	6.5	5.5
Americas	8.4	9.7	3.8	4.3	3.2	3.8
Europe	11.6	8.4	5.1	4.3	3.5	3.1
East Asia/ the Pacific	14.0	22.4	15.0	9.8	6.0	7.0
Middle East	12.3	11.5	14.9	1.8	7.2	6.7
South Asia	14.4	17.6	9.4	3.5	6.1	6.2
World	10.6	9.1	5.6	4.8	4.0	4.3

Sources: WTO (1998, 1999)

Changes in tourist preferences

Changes in tourists' tastes and preferences have significant effects on the selection of holidays and destinations. These changes are constantly altering the relative value of tourism resources across the world. As the concept of a resource is both functional and cultural, the perception of a tourist attraction does not rely on physical properties, but on a range of economic, technological and psychological factors. The value of natural attractions, for instance, changed greatly over history. In the Middle Ages Western society had very strongly held prejudices against mountain scenery, vacationing in the Alps goes back less than two centuries and emerged as an economically significant sector barely a hundred years ago (Bernard 1978). The increasing level of urbanisation and technological development will constantly appreciate the value of natural attractions such as magnificent scenery, flora and fauna, and wilderness areas.

The boom of sun and sea holidays since the late 1950s and the consequent development of the tourist sun-belt close to the major tourist generating centres, is a direct result of the mass "hunt for the sun". An increasingly educated, experienced and segmented travel market will, however, in the future more actively seek for higher quality of tourist product and expect a broader array of specialised travel services including more special trips to unspoiled environment in remote and less developed regions. Indeed, there is already a global shift from "sun and beach" holidays to more active and special interest ones such as cultural, adventure, and event holidays. Since advantages can be fleeting, "a part of judging location advantages is anticipating future needs, not just measuring current ones" (Wilbanks 1980:198).

Changes in travel patterns

Meanwhile, there have been substantial extensions of travelling distances in all developed countries. As a result of that tourism, originated as mainly a domestic phenomenon, has now spread over the whole globe. This is indicated not only by the growing share of journeys abroad, but also by the growth of long haul holidays. In the UK, for example, travel distance has been increasing gradually from the day trips to suburban attractions and weekend holidays to coast areas; to mass holidays in France, Spain and other Mediterranean destinations; to increasingly popular travel to the Caribbean, Middle East, East Europe and North America; and to the rising tourist flows to Far East and Australia. BTA (1999) figures show that the share of overseas holidays in total holidays taken by the British population increased from 14 percent in 1965 to 48 percent in 1997. The share of Western Europe in all UK visits abroad declined from 86 percent in 1987 to 81 percent in 1997, while the share of the rest of the world increased from 14 percent to 19 percent. In particular, the number of British visitors to the "remote" Latin America increased by 728 percent while the total number of British visits abroad grew only 67 percent between 1987 and 1997.

CAA (1999) data also show the same pattern of changes. The average passenger journey length of UK scheduled airlines increased from 2,043 km in 1988 to 2,464 km in 1998, an increase of 21 percent; while that of charter airlines increased from 1,854 km to 2,829 km, an increase of 53 percent. This marked trend for tourists to go further afield in search of new travel experiences can be observed over the past few decades in all developed countries. A WTO (1998) report predicts that between 1995 and 2020, the average annual growth rate of long haul travel will be 5.4 percent compared with that of the intra-regional travel of 4.0 percent. It will certainly affect some destinations more than others, and it is possible that many destinations not adjacent to the major tourist originating centres will benefit more than those traditional popular nearby destinations.

Changes in tourist destinations

Changes of tourist destinations are of two kinds: the mature of nearby popular destinations and the development of newly opened (often remote) destinations. Tourist destinations, like any other products, are subject to the influence of life cycle. Many popular Mediterranean and Caribbean destinations have reached the stage of mature and stagnation and some are even in danger of decline. Many mass tourist resorts of the post-war period, in particular, have encountered enormous redevelopment problems. This is because, over-development, growing pollution, increasing familiarity, rising prices and above all, the perception that they are "characterless, unfashionable and low in quality" (Morgan 1998:317), lead to decreasing tourist satisfaction. If these resorts do not effectively upgrade their ageing products and renew their tarnished images, they could easily follow in the footsteps of some of the declined British seaside resorts, which were deserted by many domestic visitors in favour of more attractive resorts abroad.

The global tourism market has also become increasingly competitive since more and more destinations are entering the arena. Since the 1980s, virtually every country in the world has been promoting itself as a tourist destination. As the newly opened destinations gradually move up the stages of the lifecycle and experience curve and achieve more effective and efficient promotion and development, they are likely to gain a increasingly larger share in the international tourist market. The growth in tourist flows and changes in travel patterns could also allow the new destinations to enjoy increasing economies of scale that may lead to lower price and higher volume. Many developing countries, such as Thailand, Kenya and Costa Rica, have successfully established unique images and differentiate their products to reduce the locational disadvantages as compared with destinations located close to the main tourist generating centres.

As income and mobility increases and tourist tastes change new travel routes and resorts will emerge, and the spatial structure of world tourism is expected to change. The most significant change will be the continuously increase of the share of the East Asia and Pacific region in world tourism as it is likely to retain its position as the fastest growing region in the coming decades. On the other hand, the dominant position of Europe as the main destination regions is continuing to be eroded. Its share of international tourist arrivals in the world has declined from 65.1 percent in 1980 to 59.2 percent in 1997 and is expected to be reduced further to 44.8 percent in 2020; while that of East Asia and the Pacific is 7.5 percent, 14.4 percent and 27.3 percent respectively (WTO 1998 and 1999).

Less uneven distribution of generating countries

The different levels of performance and prospects of economic development in different countries and regions will inevitably result in constant changes in the world economic map. The economic miracle of Japan and the emergence of the newly industrialised countries in East Asia, for example, have boosted international tourism in the region.

It could be said that even without its own purposeful development effort, a country's touristic locational conditions can be improved by the above-average economic performance of the neighbouring and/or nearby countries, that is by the mere increases in the value of the neighbouring countries' P and especially H of the "locational condition model". The rapid economic growth in East and Southeast Asia has greatly improved the locational advantages of the region in tourism development especially through increasingly large intra-regional tourist flows. Hong Kong or Singapore, for example, were in the periphery 40 years ago but are now well located within a new regional economic hub.

According to WTO's (1998) prediction (see Table 2), the uneven growth rates of outbound tourism in the six regions of the world will modify the current global tourist originating structure. The most noticeable change will be the increasing importance of East Asia and the Pacific as an international tourist-generating region. The locational condition of this region will be further improved by the fact that most of the large numbers of first time Asian travellers will choose close-by destinations.

Table 2   Forecast of outbound tourism by region, 1995-2020

	1995		2020		1995-2020 growth rate (% pa)
	Number (m)	Share (%)	Number (m)	Share (%)	
	17	3.02	69	4.31	5.7
Americas	115	20.43	248	15.48	3.1
Europe	333	59.15	771	48.13	3.4
East Asia/ the Pacific	85	15.10	462	28.84	7.0
Middle East	9	1.60	35	2.18	5.6
South Asia	4	0.71	17	1.06	5.5
World	563	100.00	1602	100.00	4.3

Source: WTO (1998)

Advances in transport technology

Technological advances in transportation and communications have reduced the friction of distance and led to the time-space convergence and cost-space convergence in international travel. The declined economic, temporal, social and mental distance between countries, regions and areas certainly affect the touristic locational conditions of a destination. Since the key locational disadvantage of remote destinations is its high transport cost from and to the main tourist generating countries, any reduction in long distance travel cost will have beneficial impacts for those destinations situated far away from Western Europe and North America.

An examination of air transport development during the last half a century shows that: the fastest aircraft in 1950, the DC7, travelled roughly 350 miles per hour; the Boeing 747 jumbo jets, introduced in the late 1960s, flying at 640 miles per hour; the supersonic Concorde, which made its debut in January 1976, travelling at roughly 1350 miles per hour. By the early 21st century hypersonic aircraft, burning liquid hydrogen, may fly at 4,000 miles per hour (Janelle 1991). A new double-decker jumbo jetliner, A3XX, is already being developed by Airbus. It could seat up to 900 people and offer lounges, restaurants and shops and deliver a new era of comfort which makes flying like staying in a mile-high luxury hotel (BBC 1999). Obviously, if manufacturers can come up with a hypersonic plane that can be operated economically it will undoubtedly stimulate international long-haul travel and greatly improve the locational advantage of remote destinations.

Technology developments that have shrunk the world and improved accessibility of locations have also altered their comparative spatial advantage, usually positively but sometimes negatively. For example, the Gulf region, traditionally a vital refuelling stop for airlines flying between Europe and the Far East, is in danger of being left behind by new long-range aircraft (Sheppard 1991). Major stopovers like Bangkok and Singapore on the transient routes between Europe and Australia, could also be bypassed in the future by next generations of jumbo jets.

Conclusions

So far, the present author has briefly examined the concept of locational advantage of tourism destinations and analysed its determinants, dimensions and dynamics. Every destination in the world is endowed with a specific set of locational conditions that specify the parameters within which it may development particular types of tourism in particular ways. However, these location conditions are changeable, by forces in the tourism market and tourism environment as identified above and through purposeful development effort in reducing disadvantages and creating new advantages. The decreasing importance of the physical location of a country in its tourism development may well lead to the restructuring of tourist flows, destinations and markets in the following decades. East Asia and the Pacific, with very varied tourism resources and increasing prosperity, has enjoyed the highest growth rate in the world over the last half a century, will continue to gain shares in the global tourist market. Tourism in Western Europe and North America will keep growing but their dominant position in world tourism could be gradually undermined by the relatively higher growth rate enjoyed by other regions. Eastern Europe and Latin America, in the long term, possess great potential for tourism development. The prospects of tourism growth in the other regions of the world such as Africa, South Asia and the Middle East are more difficult to predict as they are more prone to political instability and economic hardship.

It is safe to propose that the spatial distribution of world tourist activities in the future will be more even than it is at the present. However, this equalisation process in tourism development across the world will continue to be gradual and uneven. It is gradual because the shifts of tourism development from old locations which suffered significant advantage erosion to newly emerged advantageous places are slowed by huge investment costs in the latter and resistance from the former. Old resorts, like many in the Mediterranean regions, may substitute low capital costs for rising operating costs in the form of higher wages and taxes or exploit the market inertia to counteract its declining popularity. Whereas in East Asia, the cost of large scale investment in transport and accommodation facilities are much more than the low labour costs can compensate in the short term. This equalisation process is uneven because, like the spread effect in travel, the relative alterations of locational advantage of tourism destinations are rarely in the same direction or at the same pace. For instance, as can be seen from the analysis above, East Asia has significantly improved its locational advantage while South Asia and Africa largely failed to do so during the last few decades.

Every tourism destination must constantly monitor and evaluate its locational conditions and the consequent competitive advantages and disadvantages in world tourism. Based on such analyses, proper development and marketing strategies can then be formulated and implemented to capitalise its opportunities and mitigate the threats. Bhutan, a mountainous and mythical destination, for example, is very successful in turning its locational disadvantage into an advantage by limiting the number of foreign travellers and charging 2,000 dollars per person for a travel permit.

References

Ankomah, P. K. and Crompton, J. L. (1992), Tourism cognitive distance: a set of research propositions, *Annals of Tourism Research*, 19, pp.323-342.

Baloglu, S. and Brinberg, D. (1997), Affective images of tourism destinations, *Journal of Travel Research*, Spring, pp.11-15.

BBC (1999), The height of luxury, http://news.bbc.co.uk/hi/english/business, 13 March, 2000.

Bernard, P. P. (1978), Rush to the Alps: The Evolution of Vacationing in Switzerland. *East European Quarterly*, New York.

Berry, B. J. L., Conkling, E. C., and Ray, D. M. (1993), *The Global Economy: Resource Use, Locational Choice, and International Trade*, Prentice Hall, Englewood Cliffs, NJ.

BTA (1999), *Digest of Tourist Statistics*, No.22. British Tourist Authority, London.

Burton, R. (1995), *Travel Geography*. 2nd edn. Pitman, London.

CAA (1999), UK Civil Aviation Authority, http://www.caa.co.uk/.

Cater, E. (1995), Consuming spaces: global tourism, in J. Allen and C. Hamnett (Editors), *A Shrinking World?* Oxford University Press, Oxford. pp.183-231.

Cook, R. L. and McCleary, K. W. (1983), Redefining vacation distances in consumer minds, *Journal of Travel Research*, 21 (2): 31-34.

Dicken, P. and Lloyd, P. E. (1990), *Location in Space: Theoretical Perspectives in Economic Geography*, 3rd edn, Happer and Row, New York.

Goodall, B. (1991), Understanding holiday choices, in C. P. Cooper (Editor), *Progress in Tourism, Recreation and Hospitality Management*, Vol.3, Belhaven, London. pp.58-77.

Graham, B. (1995), *Geography and Air Transport*, John Wiley, Chichester.

Grant, E. G. (1987), Industry: landscape and location, in J.M. Wagstaff (Editor), *Landscape and Culture*, Basil Blackwell, Oxford. pp.96-117.

Gunn, C. A. (1994), *Tourism Planning*, 3rd edn, Taylor and Francis, London.

Heraty, M. J. (1989), Tourism transport: implications for developing countries, *Tourism Management*, 10 (4): 288-292.

Isard, W. (1956), *Location and Space-Economy*, MIT Press, Cambridge.

Janelle, D. G. (1991), Global interdependence and its consequences, in S. D. Brunn and T. R. Leinbach (Editors), *Collapsing Space and Time*, Harper Collins Academic, London. pp.49-81.

Jemiolo, J. J. and Conway, D. (1991), Tourism, air service provision and patterns of Caribbean airline offer, *Social and Economic Studies*, 40 (2): 1-43.

Jenkins, C. L. and Henry, B.M. (1982), Government involvement in tourism in developing countries, *Annals of Tourism Research*, 9 (4): 99-521.

Johnson, J. T. (1981), *Location and Trade Theory*. University of Chicago, Department of Geography, Chicago.

Kotler, P. (1997), *Marketing Management*. 9th edn, Prentice Hall, Upper Saddle River, NJ.

Kotler, P., Haider, D. H. and Rein, I. (1993), *Marketing Places*, The Free Press, New York.

Lew, A. A. (1987), A framework of tourism attraction research, *Annals of Tourism Research*, 14 (4): 553-575.

Liu, Z. H. (1994), Tourism development – a systems analysis, in A. V. Seaton et al. (Editors), *Tourism: The State of the Art*, John Wiley, Chichester. pp.20-30.

Liu, Z. H. and Jenkins, C. L. (1996), Country size and tourism development: a cross-nation analysis, in L. Briguglio; B. Archer and J. Jafari (Editors), *Sustainable Tourism in Islands and Small States*, Cassell, London. pp.90-117.

Medlik, S. (1993), *Dictionary of Travel, Tourism and Hospitality*, Butterworth-Heinemann, Oxford.

Meinung, A. (1989), Determinants of the attractiveness of a tourism region, in S. F. Witt and L. Moutinho (Editors), *Tourism Marketing and Management Handbook*, Prentice Hall, New York. pp.99-101.

Morgan, M. (1998), Homogeneous products: the future of established resorts, in W. F. Theobald (Editor), *Global Tourism*. 2nd edn. Butterworth-Heinemann, Oxford. pp.317-336.

Moutinho, L. and Paton, R. (1991), Site selection analysis in tourism: the LOCAT model, *The Service Industries Journal*, 11 (1): -10.

Murphy, P. E. (1985), *Tourism: A Community Approach*, Methuen, New York.

Pearce, D. G. (1989), *Tourist Development*. 2nd edn, Longman, Harlow.

Porter, M. E. (1990), *The Competitive Advantage of Nations*, The Free Press, New York.

Sealy, K. (1992), International air transport, in B. S. Hoyle and R. D. Knowles (Editors), *Modern Transport Geography*, Belhaven, London. pp.233-256.

Sheppard, P. (1991), Aviation in the Arabian Gulf, *Travel and Tourism Analyst*, (4), pp.5-19.

Smith, S. (1983), *Recreation Geography*. Longman, London.

Smith, S. L. J. (1995), *Tourism Analysis: A handbook*, 2nd edn, Longman, Harlow.

Srimivasan, T. N. (1986), The costs and benefits of being a small, remote, island, landlocked or ministates economy, *World Bank Research Observer* 1, pp.205-218.

UNCTAD (1992), *The Least Developed Countries*, United Nations, New York.

Vellas, F. and Bécherel, L. (1995), *International Tourism*, Macmillan, London.

Walmsley, D. J. and Jenkins, J. M. (1992), Cognitive distances: a neglected issue in travel behaviour, *Journal of Travel Research*, 31 (1): 24-29.

Wilbanks, T. J. (1980), *Location and Well-being*, Harpper and Row, San Francisco.

Williams, A. M. and Shaw, G. (1991), Tourism policies in a changing economic environment, in A. M. Williams and G. Shaw (Editors), *Tourism and Development: Western European Experiences*, Belhaven, London. pp.263-272.

WTO (1983), *The Framework of the State's Responsibility for the Management of Tourism*, WTO, Madrid.

WTO (1998), *Tourism 2020 Vision*, WTO, Madrid.

WTO (1999), *Yearbook of Tourism Statistics*, 51st edn, WTO, Madrid.

Inter-dependencies, issues and interests: Theoretical frameworks for researching tourism partnerships

Philip Long

Sheffield Hallam University, UK

Background

The importance of partnerships between the diverse range of stakeholders involved in tourism planning and development is increasingly recognised by policy makers, practitioners and researchers alike. Tourism as an industry, activity and planning field is often characterised by a fragmentation of interests and a lack of cohesion. This may, at some times and places, result in conflict, dissension and policy incoherence. In this context, it is unsurprising that some form of partnership arrangement or collaborative alliance is commonly advanced as a model for the planning and process of tourism development.

Policy, practical and ethical reasons underlie and justify the formation of partnerships for tourism development. Collaborative arrangements may be presented as being exemplary models of democratic practice, encouraging and enabling a broad range of representation. Partnerships may emerge from a genuine recognition of synergies between members, or at least, from an appreciation that a failure to act in collaboration may weaken tourism development. Collaborative alliances may form in response to development funding programmes that require a partnership approach. In such cases, financial inducements and programme requirements may result in opportunistic collaborations where partnerships may be more 'virtual' than genuine.

Partnerships for tourism development exist in a variety of forms and for a number of purposes. These include, for example; partnerships that are established with the aim of involving the private sector and local communities in public sector led developments, collaborative projects to address a particular management concern in tourism development or operation and, partnerships where tourism is part of a wider regeneration programme.

Waddock (1991) presents a classification of partnership forms and purpose that is helpful in identifying the range of organisational structures, representation and purpose that exists in tourism development partnerships. However, individual partnerships may engage in more than one kind of activity represented in figure One and they may evolve from one form to another in the course of time.

Partnership categories

	Systemic	Programmatic	Project
Nature and focus of partnership	Usually informal arrangements to promote destinations and/or tourism as an industry	Usually time-limited, but renewable partnerships that aim to develop and implement a tourism development programme	Partnerships established for the purpose of devising and implementing a specific project
Examples	National and regional level advisory groups	Local and regional tourism initiatives	Visitor and traffic management initiatives
Typical representation	Senior management from the tourism industry	Local and regional planners, politicians, businesses and communities	Specialist managers and steering groups

Figure 1   A classification of tourism partnerships (adapted from Waddock, 1991)

This paper reviews the growing body of literature on the subject of tourism development partnerships. It goes on to suggest the application of a theoretical framework which proposes research questions and methodologies derived from the broad field of organisation studies for the critical analysis of these partnership arrangements (Gray and Wood, 1991; Wood and Gray, 1991).

Bilateral or multilateral strategic alliances for purely commercial purposes, while significant in tourism sectors such as the airline and hotel industries, are excluded from the types of partnership considered here as they do not generally involve representation from a range of stakeholders. However, some of the theoretical approaches contained in the literature on tourism development partnerships may also be applied to research on strategic alliances in tourism.

Previous research on tourism development partnerships

This section outlines themes, approaches and theoretical frameworks that have been adopted in studies of tourism partnerships. It concentrates particularly on work that has applied organisational partnership and collaboration theory. Other relevant literature from the planning, economics, strategic management and politics fields, for example, is incorporated in the theoretical framework that is presented in subsequent sections.

The emergence of formal collaborative arrangements in tourism development during and since the 1980s has been associated with a number of contextual factors. These include; an increased recognition of global, national and local inter-dependencies, a blurring of boundaries between government and business, the growing call to involve stakeholders in sustainable tourism development, and the need to combine resources in development programmes. However, there are also some significant potential obstacles to collaboration and partnership in tourism development. These include, the essentially competitive nature of private sector tourism operators, bureaucratic (or democratic?) inertia in the public sector, spatial and organisational fragmentation in the tourism industry, securing the participation of interests which may be opposed to tourism development, and the difficul partnerships between operators and agencies in neighbouring districts that have viewed each other as rivals and competitors.

It is unsurprising that these critical issues in tourism development partnerships have been identified as fruitful areas for research and that theories of organisational collaboration might usefully be applied in their study. It is however surprising that such research did not appear earlier.

Selin and Beason (1991) appear to have been the first to publish a refereed tourism journal paper that makes explicit use of a partnership theory approach. Selin and Beason focused on partnerships between outdoor recreation, tourism and resource management interests in the United States. Their study involved an examination of organisational and environmental factors that might explain variations in co-operative relations. The work was based on a conceptual framework drawn from the literature on organisational exchange and collaboration (Aiken and Haige, 1968; Gamm, 1991; Gray, 1985; Gray, 1989; Levine and White, 1961, Rogers and Whetten, 1982, Waddock, 1989). Selin and Beason broke new ground in applying this literature to tourism. However, the emphasis of this early work was on bilateral, dyadic relationships rather than on network arrangements.

The literature on tourism planning, development, marketing and industry structure that preceded Selin and Beason's 1991 study did at times include a recognition of the existence or desirability of partnerships in the tourism industry or system. However, there had been no application of organisational partnership theory in any rigorous sense (for example, Gunn, 1988). Much of this earlier literature on organisational roles in the tourism industry was more concerned with describing structures and with pragmatic issues of planning and marketing than with analysing models of partnership and collaboration. Gunn (1990), for example, in an early publication on partnerships in tourism makes reference to 'increased communication – *and sometimes even co-operation and collaboration* between the fields of recreation and tourism' (1, emphasis added). Gunn identifies inter-dependencies and a need for greater organisational links between tourism and recreation interests. He goes on to present a descriptive account of research collaboration between South Africa's government tourism agency and recreation association, but there is no theoretical discussion.

In a 1993 paper, Selin noted the need to focus on the organisational domain as opposed to dyadic inter-organisational relations in tourism. He defines 'domain' here as, 'the set of actors that become involved in a common problem or interest' (1993:223). He suggests that systems in tourism are under-developed and that inter-dependencies between stakeholders in tourism are not always recognised and understood. However, there is no specific research model proposed here and the Gray and Wood (1991) theoretical framework for the study of partnerships is not mentioned. However, Selin observes that the tourism partnership theme was beginning to attract significant research attention and was adopted for the Travel and Tourism Research Association 1992 conference.

This growing research attention has developed along the lines of viewing tourism partnerships as both pragmatic management strategy and as theoretical construct. At a fundamental level, contributions have been made to the classification and categorisation of tourism partnerships. Such work has been valuable in helping to define a complex and

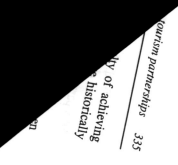

u (1995), for example, reviewed types of partnership in the
marketing. Their analytical categories were presented in terms

...ial competencies and geographical focus)

y/non-equity arrangements to joint venture structures)

f the relationship between members)

- cultural values (the seniority of participants and role of the convenor) and,

- motive (the underlying reasons for the creation of the alliance).

Other researchers have proposed models for researching partnership evolution. These suggest, for example, directing attention to:

- the antecedents to partnership formation (for example, recognition of a condition of crisis or opportunity, the existence or development of a legal mandate, the catalytic role of a broker, or following existing networks and leadership)

- problem-setting (recognition of inter-dependencies, issues and interests)

- direction-setting (identification of common goals and sharing of information)

- structuring (institutionalising and establishing frameworks, protocols and procedures)

- outcomes and feedback, emphasising the essentially dynamic and cyclical nature of activity and development (Selin and Chavez, 1995)

Attention to *who* is involved in tourism development partnerships and ways of building collaboration, with particular attention to destination community involvement, has provided another research direction. The development and use of consensus building and negotiation techniques, for example, has been the subject of other studies in the field. (Getz and Jamal 1994; Jamal and Getz, 1995; Jamal and Getz, 1997; Bramwell and Sharman, 1999). Such studies have centred on the extent to which partnerships are inclusive and they present frameworks for analysing a range of issues. These issues include; approaches to collective learning and consensus-building, the identification of power imbalances and degrees of involvement by stakeholders, the scope of the collaboration, benefits and incentives for participants, the presence and role of a facilitator, pre-existing agreements on the issues to be considered, the intensity of the collaboration, partnership practices and processes, the degree to which consensus emerges, recognition of constraints and, methods of implementation and evaluation.

Securing a 'voice' for tourism interests in partnerships concerned with wider planning processes is a further emerging research direction. Tourism may be overlooked in some situations, or present a weak voice in contrast with other industries and ministries. Williams,

Penrose and Hawkes (1998) present a framework for the design and evaluation of shared decision-making processes in these situations. They suggest attention to government and participant support for the partnership process, representation and resources, process management and design, procedural and decision-making frameworks and, partnership outcomes.

Theoretical frameworks used for researching partnerships suggest particular questions, assumptions and methodologies (Long, 1997). Some new and emerging directions in the study of tourism partnerships are presented in Bramwell and Lane (Eds.) (2000). These research approaches include models that direct attention to the processes and patterns, politics and practice of partnerships that are broadly concerned with sustainable tourism planning and development. In this volume, theoretically informed empirical studies of partnerships include the application of models that focus on process-based approaches to tourism planning, 'adaptive management' techniques, stakeholder identification, partnerships as development 'regimes', cultural dimensions of partnership practice, and collaborative learning processes.

The sections that follow consider a particular theoretical framework that has potential for informing future research in this emerging and developing field.

A conceptual framework for the analysis of tourism development partnerships

Wood and Gray's (1991) conceptual framework for the study of partnerships, or as they put it, 'inter-agency collaboration' is proposed here as being a useful and flexible theoretical structure to help shape research on partnerships in tourism. The framework is based primarily on the organisation studies literature, but concepts from political theory, economics and management are also incorporated. The purpose here is to outline the rationale for the conceptual framework, briefly discuss its components and, review its potential applications to the study of tourism development partnerships.

The framework incorporates six theoretical perspectives (Gray and Wood, 1991; Wood and Gray, 1991). The theoretical perspectives incorporate concepts and approaches to the subject of organisational partnerships from Strategic Management, Institutionalism, Economics, and Policy Studies. Other relevant theory, for example from the Political Geography and Planning literature, is implicit in the framework. The extent to which the theoretical perspectives are distinct is questioned here. The perspectives are not mutually exclusive, rather they are presented as components of an integrative analytical framework that can offer theoretical and practical insights on key questions concerning partnerships. A central issue is the extent to which these theoretical bases may be combined and integrated coherently and consistently in order to arrive at a comprehensive theory of organisational partnerships in the context of tourism development.

Elements of the conceptual framework

The six theoretical perspectives that Gray and Wood review and apply in the development of their conceptual framework are:

- resource dependence theory

- corporate social performance theory / institutional economics theory

- strategic management theory / social ecology theory

- microeconomics theory

- institutional theory / negotiated order theory

- political theory

Resource dependence, strategic management, and microeconomics have notable inter-connections in terms of their business and management emphasis. The distinctions between institutional economics, institutionalism, and political theory are also not clear.

Wood and Gray also do not discuss methodological issues that would be associated with the application to empirical research of these theoretical perspectives and of the resulting conceptual framework.

Resource dependence

This approach examines how individual organisations might reduce environmental uncertainty in their domain by seeking (and contributing) resources externally. The kinds of resources that might be considered include those that are material, human, political, structural, and symbolic. Interdependencies occur, it is suggested, because different organisations in a domain lack, possess, or control access to some resources and partnerships are one mechanism for securing access to them. Analysis of resource interdependencies within a domain, such as tourism development, may therefore contribute to an understanding of why partnerships develop and which resources partners seek out and which they are able to contribute.

Issues in the context of research on tourism development partnerships that emerge from a resource dependence perspective include:

- the interests or stakes that actual and/or potential partnership members may have in tourism development

- the circumstances and recognition of resource inter-dependencies which may encourage stakeholders in tourism development to adopt partnerships

- the patterns of inter-dependencies that result from resource exchanges between partners in a tourism development domain.

Corporate social performance/institutional economics

Theories of corporate social responsibility and performance which focus on organisational relationships and responsibilities to communities and stakeholders in an agency's policies, strategies and operations hold promise for capturing the complexities of partnerships (for example, Carroll, 1979; Freeman, 1984; Preston and Post, 1975; Wartick and Cochrane, 1985; Wood, 1991). This may include, for example, analysis of who is involved in a partnership and why, the extent to which stakeholders can inform a partnership's agenda, and how partnerships communicate with stakeholders who are excluded from direct involvement. This perspective therefore focuses on stakeholders defining and achieving (or failing to achieve) social and institutional legitimacy for their collaborative actions (Carroll 1979; Preston and Post 1975; Freeman 1984). The Corporate Social Performance approach thus moves beyond narrow organisational concerns to examine wider, societal consequences of partnerships.

Institutional economics is presented as being a theoretical approach which aims to explain economic behaviour in a wider context. 'Unlike regular economics, institutional economics presents itself as descriptive, pragmatic, anti-rationalist and reformist. It is anti-reductionist and trans-disciplinary, drawing its insights from a broad range of disciplines, including economics, sociology, biology, anthropology, political science, history, and psychology' (Pasquero, 1991:43). Institutional economics assumption that social and economic problem solving can only occur through participative institutional change provides a highly relevant theoretical base for the study of policy orientated partnerships for tourism development.

Research issues from corporate social performance and institutional economics perspectives in a tourism context include:

- how social and institutional legitimacy might be defined, agreed and achieved by the members of a tourism development partnership

- the roles that individual organisations and partnerships might play as social institutions in relation to tourism development, in seeking to promote good employment practices, or access for disadvantaged groups, for example

- how individual organisations and partnerships control and respond to their stakeholder networks in setting and implementing the agenda for tourism development

- the allocation of responsibilities for social issues involved in tourism development among partnership actors

- ways in which tourism development partnerships mediate between the interests of their participant organisations and those of the wider environment.

Strategic management/social ecology

This perspective is traditionally concerned with independent organisations charting courses of action to gain competitive advantage. In general, strategic management theory has little' room for collective action or collaborative alliances, although Astley and Brahn (1989) have adapted strategic management approaches at an inter-organisational level. More recent work has also examined various forms of alliance, collaboration and partnership as strategic tools for competitive advantage (for example, Huxham, 1996 on 'collaborative advantage'). Gray and Wood suggest that research that emphasises the benefits of collective strategy for situations in which organisations face collective problems shifts the theoretical perspective from strategic management for individual organisations to a 'social ecology' approach that places emphasis on inter-connections and dependencies in the organisation's environment.

Issues in the context of research on tourism partnerships that emerge from this perspective include:

- the extent to which members in a tourism development partnership can reduce threats and develop opportunities in relation to their shared and conflicting interests

- the trade-offs between collective and individual benefits and costs for members of a tourism development partnership

- the ways in which a shared tourism development strategy can be reconciled with individual member strategies.

Microeconomics

Applications of microeconomics theory offer another theoretical perspective that can inform research on partnership structures and dynamics. The emphasis of a microeconomics approach in a partnership context has typically focused on ways in which inter-organisational partners might overcome impediments to efficiency in their bilateral financial transactions. This would include for example, ways of reducing the costs of information, training, staff, office accommodation, and other resources from the perspective of individual organisations that are involved in partnership relationships.

Wider questions at the domain level might include an examination of the overall resource use within a partnership and any impediments to economic efficiency and resource contributions that may exist. An example is the issue of 'free-rider' effects, where stakeholders benefit from a partnership without contributing to it. Connections with a resource dependence approach are apparent and any conceptual distinctions between these perspectives are not made clear in Gray and Wood's framework. Such distinctions might start from the basis of microeconomic theory that suggests attention to single organisations (the 'economics of the firm'). A 'dependence' theory, on the other hand, implies a research focus on at least bilateral relationships.

In the context of tourism partnerships, relevant research issues from a microeconomics perspective include:

- (in)efficiencies in financial transactions between tourism development partnership members

- financial returns to members involved in tourism development partnerships.

Institutionalism

The central premise of institutional theory in the context of research on organisational partnerships is, for Gray and Wood, 'that organisations seek to achieve legitimacy from institutional actors by structurally adjusting to institutional influences. They may do this by complying with institutional directives, by copying others' responses to institutions, or by conforming to institutional norms and rituals' (1991:10). This adjustment in order to achieve legitimacy may take the form of a partnership arrangement that incorporates or consults with the 'institutional actors' in a particular domain. This perspective therefore focuses on the institutional environment within which partnerships operate, including the norms, practices, and ideologies present in it, and the ways in which partnerships might adjust to or seek to influence these dominant or latent institutional forces (Di Maggio and Powell 1983).

The research emphasis is on the context within which the partnership has emerged, developed and operates, with particular attention to the institutional demands placed on partnership members by governments, the professions, business, and communities. These institutional forces originate from more or less organised constituencies that can exert pressure on organisations to comply and adjust with dynamic institutional rules or practices in exchange for the conferral of legitimacy, resources and participation. Strong institutional forces can cause organisations in particular domains to adopt similar structures, procedures, and norms (isomorphism) (Di Maggio and Powell, 1983). In sum, institutional sanctions and incentives may represent significant constraints and encouragement for particular forms of partnership to emerge and survive. An arguably positive example is in widespread government and quasi-government economic development programmes that require partnership arrangements for their implementation.

Gray and Wood suggest that negotiated order theory is a 'slightly different application of institutional theory' (1991:10). It focuses on the symbolic and perceptual aspects of inter-organisational relationships, particularly on the evolution and negotiation of shared (and conflicting) understanding among institutional stakeholders of the partnership's structures and processes, limits and possibilities. Negotiated order theory complements institutional theory as a framework for the analysis of stakeholder perceptions and understandings of issues within a broader institutional context. It suggests attention to individual agency as well as structural factors in partnership development.

Research issues in a tourism development partnership context from institutionalist and negotiated order perspectives include:

- the particular structural arrangements adopted by tourism development partnerships, in terms of, for example, the possible replication of partnership forms (isomorphism)

- the means by which tourism development partnerships may achieve legitimacy with stakeholders

- how tourism development partnerships interact with institutional environments

- the degree to which tourism development partnerships are shaped by institutional environments or vice versa

- stakeholder and member perceptions of the purposes and priorities of the partnership.

Political theory

Access to and the distribution of power and resources is a central concern of a political theoretical approach to researching partnerships. Issues of accountability, democracy, legitimacy in the community and winners and losers from partnerships represent major research interests in this context. For Gray and Wood, the relevant issues from a political theoretical perspective for research on partnerships are, 'the power dynamics and the distribution of benefits within a network of stakeholders in a problem domain' (1991:11).

In the context of tourism partnerships, relevant issues from a political theoretical approach include:

- the degree of access to and the distribution of power and resources that affect tourism development partnership members

- the distribution of costs and benefits within a tourism development partnership and in the wider domain.

Common concerns in the theoretical framework: preconditions, process and outcomes, and the roles of individual partnership members

The previous sections have identified the kinds of research issues that are associated with each of the six theoretical perspectives that contribute to a framework for the study of tourism partnerships. Connections between some of the perspectives have also been outlined. In setting out to apply these theories as part of a framework for the study of tourism development partnerships, a fundamental consideration is the timing of the study in relation to the stage of its subject's life cycle. Put simply, research on partnerships may take place before, during and/or after a partnership is established. Different theoretical approaches suggest different questions in researching partnerships at particular stages in their emergence, development and termination. Some theoretical perspectives offer more insight than others at these different stages and some may be combined. This section considers research issues that may be associated with the stage of a partnership's existence. Following Gray and Wood, this section uses the terms, 'preconditions', 'process' and, 'outcomes' to describe these stages.

The pre-conditions that may give rise to organisational partnerships

The background to the establishment of a partnership suggests research attention to those factors that make a partnership possible and that encourage (or discourage) potential member involvement. These factors include individual, organisational, structural, and political incentives (and disincentives) that exist in the domain for partnership formation. The historical relationships between partnership members and the history of the problem domain are further considerations. Analysis of pre-conditions would also involve attention to the various definitions by members of the context and the issues that the partnership may address.

A recognition of organisational stakes and inter-dependencies within a problem domain is a feature of resource dependence theory. The identification of the nature and sources of the various resources that are required by participants may also assist in an examination of why particular partnership forms emerge. Microeconomic analysis, focusing on financial incentives, opportunities and barriers to collaboration complements a resource dependence approach.

The theoretical framework also highlights the social, political and institutional conditions that encourage partnership formation in particular contexts. These conditions include issues of representation, accountability and equity in addressing problems associated with the domain.

The extent to which an understanding of these issues is shared by participants and how this shared understanding may influence partnership form, policy and strategy is a further research consideration in relation to pre-conditions.

Partnership processes

A partnership's operational stage suggests a research focus on the nature, structure and management of the partnership arrangement and the processes by which stakeholders interact to accomplish their objectives. The language and discourse involved in the partnership process and in its statements and publications are further research topics here. Gray and Wood suggest that only three of the six theoretical perspectives address partnership processes in a systematic way; corporate social performance / institutional economics, institutionalism, and political theory. Gray and Wood suggest that they do so in a dynamic, longitudinal manner in terms of, for example, changes in 'the alignment of a partnership with its environment over time', the organisation of decision making, the duration of the partnership, and the institutionalisation of partnership structures. The institutionalist thread stands out as a common theoretical base for research on partnership processes.

The outcomes of the partnership

The identification of product and/or policy outcomes following the termination of a partnership programme may also be addressed from each of the theoretical perspectives presented by Gray and Wood. As with preconditions and process the research emphasis varies according to theoretical orientation. Issues might include whether problems were solved, whose problems were solved and, whether shared and agreed norms were realised. The definition of a partnership's success or failure and the specification of any succession arrangements that may be devised to follow the end of a partnership programme are further common concerns. The issue of whether outcomes may have been achieved in the absence of a partnership or in a different partnership form is a further theoretical consideration.

Individual partnership member roles

A partnership will typically involve a number of key individual members. These will include, in many cases, a programme manager and steering group chair. The roles that these members and managers play may comprise an important element of research on partnerships, whether focused on preconditions, processes or outcomes. Their priorities, practices and ideologies provide a further dimension that may be addressed in terms of the theoretical framework, providing insights on individual agency as well as on structural and institutional factors affecting partnerships.

The issue of individual roles in partnerships might also go beyond the convener or programme manager to an analysis of the contributions and positions of other partnership members, particularly where there is a partnership manager accountable to a chair and/or steering group. The views of these individuals are likely to be particularly significant in a partnership's strategy, priorities and programme of work.

The following, concluding section suggests applications of some propositions associated with the theoretical perspectives on partnerships to tourism development.

Conclusions

All of the theoretical perspectives reviewed by Wood and Gray may contribute to the development of a conceptual framework for the analysis of partnerships in tourism. Figure Two presents a summary of the kinds of research questions that emerge from the theoretical positions within the framework. Research issues are suggested here in relation to whether a study is focused on the pre-conditions or antecedents of a particular partnership, on partnership operation and processes or on outcomes. It is further suggested that theoretical positions may be combined into those that are primarily concerned with resource considerations and those where the main emphasis is on institutional and political systems.

Figure 2   Theoretical perspectives and common concerns of partnerships research

Partnership research issue and timing	Theoretical perspectives based on resource considerations	Theoretical perspectives based on political and institutional considerations
	Resource dependence theory Microeconomics Strategic management /Social ecology (may also apply to column 2)	Corporate social performance/Institutional economics Institutionalism/Negotiated order theory Political theory
Preconditions	Recognition of stakes and inter-dependencies in a domain Recognition that a partnership may maximise efficiencies and reduce transaction costs Fit with organisation strategy	Social, political and institutional conditions encouraging involvement Achieving a shared understanding of and response to a problem Enhancing institutional legitimacy Protecting political interests, and need for governance rules in a domain
Process	Gray and Wood suggest that process is not well addressed by these theories <u>but:</u> Identification of how interdependencies, economic relationships and strategies may change over time	Ways in which understanding of the issues, responsibilities and accountability are negotiated, agreed and shared Re-alignment of partnerships with dynamic environments Explicit member roles and responsibilities, joint decision making, agreed rules, interactive processes
Outcomes	Extent to which problems are solved by combining resources and strategies Partnership structure may lead to different problems and efficiency outcomes	Ways in which risks, costs and benefits are distributed Extent to which shared strategy is enduring and based on shared understanding

In the case of tourism development partnerships, limited budgets in the public sector and the small scale of many operators in the private sector highlights the importance of resource inter-dependencies in, for example, place marketing campaigns. The extent to which these interdependencies are accepted and recognised and their implications for partnership members may be examined from a resource dependence perspective before, during or after a partnership programme.

Achieving tourism development which is sustainable in economic, environmental and community terms is commonly high on the agenda of tourism partnerships, particularly in attempting to secure the participation of the private sector in sustainable tourism policies and programmes. A corporate social performance approach is therefore highly relevant in this context.

The extent to which tourism partnerships can mediate between their members in reconciling potentially conflicting strategic objectives would also be a relevant research approach. The issues involved with the development of a corporate partnership strategy would also be open to analysis from a strategic management perspective.

Improving transaction efficiencies within tourism domains and bilateral relationships in, for example, training and technology initiatives would also be a legitimate line of enquiry in terms of microeconomics theory. Addressing 'free rider' and other impediments to economic efficiency in the tourism development domain is a further dimension of this approach.

The institutionalist and negotiated order perspectives may also be used in an examination of the norms and ideologies which are dominant within the tourism 'policy community' and how they may change as a consequence of tourism partnership membership. The interactions between tourism development partnerships and the wider institutional environment and the achievement of legitimacy are further issues that may be addressed by this theoretical perspective.

Achieving an equitable distribution of power, resources and benefits both within tourism partnerships and spatially, within a partnership programmes' geographical boundaries, is also a highly relevant research issue in this context. Political theory offers a useful conceptual framework for the study of these issues.

The study of partnerships is itself enhanced by forging a 'partnership' between relevant theoretical perspectives. The perspectives briefly reviewed here provide the basis for a more comprehensive theory of inter-organisational collaboration in tourism. It is a framework that has proved useful in the design of previous research on the pre-conditions and outcomes of a partnership that was established to develop and manage a major festival event with tourism dimensions held in the UK in 1996 (Long, 1996; Long, 2000). The framework has also been adopted by other authors in a study of an agency established to encourage tourism on Britain's inland waterways (Fyall et al. 2000). This framework has considerable potential for further refinement and application in future research on tourism partnerships.

References

Aiken, M. and Hage, J. (1968), Organisational Interdependence and Intra Organisational Structure, *American Sociological Review,* Vol. 33, pp. 912 - 930.

Astley, W. G and Brahn, A. (1989), Organisational Designs for post-industrial strategies:The role of inter-organisational collaboration. In C.C. Snow (Ed.) *Strategy, Organisational Design and Human Resource Management.* New York: JAI.

Bramwell, W. and Rawding, L. (1994), Tourism marketing organisations in industrial cities: organisations, objectives and urban governance. *Tourism Management* (15) 6 pp425-434.

Bramwell, B. and Sharman, A. (1999), Collaboration in local tourism policy-making. *Annals of Tourism Research* 26 (2): 392-415.

Bramwell, W. and Lane, B. (2000), *Tourism, Collaboration and Partnership: Politics, Practice and Sustainability.* Clevedon: Channel View Publications.

Carroll, A. B. (1979), A three-dimensional conceptual model of corporate social performance. *Academy of Management Review* (4): 497-505.

DiMaggio, P. J. and Powell, W. W. (1983), The iron cage revisited: Institutional isomorphism and collective rationality in organisational fields. *American Sociological Review* (48): 147-160.

Emery, F. and Trist, E. (1965), The causal texture of organisational environments. *Human Relations*, 18, 21-32

Freeman, R. E. (1984) Strategic Management: a stakeholder approach. London: Pitman

Fyall, A., Oakley, B. and Weiss, A. (2000), Theoretical perspectives applied to inter-organisational collaboration on Britain's inland waterways. *International Journal of Hospitality and Tourism Administration*. 1 (1): 89-112.

Gamm, L. (1981), An Introduction to Research in Interorganisational Collaboration. *Journal of Voluntary Action Research* 10 (1): 18-52.

Getz, D. and Jamal, T. (1994), The Environment-Community Symbiosis: A Case for Collaborative Tourism Planning. *Journal of Sustainable Tourism* 2 (3): 152-173.

Gray, B. (1985), Conditions Facilitating Interorganisational Collaboration. *Human Relations* 38 (10): 911-936.

Gray, B. (1989), *Collaborating: Finding Common Ground for Multiparty Problems*. San Francisco: Jossey-Bass.

Gray, B. and Wood, D. J. (1991), Collaborative Alliances: Moving from Practice to Theory. *The Journal of Behavioural Science*. (27) 1 pp 3-22.

Gunn, C. (1990), The new recreation-tourism alliance. *Journal of Park and Recreation Management* (8) 1 pp.1-8.

Healey, P. (1997), *Collaborative Planning. Shaping Places in Fragmented Societies*. London: Macmillan.

Huxham, C. (Ed.) (1996), *Creating Collaborative Advantage*. London: Sage.

Jamal, T. B. and Getz, D. (1994), Collaboration Theory and Community Tourism Planning. *Annals of Tourism Research* 21 (3): 186 – 204.

Jamal, T. B. and Getz, D. (1997), "Visioning" for Sustainable Tourism Development: Community-Based Collaborations. In Murphy, P. E. (Ed.) *Quality Management in Urban Tourism Chichester*: John Wiley.

Levine, S. and White, P. E. (1961), Exchange As A Conceptual Framework For The Study of Inter-Organisational Relationships. *Administrative Science Quarterly*. pp.583-601.

Long, P. E. (1994), Perspectives on partnerships as an approach to local tourism development. in Seaton, A. V. et al (Eds) *Tourism: the State of the Art*. Chichester: John Wiley

Long, P. E. (1996), Inter-organisational collaboration in the development of tourism and the arts: 1996 – Year of Visual Arts in Robinson, M. et al (Eds) *Culture as the Tourist Product Sunderland*: Business Education Publishers.

Long, P. E. (1997), Researching tourism partnership organisations: from practice to theory to methodology in Murphy, P. E. (Ed.) *Quality Management in Urban Tourism*. Chichester: John Wiley.

Long, P. E. (2000), After the Event Perspectives on Organisational Partnerships in the Management of a Themed Festival Year *Event Management* Vol. 7 (1).

Nathan, M. L. and Mitroff, I. (1991), The use of Negotiated Order Theory as a tool for The analysis and development of an interorganisational field. *Journal of Applied Behavioural Science*. 27 (2): 163-180.

Palmer, A. and Bejou, D. (1995), Tourism destination marketing alliances. *Annals of Tourism Research* 22 (3): 616-629.

Pasquero, J. (1991), Supraorganisational collaboration: The Canadian environmental experiment. *Journal of Applied Behavioural Science*. 27 (1): 38-64.

Pfeffer, J. and Salancik, G. (1978), *The External Control of Organisations*. New York: Harper and row.

Preston, L. and Post, J.(1975), *Private Management and Public Policy: The principle of public responsibility*. New York: Prentice Hall.

Roberts, N. C. and Bradley, R. I. (1991), Stakeholder Collaboration and Innovation: A Study of Public Policy Initiation at the State Level *Journal of Applied Behavioural Science* (27) pp.210 - 225.

Rogers, D. L. and Whetten, D. A. (1982), *Inter-Organisational Co-ordination: Theory, Research and Implementation*. Iowa State University Press.

Selin, S. (1993), Collaborative Alliances: new interorganisational forms in tourism. In Uysal, M. and Fesenmaier, D. R. *Communication and Channel Systems in Tourism Marketing*. New York: The Haworth Press.

Selin, S. and Beason, K. (1991), Interorganisational relations in tourism. *Annals of Tourism Research* (18) pp.639-652.

Selin, S. and Chavez, D. (1995), Developing an evolutionary tourism partnership model. *Annals of Tourism Research* 22 (4): 844-856.

Selin, S, and Myers, N. (1998), Member Satisfaction and Effectiveness Attributes of a Regional Initiative. *Journal of Travel and Tourism Marketing* 7 (3): 79-94.

Waddock, S. A. (1991), A Typology of Social Partnership Organisations. *Administration and Society.* (22) pp. 480 – 515.

Williams, P. W., Penrose, R. W. and Hawkes, S. (1998), Shared decision-making in tourism land use planning. *Annals of Tourism Research* 25 (4): 860-889.

Wood, D .J. (1991), Social issues in management: Theory and research in corporate social performance. *Journal of Management* 17 pp.383-406.

Wood, D. J. and Gray, B. (1991), Toward a Comprehensive Theory of Collaboration *Journal of Applied Behavioural Science* 27 (2) 139-162.

Creating supra-brand Australia: Answering the challenges of contemporary destination marketing?

Nigel J Morgan

University of Wales Institute, Cardiff, UK

Abstract

In today's highly competitive tourism market, destination marketing (largely co-ordinated and funded by the public sector) is a highly politicised activity. Such is the difficulty of producing good, effective marketing that tourism managers are increasingly adopting branding techniques in an effort to differentiate their identities and to emphasise the uniqueness of their product. This paper discusses the role and importance of branding in destination marketing and suggests that destination managers face four unique challenges in such branding initiatives: relatively limited budgets; political considerations; a lack of control over the total marketing mix; difficulty in achieving differentiation. Focusing on the advertising activities of Australia, this paper concludes that the creation of a supra-brand in a targeted, multi-agency 'mood marketing' initiative can assist in overcoming these political difficulties facing destination brand managers.

Introduction

As tourism expands around the globe, it brings new opportunities in destination marketing, yet one of the outcomes of the increasing number of available and accessible tourist destinations is a dilution of established destination identities and increased competition amongst emergent tourism sites. The relative substitutability in tourism products is well established and destinations offering a similar product at a similar price are highly interchangeable. For example, UK tourists in search of a moderately priced sun and sand experience may accept a range of alternatives - from Cyprus, to Turkey, Spain or Greece. As a result, the need for destinations to project an unique identity - to differentiate themselves from their competitors - is more critical than ever. Yet most destinations continue to project very similar marketing images - for instance, blue seas, cloudless skies and endless golden beaches are heavily used to market the Caribbean and the Mediterranean when sun and sand are actually poor differentiators for such destinations.

This highlights the peculiar challenges of tourism destination marketing and a common problem is the persistent failure of the advertising to create a sufficiently differentiated identity for the tourist destination (Morgan and Pritchard 2000). Combine this with the highly damaging internal and external politics involved in creating destination advertising with evidence that tourism promotion does not *persuade* uncommitted potential vacationers - but rather acts to *confirm* the intentions of those already predisposed to visit (Wales Tourist Board 1994) - and destination managers have genuine problems. To counteract such challenges, many destinations, be they cities, regions or nations, are developing comprehensive identity programmes in an effort to differentiate themselves and to emphasise the uniqueness of their product in today's highly competitive market - most obviously to attract tourism and inward investment - but also to foster self-confidence and self-esteem.

The challenges of destination promotion

Destination marketing is increasingly competitive at the start of the twenty first century and public sector marketing strategies are becoming ever more sophisticated as the stakes are raised. In such a marketplace, it is becoming more and more critical for tourism destinations to be able to differentiate themselves. In the 2000s they will have to communicate with an increasingly sophisticated audience, whilst both the marketplace and the media will be even more fragmented. Mass tourism markets have been transformed into niche markets; consumer choice has exploded; and, at the same time, media choices have expanded enormously as new technology continues to push the media frontiers beyond previously established boundaries. Yet in transferring marketing techniques to destinations, destination managers face four unique challenges: relatively limited budgets; political considerations; a lack of control over the total marketing mix; difficulty in achieving differentiation.

The challenge of limited budgets

Most national tourism organisations have limited budgets and yet they have to market globally, competing not just with other destinations, but also with other global brands. Proctor and Gamble, the world's biggest advertiser, spends millions each year promoting its various products but countries such as Spain, France and Thailand still have to vie with them for consumer mindshare in a crowded marketing environment (table 1). Whilst Sony alone spends over $1.2 billion a year on global advertising, the *total* global government tourism advertising spend was just over $350 million in the mid-1990s, accounting for approximately half of the promotional budgets of national tourism organisations (Lurham 1998). Table 2 illustrates the biggest advertising spenders in 1997 (other significant spenders included Greece, Turkey, Egypt and Canada) - not including private sector spending. It is worth pointing out that this table only illustrates *national* advertising spend - where available. It does not, for instance, include countries which have no national tourism organisation. In the USA, for example, state promotion is undertaken by a variety of convention bureaux and state travel offices - whose budgets often exceed those of some countries. The Illinois state travel office budget in 1997 exceeded $35 million, that of Texas was $25 million and

Pennsylvania almost $20 million. Compare these figures with the national tourism budgets of Germany ($27 million), Hungary ($21 million) and Morocco ($18 million) (Lurman 1998).

Table 1   Tourism Destinations Versus Other Advertisers, Global Spend, 1995

Advertiser	Global Ad Spend (US$ millions)
Sony	1,277
Coca-Cola	1,146
Renault	566
Gillette	400
Tourism	*357*
Volvo	342
Fuji Film	208

Source: World Tourism Organisation and *Advertising Age*

Table 2   Top National Tourism Organisations' Advertising Spend, 1997

Country	Ad Spend (US $ millions)
Australia	30
Thailand	26
Cyprus	17
Spain	17
France	16
Puerto Rico	16
Brazil	15
Portugal	13

Source: World Tourism Organisation (figures to nearest million)

Thus, the first challenge facing destination marketers is their extremely limited budgets by comparison with the marketers of many consumer goods and services. In such circumstances, in order to compete with the global consumer brands, destination marketers have to *outsmart* rather than *outspend* the competition - and that means creating innovative, attention-arresting communications on a budget *and* maximising the media spend (Morgan and Pritchard 2000). This seems simple, but in destination advertising it is extremely difficult to achieve largely because of the peculiar political challenges facing destination marketers.

The challenge of politics

The reality of local and national state promotion is that it is about achieving a balance between applying cutting-edge communications approaches to a marketing problem and the realpolitik of managing local, regional and national politics: nowhere is the paradox of public policy and market forces more sharply defined than in the creation of destination advertising (Ward and Gold 1994: 11; Palmer and Bejou 1995). One area in which there is much debate in political terms amongst destination marketers and destination stakeholders is over the use of clichés and stereotypes in marketing and advertising. Often consumers have very cliched images about countries, yet those clichés are frequently unpopular in the countries themselves. One view is if the consumer connects with a cliché about a country, then its marketers should use it since it has recognition and therefore advertising value. That, however, is very often an advertising agency view - not one tempered by the experience of seeing the negative media reaction to advertising campaigns perceived by residents as perpetuating stereotypes which are (by definition) outdated caricatures of places and peoples (Morgan and Pritchard 1998: 175-80). The answer - which is both politically acceptable and which makes marketing sense - is to craft images which use the cliché as a hook on which to hang more detail - the cliched identity can then be reshaped and given greater complexity through effective and consistent marketing.

Beyond such issues, public sector destination marketers are also hugely hampered by a variety of political pressures - they have to reconcile a range of local and regional interests and promote an identity acceptable to a range of constituencies. As Bob Garfield, editor of *Advertising Age* and long time advertising critic, said of destination advertising in a personal interview:

> *When you look at the ads ... you can see transcripts of the arguments at the tourist boards ... the membership of which all wanted their own interests served ... you can see the destruction of the advertising message as a result of the politics.*

In addition to compromising the creative process of marketing and advertising destinations, the politicians who control public sector tourism organisations frequently demand short-term results - pressure which is inconsistent with the long term investment required by brand building. Whilst ultimately it is the politicians who hold the destination marketers' purse strings, a destination brand's lifespan is more of a long-term proposition than the careers of most politicians. Bureaucratic red-tape can also often confound effective advertising - the marketers of Valencia, Spain's third city, for instance, are obliged to issue new advertising contracts every year - a practice which can do little to ensure consistency of message (personal interview with Markets and Communication Director, Turisme Generalitat Valenciana, 1997). Frequently, political considerations within a local state can even dictate the range of photographs which are included in a campaign so that *all* the key areas, towns, or resorts within a region or country are illustrated. Whilst this has its political advantages in that it appeases local pressure groups and local residents it can seriously compromise the effectiveness of the advertising.

Even when all the internal stakeholders are satisfied with a campaign, destination advertising can run into political problems as a result of external pressures. Perhaps one of the most depressing examples of this was the *'Feast for the Senses'* campaign created for the Morocco Tourist Board in the mid-1990s. The campaign was an attempt to craft an homogeneous image for the country in all its generating markets - each of which had previously commissioned quite separate advertising on the premise that consumers in the UK, Germany, France, Italy etc. all sought different experiences from a holiday to Morocco - a disparate approach which had created a blurred and confused image of the country. Working with the Morocco Tourist Board - whose total annual tourism budget was approximately $18 million (Lurham 1998) - the agency who won the contract therefore decided to create a new logo and produced a number of visuals in a series of 10 posters and in the main brochure, followed through in television commercials - all based around the strapline *'Morocco - A Feast for the Senses'*. All the advertising was produced in seven or eight languages, so whilst consistency of brand image was achieved, the local Morocco marketing office in each of the markets was to some extent free to chose the visual it thought would best sell in that particular country (Vial 1997).

Each of Morocco's main tourism regions was featured in the campaign and such was the positive reaction in the country when the visuals were seen that in the next phase the agency even created posters for those areas where there was little or no tourism infrastructure. Yet, whilst the image building exercise was warmly welcomed in Morocco - and actually began to change regional policy-makers' attitudes to the potential of tourism - it proved extremely difficult to sell the campaign to external stakeholders. Travel agents and tour operators had to be persuaded to embrace it and a considerable effort was put into trade promotional packs, including displays, maps and a new trade magazine. Ultimately the campaign encountered problems because German tour operators lobbied the Morocco Tourist Board, concerned that the campaign was promoting the country as a cultural destination and not as the sun and sea product which their customers were seeking. Whilst the visuals and the logo were retained in the following year, the advertising agency lost the contract and the strong brand values of the original concept were diluted (Vial 1997). Whilst this is a quite recent example of the power of such pressure from international tour operators, there are many others - notably in Tunisia in the 1970s when it was German tour operators who again dictated the nature of tourism development (Vial 1997) and today on the Albanian Mediterranean coast where there is external pressure to opt for high density development rather than more sustainable alternatives (Hall 1997).

The challenge of the destination product

These examples of countries bowing to external pressures to adopt a particular type of tourism development or to change a marketing campaign, highlight the fact that destinations are not a single product but composite products consisting of a bundle of different components, including accommodation and catering establishments; tourist attractions; arts, entertainment and cultural venues; and even the natural environment. Destination marketers have relatively little control over these different aspects of their product and a diverse range of agencies and companies are partners in the task of portraying favourable brand images. These could include: local and national government agencies; environmental groups and agencies; chambers of commerce; trade associations; and civic groups (Kotler, Bowen and Makens 1996: 285). Whilst packaged goods normally have an obvious core - so that their ads can anchor themselves to product performance and attributes - with destinations the situation is much less clear.

The essence of creating a successful brand is to build an emotional link between product and consumer, but what encapsulates the emotional brand values of a destination - is it the atmosphere of a resort, the hotel the tourist stays in, or the friendliness of the local people? All of these factors can and do affect how the tourist views the vacation experience. In view of the fact that it is a composite product, can a destination ever evoke high levels of emotional commitment? Arguably it can as the potential to evoke an emotional attachment is even greater for tourism destinations than for fmcg or services - destinations have very strong and pervasive associations for tourists, which if skilfully manipulated, can provide the basis for brand-building (Morgan and Pritchard 1999). Today's tourists are not asking 'what can we do on holiday?', but 'who can we be on holiday?' - they are increasingly looking less for escape and more for discovery - and that creates the basis of an emotional connection which the marketers can exploit in advertising (Pride 1999).

The challenge of creating differentiation

Whilst there are additional political pressures in destination marketing, good advertising can still be produced. To again quote Bob Garfield:

> *Smart managers find out what is the meaning of their destination as a product to their potential consumer. They exploit that meaning in finding the value they can add to the sun and sand experience. Their advertising, when it's done well should reflect that added value ... that point of differentiation.*

Most destinations are likely to possess some unique attribute that can be translated into a unique selling proposition. The US Virgin Islands, for example, is essentially a sun, surf and sand destination which in its physical geography is identical to the British Virgin Islands 40 nautical miles away. Yet, because the US Virgin Islands' biggest market is the United States, it does have something on which to build a unique proposition. Its marketers can advertise the concept that tourists can enjoy the exotic experience of a natural paradise - yet with the comfort and security of visiting somewhere which has the familiarity of speaking the same language and using the same currency. For those Americans who want a beach holiday and are pre-disposed to try something partly exotic but mostly safe and familiar, the US Virgin Islands offer a unique opportunity and hence its marketers use the straplines *'They're your islands'* and *'The American Paradise in the Caribbean'*. These differentiate the destination from the British Virgin Islands, which uses the phrases *'Out of this world ... not out of reach'* and *'Nature's Little Secrets'*. As the US Virgin Islands brochure points out:

As an American territory, the US Virgin Islands offers United States citizens significant advantages over other Caribbean vacation getaways. Even if you are an international traveler, you will find the American system of laws and customs under which the US Virgin Islands operates to be convenient and trouble-free... Come experience the majestic beauty and friendly warmth of these American treasures ... The US Virgin Islands. They're your islands. Come see them for yourself and you'll find yourself returning (US Virgin Islands Division of Tourism 1998).

Destination marketers often focus on history, culture and beautiful scenery in their advertising but most destinations can claim to have these attributes and it is critical to build a brand on something which uniquely connects a destination to the consumer now or has the potential to do so. It must also be a proposition which the competition wants and maybe able to *copy* but which they cannot *surpass* or *usurp*. For example, other world cities can claim to be romantic or spiritual, but only Rome is The Eternal City - it has that epithet, it had it first and no other place can now claim it. Whatever proposition is used it must also have the potential to last and to evolve in a long term branding campaign. However, the point of differentiation must reflect a promise which can be delivered and which matches expectations. Good destination marketing is therefore original and different but its originality and difference needs to be *sustainable, believable and relevant* - not, for instance, in the case of Philadelphia, USA, whose promise about your vacation memories of the place living with you forever promises far too much.

One destination advertising campaign which transcends the commodity nature of the product and which promises a unique (yet credible) experience was the 1998 *'India Changes You'* campaign. There are a plethora of exotic countries which a consumer could visit and many of them have spectacular scenery and fascinating heritage, yet such is the emotional power of the sub-continent with its poignant history and diverse cultures that its advertising promise to the consumer that 'India changes you' is sustainable. Garfield describes this campaign premise as:

> among the most powerful advertising statements I have ever encountered in any category anywhere - it's not "get away from it all", it's not "escape the rat race", it's not "discover yourself" - which are all fairly familiar themes - it's better than discover yourself, it's "change yourself." It's breathtaking.

This appeal was only a part of the reason for this campaign's success. The other is that in this instance, the marketers of India also managed to transcend the politics of tourism advertising. Despite the fact that India is made up of a number of regions, all competing for tourism business, the campaign promoted the whole of India as the destination and in doing so, succeeded in preventing any dilution of the advertising message which the promotion of the individual regions would have created.

Destination branding

As discussed above, limited budgets, political pressures, the lack of overall product control, all pose unique challenges for managers of destinations. In such circumstances, some destinations are adopting strategies whose main goal is differentiation through the creation of brand saliency - the development of an emotional relationship with the consumer through highly choreographed and focused communications campaigns. Whether such strategies can truly be described as 'branding' largely depends on how branding is defined. de Chernatony's and McDonald's (1992: 18) definition is typical, describing a successful brand as:

> ... an identifiable product, service, person or place, augmented in such a way that the buyer or user perceives relevant unique added values which match their needs most closely. Furthermore its success results from being able to sustain these added values in the face of competition.

As such definitions suggest, there is a general agreement amongst academics - as well as practitioners - that places can be branded in the same way as fmcg and services (Crockett and Wood 1999, Hall 1999; Morgan and Pritchard 1999; Nickerson and Moisey 1999; Williams and Palmer 1999) and the concept of branding is increasingly being applied to destinations. However, although there is this general agreement that branding can be applied to tourism destinations, there is less certainty about how the concept translates into practical marketing activity. Certainly, provenance - where a brand comes from and where it is based - is important and influences consumer brand perceptions. Those such as Coca Cola, Microsoft and Nike are strongly seen as being American and they derive strength from the brand equity of the USA itself which is associated with independence, attitude and technological ability (Anholt 1998). In terms of tourism destination branding, provenance is even more critical because countries pre-exist any identities crafted for them by marketers and neither their advertisers nor consumers can have objective views of them.

How can destination brands be built?

The first stage in the process of building a destination brand is the establishment of the core values of the destination and its brand - these should be durable, relevant, communicable and hold saliency for potential tourists. Once these core values have been established, they should underpin and imbue all subsequent marketing activity - especially in literature text and illustrations - so that the brand values are cohesively communicated (British Tourist Authority 1997; James 1997). The brand values should also be reinforced by a logotype or brand signature and a design style guide which ensures consistency of message and approach. To successfully create an emotional attachment a destination brand has to be:

- credible;

- deliverable;

- differentiating;

- conveying powerful ideas;

- enthusing for trade partners;

- resonating with the consumer.

Such destination brand building strategies have been adopted recently by a range of countries from Greece to Thailand and, whilst there are particular challenges facing those who would brand places, more and more destinations are using brand saliency techniques in an effort to create an unique and differentiated identity. In the 1980s there were several highly successful marketing campaigns which centred on a consistent communications proposition. New York's *'I love NY'* and the *'Glasgow's miles better'* campaigns are two of the best known. In these, and in many other instances, the campaigns focused on logos and slogans but they were not truly *branding* initiatives. In building a brand for a destination, the image should not be confined to the visual and this is the essence of the latest tool adapted by today's destination marketers - 'mood brand marketing.' It is designed to create an emotional relationship between the destination and potential visitors - as in the current '*Amazing Thailand*' campaign. In this, the branding activities concentrate on conveying the essence or *the spirit* of a destination, often communicated via a few key attributes and associations (Pritchard and Morgan 1998).

Such successes in destination advertising inevitably reflect destination brands which have been able to resist the political dynamic (which is exerted at all political levels). These brands have strong advertising heritages, are consistent but at the same time are able to change, move with the times and continually refresh themselves in the minds of the consumer. This is difficult to achieve and that is why the same destinations are constantly cited as classic examples of cohesive, long-term branding - because they are a rare breed and they succeed against the odds. Thus, Ireland has been running the same basic proposition in its various campaigns for two decades - currently encapsulated in the '*Live a different life*' strapline and Spain has been pursuing a remarkably consistent branding exercise since 1983 (Parkinson *et al.* 1994).

Destination supra-brands - the case of Australia

As the above discussion illustrates, destinations can be branded and the next step in the evolution of destination branding is the creation of the suprabrand. Here, marketers of tourism destinations - primarily countries - attempt to create suprabrands which offer consumers an emotional commitment, moving beyond the mere characteristics of the product to provoke a much deeper response and identification. Crucially, however, in a suprabrand this involves a two-tier but highly integrated approach whereby the country's brand personality is consistently projected at the macro level in all the key target markets, and its sub-brands (whether states, regions or even cities) echo, but embroider in more detail the same consistent themes in their advertising messages.

Constructing emerging destination supra-brands - the case of Australia

In creating the suprabrand of Australia, the country itself is being positioned as the supra-brand, whilst its states (such as Western Australia) form the sub-brands. For Australia as a whole, the marketing challenge was that of a destination which was seen as having much to offer but with a diverse and unclear image. In order to create a unified, cohesive global Brand Australia, a number of industry experts, academics and researchers were brought together to examine the vacation needs of consumers and their perceptions of Australia. In constructing the brand, the following seven step model was adopted:

- identify the markets;

- research the brand values within the key markets and amongst the deliverers;

- evaluate the product requirements - identify any need for reinvestment;

- construct the brand architecture;

- translate the brand personality and proposition into deliverable messages;

- implement an integrated campaign;

- monitor, evaluate, review.

The first step was to concentrate on the target audience and to isolate those who were potential consumers. The marketers of Australia identified that a key target audience for the destination is a younger age group between 18-44 and especially those aged 18-35. These consumers are more likely to consider travelling to Australia now rather than seeing it as a 'once-in-a-lifetime' destination. They are looking for adventure, exhilaration, freedom and personal discovery and thus Australia's core brand values needed to reflect these attributes (table 3). In the next stage, the global brand messages in each of Australia's key generating countries were reshaped to reflect the re-crafted brand personality (tables 3 and 5). Launched in 1997, the campaign was to cost $100 million in total and was intended to generate 14 million tourists and $44 billion export earnings in markets which were estimated to have 500 million potential consumers. It was an approach based on partnership and synergy and which embraced a range of media, including television, magazines, newspapers, direct mail, cinema and the World Wide Web (see Morgan and Pritchard 1999).

Table 3   The Values and Personality of Brand Australia

Brand Values	Brand Personality
youthful	youthful
energetic	stylish
optimistic	vibrant
stylish	diverse
unpretentious	adventurous
genuine	
open	
fun	

Source: Brand Australia, video produced by the Australian Tourism Commission, 1997

A key element of the new Brand Australia was the creation of a new trademark logo. This was intended to encapsulate the personality and the brand architecture of the destination and had to be bold, exciting, energetic, vital, adventurous and sophisticated yet friendly and fun. The end result was the creation of a logo depicting a yellow kangaroo against a red sun over a background of green and a blue sea (table 4).

Table 4   The Heart of the Australia Logo

Colours	Symbolise
Red	earth, desert, centre, outback
Blue	sky, sea, cool, endless
Green	bush, rain forest, environment, clean
Yellow	warm, nights, life, energy, sun, youth, friendly

Source: Brand Australia, video produced by the Australian Tourism Commission, 1997

Whilst the core brand values of Australia remain cohesive and consistent, four different facets of its personality are portrayed in four slightly different campaigns aimed at its main tourist-generating regions - the consumers of which are diverse and seeking differing vacation experiences. To be consistent in the brand values does not mean that it is appropriate to run identical campaigns around the globe - a brand will find it difficult if not impossible to be all things to all people. Indeed, that is to erase cultural differences and ignore the fact that consumers in Asia, America and Europe respond to differing advertising appeals and are seeking a diverse range of benefits from a visit to Australia. However, what the marketers must do is to ensure that the individual country-specific campaigns reflect Australia's brand values and communicate its unique attributes. Thus, for instance, the commercial aimed at a European consumer is constructed around the centrality of emotion and the power of holiday memories, whilst the execution screened in cinemas and on television in the USA emphasises fun, adventure and discovery and features Australians 'inviting' the viewer into the destination (table 5).

Table 5   Translating the Personality of Brand Australia Globally

Region/Country	Asia	USA	Japan	Europe
Australia's Attributes	big nature, outdoors, city life	fun, diversity, active, adventure, live it	surprise, undiscovered, culture, lifestyle	activity, relaxation, intriguing, enriching, diverse, powerful memories
Campaign	*Let the magic begin*	*Holiday*	*Country of surprises*	*The sooner you go, the longer the memories...*
Message	excitement, shopping, nightlife	take a break from work and discover people and islands	fast-paced, sophisticated, cosmopolitan, modern	emotional, appealing, unique, travel now

Source: Brand Australia, video produced by the Australian Tourism Commission, 1997

Lying below the over-arching brand of Australia, each individual tourism region within the country is also pursuing an integrated sub-branding strategy which synergises with Australia the Brand. One example of a complete approach to this sub-branding exercise is that of Western Australia where tourism is a AUS$2.1 billion industry. The Western Australian' Tourism Commission (WATC) has implemented Brand Western Australia (BWA), a strategy based on intensive consumer research evaluated in Crockett's and Wood's (1999) article on the initiative (on which this section draws). Its aim is to reposition Western Australia as a premier nature-based tourism destination in the global market. Central to this repositioning has been the development of an inclusive partnership between government and industry to promote the marketing and development of the tourism product and infrastructure. Significantly, it has also prompted an organisational restructuring to better reflect its new corporate mission, increased accountability and customer focus.

BWA sought to develop a clear brand identity based on its core strengths and personality following consumer research in 1994 which revealed that Western Australia and its capital Perth lacked a meaningful identity in the international marketplace. The WATC had AUS$8.8 million over five years to develop, implement and market Western Australia to an international and Australian audience. Interestingly, BWA was not only intended to be a tourism brand - it was also to provide the state brand - hence the need for wide-ranging consultation to ensure that the actions of the Brand Strategy Group - the steering group behind the initiative - were thoroughly endorsed. Also significant was the maximisation of BWA's links with the Australian Tourism Commission's 'Big Nature-Big City' Brand strategy. The key steps in constructing the brand personality of BWA were:

- consult with possible BWA end users;

- conduct comprehensive market research in key national and international markets;

- research the key brand values amongst Western Australians and overseas visitors;

- select the appropriate target markets.

The research conducted to underpin the branding showed that Western Australia offered most of the things tourists want from their vacation, including relaxation, an opportunity for recharging and an unspoilt natural scenery; less positively, however, Perth was seen to be quiet and lacking in activity. The research concluded that Western Australia was strong on nature-based imagery and attractions but that it lacked a meaningful identity. To take this research forward, international target markets were then objectively selected using the Market Potential Assessment Formula - a model developed by WATC and the International Advisory Council. These markets (the UK, Germany, Japan, Singapore, Malaysia and Indonesia) were assessed (and continue to be reviewed) in terms of their access, growth, value and synergy with the ATC's broader Australia-wide strategies.

The personality of BWA centres around its pristine environment which then underpins the marketing of the state as a fresh, new, nature-based tourism destination with friendly, spirited people and the freedom and space to travel. BWA's core personality elements were thus defined as: fresh, natural, free, and spirited and the positioning statement *'Western Australia. Holidays of an entirely different nature'* guides the communication strategy. The visual language of the campaign was not just a logo but a set of design briefs which ensured that the visual elements of Western Australia's marketing always reflected the core personality and added to the brand's overall strengths. In constructing the advertising strategy, the overriding objective was to develop a long term campaign designed to build awareness of Western Australia as a holiday destination in what is a highly competitive and dynamic global marketplace. Celebrity endorsement was seen as an effective means of providing a point of differentiation between Western Australia and other competing destinations and TV and press advertisements as the key media. The WATC secured the services of Australian supermodel and actress Elle Macpherson who was felt to embody the personality of Western Australia. As a supermodel she also had the ability to take the message to the world in a way no paid advertising could. Her endorsement has provided Western Australia's tourism industry with high levels of recall and enquiry, as well as millions of dollars in free publicity - way beyond the state's advertising budget.

Post advertising research has revealed positive changes in attitude and belief measures in all markets and increased awareness across the board. The key evaluation indicators for BWA were:

- levels of top of the mind awareness;

- post-campaign research to establish 'perceived knowledge' and 'propensity to consider';

- industry targets for visitor nights and expenditure.

Significantly, although primarily intended to increase awareness, the initial six week UK campaign in September 1997 directly resulted in almost 6,000 visitors generating AUS$7.3 million tourism expenditure in Western Australia - a 500 percent return on the advertising outlay. Following the success of the initial TV advertisements Elle Macpherson was contracted for four additional commercials which were broadcast in the core markets from February 1999. Interestingly, in a series of initiatives similar to the '*Amazing Thailand*' campaign, BWA has also been integrated into projects with a broad community focus, including BWA vehicle number plates, vehicle registration stickers, welcome signage at state entry points and BWA 'welcome statements' on the rear windowscreens of taxicabs. A merchandise range incorporating clothing and souvenirs has also been created and distributed throughout Western Australia. A brand ownership campaign has been initiated where approved licensees use BWA's visual elements in their own advertising - and over 300 organisations had been approved by mid-1999 (see Crockett and Wood 1999).

Conclusion

It takes time to establish destination brands and it is unrealistic to expect to achieve immediate results. Building a destination brand is a long term effort, which yields incremental and not exponential results and any brand manager seeking to create an identity must have long term commitment to the brand. Moreover, destination brand managers in the public sector face four key constraints which often undermine attempts at brand building: limited budgets; political pressures; a lack of overall product control; the challenge of creating differentiation. By successfully branding a destination (which is credible, differentiating and conveying powerful ideas), however, the impact of these constraints may well be reduced.

The first problem of inadequate resources is tackled through harnessing innovation, creating powerful ideas and by employing a multi-organisational approach to constructing the brand.

In this way, relatively small individual agency budgets are pooled to underpin a targeted campaign in a very cost-effective way, yielding greater results - as in Western Australia. The second problem - political pressure - can be tackled by using an 'inclusive' approach whereby the key brand attributes and values are researched amongst the destination stakeholders and residents to ensure that they are not only relevant and credible but also acceptable, representative and not stereotypical. The final problem which often faces destination brand managers is that the actual product must correspond with the brand image and with consumer expectations, yet they are not in overall control of the product. Here, again, however, an 'inclusive' approach provides an imaginative way forward. By researching the core brand values amongst its overseas visitors and indigenous population, a tourism organisation not only ensures that the brand's associations are acceptable, but also that they reflect the product. There are significant and unique problems facing destination marketers, but these should not prevent them from persevering in their aims - successful branding brings enormous rewards. Certainly, destinations cannot afford to ignore branding as it offers an innovative and effective tool by which mangers can establish emotional links with the consumer, particularly if a multi-agency-driven suprabrand is constructed.

References

Anholt, S. (1998), 'Nation-brands of the twenty-first century', *Journal of Brand Management* 5 (6): 395-404.

BTA (1997), Living Britain. A guide to understanding the characteristics of the geographic brands of Britain, London, Scotland, England and Wales, BTA, London.

Crockett, S. R. and Wood, L. J. (1999), 'Brand Western Australia. A totally integrated approach to destination branding', *Journal of Vacation Marketing*, 5 (3): 276-289.

de Chernatony L. and McDonald M. H.,B. (1992), Creating Powerful Brands: the strategic route to success in consumer, industrial and service markets, Butterworth Heinemann, Oxford.

Hall, D. (1999), 'Destination branding, niche marketing and national image projection in central and Eastern Europe', *Journal of Vacation Marketing* 5 (3): 227-237.

Hall D. (1997), 'Tourism in Albania', paper presented at the ELRA Culture, Leisure and Tourism in Europe Conference, Dubrovnik.

James, G. (1997) 'Britain - Creating a Family of Brands', *Tourism Intelligence Papers,* BTA/ETB, London A-21.

Kotler, P., Bowen J. and Makens J. (1996), Marketing for Hospitality and Tourism, Prentice Hall New Jersey.

Lurman, D. (1998), World Tourism Organisation presentation at the 1998 International Travel and Tourism Awards, Valencia.

Morgan N. J. and Pritchard, A. (2000), Advertising in Tourism and Leisure, Butterworth Heinemann, Oxford, in press.

Morgan, N. J. and Pritchard, A. (1999), 'Building Destination Brands. The cases of Wales and Australia', *Journal of Brand Management*, 7 (2): 102-119.

Morgan, N. J. and Pritchard, A. (1998), Tourism Promotion and Power: creating images, creating identities, John Wiley and Sons, Chichester, chapter seven.

Nickerson, N. P. and Moisey, N. R. (1999) 'Branding a state from features to positioning: Making it simple? *Journal of Vacation Marketing* 5 (3): 217-226.

Palmer, A. and Bejou, D. (1995), 'Tourism destination marketing alliances', *Annals of Tourism Research* 22 (3): 616-629.

Parkinson, S., *et al.* (1994), 'Espana: an international tourist brand', *Irish Marketing Review* 7: 54-64.

Pride, R. (1999), 'Creating a Tourism Brand for Wales', paper presented at the third International Tourism and Leisure Advertising Festival, Valencia, September.

Pritchard, A. and Morgan, N. (1998), 'Creating "Wales" The Brand: Opportunities in Destination Branding Strategy', in Nahrstedt W. and Kombol T.P. (eds.) *Leisure, Culture and Tourism in Europe*. Bielefeld, Germany: 165-176

Vial, C. (1997), 'Success Stories of Tourism Campaigns', paper presented at the First International Tourism and Leisure Advertising Festival, Dubrovnik, September.

Wales Tourist Board (1994), Marketing Areas Study, Wales Tourist Board, Cardiff.

US Virgin Islands Division of Tourism (1998), US Virgin Islands brochure.

Williams, A. P. and Palmer A. J. (1999), 'Tourism destination brands and electronic commerce: Towards synergy?' *Journal of Vacation Marketing* 5 (3) 263-275.

Ward S. V. and Gold J. R. (1994), 'Introduction', 1-17 in Ward S.V. and Gold J.,R. (eds.) Place Promotion. The Use of Publicity and Marketing to Sell Towns and Regions, Wiley and Sons, Chichester: 1-17.

The changing face of retail travel: An examination of the re-emergence of franchising

Lesley Pender

University of Newcastle, UK

Abstract

This paper examines the concept of franchising as it applies to the retail travel sector. Despite having a short history the development of franchising within the sector has been rapid and has met with some success to date. This is exemplified by the case study of Canadian travel agency chain Uniglobe which is included in the paper. Using both secondary sources and original case study materials the research undertaken addresses a highly topical area yet one with a long established theoretical underpinning. Travel agency franchising is considered in the context of franchising activities in travel and tourism more generally. Motivations for the use of franchising by the retail travel sector are considered as are the implications for management of this form of business. Finally the paper critically evaluates the role of franchising in the retail travel sector together with its likely future role.

Introduction

Franchising is re-emerging as a form of partnership in the travel agency sector following previous failures in this area. Travel agents are using franchising to meet a number of strategic objectives including market growth, international market entry and access to distributions systems. Franchising agreements display both standard and unique characteristics and lead to both standard and unique management issues and critical success factors as discussed by Pender (2000).

The re-emergence of travel agency franchises follows on from the now well developed use of franchising in other industries including fast food and some areas of retailing. Other sectors of the travel and tourism industry also have more or less well-developed franchised operations. The hotel sector for example has used franchising greatly as a means of expansion and more recently airlines in Europe have followed the lead of airlines in the USA by franchising route operations. Indeed, travel agency franchising can be placed in the context of an increase in the replacement or absorption of a vast array of service businesses in a wide variety of fields by franchise chains. The service sector itself has been described as one transforming from characterisation by small unit size, local orientation, resource poverty and absence of professional management skills. (Lovelock, 1991).

The paper commences with a description of the characteristics and structure of the UK travel agency sector examining change to this and the importance of branding. The use of franchising in other parts of the tourism industry is then discussed prior to consideration of franchising in the retail travel sector including early failures and the recent revival. Case studies of franchised travel agency chains are incorporated into this work. In this way the paper illustrates ways in which the operation of franchising by travel agents varies between different organisations. Finally prospects for the future of franchising in the retail travel sector are considered. Much of the data presented in this case was obtained from secondary sources. Original case study material, based on telephone interviews, has also been used.

For the purposes of this paper the definition of franchising provided by Holloway and Robinson (1995) is adopted. Writing about tourism they define franchising as "an arrangement under which a business (whether principal or distributor) known as the franchiser grants an organisation (the franchisee) the right to use the company's name and market its products in exchange for a financial consideration." This definition is sufficient for the travel agency sector.

Background

Retail travel is one of the main components of travel and tourism distribution especially in countries with well developed outbound tourism industries such as the UK. The significance of the sector in the UK can be seen by the fact that it accounts for the sale of approximately 4/5ths of the overseas package holidays and an estimated £10.25 bn in expenditure by UK residents in 1997. (Key Note, 1998).

Characteristics and structure of the UK travel agency sector

There is a network of 7,276 Association of British Travel Agents (ABTA) travel agency offices with members having an average of 3.6 branches each. (Key Note, 1998). These agencies have a dual role, acting as a sales outlet for principals and a purchasing and information point for consumers.

Travel agencies exist in a variety of types and sizes. A key split is between retail or leisure agents, selling mainly holidays and corporate or business agents, dealing mainly with commercial clients. Travel agents can be multinationals with offices world-wide, national multiples with offices nation-wide, regional multiples or miniples with a regional presence or even smaller independents. (Renshaw, 1997) Whatever their size or type, travel agents are generally concerned with seeking appointments including ABTA and International Air Transport Association (IATA) licenses. They are also usually concerned with earning commission on sales made. This traditional method of compensating travel agents for their business usually pays between 7 and 11%. Increases to this include commission overrides and incentive payments. Fee based payments are also being introduced to replace commission in some situations.

The retail travel sector is heavily reliant on technology partly because of the importance of the flow of information to the distribution of travel services. Computer reservations systems (CRS) have been influential in travel distribution and have made significant inroads into the retail sector. The sector is one that is characterised by increasing levels of sophistication. A further significant aspect of the retail travel sector is the high degree of concentration with the top four travel agents increasing their share of the air inclusive tours (AIT) market from 48% to 54% between 1991 and 1994. Market share has long been important to organisations in the travel industry, sometimes even at the expense of profit.

A final relevant aspect in the structure of the retail travel sector is the extent to which the sector is characterised by vertically integrated companies amongst the market leaders. The with leading UK travel agency chains owned by leading tour operators. Examples include Lunn Poly, owned by Thomson and Going Places, owned by Airtours. Burns and Holden (1995) describe a key characteristic of contemporary tourism as being not only the extent to which vertical integration takes place but also the increasing tendency for this integration to be global.

Renshaw (1997) examines in detail both the role of travel agents and the structure of the retail sector in the UK.

Change to the retail travel environment in the UK

The retail travel environment in the UK has changed substantially since the sector first emerged. Structural, regulatory and other changes have all occurred. The sector today is, as a result of horizontal integration, far more concentrated than in the past. The March of the Multiples (MOM) was a phenomenon, described by the trade press, that occurred over a period of time, mainly in the 1980s, whereby larger multiple agencies took over or merged with smaller miniples and independents. This led, amongst other effects, to a far more heavily concentrated travel agency sector as described by Renshaw (1997).

In line with increased levels of concentration there has been a move towards the creation of organisations with strong power bases so increasing their negotiating power with principals. This can, in turn, lead to even higher degrees of concentration as any increase in commissions payments can now be passed on to consumers.

Branding

The development of a strong brand is often sited as a pre-requisite for successful franchising and so it is appropriate to discuss the branding of retail travel agents prior to consideration of the adoption of franchising by the sector.

Branding as a feature of marketing activity was adopted more slowly by travel firms than it was by physical goods companies but has become far more heavily used by services over the past two decades. (Seaton and Bennett, 1996) Horner and Swarbrooke (1996) describe the adoption of branding in the tourism, hospitality and leisure industries as having been speedy.

One significant aspect relating to travel agency branding in the UK is the extent to which re-branding takes place. This is in part due to increasing levels of concentration within the sector. For example the travel agency chain AT Mays and alliance partner ARTAC became ARTAC World Choice when they rebranded al of their outlets in 1998. These outlets were then rebranded following further partnership activity as Carlson World Choice and then Thomas Cook. This highlights the difficulty of establishing a clear brand identity for outlets in this dynamic industry. It has also sometimes proven difficult to create brand loyalty in an industry characterised by price competition in some segments.

An interesting aspect of brand management is the concept of brand-stretching or stepping out of your core business and using the reputation you have built to create enterprises in the manner of Richard Branson. Rogers (1998) describes some interesting examples of brand-stretching that are emerging in the travel industry. Having established a strong brand image and stretched this by stepping into another field successfully franchising is one potential means of growing this new business.

Franchising in other travel industry sectors

Hotels

Hotels have a comparatively long history of using franchising as a means of business expansion both domestically and internationally. Indeed, this sector has been used extensively, together with others such as fast food, to provide examples of franchised activities in the literature. Specific coverage of the sector is also provided by authors such as Housden (1982) and Lashley and Morrison (2000).

Hotels were, in fact, amongst the early pioneers of business format franchising with companies such as Hilton Inns and Holiday Inns in the late 1940s and early 1950s. Such firms used franchising to enter overseas markets as well as to expand in the domestic market. The success of franchising in the sector can be seen by many of the large chains operating world-wide today that have used this method of expansion. More recently franchising has also been used in the US bed and breakfast sector. Price (1997) provides the example of Choice Hotels International. The company began offering franchises to small, upscale boutique inns and hotels in 1989. The hospitality sector is however a volatile one and not without franchiser withdrawals (Price, 1997).

Airlines

Franchising in the airline sector operates in a similar manner to franchising in other sectors with smaller operators adopting the brand image and associated aspects of a major in return for some form of financial consideration. (Pender, 1999). In this way airlines can overcome some of the problems to result from the complexity of their operating environment. An example of airline franchising is provided by British Airways and Cityflyer Express.

Franchising in the scheduled airline sector has only become evident following the process of deregulation in the USA and the commencement of the process of liberalisation in Europe. Liberalisation in Europe is now complete and arguably the opportunities for further development of franchising are great in an environment that is more open to competition. The development of hub and spoke networks has also been significant with flights from smaller spoke cities feeding into hub airports at strategic locations. Longer haul trunk routes eminate from these hubs, linking them to other hub airports also fed by a series of smaller routes from spoke airports. This form of network lends itself beautifully to the operation of franchised route services on the peripheral routes.

To date there has been little evidence of the use of franchising in the chartered airline sector. A summary of some of the motivations for franchising by both franchiser and franchisee scheduled carriers, that were identified in a literature search conducted by Pender (1999), is provided in table 1.

Table 1   Indicative motivations for airline franchising

Motivations for Franchisers
To obtain traffic 'feed' from the franchisee
To gain access to domestic routes in countries the major otherwise could not enter and on routes between countries where competition is curtailed[*]
To overcome the problem that large carriers are generally not compatible with small routes (due to their fleet, cost basis and other factors)
To expand domestically and/or internationally at low cost
To avoid capital outlay when growing the company
To expand the airline's marketable network
To provide a seamless service for consumers[**]
Motivations for franchisees
To obtain access to marketing activities undertaken by the major including access to both computerised reservations systems (CRS) and frequent flyer programmes (FFPs) as well as the potential benefits of promotional spend
To increase passenger numbers (possibly leading to increased revenue)
To help new airlines establish a foot-hold in the market
To help them survive on short domestic routes
*The nature of air traffic agreements can prevent carriers from gaining access to domestic routes in some countries. Where agreement to operate in a country does exist a lack of available take-off and landing slots can still cause problems of access.
**Seamless services are those which appear as through services and thus offer a number of consumer benefits.
Source: based on Pender (1999)

Despite the above examples, franchising has not, to date, been used across the spectrum of travel and tourism businesses. Significantly, it proved difficult to find any examples of franchising in the tour operations sector other than where Airtours, a vertically integrated travel company is involved in a franchised travel agency operation. Further discussion of Airtours involvement in franchising is provided later in this paper.

The concept of franchising as it applies to the retail travel sector

Early attempts at retail travel agency franchising

The current examples of franchising in the retail travel sector is not the only experience that the sector has had with the concept. Indeed, the expansion of the multiples which began in the 1980s created a competitive environment which prompted the use of franchising. Arguably however the retail travel environment at that time was not quite ready for the concept of franchising as illustrated by the failure of Exchange Travel. Reasons for the difficulties experienced at the time are suggested in table 2 below.

Table 2   Possible reasons for franchise failures

> Travel agents offered neither a strong name nor a unique product
> Travel agents offered neither price nor product advantages
> Franchising did not guarantee the approval of principals
> IATA appointments could not be guaranteed for franchisees
> Staff training was not always adequate for franchisees
> Inappropriate appointments led to inconsistent standards and problems with quality
> Commissions could not legally be split between an agent and another organisation which the payment of royalties amounted to
> Claims in relation to potential profits were sometimes exaggerated
> There was a lack of marketing back-up
> Promises in relation to exclusivity were sometimes broken
>
> *Source:* based on Holloway and Robinson, 1995

Clearly a number of factors were involved in the failure of these early attempts at franchising some of which were obviously specific to the sector and others which were more general factors. It is interesting therefore that Floyd and Fenwick (1999) examine some of the problems and challenges encountered by franchisers during franchise system development in general.

Revival of the fittest

Holloway (1995) points out that it was only once travel agents had been granted freedom to both discount and split commission that franchising was a realistic prospect for travel agents. Indeed, the activity has increased since travel agents can now negotiate higher commission levels and improve their profit margins.

The Canadian travel agency chain, Uniglobe, was one of the first to realise the potential of franchising as exemplified by the case study below. Other travel agency chains to become involved in franchising include Bonanza Travel, a company specialising in independent travellers and the vertically integrated travel company, Airtours, which was introduced above. These two companies have been involved in a franchising since 1997 and 1998 respectively. Bonanza Travel had grown to a total of 18 franchisees in the UK by 1999 with further franchises under consideration. Bonanza Travel describes a typical franchisee's investment as £17,000 including franchise fee of £9,950 with a working capital requirement of around £5,000. (Bonanza Travel, 1998).

Franchised activities at both Uniglobe and Airtours are discussed below.

Motivations for travel agency franchising

Table 3 illustrates some possible motivations for both potential franchisers and potential franchisees to become involved in travel agency franchising.

Table 3   Indicative motivations for travel agency franchising

Motivations for Franchisers
To enter an international market(s)
To exploit market potential quickly
To obtain highly motivated branch management
To expand quickly and at low cost
Motivations for Franchisees
To retain a level of independence
To access a specialised and complex industry without necessarily having a background in the sector
To obtain access to centralised services such as back-office systems, accounting, marketing activities, distributions systems
To obtain the benefits of special deals negotiated by the franchiser for example on the purchase of equipment
To reduce the risk that is often attached to starting a new business

Management implications of travel agency franchising

The motivations for franchising in the sector outlined above are clear indications of the type of advantages that this form of business can bring. Disadvantages are also encountered when franchising however. Difficulties can for example be experienced when franchisees become too reliant on franchisers. Independence can become easily compromised in a franchised relationship. Furthermore, operational problems at the franchiser organisation can lead to difficulties for franchisees. Likewise, negative publicity relating to either a franchiser or a franchisee can potentially harm all parties.

Case study: Uniglobe sets the pace

Uniglobe provides an ideal example of an organisation which has moved into the UK market through franchising. Uniglobe has over 1000 franchised outlets/franchisees? in 18 country locations world-wide. There are now 25 agencies open in the UK with a further 6 in the process of opening and franchises awarded for 43 more. Of the 25 existing outlets, 16 are corporate agencies. Some of these franchisees have purchased multi-unit franchises and this is particularly appropriate for retail agencies for whom growth will mean that they quickly reach the maximum amount of business that their retail outlet will enable them to conduct. It is not however usually necessary to have more than one agency office in order for corporate business to expand. Details of the Uniglobe franchised operation in the UK are now discussed.

Exclusivity

Uniglobe use franchising exclusively in the UK. The Uniglobe Master Franchise for the UK is owned by one of the co-founders of the organisation and his wife. Written into the master franchise agreement is the fact that they are barred from ownership of any of the travel agency outlets.

Franchising in the UK market

The size of the UK market was attractive to the company particularly on the retail side where some of the multiple agencies have around 1000 branches. Uniglobe however always move into regions with corporate agencies prior to developing the retail, or leisure, side of the business.

The support infrastructure

Uniglobe offer franchisees a comprehensive support package in all relevant areas. Some of these are highlighted in table 4 below.

Table 4   The support infrastructure for Uniglobe franchisees

Area	Indicative Support Mechanism
Sales and Marketing	Materials and training.
Accounting	Head Office Accountants offer support
Technology	An Operations and Training Manager offers support. Whilst the company does not teach operational aspects it will bring in suppliers to do so if necessary.
Training	On-going training is provided for franchisees and their staff who are monitored closely in this area. For example owners are offered training in personnel management.

Territorial exclusivity

Uniglobe's retail franchisees are guaranteed an exclusive geographical territory organised on the basis of postal codes. This is less relevant however for corporate franchisees whose business will mainly be conducted by telephone or computer. When a corporate client moves location they often continue to use the same agent for their business travel arrangements.

Travel benefits

Whilst discounted travel is offered to franchisees any who saw this as a major motivation for purchasing a franchise would be unlikely to be suited to Uniglobe. It would also be an expensive means of achieving discounted travel.

The income source

Uniglobe franchisees pay for the franchise itself and then also pay a service fee (equivalent to a royalty). This service fee (a percentage figure) is calculated on the gross commission that the agency earns at the end of the month rather than on turnover as the percentage earned on each sale may differ. As the agency grows larger the percentage reduces, acting as a clear incentive to growth unlike the flat rate system favoured by some franchisers.

Negotiated supplies

Whilst there are no compulsory purchases, Uniglobe has negotiated good deals with suppliers but leave the purchase decision to the franchisee. Equipment is normally supplied by Gallileo or Worldspan, the major CRS companies operating in the UK.

Actively seeking franchisees

Uniglobe actively looks for franchisees in the UK and this involves placing small advertisements in newspapers. The company has found that just a few lines are necessary as serious prospects will find the advertisements.

The screening process

Once a prospective franchisee contacts Uniglobe a lengthy process has to be undertaken to ensure that they are suited to becoming a Uniglobe franchisee. The company prefers franchisees not to have worked in the industry. Rather, Uniglobe prefers entrepreneurs who have either owned a business or held a senior management position in a company previously. The idea is not to turn the owners into travel consultants which could prove detrimental to growth.

Service quality maintenance

A variety of methods are employed to ensure the maintenance of standards at Uniglobe's franchised outlets including those listed in the following table.

Table 5   Indicative service quality control mechanisms at Uniglobe

Quality Control Cards*
Robotics Software**
Visits to agencies
Customer commitments
Written manual
Awards dinner
Star agencies

*These cards, which rate agencies, are sent to customers twice a year and returned to the UK headquarters

**The robotics software, purchased with the Galileo system, checks every booking made.

Does Airtours have the advantage?

Airtours has a stake in a franchise company within the consortium of independents known as Advantage Travel. The franchise-operating subsidiary was set up on the basis of a majority vote in favour of this in a secret ballot. Airtours provides an interesting example of the establishment of a travel trade franchise operation. (Pender, 2000). Indeed, Dunscombe (1999) describes the challenge faced by the Advantage/Airtours management in the following way

> *"its tricky having to refurbish your hotel and change the house rules while attempting to keep all the paying guests happy at the same time."*

Dunscombe further describes a few of the Adventage membership leaving the consortia for the competition. Others chose to remain with Advantage but not to sign up to the new deal. Around half of the Advantage membership had however signed up to the deal by February 1999 representing 200 companies and 352 shops. (Noakes, 1999). Despite this apparent vote of confidence in the new form of business, introduction of the franchising arrangement was not problem-free (Pender, 2000).

The Airtours/Advantage franchise arrangement illustrates the use of franchising in combination with other business concepts as discussed below.

Using travel agency franchising in combination with other business concepts

Consortia formation and franchising

A popular means for independent travel agents to achieve at least some of the benefits associated with the multiples following the march of the multiples was through consortia formation. This method of grouping travel agents together was exemplified by organisations such as the former Association of Retail Travel Agents Consortia (ARTAC) and Advantage Travel. As illustrated by the case study above, Airtours involvement in a franchising arrangement with Advantage Travel has led to the creation of a franchise operating subsidiary within an existing consortium.

Vertical integration and franchising

Once again the Airtours and Advantage Travel franchising agreement illustrates the use of franchising within a business structure that has been more commonly associated with the travel agency sector in the past. Vertical integration of tour operators with travel agents and charter airlines is common amongst the larger travel companies and so perhaps it was inevitable that the spread of franchising within the sector would lead to its use by a vertically integrated company. It is, after all, these organisations that compete with one another for the leading position in terms of market share.

Conclusions and future prospects

Layers of complexity in the travel agency sector have possibly, despite failed previous attempts, led to the later development of the use of franchising by the sector in the UK. Interestingly this could also be seen to be true of the European airline sector unlike the hotel sector which in some respects has a less complex operating environment.

It is difficult to predict the likely success of travel agency franchising, particularly as the sector is a dynamic and in some respects vulnerable one. The re-emergence of franchising is occurring amid discussions about the possibility of disintermediation within the tourism industry at the same time as which suggested new forms of travel retailing have been placed on the agenda. Combating fears about the future of retail travel are suggested survival strategies including high levels of service and the development of niche markets. Much will depend on the competitive environment of the future but what is clear is that success will only be possible where franchising is implemented in an appropriate manner. One factor that is highly likely to influence the use of franchising in the travel agency sector, in the short term at least, is the international ambitions of the large integrated travel companies. On the basis of the above analysis, franchising would seem to be a highly relevant means of achieving these ambitions.

There has, to date, been little research conducted in the field of travel and tourism franchising other than the extensive coverage of the hospitality sector. The travel trade and transport sectors are worthy of further investigation as emerging areas of franchised activity.

Acknowledgements

Ms Nita Levy Uniglobe Joint Master Franchise Holder (UK).

References

Burns, P. M. and Holden, A., (1995), *Tourism - a new perspective*, Prentice Hall International.

Dunscombe, J. (1999), *TTG Columnist*, TTG, February 10th, p.13.

Floyd, C. and Fenwick, G. (1999), Towards a Model of Franchise System Development, International *Small Business Journal*, July - September, Vol.17, No.4, Issue No.68.

Harding, L. and Noakes, G. (1998), Yes vote victory for Airtours' retail plans, *Travel Trade Gazette*, 02 December, P.1.

Harding, L. and Noakes, G. (1998), Members see deal as their best Advantage, *Travel Trade Gazette*, 02 December, P.4.

Holloway, J. C. (1994), *The Business of Tourism*, Pitman, 4th edition.

Holloway, J. C., and Robinson, (1995), *Marketing for Tourism,* Pitman, 3rd edition.

Horner, S. and Swarbrooke, J. (1996), *Marketing Tourism, Hospitality and Leisure in Europe,* International Thomson Business Press.

Key Note Ltd., (1996), *Travel Agents and Overseas Tour Operators.*

Key Note Ltd, (1998), *Travel Agents and Overseas Tour Operators.*

Lovelock, C. (1991), *Services Marketing*, Prentice Hall.

Noakes, G. (1999), Advantage and Airtours tie-up attracts 350, *Travel Trade Gazette*, 10 February, P. 7.

Pender, L.J., 1999, European Aviation: The emergence of franchised airline operations, Tourism Management, 20 (5)

Pender, L. J. (2000), *Travel Trade and Transport*, in Lashley, C. and Morisson, A., (eds), Franchising Hospitality Services, Butterworth-Heinemann.

Price, S. (1997), *The Franchise Paradox - new directions, different strategies*, Cassell.

Renshaw, M. B. (1997), *The Travel Agent*, Business Education Publishers Ltd., 2nd edition.

Richardson, D. (1998), Franchising could reduce subs income, *Travel Trade Gazette*, 02 December.

Rogers, D. (1998), TTG Travel Marketing Column, *Travel Trade Gazette*, 12 April, p 13.

Seaton, A. V. and Bennett, M. M. (1996), *Marketing Tourism Products - concepts, issues, cases*, International Thomson Business Press.

Travel Trade Gazette, (1999), *CARTA blasted for dropping franchisees*, 26th April, p 88.

Uniglobe, (1999), http://www.uniglobe.com.

Bonanza Travel, (1999), http://www.bonanzatravel.co.uk.

British Airways, (1999).http://www.british.airways.com.

The Euro: Strategic implications for UK small tourism enterprises

John Pheby and Marcjanna Augustyn

University of Luton, UK

Abstract

As Pheby (1999) has indicated, UK small and medium enterprises (SMEs) are poorly prepared for the introduction of the euro. The introduction of euro notes and coins from January 2002 will pose a number of implications and challenges for UK SMEs, which are not part of the Eurozone. The launch of euro notes and coins will directly affect UK small tourism enterprises, such as BandBs, hotels, visitor attractions, restaurants and shops. Consequently, they need to prepare themselves to accommodate the forthcoming change.

The aim of this paper is to present survey results on the level of preparedness of UK small tourism enterprises to the introduction of euro notes and coins from 2002. Our research indicates that UK small tourism enterprises are inadequately prepared for this change. The research findings constitute the basis for identifying both future strategic implications for UK small tourism enterprises and some immediate steps that need to be taken.

Introduction

The euro has been introduced primarily as a response to the perceived competitive weakness of the EU economies vis-à-vis the US. The euro will have radical implications for many industries in the UK, especially the tourism sector. As Pheby (1999) has illustrated, UK SMEs generally are poorly prepared to cope with business conducted in euros. One of our objectives is to present findings of primary research into the stage of preparedness of UK small tourism enterprises for the introduction of the euro. In this respect we conducted 100 telephone interviews with selected small hotels, bed and breakfast establishments, restaurants, theatres, and various visitor attractions in York and London. As a result of this research we can only conclude that UK small tourism enterprises are very poorly prepared for the introduction of euro notes and coins. Moreover, UK small tourism enterprises seem particularly hostile to the new currency and in many cases hope that it will fail so that they will not have to bother dealing with euros. Therefore, we have developed some strategic implications for the UK small tourism enterprises that will certainly need to be embraced regardless of whether the UK joins the Single European Currency or not.

Why is the euro being introduced?

The introduction of the euro has both a political and economic dimension. The desire to avoid further conflict after the experience of the two World Wars has been the major driving force behind European integration since its very beginnings. The economic dimension has been particularly important in ensuring that political cohesiveness is attainable.

However, in recent years the term "Eurosclerosis" has been coined to describe the relatively poor economic performance of Europe vis-à-vis North America and, until very recently, Asia. Growth rates have been sluggish, unemployment high, productivity unimpressive and inflation relatively high. The usual suspects such as high government involvement in economic affairs, inflexible labour markets, lack of an enterprise culture and a poor record of innovation and investment are usually cited as being largely responsible for Europe's less than impressive economic performance.

The solution was deemed to be the establishment of the Single European Market. Through a process of eliminating border controls, freeing financial markets and enjoying greater economies of scale, Europe would be propelled on to an additional growth path estimated to be 4%. However it was recognised that this needed to be underpinned by a Single European Currency. This would virtually eliminate conversion and transaction costs between member states. Also on the assumption, and this could prove to be major, that the value of the euro is stable on the foreign exchange markets, a considerable degree of risk and uncertainty will be eliminated from overseas trading in those countries operating within the Eurozone. This has been estimated to boost growth by 5%.

Having a single currency does bring risks, but these are deemed preferable to the chaos that fixed exchange rates with their frequent competitive devaluations or the uncertainty that floating exchange rates can bring.

As Boles and McDonald (1999) indicate, there are several gains of a more microeconomic nature. The easing of transactions costs is the most obvious. They cite the example of a UK manufacturing SME with £2 million worth of exports dealing with ten different European currencies. It was estimated that with no conversion costs, at least within Eurozone, would save this company £10,000 a year plus a lot of wasted staff time.

For many commentators (e.g. De Grauwe, 1997) the euro will compel producers of goods and services to virtually eliminate price discrimination. In the absence of currency fluctuations companies within the Eurozone will be unable to arbitrarily add 20% onto prices to allow for currency fluctuations, as has sometimes been the case in the past. Consequently, competition will become keener, especially from 2002 when all prices across Eurozone will be in euros. Comparisons between different goods and services throughout Eurozone will be rendered far easier. It is also argued that the euro will encourage lower inflation, lower interest rates and consequently a lower cost in obtaining capital. This will arise from the greater economies of scale that result from greater specialisation in different areas of Eurozone that will arise along the lines of comparative cost advantage theory.

However, this is still speculative. For example, the conduct of monetary policy throughout Eurozone will be controlled by the European Central Bank. This is the single, most important institution in Eurozone.

The European Central Bank (ECB)

The European Central Bank comprises the ECB Board that consists of the President, Wim Duisenberg, the Vice president and four other members. When we add the eleven Eurozone member central bankers to the ECB Board we have the Governing Council which will take the key decisions on interest rates within the Eurozone. The ECB therefore is essentially responsible for monetary policy, that is setting interest rates and controlling money supply and influencing exchange rates within Eurozone. Under the terms of the Stability and Growth Pact, member countries face restrictions, and possible fines, on their conduct of fiscal policies. Consequently an enormous responsibility for the successful implementation of Eurozone macroeconomic policy will rest with the ECB. Therefore we need to examine the prospects of success of this institution that has set the maintenance of price stability as its main objective. However, the early indications are not very promising.

Under the terms of the Maastricht Treaty, the ECB has been seemingly well protected from political interference. This is an understandable desire, especially as the ECB has been modelled on the fiercely independent Bundesbank. However, there are some early indications that the ECB may be taking this privilege too far and alienating politicians throughout Europe. The ECB will need the support and respect of politicians if it is to succeed. The first controversy was the view of the Wim Duisenberg not to publish the minutes of ECB Governing Council meetings until sixteen years after they have been held. This contrasts sharply with the US Federal Reserve Bank that publishes its minutes two weeks after their meetings. This caused much dismay as it was construed as an attempt to be secretive and exclusive. Duisenberg is considering a compromise whereby notes are made available earlier.

We should be wary of viewing the ECB as a highly centralised bank. An important point to realise is that the ECB is part of the European System of Central Banks (ESCB). This is a far more decentralised system than the ECB would probably desire. There have been some early signs of power struggles between the ECB and the eleven central bankers. At present this is a struggle that does not necessarily favour the ECB. The central bankers can outvote the ECB by eleven votes to six at Governing Council. Indeed any feeling that the influence of the eleven central banks has been eroded may prove to be premature.

Such a highly decentralised network could undermine the smooth operation of monetary policy within Eurozone. The early history of the US Federal Reserve Bank is testimony to such problems. It was twenty years before a centralised system was operational. The cost of this delay may have been the prevention of the financial collapse of 1929. The ECB also needs to develop a pan-European supervisory role, especially as monetary issues will be more focused on European concerns. For example there are no immediate plans for the ECB to adopt a lender of last resort role in times of short-term liquidity crises.

Given the typically monetarist concern with maintaining price stability, it is important that the ECB develops a viable strategy to monitor and react to unwelcome monetary developments. The ECB needs to gain credibility within the financial markets.

The early indications are not promising. The ECB has demonstrated much uncertainty and indecision as to how it intends monitoring monetary developments. Early discussion focused upon whether the ECB would adopt an inflation target, as the Bank of England does, or a monetary target favoured by monetarists. Monetary targeting is where a statistical indicator of the likely movement of the money supply is employed. This should indicate whether the money supply is moving too quickly or slowly and whether corrective action through, for example, changing interest rates is necessary. However monetary targeting is fraught with difficulties. Has the right indicator been selected? Does it provide a reliable statistical guide as to what is happening to the money supply? Can you actually control it? These are important questions for an institution endeavouring to control a pan-European money supply within a framework of eleven different monetary systems. After much deliberation the ECB has adopted a mixture of indicators to assist in determining the conduct of monetary policy.

There are two main elements to the ECB's strategy. Firstly, a monetary reference range for M3, a broad definition of the money supply, between 3-5% is being adopted. It is argued that this is not strictly monetary targeting. The second element is focused primarily upon a harmonised index of consumer prices varying within a range of 0-2%. However a mix of other economic indicators will be referred to. This is a strange compromise position to take. The ECB has stated that it will ignore the monetary reference target if it wishes. This is a recipe for confusion. It will often appear unclear as to what stance the ECB will take in the light of certain monetary developments. For example, they endorsed the reduction of interest rates in December 1998. However there were no grounds on monetary policy terms alone for such a reduction. More recently the growth rates of the monetary reference target have been breached and no hint of an appropriate increase in interest rates was forthcoming from the ECB.

UK small tourism enterprises and their preparedness for the euro

The tourism industry is highly important to the UK economy. It is currently estimated (ETC, 2000) that 1.7 million jobs are generated by this sector. Tourism accounts for 4% of GDP, 6% of consumer spending and 5% of all exports. Overseas visitors in the UK spend approximately £15 billion each year. Nearly 50% of this spending derives from visitors from the eleven member countries who are part of the Eurozone. From January 2002 visitors from the Eurozone may wish to make payments in the UK with euro notes and coins. Indeed it is currently possible for such visitors to make payments for tourism services by Eurocheques and credit cards.

It is estimated by Middleton (1998) that small tourism enterprises (i.e. a tourism firm that employs fewer than 50 people) constitute over 95% of the UK tourism industry. Consequently, it is important to assess whether this major constituent of one of the UK major export industries is prepared for the introduction of euro notes and coins in 2002. As Pheby (1999) indicates generally UK SMEs are poorly prepared for coping with the euro.

In order to assess the situation with respect to UK small tourism enterprises we conducted a random sample of 100 small tourism enterprises split equally between York and London. We contacted small hotels, BandBs, restaurants and wide range of small tourism attractions. At every interview we spoke with either the owner or someone in a management position. We had a questionnaire prepared to enquire about the explicit preparations that the sample members had made. We were not expecting much preparation, but were nonetheless surprised by the results. We had a 100% response rate that no preparation had been made at all! We received many comments along the lines: 'I am waiting for the brochure', 'It will not affect us very much', 'Credit cards will take care of it' and 'We hate the euro and we expect it to fail, so why bother?'. It is also surprising that we obtained these results in two cities that are popular overseas visitor attractions. We can conclude, somewhat generously, that UK small tourism enterprises appear to be adopting a wait and see strategy.

Strategic implications for UK small tourism enterprises

Drucker (1977) refers to the challenges facing businesses as one of efficiency and the other as effectiveness. Effectiveness means that the focus of the business is right given its business environment. Efficiency is where the business is operating in such a way as to generate profits. Therefore efficiency can be construed as the business's short-term goal of surviving, whereas effectiveness is a longer-term aspect that ensures that the business continuous to thrive in the light of changes within its business environment and concentrates on activities that will continue to generate profits. As Rumelt (1991) argues, a good strategy is achievable given the financial and human resources available. More importantly, a good strategy will provide a business with a competitive advantage over its rivals.

It is quite apparent from our empirical analysis above that UK small tourism enterprises do not really have a strategy to deal with the euro. We feel that this is not a realistic perspective to adopt, as the euro is unlikely to collapse completely. Despite much criticism of the ECB and some currency dealers dismissing the euro as a 'toilet currency' there is still a significant economic bloc supporting it and the member countries have invested too much in the euro to abandon it. Furthermore, there are no provisions for a divorce for individual member countries from the Eurozone. By late 2002 individual members' old currencies would have been melted down and incinerated and therefore no longer legal tender. The important point to realise is that by mid-2002 all debts and transactions will be denominated in euros and there will be no way back for the old Eurozone currencies. Given that the UK is unlikely to become part of the Eurozone we will now consider some strategic implications fort UK small tourism enterprises.

1. A particular strategic weakness, i.e. a strategic competitive vulnerability is the lack of preparedness for handling euros especially from 2002. The EU has commissioned research (EC, 1998) which indicates that visitors to other Eurozone countries will be keen to make payments in euros, even prior to 2002. This implies that Eurozone visitors to the UK will probably expect, although there will be no obligation on the part of the UK businesses, to be able to make payments in euros. Over 50% of Eurozone visitor payments are expected to be made via credit cards and Eurocheques. With Eurozone visitors representing 50% of overseas visitor spending in the UK, this could pose some serious problems if large sections of the UK tourism industry are not seen to be

accommodating to the needs of such visitors. Visitors from Eurozone could very easily take their business to larger hotels, for example.

2.   An important threat to the UK tourism industry will arise from the uncertainty of currency fluctuations that will occur between sterling and the euro. This will mean that periods will occur, as now, where sterling is strong vis-à-vis the euro. Consequently, the cost of coming to the UK will be increased for Eurozone visitors. Therefore, the UK business environment will display a degree of uncertainty not experienced by the tourism industry within the Eurozone.

3.   However, there are some strategic opportunities. A strategic opportunity normally involves some cost. UK small tourism enterprises that fully embrace the euro will need to be able to accept credit cards, Eurocheques and cash payments by 2002. This will entail upgrading IT, cash registers, and opening a euro account. Indeed those UK small tourism enterprises that would take these steps could well gain a competitive advantage over those rivals that do not follow suit. Furthermore, UK small tourism businesses that begin to generate a flow of euro income would find it much easier to obtain financial backing within Eurozone. Whilst the UK remains outside Eurozone, it is likely that interest rates will remain lower in Eurozone that in the UK. This could considerably ease financial pressures on many UK small tourism enterprises.

Future steps

UK small tourism enterprises will not be able to act strategically until they are better informed than our survey indicates. Despite much governmental information on the euro and SMEs it appears that this is not being targeted at small tourism enterprises. In order to rectify this situation we recommend the following course of action.

Organise seminars/workshops that link both the e-commerce and euro implications for euro small tourism enterprises.

Initiatives should be regionally organised and led by the relevant Regional Development Agencies and Regional Tourist Boards. Normally we would suggest that local TEC/Business Link/Chamber of Commerce would play a crucial role here. However, these organisations are currently being abolished/re-organised into the Small Business Service.

Trade associations closer to specific tourism areas, e.g. hoteliers, BandBs, museums, should be at the forefront in producing straightforward literature to assist the small tourism enterprises in their respective area.

Conclusions

Our analysis has indicated that UK small tourism enterprises are essentially unprepared to deal with the euro. This applies particularly to the introduction of euro notes and coins in 2002. Given the importance of Eurozone visitors to the UK tourism industry this is an unsatisfactory state of affairs. We have highlighted some of the major strategic implications and some steps that should be taken to improve awareness among UK small tourism enterprises. The UK tourism sector is a major exporter that clearly requires much more assistance in preparing to cope with the euro. Failure to do this could severely damage its export potential. More seriously a significant number of UK small tourism enterprises could be threatened if they are not better prepared.

References

Boles, K. and McDonald, F. (1999), The euro: Paradigm shift or nominal makeover?, *22nd ISBA National Small Firms Conference Proceedings,* Leeds Metropolitan University, Leeds, pp. 161-173.

De Grauwe, P. (1997), *The Economics of Monetary Integration,* 3rd edition, Oxford University Press, Oxford.

Drucker, P. (1977), *Management: Tasks, Responsibilities, Practices,* Pan Books, London.

ETC (2000), *English Tourism Council: Useful Facts About English Tourism,* http://www.englishtourism.org.uk/market/useful_facts.htm.

EC (1998), *Final Report. Conference on the euro and tourism: opportunities and strategies for businesses*, EC, DGXXIII.

Middleton, V. T. C. (1998), Agenda 2010: A Proposed Framework for European Action in Support of SMEs in Tourism, *Tourism,* Issue 99, Winter.

Pheby, J. (1999), The euro and UK SMEs: will wait and see be a wise strategy?, *22nd ISBA National Small Firms Conference Proceedings,* Leeds Metropolitan University, Leeds, pp. 1073-1082.

Rumelt, R. (1991), How much does industry matter?, *Strategic Management Journal*, 12, pp. 167-185.

Sports tourism and the Ga
The emerging use of des
marketing with the Gay ᴊames

Brenda G Pitts

Florida State University, USA

Kevin Ayers

Western Carolina University

Abstract

The Gay Games has become one of the largest sports events in the world. Held every four years since 1982, the increasing popularity and commercialisation of the Gay Games are bringing tremendous benefits for many tourism stakeholders including the hotel, restaurant, tourism, and airline industries. Gay Games V, for example, held in Amsterdam in 1998 yielded 14,843 (42% women, 58% men) sports participants in 29 sports from 78 countries, over 800,000 spectators, 56 sports and other venues, a budget of $10 million (USD), and an economic scale of $350 million. Gay Games VI will be held in Sydney, Australia in 2002 and already organisers are predicting an economic impact of $80 million (AUS), 16,000 sports participants from 100 countries, one million visitors, and a budget of $20 million (AUS). The attraction, size, and enormity of the event is not lost on the Sydney Gay Games Organising Committee as well as national and international mainstream governing sports organisations, increasing government departments, and tourism offices. The potential economic and cultural impact for such stakeholders as the hotel, restaurant, tourism sites and offices, and airlines industries in Sydney, Australia, and around the world is enormous. However, these stakeholders will want to be involved in order to realise a return on investment. For the first time, a Gay Games organising committee is using destination marketing. With the Australian Tourism Commission involved, the Sydney Gay Games Organising Committee has embarked on a new course for promoting the Gay Games.

...ourism development

...e World Travel and Tourism Council estimated that the tourism industry world-wide generated US$340 billion in gross output and invested US$693 billion in new facilities and equipment in 1994 (Standeven and DeKnop, 1999). Sports and related recreational and leisure activity are reported to comprise approximately 25 to 32 percent of most tourism activity (Research Unit, 1994; Research Unit, 1997). If this claim is true, then sport related travel was approximately US$85 to $108.8 billion world-wide in 1994.

Sport tourism is a substantial and growing segment of both the tourism industry and the sport industry (Sports Tourism International Council, 2000; Standeven, 1998; Standeven and DeKnop, 1999). Although currently there appears to be no universally accepted definition of sport tourism, Standeven and DeKnop define it as "all forms of active and passive involvement in sporting activity, participated in casually or in an organised way for non-commercial or business/commercial reasons, that necessitate travel away from home and work locality" (1999, p. 12). Sport tourism has been described as having from two to five major categories. Kurtzman and Zauhar (1997) identified five major areas: sport tourism attractions, such as sports facilities, sports museums and halls of fame, sport theme parks, hiking trails, and sport retail stores; sport tourism resorts, such as sports and health resorts and clubs; sport tourism cruises, such as fitness cruises, golf cruises, and scuba cruises; sport tourism tours, such as those tours that bring visitors and spectators to sports events, facilities, or destinations; and sport tourism events, such as those events for sports participants or for sports spectators. Hall, (1992): Pitts, (1999), and Standeven, (1999) identify two broad sport tourism categories: sports participation tourism in which there is travel for the purpose of participating in a sports, recreation, leisure or fitness activity; and sports spectatorial travel, in which there is travel for the purpose of spectating sports, recreation, leisure or fitness activities or events. Additionally, Standeven and DeKnop (1999) set forth a sport tourist typology in which sport tourism is defined by people, or sport tourists, and are categorised by the type of sports activity in which they will participate - active or passive.

In sum, it appears that an all encompassing definition of sport tourism is that it involves all travel for the purpose of participating, spectating, or revelling in sports, recreation, fitness, and leisure activities or their related products.

Additionally, although sport tourism is a relatively new term and area for study - the recognition and study of it as an emerging industry by academics and scholars of sport studies, such as sport management, sport marketing, leisure studies, and tourism studies - the practice of travel for sports is easily traced to ancient times. For instance, throughout history, whenever there has been any sporting activity requiring travel to either participate or spectate, sport tourism was practised. One of those events recorded in history include the ancient Olympic Games, first staged in 776 B. C. in Olympia, Greece, and held every four years for a thousand years (Van Dalen and Bennett, 1971). In today's world, some sports events that many people world-wide might be most familiar with include the Modern Olympic Games and the men's and women's soccer World Cup tournament.

Research attempts are being made to define the sport tourism consumer. The Standeven and DeKnop (1999) typology is one such attempt. In this work, the sport tourism consumer is categorised into two broad groups: the active sport tourists and the passive sport tourists. Studies involving the economic impact of sports events are a method of studying sport tourism consumers by determining consumer demographic and economic elements. For example, Turco (1999) reported the results of a study of the consumers - participants - of a basketball tournament. Turco describes the consumers using a variety of terminology to categorise them, such as sports tourism participants, excursionists (who were also called day trippers), overnight sports tourism participants, sports tourism spectators, and overnight visitor groups. Pitts (1999) attempted to determine if lesbian and gay sports tourism consumers exist by determining if there were sports tourism products produced and targeted to lesbian and gay sports consumers. Pitts found a plethora of sports tourism products, such as organisations, events, travel agencies, companies, and publications offering sports participant and spectatorial tourism opportunities to lesbian and gay sports consumers. One of the findings involved a lesbian targeted travel guide book in which a calendar of events was found. In the list of 866 travel events for 1997, over a third (306, or 35%) of those were sports and recreational events. Some of those included kayaking, snow shoeing, skiing, hiking, sailing, golf, rodeo, soccer, scuba, badminton, and volleyball. Table 1 presents a sample of those events. Pitts concluded that there is a lesbian and gay sport tourism industry because there are sport tourism products and therefore consumers.

Table 1   Some examples of the sports events listed in the travel calendar

- Dogsledding in Minnesota. Offered by Women in the Wilderness, a company in Minnesota.

- International Pride Martial Arts and Judo Tournament. Offered by the International Association for Gay and Lesbian Martial Arts.

- Cross Country Skiing. Offered by Women in Motion, a company in California.

- Bighorn Rodeo in Las Vegas. Offered by the National Gay Rodeo Association.

- Dive the Great Barrier Reef. Offered by Above and Beyond Tours, a company in California.

- Austria Ski Trip. Offered by Travel Affair, a company in Atlanta, Georgia.

- Sailing Alaska. Offered by Women Sail Alaska.

- International Gay and Lesbian Badminton Tournament. Offered by Schwul/Lesbischer Sportverein Hamburg, a company in Germany.

And finally, sports tourism consumers and opportunities are being studied and identified through research involving specific sports and sports events. For instance, there have been sport tourism studies of surfing (Poizat-Newcomb, 1999), 3-on-3 basketball (Turco, 1999), car races (Burns, Hatch and Mules, 1986), boat racing (Sofield and Sivan, 1994), the Olympics (Delpy, 1997; Chalip, Green, and Vander Velden, 1998; Kang and Perdue, 1994), and, virtual sport tourism (Kurtzman and Zauhar, 1999).

To date, however, there has been no sport tourism research involving one of the largest sports event in the world - the Gay Games. The Gay Games is an international multi sports and cultural festival held every four years since 1982. The most recent one, Gay Games V, was held in Amsterdam in 1998. There were over 15,000 sports participants and an estimated 800,000 spectators and visitors. An economic scale study revealed that Gay Games V had an estimated \$350 million (USD) impact to the Amsterdam area (Pitts and Ayers, 1999). The enormity of the event and the new emphasis on the gay and lesbian consumer market is getting more attention, especially from some major corporations. Corporate sponsorship, for instance, has increased dramatically. Moreover, such stakeholders as hotels, travel and tourism companies, restaurants, and transportation are beginning to give serious attention to the event. Most recently, local, state, and national governments, national and international sport governing bodies, city sports commissions, and visitor and tourism councils and agencies are giving attention to the event. For example, during the last executive board meeting of the Federation of Gay Games (held in Berlin in November, 1999), a representative from an American city sports commission attended with the purpose of serious consideration of proposing to host a future Gay Games. (In the United States, a city sports commission is a government office whose job is to identify and bring sports events to the city.) This is worth mentioning because the sports commission is a city government office and not necessarily a gay and/or lesbian sports organisation. It is evidence that the Gay Games has commercial value to mainstream sports organisations. That is, the Gay Games is being recognised for its potential economic impact and is given serious consideration by a non-gay or lesbian sports organisation for its value.

The forthcoming event, Gay Games VI, will be staged in Sydney, Australia in 2002. Early in the proposal and planning stages, the country's travel and tourism agency, the Australian Tourist Commission, has been involved. As a city that hosts the claimed largest Gay and Lesbian Mardi Gras in the world, organisers believed that hosting the Gay Games would be a natural. That is, organisers believe that they could 'sell' the idea that because Sydney can manage the touted highly successful Gay and Lesbian Mardi Gras, then the Gay Games were sure to be a success as well. With the involvement of the Australian Tourism Commission, the promotional focus has been the city of Sydney and the country. Indeed, the marketing and promotion plans of the Sydney Gay Games Organising Committee (SGGOC) emphasise Sydney and Australia as a vacation destination using the Gay Games as the purpose for getting there. This is the first time a Gay Games organising committee has used destination vacation marketing as its primary focus. It is, however, yet to be seen if such an approach will be successful.

The purpose of this paper is to put forth a discussion of the increasing popularity and commercialisation of the Gay Games with an analysis of the emerging use of the Gay Games in destination vacation marketing. The discussion includes an overview of the growth and development of the Gay Games, the Gay Games in relation to tourism, economic impact, and commercialisation, and an analysis of the emerging use of the Gay Games in destination vacation marketing focusing on Gay Games VI and Sydney in 2002.

Growth of the Gay Games

The Gay Games is today one of the world's largest sports events. Indeed, it surpasses the Summer Olympic Games in number of participants. The first Gay Games, held in San

Francisco in 1982, yielded almost 1,300 participants in 20 sports (see Tabl... recent Gay Games, Gay Games V held in 1998 in Amsterdam, saw an amaz... participants in 29 sports from over 78 countries, over 800,000 spectators, were staged... sports and other venues, financed with a budget of over $10 million (USD), and had a... estimated economic scale of over $350 million (Pitts, 1998; Pitts, 1999; Pitts and Ayers, 1999). Gay Games VI will be held in Sydney, Australia in 2002 - exactly 20 years after Gay Games I - and already organisersare predicting an economic impact of $80 million (AUSD), over 16,000 participants from 100 countries, one million visitors, and a budget of over $20 million.

Table 2   Gay Games Facts

Gay Games Event Host Year Theme	Gay Games I San Francisco California, USA 1982 "Challenge"	Gay Games II San Francisco California, USA 1986 "Triumph"	Gay Games III Vancouver, British Columbia, Canada 1990 "Celebration"	Gay Games IV New York City New York, USA 1994 "Unity"	Gay Games V Amsterdam, The Netherlands 1998 "Friendship"	Gay Games VI Sydney, Australia 2002 "Under New Skies!"
Sports Participants	1,300	3,482	7,300	10,864	14,843	Est. 16,000
Countries Represented	12	22	28	40	78	Est. 100
Sports Events	16	17	31	31	31	30
Visitors/ Spectators	50,000	75,000	200,000	1 million	800,000	Est. 1 million
Workers/ Volunteers	600	1,200	3,000	7,000	3,042	Est. 7,000
Attendance: Opening Ceremonies Place Closing Ceremonies Place		(1) 20,000 Kezar Stadium (2) 30,000 Kezar Stadium		(2) 57,000 Yankee Stadium	(1) 50,000 Amsterdam Arena (1) 60,000 Amsterdam Arena	
Budget	$395,000.00	$885,000.00	$ 3 Million	$6.5 million	$10 million	Est. $20 million
Sponsorship	Some in-kind	$210,000	$350,000	$1 million	$2.7 million	Est. $20 million
Sponsorship Sources L/G = lesbian/gay owned	Local L/G businesses	Individuals & small L/G businesses	4 major companies	5 major & 20+ minor; some L/G businesses	50 corporate, 16 foundations, 14 government. (11 are L/G)	Est. major, minor, & L/G businesses
Estimated or actual Economic Impact	No known reports	No known reports	Est. market report: $50 million	Est. market Reports: $112- $300 million	$350 million USD; from actual study	Est. $80 million AUS dollars
Press					1,000	
Number of venues: Sports Other					56 for all	

Note: (from: Pitts, B. G. & Ayers, K. 1999. Economic Scale of Gay Games V. Paper presented at the annual conference of the North American Society for Sport Management. Vancouver, Canada, June, 1999. Pitts, B. G. & Sullivan, M. 1999. An Analysis of Corporate Sponsorship Recognition at Gay Games V. Paper presented at the annual conference of the North American Society for Sport Management, Vancouver, Canada, June, 1999. Pitts, B. G. 1995. Leagues of their own: Growth and development of sport and sport management in the lesbian and gay population in the United States, 1970s- 1990s. Paper presented at the North American Society for Sport Management, Athens, GA, June, 1995. and Pitts, B. G. 1994. Growth and development of sport in the lesbian and gay population in the United States, 1970s- 1990s. Paper presented at the First International Conference of the Gay Games, New York City, NY, June, 1994.)

The Gay Games has experienced growth in every area and also has had a major influence in and surrounding the gay and lesbian community, particularly influencing the growth and development of lesbian and gay sports events, organisations, and businesses. Earlier research on the growth and development of sports for gay and lesbian people showed that the number of sports organisations increased just prior to, during, and immediately after each Gay Games (Pitts, 1988). Today there is a gay and lesbian sports event, league, organisation, team, or business in almost every city in the United States and in many cities and countries around the world.

ation of the rising commercialisation of the Gay Games, found
ation factors are evident in the Gay Games. Among the findings
ng internationalisation, the existence of global markets for the Gay
affected the Gay Games' commercial value. There were participants
from ʃay Games V. The global nature of the Gay Games makes it attractive
to globa. ʃmmunities.

The increasing participant and visitor rates of the Gay Games represents an expanding consumer base. The average increase in participation rates alone at each Gay Games is 275%. To local and international companies, this is an opportunity to reach a specific market concentrated as a captive audience at one event.

Increasing sponsorship is evidence of the rising commercial value of the event. Sponsorship funding for the Gay Games has increased from almost nothing in 1982 to $2.7 million for Gay Games V in 1998. Already, Sydney Gay Games Organising Committee report raising almost $6 million (AUSD) in sponsorship funding for Gay Games VI in 2002.

Licensing and merchandising have increased since Gay Games I. Licensed merchandise marks the attempts of an organisation to control images and gain a source of revenue. It is also a sign of the increasing commercial value of a product. The Gay Games' organising committees have offered an increasing array and amount of Gay Games merchandise.

Competition to host the Gay Games is increasing. Spurred partially by the recognition of the Gay Games' popularity, value, economic impact, and the perceived prestige that hosting the event brings to the host community, bid committees aggressively spar for favoured status with the host selection committee. The cost of the bid process has itself become pricey. For instance, the cost to produce the five bids submitted for Gay Games VI in 2002 surpassed the cost of the first two Gay Games. The battle of the bids is a sure sign of the increasing commercialisation and value of the Gay Games.

In the same study, Pitts also found that there are two distinct categories of Gay Games sports tourism products: (1) participation, in which sport tourism products are offered to those who are going to participate in the Gay Games; and (2) spectatorial, in which sport tourism products are offered to those who want to go and participate as a spectator of the Gay Games. Pitts found that the companies offering the products included those owned and operated by lesbian/gay people and target first the lesbian and gay market, and those companies that do not appear to be lesbian or gay owned and which do not target first the lesbian and gay market. The majority of the companies were travel and tourism companies and sport tourism companies. Several of the companies offered travel packages to the Gay Games, most included tickets to the Opening and Closing Ceremonies, sports events, and cultural events. Some offered organised tours before or after the Gay Games. For example, Skylink Travel Services, a gay/lesbian company, offered travel packages that included eight nights accommodations, a Gay Games Welcome Packet, hotel taxes and service charges, daily hospitality desk, welcome party and orientation, champagne reception at the Diamond

Factory, a candlelight canal cruise with wine and cheese party, hotel porterage, and services of local lesbian and gay tour guides.

In a different but related study, Pitts and Ayers (1999) found that attendees at Gay Games V spent an average of $2,514 for the average length of stay of ten days. The individual expenditures reveal how the various stakeholders have an interest in the event. Average daily expenditures went to food, registration fees, admission fees, entertainment, retail shopping, souvenirs, lodging, private auto, commercial transportation, and miscellaneous.

Sponsorship is a sure sign of spectator recognition. Companies engage in sponsorship to build brand awareness among a specific target market. Companies are becoming more aware of the research that shows that lesbian and gay people can have high brand awareness and loyalty. This was found to be true of attendees at Gay Games IV and Gay Games V (Pitts, 1996; Pitts and Sullivan, 1999). In studies of sponsorship recall and sponsorship recognition, attendees of Gay Games IV in 1994 were found to have an average recall rate of the sponsors of 73.7% while attendees of Gay Games V in 1998 were found to have an average recognition rate of 64.2%. These rates are high when compared to similar studies which usually report rates around 20 to 40%. Additionally, the studies included what is perhaps the most important question for a sponsoring company, which is "Are you more willing to buy the products of sponsorship companies?" In both studies, the response rates to this question were also high: in 1994, 92.3% of the attendees responded yes; in 1998, 73.1% responded yes. This means, of course, that attendees are highly likely to purchase the products of a sponsoring company of the Gay Games.

Until the first academic study of the economic scale of the Gay Games was conducted at Gay Games V in 1998 in Amsterdam, economic impact of the Gay Games had been reported in newspapers and other similar media. Estimates and reports of the economic impact of the Gay Games first appeared for Gay Games III held in Vancouver, British Columbia, Canada in 1990 (see Table 2). The estimated economic impact for Gay Games III in 1990 was $50 million (USD). Two different reports for Gay Games IV in 1994 reported that its economic impact was somewhere between $112 and $300 million. The study of Gay Games V held in Amsterdam in 1998 found that visitor spending and the economic scale of Gay Games V was just over $350 million (Pitts and Ayers, 1999). It is interesting to note that each time the Gay Games is staged, the economic impact estimates double.

Whether or not the commercial value or economic impact studies are accurate, such numbers, along with the participant and spectator numbers and the gay and lesbian market data, have gained the attention of such tourism stakeholders as hotels, restaurants, transportation companies, tourist attractions, leisure activity attractions, governments, and sports venue owners. These stakeholders now appear to be working in co-operation to support, and benefit from, a Gay Games.

The Gay Games and destination marketing

Major sports events, sometimes called mega-events, such as the Olympics and soccer's World Cups, have proliferated. Many other types and sizes of sports events offered to numerous markets as participation and spectatorial events have also proliferated (Pitts and Stotlar, 1996; in press). Increasingly, this plethora of sports events is seen by government offices, destination marketing professionals, travel agencies, and commerce leaders as viable sources of tourism, economic development, and revenue (Turco, 1999). Among other things, they can boost economic development, create a tourist attraction, focus media attention on the event and the city, region, or country, generate tax revenue, provide entertainment, provide a place for business transactions, provide an advertising medium, enhance brand awareness, and rally a community for a common cause. Because an event has the potential for so many different uses, numerous people, businesses, agencies, and organisations latch onto it.

As a large and still growing event, the Gay Games, as previously noted, has become one such sports event that is attracting the attention of many of these entities. The data in Table 2 shows that every facet of the Gay Games has grown substantially since the first one in 1982 and predictions for Gay Games VI to be held in Sydney in 2002 shows continued gains. These numbers most likely played an important role in Sydney's proposal to host the Gay Games.

For the first time in the history of the Gay Games, a Gay Games organising committee has involved a country's tourism commission and is using destination marketing. Local and national entities are involved in using the Gay Games to promote the city and the country as a destination holiday. In most of the promotional literature from the Sydney Gay Games Organising Committee, it is hard to tell that the advertisement is for the Gay Games. For instance, in the two official posters, a very large picture of the famous Sydney Harbour and bridge is the full and prominent picture. In the foreground of one poster are five men in swim trunks standing and looking at the bridge. In the foreground of the other poster are two women on a motorcycle. This picture also includes the famous Sydney Opera House. Across the top left edge of each poster are the words "Dreams do come true..." and across the bottom of each poster are the words "At Sydney 2002 Gay Games." A website address is shown at the bottom and a small Gay Games logo is depicted in the bottom right corner of the posters.

One's immediate impression when looking at the posters is relaxing, holiday travel. Unless one knows what the Gay Games is, one might not truly understand that the posters are supposed to be advertisements for a sports event.

In another promotional piece, the Organising Committee has produced a fold-out colour brochure. The front page of the brochure is a picture of the famous Sydney Harbour showing both the Sydney Opera House and the bridge. In small letters in the middle of the water in the picture is printed the words "dreams do come true" and the website address. Nothing about the picture or text on the front of this brochure puts forth the message that the brochure is an advertisement for a sports event.

When opened fully, the inside layout of the brochure contains four pictures: one depicts two women standing and looking at the Sydney Harbour; one shows four men in a small rowboat in the surf; one is a picture of a track and field sports facility; and one is a picture of three native Aboriginal men doing what appears to be a ritual dance. At first glance, it appears that the brochure is advertising a place (destination) that has a variety of activities. There is nothing in the pictures that suggests that the brochure is an advertisement for a sports event.

In very large letters on the right side are the words "dreams do come true." Along the bottom edge of the brochure are three words: inclusion, participation, and personal best. Along the left side is the official Gay Games VI logo banner with the words "Gay Games VI 2002 Cultural Festival Sydney." At various locations amongst the pictures are two lists of cultural activities and sports activities, but with no explanation about what they are. Alongside two of the pictures are the following texts:

> *"A beach party at bondi! The most famous beach in the world with lifesavers of every sex, sun, surf, music and more beautiful bodies than you have ever seen."*

> *"Lesbians and gay men have always contributed an enormous amount to the world. In Sydney our skills and abilities will be on show in everything we do as creative, inventive people. Join us!" and,*

> *"Sydney Olympic Park is a fantastic site. Many of the sporting and cultural events will be within walking distance of each other in venues used by the world's best athletes in the 2000 Olympics. The opportunity to reach your personal best in these surroundings will only come once. Don't miss it!"*

On the back full layout of the brochure are three pictures: one of a person snorkelling; one of five men looking at a harbour; and one very large picture of a Qantas airplane in flight. At bottom left are Sydney Gay Games addresses and phones information. In one small spot is what appears to be the dates of the events: 25 October - cultural launch; 2 November - Opening Ceremony; and 9 November - Closing Ceremony. There are three areas with text, which states the following:

> *"Watch our website www.gaygamesVI.org.au for updates on sport details, the cultural program, registration, general information." and,*

> *"Sydney is a fantastic gay and lesbian destination. New South Wales outlaws discrimination on the grounds of homosexuality and recognises gay relationships. It's a tolerant open city where having a good time is a religion. The Gay Games are a wonderful event wherever they're held, but they are only going to be in Sydney once - in 2002. If you make one dream in your life come true, make it Gay Games VI in Australia."*

In the picture of the Qantas airplane is the caption "Qantas is the official airline of Gay Games VI and Cultural Festival Sydney 2002."

Again, the viewer of this brochure is presented with more illustrations and text about visiting a place, rather than being presented with information promoting the largest lesbian and gay sports event in the world.

Interestingly, the word 'destination' actually appears in the text in the brochure. In tiny print on the back of the brochure is printed "Australian Tourist Commission." Unless one is conducting research such as this, it is small and practically unnoticeable.

In a promotional video for Gay Games VI, the same focus on visiting the many famous and not so famous sites of Sydney and Australia is painfully obvious. Throughout the almost 10 minutes, the viewer is bombarded with scenes, sights, places, attractions, and sounds of Sydney and greater Australia. The video makes it very clear that the focus of this Gay Games organising committee, working in conjunction with the Australian Tourist Commission, is on the destination and not necessarily on the sports event.

It is obvious, therefore, that the primary focus of the promotional literature is visiting the destination of Sydney and Australia, and promoting the Gay Games is secondary. So much secondary that members of the executive board of the Federation of Gay Games have raised questions and voiced complaints about the overwhelming lack of focus on the sports events and the Gay Games in the literature. At each annual board meeting of the Federation of Gay Games, the governing body of the Gay Games, the organising committee must present reports and updates. At the annual meeting in Berlin, in October, 1999, the Sydney Organising Committee unveiled the new logo, the posters, banners, other promotional literature, and the video. Almost immediately, there were questions regarding the lack of illustrations and focus on sports and the Gay Games (notes, 1999). Representatives of the organising committee explained that their focus came from the fact that they believe the majority numbers of Gay Games participants and attendees have been and will most likely be from North America - specifically, the United States - and eastern Europe. Australia will be a very long trip for most. In order to make the trip enticing, the committee believes that they must promote the destination as heavily as the Gay Games. Additionally, the committee remarked that they believe that most travellers will want to make the most of such a long trip by planning to be in Sydney and/or Australia for several extra days to see the city or the country. Their promotional literature, they believe, is an attempt to put forth information about the city and country for the potential traveller.

Summarily, the Sydney Gay Games Organising Committee is most likely on the right track with their thinking. The Pitts and Ayers (1999) economic impact study of Gay Games V in Amsterdam in 1998 revealed that visitors stayed ten nights in Amsterdam, for the Gay Games, and stayed an additional five nights in other places in the surrounding region including Paris, London, Austria, Belgium, and Italy.

In addition, the Sydney Gay Games Organising Committee is doing something else that represents a move away from the traditional protocol of the Gay Games. The Gay Games includes a cultural festival which includes such art forms and exhibitions as music, choir, band, theatre, film, print art, photo art, sculpture, painting, and many other. The cultural festival was not an originally planned event within the Gay Games. It emerged as gay and lesbian people from around the world wanted to share and celebrate their culture. It is now officially recognised by the Federation of Gay Games. Indeed, the full title of the Gay Games is "Gay Games and Cultural Festival."

The traditional protocol is that the cultural festival events take place during the same eight-day period of time as the Gay Games. Sydney, however, will break that tradition. Sydney will start the cultural festival a week in advance of the Opening Ceremonies of the Gay Games. This move ensures that some visitors and participants for the Gay Games will arrive in Sydney a week before the Gay Games start, thus ensuring that some visitors and participants will be in the city, or the region, for two weeks.

This move is in line with current sport marketing practices involved in enhancing the entertainment and commercial value of sports events. For example, one of the most extreme cases is the Kentucky Derby. The Derby, a horse race, is a sports event that lasts about two minutes. Yet, Kentucky Derby festival events surrounding the two-minute sports event now start four weeks in advance of the event and involved more than 80 events (Pitts and Stotlar, 1996).

Comparatively, some consumers complain that entertainment events surrounding sports events actually distract from the event and add nothing to the value of the sports event. However, there is compelling evidence in the literature that most consumers of sports events expect and want the entertainment events as part of the sporting experience.

The Federation of Gay Games organisational structure includes a sports committee and a cultural committee. Each committee has members whose special interest is either in the sports events of the Gay Games or the cultural events. Each committee is responsible for the planning, rules, policy, and staging of their events. There is increasing pressure from each committee for more funding for their events. There is also increasing discussion about which is the key focus of the Gay Games - the sports or the cultural events. The sports committee has a point, however, in that the primary mission of the Gay Games is sports participation. Yet, they also recognise the importance of culture and its place as both an entertainment factor and a celebration of the lesbian and gay culture world wide.

Summary discussion

The emerging use of the Gay Games for destination marketing is inevitable. Mega sports events such as the Gay Games are very expensive events and require millions in funding. The majority of sports events today have to have sponsorship funding and the support of communities, cities, and governments, as well as the support and co-operation of other such stakeholders as hotel, travel, and transportation industries and sports governing bodies in order to ensure success. These stakeholders rely on the commercial and entertainment value of the event in order to realise a return on their investment. Thus, the sport management professionals responsible for the event must promote to ensure the success of the event so that all stakeholders might be satisfied. It is also important, however, that the Gay Games organisers remember that perhaps the most important stakeholder of the Gay Games is the sports participant. Finding a balance in satisfying the many different stakeholders through promotional and marketing efforts will be a real test of the success of future Gay Games.

References

Burns, J. P. A., Hatch, J. H., and Mules, T. J. (1986), *The Adelaide Grand Prix: The impact of a special event. Adelaide*: Centre for South Australia Economic Studies.

Chalip, L., Green, B. C., and Vander Velden, L. (1998), Sources of interest in travel to the Olympic Games. *Journal of Vacation Marketing*, 4 (1): 7-22.

Delpy. L. (1997), A profile of the 1996 Summer Olympic Games Spectator. Paper presented at the 12th annual conference of the North American Society for Sport Management, San Antonio, Texas, USA.

Hall, C. M. (1992), Review, adventure, sport and health tourism. In B. Weiler and C. M. Hall (Eds.) *Special Interest Tourism*. Belhaven Press, London, p. 147.

Kang, Y. X., and Perdue, R. (1994), Long-term impact of a mega-event on international tourism to the host country: A conceptual model and the case of the 1988 Seoul Olympics. In M. Uysal (Ed.), *Global tourist behaviour*, International Business Press, New York, pp. 205-225.

Kurtzman, J. and Zauhar, J. (1997), A wave in time - The sports tourism phenomena. *Journal of Sport Tourism*, 4 (1): 1-13.

Kurtzman, J. and Zauhar, J. (1999), The virtual sports tourist. *Journal of Sport Tourism*, 5 (4): 21-30.

Notes. (1999, October), Notes taken at the annual board meeting of the Federation of Gay Games. Berlin, Germany.

Pitts, B. G. (1998), Let the Gaymes begin! A case study of sports tourism, commercialisation, and the Gay Games V. Paper presented at the 2nd Gay Games Conference: Queer Games? Theories, Politics, Sports. Amsterdam, July 28-30, 1998.

Pitts, B. G. (1999), Sports tourism and niche markets: Identification and analysis of the growing lesbian and gay sports tourism industry. *Journal of Vacation Marketing*, 5 (1): 31-50.

Pitts, B. G. and Ayers, K. (1999), An economic scale analysis of Gay Games V, Amsterdam, 1998. Paper presented at the annual conference of the North American Society for Sport Management, Vancouver, British Columbia, Canada, June, 1999.

Pitts, B. G. and Stotlar, D. K. (1996), *Fundamentals of sport marketing*. Morgantown, WV: Fitness Information Technology, Inc.

Pitts, B. G. and Stotlar, D. K. (in press), *Fundamentals of sport marketing (2nd Edition)*. Morgantown, WV: Fitness Information Technology, Inc.

Poizat-Newcomb, S. (1999), The genesis of a sports tourism activity - Surfing (Part I). *Journal of Sport Tourism*, 5 (4): 4-12.

Research Unit, Sports Tourism International Council (1994), Sports as an economic generator. *Journal of Sport Tourism*, 1 (2): 21-33.

Research Unit, Sports Tourism International Council (1997), STIX - Sports tourism impact index, as an economic generator. *Journal of Sport Tourism*, 3 (4): 13-14.

Sofield, T. and Sivan, A. (1994), From cultural event to international sport - The Hong Kong Boat Race. *Journal of Sport Tourism*, 1 (3): 5-22.

Sports Tourism International Council. (2000), Developing the sports tourism profession. http://www.sportquest.com/tourism/index.html

Standeven, J. (1998), Sport tourism: joint marketing - A starting point for beneficial synergies. *Journal of Vacation Marketing*, 4 (1): 39-51.

Standeven, J. and DeKnop, P. (1999), *Sport tourism*. Champaigne, IL: Human Kinetics.

Turco, D. (1999), Travelling and turnovers: Measuring the economic impact of a street basketball tournament. *Journal of Sport Tourism*, 5 (1): 6-11.

The value of internet tourism sites from a research viewpoint

Jeff Pope

Curtin University, Australia

Introduction

World-wide, tourism internet (Net) sites are very numerous, growing daily and are increasingly important to potential tourists, actual tourists, business, the professional community, particularly in government and universities, and students. Much research attention is on the use of the Internet for business, and the realm of electronic commerce (see, for example, Weber and Roehl, 1999, for a useful summary of primarily US literature on this aspect; TravelTalk Asia-Pacific, 1999, p39). This research focuses on the identification of leading (English-language) sites world-wide, and their value and qualities from a research viewpoint. For the purpose of this paper research is widely defined, and includes undergraduate seminar, essay and project work.

In an Australian tourism business context, the use of net technology by travel agents in Perth, Western Australia, has been investigated by Vasudavan and Standing (1999). The findings are disappointing; travel agents 'have not whole-heartedly embraced the www', most of them have a 'paper based mentality' and the benefits of electronic commerce are not being realised (*ibid.*, p109). Further, the Australian Tourism Commission revised its net site policy in early 2000, and currently has three sites. These are divided into three: a user site for Australian holiday information for international markets; a corporate site primarily for business and government, with marketing information, statistics and research reports; and an exclusive site for the international and domestic media. These are: www.2000.australia.com; www.atc.net.au; and www.media.australia.com respectively.

In an academic context, few books have recognised the potential of the Net as a reference source, until a few years ago. One of the best current examples is Pearce *et al* (1998), who list around 300 relevant tourism net sites. This topic is in its infancy from an academic research viewpoint. Initial work includes Williams *et al* (1996), Pedrazzini and Weeks (1998), the more technical paper by Hyun and Youn (1999), Pope (1999), and an ongoing Australian CRC (1999) study. Journals are now taking an increasing interest in this field e.g. *Journal of Teaching in Travel and Tourism* (2000). However, many studies approach this topic in terms of an overview of available information, data and sources rather than an evaluation of the quality of specific sites.

One of the major problems in this emerging field is that www addresses change from those listed, reflecting the speed of change on the Net. One example is the World Travel and Tourism Council site in Pearce *et al* (1998). Nonetheless, a reasonable assertion is that at a grass roots level many academics and students are increasingly using the Net as a source, possibly a major source, of data and information. One can further speculate that accessing such information is rather haphazard and inefficient for the vast majority of users in universities and possibly the government sector. Research studies such as this will hopefully reduce that information search time.

The key questions include:

(i)   Of the many tourism sites, which are the most useful from a research viewpoint? Which are the leading organisations and countries in the world?

(ii)   What criteria should be used to make such an evaluation or assessment?

(iii)   What is current 'best practice' and what improvements, if any, are needed?

(iv)   Can some of the worst sites be improved? Is it in their interest?

(v)   What are research user perceptions and how much are Net tourism sites being used for research purposes? How much do attitudes and use vary between different types of users?

Evaluation criteria

Evaluation criteria from a user viewpoint for commercial tourism business sites are likely to be different from evaluating all tourism sites from the academic viewpoint of the provision of data and information. For example, Vasudavan and Standing (1999, p108) used six criteria in their study of Net sites of travel agencies in Western Australia. These comprised: customer interaction (site navigation/relevance to enquiry); creation of (user) profiles; partnerships i.e. links with other sites; transactions e.g. via credit card; adaption to user profile; downloading of information possible.

It is important to distinguish between differences between tourism sites and differences in user purpose. Of course each user will have his or her own evaluation criteria. The presumption of this research is that academics, researchers, government officials and students are seeking data and information, and that their major if not sole evaluation criteria is the quality of that information. The criterion 'ease of access' (to the site) might be added, although for the purpose of this study this is not considered to be a problem or vary between users.

Another possible criterion is 'fee payment'. This is recognised as an issue of increasing importance. One site, that of the World Tourism Organisation, stands out for its high pricing policy for tourism data, and should consider recognising and addressing the needs of the academic community for reasonable cost internet data access via libraries (in line with many other data providing bodies, at least in Australia).

As a pioneering study in a new and rapidly evolving field, this research has used straightforward, basic evaluation criteria of its assessment of tourism sites from an academic viewpoint. Other more sophisticated evaluation criteria can be derived in future work.

The major evaluation criteria used in this study are:

(i) Ease of accessing the site

(ii) Provision of statistical data, and its quality, quantity and explanatory notes e.g. tourism trends and historical data, profiles of tourism markets, and impacts of tourism on the economy, particularly in economic terms

(iii) Provision of information, and its quality and quantity

(iv) Full research reports, journal articles and/or annual reports available

(v) Downloading of data/information/articles, particularly in PDF

(vi) Links to other sites (quantity and ease of use)

It must be stressed that sites were evaluated on what their focus was. Thus a regional site was assessed on the quality and quantity of data and information that it contained on tourism in its designated region, and an eco-tourism site on data held for an academic interested in that particular field, and so on. Any comparison of sites should therefore be made with caution, and as a principle it is inappropriate to compare sites across different groups, other than in terms of broad quality categories.

This paper does not list every site of the 233 which were evaluated, because of the constraint on length and also the degree of subjectivity. Rather, the focus of this paper is on the leading sites in four geographical categories (a proxy for purpose), namely world, (world) region, country and state.

Method

The research method may be summarised as follows:

(i) Identification of the (English-language) sites to be evaluated. This is not meant to be comprehensive, but rather illustrative, with a spread of sites by type e.g. international or regional tourism body, government tourism office, government research agency, university department, university library, and by country.

(ii) Identification of data and information available.

(iii) Any comments related to (ii), such as charging for data, members access only, difficult to find, links to other sites, overall quality e.g. 'too general'.

(iv) Geographical classification: for world, region i.e. group of neighbouring countries, country, and state or smaller region within a country.

(v)   Subjective quality score on a scale of 10 (best) to 0 (worst).

(vi) Most sites were only visited once (in mid 1999).

In terms of representation, national sites accounted for around half of all sites investigated, with (world) regional sites the least (12%). The site data is available on an Excel spreadsheet and can be classified in alpha order by organisation or site address, or by geographical category, or by ranking order of quality.

It is recognised that the sites selected are not a representative or random sample in the usual sense of academic research. Rather, leading tourism and travel sites have been targeted, from available public information, current own research and student use, and use of search engines, particularly Yahoo. Flow on (linked) sites from each of these were an important source. As the study progressed, it became more difficult to access new sites i.e. significant diminishing returns to scale in economic terms.

This study has attempted to obtain a geographical balance throughout the world and remain unbiased. However, one unavoidable bias and major weakness of this study is that only English-speaking sites have been evaluated, because of a lack of foreign language skills. Although unintentional, there may be some small bias towards sites in the researcher's home country, Australia, and the leading country in the world for Net sites and e-commerce, namely the USA. There may also be some additional focus on sites in the Asia-Pacific region.

The weaknesses and limitations of this research are recognised, particularly the rapid dating and diminishing relevance of its findings over time. However, in an emerging field where the great emphasis is *from a commercial and/or user's viewpoint*, it is hoped that this study makes a small but useful contribution to tourism research in this rapidly developing and important field. This study should be seen as ongoing rather than as a finalised project.

Findings

The major overall findings of the quality of (English-language) tourism Net sites world-wide *from a research user's viewpoint*, are:

(i)   There is a wide range in the quality of sites.

(ii)   The quality of sites appears not to follow a normal distribution. Overall, only 12% are considered to be good or very good, with the vast majority (62%) classed as poor.

(iii) Leading quality sites comprise: World Travel and Tourism Council (WTTC); Tourism Industries (USA); Hawaii Tourism Authority; Tourism Tasmania; Tourism Research Laboratory (USA). Sites located in the USA dominate.

(iv)   The poorest quality sites include mainly National and State Tourism Offices e.g. Britain, Canada, Cayman Islands, Germany, India, Indonesia, Japan, Korea, New Zealand, Northern Ireland, Western Australia; travel agents' associations e.g. in USA, UK; regional government/political organisations e.g. ASEAN, Caribbean Tourism Organisation; tourism consultants.

(v) The worst sites contained little or no information of use to a researcher. Some are essentially just a marketing vehicle rather than there to provide useful information. This is particularly true of tourism consultant sites.

(vi) Research organisations also had a wide range in quality, from leading sites such as the Tourism Research Laboratory (Illinois, USA) to the poorest such as the European Tourism Research Institute.

When categorised in terms of (geographical) type of site, state sites have proportionately more better quality sites than do (world) regional sites. The latter may reflect fewer resources, particularly financial, or possibly expertise in bringing together and integrating disparate data and information from different countries. However, world regional sites have a significant 43% of sites in the average or mid-range category, and this augurs well for future improvement in quality.

Out of the 233 sites evaluated, only five scored the highest assessment of 9 out of 10. This represents around two per cent of sites. Three of these came from state run or state focused sites. Whilst this is of course totally subjective, it does suggest that, as a major quality source of tourism research data, the Net overall is still in its infancy. However, whilst this finding is true overall, that is not to say that researchers in particular fields, and many students – whose requirements may be less demanding – may not enjoy a far higher use and personal quality assessment of Net sourced data and information.

The leading sites

The major features of the sites with current 'best practice' include:

- large amounts of statistical data, with explanations or reports on what the data means;

- annual reports, trends and past tourism information;

- profiles of the tourism markets;

- impact of tourism on the economy;

- ability to download in PDF;

- free access i.e. no user fee.

The leading five sites (of those investigated and in alpha order) by organisation are considered to be: Hawaii Tourism Authority (USA); Tourism Industries (USA); Tourism Research Laboratory (USA); Tourism Tasmania (Australia) and WTTC (USA).

In terms of the top sites by country of location of the Net site, the USA dominated overwhelmingly (with 22 out of 40 of the leading sites, including 9 of the top ten world sites), followed by Australia (9) and Canada (3). The UK and Europe overall ranked poorly in comparison, although note that only English-language sites were evaluated.

The leading South East and North Asian sites comprise Singapore Tourism Board Homepage, Tourism Authority of Thailand, Tourism Malaysia, Travel News Asia, Asia Pacific Journal of Tourism Research, and Pacific Asia Travel Association.

The leading Australian sites are Tourism Tasmania, Australian Bureau of Statistics, Office of National Tourism (Australia), Tourism Queensland and Tourism Victoria.

In Canada, the best sites are EDT Tourism Nova Scotia, Canadian Tourism Statistics, Ontario Canada Tourism and Rene Waksberg's Tourism Research Links.

The only European site worth noting is the highly ranked Austrian National Tourist Office site. It is disappointing that, in spite of its importance in international tourism and its number of academic tourism courses, no UK sites featured in the leading sites. The most noteworthy UK site (in the mid-quality group) is that of the British Airports Authority (BAA).

A noteworthy finding is the importance of transport sites, especially air transport, as a tourism research source, comprising Air Transport Association (ranked good), Airports Council International, Bureau of Transportation Statistics (USA), and BAA (UK).

The leading sites, with their addresses, are presented in Appendix A.

It is perhaps not surprising that many national and state tourism office sites are of poor quality from an academic viewpoint as their primary purpose is to entice potential tourists to their country or region. However, such sites can be of high quality from a researcher's perspective, and some US, Australian and Canadian sites offer an insight into current best practice e.g. Hawaii, California, Tasmania, and Nova Scotia.

A surprising finding is the poor site quality of tourism research organisations e.g. Canadian Tourism Research Institute, Centre for Regional Tourism Research (Australia), and especially international ones e.g. European Tourism Research Institute, Co-operative Research Centre for Sustainable Tourism. Whilst sites of a more general nature cannot be expected to cover a multitude of business activities, it seems reasonable to expect that tourism, as one of the leading industries, should feature more prominently on some sites. For example, the ASEAN site has little of (academic) use on tourism. Even the United Nations, with vast resources, ranks poorly.

Another possibly surprising finding is that some relatively poorer countries (in terms of per capita income) have much better tourism sites than those in richer countries. For example, in the Asia-Pacific region, China's National Tourism Administration site and that of the Philippines Department of Tourism rank far better than those of the Tourism Boards in New Zealand and Japan. Singapore, Malaysia and Thailand are amongst the leading Asia-Pacific (national tourism office) sites.

An expected problem is that of charging for data and information. Whilst this may be a reasonable practice for commercial consultancy organisations who can recover such fees from clients, generally academics and certainly students have insufficient financial resources. In short, charging for access to data and information is a barrier to learning at the university level. The best known and current worst offender is the World Tourism Organisation. Other leading sites which charge include the Pacific Asia Travel Association and Australia's Bureau of Tourism Research. In the future, it is to be hoped that they will introduce academic access to their valuable data sources for *bona fide* academics and students (using passwords as appropriate) via university libraries for a reasonable one-off annual fee payable by the institution. For example, the Australian Bureau of Statistics currently does this.

Specialist bodies such as The Ecotourism Society, Air Transport Association, Rene Waksberg's Tourism Research Links and Airports Council International all rank well.

Student perception and use of tourism net sites

The second stage of this project comprises an evaluation of student use of and perception of the quality of Net sites. A survey of Tourism Management undergraduates within the Bachelor of Commerce degree at Curtin University was undertaken in the second semester, 1999.

A four-page questionnaire (survey instrument) was distributed to students attending four tutorials and one lecture in various first, second and third year tourism classes. All were completed, although the response rate represents 70% of all students enrolled because of absentees and late arrivals (who were excluded). A total of 78 responses were analysed: 34 from Tourism Management Year 1, 29 from Tourism Management Year 2, nine from Tourism Management Year 3 and six from Tourism Economics Year 2. It should be noted that student numbers vary between semesters, and the latter two classes are under-represented. Each student did not necessarily answer every question.

The major findings from this small survey are:

1. Students had access to and used the internet for around 25% of their total time spent on research.

2. Local (Australian) students spent 4% less time than international students on the net for study purposes.

3. Around 70% of all students used university computer and internet facilities rather than using their own private facilities e.g. at home.

4. Students strongly believed that the internet was a useful research tool for all areas of tourism.

5. Students would use the internet even more if lecturers supplied them with relevant and useful site addresses. Potential growth in research use is therefore high.

6. Perceptions of good net tourism sites were reasonably similar between different types of students. Reasons included high quality statistics, reports, links, contacts and organisational features. There were no notable differences in perceptions between light and heavy users.

7. For the worst tourism Net sites, the majority of students (who use the internet relatively less) indicated that access fees were the main deterrent for them accessing information. However, heavy users did not see this as a major weakness of sites. This probably reflects their greater experience, and their ability to find free sites with high quality data sources on the internet.

8. Heavy users tended to be international students (57%), particularly Malaysian and Singaporean, although they comprised only a small proportion of the sample. Heavy users are more likely to be in their final year of study. There is no correlation between heavy use and academic ability, with an even distribution over the academic scale. Heavy users are much more likely to have visited some or a number of 'top' net sites than average and light users.

9. There was an observable but non-statistically significant correlation between lecturer recommendation of internet sites and student use.

10. Students were found to be more critical of the 'top' sites than earlier research (discussed above) had rated them. On average, students had visited 1.7 of the 'top' 40 sites, as listed in Appendix A, and such visits comprised 11% of all sites visited. It should be noted that only one small class, Tourism Economics, had received the list of top sites given in Appendix A, although some students may have obtained it from an earlier class or from friends.

11. Of specific sites, the *Australian Bureau of Statistics* and *World Travel and Tourism Council* were visited most, accounting for 32% of all visits. The only site to be more highly ranked for quality by students than in our previous research ratings was that of the *Airports Council International*.

12. Of all sites visited, 'well-known' sites were by far the most frequently visited, even though they were not ranked as the best of sites from a research viewpoint.

13. Students also used a small number of sites not listed or given to them by lecturers, particularly local and national tourism authority sites. These included those of the *West Australian Tourism Commission, Qantas* and *Singapore Airlines*.

Overall, international (Asian) students have so far adapted much better than Australian students to using internet sites for tourism research. User access fees remain an ongoing problem. The prognosis for much greater academic and student research use of the internet is good, although it should not be assumed that all students are comfortable with and fully understand the internet's functions and capabilities.

Conclusion

This research project is a continuing part of a journey rather than a destination. It provides a 'snapshot' of the quality and student use of sites from an Australian perspective in mid/late 1999. Hopefully the sites investigated and identified as 'leading', 'best', 'very good' or 'good' provide a sound and time-saving start for anyone using the Net as a data and information research source. Larger international surveys of student users should be undertaken.

The next stage of this research project involves an international email survey of tourism academics' use of the internet and perceptions of leading, quality sites. It is hoped that findings from this survey can be presented at the *Tourism 2000: Time for Celebration?* Conference. Hopefully, some consensus on 'best tourism site practice' may emerge.

Overall, there is undoubtedly a great volume of tourism information on many Net sites; the bad news is that most of it is of little use to an academic user. However, there are a few tourism Net site 'gems' available, and this study points the way to some of them.

Ideally, further research should include a much larger and up-to-date survey, including non-English language sites. In the meantime, the feedback from an international range of users should be obtained, probably on an informal basis to begin with. Also, particular attention needs to be focused on detailed analysis of the characteristics of the leading tourism sites.

It is hoped that the *Tourism 2000: Time for Celebration?* Conference generates stimulating comments and constructive criticism from international peers, and a good starting point for further work in this exciting and fast-evolving field.

References

Co-operative Research Council [CRC] (1999), '[Australian] Tourism Industry Information System' project, current.

Hyun, J. P., and Youn, G. K. (1999), *'Analysis of Easy-To-Use Navigation for Tourism Information Web Sites Based on the Types of Organising Information for Users'*, Asia-Pacific Tourism Association Fifth Annual Conference, Hong Kong, August and Conference Proceedings, Volume 1, pp70-76.

Journal of Teaching in Travel and Tourism (2000), Special Issue on 'The Internet and Travel and Tourism Teaching', forthcoming.

Pearce, P. Morrison, A. and Rutledge, J. (1998), *Tourism: Bridges Across Continents*, McGraw-Hill, Sydney.

Pedrazzini, T. and Weeks, P. (1998), *'Tourism and Hospitality Research on the Internet'*, Abstract in Proceedings of the 8th Australian Tourism and Hospitality Research Conference (Part One), Gold Coast, Queensland, February, Bureau of Tourism Research, pp210-211.

Pope, J. (1999), *'The Quality of Internet Tourism Sites from an Academic Users'* Viewpoint', Asia-Pacific Tourism Association Fifth Annual Conference, Hong Kong, August and Conference Proceedings, Volume 1, pp77-85.

TravelTalk Asia-Pacific (1999*), 'Electronic marketplace - diminishing roles for travel agents and CRSs'*, p39.

Vasudavan, T. and C. Standing (1999*), 'Web Technology Diffusion and Service Offerings by Travel Agencies'*, in Proceedings of the 9th Australian Tourism and Hospitality Research Conference (Part One), Adelaide, February, Bureau of Tourism Research, pp99-111.

Weber, K. and Roehl, W. (1999*), 'Profiling People Searching and Purchasing Travel Products on the World Wide Web'*, Paper presented at the 9th Australian Tourism and Hospitality Research Conference, Adelaide, February 1999.

Williams, P. W., Bascombe, P., Brenner, N., and Green, D. (1996), 'Using the Internet for Tourism Research: "Information Highway" or "Dirt Road"?', *Journal of Travel Research*, 34 (4).

Appendix A

Leading English-Language Tourism Net Sites for Research Use, 1999 (by Category)

Site address	Organisation
World	
http://www.wttc.org	World Travel and Tourism Council
http://www.air-transport.org	Air Transport Association
http://www.ecotourism.org	The Ecotourism Society
http://www.fourseasons.com/index.html	Four Seasons Hotels and Resorts
http://www.tourism-montreal.org/main1.htm	René Waksberg's Tourism Research Links
http://www.airports.org	Airports Council International
http://darkwing.uoregon.edu/ ~ ginger	Dr Greg's Homepage
http://www.cyberwonders.com	Cyberwonders Travel
http://www.findat.com/cats/cat01/top02/HOR/tourism.htm	Horwath Hotel, Travel and Tourism Group
http://www.oecd.org	Organisation for Economic Co-operation and Development

(World) Region	
http://www.tourismfuturesintl.com	Tourism Futures International
http://web3.asia1.com.sg:80/timesnet/navigtn/tna.html	Travel News Asia
http://www.bigvolcano.com.au/ercentre/ercpage.htm	Ecotourism Resource Center
http://www.geocities.com/Paris/9842/tourism.html	Tourism Research
http://www.hotel-online.com/neo/trends/asiapacificjournal/index.html	Asia Pacific Journal of Tourism Research
http://www.pata.org	Pacific Asia Travel Association
http://aacvb.org	Asian Association of Convention and Visitor Bureaus
http://www.cowan.edu.au/pa/ioto/about/regional/regional.html	Regional Tourism (ECU)
http://www.iaato.org	International Assoiation of Antartic Operators
http://www.travel-asia.com	Travel Asia

Country	
http://tinet.ita.doc.gov	Tourism Industries (USA)
http://www.abs.gov.au	Australian Bureau of Statistics
http://www.austria-tourism.at	Austrian National Tourist Office
http://www.canadatourism.com/tourism/stats	Canadian Tourism Statistics
http://www.tourism.gov.au	Office of National Tourism (Australia)
http://www.btr.gov.au	Bureau of Tourism Research (Australia)
http://www.hvs-intl.com	HVS International
http://www.restaurant.org	National Restaurant Association
http://www.stb.com.sg	Singapore Tourist Board Homepage
http://www.tat.or.th	Tourism Authority of Thailand

State	
http://www.hawaii.gov/tourism	Hawaii Tourism Authority
http://www.tourism.tas.gov.au	Tourism Tasmania

http://www.tourism.uiuc.edu	Tourism Research Laboratory
http://gocalif.ca.gov/research/index.html	California Tourism Research
http://www.gov.ns.ca/ecor/tns/index.htm	EDT Tourism Nova Scotia
http://www.qttc.com.au	Tourism Queensland
http://www.touirsm.vic.gov.au	Tourism Victoria
http://www.canberratourism.com.au	Canberra Tourism
http://www.forestry.umt.edu/itrr	Institute for Tourism and Recreation Research
http://www.ontario-canada.com	Ontario Canada Tourism

Tourism in Nunavut: Problems and potential

John Selwood and Stephanie Heidenreich

University of Winnipeg, Canada

Canadian writer Robert Kroetsch captures the sense of the North as what some consider Canada's ultimate travel frontier: "To go North is to slip out of the fastenings of night and day into other versions of light and dark" (Kroetsch, 1996). Indeed, when one pauses to reflect what might draw visitors more than 1000 kilometres to see a barren landscape with only a few scattered nodes of human settlement, one falls back on this shift in perspective, the "turning upside-down [of] assumptions about time, about direction, about urban ambition, about America" (Kroetsch, 1996). The appeal of the North does not lie in a concentration of diverse attractions as it might for metropolitan destinations or mass tourist resorts. Rather, it may be attributed to an intangible sense of *difference* from the South, which is the result of the region's remoteness, isolation and extreme environment. Geographically, much of Nunavut is located above the Arctic Circle (figure 1). However, the North is more than just latitude; its essence lies in what Louis Hamelin has called "nordicity." This term refers to a more complex appreciation of the North that is based on a variety of criteria and premised on the notion that northernness is a state of mind; "more than an area, it is a passion" (Hamelin, 1978). Certainly, the region has significant attractions in the form of cultural artefacts and natural sites. However, the time and money required to experience these resources hardly seems to justify the journey if the aura of the "North" does not come into play. Nunavut's official travel publication, *The Arctic Traveller* (Nunavut Tourism, 1999), asserts: "Nunavut is caribou on a distant horizon, and polar bear tracks in newly fallen snow.... Nunavut is quiet time near a rushing waterfall, learning ancient stories from an elder, and a night in a cozy igloo." Nunavut must capitalise on its image and mystique to capture a tourist segment willing to make the significant investment required to reach the region.

The Canadian North appeals most to those in search of "pristine" wilderness, allocentrics who shun destinations promoted by travel agencies offering inexpensive packaged tours (Plog, 1991). However, the isolation, which enables this experience, also makes travel to the area time-consuming, difficult and costly. While local commitment to tourism is high, and the industry is seen as a promising way to broaden the base of the northern economy, it is difficult to develop the necessary infrastructure in the small, widely scattered communities. Nevertheless, the growing interest in eco- and adventure tourism, as well as increased government involvement in promoting tourism in the North, have contributed significantly to the industry's expansion over the years. The creation of Nunavut, in particular, has boosted the region's visibility on both a national and international level. This paper will examine the steps being taken to promote tourism in Nunavut, as well as the difficulties in marketing the region as a major destination.

Figure 1   Nunavut's Relative Location

Overview of Nunavut

Once considered the eastern part of Canada's Northwest Territories, the area now known as Nunavut became its own administrative district on April 1, 1999. The territory covers 1.994 million square kilometres, or an area roughly three times that of France, the largest country in Europe (figure 2). Yet the total population of the entire territory is approximately that of a small town, and Iqaluit, the territorial capital, has under 5000 inhabitants (Nunavut Tourism, 1999). Approximately 85 per cent of the territory's 25,000 inhabitants are Inuit, resulting in *de facto* self-rule for its Aboriginal people (Nunavut Tourism, 1999). Major industries include mining, tourism and the production of Inuit art and crafts (Geddes, 1999).

Nevertheless, the area is marked by high levels of unemployment (29 per cent), and 95 per cent of Nunavut's operating budget comes from the federal government. Great hopes are placed on tourism as a means to achieve greater economic independence, with the most optimistic statistics recording 17,000 visitors to the territory each year, contributing a total of $30 million to the Nunavut economy (Lanken and Vincent, 1999). Although estimates of the number of tourists visiting Nunavut vary significantly, sources agree that tourism is expected to increase dramatically over the next several years.

Figure 2   Nunavut's Relative Area

FRANCE
(543,030 sq km)

NUNAVUT
(1,994,000 sq km)

Marketing the region

Nunavut's improved position in the tourism industry may be attributed to a growing number of travellers seeking new destinations and willing to pay substantial sums to visit them. Given its rudimentary tourism infrastructure and high costs, Nunavut lends itself well to adventure-type tourism which tends to draw an affluent clientele (Van Houten and Boldt, 1998). For instance, a two-week excursion in Auyuittuq Park, described as "one of the tourist jewels of Nunavut", costs $3,150, airfare to Iqaluit not included. Visitors must carry their tents and equipment with them as the park's facilities are limited to a few official campsites and several emergency shelters (Geddes, 1999; McArthur 1999). Because of limited capacities to accommodate visitors, the territory's focus is on small groups that can be handled by small tour operators (*Marketing Magazine*, 1999).

Increased promotion of Nunavut during the time leading up to and following its creation has had a positive impact on the local economy. The territory now has its own tourism organisation, Nunavut Tourism, which is actively marketing the territory as a destination. Much of the organisation's budget has been directed toward advertisement and promotion, although the budget for these initiatives was cut by one-third in 1999 so as to provide more funding to train tour operators and develop the tourism product. Some have found fault with the deployment of funds allocated by the territory for tourism promotion (*Marketing Magazine*, 1999). Nevertheless, an impressive body of travel information has been developed, both in printed form and on the Internet. *Marketing Magazine* (1999) cites Nortext's *Nunavut Handbook*, most of which is available on the Internet (www.arctic-travel.com), as one of the most significant promotional initiatives for the region. E_commerce also has appreciable benefits for small-scale operators, providing them with access to large markets at little cost. Because communications is a priority in a territory with a population density of 1.3 people per square kilometre, local Web sites are well developed and organised, and provide visitors with comprehensive information about the region. Large government sites such as Nunavut Tourism and smaller local initiatives like Rankin Inlet's Web site display a consistently high quality that cannot be taken for granted with such an unregulated medium.

Infrastructure in the North

Concerted efforts to market the region have met with some success. A number of partnerships and plans are being developed, including a series of federal-provincial agreements for infrastructural improvements in the areas of transportation, industry, education and training, as well as trade. Feasibility studies into power transmission and the development of a road from Churchill into the Kivalliq region are being conducted (Canada-Manitoba Economic Development Partnership, 1998). More recently, Nunavut and Manitoba have signed a Memorandum of Understanding which lays the groundwork for future co-operation in developing the northern region (Manitoba Government, 2000). However, as Jan Lundgren has observed, the area's much lower population density and small population severely hamper economic development relative to other northern regions such as Scandinavia (Lundgren, 1995). As one Iqaluit-based tour operator points out: "The government can print up glossy brochures, but the fact is, you can go to... Paris for less money" (Geddes, 1999).

Transportation

Travelling to the North presents challenges because of the distances involved and environmental factors that result in high costs. Nunavut has only 21 kilometres of road, running from Arctic Bay to Nanisivik, precluding visitors from using ground transport to gain access to the area (*Maclean's*, 1999). The tundra soil is constantly shifting due to permafrost, which makes road construction problematic. Although plans are on the table to build a road linking the Kivalliq region to Churchill, Manitoba, it will be some years before such a project materialises because Churchill itself is not yet connected to southern Manitoba's road network (Selwood and Lehr, 1999). Currently therefore, almost all visitors reach Nunavut by air, although during the summer some travel is possible by sea. Flights depart from the gateway cities of Yellowknife (linked to Edmonton and the West),

Winnipeg, Ottawa and Montreal (figure 3). There are also several international flights to Iqaluit from Nuuk and Kangerlussuaq in Greenland. Once in the territory, travel does not become easier and consists of smaller planes servicing communities from the territorial transportation hubs of Cambridge Bay (in the Kitikmeot region), Rankin Inlet (in Kivalliq) and Iqaluit (in Qikiqtaluk). Needless to say, the distances and relatively small passenger loads result in high airfares (Lundgren, 1999). A round trip from Montreal or Ottawa to Iqaluit, the territorial capital, usually costs more than $1000 (Crary, 1999). Furthermore, smaller communities often have only two or three scheduled flights a week, and these can easily be delayed by poor weather conditions or mechanical problems (Crary, 1999 and *Winnipeg Free Press*, 1998a). Not only is travel to and within the area extremely expensive, but the infrequency of flights on some routes and schedule irregularities make it very difficult for individuals or tour organisers with tight itineraries to arrange excursions to the region.

Figure 3   Nunavut Localities and Air Links

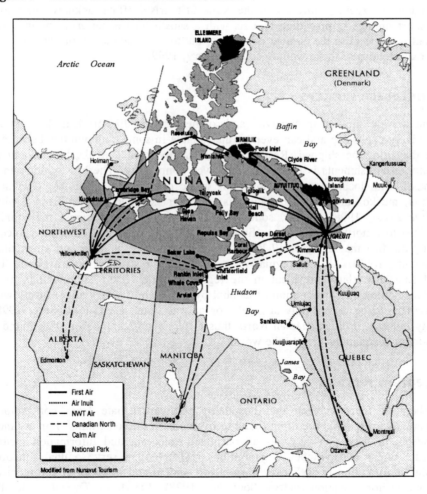

Accommodation

Once travellers arrive at their destination different problems arise. While Iqaluit boasts some 175 hotel rooms (Crary, 1999), Rankin Inlet has only a single hotel that accommodates 130 guests in 65 rooms. What is more, most hotels and motels originally catered to construction workers and government employees, rather than to leisure travellers. Much of the accommodation is therefore quite rudimentary, despite which rates are very high, ranging from $150 to $200 per person per night. The poor ratio of quality to price when compared to other travel destinations is striking. In smaller communities lodgings are generally more informal: shared bathrooms are the norm, and it is not unusual for single travellers to have to "double up" and share a room with other guests if a large number of visitors arrive at the same time (*Winnipeg Free Press*, 1998). Another alternative is the "homestay," similar to Bed and Breakfast, allowing visitors to get a better appreciation of how Inuit families live today. However, the accommodations are often relatively crowded and lacking in amenities. They can also be at odds with visitor preconceptions about authentic Inuit lifestyles. Madeleine Redferne, executive director of the Nunavut tourism office, acknowledges some of the local shortcomings in providing tourists with a satisfactory experience, noting "Our short term goal is not to raise the number of tourists, but to raise the quality of what we offer to match the expectations of those who do come" (Crary, 1999).

Food and beverage services

Dining options are also limited in Nunavut, and southern staples like fresh milk, eggs and bread are relatively expensive and can even be unavailable in some communities because of the distances they must be shipped. Restaurants are usually located in the hotels, and the choice of dining establishments is limited in any given community. The best option can be "country foods," with local specialities including arctic char, turbot, scallops, Greenland shrimp, caribou, muskox and maktaaq, which is the outer skin and blubber from a whale (*Winnipeg Free Press*, 1998). Again, some visitors (especially vegetarians) may find it difficult to adjust to a northern diet, or to find acceptable alternatives. Consumer choice is also limited by the fact that many small hotels serve meals cafeteria-style and at set times (Nunavut Tourism, 1999). Alcohol regulations pose another restriction on travellers. The high rates of substance abuse prevalent in the region have led some communities to go "dry," either forbidding all consumption of alcohol by locals and visitors alike, or allowing alcoholic beverages to be served only at hotels, or only to hotel guests (Soublière, 1998). The hospitality industry in the Canadian North thus differs significantly from that found in most other tourism destinations around the world.

Visitor reception services

Limited numbers of tourists mean that hospitality services deviate from conventional patterns, and creative responses are often found to overcome local constraints. For instance, a hotel establishment may also serve as an outfitter, restaurant and information centre. Similarly, local Hunter and Trapper Organisations (HTOs) often serve a dual function, providing visitor information as well as resources for hunters and trappers in communities that do not have visitor reception centres (Soublière, 1998). *The Arctic Traveller* cites the Royal Canadian Mounted Police (RCMP) as another potential source of tourist information

(Nunavut Tourism, 1999). Clearly, the industry is structured differently in the North to accommodate travellers to the best of the region's ability, even when the conventional infrastructure is not economically feasible. In some localities, however, it is difficult to provide comparable service in the North. There are few banks or automated teller machines (ATMs), and credit cards are only accepted at major hotels and some stores (*Winnipeg Free Press*, 1998). Furthermore, communications service is not consistent, and some communities do not have pay phones, or telephone service in hotel rooms. Very remote communities or lodges might simply be serviced by a radio telephone service or daily high-frequency radio communications (Nunavut Tourism, 1999). Thus, tourists to the North must plan ahead more than if they were visiting more developed destinations.

Cruises

Given the rudimentary state of tourist amenities in Nunavut, cruises may provide travellers with greater comfort and convenience than land-based travel. The *Nunavut Handbook* (Soublière, 1998) refers to this option as "a kinder, gentler northern experience," but notes that even cruise ships are susceptible to unforeseen contingencies, as was the case in 1996 when a cruise ship ran aground in shallow water. Passenger vessels began to ply the region in 1987, when ice-breaking, ice-strengthened ships travelled routes between Siberia and Greenland, often via Alaska and Canada's Far North (Marsh and Semple, 1995). Since then, cruising has increased in popularity. However, it is an expensive proposition since most cruise excursions last 10 to 14 days, costing an average of $11,000 per person. The most recent addition to the route is The Radisson Seven Seas' *MS Hanseatic*, currently the most luxurious ship in the region.

Tourist attractions

Nunavut's attractions may be identified broadly as nature-based activities and those relating to Inuit culture. While the former are currently the more lucrative, drawing sports enthusiasts and adventurers in search of new challenges, the latter have significant potential for further development, with the growing interest in Aboriginal heritage. Most communities provide opportunities for both types of experiences, and package tours often include both nature-based activities and cultural components.

Nature-based activities

A host of summer and winter sports, as well as various types of wildlife viewing are offered in Nunavut. Traditional activities such as dog-team expeditions, kayaking and igloo-building are complemented by less culturally specific activities such as hiking, cross-country skiing, hunting, fishing and snowmobiling. Because Nunavut is so sparsely settled, tourists may experience "wilderness adventure" no matter where they are staying, and a large variety of excursions are available even out of Iqaluit itself. However, increasing numbers of hunting lodges and "outcamps" provide more complete wilderness experiences (Soublière, 1998).

Parks

Parks and nature reserves constitute significant attractions in Nunavut. In addition to 11 territorial parks, designed primarily for local use (Government of Nunavut, 2000), the region contains a number of wildlife sanctuaries and heritage rivers as well as three national parks, namely Auyuittuq, Quittinirpaaq (Ellesmere Island) and Sirmilik. Significantly, all three were established at the time of Nunavut's creation, although Quittinirpaaq and Auyuittuq had been previously designated as national park reserves (*Canadian Geographic*, 1999). Thus, the very creation of parks in the area draws in significant amounts of money. The boundaries were negotiated in conjunction with the Inuit land claims settlement, and special terms were laid out to ensure Inuit involvement in park management and other benefits to the community through their creation (McNamee, 1999). The federal government has granted six communities a total of $4.4 million to examine park-related economic opportunities and to train locals to participate in park management (*Canadian Geographic*, 1999). The very creation of parks is bringing a significant amount government funding into the area. The parks currently receive an estimated 1,000 visitors per year, and are making a sizeable contribution to eco-tourism in the region. Negotiations are presently underway for two additional national parks in Nunavut (Aubry, 1999).

Heritage sites

The development of heritage attractions is rather more complex than interpreting natural sites, since most Inuit culture is preserved either in archaeological remains or through "living culture." The Fall Caribou Crossing and Arvia'juaq National Historic Sites, both located in the Kivalliq region, highlight some salient issues in the development of northern heritage sites. Situated approximately 75 kilometres south of Baker Lake, Fall Caribou Crossing "commemorates the importance of the fall caribou hunt at water crossings" (Government of Canada, 2000b). While the site is certainly integral to the region's heritage and local outfitters are being encouraged to develop tours that include visits to the site, the average visitor has little reason to go to the actual location, since there is little at the site to identify its significance. Instead, the crossing is interpreted through exhibits at the Inuit Heritage Centre in Baker Lake, and through a Web Site that is being developed (Government of Canada, 2000b). The area has been "chosen to represent [a] significant historic story," but contains few landmarks that would encourage tourists to visit the site itself.

Arvia'juaq, meanwhile, is significant to Inuit culture because it served as a fishing camp for many generations. Oral traditions, archaeological evidence and traditional Inuktitut place names are the main reasons for the site's significance. Again, although the site is commemorated, interpretation takes place at the Margaret Aniksak Visitor Centre in Arviat, as well as over the Internet. Although it seems dubious that the sites themselves will develop into well-frequented tourist attractions, their development preserves Inuit heritage by researching and documenting oral tradition related to them, and injects federal funds into the community through heritage-related cost-sharing agreements and grants (Government of Canada, 2000a). A Geographic Information System (GIS) data base is currently being set up for the region in order to identify and document the cultural significance of these and similar sites.

Community-based cultural attractions

Within the communities, tourists have plenty of opportunities to experience different aspects of Inuit culture. In addition to taking in interpretive centres, visitors are able to "participate" in the local culture by wearing caribou-skin clothing, learning traditional dances or listening to Inuit singing and storytelling (Nunavut Tourism, 1999). Inuit art and crafts may well be the most recognised hallmark of Inuit culture in southern Canada and indeed around the world. Studio visits are often an integral part of touring a community, and most communities offer such experiences since some 1,500 to 2,000 people in Nunavut work as artists, at least part-time (Nunavut Tourism, 1999; Geddes, 1999).

Because much of the heritage component of Nunavut's tourism experience relies on cultural immersion rather than on historic artefacts, unrealistic visitor expectations pose a significant problem in using Inuit heritage as a tourism resource. Ann Meekitjuk Hanson explains: "It has been our experience that some visitors expect us to be historic pieces. They expect us to always be smiling. Their romantic notion is that we still live in snowhouses and have been frozen in time" (Soublière, 1998). Given the widespread stereotypes about the North and the relatively limited knowledge most people have of its contemporary realities, traveller education is essential to ensure a mutually satisfying experience for visitor and host. As yet, residents have not made significant changes to their way of life or communities to accommodate visitor expectations of "authentic" Inuit lifestyles.

Discussion

Nunavut seems poised to embrace tourism as a promising way to develop its economy and improve local infrastructure and services by expanding the user base. The industry contributes to the economy through tourist dollars as well as federal money spent on developing sites and creating parks and other facilities. While capacities remain limited and cannot be expected to grow significantly over the next several years, the territorial government is committed to developing the industry through concerted marketing initiatives and wide-ranging product development. High costs and the very rudimentary tourist amenities remain key deterrents to potential visitors. However, current trends reflect people's growing desire to explore new travel frontiers and journey into little-known regions of the world, whatever the practical obstacles and costs.

Although absolute visitor numbers are small, Margaret Johnston and others have pointed out that issues of capacity and sustainability are already of particular concern in the delicate northern environment (Johnston, 1995). These concerns carry over to the social fabric as well, as commodification of culture poses particular problems for Aboriginal cultures which are often romanticised and otherwise misrepresented in the minds of outsiders. At present, the people of Nunavut are seeking to recapture their traditions, while at the same time rapidly incorporating information technology and other modern conveniences they perceive as beneficial to their way of life. On the one hand, the hunting tradition is enjoying a revival with the Inuit community seeking federal government approval to hunt the giant bowhead whale. Once a staple of the Inuit diet, the bowhead is now making a comeback after being hunted to near extinction in the late 19th century (*Winnipeg Free Press*, 2000). On the other hand, the residents of Nunavut are not prepared to ossify themselves in catering to the tourist's search for "authenticity." Theirs is a living culture that is changing rapidly and which, with continuing increases in visitor numbers, can be expected to change even more quickly as the local population seeks to accommodate them. However, traditional Inuit culture is only part of the "northern experience." The sheer vastness of the territory, its pristine beauty, its unique flora and fauna, the Aurora Borealis, and the sense of difference arising from its remote location will continue to lure the tourist, although in relatively limited numbers. Conversely, Nunavut's remoteness, its harsh environment, the limited number of settlements and the great distances between them, will act as constraints on growth and, one hopes, permit development to occur at sustainable levels.

References

Aubry, Jack (1999), Nunavut's land that never melts to become national park, *Ottawa Citizen*, July 3, p. A1

Canada-Manitoba Economic Development Partnership (1998), Co-ordinated Economic Plan for Manitoba Bilingual Communities to be Funded by Federal-Provincial Funds, *News Release*, September 25.

Canadian Geographic (1999), *National Parks for Nunavut*, 111, (7), p. 17.

Crary, David (1999), Nunavut opens its doors to tourism, *Winnipeg Free Press*, April 3, p. C3.

Geddes, John (1999), *Northern Dawn: The Inuit prepare to embrace self-government with hope, fear and fierce determination*, Maclean's, 112, (7), p. 26.

Government of Canada (2000a), Arvia'juaq National Historic Site, Government of Canada, Canadian Heritage-Parks Canada, National Historic Sites, http://www.newparksnorth.org/arviajua.htm, April 10.

Government of Canada (2000b), Fall Caribou Crossing National Historic Site, Government of Canada, Canadian Heritage-Parks Canada, National Historic Sites, http://www.newparksnorth.org/fall.htm, April 10.

Government of Nunavut (2000), A New Nunavut Parks Program, Government of Nunavut, Department of Sustainable Development, Parks, Trade and Tourism, http://www.newparksnorth.org/newpark.htm, April 10.

Hamelin, L. (1978), *Canadian Nordicity: It's Your North Too*, Harvest House, Montreal.

Johnston, Margaret E.(1995), Patterns and Issues in Arctic and Sub-Arctic Tourism, in C. M. Hall and M. E. Johnston (Editors), *Polar Tourism*, Wiley, Chichester, pp. 27-42.

Kroetsch, Robert (1995), *A Likely Story: The Writing Life*, Red Deer College Press, Red Deer, Alberta.

Lanken, Dave and Mary Vincent (1999), Nunavut Up and Running: On April 1, Canada's youngest population takes control of 'our largest territory, *Canadian Geographic*, January/February, 119, (1), p. 34.

Lundgren, J. O. (1995) The tourism space penetration processes in northern Canada and Scandinavia: a comparison, in C.M. Hall and M.E. Johnston (Editors), *Polar Tourism*, Wiley, Chichester, pp. 43-61.

Lundgren, J. O. (1999), Accessing the Canadian North and Arctic for Tourists-Past to Present, *Téoros*, 18 (2): 44-51.

Marsh, John and Susan Semple (1995), Cruise Tourism in the Canadian Arctic and its Implications, in C.M. Hall and M.E. Johnston (Editors), *Polar Tourism*, Wiley, Chichester, pp. 63-72.

McArthur, Douglas (1999), A Breathtaking Slog: A motley crew of city slickers face down Auyuittuq National Park Reserve, *Globe and Mail*, March 31, p. C6 and p. C4.

McNamee, Kevin (1999), CNF welcomes new Arctic national park, *Nature Canada, Fall*, 28 (4): 4.

Maclean's (1999), *The Birth of Nunavut*, 112 (26): 32.

Marketing Magazine (1999), *Nunavut tentative on tourism push*, 104 (9): 2.

Manitoba Government (2000), Premier to Travel to Nunavut for Signing of Co-operation Agreement, *News Release*, February 20.

Nunavut Tourism (1999), *The Arctic Traveller Nunavut Vacation Planner, in partnership with the government of the Northwest Territories.*

Peryman, Lisa (1997), How to eat seal and other tips: a Nunavut publisher (Nortext Multimedia) offers the last word on arctic travel, *Quill and Quire*, September, 63 (9): 14.

Plog, Stanley C. (1991), *Leisure Travel: Making it a Growth Market ... Again!* Wiley, New York.

Selwood, H. John and John Lehr (1999), Tourism in Manitoba 'North of the Fifty-Third, *Téoros*, 18 (2): 30-36.

Soublière, Marion (1998), *The Nunavut Handbook*, Nortext Multimedia, Iqaluit.

Van Houten, Ben and Ethan Boldt, (1999), Expanding to... Nunavut? *Restaurant Business*, 98 (5): 15.

Winnipeg Free Press (1998), "*Nunavut no Disneyland, guide warns*, August 15, p. C4.

Winnipeg Free Press (2000), *Inuit seek OK to hunt endangered bowhead whale*, March 20.

Winnipeg Sun (1999), *Doer discusses deal to build highway to Nunavut*, November 29.

Travel agencies' perception of students as a viable market

Tekle Shanka

Curtin University of Technology, Australia

Abstract

This paper reports the findings of a survey of 610 travel agencies about their perception of students as a viable market. Results indicate that holiday/leisure travellers are the most significant markets (80%) mainly through international airfare /packaged tour bookings (66%) student market contributes only marginally (< 2%). While the 35-49 year age group contributes 56% for the business student market contribution to the business is less than 3%. According to the results the significance of student markets both at present and in the future is very low (means of 1.9 and 2.4 respectively). The insignificance of student market is attributed mainly to two reasons: students looking for the cheapest possible discounted airfares (37%), and travel agency offices' geographic distances from higher education institutions (21%). Over a third of the respondents (36%) indicated that they do not promote their products to student market specifically. Detailed analysis of the findings and implications to the service providers are presented.

Introduction

Travel agencies play a central role in the marketing of travel and tourism products by serving as both information providers and planning/booking providers for a large share of travellers, particularly in the international context (Oppermann, 1999; Ryan and Cliff, 1997). According to Harris and Howard (1996) travel agencies act as links between suppliers of tourism services with consumers through the provision of reservation, ticketing and other services. They are the front ends of the distribution of travel and tourism business; they meet more of the customers than any other distribution channel and they do more of the selling (Richardson, 1996). As Goeldner, Ritchie and McIntosh (2000) put, travel agencies are experts who are knowledgeable in all aspects of travel and travel opportunities. Travel agencies are considered experts in their field and once the question of getting to a destination becomes a technicality, the agent's most important role is guiding the customer through the emotive decision on where to go (The Economist, 1998). For example, King and Choi (1999) observed that the Korean travel agency sector is a core element of the tourism industry in Korea with the agencies constructing and packaging holiday products and selling predetermined itineraries to Korean consumers. Michie and Sullivan (1990) noted that travel agents can play various roles in their clients' travel decision processes, including the roles of gatekeeper, influencer, and decision maker because of their knowledge of tourism products world-wide (Ross, 1997). Such information is supplied to the travel agency by various tourism authorities of the destinations including the national tourism authorities (Lewis and Meadows, 1995). Travel agencies need to segment their markets and develop marketing strategies targeted towards specific groups of customers (Goldsmith and Litvin, 1999).

This study

The aim of this study was to determine the student market contribution to travel agency businesses. It was also intended to see how travel agencies promote to student market. In this regard the mode/s of promotional mix elements applied by travel agents were investigated.

Methodology

A list of 610 travel agencies in three states, namely, Western Australia, Northern Territory, and South Australia, was generated from the March 1998 Travel talk Directory. An 11-item structured questionnaire with a cover letter and pre-paid, return envelopes was mailed to the 610 addresses in April 1999. A follow-up letter was sent four weeks after the initial mailing. A total of 204 questionnaires (33% of total) were returned. Of these 184 (30% of total) were useable and were analysed. Using SPSS statistical package (version 8.0)

Results and discussion

Of the respondents 50.3% were males, 33% 50 years of age or older, worked in the travel industry for an average of 14.75 years. Table 1 shows the profiles of respondents.

Table 1   Respondents' profiles

	Count	Per cent*
Gender	*179*	*100*
Male	90	50
Female	89	49
Age group	*183*	*100*
<25 years	11	6
25 - 29 years	23	13
30 - 39 years	35	19
40 - 49 years	53	29
50+ years	61	33
No. of years in the travel industry (mean 14.75 years)	*127*	*100*
1 - 5 years	32	25
6 - 10 years	25	20
11 - 15 years	16	13
16 - 20 years	18	14
21+ years	36	28

* Decimal places have been rounded to 1

About 30% mentioned that their business has been running for an average of 16.16 years, 65% of respondents mentioned 'travel agency' as the business they are in, 71% of businesses in Western Australia, 38% of businesses two km. from any higher education institution, average number of full-time and part-time staff being 10.98 and 4.96 respectively. Details are presented in Table 2.

Table 2   Business Profiles

	Count	Per cent*
No. of years business has been running (mean 16.16 years)	*131*	*100*
1 - 5 years	20	15
6 - 10 years	39	30
11 - 15 years	25	19
16 - 20 years	15	12
21+ years		
	32	24
Type of business	*179*	*100*
Travel agency	117	65
Tour operation	35	20
Both	27	15
Business location	*184*	*100*
Western Australia	130	71
Northern Territory	18	10
South Australia	30	16
Other	6	3
Distance from higher education institution	*182*	*100*
<500 m.	16	9
500m. - 1km.	27	15
1km. - 2km.	47	26
2+km.	69	38
No higher education institution nearby	23	12
No. of full-time staff (mean 10.98)	*92*	*100*
One to two	31	34
Three to five	40	43
Six or more	21	23
No. of part-time staff (mean 4.96)	*64*	*100*
One	34	53
Two to three	19	30
Four or more	11	17

* Decimal places have been rounded to 1

Respondents' main products include international packaged tour/holiday bookings and international airfare bookings (66.3%). They cater mainly for holiday/leisure travellers (79.9%) aged between 35 49 years (56%). Student market contributes only 2.7% for the business and its significance is very minimal (1.6%). One-way ANOVA results indicate that there exist significant differences in the percentage contribution of target market and student market as well as in student market significance in the present time and in the future. These differences were noted in relation to business location, staff size (part-time staff), age group of respondents and the number of years business has been in operation. Table 3 shows the ANOVA results.

Table 3   One-way ANOVA results

Respondent variables	Percentage contribution of target market	Percentage contribution of student market	Student market significance today (a)	Student market significance in future (a)
Business location	*57.44 (18.27)*	*9.49 (13.13)*	*1.91 (1.04)*	*2.36 (1.17)*
Western Australia	57.47 (17.32)	8.84 (12.90)	1.86 (1.02)	2.26 (1.08)
Northern Territory	48.59 (22.23)	16.53 (18.10)	2.71 (1.45)	3.29 (1.36)
South Australia	63.07 (18.56)	8.52 (10.83)	1.73 (0.69)	(1.13)
Others	54.67 (18.89)	6.83 (3.76)	1.67 (1.03)	2.67 (1.63)
F-value	**2.345**	**1.888**	**3.961 ***	**4.506***
Part-time staff	*56.22 (19.13)*	*8.00 (12.04)*	*1.77 (0.92)*	*2.20 (1.01)*
One	58.97 (18.33)	10.03 (15.80)	1.85 (1.05)	2.24 (1.07)
Two to three	59.47 (20.67)	5.58 (5.03)	1.53 (0.61)	2.00 (0.82)
Four or more	42.09 (12.77)	6.30 (6.09)	1.91 (0.94)	2.45 (1.13)
F-value	**3.966***	**0.923**	**0.925**	**0.735**
Age group	*57.65 (18.11)*	*9.53 (13.15)*	*1.91 (1.04)*	*2.36 (1.17)*
< 25 years	60.00 (13.33)	9.70 (8.74)	2.27 (1.10)	3.09 (0.94)
25-29 years	55.78 (20.14)	11.43 (14.66)	2.09 (1.16)	2.48 (1.24)
30-39 years	58.43 (17.61)	7.94 (7.08)	2.03 (1.10)	2.71 (1.25)
40-49 years	56.80 (19.66)	11.75 (18.66)	1.89 (1.07)	2.19 (1.04)
50+ years	58.23 (17.37)	7.75 (9.84)	1.74 (0.93)	2.13 (1.16)
F-value	**0.159**	**0.837**	**1.031**	**2.932***
No. of years business has	*54.96 (61.41)*	*6.50 (11.39)*	*1.69 (2.05)*	*2.09 (2.49)*
been operating	55.75 (72.75)	5.75 (28.98)	1.64 (2.98)	2.24 (3.46)
1-5 years	50.58 (61.98)	4.61 (13.07)	1.46 (2.03)	1.97 (2.65)
6-10 years	49.60 (66.40)	3.14 (6.69)	1.42 (2.02)	1.64 (2.44)
11-15 years	47.59 (64.01)	1.74 (7.18)	1.11 (1.82)	1.24 (2.38)
16-20 years	50.47 (65.46)	4.52 (13.27)	1.65 (2.47)	1.91 (2.78)
21+ years	**0.599**	**2.817***	**2.123**	**2.309**
F-value				

Standard deviations are in parentheses.
*Significant at .05 level, **Significant at .01 level.
(a) On a scale of 1 to 5 (1 = not significant at all; 5 = extremely significant).

Percentage contribution of target market

As Table 3 shows percentage contribution of target market was higher in South Australia compared with other states; was higher in relation to the less than 25 years age group and higher in relation to businesses that have been in operation for 1-5 years. However, these differences were not statistically significant. On the other hand, a statistically significant difference was shown in relation to the size of part-time staff (F=3.97) as businesses with one part-time staff showing higher percentage contribution compared with those employing four or more part-time staff.

Percentage contribution of student market

The 1-5 year old businesses showed significantly higher (F=2.817) student market contribution compared with other businesses. Although Northern Territory respondents, respondents with one part-time staff and those aged between 40-49 years showed a higher percentage of student market contribution, it was nevertheless not statistically significant.

Student market significance today

Statistically significant difference (F=3.961) was noted between business locations with the Northern Territory showing significantly higher value. Although businesses with four or more part-time staff, younger respondents (<25 years old), and businesses in their first 5 years of operation or those operating over 20 years have registered slightly higher percentage values these values did not show statistically significant differences.

Student market significance in future

Statistically significant differences were noted in regard to business location and age group of respondents. Northern Territory respondents and those in the age group less than 25 years tend to be more optimistic about student market contribution to the business in the future (F=4.506; F=2.932).

Promotional approaches

While over a third of the respondents mentioned they were not promoting their services to student market specifically, those who did promote the services used a combination of approaches, the major ones being print media such as newspapers, brochures, magazines, direct mail, etc. While tour operators mainly use tourism brochures and the Internet to promote their services to the student market travel agencies on the other hand mainly use major newspapers/community newspapers. Table 4 shows the breakdown of the promotional approaches.

Table 4   Promotional methods used by type of business

Promotional type	Tour Operator	Travel Agency	Both	Total
Major/community newspapers	8 (22.9)	23 (20.0)	6 (22.2)	37 (20.9)
Internet web site	13 (37.1)	14 (12.2)	6 (22.2)	33 (18.6)
Shop front/in-office display	7 (20.0)	16 (13.9)	6 (22.2)	29 (16.4)
Tourism brochures	15 (42.9)	8 (7.0)	2 (7.4)	25 (14.1)
Other publications	8 (22.9)	5 (4.3)	4 (14.8)	17 (9.6)
Other	1 (2.9)	14 (12.2)	0 (0.0)	15 (8.5)
Direct mail	4 (11.4)	7 (6.1)	2 (7.4)	13 (7.3)
TV advertisements	2 (5.7)	7 (6.1)	1 (3.7)	10 (5.6)
Total	35 (19.8)	115 (65.0)	27 (15.3)	177 (100.0)

Percents and totals based on multiple responses.
Figures in parentheses are column percentages.

Respondents from Western and South Australia mainly use major/community newspapers (20.3% and 23.3% respectively) for promotional purposes while those in the Northern Territory mainly use tourism brochures (50.0%) for the purpose. Internet and shop front/in-office display also feature prominently in Northern Territory as can be seen in Table 5.

Table 5   Promotional methods used by business locations

Promotional type	Western Australia	Northern Territory	South Australia	Others	Total
Major/community newspapers	26 (20.3)	4 (22.2)	7 (23.3)	1 (16.7)	38 (20.9)
Internet web site	22 (17.2)	7 (38.9)	4 (13.3)	1 (17.7)	34 (18.7)
Shop front/in-office display	20 (15.6)	7 (38.9)	3 (10.0)	0 (0.0)	30 (16.5)
Tourism brochures	16 (12.5)	9 (50.0)	2 (6.7)	0 (0.0)	27 (14.8)
Other publications	9 (7.0)	6 (33.3)	2 (6.7)	1 (16.7)	18 (9.9)
Other	11 (8.6)	2 (11.1)	3 (10.0)	0 (0.0)	16 (8.8)
Direct mail	10 (7.8)	1 (5.6)	3 (10.0)	0 (0.0)	14 (7.7)
TV advertisements	7 (5.5)	1 (11.1)	1 (3.3)	0 (0.0)	10 (5.5)
Total	128 (70.3)	18 (9.9)	30 (16.5)	6 (3.3)	182 (100.0)

Percents and totals based on multiple responses.
Figures in parentheses are column percentages.

Reasons for not promoting to student market specifically

According to respondents the two main reasons why student market would not be significant at present or in the future were: 'students look for cheap fares', and 'geographic locations of the businesses i.e. Businesses operating far away from where the higher education institutions are located. Other reasons include respondents' main product being up-market products, student market being of low profit, etc. as shown in Table 6.

Table 6   Reasons for Student Market Insignificance (N=87)

Reasons	Percent mentioning
Students look for cheap fares	37.9
Geographic location	21.9
Student market is of low profit	9.3
We provide up-market products	9.2
We Serve repeat clients	8.0
We are corporate travel agency	5.7
We are travel wholesalers	3.5
We offer guided tours	2.3
We are ethnic travel specialist	1.1
Lack of backpacker accommodation and limited public transport	1.1

Implications and conclusion

The findings suggest that travel agencies/tour operators are not keen to attract student market even though currently this market contributes approximately 8% of the business. The perception that 'students look for cheap fares' needs to be addressed. It is true that other market segments would also shop around for cheaper fares. In this context, travel agencies should not discard the student market as unapproachable. Promotional approaches need to be addressed as to how best communicate to the student market. While STAs (student travel agencies) operate on campuses students may not discount the opportunity to compare fares with STA offerings. For this reason travel agencies must be proactive in marketing their offerings to students. One best method growing in popularity is the Internet and as students use the Internet very frequently, it would be a good opportunity for travel agencies to reach this audience via the Internet. As shown in the preceding pages, younger travel agency staff seems to look favourably the future significance of the student market. As this is a positive sign further research in this regard is necessary to come up with a more solid view with bigger sample size from different locations.

References

Goeldner, C. R., Ritchie, J. R. B. and McIntosh, R. W. (2000), *Tourism: Principles, Practices, Philosophies*, 8th edition, John Wiley and Sons, New York.

Goldsmith, R. E. and Litvin, S. W. (1999), Heavy users of travel agents: a segmentation analysis of vacation travellers, *Journal of Travel Research*, (November), 38 (2): 127-133.

Harris, R. and Howard, J. (1996), *Dictionary of Travel, Tourism and Hospitality Terms*, Hospitality Press, Melbourne.

King, B. and Choi, H. J. (1999), Travel industry structure in fast growing but immature outbound markets: the case of Korea to Australia travel, *International Journal of Tourism Research*, (March-April), 1 (2): 111-122.

Lewis, P. G. and Meadows, A. J. (1995), Canadian tourist information and the UK: plans and perceptions, *Tourism Management*, (February), 16 (1): 67-72.

Michie, D. A. and Sullivan, G. L. (1990), The role(s) of the international travel agent in the travel decision process of client families", *Journal of Travel Research*, (Fall), pp.30-38.

Oppermann, M. (1999), Data based marketing by Travel Agents, *Journal of Travel Research*, (February), 37 (3): 231-237.

Richardson, J. I. (1996), *Marketing Australian Travel and Tourism: Principles and Practice*, Hospitality Press, Melbourne.

Ross, G. F. (1997), Travel agent employment perceptions, *Tourism Management*, (February), 18 (1): 9-18.

Ryan, C. and Cliff, A. (1997), Do travel agencies measure up to customer expectations? An empirical investigation of travel agencies' service quality as measured by SERVQUAL, *Journal of Travel and Tourism Marketing*, 6 (2): 1-31.

The Economist (1998), *Vanishing Breed? A Survey of Travel and Tourism* (January 10), p. 9.

Maximising the ticket reve   major sports events

Harry Arne Solberg

South Trøndelag College, Norway

Introduction

The interest for hosting major sports events seems to be growing, and one find several examples where regions and countries spend substantial resources to achieve the most attractive events. Considering the financial experiences, one can regard this growing interest as a paradox. There are many former organising committees which have met severe financial problems and been unable to reach the financial break even. Many events are able to gather a large number of visiting spectators and can therefore be regarded as tourist attractions. It is also well documented that they can be profitable for regions, although one also will find examples which reveals the opposite results (Andersson 1996), (Getz 1992), (Hall 1992), (Crompton 1995), (Gratton, Dobson and Shibli 1999).

However, it is a fact - and often a problem for the organisers - that the tourists spend most of their expenditures "outside" the arenas. Even if the local travel and tourism industry benefit substantially and often is the one which receive the lions share of the visitors expenditures, they are not automatically willing to support the organisers. In fact, the travel and tourism industry often behave as free-riders, and leave to the organisers to achieve the financial revenues which are necessary to cover their costs.

From a regional perspective, such events are beneficial if they lead resources into the region which not would have occurred without the event. The potential organising committees, however, will have to consider whether they will achieve enough financial support to balance their own costs. If this seems unlikely, one cannot expect them to apply for such events, even if they are profitable for the region. Therefore it is obviously a risk that negative financial results may frighten potential future organisers from applying, even if the events are likely to be profitable for the local travel and tourism industry, and/or for the region.

It is also important that the organisers are able economise their activities and achieve the revenues and financial support which are sufficient to cover their costs. Their sale of tickets is one of their sources, and for the organiser it does not matter whether the tickets are sold to locals or to visitors. The purchase of tickets and beverages are the only expenditures that the visitors spend at the arena, and which falls to the organiser. In many cases a considerable the spectators have a very high willingness to pay (hereby called WTP) for the ckets. It is well known that international championships and similar sports events are popular objects among black market agents, who sell tickets. On some occasions, the black-market ticket prices can reach extremely high values. Which, also illustrates that the organisers could have increased their own ticket revenues, if they have improved the price policy.

In many cases, however, the organisers meet several obstacles which complicate this task. International sports events are hosted at different places, and the typical spectators at one event are not necessarily the same as those who attend the following event. Therefore the experiences regarding the spectators WTP for tickets are not always transferable. The ticket sale is often launched several months (in some cases even years) in advance of the event. At such an early stage organisers obviously lack information about the market conditions.

It has become very common that the tickets to sports events are sold as bundles, where the tickets give admittance to several happenings. At team tournaments the bundle may include several matches for specific teams, or several matches that are played in the same arena - on the same day. Bundling is generally a profitable price-strategy in cases when the products being bundled are negatively correlated in demand. In other words: when consumers who have a very high willingness to pay for good 1 have a low willingness to pay for good 2. Such circumstances are common at many sports events. Many spectators are mainly interested in watching their "own" team, such as their national teams, or club teams from their own country or region.

This paper is divided in two sections. The first one presents the general principles for the bundling strategy. It will illustrate how organisers of sports events can use it in their sale of tickets at sports events, and how it can increase their revenues. The purpose is to clarify under which circumstances bundling is more profitable than individual sale. The paper will only focus on the case when the bundle consists of tickets to the subsequent matches which are played in the same arena, and on the same day. There will also be presented some figures which illustrate the different scenarios.

The second section is a case study, based on empirical data from the World Championship in Ice hockey, which was hosted in Norway, May 1999. It will use the framework which is presented in the first section, and analyse whether bundling was able to increase the ticket revenues, compared to individual ticket sales. The analysis is based on surveys where the spectators were asked for their maximum WTP for tickets, for the two matches the day they were interviewed. The organiser based their ticket sale completely on the bundling principle, and did not sell tickets for individual matches, except for the very last day when there was only one match played (the second leg of the final).

Bundling – some general theory

Broadly defined, bundling is the practice of marketing two or more goods in a single "package" at a special price (Guiltinan 1987). Firms often sell their goods in packages: sporting and cultural organisations offer season tickets, restaurants provide complete dinners, and tour-operators offer package-tours including transport and overnight stays. Bundling makes sense when customers have heterogeneous demand, and when the firm cannot price discriminate. In general, the effectiveness of bundling depends on how negatively correlated demands are. In other words, it works best when consumers who have a high reservation price[1] for good 1 have a low reservation price for good 2, and vice versa. If the demands are positively correlated, bundling will not be profitable, and firms will earn the same profit by selling the goods separately.

The profitability of bundling comes from extracting the *consumer surplus*. If the goods are independent in demand, some customers who would buy only one of the products if they were priced individually, may buy both if the goods are bundled together. The reason is that the value these customers attach to one good is so much higher than its price that the combined value of the two goods exceeds the bundled price. In economic terminology, the consumer surplus from the highly valued good is transferred to the less valued good. In fact, the basic economic rationale for the success of bundling relies on this transfer of consumer surplus.

From a managerial perspective, the rationale for bundling is based on two realities. First, the cost structure is characterised by a high ratio of fixed to variable costs and by a high degree of cost sharing. This means that the same facilities, equipment, and personnel are used to provide multiple services (Dearden 1978). Second, the goods offered are generally interdependent in terms of demand. The customers are often potential buyers of a range of goods from the same supplier. The effectiveness of price bundling, then, appears to be a function of the degree in which it stimulates demand in a way that achieves cost economies.

In general the seller may have two aims. The first is to stimulate customers of one good to buy more of the other goods, and vice versa. The second is attracting new customers, which means customers that initially bought neither of the goods.

A firm that sells goods only in package form has adopted a *pure* bundling strategy. Firms that sell the same goods separately as well as in packages has adopted a *mixed* bundling strategy. Mixed bundling is often the ideal strategy when the demand from different segments are only somewhat negatively correlated, and/or when marginal production costs are nil. Mixed bundling strategy includes two alternatives. In *mixed-leader* bundling, the price of one of the two products is discounted when the other product is purchased at the regular price. That is, given P_1 and P_2 (the ordinary market prices), customers can only buy good 1 at P_{1*} (where $P_1 > P_{1*}$) if good 2 is purchased at P_2. Such a strategy is proper if one of the goods is significantly more popular (in terms of WTP), than the other. Usually it is the popular good which is discounted. In the *mixed-joint* form, a single price P_B is set when the two products are purchased jointly (where $P_B < P_1 + P_2$). This strategy is usually profitable if the popularity of the goods is approximately equal.

Let us look at an example which illustrates how bundling can be used at the ticket sale at sport events. We imagine the following assumptions are present:

- There are two matches which are played on the same day (M_1 and M_2) and on the same arena. The second match follows subsequently after the first match. However, it is possible to remove all the spectators in the first match from the stands, and let in a totally different group to the second match.

- There are five groups of spectators. Each or the four teams have their own supporters, and there is a group of neutral spectators. It is assumed that the spectators within each of the groups have identical reservation prices, which means their WTP for tickets is equal.

- The potential spectators will attend matches where their reservation prices equal, or exceed the market prices.

- Ordinary price discrimination is out of the question, and the organiser is obliged to set (only) one price for each match (or bundle).

- The spectators' utility from watching the separate matches is independent of each other. If they attend one match, it will not influence their reservation price for the other match.

- For the organiser, the costs are invariant of the matches.

Variables:

S_1 = supporters of one of the two teams playing in the first match

S_2 = supporters of one of the two teams playing in the second match

N = neutral spectators

P_1 = market price at match 1

P_2 = market price at match 2

P_B = price on bundle

R_1 = reservation price at match 1

R_2 = reservation price at match 2

An organiser which maximises the ticket revenues will consider the following three alternatives:

1. Setting a single price for each of the matches separately, hereby called the *pure component* strategy (PC). This is the same as traditionally monopoly pricing.

2. Offer the two matches for sale only in a package, and at a price P_B. This is known as *pure bundling* strategy (PB).

3. Combine strategy 1 and 2 and offer each match separately, or a package of both, at a set of prices (P_1, P_2, P_B). This is known as *mixed bundling* strategy (MB).

The figures 1-3 illustrate the three alternatives. In all of them it is assumed that the potential spectators will by a ticket if the reservation price(s) (at lest) equals the market price. This means M_1 is bought if $R_1 \geq P_1$, M_2 if $R_2 \geq P_2$, M_1 plus M_2 if $R_B \geq P_B$. This means that one will buy if the market prices equals equal or are higher than their reservation prices. If this assumption does not hold, the seller can solve the problem by offering the tickets slightly below the reservation prices (99,95 instead of 100).

In *figure 1*, spectators with reservation prices below P_1 and P_2 will not by ticket for any of the matches. Those with $R_1 \geq P_1$ and $R_2 < P_2$ will attend the first match but not the second, while those with $R_2 \geq P_2$ and $R_1 < P_1$ only will attend the second match. Those with $R_1 \geq P_1$ and $R_2 \geq P_2$ will attend both matches. *Figure 2* illustrates a situation where the tickets only are offered in bundles. The spectators will have to buy a ticket for both matches, even if they only are interested in one of them. *Figure 3* presents the mixed bundle alternative. Individuals in the south-west region of the "P_2cdP_1" will not attend any of the matches. Their reservation prices are all below the market prices, $R_1 < P_1$, $R_2 < R_2$, and $R_B < P_B$. Individuals in the south-east region of "P_1de" will attend the first match, but not the second. For them, $R_1 \geq P_1$ and $R_2 < (P_B - P_1)$. The equation in the bracket represents the implicit price of match two for an individual who already is prepared to buy a ticket for match one. Individuals in the north-west region of "P_2ca" will only attend the second match, but not the first one. Individuals in the region north-east of "$acde$", or on the curve, will attend both matches. For them, $(R_1 + R_2) \geq P_B$, $R_1 \geq (P_B - P_2)$ and $R_2 \geq (P_B - P_1)$. The bundle is consumed not only by those who derive a positive consumer surplus from watching both matches, but also by those who derive a larger consumer surplus from the bundle, $(R_B - P_B)$, than from purchasing either matches separately, $(R_1 - P_1 + R_2 - P_2)$.

An organiser that aims to maximise the income, will choose among these alternatives by calculating the most remunerative configuration of prices under each strategy and then compare the resulting net-income from the different alternatives. The relative profitability of the three strategies depends on the distribution of potential spectators in the reservation price space.

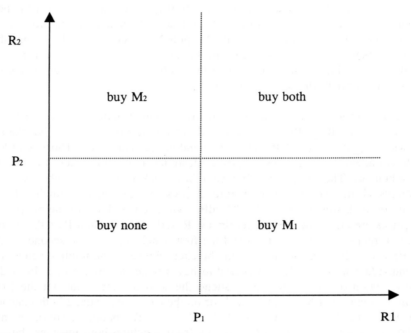

Figure 1   Reservation prices

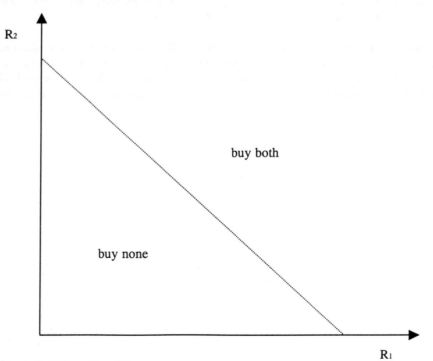

Figure 2   Pure bundling

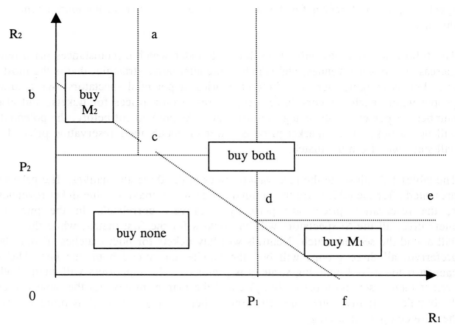

Figure 3   Mixed bundling

Pure bundling will always be the optimal strategy which maximises the revenues when the reservation prices are perfect negatively correlated. In such cases, the mixed bundling strategy is able to equal the revenues, assuming the spectators prefer bundles instead of tickets to separate matches.

In many cases the reservation prices are not perfectly negatively correlated. This can make the mixed bundling strategy more profitable than the pure bundling strategy. In Fig. 3, people who have reservation prices in the P_2cb and P_1fd areas will not by tickets if they only are offered bundles. If the seller uses a mixed bundling strategy, those which have reservation prices in the P_2cb area, will buy M_2, while those with reservation prices in the P_1fd area will buy M_1.

The preference structure which is described above, is common at many sport events. Team-tournaments, e.g. international championships, usually contain several matches. Very often there are several matches/competitions on the same day in the same arena, which follow sequentially. For the organisers, the variable (and marginal) costs related to the hosting of the matches are often low, and the costs are usually independent of the matches. It is very common that a major part of the staff consist of volunteers who are working for free.

It is a well-known phenomenon that many spectators mainly are interested in watching their own teams. Some of them are willing to spend considerable amount of money on following their favourites, but their WTP for watching the other teams is usually substantially lower. There are also those who are mainly interested in watching good sports and/or exciting matches. Such spectators tend to prefer the most exciting teams, e.g. Brazil in soccer and US (dream-team) in basketball. Another pattern, which also very is common among the spectators, are preferences for the matches in the second part of the tournaments – especially the finals.

The following examples will try to illustrate under which circumstances price bundling can increase the ticket revenues, and which of the alternative strategies that is the most profitable one. Let us imagine there are three categories of potential spectators. We assume that the people within each category have identical reservation prices for tickets, and also that the numbers of persons in the categories are equal. As pointed out before, the potential spectator will buy a ticket if the market price is lower or equals their reservation price. If not, they will stay away from the match.

The tables 1-3, illustrate the reservation prices in the three alternatives. The prices which are presented after the tables, are the optimal prices which maximise the ticket revenues. In table 1, the reservation prices are perfectly negatively correlated. In the pure component alternative, all the S_1 spectators will buy tickets for the first match, while the S_2 supporters will attend the second match. Neutrals will buy tickets for both matches. If pure bundling is preferred, all three groups will buy the bundle and attend both matches. The same will happen if the mixed bundling strategy is preferred. The supporters will attend both matches even if their reservation prices (only) equal the market prices. As the table reveal, both of the bundle alternatives give the organiser higher revenues, as well as more spectators, than the pure component strategy.

Table 1   Perfect negative correlation in WTP

	S_1	N	S_2
R_1	90	50	10
R_2	10	50	90
Aggregate	100	100	100

Pure component strategy: $P_1 = 50$ and $P_2 = 50$, $=> TR = 4*50 = 200$

Pure bundling strategy: $P_B = 100 => TR = 3*100 = 300$

Mixed bundling strategy: $P_1 = 90$ and $P_2 = 90$ or $P_B = 100 => 3*100 = 300$

In table 2 the reservation prices are not perfectly negatively correlated any more. Neutrals now have a lower WTP compared to the first example, while the other two groups are identical. If the pure component strategy is preferred, the S_1 supporters will buy M_1, while the S_2 supporters will buy M_2. The neutral spectators will stay away from both matches. The bundling alternatives give the same result, namely that both the supporter-groups buy bundles while the neutrals will stay away. This example illustrates the risk for few spectators on the stands.

There is obviously a risk that supporters may only attend the matches which include their favourite teams. Their choices are likely to be influenced by the alternative ways of spending the time on the places where the events are hosted? One should not expect the visiting spectators to find the "other matches" tempting if the local travel and tourism industry offers them a number of attractive alternatives. In such cases, the travel and tourism industry may represent a further obstacle for the organiser, in their efforts to achieve the necessary financial revenues.

Table 2   Neutrals are less interested

	S_1	N	S_2
R_1	90	30	10
R_2	10	30	90
Aggregate	100	60	100

Pure component strategy: $P_1 = 90$ and $P_2 = 90$, $=> TR = 2*90 = 180$

Pure bundling strategy: $P_B = 100 => TR = 2*100 = 200$

Mixed bundling strategy: $P_1 = 90$ and $P_2 = 90$ or $P_B = 100 => TR = 2*100 = 200$

Table 3 illustrates a situation where the neutrals are more eager to attend, compared to previous two alternatives. Their aggregate WTP is now higher than the supporters. In the pure component case, the S_1 spectators will buy M_1, while the S_2 supporters buy M_2. The neutral spectators will attend both matches. In the pure bundling strategy all, the three groups will prefer bundles. The optimal bundle price is 100, and the neutral spectators will therefore obtain an aggregate consumer surplus of 40. Mixed bundling turns out as the optimal strategy which maximises the ticket revenues. In this alternative the S_1 spectators will only buy M_1, while S_2 spectators only will buy M_2. The neutrals will buy the bundle. The mixed bundling alternative leaves the spectator with no consumer surplus.

So far we have assumed the size on the groups to be equal. Whether this is a realistic assumption will vary from match to match, and from event to event. In some cases it may correspond very well with the realities, while it can be very unrealistic in other cases. At certain events the organisers may have to consider the matches individually, and make separate predictions regarding the expected number of spectators. It is likely that local spectators will dominate on a total basis, due to significantly lower travel costs. On the other hand all locals are not necessarily interested in watching teams from other nations. Therefore (only some) few of them may attend the matches between neutral teams, unless the visiting teams have a reputation for being very exciting or of extreme good quality. One must also bear in mind that the most popular international championships are able to gather a large number of visiting supporters. Especially from the neighbour countries, if the sport is popular here. Information about these and similar circumstances, can be extremely important when the organisers try to predict the number of locals and visitors that will attend.

Table 3   Neutrals have a higher WTP

	S_1	N	S_2
R_1	90	70	10
R_2	10	70	90
Aggregate	100	140	100

Pure component strategy: $P_1 = 70$ and $P_2 = 70$, $=> TR = 4*70 = 280$

Pure bundling strategy: $P_B = 100 => TR = 3*100 = 300$

Mixed bundling strategy: $P_1 = 90$ and $P_2 = 90$ or $P_B = 140 => $ Income $= 320$

The bundling strategies turned out as more profitable than the pure component strategy in all the three alternatives. Pure bundling maximised the revenues when the reservation prices were perfectly negatively correlated. Mixed bundling was most profitable when there were many neutral spectators, assuming these had a higher aggregate WTP for both matches than the supporters. The bundling strategies gave the same result in the case when the neutrals had lower aggregate WTP than the supporters.

The example in table 2 presented a situation where the supporters outnumbered the neutral spectators. Therefore the most profitable price policy required bundling prices above the reservation prices for the neutral spectators. However, if the neutral spectators have been in majority, this may not have been the most profitable strategy. If so, the optimal bundle price (P_B) may be 60.

The examples also illustrated the conflict between the maximising of revenues and the maximising of spectators. There is a risk that neutral spectators may find the prices to expensive, especially if the pure bundling strategy is preferred, assuming a large number of supporters have a extreme high WTP for matches were their favourite teams are involved. The maximising of the ticket revenues may require expensive prices, depending on the price elasticity.

On the other hand, the maximising of spectators requires cheaper prices. In many cases the organisers earn the majority of their revenues from other sources, such as sponsorship deals or by selling TV-rights. It is likely that both the latter two sources are positively correlated with the number of spectators. Sponsors want maximum reach, both on the stands and in terms of TV-viewers. The TV-channels will prefer crowded audience, which makes the programs more attractive as viewing objects. Such circumstances can motivate the organisers to lower the prices in order to increase the revenues from other sources. The maximising of their total revenues logically requires that the marginal revenues from the different sources equal each other.

Misjudging the reservation prices

Many organisers find it difficult to decide the optimal prices which maximise the ticket revenues. It requires substantial information to find the exact reservation prices for the various groups of spectators. For events such as international championships which move from place to place, the experiences at one occasion are not necessarily relevant if the next event takes place under different circumstances. The spectators which attend a world championship in Japan, can be quite different from those who attend the championship next year in Scandinavia. The organiser will have to make several guesses when they try to predict the number of spectators and/or their WTP for tickets. Therefore it is likely that they also make some mistakes and misjudge the WTP, at least for some of the categories of spectators. To illustrate the consequences, let us imagine that the organiser anticipate the supporters are more interested in the matches which not include their own team, than they really are. Let us assume that their real WTP for these matches is 5 and not 10. This means that the supporters real aggregate WTP is 95, and not 100. If the pure bundling strategy is preferred and the organiser predict the aggregate WTP to be 100, the consequences will be catastrophic. There will, in fact, be no spectators in alternative 1 and 3, as also the supporters will find the prices too expensive. There will only be neutral spectators in alternative 2. The total ticket revenues will be reduced by 200 in all the three alternatives. Such misjudges can also cause substantial consequences for the local travel industry if the number of visiting spectators is reduced.

The negative impact are of less importance in mixed bundling strategy scenario. Here the S_1 spectators will still attend the first match, while the S_2 supporters still will attend the second. The revenues will now only be reduced by 20. This example illustrates a severe disadvantage with the pure bundling strategy, namely that one mistake may "damage" the demand for both products. To allow for individual sales, in addition to offer bundles, is thereby a way the organisers can reduce the risk.

The quality on the matches, at such tournaments, does often vary substantially. Some may be very good, while others are (very) poor, even in world championships. Spectators from the "best" countries may have plenty of opportunities to watch matches of good quality in their domestic leagues at home. Therefore they may not find the matches between secondly rated teams attractive. One should not expect them to have a high WTP for watching the matches that not include their own country. The spectators from the secondly rated countries may have other preferences. For them, the championship also represents a rear opportunity to watch sport of good quality, in addition to the possibility to follow their own team.

A case study of the bundling strategy from the world championship in Ice-hockey in 1999

The last section is a case study from the World Championship in ice-hockey in 1999, which was hosted in Norway. It is an empirical analysis of the issues which was illustrated in the first section, based on interviews with the spectators.

Methods

The survey achieved totally 1413 interviews. Of these were 1027 carried out at the arena, while 396 were follow-up interviews via phone, one to two months after the event. There were established routines during the arena interviews in order to achieve random samples during the specific days, but not on overall basis. This means that the proportion of spectators at the different rounds were not 100 % reflected in the interviews. Neither did the interviews reflect the geographical distribution of spectators 100 %. The arena interviews were very short. The questionnaires concentrated on some few background variables, and in addition the respondents were also asked about their WTP for ticket to the separate matches, on the day when the interview took place. These questions were constructed as "open-end" questions, based on the contingent evaluation method (Mitchell & Carson 1989). The method corresponded with the sale-strategy used by the organiser. Practically all the tickets were sold as bundles, in packages which consisted of the two matches at the same arena on the same day. The follow-up interviews focused on further background variables. In addition there were questions related to other issues than the WTP, such as the interest for sport and ice-hockey, the expenditures during the championship (only for visiting spectators), and also whether their financed their own expenditures (including tickets) or not. The analysis, which is presented in the following sequence, is based on the WTP answers from the arena-interviews, while the background variables came from both surveys.

Results

Table 4 present the spectators aggregate WTP for the two matches on the day the interview took place. The statistical analyses revealed that people were significantly more interested in watching their own countries – in terms of WTP (no big surprise). People also became more interested as the tournament continued to the second round, and later to the semi-finals and finals. The exception was the second round matches between the teams that became 3rd. or 4th. in the preliminary round (hereby called B-countries). The supporters were significantly less interested in these matches, which decided the ranking from 9-16 in the tournament, compared to the matches these countries played in the preliminary rounds.

Table 4   Aggregate WTP for tickets to the two matches at the interview

	Preliminary round	Second round	Final round
25 % quartile:	150	209	300
50 % " :	350	415	600
75 % " :	515	650	1000
Mean:	398	503	864

Table 5 shows the distribution between supporters and neutral spectators at the three stages in the tournament, based on data from the interviews. Supporters are here defined as spectators who had their own country playing in one of the two matches. Neutrals were the spectators who did not have their country playing in the arena, on the day they were interviewed, as well as spectators from countries that did not participate in the tournament.

Table 5   Distribution - supporters vs. neutral spectators

	Preliminary round	Second round	Final round
Supporters:	72	47	77
Neutrals:	28	53	23

Table 6 shows the average willingness to pay for the different rounds. "The other match" is defined as the match before or after the one which included their own country. The finals include the semi-finals (four matches), bronze final (one match) and the gold finals (two matches). The table illustrates that the WTP-ratios between "own match-other match-neutral match" were quite stable in the three rounds. We also see that the WTP increased from the preliminary round to the second round, and further to the finals. The strongest WTP-increase found place between the second round and the final round, both nominally and relatively.

Table 6   Average WTP – individual matches - different rounds

	Preliminary round	Second round	Finals
Match including own team	328	434	639
The other match	100	129	189
Neutral match	177	222	392

Was bundling the optimal price setting strategy?

The following sequence will analyse whether the market condition were in favour of bundling. Which price strategy gave the highest revenues – bundling or the pure component strategy? The analysis is based on the same framework as in the previous section which presented the examples. The spectators within the respective groups are assumed to have the identical reservation prices. This means that all the spectators within a group would buy a ticket if their reservation prices equalled or were higher than the market prices. If the market prices were set higher than the reservation prices, no one in the group would buy a ticket. If they were set lower, everybody would buy. This means that the there were no ordinary demand curves. The mean values are used as reservation prices, which is a very dramatic (and unrealistic) assumption. Such a strong assumption did obviously correspond with the data, as these revealed ordinary downward sloping demand curves. However, the main aim of this analysis was to investigate whether the bundling were able to increase the ticket revenues, compared to the separate sale of single matches. From such a perspective, the assumption can be defended.

The following presentations contain some adjustments which not correspond with the pattern that was found in the surveys. These adjustments are made for pedagogical reasons and they should lead to results which can cause some misunderstandings. Firstly, the size on the two groups (fans and neutrals) are adjusted, compared with the original distribution. In the preliminary round and the final rounds, the ratio is set to75/25, while the surveys showed 72/28 and 77/23. In the preliminary round a 50/50 is assumed, while the surveys showed 47/53. Secondly, it is also assumed a perfectly inverse relationship for the reservation prices in mach one and two for the two groups of supporters. The same assumption also applied the two groups of supporters in the same match. The ratio between the supporters in the first and second match were not as the tables present. The size of the supporter groups varied substantially between the matches, depending on which teams were playing. Norway, Sweden and Finland had the largest number of supporters, and the matches including these teams gathered more supporters than the other matches.

Pure bundling and mixed bundling turned out to be the most profitable strategies in the preliminary round, as the figures in table 7 presents. The neutral spectators would have been displaced as their reservation prices were below the optimal market price. If the bundling prices were reduced to 314, it would have reduced the revenues to 1256. It is worth to note that this would increased number of spectators as also the neutrals would have attended. There was no point in reducing the bundle prices to 314 in the mixed bundling scenario, as this would have led all the supporters to buy bundles for 314, instead of individual matches for 328. The pure component strategy would have resulted in less income and fewer spectators, as only 3 of the 8 groups would have attended the matches. The neutrals would have stayed away, and the supporters not would have bought tickets to "the other match".

The pure bundling strategy was adopted by the organisers during the event, and it caused some controversies in the preliminary round. According to some newspapers, several potential spectators found the prices to expensive and went home instead of buying the bundles which would have given them admittance to the Norwegian matches.

Table 7   Reservation prices - preliminary round

	S_1	S_1	S_2	N
R_1	328	328	100	157
R_2	100	100	328	157
Aggregate	428	428	428	314

Pure component (PC): $P_1 = P_2 = 328 => TR = 3*328 = 984$

Pure bundling (PB): $P_B = 428 => TR = 3*428 = 1284$

Mixed bundling (MB): $P_1 = P_2 = 328, P_B = 428$, TR(total revenues) $= 3*428 = 1284$

The matches in the second round gathered a larger part of neutral spectators than the other matches. One reason may have been that spectators from B-countries preferred matches of good quality instead of following their own teams playing for the places from 9 to 16. This applied the home team supporters since Norway became 3 rd. in their preliminary group. The surveys revealed that the spectators from A-countries (teams which qualified from the preliminary round) had significantly higher WTP for watching their own teams than the spectators from B-countries, as it is illustrated in table 8. On the other hand, spectators from A-countries were less interested in watching "the other match" and "neutral matches", compared with the spectators from B-countries in the preliminary round. It is worth to note that as much as 53 % of the spectators from A-countries were not willing to pay at all for watching "the other match" in the preliminary round. As pointed out before, the quality of the matches in this tournament varied significantly, even in a World Championship. Many of the A-countries have national leagues of very good quality. Therefore the spectators from these countries may not find the matches between B-countries interesting. Visitors from B-countries may have gone to the championship with a different attitude. For them the championship also represented a rare opportunity to watch sport of quality. The spectators from B-countries seemed to have lost much of their interest for watching "the other match" in the second round. The teams which became 3rd. or 4th. in the preliminary round were packed together in the following matches, and therefore the "other" matches in this round did not include the most attractive teams.

Table 8   Aggregate WTP – spectators from A and B-countries (mean value)

	Preliminary round		Second round		Final round	
	A-country	B-country	A-country	B-country	A-country	B-country
Own country + the other match	436	425	580	227	828	-
Neutral matches	354	301	505	432	511	376

The prices in table 9 would have led the supporters to buy bundles instead of separate matches. This would have left them with an aggregate consumer surplus on 2*119 = 238. It is also worth noting that all the matches would have been sold out in both of the bundling alternatives.

Table 9   Reservation prices – second round

	S	N	N	S
R$_1$	434	222	222	129
R$_2$	129	222	222	434
Aggregate	563	444	444	563

Pure component: $P_1 = P_2 = 222 => TR = 6*222 = 1332$

Pure bundling: $P_B = 444 => TR = 4*444 = 1776$

Mixed bundling: $P_1 = P_2 = 434, P_B = 444 => TR = 4*444 = 1776$

The bundling strategies turned out as the most profitable alternatives also in the final rounds. The optimal price strategy would have displaced the neutrals, as these would have found the price too expensive and preferred to stay away. The pattern and results in this round were practically identical with the preliminary round. A bundle price on 606 would have reduced the revenues slightly. On the other hand it would have increased the number of spectators, as also the neutral would have attended.

Table 10   Reservation prices – final round

	S_1	S_1	S_2	N
R_1	639	639	189	303
R_2	189	189	639	303
Aggregate	828	828	828	606

Pure component: $P_1 = P_2 = 639 => TR = 3*639 = 1917$

Pure bundling: $P_B = 828 => TR = 3*828 = 2484$

Mixed bundling: $P_1 = P_2 = 639, P_B = 828 => TR = 3*828 = 2484$

Invited spectators

Nowadays it has become common that firms and similar organisations invite each other as guests to popular sport events as a method of cultivating their business relations. The surveys revealed that the phenomenon also was present at this championship. According to our material, 72,4 % of the spectators paid for their own tickets (also including children who received the tickets from their parents, as well as those who got tickets from friends), while 27,6 % where sponsored by firms/organisations. The surveys revealed that those who paid for their own tickets had significantly higher WTP for their own teams than those who were invited. This difference was not found for "the other match" or for the neutral matches. The survey also revealed other differences between the two categories. While those who paid for the tickets them selves increased their personal WTP in the second round and in the finals, this pattern was not found among the invited guests. Their willingness to pay hardly increased at all. The surveys also revealed that the sponsored guests were less interested in the sport, and that they saw fewer matches during the championship, compared with those who paid for their own tickets.

Discussion – some methodological considerations

The assumption of equal reservation prices in the respective groups can be regarded as controversial. It was a very strong simplification, and the surveys revealed that the spectators within the various categories were not "that" heterogeneous. In fact the demand curves showed the downward sloping pattern. This means that there was no common reservation price which made *all in the groups* withdraw from the market (except from the maximum WTP). The number of potential spectators would have been reduced gradually if the prices were increased. This is the normal "procedure" almost in all markets, as well as in most market segments. It is in fact very unusual that all (or the majority) within a market segment have the same reservation price, and drop out collectively if the market price increase above a certain level. Alternatively the spectators could have been split in more groups which also were more homogenous. The disadvantage is that such an analysis would not have given more information for the organisers, probably the opposite. The mean WTP value should only be regarded as an indication on the reservation prices within the groups.

However, the mean value is not necessarily the best variable. In fact there are arguments for preferring one of the percentiles instead of the mean. A potential weakness is that it may be considerable influenced by extreme values. Some few high extreme values are able to cause a substantial skewed distribution. In fact the data revealed some skewed distribution, as some spectators revealed extreme high WTP-values. This pattern especially appeared in the final rounds. In that way it does not necessarily reflect the WTP for the majority in the sample. The quarter percentiles (25, 50 or 75), can therefore be regarded as alternatives.

On the other hand, table 11 illustrates that the aggregate WTP ratio between "the match including own team + the other match" and "two neutral matches" are mainly the same for percentiles as well as for the mean values. The supporters had higher aggregate WTP (for both matches) than the neutrals had for two matches. Roughly the ratio were not influenced by which of the variables one used in the analysis. Consequently, the results would roughly have been the same if one of the percentiles had been used instead of the mean value.

Table 11   Willingness to pay – distribution quarter percentiles

	Preliminary round			Second round			Final round		
	25 %	50 %	75 %	25 %	50 %	75 %	25 %	50 %	75 %
Own team + the other match:	250	400	515	300	500	700	302	516	888
Two neutral matches:	150	280	400	250	400	550	138	250	550

Organisers of such event will have to consider which of the classification alternatives that are the most convenient when they decide the price policy. In this analysis the categorisation was very roughly, as it only differed between the three rounds. An optimal price policy which had maximised the ticket revenues, would probably have required separate prices for the different matches. Teams from countries "near by" are more likely to have a large group of supporters, while teams from "far away" likely will have few supporters. This pattern was also at this championship. The majority of spectators came from the Nordic countries. Sweden and Finland dominated the group of foreigners, while there were few spectators from Russia, Czech, Slovakia, Canada and US, which all had teams of good quality.

There are some additional methodological assumptions which need a comment. The prices at the championship differed, and most matches had three alternatives. Such circumstances were not taken care of in the analysis, as the spectators were asked for "one WTP", and not for their eventually various WTP at the different places in the arena. This simplification should not be regarded as a severe weakness at this championship. Two of the arenas had a capacity on 5000 spectators, while the capacity in the arena where the final round was played were on 10000. On such smaller arenas the quality between the different seats should not be considerable, especially at the first two arenas. At larger arenas, however, such concerns may be of bigger importance.

There will usually be some special uncertainties related to the matches after the preliminary round. In major tournaments the teams are moved from place to place, and knock-out competitions the spectators will not know where their team will play until shortly before the matches. The teams which win their group, may be allowed to continue to play their matches at the same arena, while those that become second, may have to move to another arena (and sometimes to a different part of the country). Such circumstances can reduce the spectators' willingness to travel to the tournament, or motivate them to attend fewer matches than they would have done if it was easier to predict. It also makes it more difficult for the organiser to predict the demand for tickets.

Conclusions

The results from the WC-surveys revealed that the bundling alternatives were more profitable and increased the ticket revenues in all the three rounds, compared to individual sale of tickets. The bundling alternatives also gathered more spectators. Mixed bundling will generally be more profitable when there is a large group of neutral spectators, and if these have a higher aggregate WTP than the supporters. Table 3, earlier in the paper illustrated, such a case. This could have been the case in the final rounds if countries such as Russia, Canada and US had reached the finals. If so, there would obviously have been more neutral spectators at the last matches, which could have made mixed bundling the most profitable strategy.

As this paper have shown, the organisers of such events meet several difficulties in their efforts to establish the price policy which maximise the ticket revenues. This may even require a separate price policy for each of the teams. If this is carried out 100 %, it is likely to cause controversies among the spectators. The organisers may have to balance the financial benefits up against the potential negative attitudes, which are likely to emerge among the spectators.

Endnotes

1. The maximum price a potential customer is willing to pay for a specific good.

References

Adams, William J. and. Yellen, Janet L (1976), "Commodity Bundling and the Burden of Monopoly", *Quarterly Journal of Economics*, 90 (August), 475-498.

Andersson, Tommy (1996), "Vem vann på VM? Effektivitet og fordelingseffekter av evenemang" I *"EVENEMANG - Affärsmöilighet och imageskapare - DOKUMENTATION.* Gøteborgs Universitetet.

Dearden, John (1978), Cost Accounting Comes to Service Industries, *"Harvard Business Review"*, 56 (September-October) 132-140.

Crompton, John L. (1995), Economic Impact Analysis of Sports Facilities and Events: Eleven Sources of Misapplication. *Journal of Sport Management*, 1995, 9, pp. 14-35.

Getz, Donald (1995), "Event Tourism - evaluating the Impacts", *Travel, Tourism and hospitality research*, John Wiley and Sons, Inc.

Getz, Donald (1992), *"Festivals, Special Events, and Tourism"*, Von Nostrand, New York.

Gratton, Chris, Dobson, Nigel and Shibli, Simon (1999), The economic importance of major sports events: a case-study of six events. *Managing Leisure* 4, 1-12, (1999).

Guiltinan, Joseph P. (1987), The Price Bundling of Services: A Normative Framework. *Journal of Marketing*, April 1987, Volume 51, Number 2.

Hall, C. M. (1992), *"Hallmark Tourist Events"*, Bellhaven Press, London.

Mitchell, Robert Cameron, Carson, Richard T. (1989), *"Using Surveys to Value Public Goods: The Contigent Valuation Method.*

Rubinfield, Robert S., and Pindyck, Daniel L. (1995), Microeconomics. Fourth edition. Prentice Hall. New Jersey.

The growth and trends of conference centres: A case study of the UK

Julie Spiller and Adele Ladkin

Bournemouth University, UK

Introduction

The meetings incentives conferences and exhibitions (MICE) sector of the tourism industry has experienced tremendous growth throughout the world, with many cities having already invested in major MICE facilities. The first conference cited was held in 1896 in Detroit, Michigan when a group of businessmen first realised the economic value of hosting meetings (Gartell, 1991). However the growth of the MICE industry throughout the world did not occur until much later. In 1959 the Pollizer Committee enquiry investigated the lack of quality exhibition venues in Britain. The committee reported that trade exhibitions would play an increasingly important part in the promotions of export trade and that facilities for such activities should be of the highest standard (N.E.C. report, 1998). In 1980 the first convention bureau was built in London, this was the start of the major growth of the MICE sector in the UK.

Growth in the MICE industry has occurred on a global scale. In 1998 the UIA identified over 184 countries which have held MICE events. The most rapid growth has occurred in Asia. Africa and Eastern Europe have recently entered the MICE market, the USA has the maturest MICE market. Since the 1980's the USA has experienced a decline in the number of international conferences hosted, from 19% to 12%. (ICCA 1999). The USA has lost part of its market to newly developing MICE destinations such as Asia. The ICCA relative figures for the market share (%) per continent predict that in the year 2000, 56% of international meetings will be held in Europe, 15% in Asia, 11% in North America, 6% in South/Central America, 10% in Australia/Pacific and 2% in Africa (ICCA, 1999).

Limited research

The MICE sector is an important generator of tourism expenditure, investment, foreign exchange earnings and employment. There is an inability to calculate the exact size of the MICE industry due to the lack of comprehensive accurate data. Many attempts to estimate the economic importance of the industry have proceeded in a rather piecemeal fashion and in some cases, the assumptions upon which they are based may be challenged.

As a consequence, it is difficult to estimate the size of MICE industry throughout the world, particularly in newly developing MICE regions such as Asia, Africa and Eastern Europe where the data collection is even more problematic than in developed MICE countries. Not all MICE venues have the technology or facilities to tabulate data on the number of events or conventions held, or the total revenue generated. In order to correct the deficiencies in the collection of data, definitions, methods of data collection and finding should be standardised and collated. However, in view of the rapidly developing industry, the time taken to carry out surveys and costs occurred. This will probably not take place for a number of years. This lack of present research and data collection is seen as a significant limitation to the long-term development of the MICE sector throughout the world.

Aims and objectives

The overall aim of this paper is to identify trends within the UK conference industry. Using secondary sources, the paper reviews the growth and key characteristics of the UK conference market. This includes trends in opening of centre, the number of conferences held in the UK, and the average length of conferences. The costs and benefits of the UK MICE industry are also outlined. Specifically, the primary research explores the relationships between the year of opening the conference centre, the size of the conference venue, and ownership of the venue (public and private).

In pursuit of its aims, the paper is organised in the following way. The initial section shall concentrate specifically on the MICE industry in the UK. The second section of the paper identifies the methodology used to carry out the research on the UK MICE industry, followed by the results section. The results are discussed in order to identify general trends within the conference industry, and a number of conclusions are drawn.

Key concepts: an overview

It is essential that the key concepts used in this research are defined, as the different array of terms can lead to confusion. For this paper, a conference is understood to be a generic term for all meetings.

The Meetings, Incentives, Conventions and Exhibitions (MICE) sector consist of activities including conventions, trade shows, seminars, events, exhibitions and incentive travel (Dwyer & Forsyth, 1996). Lawson (1982) extends the number of activities included in the MICE sector to include workshops, symposiums, forums, panels, lectures, and colloquiums. Throughout this paper the MICE sector will predominantly refer to conference centres.

"Conference" – As far back as 1977, The British Tourist Authority define a *conference* as:

- a meeting held in hired premises;

- lasting a minimum of six hours;

- attended by a minimum of 25 people; and

- having a fixed agenda or programme.

In recent years the BTA have changed their definition of a conference. Between 1994 and 1997 the definition of a conference was restricted to a minimum of 15 delegates. In 1998 it was extended to include smaller meetings with between 8-14 delegates (British Conference Market Trends Survey (BCMTS) 1998).

"Convention" - is defined as an assembly of persons for some common object, or for the exchange of ideas, views and information of common interest to the group. The term *convention* is widely used in America, Australia and Asia to describe the traditional form of annual or total membership meetings. Over 80% of associations in the USA hold an annual convention for their total membership and many companies provide similar opportunities for work-related and social purposes in attractive surroundings. These are meetings which are often linked to incentive travel (Lawson 1982).

The United Kingdom

The MICE sector accounts for £12 billion of the total value (£37 billion) for leisure and business tourism generated in the UK (Scarborough Borough Council, 1998). According to the British Tourist Authority, the conference industry generates approximately 27% of the total income from tourism for the UK (BACT, 1996). The UK has between -4,000 and 5,000 MICE venues, with an estimated income generation of £2 billion (BCMTS 1998).

During the 1990's there has been a rise in the number of conference centres which have opened throughout the UK. There were 29% more conferences in 1995 than 1994, with an increase again in 1996. An increase in the number of delegates also occurred. Today most major cities have well-established conference bureaus, of which, many are part funded by the private and public sectors. Increasingly local authorities are recognising the value of the MICE business (White 1995).

The most recent findings on the UK conference market come from the British Conference Market Trends Survey (1998). The figures relate to both international and domestic conferences. During 1998, an estimated 658,900 conferences and meetings took place in Great Britain. The average duration of non-residential conferences was 1.24 days, while residential conferences lasted an average 2.37 days. The majority of conferences were corporate events (73%). On average 38 delegates attended corporate events, who spend on average £46 per day. The average number of conferences held by a venue was 160, although residential centres held on average 300. Purpose built venues held on average 259, and urban hotels 252. The average total revenue earned per conference (through daily rate charges) was £2,949, with average total revenue per delegate of £66.

The 1990s witnessed an increasingly competitive market that is currently still growing. As competition increases, UK towns and cities have to become increasingly competitive in order to win lucrative conference businesses. In today's climate there is great competition in the MICE sector throughout the world. Delegates chose to go to conferences overseas as other countries offer competitive conference packages, high tech facilities that often can not be matched by the UK market. Additionally, flight times and prices have reduced, making it easier and cheaper to go abroad, especially as business class facilities are available on most flights. Many overseas countries have a competitive edge over the UK and particularly London because of their environmental quality, improved weather conditions and the cultural aspects offered to the delegates. However, the UK remains an attractive market for overseas visitors due to its cultural heritage. In addition, it must be pointed out that in the UK, it is domestic conferences that form the majority of the conference market.

London remains the dominant destination attracting more meetings than almost any other capital. This popularity is due to ease of access, and it is the world centre for finance, insurance, commodity trading and communications. Additionally London offers some outstanding conference facilities, including the Business Design Centre in Islington, Olympia, Wembley, Alexandra Place, the Barbican, Sedgwick Centre, St. James Court, and Elizabeth II Conference Centre.

Within the UK, the highest level of revenue was generated in London, with the average conference centre generating £343,574 in the first three months of 1998. This gives a projected average income for a typical London conference centre of over £1.37 million for 1998. When the UK multiplier is employed London generates approximately £1billion from conferences alone.

The growth in the MICE sector in the UK continues with much construction and a wealth of plans for improvements of purpose-built centres. Within London, the construction of the new ExCel exhibition centre should improve the chances of London holding some of the largest events in Europe, putting the UK firmly on the world's convention map.

Costs and benefits of the MICE industry in the UK

One of the reasons why the UK and other countries have invested into the MICE tourism sector is that it is least responsive to price changes and seasonality than other industry sectors. The MICE sector is potentially able to attract high spending, longer staying visitors to a destination.

There is a wealth of literature that explores the relative costs and benefits of the MICE industry (Dwyer & Forsyth 1997, Mistilis & Dwyer 1997). Fench 1992 has summarised the costs and benefits relating to conference centre development. Fenich (1992) summarised the advantages and disadvantages of developing convention centres, which is shown in Table 1.

Table 1   The advantages and disadvantages of conference centre development

Advantages	Disadvantages
Direct	**Direct**
Local government/private sector investment	High development costs
High level of delegate spending	High carrying costs
Increased employment	High operation costs
Indirect	**Indirect**
Economic gains to the local community	Losses in operations
Impact on occupancy hotel bookings	Infrastructure costs
Enhanced urban image	Opportunity costs
Redevelopment of blighted areas	Loss of property taxes
	Continuing costs for police, firemen
	High debt service

Source: Fenich, (1992, p.194) (modified)

Methodology and primary research

The primary research for this paper was collected using a sample of 66 conference centres in the UK. The information was collected to identify trends in ownership of UK conference centres, the changes in the physical size of conference centres, the capacity of the conference centres and the trends in the length of UK conferences. The research explores the relationships between the year of opening the conference centre, the size of the conference venue, and ownership.

Initial address list

In order to obtain a definitive address list a number of sources were utilised. The major sources of addresses were collected from the "Venue: The World-wide Guide to Conference and Incentive Travel Facilities 1998/99", which contains information on over 4000 venues throughout the United Kingdom. Venues are listed in order of major town's, with separate sections for exhibition and conference centres, unusual venues, hotels, academic and management training centres and hotels in the surrounding area.

Due to time and financial constraints to reduce the size of the mail drop, only the venues under the section of "Exhibition centre and conference centres" were used. All other venues within other sections were dismissed due to lack of clarity of the initial use of the facilities. A total of the 215-conference centre addresses were established from the 'Venue Directory'.

The postal questionnaire

The postal questionnaire was sent to 215 conference centres in the UK. The questionnaire comprises three sections; the first section (questions 1-2) seeks information from the respondent, including questions concerning the respondent's responsibilities. This was to establish whether or not an appropriate individual (i.e. the conference manager) had completed the questionnaire.

The second section, questions 3-7, identifies the name and location of the centre for future reference. This section also collected data concerning the date of opening, cost of construction, and whether or not refurbishment or extensions to the centre had been undertaken, and the ownership of the conference centre.

Section three (questions 8-16) identifies the size of conference centre expressed as the total conference floor space, number of auditoria and meeting rooms as well the maximum capacity for delegates. This section also identifies staffing levels for the centres, with regards to full and part time employees, the number of events undertaken in the financial year of 1997-8 and the estimated percentage of delegates who were local/non local.

The survey allocated one month for completion from, the 15th June to 15th July 1998 inclusive. The 215 questionnaires, with a further 215 returning stamped addressed envelopes and covering letters were sent out at the beginning of this period.

To those conference centres who had not returned their questionnaire, a telephone reminder was undertaken. A second questionnaire with covering letter and a stamped addressed envelope was sent at the beginning of July 1998, with a further three weeks returning period. After this period no more questionnaires were returned. With the total survey population being 215, and the number of useable questionnaires returned being 64, the return rate of useable questionnaires was 29.8 %.

Analysis of data

The questionnaires returned completed and considered useable were coded and entered into SPSS (version 6.0) for analysis.

Results - general characteristics

Although the questionnaires were completed, it is important to establish whether an appropriate individual has completed the questionnaire. To this effect, the corporate responsibility of the respondent was requested and the results are shown in Table 2.

Table 2   Respondents responsibility (N=64)

Responsibility	Number of respondents citing responsibility (%)
Conference Manager	18 (28.1)
Director	7 (10.9)
Events Manager	7 (10.9)
General Facilities Manager	7 (10.9)
Operations Manager	6 (9.3)
Sales / Marketing Manager	6 (9.3)
Exhibitions Manager	1 (1.5)
Other	12 (18.7)
Total	**64 (99.6)**

Note: Percentage does not add up to 100 due to rounding.
Source: Author

The largest number of respondents stated that they were Conference Managers. This was followed by Director, Events Manager and General Facilities Manager each having seven respondents. The 'Other' category was composed of a number of responsibilities including accountant, administrator and partner, all of the responsibilities disclosed could be considered as relevant with respect to their ability to give accurate, informed responses to questionnaire.

Date of conference centre opening

The growth of the conference centre industry in the UK began in the 1960s'. From the 1960s until the 1980s the industry experienced steady growth. The 1980s and 1990s experienced rapid growth, which peaked in the 1990s with 24 centres opening.

Table 3   Decade of conference centre opening in the UK

Pre 1960s	1960s	1970s	1980s	1990s
4	3	12	21	24

Source: Author

From 1960 to 1998, 64 conference centres were opened. In the 1960's, there were 3 (4.7%) and in the 1980's 12 (18.8%). It was during the 1980's that the UK experienced a rapid rise in the number conference centres being opened, with 21 or 32.8% centres opening during this decade. Of these 21 conference centres the vast majority, 15 (71.4%), opened between 1985 and 1989, causing a period of economic prosperity within the UK. In the 1990's, more centres have been opened in the first seven and a half years, up to the closing date of the questionnaire than in the entire decade of the 1980's. During the 1990's, 24 conference centres opened (37.5% of the survey responses). Differentiating between the initial half of the 1990's and the latter half of the 1990's, it can be seen that 14 (58.3%) conference centres were opened in the first five years of the decade, while 10 have opened from 1995 to mid way through 1998. This may reflect the economic recession.

Ownership

Table 4 shows the ownership of the conference centres in the UK.

Table 4   Conference centre ownership in the UK

Local authority	50.0 %
Private Ownership	34.8 %
Joint Ownership	6.1 %
Other	9.1 %

Source: Author

In the UK local authorities own 50% of convention centres, compared to 34.8% which are owned by the private sector. The 'other' category includes those owned by charities.

During the 1960 to 1980s a high proportion of conference centres were owned by the public sector. However by the 1990s this pattern had changed, and now a greater number of conference centres are owned by the private sector. During the 1980s Local Authorities gave the largest number of grants to convention centres (41.1%). This occurred during a period of political belief that such public funding would create economic regeneration of blighted areas. The 1990s have seen a reduction of Local Authority funding (23%) due to a change in the UK Government policies. The 1990s can be seen as an era of private funding.

Table 5   Decade of Conference Centre Opening/Ownership in the UK

		Ownership				
		Public	Private	Joint	Other	Total
	< 1960's	3	1	0	0	4
Decade	1960's	3	0	0	0	3
Of	1970's	5	7	0	0	12
Opening	1980's	12	6	1	2	21
	1990's	9	8	3	4	24
	Total	32	22	4	6	64

Source: Author

An important part of a conference centres income may come from a Local Authority subsidy. However 69.6% of the respondents stated they received no such grant. The centres in the UK that did receive a grant received between £108,000 and £20 million from their Local Authority.

The expansion of conference centres in the 1980's was from Local Authorities (Public Ownership) with 12 conference centres (57.1%). This compares to 6 (28.5%) conference centres, which are privately owned. The 1990's have seen an increase in the proportion of privately owned centres at 33.3% compares to 37.5%, which are publicly owned. The 1990's represent a decade of increased private funding.

Two conference centres opened before 1960, they both received a Local Authority subsidy. During the 1960s, three convention centres opened, of which none of them received local authority subsidy, whereas of the 17 conference centres opened in the 1980's seven of them (41.1%) received such a grant. This proportion reduces to just 23% for the 1990's. Please note that only 44 respondents completed this question This data support the theory that conference centres were established and/or supported by Local Authority finances in the 1980's, while the 1990's is an era of private funding.

Table 6   **Decade of Conference Centre Opening/Local Authority Subsidy in the UK**

		Local Authority Subsidy		
		Yes	No	Total
	<1960's	2	0	2
Decade	1960's	0	3	3
Of	1970's	2	7	9
Opening	1980's	7	10	17
	1990's	3	10	13
	Total	**14**	**30**	**44**

Note: 20 not completed
Source: Author

Size of conference centre

The survey findings indicate that throughout the 1970's the majority of conference centres had a total exhibition floor space of 4,000 square metres (sq. m) or less. The 1980's were a decade of 'large centres' defined as being 4,000 sq. m or larger. The 1990's were a decade of smaller centres with 78.6% of the responding centres having a floor space of 4,000 sq. m or less.

Cost of conference centre

The costs of building a conference centre range between £335,000 and £186 million, with the average cost on construction being approximately £20 million. This can be compared with research by Scarborough Borough Council (1998) which states that the cheapest conference centre opened in the UK between 1991 and 1997 and cost £6 million. However the most expensive centre cost £180 million. This research shows that the largest number of conference centres (13 or 39.4%) cost over £10 million to construct. However 11 centres (33.3%) cost under £2.5 million to construct. The 1980's had twice as many centres being constructed which cost £10 million or more than those costing under £2.5 million. The 1990's have seen the construction of cheaper conference centres (8 centres costing below £5 million and only 5 costing over £10 million).

Renovation to conference centres

In addition to the building of new convention centres, existing facilities can be re-furbished to compete with the more modern facilities of the 1990's. The majority of conference centres in the sample had not undertaken any such refurbishment or extension. However 18 conference centres had undertaken re-furbishment, of which, 11 centres (61.1%) had done so during 1996 to 1998. During the same period 7 new conference centres opened. These results can be compared to Tagungs-Wirtschaft (1992) findings which show that 42% of all (from a survey of 70 conference centres) have been extended at one time or another, some of them even twice. There research suggests that they were not adequately dimensioned in the first place or that actual demand was wrongly assessed.

Conference centre infrastructure

The average conference centre will have 2 auditoria, with an average capacity of the largest auditoria of approximately 1,600 individuals and the average number of meeting rooms being 17. Overall the typical conference centre will have a total exhibition floor space of 5,971.98 sq. metres and an average maximum capacity with regards to delegates of 1,910. Based on these findings, the characteristics of the typical UK conference centre can be established, which are shown in table 7.

Table 7   The minimum, maximum, mean for auditoria, meeting rooms, total floor space and number of delegates of a typical UK conference centre

Variable	Minimum	Maximum	Mean
Number of Auditoria	0	14	2.07
Maximum Capacity of Largest Auditoria	0	12,500	1,645.20
Number of Meeting Rooms	1	510	17.25
Total Conference Floor Space	93	100,000	5,971.98
Maximum Number of Delegates	50	15,500	1,910.40
Total Number of Conferences 1997-98	1	2,900	200.94
Total Number of Business Meeting 1997-98	0	1,440	144.90
Total Number of Trade Shows 1997-98	0	60	5.59
Total Number of Public Exhibitions 1997-98	0	100	11.43
Total Number of Performances 1997-98	0	922	63.80
Total Number of Other 1997-98	0	1,000	86.94
Average Number of Days Per Conference	1	5	1.57
Number of Full-Time Employees	2	297	44.58
Number of Part-Time Employees	0	600	39.03

Source: Author

With regards to the number of conferences held in the financial year 1997-98 a typical conference centre will host 356 events, each lasting on average 1.5 days. In order to undertake such events the staffing levels will be on average 44 full-time employees and where required the centre will employ an additional 39 part-time staff.

The majority of centres employ relatively few full-time employees. Approximately 31% of responding centres employ 10 or fewer such individuals, with 63% employing 30 or fewer and approximately three quarters (74%) employing 40 or fewer individuals. This suggests that the actual conference venue itself is not a significant employer. Conference centres do not directly employ high numbers of people compared to the size of the building. Greater numbers of people may be employed indirectly due to the employment multiplier as many industries will supply and service for the conference centre.

With regards to part-time employees, 20.3% of conference centres who responded stated they employed three or fewer part-time individuals, with 56.2% employing 20 or less. However 26.5% employ over 40 part-time individuals. Conference centres either utilise part-time employees extensively or there is minimal use of them.

Conference delegates

The findings relating to conference delegates show that 37 (62.7%) of centres responding state that the majority of delegates were considered local (60%), leaving 37.3% of centres having a majority of non-local delegates. This is a reflection of the nature of the domestic market.

The average length of a conference is between 1 and 1.9 days of which 75% of all delegates are local. This would suggest that the turn over of delegates is high, as they do not stay long at the conference. To generate more money to the local economy the conference centre should promote conferences to non-local delegates who are more likely to stay in the host community for longer. Countries such as Singapore have a high rate of international delegates which stay longer in the host community. Therefore the UK should consider greater overseas marketing to encourage long stay overseas delegates. Due to the large number of delegates attending conferences for a short period of time a trough peak trough pattern in occupancy may occur. To reduce this, the marketing of conference centres to increase number of conferences is required.

Conclusion

The research identifies that the UK has a mature and extensive MICE industry. Since 1970's there has been considerable growth in the UK MICE industry, and also in the number of conference centres built. Those conference centres built in the 1980's were characterised by local authority ownership, having large exhibition space, defined as being over 4,000 square metres, and costing over £10 million to construct. They were often developed as loss-leaders to attract further business to an area. The 1990's saw a shift to smaller privately owned centres that are run as commercial enterprises. Typically, they have less than 4,000 square metres, and cost less than £5 million in construction costs.

The research concludes that with the expansion of both the quantity and size of conference centres, there is a danger that too many centres will be established leading to over capacity within the industry. This increased competition may also lead to a reduction in both prices and profit margins.

References

BACT British Association of Conference Towns (1996), *Findings for the UK Conference Industry*.

The British Conference Market Trends Survey (1998), *Annual Report*.

Dwyer, L., and Forsyth, P. (1996), *Mice Tourism To Australia: A Framework To Assess Impacts, Proceedings of the Australian Tourism and Hospitality Research* Conference, pp. 313-323. Coffs Habours.

Dwyer, L., and Forsyth, P. (1997), Impacts and Benefits of MICE Tourism: A framework for Analysis. *Tourism Economics*. Vol 3 No. 1. pp.21-38.

Fenich, G. G., (1992), Convention Centre Development; Pros Cons And Unanswered Questions. *International Journal of Hospitality Management*. Vol. 11 (3), pp.183-196.

Gartrell, R. B. (1991), Strategies Partnerships For Convention Planning; The Role Of Convention And Visitor Bureau's In Convention Management. *International Journal of Hospitality Management*. Vol. 10 (2), pp. 157-165.

The International Meetings Market (1991-2000), *ICCA. in conjunction with Association Meetings International*, 1998.

Lawson, F. (1982), *Conference and Convention Centres*, Routledge, London.

Mistilis, N. and Dwyer, L. (1997), Capital cities and regions: economic impacts and challenges for development of the MICE industry in Australia. *In Tourism and Hospitality Research Conference: Building a Better Industry*, Sydney, Bureau of Tourism Research, Canberra.

The NEC Group (1998), *National Exhibition Centre NEC Arena*, The NEC Group.

Scarborough Borough Council (1998), *Leisure and Amenities Committee*, Report of the Acting Director.

TW Tagungs-Wirtschaft (1992), *"Investment of conference centres up to the year 2000"*. November.

Union of International Association (1999), http://www.uia.org/uiastats/stcnf98.htm.

Venue: The Worldwide Guide to Conference, Incentive Travel Facilities (1998/99), Haymarket Business Publications Ltd, London.

White, S. (1995), Battle of the UK Destinations. *Conference and Incentives Travel*. September. pp. 27-32.

Ethical values in tourism: A look at core principles in major lodging properties in the United States

Gary Vallen and Matt Casado

Northern Arizona University, USA

Introduction

Customer service has received total attention by government and business entities in the last two decades. Most hospitality and tourism jobs are under the constant scrutiny of the public, hinging on a face-to-face relationship where the inefficiency of one employee or the lack of attention to the guest by management may lose a guest forever (Casado, 2000). Indeed, "all the [costs of] advertising and representations made by the hotel come down to the quality of service delivered at one moment of truth" (Vallen and Vallen, 2000). While management's energy has been focused on customer service, little attention has been given to the concept of business ethics--at least until recently.

Increasing awareness on the part of the public about ethical practices is forcing official institutions and private corporations to adopt and follow those lines of action that are acceptable in terms of values to society. For this reason, ethical principles should be an intrinsic part of the social responsibility of managers. Because of the widespread use of technological information, more and more people are getting the message that low standards of professional conduct, blatant disregard for the environment, and uncontrolled corporate greed are not acceptable. Such conduct may even be penalised by potential customers refusing to patronise products and services and, in some cases, by boycotting entities guilty of unethical practices.

Tourism enterprises are by no means immune to this possibility. For instance, customers avoid airlines that, according to press reviews, place too few resources towards airplane maintenance in order to increase corporate profits. People choose not to book cruises with certain companies whose ships have been found guilty of dumping garbage into the ocean to avoid paying dumpster fees at ports of call. And large numbers of travellers decide to avoid certain countries that allow pristine forests to be decimated by unscrupulous logging companies. The list goes on.

Ethics research institutions and resources

The world of business is concerned with creating awareness of its ethical principles in part because of the fear of bad publicity and potential loss of customer confidence. Conferences are held annually on applied ethics, where conceptual and empirical papers are presented to business professional and education audiences. The emphasis of some topics is to bridge the gap between ethical principles and corporate profits.

An annual publication on business ethics is printed at Pepperdine University, where articles dealing with ethics topics published in journals, newspapers, and magazines are selected, reviewed, edited and made meaningful to business professionals (Martin, 1998). The Josephson Institute for the Advancement of Ethics, based in Marina del Rey, California, provides government, business, journalism, and education agencies with instructional materials and trainer-training workshops for the dissemination of ethics (Casado, Miller, and Vallen, 1994).

Two institutions dedicated to the advancement of ethics in the hospitality industry are: The International Institute for Quality and Service in Ethics and Tourism (IIQUEST) and the Marion Isbell Endowment for Hospitality Ethics Centre. Both are non-profit organisations dedicated to the promotion of ethics in hospitality and tourism. Based at the Glion Management Centre in Bulle, Switzerland, IIQUEST conducts periodic surveys to determine progress in ethics within the industry and organises contests for published articles and essays written by students from hospitality and tourism schools around the world. The Marion Isbell Centre was created in 1988 by the founding family of Ramada Inns. Housed in the School of Hotel and Restaurant Management at Northern Arizona University in Flagstaff, its mission is the study and promotion of hospitality and tourism ethics.

The cost of ethics breaches

Today's global marketplace, including most tourism companies, is based on an economic system in which the major portion of production and services are privately operated and therefore are for profit. Line employees reporting to managers, managers reporting to senior officers, senior officers reporting to owners and/or stockholders are evaluated on their ability to generate a bottom-line profit. This profit-driven approach views corporate ethical policies as contrary to profit-making goals. And yet, most business executives would try to avoid at all costs the possibility of their companies making newspaper headlines for some uncovered ethical breach. One could imagine how badly the CEO of an airline would wish to trade proper integrity regarding aircraft maintenance for the hundred of lives lost in a crash. One could easily envision the president of a cruise-ship line wishing to trade a law-abiding respect for the ocean for the corporate reputation-damning articles published about the company's ships dumping rubbish in the high seas.

There may be substantial costs associated with doubtful ethical practices in every company. And though it is impossible to place a cost on the hundreds of lives lost in an airplane accident or to calculate the value of a polluted ocean, it is less difficult to imagine what ethical breaches may cost companies in the long run. The purpose of this paper is to explore the perceptions of managers of lodging properties of US hotels on ethical principles.

The study

This study ranks the perceptions of hospitality lodging general managers on the importance of twelve core ethical principles suggested by the Josephson Institute of Ethics (Josephson, 1988). These principles establish the standards or rules of behaviour within which an ethical person functions and could be adopted as the basis of the formation of future business leaders. Based on the search for what constitutes right or wrong in a business context in general, and the hospitality/tourism business in particular, the study investigates the following ethical principles:

Accountability: The holding of people morally accountable for some past action or for the treatment of others as derived from the specific professional position that one holds. Morally responsible tourism managers should be accountable for the welfare of the employees they supervise given that, in most cases, the workers' livelihood depends on them.

Commitment to Excellence: Commitment to excellence determines the necessity to deliver the best service possible for the price obtained. Tourism managers that deviate from this principle actually cheat their guests of the right to have their money's worth for services received.

Concern for Others: The need to do unto others as you would have them do unto you. This principle is hard to observe from the lofty position of managers vis-à-vis hourly workers performing menial jobs.

Fairness: The basic policy of equal treatment for equal production. Tourism managers, as do managers in other industries, tend to be unfair in the treatment of minorities such as women, the young, the old, and, in the US, undocumented aliens.

Honesty: Although the Italian Renaissance statesman and writer Niccolo Machiavelli, insisted that those that trick men with their cunning overcome those abiding by honest principles, his theory would not be applicable to modern times, at least not in an ethical sense. Deceiving or misleading others often results in costly lawsuits and, in some cases, jail sentences.

Integrity: Soundness of moral principle and character may be qualities of an individual's moral code. Sometimes, however, there exist conflicting pulls of moral conscience and self-interest. Tourism corporations can be relevant examples of situations that can damage individual integrity and responsibility. For instance, the willingness by the manager of a company to continue daily operations when a resort is polluting the local environment in exchange for keeping his/her job, status, and benefits.

Law Abiding: Often, the legality of an action does not guarantee that the action is morally right. While laws codify customs, they are not sufficient to establish the moral standards that should guide individuals or professions. Although abiding by codes of law, tourism mangers may be acting against their values. For instance, taking advantage of bankruptcy laws to undercut the competition's fair market prices.

Ethical Leadership: To seek and adopt the function of leaders in moral principles requires courage on the part of committed individuals. An example of ethical leadership in the tourism industry would be to support any statutes or regulations fostering workers' opportunities to advance socially; for example, supporting universal health coverage for all employees.

Ethical Loyalty: The faithfulness to engagements and obligations towards laws, companies, guests, and employees should be part of the moral behaviour of all professionals. This faithful adherence may be difficult if one's own benefit or social comfort is at stake. A tourism manager might find it difficult to abide by legal or company principles if his or her quarterly bonus for improving the bottom line is in jeopardy.

Promise Keeping: Some time ago, a business deal made verbally with another person was assurance that the expectations would be fulfilled. Today, most business deals must be closed in the presence of attorneys lest one of the parties involved break the original promise. Tourism managers intending to make use of another person as a means to an end would be acting untrustworthily. For instance, signing a promissory note knowing that the company is going into chapter eleven.

Reputation: The estimation by which a company is held by the community and guests is important for conducting business. Attempts by tourism companies to bust a fair attempt by employees to unionise could cast an unfavourable shadow on the company's ethical values.

Respect: One of Kant's categorical imperative principles states that everyone should be treated as an end, not merely as means. Every human being deserves to be treated with respect, as an independent moral agent. A tourism company would break this principle by hiring illegal immigrants at lower hourly wages knowing that these workers are unable to legally complain about the wage difference.

Methodology

Population: The population for this study was general managers of lodging properties in the fifty US states. The sample consisted of general managers from the ten largest lodging establishments in each state, or 500 executives in total. The sample was selected by identifying the largest ten properties by state as printed in the Spring 1999 edition of the Hotel Travel Index. Because of the disparity between states, the sample property size ranged from under 200 to over 5,000 rooms. The average property size for all respondents was 554 rooms. The survey instrument was sent to these industry leaders by mail. The questionnaire asked respondents to rank their perceptions on ethical issues and to provide demographic and psychographic information about themselves and their properties. The number of returned valid questionnaires was just nine percent of the sample. This limited number of answers can be attributed to the traditionally poor response of busy hospitality executives to surveys of any kind.

Design: The study has the characteristics of descriptive/analytical research, in that it is concerned with analysing the perceptions of respondents. The data collected from the survey were processed using the Statistical Package for the Social Sciences (SPSS) procedures for frequencies.

Findings

Respondents were asked to rank the twelve ethical characteristics identified in this study in two separate ways. *Exhibit 1* lists the twelve ethical characteristics ranked by their impact on hotel profitability. Four characteristics for operational success were ranked with percentages above ten: leadership, accountability, commitment to excellence, and integrity. The rest scored between 8.9 percent for honesty, to 0.0 percent for concern for others.

Exhibit 2 shows the ranking general managers gave to the same attributes in terms of ethical breaches they had most often observed (observed unethical behaviour). Three characteristics were ranked above ten percent: accountability, commitment to excellence, and respect for others. The rest were ranked from 8.9 percent for concern for others to 0.0 percent for law abiding.

Exhibit 3 lists selected qualitative comments of respondents specific to breaches of the twelve core ethical principles. This exhibit provides examples of comments submitted by respondents detailing breaches for each of the twelve core ethical principles researched in the study.

Exhibit 4 shows demographical data of the respondents. Most executives had been in the industry over 26 years, worked in the current property between 2 and 5 years, and earned between $120,000 and $ 159,999. Eighty-seven percent of the respondents were male; their age was 46.2 years on average, held a college degree, and were married with at least one child.

Exhibit 5 (psychographics) describes the majority of the respondents as being ideologically conservative, believers of God and attending church regularly, and holding the perception that they had higher personal ethical traits than other people in general and other hoteliers in particular. The perceptions of most respondents were that ethical behaviour in the hospitality industry ranks about the same as in other industries. A fascinating finding discussed in Exhibit 5 is respondent estimates related to cost of ethical breaches. According to general manager respondents, the annual cost to the hotel from breaches of ethical principles averaged $102,000. Two respondents estimated such costs in excess of $500,000 per year!

Discussion

The results of this study indicate that the general managers of lodging properties who responded to this survey are concerned with the breach of ethical principles by industry operators. Some of the comments expressed by the respondents were: "Owners routinely lie and deceive employees. For example, owners have denied knowledge of 'sticky' issues despite irrefutable evidence to the contrary;" "a large number of associates are more concerned about 'what is in it for me' versus dedication and loyalty for the long-term;" "too many junior managers want the rewards without the accountability. A recent example is a manager on duty leaving the hotel at the end of his shift even though a tornado was heading in our direction."

It seems to be plausible to suggest that the practice of ethical principles by hospitality and tourism companies is desirable. It is desirable not only because it is the right way to act, but also because the general public is becoming aware that unethical behaviour can be punished by refusing to buy such company's products and services. Because acting ethically requires certain intellectual skills that develop with both maturity and formal education, the preparation of hospitality and tourism future managers should include classroom instruction on ethical practices. If ethical principles were internalised during college years, they would be readily carried into the workplace. The approach to ethical decision-making should be grounded on the twelve principles used in this study, as ranked by industry operators. They should form the basis for an integrated hospitality and tourism ethics program. Integration of these topics into the curriculum should result in an increased awareness of ethical considerations among future hospitality and tourism managers (Casado, Miller, and Vallen, 1994).

Business concerns for sound ethical practices that help ensure fair treatment for guests and employees, and preservation of the environment, are a benefit to all of society. Clearly, the business community, established primarily to obtain financial profits, sees the equation: good ethics = good business = high profits. In this paper, though some respondents have estimated a quantitative cost for ethical breaches (see Exhibit 5), costs do not always result from ethical breaches. If good ethics always brought high profits over the long term, there would be no unethical behaviour to discuss in the first place. Ethical treatment of guests, employees, and the environment will, at times, be costly. It is at those times that a company's real character is tested. It is at those times, society hopes the motivation of company management is towards doing the right thing.

Exhibit 1

Twelve Ethical Characteristics Ranked by Major Lodging Property General Managers According to Their Impact on Hotel Profitability

Respondents were asked to rank twelve ethical characteristics, ranging alphabetically from Accountability to Respect for Others. Respondents were asked to rank the characteristics in terms of the importance they perceive such ethical characteristics have on the successful continuing operations of their hotel. In other words, general managers were asked to rank the twelve ethical characteristics in relation to the importance such characteristics have on operating a profitable hotel:

Results to this first ranking question (characteristics for operational success) were:

1. Leadership was considered most important by 24.4 percent of general manager respondents;

2. Accountability was considered most important by 20.0 percent of general manager respondents;

3. Commitment to Excellence was considered most important by 15.6 percent of general manager respondents;

4. Integrity was considered most important by 13.3 percent of general manager respondents.

5. Honesty was considered most important by 8.9 percent of general manager respondents;

6. Fairness was considered most important by 4.4 percent of general manager respondents;

7. Law Abiding was considered most important by 4.4 percent of general manager respondents;

8. Respect for Others was considered most important by 3.5 percent of general manager respondents;

9. Promise Keeping and Trustworthiness was considered most important by 2.6 percent of general manager respondents;

10. Reputation and Morale was considered most important by 1.7 percent of general manager respondents;

11. Loyalty was considered most important by 0.9 percent of general manager respondents;

12. And Concern for Others was not considered most important by any (0.0 percent) general manager respondents.

The second way respondents were asked to rank characteristics was in terms of ethical breaches they had most often observed. In other words, general managers were asked to think back to breaches of ethical conduct (unethical behaviour) they had observed and rank the twelve ethical characteristics in relation to the frequency with which they had observed these breaches.

Results to this second question (observed ethical breaches) were:

1. Accountability was seen breached most regularly by 17.4 percent of general manager respondents;

2. Commitment to Excellence was seen breached most regularly by 17.4 percent of general manager respondents;

3. Respect for Others was seen breached most regularly by 15.2 percent of general manager respondents;

4. Concern for Others was seen breached most regularly by 8.9 percent of general manager respondents;

5. Fairness was seen breached most regularly by 8.9 percent of general manager respondents;

6. Honesty was seen breached most regularly by 8.9 percent of general manager respondents;

7. Leadership was seen breached most regularly by 8.9 percent of general manager respondents;

8. Loyalty was seen breached most regularly by 4.4 percent of general manager respondents.

9. Promise Keeping and Trustworthiness was seen breached most regularly by 4.4 percent of general manager respondents;

10. Integrity was seen breached most regularly by 2.2 percent of general manager respondents;

11. Reputation and Morale was seen breached most regularly by 2.2 percent of general manager respondents;

12. And Law Abiding was not considered most important by any (0.0 percent) general manager respondents.

Cross-Tabulations

A number of more interesting cross-tabulations were developed in an attempt to understand the relationships between some of the demographic and psychographic variables. Those findings are shown here:

- *Annual Cost of Ethical Breaches by Property Size*. This cross-tabulation ran property size (number of rooms) by perceived annual overall cost to the hotel from ethical breaches of conduct by hotel managers and employees. The study produced expected results - namely, the larger the property the higher the perceived annual cost assigned by respondent general managers.

  Specifically, respondents who perceived annual overall costs to the hotel from ethical breaches of conduct as $25,000 or less came from hotels averaging 513.1 rooms. As the perceived annual cost rose to between $26,000 and $100,000, the property size rose to an average 534.8 rooms. Those managers who perceived annual costs ranging above $100,000 came from properties averaging 777.4 rooms; and

- *Ethics in Hospitality Industry versus Other Industries by Years Employed in Industry*. Although the demonstrated trend was imperfect, the results from this cross-tabulation were still quite interesting. The trend seemed to indicate that the longer a manager was employed in the hospitality industry, the less ethical he/she perceived hospitality as compared with other industries.

  Specifically, respondents who considered hospitality ethics much higher than ethics demonstrated in other industries had worked in hospitality 15.2 years. Those who considered hospitality industry ethics higher than other industries had worked in hospitality 26.4 years. Those who considered hospitality industry ethics about the same as other industries had worked in hospitality 22.0 years (this response category balked the trend a bit). Those who considered hospitality industry ethics lower than other industries had worked in hospitality 29.0 years. And those who considered hospitality industry ethics much lower than other industries had also worked in hospitality 29.0 years.

Exhibit 2

Twelve Ethical Characteristics Ranked by Major Lodging Property General Managers According to Their Frequency of Breach

Respondents were asked to rank twelve ethical characteristics, ranging alphabetically from Accountability to Respect for Others. Respondents were asked to rank the characteristics in terms of ethical breaches they had most often observed. In other words, general managers were asked to think back to breaches of ethical conduct (unethical behaviour) they had observed and rank the twelve ethical characteristics in relation to the frequency with which they had observed these breaches.

Results to this second ranking question (observed ethical breaches) were:

1. Accountability was seen breached most regularly by 17.4 percent of general manager respondents;

2. Commitment to Excellence was seen breached most regularly by 17.4 percent of general manager respondents;

3. Respect for Others was seen breached most regularly by 15.2 percent of general manager respondents;

4. Concern for Others was seen breached most regularly by 8.9 percent of general manager respondents;

5. Fairness was seen breached most regularly by 8.9 percent of general manager respondents;

6. Honesty was seen breached most regularly by 8.9 percent of general manager respondents;

7. Leadership was seen breached most regularly by 8.9 percent of general manager respondents;

8. Loyalty was seen breached most regularly by 4.4 percent of general manager respondents;

9. Promise Keeping and Trustworthiness was seen breached most regularly by 4.4 percent of general manager respondents;

10. Integrity was seen breached most regularly by 2.2 percent of general manager respondents;

11. Reputation and Morale was seen breached most regularly by 2.2 percent of general manager respondents;

12 And Law Abiding was not considered most important by any (0.0 percent) general manager respondents.

Exhibit 3

Major Lodging Property General Managers' Qualitative Comments Specific to Breaches of the 12 Core Ethical Principles

Accountability: (a) Hourly employees do not accept responsibility for their part in building business for the property. (b) Managers are not accountable for their areas of responsibility. Instead, they tend to blame others when things go wrong.

Commitment to Excellence: (a) Hourly employees do not (or cannot) understand the importance of excellent service to generating return customers. (b) People aren't committed to growing in their positions. Will do only what is asked of them.

Concern for Others: (a) Owner told the Director of Sales that she was doing a fine job, then told the General Manager to terminate her for non-performance. (b) Hourly employees do not accept responsibility for their part in building business for the property.

Fairness: (a) Managers sometimes disregard fairness due to the need to make a decision that may be advantageous to their needs. I.e. promoting somebody they like without going through the proper selection process. (b) Hardworking members of the team feel unfairly overworked when the laziness of family owners creates additional burdens.

Honesty: (a) There are double standards at our hotel. Owners expect employees to be honest, but employees see dishonesty among the owners. (b) When a manager makes the wrong decision, he/she tends to stretch the truth so that he/she doesn't appear incompetent.

Integrity: (a) In the hospitality industry, we are so desperate for business that we will sell our soul (integrity) to book the business. (b) Not keeping information confidential, even after being told to do so.

Law Abiding: (a) Stealing of cash or not charging for food products in order to improve tips. (b) Diversity applies to someone else. Comments made out of context (you are too old...) come back to haunt the organisation.

Leadership: (a)Youthful managers tend to leave decisions to higher management even though they are empowered to make things happen themselves. (b) Not setting a good example (e.g. when a department head parks in a guest parking space).

Loyalty: (a) Excessive gossiping and searching for "the guilty party" prohibits loyalty - upper management recently told a manager to call in sick and take an extra vacation day without advising that manager's boss. (b) Sharing trade secrets with newly opening hotels or going to work for them after spending years being trained by a hotel family.

Promise Keeping and Trustworthiness: (a) The general manager before me violated the trust of dozens of employees by making any promise necessary at the time to solve the current crisis. (b) Meeting planners are not receiving the same level of service promised to them (and expected) at the time the contract was signed.

Reputation and Morale: Our employees do not show pride in their work; approaching their responsibilities as another 8 hours to survive rather than a challenge to make the best presentation they can.

Respect for Others: (a) Due to increasing pressure to perform, managers act in a way which can be perceived as lacking respect for hourly employees. This may be a result of how senior management is treated by the corporate office, which then translates into the behaviour they take out on their staff. (b) This is the number one human resource issue due to the very diverse employee population (over 1,000 minority employees in our hotel). Customers still have numerous stereotypes about our industry (i.e. addressing a housekeeper as maid).

Note: *Listed in alphabetical order, this exhibit provides examples of comments submitted by respondents detailing breaches for each of the twelve core ethical principles developed in the study. Comments read as they were provided by respondents, they have generally not been edited for content or verbiage.*

Exhibit 4

Major Lodging Property General Managers; Demographical Findings

The survey asked a series of demographic and property-specific questions to better understand characteristic traits of general manager respondents. Those results are shown:

Years in the industry. The average respondent had been working 25.96 years (assuming midpoints) in the hospitality industry.

- Specifically, 0.0 percent had been in the industry less than 6 years, 4.3 percent stated they had been in the industry 6 to 11 years, 23.9 percent stated 12 to 18 years, 23.9 percent stated 19 to 25 years, and 47.8 percent stated they had been in the industry 26 or more years;

Years at current property. The average respondent had been working 6.5 years at their current property.

- Specifically, 13.0 percent had been at their current property 1 year or less, 43.5 percent had been at their current property 2 to 5 years, 13.0 percent stated 6 to 10 years, 13.0 percent stated 11 to 15 years, and 10.9 percent had been at their current property 16 years or longer;

Rooms at Hotel. Results showed a wide range of property sizes from as little as 153 rooms to as large as 2,019 rooms. The average property size for this study was 554 rooms.

- Remember this study was designed to look at the ten largest hotels in each of fifty United States. In some states (e.g. Montana, Alaska, etc.) the largest hotels were relatively small when compared to states (e.g. Nevada) with dozens of hotels boasting 1,000 to 5,000 rooms;

Gender. Some 87.0 percent of the respondent general managers were male. Just 13.0 percent were female;

Age. The average respondent was 46.2 years of age.

- Specifically, 0.0 percent of all respondents were younger than 31 years of age, 23.9 percent were between 31 and 40 years of age, 43.5 percent were between 41 and 50 years of age, 30.4 percent were between 51 and 60 years of age, and 0.0 percent were 61 years of age or better;

Overall Salary and Compensation. The average respondent earned $119,535 annually.

- Specifically, 0.0 percent of all respondents earned less than $40,000 annually, 21.7 percent earned between $40,000 and $79,999 annually, 23.9 percent earned between $80,000 and $119,999 annually, 28.3 percent earned between $120,000 and $159,999 annually, and 19.6 percent earned $160,000 or more annually;

Education. The average respondent had 3.2 years of education beyond high school.

- Specifically, 2.2 percent of respondents had not finished high school, 17.4 percent had some college (no degree), 63.0 percent of respondents had either a 2- or 4-year degree, 8.7 percent had begun a graduate degree, and 8.7 percent had earned a master's or doctorate degree;

Marital Status. The vast majority of all respondents (80.0 percent) were married.

- Exactly 6.7 percent stated they were divorced, another 6.7 percent said they were re-married, and another 6.7 percent were never married; and,

Family Size. Exactly 89.1 percent of all respondents stated they had at least one or more children. Some 10.9 percent of respondents had no children.

Exhibit 5

Major Lodging Property General Managers; Psychographical Findings

In addition to understanding demographic characteristics, the study sought to understand psychographic and lifestyle habits of respondent general managers. Those findings are shown:

Political Ideology. The average respondent scored 3.6 (between neutral and conservative, but closer to conservative) on a 1 to 5 scale of political ideology where 1 is very liberal and 5 is very conservative.

- Specifically, 0.0 percent of respondents were very liberal (Likert score of 1), 13.0 percent were liberal (Likert score of 2), 17.4 percent were neutral (Likert score of 3), 65.2 percent were conservative (Likert score of 4), and 4.3 percent were very conservative (Likert score of 5);

Religious Beliefs. Because religious convictions often impact ethical behaviour, the research sought a deeper understanding of the religious and church-attendance psychographic characteristics of respondents. The average respondent scored 4.2 (between believing in God but seldom attending church versus believing in God and regularly attending church) on a 1 to 5 scale of religious beliefs where 1 is an unbeliever and 5 is a committed believer.

- Specifically, 4.4 percent of respondents did not believe in any higher being (Likert score of 1), 2.2 percent believed in a higher being but it was not "God" (Likert score of 2), 17.4 percent believed in God but did not attend church (Likert score of 3), 23.9 percent believed in God but seldom attended church (Likert score of 4), and a full 50.0 percent of respondent general managers believed in God and regularly attend church (Likert score of 5);

Personal Ethics versus General Population. Respondents were asked to compare their own personal ethical behaviour with other people in general. Results suggested that general managers perceived their own ethics to be substantially higher than the average population. The average respondent scored 4.0 (my own personal ethics are "higher" than other people in general) on a 1 to 5 scale of personal ethical ranking where 1 is "my ethics are much lower than other people in general" and 5 is "my ethics are much higher than other people in general."

- Specifically, 0.0 percent of respondents thought their own ethics were much lower than other people in general, 0.0 percent thought their ethics were lower, 17.4 percent thought their ethics were about the same, 65.2 percent thought they were higher, and 17.4 percent thought their own ethics were much higher than other people in general;

Personal Ethics versus Hospitality Industry Managers. Similarly, respondents were asked to compare their own personal ethical behaviour with other industry managers. Results suggested that general managers perceived their own personal ethics to be substantially higher than the rest of the hospitality industry. The average respondent scored 4.0 (my own personal ethics are "higher" than other industry managers) on a 1 to 5 scale of personal ethical ranking where 1 is "my ethics are much lower than other industry managers" and 5 is "my ethics are much higher than other industry managers."

- Specifically, 0.0 percent of respondents thought their own ethics were much lower than other hospitality industry managers, 0.0 percent thought their ethics were lower, 26.1 percent thought their ethics were about the same, 52.2 percent thought they were higher, and 21.7 percent thought their own ethics were much higher than other hospitality industry managers;

Ethics in Hospitality Industry versus Other Industries. Unlike the previous two questions, where managers perceive their own ethics to be higher than their peers' or the general population, the industry fared less well. Managers were asked to rank the hospitality industry's ethics with other industries. The hospitality industry scored just 3.2 (just slightly higher than hospitality industry ethics are about the same as other industries) on a 1 to 5 scale of industry ethical ranking where 1 is "the hospitality industry ranks much lower for ethics than other industries" and 5 is "the hospitality industry ranks much higher for ethics than other industries."

- Specifically, 2.2 percent of respondents thought the hospitality industry ranks much lower than other industries, 8.7 percent thought the hospitality industry ranks lower than other industries, 65.2 percent thought it ranks about the same, 17.4 percent thought the hospitality industry ranks higher, and 6.5 percent thought the hospitality industry ranks much higher than other industries; and

Cost of Breach. Respondent general managers were asked to assign an annual overall cost to the hotel from ethical breaches of conduct by hotel managers and employees. The average annual cost from ethical breaches of conduct was $101,794.87.

- Specifically, 20.5 percent of respondents projected the cost to their hotel from ethical breaches of conduct at $10,000 or less per year, 10.3 percent thought the cost was between $11,000 and $25,000 per year, 10.3 percent thought it was between $26,000 and $50,000, 30.8 percent thought between $51,000 and $100,000, and 28.2 percent of respondents projected the cost to their hotel from ethical breaches of conduct at $100,000 or more per year.

- Respondents who believed the projected cost of ethical breaches was over $100,000 were asked to indicate at exactly how much they perceived this annual cost. Two of the respondents stated their perception was an average annual cost of $500,000 per property per year!!

References

Casado, M. A. (2000), *Housekeeping Management*. New York: John Wiley and Sons.

Casado, M. A., Miller, W. and Vallen, G. K. (1994), Ethical Challenges of the Industry: Are Graduates Prepared? FIU *Hospitality Review*. 2.

Casado, Matt A., Miller, William and Vallen, Gary K. (1994), Ethical Challenges of the Industry: Are Graduate Prepared? *FIU Hospitality Review*. 5.

Josephson, M. (1988), Teaching Ethical Decision Making and Principled Reasoning. *Ethics: Easier Said than Done,* Winter, 27-33.

Martin, L. (1998), Integrating Ethics in the Hospitality Curriculum. *Journal of Hospitality and Tourism Education,* Volume 10, Number Two, 25.

Vallen, G. and Vallen, J. (2000), *Check-In Check-Out*. Upper saddle River, New Jersey: Prentice-Hall, Inc.

Sustaining the economic benefits of tourism: The case of Macau

Aliana Leong Man Wai

University of Macau, Macao

Abstract

In 1999, Travel and Tourism is expected to generate some $3.5 trillion of Gross Domestic Product (GDP) and almost 200 million jobs across the world economy.[1] Tourism can be considered as one of the Macau's principal industries, generating some 40 percent of the territory's GDP. As an indication of the importance of tourism, the yearly influx of visitors averages twenty times that of the resident population. As Macau's principal industry, it employs a third of the territory's workforce.[2]

The economic importance of the tourism and travel industry, however, has been the subject of little research or documented studies concerning the sustainability of the tourism industry in Macau. To take advantage of the fast-growing tourism phenomenon, Macau cannot be a follower, but must be proactive to the rapid changing market needs. This paper seeks to identify the characteristics of the tourism market, to classify the tourism product, to analyse the strengths, weaknesses, opportunities and threats of the Macau tourism industry.

Ultimately, the study applies the strategic models used in Singapore proposing a set of strategies for the long term flourishing of Macau tourism industry in the new millennium.[3] These strategies include redefining tourism, reformulating the product, developing tourism as an industry, configuring new tourism space, partnering for success, creating positive images, restructuring tourism education and developing competitive gambling industry.

Introduction

With its centuries-old tradition as a meeting point of cultures and civilisations, tourism generated some 40 percent of the territory's gross national product in 1999. As an indication of the importance of tourism, the yearly influx of visitors averages twenty times that of the resident population. Tourism is Macao's principal industry, employing close to a third of the territory's workforce. Approximately 30 percent of the working population are employed in' hotels, casinos, restaurants and the transport system.

The economic impacts of the tourism and travel industry, however, has been the subject of little research or documented studies concerning the sustainability of the tourism industry in Macau. To take advantage of the fast-growing tourism phenomenon, Macau cannot be a follower, but must be proactive to the rapid changing market needs. This paper seeks to identify the characteristics of the tourism market, to classify the tourism product, to analyse the strengths, weaknesses, opportunities and threats of the Macau tourism industry.

Ultimately, the study applies the selected strategic models used in Singapore proposing a set of strategies for the long term nourishing of Macau tourism industry in the new millennium. These strategies include redefining tourism, reformulating the product, developing tourism as an industry, and configuring new tourism space, partnering for success, creating positive images, restructuring tourism education and developing competitive gambling industry.

Tourism's role in economic development

According to the World Travel and Tourism Council (WTTC)'s[4] report in March 1999, World Travel and Tourism has largely weathered the Asia/Pacific financial crisis, thanks to the economic strength of the North American and European Union regions. In 1999, Travel and Tourism is expected to generate some $3.5 trillion of Gross Domestic Product (GDP) and almost 200 million jobs across the world economy – approximately one third of this comes from the industry itself and the remainder from its very strong catalytic flow-through effect in other sectors such as retail and construction.

WTTC estimated Travel and Tourism generating, directly and indirectly, across the global economy 11.7 percent of GDP, 192.3 million jobs, 8.2 percent of total employment and 5.5 million new jobs per year until 2010.

Across the Southeast Asia economy, Travel and Tourism, directly and indirectly, generates 10.6 percent of GDP, 15.3 million jobs, 7.3 percent of total employment and 4.7 million new jobs per year until 2010.

WTTC's projections for 2010 indicated that Travel and Tourism generates, across the global economy 11.6 percent of GDP, 9.0 percent of total employment and looking forward, world Travel and Tourism GDP is forecast to increase in real terms at 3.0 percent per annum in the decade to 2010. In the same period, employment in Travel and Tourism is expected to grow at 2.6 percent per annum.

Projection of Travel and Tourism employment generating, across the Southeast Asian economy: 12.5 percent of GDP and 8.2 percent of total employment. Looking beyond the financial crisis, individually and collectively, the Asia Pacific Economy Co-operation (APEC) member countries remain poised to be among the largest and fastest growing Travel and Tourism economies in the world.

In addition, World Tourism Organisation (WTO)'s[5] projections for 2000 and 2020, by 2020, the Tourism 2020 Vision study forecasts that there will be 1.6 billion international visitor arrivals world-wide. These visitors will spend over US$ 2 trillion. These figures represent sustained average annual rates of growth of 4.3 percent and 6.7 per cent respectively.

Europe will remain the largest receiving region through its market share is forecasted to decline from to 45 percent in 2020. East Asia and the Pacific will surpass the Americas as the second largest receiving region, holding a 27 percent market share in 2020 as against 18 percent by the Americas. The respective shares of Africa, the Middle East and South Asia will record some increase to 5 percent, 4 percent and 1 percent by 2020.

Literature review

The economic advantages and disadvantages of tourism have been extensively documented (Theobald, 1994, p.75-78; Hudman, 1989, p.211-220; Holloway 1995, p.38-42; Mathieson, 1993, p.35-92, Edgell, 1990, p.19-36; Frechtling: 1987, p.330). The economic benefits of tourism, which have been documented in the literature, include the following:

1. the contribution of tourism to foreign exchange earnings and the balance of payments;

2. the generation of income;

3. the generation of employment;

4. the improvement of economic structures;

5. the encouragement of entrepreneurial activity.

Costs mentioned in the literature include:

1. the danger of over-dependence on tourism;

2. increased inflation and higher land values;

3. an increased propensity to import;

4. the seasonality of production and the low rate of return on investments;

5. the creation of other external costs, such as crime.

Inskeep (1991, p.368-374) further elaborated the economic benefits of tourism as serving as a catalyst or the development or expansion of other economic sectors, such as construction and certain types of manufacturing and handicrafts, throughout their supplying the goods and services used in tourism. Tourism can create employment opportunities for women. Tourism can also be a major stimulus for conservation of important elements of the cultural heritage of an area because their conservation can be justified. A sense of pride by residents in their culture can be reinforced or customs renewed when they observe visitors appreciating it. Tourism can promote cross-cultural exchange of visitors and residents. However, this also raised points that tourism may accrue few potential economic benefits to the local area and local resentment can sometimes be generated if many visitor facilities are owned and managed by outsiders.

Therefore, the magnitude of economic impact is governed by a multitude of factors (Mathieson, 1993, P. 52). Some of the more pertinent ones include: The nature of the main facility and its attractiveness to visitors; The volume and intensity of visitor expenditures in the destination; The level of economic development of the destination areas; The size of the economic base of the destination area; The degree to which the destination has adjusted to the seasonality /propensity of visitor demand.

Archer (1996, p. 6-18) advocating that a government wishing to maximise the income levels or employment opportunities for its resident population, must see an economist's task as recommending an optimum allocation or redistribution particular constraints or conditions governing resource usage, then an economist's task is to work within such limitations. He further raised the point of cost-benefit analysis. Financial analysis places the emphasis on the financial revenue and costs accruing to the developers, not to the affected community or to the country as a whole.

Economists frequently use input-output analysis to measure the direct and secondary economic effects of additional tourism expenditure on an area or for measuring the overall economic impact of total tourism expenditure (Archer, 1977; Fletcher, 1989). The input-output models, which produce different types of multipliers, allow for the examination of inter-industry linkages (Gartner, 1996, p. 106)

The viewpoint of Archer (1996) can be summarised into 5 aspects. First, it is important to remember that tourism is a major world industry, perhaps already the largest single generator of foreign currency flows internationally. Second, it is equally apparent that many tourism developments undertaken in developed, as well as developing economies, have done considerable long-term damage both to the environment and to the socio-cultural effects as well as the more readily observable economic costs and benefits. Third, many of the proposed "alternative forms" of tourism, because of the small scale of their operations, would not be financially viable unless they are able to exist in parallel with more mainstream forms of tourism. Fourth, in the case of independent islands and small-state economies, the problems of tourism development are exacerbated by the relatively small size of the resource base and over-dependence on the production and export of a limited arrange of products. Typically small economies have developed relatively few trading linkages between the different sectors of the internal economy and are unable to supply sufficient goods and services to satisfy both the domestic market and the export sectors. Fifth, there is a strong onus on academics in all disciplines to make a determined effort to devise methods of identifying, assessing and quantifying the direct and secondary effects on tourism developments.

Mill and Morrison (1994, p. 285-306) suggested three major categories of economic impacts on tourism. These criteria included foreign exchange earnings, increasing income, and increasing employment. A variety of techniques can be used to measure such impacts, such as multiplier calculations, input-output analysis, and cost-benefit analysis. To maximise tourism's economic effect, they further proposed the strategies of growth philosophy, minimising leakage by using import substitution, incentive programs, multinational control and restrictions on spending.

Gunn (1988, p. 208) argued that economic development cannot be an exclusive goal for tourism development. Tourism planning must integrate tourism into ongoing area social and economic life. Without a balance of all four goals –economic gain, visitor satisfactions, resource protection, and local integration – planning and development is destined to be less successful. He further advocated that a mix of planning processes is most effective. Projected here are three levels of process: continuous, regional strategic and community (Gunn 1988, p. 238).

Visitors' profile of Macau's tourism

Visitors

Visitors to Macao have been increasing in the 90s until the year 1997 and 1998 due to the negative media coverage and the Southeast Asia financial crisis. The number of visitors declined to 7 million in 1997 and 6.95 million in 1998. Referring to Table 1, they are mainly from Hong Kong, PRC, Taiwan and Japan. Meanwhile, we can see that Macau tourism is heavily reliant on Hong Kong visitors, but Hong Kong visitor's arrivals have had the tendency of declining. As far as Macau tourism development is concerned, to depend on a single market may result in lower resistance to market risks. For example, in 1998, visitors from PRC were claimed to be the second biggest source of market for Macao, while the Taiwanese and Japanese markets have declined substantially. Our strategies must seek to expand the PRC market, meanwhile to sustain the Hong Kong; Taiwanese and Japanese markets in the future.

Table 1   Visitor Arrivals by Place of Residence

	1990	1996	1997	1998
Visitors (000s)	5,942.210	8,151.1	7,000.4	6,948.5
Arrival from:				
East Asia	**5,2555,510**	**7,5040,091**	**6,517,679**	**6,535,462**
Hong Kong	4,803,8	5,520,701	4,702,475	4,721,762
PRC	2,226	607,561	529,829	816,816
Taiwan	N/A	756,690	908,907	816,640
Japan	449,530	497,523	286,060	155,697
S. Korea	N/A	117,499	88,863	22,881
Others	6,866,60	1,117	1,545	1,666

Source: Year book of statistics 1991, 1997 and 1998, Census and Statistics Department, Macau

According to Table 2, visitors entered Macao via sea, land and airways. For example, in 1998, 6.95 million visitors visited Macao. There were 4.7 million or 68 percent were from Hong Kong; 1.7 million visitors or 25 percent arrived by land from China; while 5 million or 7 percent arrived at the Macau International Airport by air. Arrivals by sea have been declining since 1997, this phenomenon maybe due to the decline of Hong Kong visitors and the increase of visitors from PRC as indicated in Table 1.

Table 2   Markets Profile: Arrivals for all Markets

	1996		1997		1998	
1. Arrivals		Percent Share		Percent Share		Percent Share
Total	8,151,055		7,000,370		6,948,535	
Sea	6,041,204	74 percent	4,838,576	69 percent	4,687,055	68 percent
Land	1,700,856	21 percent	1,624,585	23 percent	1,749,300	25 percent
Air	408,995	5 percent	537,209	8 percent	512,180	7 percent

Source: Macau Travel and Tourism Statistics as at 1999, Macau Government Tourist Office (MGTO), p. 16

As shown in Table 3, for visitors who arrived by land or by sea, visitors from PRC were claimed to be the biggest spenders averaged MOP 2,822 per capita, in 1998. The reason for that could be viewed that the larger amount of spending on shopping, food and beverage.

Table 3   Visitors' Per-Capita spending (1996-1998)

	Departed from Macau by land			Departed from Macau by sea			Departed from Macau by air	
Expenditure Items	PRC visitors			All visitors			All visitors	
Total	'96*	'97	'98	'96	'97	'98	'97	'98
Total	1,806	2,374	2,822	1,274	980	978	1,064	974
Non shopping	607	1,099	1,091	974	794	778	557	474
Accommodation	59	504	414	329	228	233	247	207
Food and beverage	507	497	534	392	327	284	229	192
Shopping	1,136	1,275	1,731	300	186	200	508	500

*Excluding the accommodation expenses of the group visitors.
Source: Census and Statistics Department, Macau, (Tourism Statistics 1997, 1998)

Table 4 and Table 5 indicated that Southeast Asian, Australian, New Zealanders and Europeans were among the biggest spenders per diem by sea. For visitors who arrived at Macau by air, the biggest spenders were the Europeans, averaged MOP 5600 per capita in 1998, succeeded by the Southeast Asia visitors, averaged MOP 3245 per visit. While the PRC visitors were the third biggest spenders, averaged MOP 2464.

Table 4   Major Visitor Markets per diem spending by Sea (1998)

Item	HK	Japan	Taiwan	S.E. Asia	Europe	USA & Canada	Aust. & NZ	Others
Total	895	1,259	1,112	1,576	1,336	1,195	1,573	1,244
Non Shopping	743	699	859	1,178	988	902	1,081	1,091
Accom.	201	274	287	450	440	276	545	395
FandB	279	207	289	420	304	362	333	424
Shopping	152	560	253	398	348	293	491	153

Source: Census and Statistics Department, Macau, (Tourism Statistics, 1998)

Table 5   Major Visitor Market per Capita spending by Air (1998)

Item	PRC	Taiwan	S. Korea	SE Asia	Europe	Others
Total	2,464	610	943	3,245	5,600	1,658
Non Shopping	1,190	233	917	2,184	3,621	1,267
Accom.	598	84	640	787	2,280	556
FandB	442	101	277	1,097	963	518
Shopping	1,274	377	26	1,062	1,979	391

Source: Census and Statistics Department, Macau, (Tourism Statistics, 1998)

Table 6 indicates that there were only 58 percent visitor who arrived by sea had stayed in Macau in 1998. For the visitors left by air, there were only 21 percent who arrived had stayed in Macau. However, 100 percent visitors from PRC chose to stay in Macau overnight. For the average length of stay, PRC visitors stayed 2.3 days, in which visitors left by sea, stayed 1.7 day and visitors left by air stayed comparatively longer, 3.4 days.

Table 6   Purposes of Visit and Length of Stay for Major Visitor Markets (1997-1998)

Purpose	By land PRC		By sea All		By air All	
	1997	1998	1997	1998	1997	1998
Holiday	82 percent	88 percent	53 percent	51 percent	18 percent	17 percent
VFandF	16 percent	9 percent	14 percent	13 percent	3 percent	3 percent
Business	1 percent	2 percent	14 percent	13 percent	5 percent	5 percent
Gaming	1 percent	2 percent	10 percent	11 percent	1 percent	.2 percent
In-transit	1 percent	2 percent	10 percent	11 percent	52 percent	51 percent
Others	1 percent	1 percent	10 percent	12 percent	21 percent	24 percent
Average Stay						
Days	2.3	2.3	1.7	1.7	3.5	3.4
Nights	2.1	2.2	1.9	1.8	3.5	3.4

Source: Census and Statistics Department, Macau, (Tourism Statistics, 1998)

According to the surveys conducted by the Census and Statistics Department, Macau, the purposes of visit to Macau were for holidays, visiting friends and families, business, gaming, in-transit and others. For the visitors who arrived by land, 88 percent indicated it was for holiday purposes. For the visitors who arrived by sea, about 58 percent were for holidays. For visitors who arrived by air, it was only 17 percent who were for holiday purpose, while in-transit visitors accounted for 51 percent. For the visitors who visited Macau for gaming purpose, those arrived by sea were the most, 11 percent. Some argued that the low percentage of those from Hong Kong / by sea for the purpose of gaming. It is highly under-reported the actual figure of visitors for the purpose of gaming.

It is apparent that the gaming visitors were not the majority of Macau visitors. It will be a big challenge for Macau to attract more in-transit visitors to stay in Macau for a longer period of time.

There are two major criteria to measure quality of travel industry, which is the length of stay and spending per capita. We can preview that the quality of travel is not very satisfactory in Macau. For the short length of stay, 2.9 days in 1998, compared to 4.1 days in Singapore in 1995, and the difference is very appealing (Ng et al, 1997). For the lower visitor spending per capita, in 1998, the biggest spenders were the Europeans (MOP 5,600), Southeast Asians (MOP 3,245), and PRC visitors (MOP 2,464). In Hong Kong, the average spending per capita was HK$ 7,747 in 1996 (Ng et al, 1997, p.52). It is the 6.3 times compared to Macau visitors' expenditure per capita.

The short stay of visitors may imply a lower visitor spending per capita. That means Macau tourism belongs to the low cost effective type of destination. How to maximise the expenditure and extend the length of stay could be the core problem for Macao's tourism strategic development.

Table 6 showed that the majority of visitors visited Macau for holidays, followed by visiting friends and families and business. Gaming visitors did not play a major role in total arrivals. However, they contributed most to the economy of Macau. For the visitors who arrived by air, over half were for in-transit purposes. How to make this in-transit visitors stay longer cold be a potential market for development. In fact, there is great potential to increase the expenditure of the visitors.

Macau tourism products

Macau is a vibrant modern city that is also rich in culture and heritage. A visitor can take a stroll along cobbled streets and admire typical Portuguese mansions and Chinese temples. Some popular tourism attractions include the 17th century Barra fort which is now know as the "Pousade de Sao Tiago", and the 100 year old "Bela Vista" Hotel (now it has been renovated to be the residence of Portuguese Consulate). Macau is unique due to the rich heritage accumulating over 400 years of the coexistence of the Portuguese and the Chinese. Not only do we have historic buildings, but also there is a living blend of Portuguese and Chinese elements in our everyday life, our customers and our cuisine.

According to a study from MGTO, the opening of the Macao International Airport has enabled tourism in Macau to enter a new era. In 1997, over half a million visitors entered

Macau via air, accounting for 7.3 percent of the total visitors in Macao. Compared to year 1996, there was a significant increment of 32 percent.

Derived from the Macau Government Official Homepage,[6] Macao's approach has been to emphasise its unique character. Efforts have been made to attract customers in new markets through initiatives aimed at establishing an image of the enclave that better reflects its distinct identity.

New hotels have opened and the inauguration of the Tourism Activities Centre, provided meeting, conference and exhibition facilities. The Cultural Centre inaugurated in 1999 is located on reclaimed land in the outer part area and covers a total area of 16,000 square meters. A theme park on the island of Taipa has two schemes, which is supposed presently under construction. However, the construction work has been ceased for almost two years. If the theme park is complete, it will include a square, gardens, an amphitheatre, a wax museum and sports and culture facilities. Other attractions will be an aquarium with dolphins; a lake and an area dedicated to dragon boat racing.

The Macau Museum, officially opened in April 1998, recounts the historical evolution of the territory. The museum is divided into three main sections: early history, the golden age and following decline, and the modern era.

Through the creation of new visitor attractions, primarily on the islands, and the promotion of new cultural and gastronomic events, the aim is to increase visitors' per capita spending and length of stay in the territory, maximising the value of Macao's historical and cultural heritage through the preservation of traditional areas.

Of the two buildings that will comprise it, one will house the archaeological and historical collections from the old Camoes Museum and a museum solely dedicated to the history and architecture of Macau. The second building will contain two auditoriums with capacity to hold, respectively, 1,200 and 400 people.

Visitors attractions of note which are already open to the public include the Maritime Museum, and the Grand Prix and Wine Museums. A further attraction is the largest cybernetic fountain in Asia, which had been installed in the outerport reservoir in 1996. Then, it has been moved to Nam Van Lake since 1999 for more visitors and Macau residents to appreciate.

Since 1993, the government has initiated the construction of several monuments symbolising the centuries long friendship between the Portuguese and Chinese peoples. These works can be found in different areas all over Macau and the islands. The most recent are an 18-meter-high statue in white marble of the Chinese goddess A-Ma, unveiled on the highest point of Coloane island and a statue of the goddess Kun Iam which, along with an ecumenical centre, has been constructed on a small islet next the NAPE land reclamation zone.

MGTO developed the theme " Dynamic Macau, Events All Year Around" as the focus of their promotions. Besides interest generated by the traces of cultural miscegenation (the old architecture, Chinese Temples, Portuguese forts and baroque churches), visitors also make the trip to Macau to attend specific events: the Arts Festival, Grand Prix, Chinese New Year festivities, the International Fireworks Festival, the International Music Festival, the Dragon Boat Races, greyhound and horse racing and the wide variety of other attractions available in the leisure and entertainment industries.

In the last three years, the government has overseen the rejuvenation of over 250 historical buildings, including 15 temples. Of these tourism projects that have recently been completed or are still in progress, of note are the special cases of architectural rejuvenation or beautification and the creation of new park areas. These include the renovation of the traditional "Bairro do Lilau" area, ST. Dominic's Church and the "Rua da Felicidade" and the "Seac Pai Van" Park project on Coloane island.

There are 105 hotels, inns and villas in Macau as of 1998. There are fifteen 4-5 star hotels; eleven 3 stars hotels; seventeen 2 stars and 62 villas in Macau. There are 9015 rooms available in 1998 employing 7138 staff. Among the employed staff, there are 4770 people were employed by 4-5 star hotels, compared to the year 1997, there had been 2.6 percent decline.

In 1998, the hotel occupancy rate was 51.3 percent. The average stay was 1.34 night. (Census and Statistics Department, Macau: Visitor Statistics 1997, 1998)

SWTO analysis of Macau tourism industry

Synthesising the studies by (Ng et al 1997, p.49-80; Wong et al 1999, p.26; Fang, 1998 p.165-170; Berlie, 1998, p.171-182; Liu, 1999, p.341), they advocated that Macau tourism industry has the following Strengths, Weaknesses, Opportunities and Threats:

Strengths

1. The open policy of being a free port, the comprehensive international relations and international capital flows are the direct motivations to promote Macau tourism.

2. Macau government's internal policy to promote and to preserve the fragile tourism destination and heritages. For instance, the promotional campaign of shaping Macao as the "city of culture and non stop events", International Firework Competition, music festivals, Grand Prix car racing, international Marathon, International Dragon Boat competition so on. There are all activities to enhance the awareness of Macao and to attract visitors to visit Macao.

3. The simplified immigration procedures and visa application procedures and aggressive marketing are some of the strong means to tourism development. Macau government has dedicated to establish information organizations in Hong Kong, Malaysia, Singapore, Sydney and London etc; to promote Macau via news, hotline, brochure, pamphlet and Macau Travel Talk monthly magazine; to expand travel agencies, from 60 in 1994 to 104 in 1997.[7]

4. The location of Macau itself is an undisputed strength. It is located in the center of the West Pacific coast.

5. Strong and established gaming industry.

6. Good supply of hotel rooms with reasonable prices.

7. Unique culture and gourmet attraction.

8. Macau Government invested MOP fifty six million on tourism education in 1998.[8]

9. Macau International Airport has benefited from the Taiwanese in-transit visitors who wish to visit China.

10. The Chief Executive of Special Administrative Region (SAR), Mr. Edmond Ho, indicated that Macau government will make it more convenient for Taiwanese to visit Macao. He is very optimistic about Macao-Taiwan relationships.[9]

Weaknesses

1. Macau tourism has been heavily dependent on Hong Kong visitors, over 70 percent of the total arrival in 1998 (Fang, 1998, p.167).

2. There are two essential criteria to measure a country/region's tourism quality. These are the lengths of stay and the average spending per capita. Looking into these two criteria, the tourism quality in Macao is not very high because the average stay was only 1.8 night in 1998 and average spending per capita was 2822 in 1998 and 2374 in 1997.[10] This was only 1/6 compared to Hong Kong.

3. There are limited natural resources for tourism development in Macau as what Singapore is facing. Most visitors have the idea of spending half a day to see Macau. Attractions are of small size and lack systematic organization. Thus, visitors have the impression that Macau can be toured in half-day (Ng et al, 1997).

4. Tourism education in Macau has been criticized as not utilizing resources effectively on professional training.[11a] Some councilor advocated to enhance the quality of Macau tourism. He further raised the concern on if the investment and training conducted in Institute of Tourism Education is equivalent.[12b] The fact that the managerial staff there enjoys some of the most privileged benefits and the highest government subsidies per student per year (Appendix I).

5. The triad related incidents and negative media coverage about Macao City.

6. For many medium to long haul visitors, there is lack of direct air links. For instance, from Macau International Airport, this is no direct flight to Japan, S.

Korea, Portugal, USA, Canada, Germany... etc. These are all-important potential markets for Macau tourism.

7. The language barrier has been an on-going problem for tourism development. The insufficiencies in English and Putongua are mainly twofold: 1. Cantonese is widely spoken in Macau society and is the media of instruction in Chinese high schools, which accounted for 84 percent of all high schools in Macau (Chan, 1999, p.600). 2. There are only 8.8 percent high schools using English as media of instruction (Chan, 1999, p.600). It is a challenge for the travel industry to be able to recruit personnel who are proficient in both Putongua and English.

8. Lack of initiatives to promote Meetings, Incentive Travel, Conferences and Exhibition (MICE) Market and business travel, while over emphasizing gaming and cultural attractions. Leong (1999)'s study indicated that the newly developed MICE market, such as the Macau International Fairs, failed to attract affluent neighbors such as Hong Kong, Taiwan and Japan players. In addition, the Macau International Airport did not play an important role in this important market.

9. There might be potential political tension between Macau and Taiwan after handover.

10. Over dependency on a single industry, gaming, lack of diversification.[12]

11. There are fraudulent travel agencies which deliberately cheat visitors by means of selling imitation goods, inferior quality of commodities and making shopping activity an excessive part of traveling in Macau in order to combat the intensified competition and to make up the prices offered below cost.[13]

12. Lack of large-scale travel agencies in Macau. There were only 4 travel agencies, which hired more than 50 staff.

13. The tourism industry has not been able to retain professionals to stay, such as tour guides. Recruitment has to be done annually.[14]

14. Entertainment development does not correspond to market needs. For instance, the newly inaugurated Cultural Center has suffered MOP 4 million loss in the year 1999.[15]

Opportunities

1. The hand-over events at the end of December 1999 have greatly enhanced the international awareness of Macau. We will forecast more cooperation with Chinese trade being the bridge and window of China. China National Tourism Administration has announced the regulations for an experimental Chinese and foreign joint venture on travel agencies. We believe that a lot of curious visitors will visit Macau in the coming year.

2. The high quality golf niche market is attractive to Japanese visitors. The strong GDP and Yen are also motivators for more Japanese to travel aboard.

3. Capitalize on the Pearl River Delta Joint promotion to complement the restriction of limited resources and tourist destinations in Macau. With this Canton, Hong Kong and Macau triangle, Macau appeals to the capital of gaming, nightlife, and possessing the religious advantages. Hong Kong is the shopping paradise and a modern cosmopolitan, while Canton has her own Southern Cantonese Culture and wide hinterlands.

4. The gradual economy recovery of our major markets, Hong Kong, Japan, Taiwan, S. Korea and PRC.

5. The new Secretary of Social and Cultural Affairs indicated that he would study the allocation of higher education resources and intends to elevate the educational standard based on the current education policy.[16]

6. Diversification of industries, such as developing heritage tourism, souvenir markets and kinship markets.

7. The confirmation of establishing the World Disney World in Hong Kong will promote the triangle of (Guangzhou), Hong Kong and Macau to a new stage. This will enhance the confidence of making this triangle an internationally renowned modern tourism destination in 2005.[17]

8. According to the WTO's forecast, Asia will be the major tourism destination in 2020. PRC will be the first tourism receiving country in the world in stead of the 6th in 1999. Hong Kong will be elevated into 5th position instead of the 18th.[18a]

Threats

1. The increasing competition from other destinations in gambling, compatible attractions, and more competitive visitor packages, especially South Korea competing for our Japanese visitors, Hong Kong competing for our PRC visitors and PRC competing for our Taiwanese visitors.

2. The Chek Lap Kok (CLK) Airport competition in terms of number of flights and departure taxes. For instance, CLK Airport charges HK 50 for adults and children under 12 is exempted from July 6, 1998 onward.[19b] However, Macau International Airport charges MOP 130 for adults and from MOP 50 to MOP 80 for children depending on the origination of passengers.[19c]

3. The Asian economic crisis has reduced many travel opportunities for the Southeast Asian visitors. The devaluation of Taiwanese dollar, and Korean Won has de-motivated visitors from those two regions.

4. The tight visa issuing policy to PRC visitors could be a barrier for many visitors who plan to visit Macau. Although this policy is effective in controlling illegal immigrants, it will also have certain side effects on the affluent Chinese residents who intend to visit Macau.

5. After the hand-over, we would expect Portuguese visitors; both business travelers and leisure travelers will decrease.

6. The China-Taiwan issues may affect the Taiwanese visitors visiting Macau and or using Macau International Airport as a transit point. In addition, most visitors from Taiwan tend to use Macau as a transit point.

7. Higher competition from Hong Kong, under the Neighborly Pact, Hong Kong provides visa-free access for overseas visitors from Hong Kong entering Shenzhen extended to Zhuhai; visitors are allowed to visit six other cities within Guangdong and depart from different points.[19] In this way, there is a possibility to reduce Macau's potential in-transit passengers.

8. There is no pricing control on the travel agencies charging visitors. Partially this is due to the loss of substantial Southeast Asian visitors; the source of Macau visitors has shifted to more reliance on the visitors from China. To fight for more visitors, the travel agencies started to recruit visitors by means of charging fees below their costs. In return, they will bring them to shop in delegated places to compensate the cost, while sightseeing and tourism become second to shopping. In long run, this activity will have serious negative effect on the image and quality of Macau tourism.[20]

9. The former Portuguese administration government has been highly criticized for failing to ensure that educational resources were properly allocated. Higher education organizations are under different under-secretaries. Education resources are scattered. Under different centers of power, it is very difficult to concentrate resources on education aspects,[21]. For example, staff belonging to the same rank can enjoy much better benefits under different higher institutes. According to the Macau Government Official Bulletin,[22] , the President, Vice-president, the Head of Vocational School and the Head of Higher Education Program all enjoy special academic allowances for the duties which they are supposed to perform. The range is from MOP 10,000 (ten thousand) to MOP 6,500 (six thousand five hundred) per month, payable 14 months a year. In other words, the head of a department would be paid MOP 45,000 per month instead of MOP 38,500 per month.

Strategic development for sustaining tourism economic benefits

Referring to the Singaporean experience, Macau has a lot in common, such as the limited resources, the limited land spaces, over-population and geographical location. These experiences and successful steps taken can be substantially applied to Macau's current situation with properly modifications, according to our actual situation.

Redefining tourism

Tourism is all encompassing. Directly and indirectly, it reaches into the myriad aspects of life-from a visitor on a group tour to a waiter in a restaurant, tourism is found in one form or another. Tourism is undoubtedly a significant component of everyday life and this translates into a significant contribution to the economy.

To approach tourism from the point of destination marketing alone is thus no longer sufficient. To realise the full potential of this dynamic industry for the good of the Macau City economy, a wider perspective is crucial. In terms of positioning Macau as a Tourism Destination in the 21st Century, this means additional roles and efforts.

Macau has always been presented as a capital of gaming/casinos/gambling. This role is traditional but still important, which must not only be retained, but also improved upon – thorough the reformulation of the Macau tourism product into a truly competitive one. There two other important roles that Macau can play. As a tourism business center, Macau will concentrate on the business aspects of tourism, ensuring that the industry's economic contribution is enhanced through product innovation and promotion of tourism-related investments. And with a strategic location and reasonably supporting infrastructure, Macau is also well-suited to be a tourism hub – not just for visitors using Macau as a base to explore the region but also as a headquarters for regional tourism businesses. To attract in-transit travelers, Macau may offer very attractive stopover packages to various airlines, especially during weekdays. Addressing the low occupancy rate of Macao hotels, we may offer US$ 50 for a first night stop over package, while the second night may charge US$ 90 etc to make it irresistible for in-transit visitors to stay at least the first night. During daytime, package tours can be offered to maximize the expenditure. Special tours can be designed based on the themes of cultural tourism, gaming tourism, and gourmet tourism. Golf tourism, shopping tourism, artifact shopping and manufacturing tourism, oriental furniture purchasing and appreciation tourism, real estate purchasing and investment tourism and much more to enhance the attractiveness for visitors to stay and to maximize the economic benefits of tourism to all levels of Macau business.

Redefining tourism is timely. Macau is a renowned gaming city. With increasing awareness of the region's potential, adopting a wider perspective in promoting the industry will ensure full capitalisation of Macao's existing strengths to create new opportunities for Macau. A new approach will also come with a new legend – a legend that depicts the exciting potential of Macau as it stands today, an the bright future it strives for through integrating their five roles of the Las Vegas of the Orient, visitor destination, tourism business centre, tourism hub, and the Eastern-Western cultural exchange centre.

Reformulating the tourism product

Macau is a small city with limited resources and facilities. It would be difficult to be positioned as a world-class city like Paris, New York and London. From food to fashion to culture, they appeal to visitors in their own unique ways. More than a visitor attraction, these cities possess that magical sense of place, an evocative mixture of factors that spell the difference between a must-stay and stopover.

Macau is not a successful must-stay visitor destination. To reformulate the Macau product is about building upon existing strengths and closing in on the weaknesses. It is about catering to the myriad interests of the visitors while ensuring that local's needs are met. Possibilities abound:

1. Developing non sight-seeing tourism products. Macau does not have the conditions to compete with world-class cities like Paris, London and Tokyo. Developing non-sightseeing tourism products can be a viable way to attract repeated visitors. Non sightseeing tourism may include Meeting, Incentive travel, Conference and Exhibitions (MICE), Sport tourism, Trade and Business tourism, Religious tourism and Cultural tourism etc. Davidson (1996, p. 5) and Rogers (1998, p.21) advocated the advantages of business tourism for the destination. Business tourism can generate greater profitability, offset the effects of seasonality, the most environmentally friendly type of tourism, and business visitors can also be the unpaid ambassadors for that place to promote business and cooperation possibilities. Macau can be developed as a MICE center among China and the South East Asia, even the world, given her geographical and plentiful conference infrastructures.

2. Developing more and better events.

3. Promoting hassle-free travel thought seamless transfers and efficient transfers and linking our products to regional developments.

4. Creating a conducive environment in which sports, cultural and arts events can be staged.

By reformulating the Macau product, we are investing in the continued success of our own tourism industry. It will require close involvement and collaboration of many parties, and the intricate orchestration of these parties' respective interests. The success of this effort will take the Macau product well into the 21st century, and ensure Macau a prominent place on the world tourism map for many years to come.

Developing tourism as an industry

The diversity of tourism sectors underscores the intrinsic uniqueness of industry-the multi-component nature of the visitor experience. It also means that memorable experiences are all the harder to bring about. If a visitor encounters any unpleasant experiences in part of his/her trip, he will always remember the negative aspects.

Developing tourism as an industry is thus critical, and an effective and far-reaching industrial strategy is required. For Macau to be a tourism business centre, this is doubly important. What should a strategy for the tourism industry entail?

The following elements are essential:

- Adopting a cluster development approach in order to ensure a higher-level perspective of industry development is taken. By identifying gaps in the tourism cluster and forging horizontal integration across sectors and business to create synergy, new products and services can be created and a new level of competitiveness achieved; Developing senior travel market could be a potential market for Macau to develop/explore; Macau can also be a place where overseas Portuguese descendents relive old memories, revisit old haunts and meet up with old friends and relations (Chaplin and Leong, 1999). The outgoing government of Macau is committed to reinforcing the value of Portuguese and Macanese patrimony not only to the economy of the territory through tourism, but also to the assertion of an unique identity in a region which is relatively homogeneous. As a tourism destination in the Pear River Delta of South China, Macau is marketed with allusions to its 'Mediterranean ambiance', 'A little bit of Europe in Asia', and 'Asia's timeless inter-cultural treasure'. This can be another visiting friends and families (VF and F) potential market for Macau. In addition, Macau can be the market for Oriental Antique furniture for Europeans with her geographical and free port advantages. Knowledgeable sales persons and appreciation of oriental ancient culture will have to be developed before successful selling.

- Encouraging upgrading efforts by local companies, to ensure that they are continually at the forefront in areas such as business know-how, product development and regional expansion.

- Attracting world-class players to invest in Macau and enhance the range of world-class products available locally; The establishment of Walt Disney Land in Hong Kong could bring some visitors to extend their visit to Macau, especially those from PRC and Taiwan.

- Enhancing the existing operating environment requires putting in place an attractive tax and incentive structure in order to encourage companies to invest and upgrade, reviewing the mechanism for land sales and licensing procedures, and developing new infrastructure such as a new exhibition center and a international cruise passenger terminal.

- Building superior information networks, through promotion of greater usage of information technology in the industry and development of a computer network to enable electronic link-ups between players in the industry. In this aspect, professional associates such as Macao Hotel and Travel Association can play an important role on fostering and upgrading the industries' technologies and to communicate among the government organizations and players.

- Developing a competent tourism workforce requires nurturing a pool of creative, capable and internationally-oriented mangers, development of a comprehensive skills and attitudinal training program, and encouraging automation and re-engineering of work processes which can improve efficiency. To entice more people to join the tourism workforce and therefore alleviate the shortage of manpower in the industry, an image-building initiative will also be organized, so as to attract and retain capable entrants; These were only 33 percent of the Institute of Tourism Education Bachelor degree graduates who are engaged in the industry in 1997/98.[23]

The MGTO will play a key role in implementing the above measures together with other relevant government agencies, and of course in close association with members of the industry.

Configuring new tourism space

Regionalisation is a key strategy for Macao's continued economic development. By looking beyond our own shores, the city economy itself is strengthened through enhanced opportunities for growth via enhancing free trade, division of major industries to avoid repetition, and the integration of basic infrastructures.

For tourism, regionalisation is logical. The plethora of culture, history and natural wonders of our neighbour's complement Macao's offerings very well, and portend vast opportunities. Not just for Macau companies, but also for any companies using Macau as a regional base or headquarters for the region. Tourism has been one of the most popular areas of investment for Macau companies venturing into the region in recent years. In 1997, Macau companies invested over US$ 10 billion, split between 6,333 projects in the PRC.[24].

Regionalisation is thus central to Macao's role as a tourism hub – a springboard both for home-grown and foreign companies tapping the region's tourism potential and for visitors exploring the region.

Configuring new tourism space entails more than just encouraging tourism-related investments overseas. Inherent in our strategy is a conscious effort to complement the attractiveness of respective countries and to produce a stronger collective product to the benefit of all parties involved. Blending Macao's city-sophistication with Hainan's rustic beach charms in one example of this collective attractiveness; attracting MICE participants from Zhuhai and Shenzhen to extend their trip to Macau could be another viable cost-effective project,[25] Macau – Qingdao,[27] tourism development based on economic and trading co-operation in shipping, and other aspects. Macau, Hong Kong and Canton triangle alliances is also a powerful tool complement Macau tourism products. A well-rounded regional offering that arises from countries capitalising on their own strengths and working together in a win-win manner. Such products can be linked in a complementary manner, with seamless connections provided, thereby widening the range of attractive products the region as a whole can offer to the international traveller.

Partnering for success

The sprit of partnership is necessary pervasive. For tourism development to be invigorated, partnerships must exist at every level from the highest to the operational. Thus, partnerships can begin at government to government level, where tourism co-operation agreements have been signed to set the necessary framework. With this background, partnerships at the other levels can then be formed to carry out actual tourism development-multi-agency for supporting infrastructure, intra-private for collaborative marketing and public-private for software development, to name only a few.

For a start, the MGTO can form a Destination Marketing Committee involving members of the pubic and private sectors, to serve as an integrated marketing platform to address the need for a consistent image and to leverage on the promotional resources of the industry. The MGTO can organise a series of Macau/Asia tourism conferences on an annual basis, to create a platform for public and private sectors to deliberate on macro-policy matters and chart new directions for the tourism industry on a regular basis. With partnerships, seemingly insurmountable obstacles can be overcome and the tourism industry can be assured of sustainable growth well into the 21st century.

Creating positive image of Macau City

Macau's rank in the best living city in Asia has sharply dropped form the 11th in 1998 to the 24th in 1999.[28] It has led to worrisome states for both Macau residents and visitors. According to Maslow's (Macintosh, Goeldner and Ritchie, 1995, p. 175) hierarchy of needs (physiological, safety/security, relationship, self-esteem, and self-actualisation), safety is the second level of needs while travel belongs to the highest level of self-actualisation. Before the lower level of needs is satisfied, people will not move higher levels of the ladder. Therefore, nobody will travel to an unsafe city. Ensuring a secure and harmonic tourism atmosphere in Macau City is a key point for tourism development. This should start with solving the long disturbing security problems and to present a peaceful picture to the mass media. Friendly people, clean city, comfortable facilities, efficient services and professional attitudes are essential traits for good tourism practice. All these need to be properly addressed with limited resources. Reducing tourism taxes, such as airport tax, will be an incentive for people to visit Macau.

As for the fraudulent travel agencies and merchants, Macau government should adopt strict policies to reinforce the punishable acts, to revoke the licenses of badly reputed shops, event to consider prosecutions for those serious cases. For some softer polices, Ho suggested that reinforcing a minimum charge per visitor to Macau could be an alternative to ensure the travel agencies will not attract visitors to Macau below cost.[29]

Practitioners in the tourism industry should join together to upgrade the standard of the services, to explore potential sources of markets and to grasp the golden opportunity of the historical moment, the hand over, to maximise tourism expenditures.

Restructuring tourism education

"To state what is, perhaps, the obvious, tourism is about people" (Baum, p.3). As stated above, tourism is an integrated industry involving in all industries. Macau has been investing abundant resources on tourism education which accounts for over half of the expected income from tourism fund, 49 million over 97 million per year, for less than 200 full time students. The return on investment has been highly concerned by the Councillors in the legislation council. As tourism fund is one of the local public resources, Macau must pay full attention to the effectiveness of its application. Ng was concerned about if ITE's continuing education programs have contributed to the local labour retraining and if the degree graduates would be engaged in tourism industry to serve Macau, even if they were employed by Macau tourism industry.[30] It was only 33 percent ITE bachelor graduates who are engaged in tourism industry in 1997/98 as indicated in the ITE prospectus 1999/2000. Out of their approximately 50 graduates per year, it was only about 15 practitioners were trained for the tourism industry for the entire year.

Appendix I, namely Budget and Student Numbers from 1996/97 to 1998/99, indicates the annual budget (including the annual budget and supplementary budget), number of degree students (including Ph.D., Master, Bachelor and Professional Degrees), number of students in training and special programs for UM, MPI and ITE from 1996 to 1998. Based on the calculation from Appendix I, Table 7 summarises the investment per student per year for UM, MPI and ITE. ITE's investment per full time student per year was about 9 times higher than UM and 4.4 times higher than MPI in 1996/97; 6.5 times higher than UM and 5.4 time higher than MPI in 1997/98; and 2.7 times higher than UM and 2.5 times higher than MPI in 1998/99.

Table 7   Comparison of Full time student investment per student per year

Organisation	1996/97	1997/98	1998/99
University of Macau	57,141	77,684	86,024
Macau Polytechnic Institute	115,827	93,304	95,714
Institute of Tourism Education	513,333	508,301	234,712

Source: Appendix I

Referring to the Hong Kong experience, tourism is their second large industry attracting over 1,400 million visitors in 1997 while they do not have a financial independent institute for tourism education. During the very difficult financial situation in Macau, does this deserve our second thought for continuing to invest in the much needed tourism fund of such an organisation? Would the tourism industry in Macao be able to generate sufficient employment opportunities for the graduates in the coming years? Would the Macau economy be able to afford this "luxury"?

In 1996, the combination of promotional expenses for hotels and travel agencies, Art Festivals, Dragon Boat Competition, Firework Competition and the Grand Prix Car Racing were about 50 million patacas. As it was published in Macau Official Bulletin,[31] Institute of Tourism Education (ITE)'s annual budget was over 50 million for the year 1997 with about 106 full time students[32] at that time. Tourism industry was once very prosperous right after the inauguration of Macau International Airport and before the economic crises. Investing in tourism education seemed to be appealing and needed. However, with the change of winds in economy, should the investment in this regard be shifted to more immediate needs? Merging ITE with MPI (Wu, 1999a; Wu, 1999b, p. 53; Leong b, 1999) appeals to be a sensible thought to maximise utilities on funding. In fact, the ITE has never been academically independent because the diplomas for both Bachelor degree and professional degree have to be jointly issued with Macau Polytechnic Institutes (MPI).[33] For higher education or equivalent programs, ITE has to gain pedagogic opinions from MPI. In other words, all diplomas are having the logo of MPI and have to be signed by the president of MPI according to the related Decree of Law. With this precondition, the agony of transition can automatically be minimised.

Looking into the on-going acclaims of high quality in terms of its administration, curriculum, academic staffs' credentials and the facilities.[33a] Table 8 shows the comparison of *full-time* academic staff credentials as of the year 1999/2000 from the University of Macau (UM), MPI and ITE. The comparison indicates that UM has total 270 staff with 23.3 percent Ph.D. holders, 48.5 percent master holders, 26.6 percent bachelor holds and 1.9 percent others. MPI has total 113 academic staff with 3.5 percent Ph.D. holders, 39 percent master holders, 50 percent bachelor holders, 6.6 percent higher diploma holders and .9 percent diploma holder. ITE has total 16 academic staff: 0 percent Ph.D. holders, 19 percent master holders, 63 percent bachelor holders, .6 percent higher diploma holders and 13 percent diploma holders. We can conclude both the quality and quantity of academic staff at ITE are inferior to UM and MPI and need major improvement.

Table 8   Comparison of Full Time Academic Staff Credentials as of the Year 1999/2000

Higher Education Organisations	Total Academic Staff	Ph.D. Holders (percent)	Master Holders	Bachelor Holders	Higher Diploma Holders	Diploma Holders
UM	270	63 (23.3 percent)	131 (48.5 percent)	72 (26.6 percent)	5 (1.9 percent)	N/A
MPI	113	4 (3.5 percent)	44 (39 percent)	57 (50 percent)	7 (6.6 percent)	1 (.09 percent)
ITE	16	0	3 (19 percent)	10 (63 percent)	1 (.6 percent)	2 (13 percent)

Source: UM Document provided by UM Personnel Department
IPM Document No. 104/SAG/PES/00
ITE Prospectus 1999/2000, p. 101 – 108

Furthermore, Table 9 outlines the part-time teaching positions in the degree programs of ITE held by full-time administrative staff. From this can be seen that there are a total 28 part-time teaching staff, with about 25 percent of the administrative staff from various departments of ITE are teaching in the degree programs. Compared to the number of full time academic staff, 16, we see that the part-time academic staff in ITE is 1.75 times more than full-time academic staff with 25 percent of them involved with full-time administrative responsibilities. It could be a reasonably doubt on the quality of teaching and administration regardless the repeated payments to the staff doing part-time teaching jobs within ITE. Upon reviewing the credentials of these internal part-time academic staff, it would not be a problem to recruit equally qualified persons from outside. Besides, there are also potential conflict of interests to be in charge of a department and to teach within this department.

Table 9   ITE Part Time Academic Staff in Degree Programs Holding Full Time Administrative Positions as of the year 1999/2000

Subjects Areas	Department Involved	Highest Degree Obtained
Hotel Management	Vocational Training	Bachelor obtained in ITE
Cost Accounting	Personnel and Account	Bachelor obtained in USA
Hotel Management	Public Relations	Bachelor obtained in UEA*
Hotel Management	President's Office	Bachelor obtained in ITE
Housekeeping	Vocational Training	Bachelor obtained in ITE
Management	President's Office	Master obtained in UEA
Management	Degree programs (EST)	Master obtained in UEA

Source: ITE Prospectus 1999/2000, p. 102-108
* University of East Asia (UEA)

Advertising for teaching position openings and hiring the best-qualified people for the jobs can be the first step for quality teaching initiatives. In fact, the Equal Employment Opportunity (EEO) has been a common practice in the developed countries, such as USA, United Kingdom (UK) and Australia. There is an urgent need for tourism education to do the same so to enhance the competitiveness of its academic team. The second step is to recruit a stable team of full time faculty members to be fully dedicated to teaching responsibilities but not inviting within its internal administrative staff, given the fact the ITE possesses the highest expenditure per student per year, MOP 234,712, in 1998/99 according to Appendix I. If the tourism fund is not applied to enhancing teaching and learning, where best can public funds be invested? It also shows that the majority of the Institute's budget is spent on administrative and other expenses rather than academic and teaching purposes.

Encouraging competition can be the best way to improve efficiency, especially for the continuing education programs in tourism. All higher education institutions, both public and private, should be empowered to launch programs, which flexibly respond to the industry needs and based on self-financing principles instead of the current practices of the tourism education monopoly. The alternative usage of the tourism fund could be applied to more immediate needed aspects, such as reduce tourism tax (including airport tax, embarkation and disembarkation taxes for maritime transportation), invest in high technology and sciences research, and fighting corruption etc.

Given the fact the tourism is an all-encompassing industry, what Macau needs are integrated Universities/Institutes, but not just a single tourism institute!

Developing competitive gaming industry

Fong (1998: p.167-169) indicated that the problems that exist in the tourism and gambling industry are relatively easy to solve, and the transformation and upgrading of the industry will lead to further development. He pointed out the problem is that Macau's gambling facilities are underdeveloped, which has led to an erosion of the client bases. He further criticised Macau's gambling industry as not refined. The crude represents in the deficiencies of limited intellectual and entertainment values, chaotic atmosphere, inadequate services, worn out machines and lack of excitement and novelty. He suggested using laser technologies to equip the gambling industry to provide the needed excitement and novelty and to attract high-class clientele.

Concerning policies, Liu (1999: p.339) proposed policies. These policies include 1. The SAR government should adopt strict policies to control gaming industry and to strengthen the power of the Independent Commission Against Corruption in Macau; 2. To empower the Department of Supervision and Co-ordination for Gambling; 3. To adjust and clarify the entertainment companies, gambling VIP room brokers and other concerning parties' responsibilities and conflict of interests; 4. To complete the taxation systems of gambling industry and to consider taxing those peripheral industries; 5. To diversify other visitors markets; and 6. To train qualified persons for the long term flourishing of the industry.

To attract more visitors from Hong Kong, the jetfoil tickets fares have to be reduced to a substantial level in order to combat the competitions from Taiwan, Thailand, the Philippines and Malaysia. To waive the tourism tax on selected industries, such restaurants and hotels, could be a viable strategy to boost up the sales and to make travelling to Macau better value for money.

Conclusion

Sustaining Macao's economic benefits will adopt eight specific thrusts: redefining tourism of Macau; reformulating tourism product; developing tourism as an industry; configuring new tourism space, partnering for success, creating positive image of Macau City, restructuring tourism education and developing competitive gaming industry. The main strategies behind these marketing thrusts are the recognition of tourism as an experience industry, the need for a strong branding consistent with Macao's current position, and the need to use more than just traditional means to reach our customers. Cost effective tourism education is needed in all sectors for the multi-faceted tourism industry to continue thriving in Macau. MGTO should no longer focus on visitor promotion alone. It will serve its role as the main co-ordinator, ensuring that the champions of the industry are supported in their drive for greater tourism development.

Endnotes

1.   http://www.wttc.org.

2.   http://www.macautourism.gov.mo.

3.   Ibid.

4.   www.stb.com.sg/t21/strategic.st.

5.   http://www.wttc.org-Travel and Tourism's Economy Impact Highlights –March 1999.

6.   WTO's Projects for 2000, 2010 an 2020-WTO-Tourism 2020 Vision (revised) as at June 1998.

7.   http://www.macau.gov.mo.

8.   Tourism Statistics, Census and Statistics Department, Macau, 1994-1997.

9.   Macau Government Official Bulletin (MGOB): Series I, April 6, P. 409, 1998; MGOB: Series I, July 20, P. 855. (The total budget included the annual budget (MOP 51.6 million plus the supplementary budget MOP 5.1 million).

10.   Macau Daily News, January 2, Sunday, 2000

11.   Tourism Statistics, Census and Statistics Department, Macau, 1997-98

12.   Va Kao Po, December 26, Sunday, 1999

13.   Macau Daily News, January 2, Sunday, 2000

14.   Macau Daily News, December 29, Wednesday, 1999

15.   Macau Daily News, August 21, Saturday, 1999

16.   Macau Daily News, January 5, Wednesday, 2000

17.   Macau Daily News, November 15, Monday, 1999

18.   Va Kao Po, December 26, Sunday, 1999

19a. Macau Daily News, November 1, Monday, 1999

19b. http://www.travel.com.hk/hong kong/airport 2.htm

19c. http://www.macau-airport.gov.mo/english/faq.html

20.   Macau Travel and Tourism Statistics as at 1999(Jan – Jun), MGTO, p. 10.

21. Macau Daily News, December 29, Wednesday, 1999

22. Macau Daily News, November 15, Monday, 1999

23. Macau Government Official Bulletin December 6 ,1999, Section I

24. ITE Prospectus 1999/2000, p. 99

25. http://www.macau.gov.mo/eng_txt/economy.html

26. Macau Daily News, July 17, 1999

27. Macau Daily News, June 5, 1999, Saturday

28. Macau Daily News, January 1, 2000

29. Macau Daily News, December 29, 1999

30. Va Kao Po, January 7, 1999

31. Macau Government Official Bulletin, Series I, April 21, 1997, P. 521; MGOB Series 1, August 4, 1997, P. 912.

32. Macau Government Official Bulletin, Series I, July 29, 1996, No. 31, p. 1319 and 1320.

33. Education and Training in Numbers 1998/1999, Department of Education and Youth Affairs, P. 10

33a. WTO visited ITE, giving high regards on teaching quality and facilities, indicating the obtained teaching quality certification is the first case in the world, Macau Daily News, March 29, 2000.

34. MGOB Series I, March 25, 1996, P. 703; MGOB Series I, July 22, 1996, P. 1301

35. MGOB Series I, July 4, 1997, No. 14; MGOB Series I, October 13, 1997, P. 1203

36. MGOB Series I, March 16, 1998, No. 11; MGOB Series I, July 27, 1998, No. 30

37. MGOB Series I, March 11, 1996, P. 649; MGOB Series I, September 23, 1996, No. 39.

38. MGOB Supplementary pages, March 31, 1997, P. 425; MGOB Series I, August 25, 1997, No. 34.

39. MGOB Series I, January 26, 1998, P. 41; MGOB Series I, July 13, 1998, No. 28.

40. MGOB Series I, February 22, 1996, P. 285; MGOB Series I, September 9, 1996, No. 37

41. MGOB Series I, April 21, 1997, P. 521; MGOB Series I, August 4, 1997, No. 31

42. MGOB Series I, April 6, 1998, P. 409; MGOB Series I, July 20, 1998, P. 855

43. Pre-University students only paid MOP 20000 per year, however, the full time students from China paid about MOP 80000 per year. We disregarded the difference of Pre-University and full fee paid students to get the estimated tuition fee of MOP 36000 per student per year.

References

Archer, B. (1996), Sustainable Tourism: an Economist's Viewpoint, in Briguglio L. et al, (editors), *Sustainable Tourism in Islands and Small States: Issues and Policies*, A Cassell Imprint, NY.

Archer, B. (1977), *Tourism Multipliers: the State of the Art*. Cardiff: University of Wales Press, UK.

Berlie, J. (1998), Macao's society and economy: essay on political economy, social change and prospects, in Ramos R. et al (editors), *Macau and its neighbours toward the 21st century*, University of Macau and Macau Foundation.

Baum, T. (1993), *Human Resource Issues in International Tourism*, Butterworth Heinemann, Oxford, London.

Chan, I. S. (1999), *Handbook of Macau Society*, CUIP, Hong Kong.

Chaplin, I. and Leong, M. W. (1999), *"Conservation and Interpretation of Cultural Legacies for Ethnic Tourism"*, Paper presented in International Conference on "Anthropology, Chinese Society and Tourism", from September 28 to October 3, 1999, held in Yunnan University, China.

Davidson, R. (1996), *Business Travel*, Third Edition, Longman Singapore Publishers Pte Ltd., Singapore.

Edgell, D. (1990), *International Tourism Policy*, Van Nostrand Reinhold, NY, USA.

Fang, Y. T. (1998), "An opinion on the choice of the leading sector in Macao's current economic development", in Ramos R. et al (editors), *Macau and its neighbours toward the 21st century*, University of Macau and Macau Foundation.

Fletcher, J. (1989), Input-output studies and tourism impact studies. *Annals of Tourism Research*, 16 (4): 541-556.

Frechtling, D. (1987), "Assessing the impacts of Travel and Tourism – Introduction to Travel Impact Estimation" in Ritchie and Goeldner (editors), *Tourism and Hospitality Research,* John Wiley and Sons, New York,

Garnter W. (1996), *Tourism Development: Principles, Processes, and Policies*, Van Nostrand Reinhold, NY.

Gunn, C. (1988), *Tourism Planning*, 2nd Edition, Taylor and Francis, Washington D. C., USA.

Holloway C. (1995), *The Business of Tourism*, 4th Edition, Harlow, Essex: Longman.

Hudman, L. (1989), *Tourism in Contemporary Society*, Prentice –Hall, Inc. New Jersey, USA.

Inskeep, E. (1991), *Tourism Planning: An Integrated and Sustainable Development Approach,* Van Nostrand Reinhold, New York, USA.

Lei Heong Iok, "*The Development of Higher Education after Hand-over*", paper presented in the Conference entitled The Direction of Macau Education after Hand-over, November 14, 1999, Macau.

Leong, M. W., Aliana (1999a), "*A Study on Providing Satisfactory Customer Services to Business Travellers: The Case on Macau International Fairs*", Paper presented in the international conference titled: " Customer Service and Service Quality", hosted by the Fachhochschule Munchen University and ATLAS, Munich, Germany, September 9-11, 1999.

Leong, M. W. , Aliana (1999b), "Thoughts of Hand-over", in Ieong W. H. and Wong H. K. (editors), *Thinking of Tomorrow*, Macau University Celebration Committee for Macau Hand-over to China.

Liu P, L. (1999), The Direction of Gaming Development, in Yuan J. (editor), *Problems and Solutions: Before and After Macau Hand-over*, Notable Policy Institute, Hong Kong.

Macintosh R., Goeldner C. and Ritche J. (1995), *Tourism Principles, Practices, Philosophies,* Seventh Edition, Wiley, Singapore,

Mathieson, A. (1993), *Tourism: Economic, Physical, and Social impacts*. Current edition, Longman Singapore Publishers Ltd. Singapore.

Mill, R. and Morrison, A. (1994), *The Tourism System an Introductory Text*, 2nd Edition, Prentice-Hall International Editions, Singapore.

Ng L. S. et al (1997), editors, *Stability and Prosperity: Macau Economic Development Strategy Studies beyond the 21st Century*, Wen Wei Publishing Co. Ltd., Hong Kong.

Rogers T. (1998), *Conferences- A Twenty-first Century Industry*, Addison Wesley Longman, Singapore.

Theobald, W. (1994), *Global Tourism: The Next Decade*, Butterworth-Heinemann, Oxford, UK.

Wong, H. K. (1999), *Macau Economy*, Xinhua Publishing Co., Beijing, China.

Wu Zhiliang (1999a), Thoughts on the Governmental Organisations in the Macau Special Administrative Region, *Macau Policy Study*, Volume 4, February.

Wu Zhiliang (1999b), Thoughts on the Governmental Organisations in the Macau Special Administrative Region, in Yuan J. (editor), *Problems and Solutions: Before and After Macau Hand-over*, Notable Policy Institute, Hong Kong.

Appendix I   Budget and Student Numbers from 1996/97 to 1998/99

University of Macau				
	96/97	97/98	98/99	Remarks
Budget (MOP in million)	330[34]	373[35]	364[36]	
Full time Programs:				
Post graduate students	401	466	420	
Bachelor/professional degree students	2,799	2,492	2,249	
Pre-university	343	323	314	
Sub-total	*3,543*	*3,281*	*2,983*	
Investment per full time student per year *	57,141	77,684	86,024	
Non Degree programs:				
Teachers' training	537	560	566	
Continuing Education and Special Programs	390	514	2,137	
Subtotal	*927*	*1,074*	*2,703*	
Total	4,470	4,013	5,686	
Macau Polytechnic Institute				
	96/97	97/98	98/99	
Budget (MOP in million)	138[37]	132[38]	162[39]	
Degree Programs:				
Post graduate students	nil	Nil	Nil	
Bachelor/ professional degree students	1,016	1,165	1,400	
Investment per degree student per year **	115,827	93,304	95,714	
Non Degree programs:				
Continuing Education and Special Programs	3,961	4,146	1,988	
Total	4,977	5,311	3,388	
Institute of Tourism Education				
	96/97	97/98	98/99	
Budget (MOP in million)	48[40]	56[41]	54[42]	
Degree Programs:				
Post graduate students	Nil	Nil	Nil	
Bachelor/ professional degree students	90	106	212	
Investment per degree student per year **	513,333	508,301	234,712	
Non Degree programs:				
Continuing Education and Special Programs	N/A	N/A	N/A	

Source: Education and Training in Numbers 1998/99, Department of Education and Youth Affairs.
* Total budget divided by the full time student numbers minus tuition fees paid by students, MOP 36,000, per student per year.[43]

** Total budget divided by the full time students numbers minus tuition fees paid by students, MOP 20,000, per student per year.
N/A: Official figures are not available.

The holiday brand – what does it mean? Towards an experiential approach to the exploration of brand equity in the UK package tour industry

Sheena Westwood

University of Wales Institute Cardiff, UK

Abstract

The significance of branding as a key marketing initiative is beyond dispute, and it is predicted that in the future, the brand will become an even more important factor in consumer decisions, therefore the future of brands is of prime importance for tourism marketers. However, within the tourism industry, research and academic focus on branding related issues is primarily confined to hotels and destinations. The mainstream UK package holiday industry is characterised by a virtual oligopoly, ruthless competition and price wars, in an environment of continual change. The paper considers the package holiday as an 'experience', with specific characteristics that add an extra dimension to the building, communication and delivery of an identifiable value-laden brand. Based on interviews and focus groups it explores the concept of branding within this experiential context. In particular, the paper focuses on the level of expectations, some of the criteria in holiday decision-making, the role and significance of brands, brand awareness and brand loyalty. The findings indicate that, despite costly initiatives to raise awareness and promote loyalty, in the tour operating sector the brand messages are failing to reach their target. Consumers are increasingly seeking real value and are confused by weakly differentiated products and sceptical of similar promises that often fail to be delivered. While this is an exploratory study, the findings have implications both for tour operators and for the tourism industry in general. The paper concludes by drawing attention to some of the gaps in the current situation, and discusses a research agenda for the way forward in tourism branding.

Introduction

Described as '*the* most important phenomena of the 20th century' (Lury, 1998:xi), brands have arguably become today's most effective, and certainly most visible, marketing tool. During the last two decades, branding has taken on an increasingly significant role, both within the wider function of marketing, and sociologically as a force that, while not always fully understood, permeates daily life to a greater or lesser degree on a global scale. Whether as an organisation, an academic, a consumer or merely an observer, the power of successful branding cannot be ignored, and the concept has developed as both a valuable financial equity and a sophisticated science, incorporating both rational and emotional values (James, 1997A-21, East, 1997:29, Gilmore, 1997:1). It is generally asserted that the power of branding is in its competitive potential (Brown, 1997) - that is by the communication of the associated intangible values and attributes that differentiate it from competitors' offerings, and lead to the increasingly recognised 'holy grail' of customer loyalty (Mitchell, 1998). Although brands tend to be associated with commodities such as fast moving consumer goods, the brand concept is no less important for services - as Lumsden (1997) states, the essence of a brand is to add value to 'what otherwise would be a service with no name'. In this context, 'value' is complex – it consists of some 'hard', functional elements, but it is the essentially 'soft' issues such as emotional attachment, trust and commitment, which are difficult to evaluate and even more difficult to create and sustain, that count. In today's highly competitive market, the key is to build and maintain a brand that engenders loyalty and forms 'a psychological contract between customer and company' (Gilmore, 1997:3).

For an organisation, positive consumer associations with brand values enable premium pricing and help develop consumer loyalty – indeed, there are no shortage of documented evidence of the value of successful branding as a marketing strategy. Blumenthal (1995:30) asserts that it can increase gross profits by up to 50 per cent, and in terms of financial equity, there have been widely publicised cases of organisations paying several times the balance sheet asset value for brand names (de Chernatony and McDonald, 1998:13). Research has even shown that consumers are more likely to trust some of the big brand names than British institutions such as the Church and the police (The Henley Centre, cited in Lury, 1998:20). However, while branding has become the subject of much research and discussion by practitioners and academics alike, the main focus is on the retail sector - primarily fast moving consumer goods (fmcg) and grocery products. A recent survey of 'the most popular brand name products in the UK' (Bainbridge, 1999:22) was comprised entirely of grocery products. The tourism industry, despite its size, economic importance and interest value, is under-represented in terms of branding-related research and academic attention. While there is some attention paid to branding in relation to tourism, it is primarily limited to the areas of destinations and hospitality (Nickerson and Moisey, 1999:219; Hall, 1999:227; Rompf, 1999:253). Within the wider arena, as Morgan and Pritchard (1998:142) point out, there is little empirical research that explores the application of branding to tourism products.

The tourism industry is huge, diverse, complex and many faceted. It is generally accepted that it exhibits certain special characteristics, and it is this combination of intangibility, heterogeneity, inseparability and perishability that sets tourism products apart from typical 'hard' manufactured goods, and presents specific challenges for marketers in the development of a marketing strategy. Within the UK tour operating industry, concern has been expressed (Rogers, 1998:17) about the lack of customer loyalty. This is hardly surprising in an industry that is very price led – characterised as it is by lack of differentiation, fierce competition and highly publicised price-wars. This paper seeks to explore the role and significance of branding in the mainstream UK tour operating market, arguing that the particular characteristics of the tour operating industry add an extra dimension to any marketing strategy involving the building of a strong, identifiable brand. It considers whether branding concepts apply equally to 'hard' manufactured products, as they do to complex, composite tourism products and examines the significance of the tour operator brand in consumer choice and decision making for package holidays. Finally it discusses some areas of development for branding the 'fully extended [tourism] product' (Gronroos, 1980:36).

Branding: understanding the concept

Although Lury (1998:xi) describes branding as a phenomenon of the 20th century, it is far from being a new concept. Over 2,000 years ago, marks and symbols were used to identify and differentiate goods. In modern marketing terms, branding began in the 18th century when advertising was used to promote goods as social status indicators – a brand association that is highly significant today (de Chernatony and McDonald, 1998:24, Westwood et al, 1999b:242). Since then the concept of branding has developed into a sophisticated science and a highly valuable asset, with benefits for both the organisation and the consumer. While the basic principles of branding – that is as a means of identification and differentiation through a recognisable name, term, symbol or design, (Kotler and Armstrong, 1980:283) still apply, it is increasingly acknowledged that the value of brands is both rational and emotional (Gilmore, 1997:1). Rational values include value for money, convenience, reliability, safety and functionality, while emotional values are those difficult to evaluate, intangible, 'soft' issues such as psychic benefits (as discussed in Westwood et al, 1999b:238), self expression, emotional affinity, trust and commitment which should be nurtured into brand loyalty and customer retention – ultimately leading to an increase in profits (East, 1997:40). The term 'brand equity' is used to express the elements of consumer brand knowledge, which are deemed intrinsic to the measurement of a brand's success, that is, awareness, brand personality or image, brand associations, and brand loyalty (Keller, 1993, Aaker and Joachimsthaler, 1999:137).

Brand loyalty

The value of retaining customers, and the cost of customer defections is well researched and documented (Reichheld and Sasser, 1990, Reichheld, 1993, 1996), and it is often asserted that it is five times more costly to recruit a new customer, than to sell to an existing one (Kotler and Armstrong, 1994:560; McLuhan, 1999:29). Throughout the last decade, there has been an increasing emphasis on the marketing quest for customer loyalty – that is true loyalty as opposed to repeat purchase (Mitchell, 1998:104). The topic has been the focus of much research and discussion, with Perry (1994), Gilmore (1997), Day (1969) and Dick and Basu (1994) in agreement that a successful brand does not just happen, it is essential to build and maintain a brand which engenders loyalty and forms a 'psychological contract between customer and company'. Similarly, McWilliam, (1992, cited in Knox, 1996:36) argues that the reasoning behind most branding is the encouragement of consumer commitment in order to promote positive discrimination. Increasingly, the emphasis is on differentiation through loyalty and the emotional appeal of brands, rather than through discernible tangible benefits. As Lury (1998:4) says 'it is our perceptions - our beliefs and our feelings about a brand that are most important'. Recent research has shown that traditional brands, which are concentrating on 'hard' values such as function, features and attributes, are losing ground to those, which have recognised that 'soft' values are more likely to engender emotional attachments and promote involvement and loyalty.

However, in the last few years there has been considerable concern over the decline in customer loyalty, particularly in the fmcg and grocery markets (Knox:1996:35, Christopher, 1996:55). This is partly attributed to the increase in consumer sophistication and a more discerning, demanding consumer with progressively higher expectations, and a high level of marketing literacy – that is, they are much more inclined to be cynical about the brand claims that are made (Southgate, 1996:16, Christopher, 1996:55). Perry (as cited by Yiannis and Lang, 1992) asserts that with the breaking down of class and social barriers, consumers are becoming 'simply consumers - with tastes, lifestyles and aspirations that are very different'. The implication being that organisations face an even bigger challenge in terms of understanding consumers and their behaviour in order to establish meaningful, sustainable, consumer-provider relationships. Similarly, within tourism, research has shown that consumers are becoming increasingly discriminating, confident and sophisticated (Poon, 1993:116-122). The tour operating industry, as discussed below, is characterised by complex, substitutable products, and a highly competitive, price sensitive market. The rise in consumer confidence and sophistication is underlined by trends which bear testimony to increasing proclivity to exercise choice. These include late booking trends and bargain hunting - both with implications for price sensitivity; independent booking - driven by emerging technology; a willingness to complain - fuelled by television consumer programmes; and the search for 'exotic'- but affordable - destinations.

UK tour operating – the nature of the industry and the market

A consumer durable or a fast moving consumer good, although increasingly containing a 'soft' service element, is primarily a tangible commodity where production is tightly controlled, and which can be felt, tested and seen before purchase, used and appraised afterwards, and if necessary, repaired or replaced if found faulty. Inclusive air tours, and indeed, tourism 'products' in general, are a complex and dynamic amalgam of various components - some 'hard' tangible 'good' elements combined with a high proportion of 'soft' - intangible, subjective and service - elements. The parent company exercises varying degrees of control over these components, which are often branded in their own right. From a consumer's point of view, the 'hard', tangible elements of an inclusive air tour include, for example, the brochure, price, aircraft seat, hotel room and destination, and the 'soft' intangible elements include expectations, quality, attitudes, emotions and symbols - all packaged into a 'holiday experience', which, by its very nature is intangible. Therefore, it is the experience in its entirety – or as Gronroos (1980:36) has termed it, 'the fully extended product' that is important. As Ryan (1993:25) argues - there is nothing remaining afterwards except memories evoked by souvenirs and photographs, memories that are stimulated by anticipation of the next holiday experience. Anholt (1999:290) stresses the importance of the consumer sharing the brand-owners vision and understanding of the brand, and argues that in order for them to 'buy-in' to its values – feeling emotional attachment to 'their' brand - it is necessary for them to have close experience with it. This view is supported by East (1998:122) who argues that attitudes learned through direct experience have strong associations with behaviour.

However, within a holiday package there are many experiences – a number of which, as previously mentioned, are beyond the control of the operator, the implication being that if certain elements of the experience fail to meet expectations, it will affect perceptions of the brand as a whole, thus influencing future decisions.

The holiday experience

Despite the trend towards late booking, for many consumers, the holiday experience begins some months before the actual consumption of the 'product', and could be divided into three stages - pre-consumption, consumption and post-consumption. Using the loose framework of Mathieson and Wall's (1982) sequential model of consumer decision making, the 'pre-consumption' stage encompasses a 'felt need or travel desire' through information and evaluation, travel decision, purchase and travel preparation stages. Driven by advertising to raise awareness and desire, here, the main 'soft' elements would be anticipation and expectation, with the main 'hard' element being the brochure and other advertising material, which as previously mentioned, is also used to reinforce the choice and eliminate doubts (de Chernatony and McDonald, 1998:72-73). The consumption stage of 'travel preparation and travel experience' (Mathieson and Wall, 1982) could be said to begin with the journey to the airport, through the actual holiday, and includes the return journey. At the post-consumption stage, as previously mentioned, the consumer is left with largely intangible, emotional elements - memories, photographs and souvenirs of the experience. 'Travel satisfaction evaluation' takes place now - appraisal and re-appraisal of the entire experience, which, as Mathieson and Wall (1982) state, has a strong influence on subsequent travel decisions - allegiance to the brand manifesting in brand loyalty, repeat purchase and recommendation to friends and colleagues, or, conversely, disappointment and disillusionment with all, or part, of the experience will result in negative attitudes towards the overall brand.

Within the package holiday experience there is a predominance of 'soft' intangible characteristics that are difficult to evaluate, standardise and control. However, it is these very characteristics that have the potential to affect consumer experience and brand associations, thus adding an extra dimension to any marketing strategy involving the building of a strong, identifiable air tour brand. It can be argued that if, as both research and industry experience suggest (de Chernatony and McDonald, 1998:9; Lury, 1998:22), the strength of a brand is in its relationship with the consumer, and the value of the brand exists in the mind of the consumer (Anholt,1999:290;Lury, 1998:4), then in order to reinforce that relationship the brand needs to be associated with all elements of the experience. That is, from the symbols and images communicated in the advertising, through the information search process, the booking process, the holiday itself, through to the return journey, remaining in the mind of the consumer during the appraisal stage. However, while vertical integration has increased the level of control for the major operators to some extent, with some of the various components of the 'experience', such as travel agents, airlines and accommodation being owned by the same organisation, they tend to be branded in their own right. This factor, combined with the constant re-structuring, means that the communication of coherent, consistent, enduring brand values and 'personality' (Aaker, 1996, Christopher, 1996) is hindered by fragmentation and consumer confusion.

The market

Since the 1960s and the early days of mass overseas holidays, UK tour operating has expanded and developed into a major, international and multifaceted industry that is characterised by acquisition, consolidation and vertical integration. Although it is comprised of hundreds of diverse operators, it is heavily dominated by a few major, vertically integrated companies. The market situation is extremely dynamic, with the top four operators increasing their grip on the industry almost on a daily basis. Although ten companies currently control 69 per cent of the market, the 'top four' companies account for 57 per cent of market share, and account for over 16 million holidays a year (Noakes, 1999:3).

Table 1   **The top four UK tour operators source: Travel Trade Gazette 2000**

THOMSON 18 *per cent UK market share*	AIRTOURS 15 *per cent UK market share*	THOMAS COOK 13 *per cent UK market share*	FIRST CHOICE 10 *per cent UK market share*
TOUR OPERATIONS: Thomson Holidays Portland Direct Budget travel (Ireland) SkyTours Freestyle ***ThomsonBreakaway:*** Crystal Travel Ausbound Austravel Jetsave Jersey Travel Service Tropical Places Greyhound International American Holidays ***Thomson Independent Holidays Group:*** Holiday Cottages Group Something Special Holidays Spanish Harbour Holidays Chez Nous Blakes Holiday Boating Magic Travel Group Simply Travel Headwater Holidays **RETAIL:** Lunn Poly (794 branches) Callers-Pegasus (34 branches) Sibbald Travel (11 branches) Travel House (59 branches) Team Lincoln Manchester Flights Budget Travel Thomson Preferred Agents (not wholly owned – approx. 1,600 branches) **AIRLINE** Britannia Airways **CRUISES** Thomson Cruises	**TOUR OPERATIONS:** Airtours Holidays Panorama Bridge Travel Cresta EuroSites Tradewinds Jetset Vacation Canada Freedom Breaks Jetset Flights Airline Consolidation Centre Direct Holidays Escapades **RETAIL:** Going Places (730 branches) Travelworld (132 branches) Advantage Travel Centres franchisees (321 branches) Late Escapes Go Direct Space Flightdeck **AIRLINE:** Airtours International **CRUISES:** Carnival Cruises (an Airtours shareholder) Airtours Sun Cruises Direct Cruises Costa Cruises	**TOUR OPERATIONS:** JMC Thomas Cook Holidays Neilson Club 18-30 Time Off Style Holidays/Cachet Travel Skiers World **RETAIL:** Thomas Cook (750 branches) ARTAC Worldchoice partnership (770 branches) Thomas Cook direct Orchid Travel **AIRLINE:** JMC Airlines	**TOUR OPERATIONS:** First Choice Holidays Eclipse 2wentys Sovereign First Choice Ski, Lakes & Mountains Unijet Viking aviation Hayes & Jarvis Meon Travel Suncars Rainbow Holidays Sunsail Globesavers Falcon (Ireland) JWT (Ireland) Flexiski **RETAIL:** Travelchoice Travelchoice Express Travelchoice Direct Bakers Dolphin Holiday Hypermarkets Hays Travel Holiday Express **AIRLINE:** Air 2000 **CRUISES:** First Choice Cruises

A major catalyst for the escalating power of the top four companies was the Monopolies and Mergers Commission ruling in December 1997 in favour of the tour operators on the issue of restriction of consumer choice through vertical integration. This paved the way for a massive, ongoing programme of consolidation by the major players in the industry – the market share of the top four having increased by 17 per cent since then (Noakes, 1999:3). These operators are heavily integrated - linked both horizontally across the various holiday types and vertically, through transport via their charter airlines, to retail distribution via their travel agencies, and accommodation via cruise ships, time-shares and holiday cottages. Their strategy of the pursuit of growth and market share through a programme of acquisition and consolidation continues. As table 1 illustrates, currently the companies are focusing their efforts on the acquisition of specialist and niche markets, and between them cover virtually the whole gamut of mainstream and specialist package holidays.

There is evidence that some of the major operators are waking up to the fact that branding is a key marketing issue, and are investing in brand building initiatives (Rogers, 1998:13). In September 1999 Thomas Cook launched a re-brand of its products under the umbrella brand name JMC, with the aim of promoting the brand rather than the price. Industry sources (Dunscombe, 2000:13; Vincent, 2000) indicate some success in terms of increased awareness and numbers of bookings. However, very often short-term sales tactics deemed necessary to reduce surplus capacity undermine these longer-term strategies aimed at building brand identity. It remains to be seen as to whether JMC can deliver the brand promises or whether it is just a case of 'bolt-on marketing' (Southgate:1996:16), something that consumers are becoming increasingly sceptical of, and which, while it may increase bookings in the short term, does nothing to generate loyalty.

As previously discussed, while brand loyalty is recognised as becoming harder to gain, marketing focus in general is on building long term customer-provider relationships. Within the industry brand loyalty is notoriously low (Noakes, 1999:29), and Rogers (1998:7) suggests that this is partly due to the industry practice of price-cutting. The price-led nature of the product is difficult to escape and the industry has been concerned for some time about the increasing numbers of consumers now well practised in the art of last minute bargain hunting. Despite the attempts of operators to discourage this trend through initiatives such as such as early booking discounts together with reducing supply, price, rather than brand-loyalty is still the main factor in holiday decision-making (Banerjee,1999:6). Citing industry research, Banerjee supports the findings of this study, suggesting that there is a general distrust of operators, very low awareness of operators and confusion between operator and agent brands.

Another significant factor in the lack of loyalty is that of product parity. Brown (1997:16) argues that successful branding reduces and simplifies the decision making process by eliminating the consideration of alternatives. In the UK package tour industry there are very few barriers to imitation by competitors - companies offer the same destinations, very often using the same accommodation, the same flights and, on occasion, the same transfer transportation. The response of the major tour operators is to flood the market with sub-brands in an apparent attempt to provide differentiation when in actuality, non applies, resulting in a plethora of 'segmented' products. This similarity between brands means that the distinctiveness of any single brand is blurred. Rather than reinforcing brand values, and simplifying decision making, consumers are saturated by the resulting 'brand-clutter'. The result is that consumers are confused and there is an absence of emotional association with any particular brand. Carey and Gountas (1999:70) state that within the tour operating industry, differentiation is one of the most difficult things to achieve. However, while Allen et al (1992:493) support the theories that emotions serve as primary motivators of behaviour, as Hallberg (1995:18) asserts, mere emotion is not enough, 'while emotion has always been an important component of branding, emotion in the absence of a point of difference that can be articulated and firmly seated in the memory is arguably a recipe for consumer confusion'. He argues that the communication of added values such as security, consistence, dependability, and even status symbolism, via identifiable brand image, are of prime importance.

Methodology

A service has been described as 'an act, a process and a performance' (Gilmore and Carson, 1996:21), complex, dynamic and occurring through human interaction. This description can be applied aptly to the inclusive air tour product, which consists of an integration of components, many of which involve the delivery of service, and therefore human and other processes out of the control of the brand manager. The aim of the primary research was to gain an insight into holiday decision considerations, focusing on the awareness and influence of brands in the process. As such, it required research methods offering flexibility and a wider, more in-depth understanding of brand perceptions - that is, the process by which the consumer selects one holiday product over another very similar product.

Qualitative methods were considered highly suitable, as they offer a variety of methods that are particularly relevant when looking at actions, behaviour, attitudes and perceptions rather than rather than more structured approaches, used when looking at frequency. As Patton (1980:7) and Maxwell (1998:84) suggest, the strength of a qualitative approach is 'an understanding of the processes by which phenomena take place'. In this study, the major advantage was that the methods could be selected and adapted to comply with the particular research aim, while allowing the opportunity to build on and develop understanding of issues throughout the research project, and not just from the final results. Ryan (1995) and Moutinho (1989, cited by Ryan, 1995) suggest that the less structured approach will evoke the emotion associated with the topic 'by bringing hidden stimuli up to the level of conscious awareness', therefore a combination of in-depth, semi-structured interviews and focus groups were used.

The research was conducted in two stages. The preliminary stage comprised five semi-structured interviews, which were held prior to two focus groups. The interviews were designed to generate ideas and provide a focus for the subsequent groups and stage two. The participants were varied in age, gender and partnership status, from various geographical locations within the UK, and all were on holiday with mainstream air tour operators. The questions were 'conversations with a purpose' (Lofland and Lofland, 1971), phrased according to the path of the conversation, but within the loose framework of the research question. Interviewing holidaymakers 'in situ' on the topic of tour operators proved to be ideal, selection was not difficult and participants were relaxed and willing to respond openly. Two focus group sessions, each comprising six participants, were held in Cardiff. The geographical location was chosen from convenience due to time limitations on the study,, rather than for other specific reasons, however, location was considered unimportant at this stage of the study. The participants were varied in gender and age, from socio-economic groupings B and C1, and were purposively selected (Fournier, 1998) in order to gauge the responses from different ages and genders, as a guide in the selection of further groups. They had all taken, or were planning, at least one mainstream (i.e. not group, tailor-made, specialist, independent or niche activity) UK air package holiday during the past three years.

The quality of the information gained in the first stage guided the choice of location for stage two. In this stage, a combination of 15 in-depth interviews and 5 focus groups were carried out at various locations in Spain. The same sampling criteria were used as in stage one, again, the respondents were all on holiday with mainstream operators and were of varied in age, with a slightly wider social class range - from B to C2. The question frameworks were further refined according to the findings of stage one, with increased focus on expectations, decision making and choice criteria.

The research objectives were deemed entirely suited to the synergistic and dynamic nature of focus groups, as mentioned above, the findings of the focus groups in stage one were then used as a basis for refining the framework of the interviews and of stage two. A variety of projective techniques were used in the focus groups, including word association, sentence completion, brand personality, brand recognition and brand awareness. Projective techniques are based on the Freudian belief that anxiety is easily dealt with if it is externalised and projected onto a third party (Murray, 1943). Possibly the most revealing and successful technique was the brand personality activity. In a marketing context, a 'personality' is ascribed to a brand according to certain values associated with it by the consumer (Aaker, 1996:138). Christopher, (1996), asserts that it is the brand's personality that 'makes a brand a brand', and differentiates it from the competition. Introduced towards the end of the session, when participants were relaxed within the group and the discussion was flowing freely, the participants were asked to describe major tour operators as personalities, and to describe the type of person the major tour operators would be if it were alive- the way it dressed, behaved, the type of house it lived in, the car it drove, and so on. Like many research techniques, they are open to criticism, however, while their limitations were recognised, in this instance their suitability in terms of eliciting wider, deeper feelings, thoughts and brand associations, and the avoidance of 'diplomatic' responses (Ryan, 1995), was considered to over-ride any weaknesses. Although some techniques were more successful than others as inhibitions and embarrassments in focus group research can be serious barriers, putting constraints on natural responses, the results generated through the general discussion and the projective techniques were, on the whole very revealing. Throughout the study, data was recorded on audiotape and observational notes were made during the course of the session. The following section discusses the findings of the study within the context of the themes explored in the review of the literature.

Consumer perceptions of brands

Attitudes Towards Brands

When asked about the importance of brands when making general purchases, participants made two main associations - risk aversion and quality. The responses of the majority of respondents supports literature on the benefits of brands in that brands speed up and simplify purchase decisions, reduce risk, and provide expected standards. It was generally felt that even low involvement purchases (Westwood et al, 1999b:241) such as groceries, can be time consuming and stressful. Key words associated with this line of questioning were *'trust'* *'knowledge'* *'quality'* *'familiarity'* *'guarantee'* *'tried and tested'*.

The responses in reference to tour operator brands, illustrate the weak product differentiation and lack of identification with brand values. Overwhelmingly the brand was considered insignificant and was not a factor in decisions. Comments such as *'all of a kind'*, were repeated frequently, with most respondents stating that they did not consider it important, nor that it held any particular values or meaning for them, although one respondent did associate 'Skytours' with *'lots of children'*. The general attitude of distrust of tour operators is summed up in the following quotation:

> *'to be quite honest, I wouldn't trust any of the operators. You haven't got much choice sometimes – if you're going to Spain and the Canaries – they are all pretty much the same – hotels and the like, and generally speaking, I mistrust them'.*

Brand expectations

When talking about brands in general, brand expectations were quite high, and generally respondents felt that expectations were met. On occasions when brand expectations had not been met, several respondents had experienced disappointment, and admitted that it would affect their choice in future. However, in contrast, expectations of package holidays were quite low, with the view that things were not expected to be as depicted in the brochure being repeated several times. A significant number of respondents were quite pragmatic – the attitude being that things would inevitably go wrong and that if they did – it was no surprise, but if they didn't – then it was a bonus, for example:

> *'What we do, and what I think most people do is, they travel hopefully ... it's better to travel hopefully than to arrive sometimes. And when you get there you're either pleasantly surprised, or you're not surprised.'*

This not only illustrates the general notions of low quality, but also of low involvement in the purchase. This is surprising considering the nature, cost and significance of holidays, particularly when compared to other similar high involvement purchases, where expectations of performance were much higher.

Despite low expectations, unprompted recall of a disappointing holiday experience provoked an emotional response from many respondents. Whereas the overall indications were that brand had no positive significance in decisions, bad experiences tended to be remembered and recalled easily. As with products in general, the association always resulted in negative perceptions. However, in the case of holidays, although it was often just one or two elements of the experience that did not meet expectations, beliefs and attitudes were formed towards the brand as a whole, and tended to be remembered – which adversely affected future brand choice, for example:

> '....with Sunworld – I mean, it was a disaster from start to finish with them because when we got to the airport they said they didn't have us on the list for the bus, and that's how it started – the holiday! We don't take much notice of the other operators – it wouldn't matter which one, we only know we wouldn't use Sunworld again!'

If, as previously discussed, behaviour is likely to be affected by attitudes learned through direct experience, the implication is that the failure of certain elements of the experience will adversely affect attitudes towards the brand as a whole, and thus influence decisions (East 1998:122). In addition, 'holiday conversation' with friends, neighbours and colleagues was considered by many respondents to be an important part of the experience – not only at the 'post-consumption' stage in terms of 'memories and souvenirs' (Ryan, 1993:25) but as discussed below, as an important source of first hand information.

Areas where expectations had not been met covered all the experience – including aircraft punctuality, safety and standards, accommodation, overall organisation, the destination itself and, in particular, staff attitude. Research by Westwood et al (1999a:179) on consumer sensitivity to staff attitudes is supported by more recent findings by MORI (cited by Rogers, 1998:13), which strongly indicates that staff attitude is more important than quality or price when consumers are considering a branded product. Indeed, increased investment in internal marketing and staff training to engender brand commitment and understanding is becoming a key initiative for leading service companies such as British Airways (Gofton, 2000:29).

Awareness of tour operators

while all respondents were able to name at least three mainstream operators, overall, there was very low awareness. Interestingly, throughout the research, Thomson emerged as being the most salient, and appeared to be the standard by which other mainstream operators were judged. It was perceived as being superior to the others, although this was for a number of reasons - some tangible such as reliability and breadth of choice and some less so - simply a perception of general superiority. This was confirmed by the findings in the brand personality activity, which revealed a significant lack of awareness of other tour operators. Interestingly, the focus groups ascribed virtually the same characteristics to several of the operators, while participants struggled at times to attribute any characteristics at all to some operators. Thomson and Thomas Cook are two of the longer established operators, and the response of the participants reflected this. They were perceived as being very similar, and were personified as 'middle aged, middle class, male, sensible, boring, well mannered living in a detached house with neat gardens, driving a Rover/Mondeo car and playing golf (Thomson) and 'middle aged, tweed suited, male, very sensible, well educated and experienced - 'similar to Thomson but more experienced' (Thomas Cook). In contrast, Airtours was perceived as being younger and less dependable, and was personified as 'Essex Man' - flashy, wearing branded casual clothes, slightly cheap, male, in his 30's, not highly educated and driving a Ford Escort. The lack of perceived difference, or any definable image of other operators was evident in other descriptions -. Unijet was described as 'cheap, boring, no personality', First Choice were perceived as similar to Airtours, while Cosmos was perceived as being similar to Thomson but 'living in a flat, not a house'.

Consumer confusion and decisions

Theory of branding asserts that it aids in decision making by simplifying choice and reducing time, through identification with known and expected values.

As discussed earlier, the study revealed a lack of awareness of, or association with any brand values. In fact, there was a great deal of confusion between tour operators, and between tour operators and agents, and a complete lack of knowledge about their relationships. Very often respondents were confused between brands, and, perhaps more significantly, between tour operators, airlines and travel agents. Rather than simplifying the process, several respondents stated that the number of similar brands made decision making much more complicated and time consuming, for example:

> *'If everything was in one brochure..they wouldn't need Airtours..oh, well, Airtours isn't Thomson, but all these – they all belong to Thomson, if they had one brochure, it might be thick, but you could go through the lot in one night, it is very confusing –why do you need five or six different ones?'*

Again, distrust was evident in the comment of another respondent who felt that the reason for such a large number of similar offerings was to enable operators to charge varying prices for the same holiday.

Loyalty

There is an ongoing debate among academics and practitioners about what 'loyalty' actually is, and it is generally agreed that repeat purchase does not constitute loyalty (McLuhan, 1999:29). Although a few respondents admitted to being loyal to brands of certain products, only a very few perceived themselves as loyal to particular tour operators. Some activities and questions revealed patterns of repeat purchase, however, by their own definition, this repeat purchasing was not due to tour operator brand loyalty but a reflection of satisfaction with elements of the product – particularly loyalty to tangible elements such as destinations, hotels , convenience of schedules and departure airport. Indications of emotional attachment and loyalty to destinations and hotels were evident with several respondents, in addition to returning themselves they had had recommended them to family, friends and colleagues - one respondent had returned to the same hotel 23 times - but not with the same operator. In this particular case, the choice criteria were flight schedules and departure airport, similarly the response of others indicated strongly that when making holiday decisions, the prime considerations were destination, accommodation, price and departure airport, with choice of tour operator being of low significance.

Howard-Brown (1999:58) cites the result of recent research, which suggests that a significant proportion of respondents considered that recommending a company to friends and family was a sign of loyalty. Certainly this study has shown that word of mouth recommendation and information is considered valuable and reliable. Despite the predicted technological wave, the need for dialogue with a more 'experienced' third party emerged as still being an important factor, in terms of providing a reference point and security. Very significant was the reliance placed on word of mouth recommendations, both in choice of destination and operator. Many respondents agreed that it was important to exchange views with people, both for information before making a decision, and for reassurance after purchase, for example:

> *'that's how you find out about good and bad operators and places worth visiting ... you can find out a lot about how they feel about places then you go back and look in the brochure'.*

This corresponds with 'dissonance reduction' type of brand buying behaviour – where, despite the fact that holidays are a relatively high involvement purchase, due to the lack of differentiation, the purchase decision is based on factors such as word of mouth recommendation and advice from other sources such as travel agents, rather than any firm brand beliefs (de Chernatony and McDonald) 1998, cited in Westwood et al, 1999b). Additionally, it indicates a lack of confidence in the brands, underlining the need for information, support and confirmation from another source. A pattern emerged regarding trust and loyalty - participants felt more loyalty to the travel agent than to the tour operator. This strongly supports the argument of Fournier (1998:347), Bendapudi and Berry (1997) on the importance of the customer/provider relationship in brand loyalty. It also further emphasises the level of confusion through a lack of awareness of vertical integration, directional selling practices and the relationships between tour operators and agents.

Information sources

The brochure was mentioned as being important and the main source of information, particularly in the 'pre-consumption' stages, for the majority of participants – whether they booked direct through the brochure or with a travel agent. When asked about other methods, Teletext was generally perceived to be for last minute bookings, and some distrust was voiced, particularly regarding pricing. Of those who had experienced booking via Teletext, the majority stated that they would not do it again – citing 'hidden extras' and 'unknown accommodation' as the main reasons. This is particularly interesting considering future predictions of increases in bookings via the Internet, indeed, the Internet was considered as a possible form of future booking by a only few respondents – the majority preferring to '*stick to tried and trusted methods.*' One respondent had used the Internet to search for destination information, however, both brochures and the Teletext were widely used to provide information on destinations, accommodation, availability, and prices – sometimes used after the actual booking was made in order to reinforce and reassure – and as a tangible 'guarantee'. Again the level of general distrust is evident in the admission by a respondent that she always took a copy of her brochure with her on holiday to refer to in case anything went wrong.

Marketing implications

This exploratory study supports general theories (Kotler and Armstrong, 1980:283; Keller, 1993, Aaker, 1996; Gilmore, 1997:1) that for many types of goods, brands are used as benchmarks of differentiation, quality and reliability; consumers attribute certain values to brands, they offer a 'short-cut' and reduce risk in the decision process. Yet, as the study has clearly shown, despite attempts by the major tour operators to engender loyalty and awareness of their brands through expensive and sophisticated promotional activities, there are strong indications that they are missing the target. Tour operators are failing to reach the consumer in terms of both the 'hard' and the 'soft' issues identified in the literature discussed earlier. Failure to build valuable relationships and create emotional bonds is evident in the overall distrust, low expectations and confusion. In holiday choice, 'functional' factors such as destination, accommodation, price and accessibility to departure airport were considered important – a case of *'where, when and how much?'* rather than *'who?'* with the actual tour operator considered as being substitutable and of little significance. The comment of one focus group participant summed up the general attitudes towards tour operator brands when she said:

> *'We don't really care who the holiday is with as long as it is somewhere we want to go at the lowest price - all the companies are pretty similar - same hotels quite often'.*

With the increasing spread and dominance of the top four companies, the industry is heading towards an oligopoly. The longer-term implications for this are that, with too few players in control there will be less price competition - a virtual cartel headed by these large, vertically integrated, international groups and consortia. Given this scenario, it is likely that there will be less price competition, and that the focus will shift from price competition to brand competition. This surely highlights the need to develop brands with which consumers can identify, which means much more than price need values.

However, the more immediate picture is one of confusion for the consumers and significantly, with business customers such as agents within the industry itself (Blocksidge, 1999:18). A basic tenet of branding theory is that of the brand as a mark of differentiation and identification. Yet, despite – or because of - the proliferation of package holiday brands, the study has highlighted the lack of differentiation between products – not only between those of competitors, but with those belonging to the same organisation. Nonetheless, the study supports Carey and Gountas 1999:70 in that establishing a true basis for differentiation of a product as complex and variable as a package holiday is a very difficult task. Currently consumers feel the need for a physical reference point – friends, family or colleagues for information and reassurance, and a travel agent for information, booking facilitation and security. With brand confusion and brand scepticism rife within the industry, promises of value are not enough - benefits must be communicated effectively and delivered consistently to an increasingly individual and discerning consumer.

Concluding thoughts on a research agenda for tourism branding

Although the focus of the study was the tour operating industry and the package holiday experience, it has equal application to many other tourism products. Consumer concepts of quality are changing, and as their confidence continues to grow they will seek 'real values' (King, 1991) rather than superficial styling. The inexorable advance towards direct interaction via the Internet - and perhaps more significantly - digital television means that there will be increased choice and independence for the consumers - a scenario that has very serious implications for the tourism industry. As the study revealed, 'functional' elements such as accessibility are as significant as 'soft' elements, and just one element of the experience that does not live up to expectations, or that conflicts with the values that are being communicated can result in confused messages and adversely affect perceptions of the overall brand value.

Although this is an exploratory study, the message is clear - there is much more work needed to understand the role and significance of brands in tourism in general. It is time to move beyond short term 'snapshot' research and to fully engage with consumers. Only then will it be possible to develop distinctive and credible brands that mean more than just empty advertising rhetoric. A deep understanding of the experiential aspects of tourism products has a much greater role to play in future, that is taking a holistic view of the experience within a contextual setting - considering the experience within the 'life-world' (Satre, 1962; Valle and King, 1978). This calls for the development and adoption of diverse methodologies and techniques to give insights into the tourism life experience - then tourism branding can move forward and come into its own.

References

Aaker, D. A. (1996), *Building Strong Brands*, The Free Press, London:138.

Aaker, D. A. and Joachimsthaler, E. (1999), The Lure of Global Branding, *The Harvard Business Review*, November-December:137.

Allen, C. T., Machleit, S and Schultz Kleine, S. (1992), A comparison of attitudes and emotions as predictors of behaviour at diverse levels of behavioural experience, *Journal of Consumer Research*, 18 (4):March:12.

Anholt, S. (1999), Travel and tourism companies: global brands, *Journal of Vacation Marketing*, 5 (3):July:290.

Bainbridge, J. (1999), *Biggest brands*, Marketing, 19 August:22.

Banerjee, T. (1999), Holidaymakers put cost before brand loyalty, *Travel Trade Gazette*, 22 March:6.

Bendapudi, N. and Berry, L. (1997), Customers' motivations for maintaining relationships with service providers, *Special Issue: Service Marketing*, Spring 1997, 73 (1):15.

Blocksidge, C. (1999), More lost bookings are verging on the spiteful, *Travel Trade Gazette*, 19 July:18.

Blumenthal, I. (1995), What's in a Name?, *Hospitality Industry International*, 5: 30.

Brown, A. (1997), Brand of Gold, *The Leisure Manager*, 15 (6): 16-18.

Carey, S. and Gountas, Y. (1999), Changing attitudes to 'mass' tourism products-the UK outbound market perspective, *Journal of Vacation Marketing*, 6 (1): December:68.

Christopher, M. (1996), From brand values to customer value, *Journal of Marketing Practice: Applied Marketing Science*, 2 (1):55-66.

Crask, M., Fox, R. J. Stout, R. G., Hall, S. P. (1994), *Marketing Research Principles and Applications,* Allyn and Bacon, USA, 34, 41.

de Chernatony, L. and McDonald. M. (1998), *Creating Powerful Brands*, 2nd edition, Butterworth Heinemann, Oxford: 24-25.

Day, G. S. (1969), A two dimensional concept of brand loyalty, *Journal of Advertising Research*, 9, September:29-35.

Dick, A. S. and Basu, K. (1994), Customer Loyalty: towards an integrated conceptual framework, *Journal of Academy of Marketing Science,* 22 (2):99-113.

Dunscombe, J. (2000), Advantage members are rowing over the extent of support for Airtours, but the factions must recognise their mutual needs, *Travel Trade Gazette*, 7 February:13.

East, R. (1997), *Consumer Behaviour*, Prentice Hall, London: 29; 122.

Fournier, S. (1998), Consumers and Their Brands: developing Relationship Theory in Consumer Research, *Journal of Consumer Research,* 24, March: 343.

Gilmore, A. and Carson, D. (1996), Integrative qualitative methods in a services context, Special Issue: Qualitative Market Research, *Marketing Intelligence and Planning,* 14 (6): 21–27.

Gilmore, F. *ed.* (1997), *Brand Warriors,* Harper Collins, London: 1.

Gofton, K. (2000), Putting staff first in brand evolution, *Marketing*, 3 February:29.

Gronroos, C. (1980), Designing a long range marketing strategy for services, *Long Range Planning*, 13 :36-42.

Hall, D. (1999), Destination branding, niche marketing and national image projection in Central and Eastern Europe, *Journal of Vacation Marketing*, 5 (3): July:227.

Hallberg, G. (1995), *All Consumers Are Not Created Equal,* Wiley, New York.

Howard-Brown, J. (1999), Customer evaluation of direct mail in the travel and leisure sectors, *Journal of Vacation Marketing,* 6 (1).

James, G. (1997), *Britain - Creating a Family of Brands*, Tourism Intelligence Papers, BTA/ETB, London:A-21.

Keller, K. L. (1993), Conceptualising, Measuring and Managing Customer-Based Brand Equity, *Journal of Marketing*, 57 (January) : 1-22.

King, S. (1991), Brand-building in the 1990's, *Journal of Marketing Management*, 7:3-13.

Knox, S. (1996), the Death of Brand Deference: can management stop the rot? *Marketing Intelligence and Planning* , 14 (7): 35-40.

Kotler, P. and Armstrong, G. (1994), *Principles of Marketing*, Prentice Hall, London:560.

Kotler, P., Armstrong, A., Saunders, J. and Wong, V. (1996), *Principles of Marketing, European Edition*, Prentice Hall, London: 588.

Lofland, J. and Lofland, L. H. (1971), *Analysing Social Settings,* Wadsworth, California.

Lumsden, L. (1997), *Tourism Marketing,* Thomson Business Press, London.

Lury, G. (1998), *Brandwatching*, Blackhall, Dublin:xi.

Mathieson, A. and Wall, G. (1982), *Tourism: Economic Physical and Social Impacts*, Longman, London 1982, cited by Cooper et al, 1998:56.

Maxwell, J. A., Designing a Qualitative Study, *in* Bickman L. and Rog D. J., *eds.* (1998), *Handbook of Applied Social Research*, Sage, London, 84.

McLuhan, R. (1999), Seeking the truth about real loyalty, *Marketing,* 23 September:29.

McWilliam, (1992), "Consumers' involvement in brands and product categories" in Baker, M. J., *Perspectives in Marketing Management, 2ⁿᵈ ed.*, John Wiley and Sons, Chichester.

Mitchell, A. 1998, Loyal yes, staying no, *Management Today*, May: 104

Morgan, N., and Pritchard, A. (1998), *Tourism, Promotion and Power,* Wiley, Chichester: 142.

Morgan, D. (1993), Focus Groups as Qualitative Research, in *Advancing the State of the Art, Successful Focus Groups:* Morgan, D. (Ed.) Sage, London: 10.

Moutinho, L. (1989), Tourism marketing research, in *Tourism Marketing and Management Handbook*, Witt, S. and Moutinho L. (eds.) Prentice Hall, London,

Murray, H. A. (1943), *Manual of Thematic Apperception Test,* Harvard University Press, Cambridge, Massachusetts, cited by Ryan, C. 1995, *Researching tourist satisfaction,* Routledge, London

Nickerson, M. and Moisey, N. (1999), Branding a state from features to positioning: Making it simple? *Journal of Vacation Marketing,* 5 (3): July:217.

Noakes, G. (1999), Top four operators tighten grip on trade, *Travel Trade Gazette,* 5 July:3.

Patton, M. Q. (1980), *Qualitative Evaluation Methods,* Sage, Beverley Hills: 7.

Perry, (1994), as quoted in Yiannis and Lang, 1995:36.

Poon, A, (1993), Tourism, *Technology and Competitive Strategies*, CAB International, Wallingford: 116-122.

Rompf, P. D., (1999), Consumer's evaluation of a new product bearing a familiar name: An exploratory study on brand equity extensions in the hospitality industry, *Journal of Vacation Marketing*, 5 (3): July:253.

Rogers, D. (1998), Sun, sea and brands, *Marketing*, March: 17.

Rogers, D. (1998), Travel Marketing Column, *Travel Trade Gazette*, 14 June;13.

Rogers, (1999), Travel marketing column, *Travel Trade Gazette*, 13 September:13.

Room, A., in Hart, S., and Murphy, J., (eds.) *Brands, The New Wealth Creators*, Macmillan, Basingstoke: 14.

Ryan, C. (1993), Recreational Tourism A Social Science Perspective, Routledge, London:25.

Ryan, C. (1995), Researching Tourist Satisfaction, Routledge, London.

Satre, J. P. (1962), Being and Nothingness, Washington Square Press, New York.

Statt, D. A., (1997), *Understanding the Consumer*, a Psychological Approach, MacMillan, Basingstoke: 162.

TTG's Guide to the Big Four, (2000), *Travel Trade Gazette*, 17 January:44.

Valle, R. S. and King, M. (1978), An Introduction to Existential-Phenomenological Thought in Valle, R. S. and King, M. (eds.)Psychology, in *Existential-Phenomological Alternatives for Psychology*, Oxford University Press, New York:6-17.

Vincent, S. (2000), Travel is more than smoke and mirrors, *Travel Trade Gazette*, 7 February:4.

Westwood, S., Pritchard, A. and Morgan N. J. (1999a), Businesswomen and Airlines: a case f marketers missing the target? *Journal of Targeting, Measurement and Analysis for Marketing*, 8 (2): 179-198.

Westwood, S., Morgan, N. J., Pritchard, A. and Ineson, E. (1999b), Branding the package holiday - the role and significance of brands for UK air tour operators, *Journal of Vacation Marketing*, 5 (3): July, 238-252.

Yiannis, G. and Lang, T. (1995), *The Unmanageable Consumer*, Sage, London: 34.

Authenticity in promotional information: Do package holidaymakers seek it – should tour operators promote it?

Eugenia Wickens and Aileen Harrison

Oxford Brookes University, UK

Introduction

Greece is promoted primarily as a sun, sea and sand rather than as a cultural destination. Brochures and other printed information thus convey information about beaches, number of hours of sunshine and average temperatures, location and facilities of the accommodation and details of the nightlife (Wickens, 2000). Less emphasis is given to details of special interest tours to nearby cities or ancient sites or museums, which might inform the foreign, northern European visitors to Greece.

Drawing upon ethnographic evidence from a broader research project on tourism in Chalkidiki, Northern Greece, this paper argues that certain tourist types (Wickens, 1999) are attracted to Greece for its historical and cultural heritage as well as its sunny weather. These tourists want to experience the authentic 'other'. *Authenticity* is the primary motive of tourism for these categories of tourist and plays a key role in shaping tourists expectations and thus behaviour. Since travel brochures are one of the key elements in communicating the tourist 'product' (Boyer and Viallon 1994), for a destination such as Chalkidiki, brochures and other printed images form the initial impressions and thus travel and holiday expectations (Foxall and Goldsmith, 1994).

The tourist industry, especially tour operators and retailers, needs to rethink marketing strategies by conveying authenticity in their promotional information. Marketing authenticity, that is promoting the traditional aspects of Greece, could attract an upmarket clientele. Such marketing will provide a sustainable business opportunity for tour operators as well as providers of facilities in the tourist destination by delivering the best match of resources with the identified needs for this target group of tourists.

Promoting Greece as a tourist destination

Greece is a country of around 10 million inhabitants. It covers an area of approximately 132,500 square kilometres and about 80% of its landmass is mountainous (Pettifer, 1993). In terms of historic sites, Greece is undoubtedly one of the richest in the world, with a plethora of ancient and Byzantine monuments and artistic treasures. It 'represents something infinitely desirable to most visitors, a combination of unsurpassed natural beauty and antiquity and perhaps most of all, warmth and sensuality - Byron's sweet south' (Pettifer, ibid.: 70). With around 9000 miles of coastline, about 2000 islands, and its mild climate, Greece is very attractive to foreign visitors seeking a relatively inexpensive holiday (Wickens, 1999).

A number of recent studies have shown that over the last two decades, the natural beauties of Greece, particularly its sunny beaches, have been preferred to its historical monuments (Leontidou, 1991; Komilis, 1987 and 1994; Coccossis and Parpairis, 1996). For instance, Leontidou (ibid: 84) writes:

'If Greece is one of the cradles of Western civilisation... this is hardly evident in the nature, destination and seasonality of tourist flows. Instead, the country's mild climate...its natural beauty and especially the clear sea are preferred to its culture, heritage, myths and historic monuments.'

Likewise, Komilis (1994) argues that 'sun-lust' tourism is the predominant form of tourism in Greece. For the overwhelming majority of foreign visitors the main attractions of Greece appear to be 'the gorgeous blue skies, relaxation, cheap wine and that enduring Greek sense of freedom' (Smith, 1996). These sun-seekers originate from Northern Europe, with the UK, Germany, Austria, France, and Italy being the 'major tourist-generating countries'. The average length of a visitor's stay is 14 days. A high proportion of sun-seeking tourists are drawn from lower-income brackets (EOT, 1990). More than half of all arrivals to Greece occurs in the summer months of July and August. The seasonality of tourism is among the most extreme in Europe (Komilis, 1994).

In recognising some of the problems associated with mass tourism (e.g., air pollution, traffic congestion), the Greek authorities have recently begun promoting the off-peak months, and alternative forms of tourism. For instance, winter sports holidays, or visits based on ecological attraction are now being promoted through overseas advertising campaigns (Kenna, 1993; Komilis, 1994 and 1996). In an attempt to disperse tourism away from the coastal areas, both the Greek authorities and tourist operators, as an alternative to the traditional beach holiday have, for example, recently promoted villages located on the slopes of the Pindos Mountains in Epiros.

'There is an alternative to ... overcrowded beaches this summer - head inland to cooler, loftier climes ... If it is not to be the sea in Greece then it should be the mountains: just about the only other place where keeping cool is not likely to be a preoccupation in high summer.' (Ottaway, 1997: 4)

Overseas promotion by EOT has been intensified, with the aim of attracting off-season and higher income tourists (Kenna, ibid.; Komilis, ibid.).

'We are not interested in Greece being the summer resort of Europe for millions of visitors with little money to spend... by upgrading our services and expanding our image as a year round tourist destination, we hope to attract up-market holidaymakers.' (Kefaloyannis, 1990: 16)

The Greek Tourist authorities are attempting to change Greece's image away from that of a land of sun and sea. Emphasis is being placed on quality rather than quantity. Despite this new approach however, Greek seaside resorts, including Chalkidiki, still remain a magnet for millions of sun-seekers (Komilis, ibid.). The sun is still a key 'selling point' for Chalkidiki as a holiday destination and is commonly used by travel operators to market their package holidays. Fieldwork shows that Kalimeria a village resort in Chalkidiki is perceived by many participants as the perfect seaside resort which 'guarantees' that they will obtain 'the ideal tanned body', a fashion ideal pursued by many Western Europeans. As Urry (1991:38), points out, 'beaches in Britain cannot guarantee the sun. Nor can they guarantee clean water, if one wishes to swim in the sea'. It is not therefore surprising that Kalimeria with its promise of an experience of a 'real' seaside with 'warm, beautiful and clean' waters, together with long hours of sunshine attracts many sunseekers. However, evidence from Chalkidki also indicates that certain tourists are attracted to this place because they want to sample the Greek culture (Wickens, 1999).

Figure 1   Narrowing Down to Target Markets, Kotler 1989

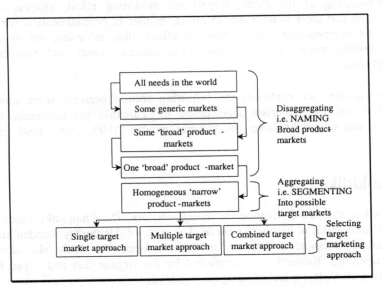

This paper focuses on the unique ability of a popular destination such as the beautiful area of Chalkidiki in Northern Greece to appeal to a variety of target markets. It shows also how these target market segments can be developed discretely by a unique combination of marketing messages - the marketing mix - specifically targeted for those segments.

Figure 2   The Segment, Target, Position Process, Kotler 1984

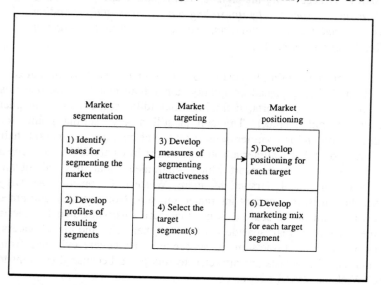

We contend that this is the only sustainable approach in increasingly competitive markets, with increasingly demanding and sophisticated consumers. The organisation builds up their knowledge and understanding of the client, targets the marketing effort, shaping and portraying the product so that there is no waste of effort, neither in communication nor in alienating customers by inappropriate and ill targeted effort, thus achieving the mutual benefit of a happy holiday maker and an organisation making money and providing satisfaction to its employees.

However, before we consider the evidence, the following section presents some useful background information concerning tourism development in Chalkidiki and Kalimeria, the place where fieldwork was undertaken over the summer months (1993, 1994, 1995, and 1996).

Tourism in Chalkidiki

Chalkidiki is now a well-established destination for foreign visitors. The Chalkidiki region is situated southeast of Thessaloniki, in Northern Greece. The coast of this thickly wooded area comprises three peninsulas: Kassandra, Sithonia, and Mount Athos (the 'Holy Mountain', which is a monastic republic). Kassandra is surrounded by the Aegean Sea and edged by curving beaches that give the visitor a feel of being on an island.

The region of Chalkidiki has undergone extensive and rapid development since the 1970s. In particular, Kassandra has developed fast and evolved into one of the largest tourist destination in Northern Greece. It has a number of thriving beach resorts (e.g., Kallithea) with extensive modern tourist accommodation, including several small family-run hotels and lots of self-catering apartments/studios. In addition, there are a number of large hotel complexes, for example, Acti Sani, Palini and Gerakina. These provide the visitor with amenities such as restaurants, bars, nightclubs and discotheques, as well as tennis and volleyball courts, and all kinds of water sports. Most of these hotel complexes or, to use Cohen's (1972) phrase, 'touristic bubble', are isolated from the village/resorts located along the coast of Kassandra and Sithonia (e.g., Acti Sani).

Chalkidiki is full of contrasts. Travelling around this area of Greece, one can see that much of the inland region of Chalkidiki, as well as some of the southern parts of Kassandra, are still wild and 'unspoilt'. The whole region has a plethora of attractions, including: the Petralona caves with its paleontological interest; the ancient site of Stagira, the birth place of Aristotle; and several traditional villages such as Arnea, found on the slopes of Mount Holomon, and Afitos built on the slopes of an ancient citadel. Other attractions include its sandy beaches, and its clear, pollution-free, seawater (Wickens, 1999).

Chalkidiki is marketed as an area of 'a 'hidden paradise'. It seeks to attract those people looking for long golden beaches. In a revealing comment, Andreas Andreadis, (President of the Chalkidiki Hotel Association), said:

> *'We've done a good marketing campaign and we're very family orientated, with clean beaches and good quality accommodation. The area is also very popular with Greek people, which must say something about the region'* (Andreadis, 1994: 60).

Figure 3   The Tourism product, after Middleton, 1988

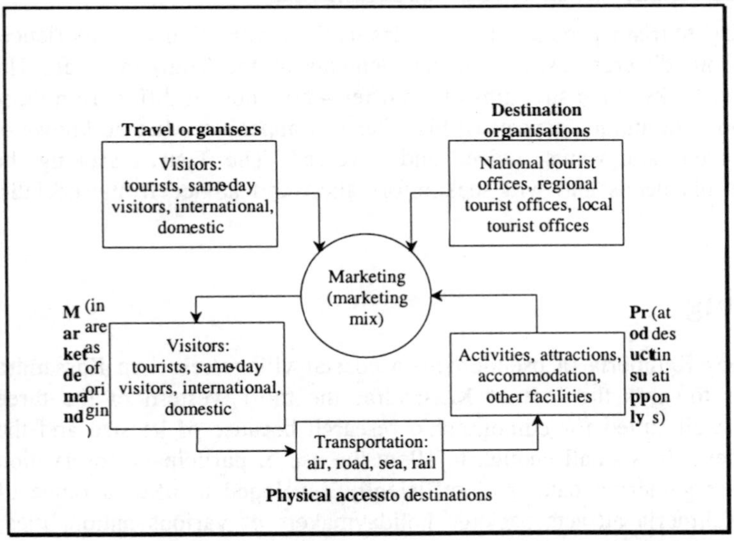

The offer to the tourist consists of a whole range of elements - each with features which convey their own mixture of messages and benefits, tangible and intangible.

Chalkidiki, like other holiday regions in Greece, can 'guarantee' the sun. It is not surprising, therefore, that Chalkidiki, becomes congested during the summer months with both foreign and domestic visitors. Extreme peaks occur between mid-July and mid-August. This particular period places stresses and strains upon the transport system, which has to cope with a sudden and enlarged volume of motor car traffic (see Wickens, 1999).

Figure 4   Different Segmentation Approaches in a market, after Kotler and Armstrong (1989)

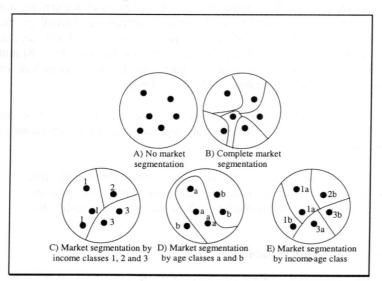

Every customer, for every tourism product, be it a destination, attraction or experience, seeks different benefits from different aspects of the elements of the Tourism offer. The judicious planner therefore, looks at the strengths of his offer – how does it differ from those around- and determines how the unique aspects of his offer can appeal to what he knows of his customers and their needs and wants, voiced and unvoiced. The Tourist seeking the authentic will be clear in his needs and will seek information and advice from specialist sources of information.

The research setting

The locus of fieldwork was Kalimeria (a pseudonym) a coastal village/resort in Kassandra Chalkidiki. Kalimeria lies towards the foot of Kassandra, the most western of the three peninsulas. This resort is well suited for ethnographic research because of its size and the level of tourism development. It is small enough to allow the use of participant observation as the primary methods for gathering data, and sufficiently developed to offer a range of experiences of tourists. Kalimeria attracts package holidaymakers of various nationalities, primarily British, Austrian and Germans. This meant that semi-structured interviews could be conducted with both English and German speaking respondents (see Wickens, 1999).

In the last twenty-five years Kalimeria has experienced a radical transformation from a quiet fishing and farming village into a bustling summer seaside resort. This transformation is a direct consequence of the increased demand for small, affordable accommodation units close to the beach. Today in Kalimeria, there are hotels, self-catering apartments and other rented accommodation. Large hotels (of ninety beds and more) are equipped with a swimming pool, and a bar providing foreign visitors with a programme of evening entertainment, including 'Greek nights'. The majority of hotels have less than fifty beds and the largest hotel unit has a capacity of 120 beds. There are no large hotel complexes in this resort. The nearest one is located approximately 15 kilometres from the village.

The recently developed coastal part of Kalimeria is separated from the site of the original village by the coast road. The original village was built away from the sea, at the fringe of the pine forests which still largely covers the steep hills lying directly behind the village. A large number of bee hives are scattered throughout Kalimeria's pine forests. Indeed, the whole region of Chalkidiki is well known for the quality of its honey. Walking through this old part of the village, one can see a small number of old but still inhabited cottages as well as some derelict properties built in the traditional simple manner. These old dwellings are sited completely irregularly with the 'stena' - narrow streets and alleys - occupying the spaces between them, hence their fluctuating width and characteristic twists and turns. The village's 'stena' as well as the roads in the modern part of the village have recently been paved with flagstones in patterned red and grey bricks (see Wickens, 1999).

Charter tourists in Kalimeria

Official statistics (EOT, 1996) indicate that the majority of foreign tourists arrive in Kalimeria as part of a package holiday organised by tour operators. The package often includes air transport, accommodation with breakfast and transfers to/from the airport. These charter holidaymakers arrive at the airport in Thessaloniki and from there, are transferred by coach to their allocated hotel or self/catering accommodation. British, Germans and Austrians constitute the majority of these institutionalised tourists. Over the last two years, package holidaymakers from Eastern European countries have also begun to visit Kalimeria.

A tourist typology

Wickens (1994) presents a tourist typology which challenged the assumption that the tourist is a homogeneous category. The five types of tourists distinguished -the Lord Byron, the Cultural Heritage, the Heliolatrous, the Raver and the Shirley Valentine - are in effect sub-divisions within Cohen's category of 'institutionalised tourist' (Cohen, 1972). The typology is based on analytically separate motivation/behaviour patterns which reflect the primary characteristics of a particular tourist types (see also Wickens, 1997).

Two of these tourist types: the Lord Byron and the Cultural Heritage will be discussed here.

The case of the Lord Byron

The defining characteristic of the Lord Byron tourists is the annual ritual return to the same place and, sometimes, to the same accommodation. They seem to have a kind of love affair with Greece, with what they see as a 'relaxed, laid-back and out-doors way of life'. Feeling that they were treated as a 'friend', as a 'member of a family', and not as a tourist, was a common theme amongst these participants. These repeat visitors are more likely to have protracted contacts with locals, often being invited for a meal either in their 'friends' homes or in a taverna. In this way the Lord Byron type is likely to have an intimate and direct experience of Greek hospitality.

Although they expressed concerns about the changes that have been taking place in Kalimeria as a result of mass tourism, they still saw their hosts as 'spontaneous', 'child-loving' and 'hospitable', 'genuine', typically Greek' and claimed that 'Greeks haven't changed'. This theme of 'Greeks haven't changed' was common in conversations with the Lord Byron type. A retired female participant, who has been visiting Kalimeria on her own for the last ten years, said:

> *'I like the Greek way of life. So I've noticed a big difference in tourism, but not in the people, they haven't changed. They are still very courteous, friendly and nice....I mean, I still find them hospitable, in that you'd even go in just to buy a stamp, in a little shop and I know they'd say 'sit down' and they would come out with a little glass of something and all I bought is one stamp... That's Greek hospitality. It's not changed even though the tourists are here. It is the same friendliness and hospitality'.*

Figure 5   The Pyramid of Needs, Maslow, 1954

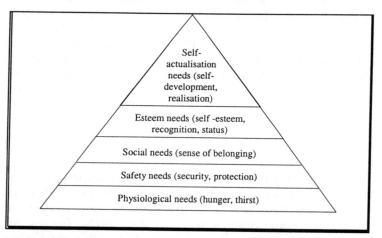

Abraham Maslow suggests that there is a hierarchy of needs. Individuals in modern day societies, in the main, will not seek to satisfy their higher level needs until the more basic and pressing needs of safety and security have been satisfied. The Lord Byron, the Cultural Heritage and the discerning Heliolatrous will be found to be seeking to satisfy the higher level needs of esteem and self actualisation. The 'product' and all the promotional messages must acknowledge this and communicate accordingly.

The Lord Byrons clearly felt that they could have an authentic experience, i.e., human spontaneity and genuine hospitality, by interacting with local people in this host community. This desire for human authenticity, rather than cultural/material or physical/natural authenticity, seems to form the focus of their holiday experience (see Wickens, 1999).

This expectation of human authenticity is reflected in several of the Lord Byron's activities. 'I prefer doing things that are Greek', 'I prefer eating out in a real Greek taverna', 'we prefer to use the pantopoleio and the kreopoleio[1] where locals do their shopping', 'we prefer to have our meals where the locals go', are participant statements, which reflect their desire to 'go native'. They also enjoy intermingling with the Greeks in the evening parade along the seafront, and sampling local entertainment in tavernas located in the old parts of Kalimeria.

Statements such as these indicate that these participants wish to go native in Kalimeria.

Typical expressions of this are: 'I prefer doing things that are Greek'; 'I prefer eating out in Greek tavernas, where the locals go'; 'We enjoy local life and cuisine'. Lord Byrons often reported that, 'the novelty is to go away and do something that is typically Greek'. Indeed, 'going native' is reflected in several of their activities, such as using public transport to visit other villages in the peninsula, shopping and buying 'Greek things', and intermingling with Greeks in the evening ritual stroll along the seafront. This represents the sacred' part of their role in this host community, which denotes the parts that these participants wish to play, while on holiday in Kalimeria.

The case of the cultural heritage type

Although this was their first visit to Kalimeria, all of these participants had some previous holiday experience of Greece and knowledge of Greek culture and ancient history. The majority had visited Greece at least twice in the previous six years. They identified the natural beauties of Greece, its culture and history as the primary reasons for their visits. As one female participant (her travelling companions included her husband, two young sons and her elderly mother) put it:

> '*The classical sites, Epidorous, Sparta, the Greek way of life, the food, the language, the music, ...the plant life, the animal life.. a lot of wild birds, some of them en route, on migration.....the beautiful sunsets, Greece has so many things to offer... Because of these special sites, ..the classics archaeology is a particular draw for people who are specifically interested in that type of holiday - an interest holiday. ... And so Greece can provide a number of things - the interest holiday side of things - sailing and water sports, as well as the conventional, sunbathing type - it has a lot to offer to people.*'

Organised excursions to the historical monuments of Thessaloniki, to Stagira (the birthplace of Aristotle), and to the Petralona caves were also undertaken by Cultural Heritage tourists. As one female participant who was travelling with her husband expressed it:

> '*You can always escape. .....we try to get about on the local bus and that's quite a good experience......it's also nice listening to the Greek people, yapping to each other, especially the old women in their black clothes.... yesterday, we were in Aghia Paraskevi ... the scenery was fantastic, breathtaking... oh yeah, we spend most of our time sightseeing and visiting other villages.*'

In actively seeking to sample the village life in Kalimeria, the Cultural Heritage type also comes into contact with locals and Greek holidaymakers[2]. Interactions with their hosts occur in tavernas, cafes, zaharoplasteios shops, but also on the beach. The 'unexpected friendliness' and hospitality of their hosts was a common theme to arise in our conversations. This is illustrated in the following extract from a conversation with a female participant who was holidaying with her husband in Kalimeria.

> *'Last night we just happened to be getting off the boat and walking up along the beach and these people...just dragged us - me and my husband- into their party. There were lots of Greek people dancing on the beach and they were cooking the little fish - and they shared the fish with us and it was a wonderful experience, it was just wonderful. So you still get the spontaneity here and I like that... Oh, it was a lovely experience......That wouldn't happen in England.'*

The Cultural Heritage tourist clearly is not isolated from the host environment as has been suggested in previous studies, including Cohen's work. When asked if they would return to Kalimeria, a common response from participants in this category was that they would like 'to visit other parts of Greece'. For example:

> *'Oh I'd come again, perhaps, in a few years time, to another resort in Chalkidiki, yes, but I'd like to see other places in Greece as well. I'd come to Greece in May or early June, or late September when it's not that hot.'*

Similarly

> *'We will come to Greece. We'd like to see some other parts of Greece, maybe some of the islands. We'd very much love to visit Crete next year. One of our friends who's been to Crete, said it was a lovely island, not very touristy - lots of historical monuments to see.'*

The majority said that they were specifically interested in 'the very special sites of Greece', the 'classics' and 'archaeology', and that it was the promise of an experience of Greek village life that had drawn them to Chalkidiki. Their experiences of exploring the whole of the Chalkidiki region, and travelling as far as Meteora (monasteries located in the central part of Greece) was a frequent topic in my conversations with this tourist type.

The majority of participants (ten out of eighteen) told me that they enjoyed 'travelling around in buses to little places like Aghia Paraskevi'; 'travelling around independently because they were interested in the Greek culture'. This theme is illustrated in the following extract from a conversation I had with one Cultural Heritage type.

> *'.. Chalkidiki is very beautiful.....we've visited Petralona caves and Afitos..Most people we bumped into were locals or holidaying Greeks not tourists....yes they were extremely polite and friendly and hospitable.'*

> *'Yes, we did travel around the peninsula and although some parts are touristy - e.g., Kalithea is very commercialised - you can go two or three miles away from the main coastal road - and find places which I can describe as the true Greek*

way of life....Aghia Paraskevi was very casual, friendly and very quiet - no discos.'

Analysis indicates that participants in this cluster use Kalimeria as a base to explore Chalkidiki. Visiting other villages and historical monuments, taking 'walks amongst the hills in the hinterland' and/or doing 'a lot of foot-slogging in the evenings around the back streets' to see the 'true way of life' seem to be the main holiday activities undertaken by them. As this retired male participant and his wife stated:

'we enjoy travelling around Chalkidiki....not just to see the sights but also to try and get a feel of the country and the culture.... No we're not here for watersports or whatever.... We've seen some of the ancient sights...and we're going on an organised trip to Meteora tomorrow,.... but some days we are just as happy sitting in a cafe, along the waterfront, listening to Greek music, and mixing with Greeks.....'

The following is an extract from a conversation with a male participant who was holidaying with his wife. It describes his encounter with Greek hospitality.

'this place has a great deal of character.......The food and service are also good.....We enjoy going to the tavernas and having a nice Greek meal - fish, or soublaki, mousaka and kleftico....and then we wander back to our hotel about eleven o'clock and go to bed.... Last night, we [he and his wife] had a three-course meal at this taverna .....and we had a coffee and a Metaxa on the house. You wouldn't get that in England......This is what we like best in this place.'

Such encounters with Greek hospitality, as well as seeing places of cultural and historical interest in Chalkidiki, seems to form the basis of the 'sacred' part of the Cultural Heritage types Chalkidiki experience. The case of the Cultural Heritage type provides evidence that these tourists are interested in the authentic 'other' (Wickens, 2000). All participants in this category had previous experience of Greece. The majority of them reported that they were specifically interested in the special sites of Greece, the classics and to sample Greek village life. The theme of 'travelling around independently' because they were 'interested in the Greek culture' Throughout fieldwork, the theme 'we want to sample the Greek culture' was commonly encountered in conversations with participants in this category. Clearly like the Lord Byrons, the Cultural Heritage expects to experience the culture of Kalimeria. Their narratives reveal that they are interested in the 'other', that is, in the history and culture of the whole region of Chalkidiki, including local food, Greek folk music, handicrafts, architecture and the Greek language.

Figures 6 and 7 The Role of Promotion Information Search – Types of Information Search

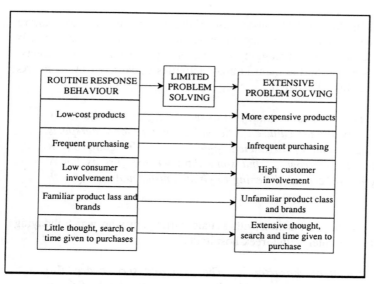

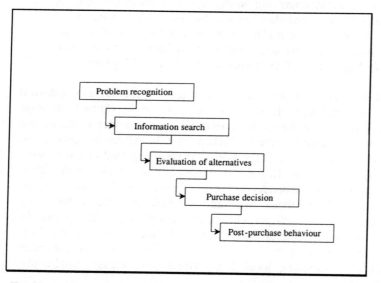

For the people in this target market, the purchase of such a holiday will be deemed to be a "problem" (resolution of a situation) requiring some limited information – a limited search and they will filter out irrelevant or inappropriate commercial and non-commercial information. The tourism experience starts before the holiday and the search will concentrate on information which reinforces the concept of authenticity being available as part of the package. The importance of reliability, i.e. authenticity of information, is crucial as it shapes expectations and affects perceptions and thus the memories and of the whole holiday.

Advertising narratives often 'invite the reader to select an "unspoiled Greek island" (Kenna, 1993: 78). The theme of 'Escape to the Greece of the Greeks' is also common in newspaper advertisements (e.g., the Weekend Guardian, April, 1997).

In addition, the word authenticity has been used to describe a landscape that is virgin, beaches that are natural, but not people or Greek hospitality.

> *'The Gods could have made their beaches anywhere. They chose the coastline of Greece'. (in Boniface and Fowler, 1993: 8)*

These advertisements show that tourists are sold images of places in Greece as being 'natural' and 'undiscovered'. Tourists are also sold images of Greece as an area governed by the 'Four S's' - sun, sea, sand and sex.

'The magic that is Greece,... Naked hills and naked girls.... sunshine's free of charge...Simplicity? Miracle? Offering of the gods? Yes, but Zeus is like that...Come on then, why delay, come to our land. Come and place yourself at the service of magic. At the essence of Beauty' (EOT, 1988). Or again: 'Greece voted the most erotic place in the world..... In the untainted landmarks of Greece eroticism is present in its purest form' (EOT, 1997).

Product and promotional information is critical in the search process if the mutual benefit (profit for the organisation and satisfaction for the customer) is to be maintained.

There are several studies which show that an increasing number of foreign visitors to Greece, including Chalkidiki, are attracted by its sunny beaches rather than by its historic monuments, and heritage (cf. Leontidou, 1991; Komilis, 1994). However, the evidence from Chalkidiki shows that although foreign visitors are primarily concerned with the 'authentic' Greek sunny weather, and the clear sea, there is also evidence which shows that certain tourist types are interested in the cultural authenticity of this sunny resort. The Chalkidiki study shows that tourists are characterised by a highly diversified pattern of interests and activities (Wickens, 2000).

Figures 8 and 9 A Basic Model of Buyer Behaviour (showing some categories of factors which influence behaviour)

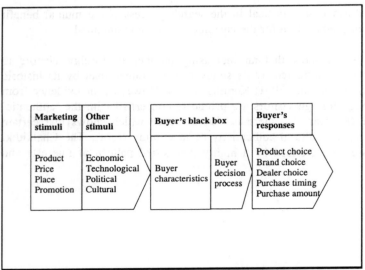

Cultural	Social	Personal	Psychological	
		Age and life cycle stage	Motivation	
	Reference groups	Occupation	Perception	Buyer
Culture		Economic circumstances	Learning	
Subculture	Family	Lifestyle	Beliefs and attitudes	
Social class	Roles and statuses	Personality & self-concept		

What then is of prime importance to tour operators who are competing in the increasingly competitive and price competitive market of short haul, mid price package holidays is to

Marketing stimuli	Other stimuli	Buyer's black box		Buyer's responses
Product Price Place Promotion	Economic Technological Political Cultural	Buyer characteristics	Buyer decision process	Product choice Brand choice Dealer choice Purchase timing Purchase amount

establish an identification and an understanding of the characteristics of their target holiday makers. Then to build up the profile of knowledge and understanding of the different needs and expectations of the various potential target market segments so as to better communicate the message of the reality of the experience, the authenticity to match the personal and social characteristics of the tourists.

Conclusion

The interaction of all the factors, internal, external and situational which lead to the satisfactory conclusion of the purchase of a satisfyingly authentic holiday – with expectations wholly in line with the promises made at every stage of the search and purchase decision – need to match with the reality of the experience. The promise, the portrayal of the image of the authentic, the packaging of the experience and all of the roles of the players in the provision of the holiday combine in the experience of the tourist to shape what is real. The authentic holiday is the sustainable future for the package holiday organisation. The reality of the holiday itself, the memories and any follow up when the holiday is over all shape the experience during and after the holiday and ensure a authentic experience to be shared and remembered, becoming its own authenticity for the tourist and his peers for years to come.

Endnotes

1. A Pantopoleio is a grocer's shop and a Kreopoleio is a butcher's shop.

2. Kalimeria is a popular seaside resort for Greek holidaymakers.

References

Andreadis, A. (1994), quoted in 'Tourism in Greece', *Travel Weekly*, March, 30th, p.60.

Boniface and Fowler, (1993), *Heritage and Tourism in the 'Global Village'*, London, Routledge.

Boorstin, D. (1964), *The Image: A Guide to Pseudo-Events in America*, New York: Harper and Row.

Buck, R. C. (1977), 'The Ubiquitous Tourist Brochure: Explorations in its Intended and Unintended Use', *Annals of Tourism Research*, 4, (4): 195-207.

Cohen, E. (1972), 'Towards a Sociology of International Tourism', *Social Research*, 39, (1): 164-182.

Cohen, E. (1974), 'Who is a Tourist? A Conceptual Clarification', *Sociological Review*, 22, (4): 527-555.

Cohen, E. (1984), 'The Sociology of Tourism: Approaches, Issues and Findings', *Annual Review of Sociology*, 10: 373-392.

Coccossis, H. and Parpairis, A. (1996), 'Tourism and Carrying capacity in Coastal areas; Mykonos, Greece', in Priestley, G. et al. (eds.) *Sustainable Tourism? European Experiences*, Wallingford: CAB International and Responses, London: Pinter.

Crick, M. (1989), 'Representations of International Tourism in the Social Sciences: Sun, Sex, Sights, Savings, and Servility', *Annual Review of Anthropology*, 18, (1): 307-344.

Culler, J. (1981), 'Semiotics of Tourism', *American Journal of Semiotics*, 1: 127-140.

Dann, G. M. S. (1977), 'Anomie, Ego-Enhancement and Tourism', *Annals of Tourism Research*, 4, (4): 184-94.

Dann, G. M. S. (1981), 'Tourist Motivation: An Appraisal', *Annals of Tourism Research*, 9, (2): 187-219.

Dann, G. M. S., Nash, D. and Pearce, P. L. (1988), 'Methodological Issues in Tourism Research', *Annals of Tourism Research*, 15, (1): 1-28.

Dann, G. M. S. and Cohen, E. (1991), 'Sociology and Tourism', *Annals of Tourism Research*, 18, (1): 155-69.

Engel, J. F., Warshaw, M. R., Kinnear, T. C. (1967), *Promotional Strategy*, 6th Ed, Illinois, pub. Irwin

EOT (Greek National Tourism Organisation) (1990), 'Statistical Year Book of Greece', Athens: EOT.

EOT (1996), (Thessaloniki Tourist Organisation), *Personal communication*, September, 10th.

EOT (1997), Tourist Advertisement in the *Telegraph Magazine*, April 19th, p.31.

EOT (1997), Tourist Advertisement in the *Weekend Guardian*, April 19th, p.19.

Foxall, G. R., and Goldsmith, R .E., (1994), *Consumer Psychology for Marketing* London, pub. Routledge.

Kefaloyannis, (Minister of Tourism) (1990) quoted in Palmer, G. 'Tourism in Greece', *the Guardian*. April 30th. p.16.

Kenna, M. (1993), 'Return Migrants and Tourism Development: An Example from the Cyclades', *Journal of Modern Greek Studies*, 11: 75-95.

Komilis, P. (1987), The Spacial Structure and Growth of Tourism in Relation to the Physical Planning Process: The Case of Greece, University of Strathclyde: Unpublished Ph.D.

Komilis, P.(1994), 'Tourism and Sustainable Regional Development', in Seaton, A. et al. (eds.) Tourism the State of the Art, Chister: Wiley.

Komilis, P. (1996), 'Developing Cultural Tourism in the Greek Aegean Islands', in Robinson, M et al. (eds.) *Tourism and Culture, Towards the 21st Century, Conference Proceedings: Managing Cultural Resources for the Tourist*, Newcastle: University of Northumbria.

Kotler, P., (1984), *Marketing Management*, 5th ed, New Jersey, pub. Prentice-Hall.

Kotler, P. and Armstrong, G. (1989), *Principles of Marketing*, Prentice-Hall.

Leontiduou, L. (1991), 'Greece: Prospects and Contradictions of Tourism in the 1980s', in Williams, A. and Shaw, G. (eds.) *Tourism and Economic Development, Western European Experiences*, London: Belhaven Press.

MacCannell, D. (1973), 'Staged Authenticity: Arrangements of Social Space in Tourist Settings', *American Journal of Sociology*, 79, (3): 589-603.

MacCannell, D. (1976), *The Tourist: A New Theory of the Leisure Class*, Basingstoke: MacMillan.

Maslow, A. (1954), *Motivation and Personality*, Harper and Row, New York.

Middleton, V. T. C., (1988), *Marketing in Travel and Tourism*, London, pub. Heinemann.

Ottaway, M. (1997), 'There is an Alternative to Baking', *The Sunday Times*, March 30th. p. 4.

Pearce, P. L. (1982), *The Social Psychology of Tourist Behaviour*, Oxford: Pergamon Press.

Pearce, P. L. (1993), 'Fundamentals of Tourist Motivation', in Pearce, D. and Butler, R. (eds.) *Tourism Research: Critiques and Challenges*, London: Routledge.

Pettifer, J.(1993), *The Greeks: The Land and People Since the War*, Harmondsworth: Penguin.

Selwyn, T. (ed.) (1996), *The Tourist Image: Myths and Myth Making in Tourism*, Chichester: Wiley.

Smith, H. (1996), 'God's Own Country', *The Guardian*, February 11th, p.24.

Urry, J. (1991), *The Tourist Gaze: Leisure and Travel in Contemporary Societies*, London: Sage.

Watson, G. and Kopachevsky, J. (1996), 'Interpretations of Tourism as Commodity', in Apostolopoulos, Y. et al. (eds.) *The Sociology of Tourism: Theoretical and Empirical Investigations*, London: Routledge.

Wickens, E. (1994a), 'A Flight from Everyday Life: The Tourist Experience in Chalkidiki, Northern Greece', School of Social Sciences, Oxford Brookes University. (Paper presented at the BSA Annual Conference, University of Central Lancashire, Preston.)

Wickens, E. (1994b), 'Consumption of the Authentic: The Hedonistic Tourist in Greece', in Seaton, A. et al. (eds.) *Tourism: The State of the Art*, London: Wiley.

Wickens, E. (1995), 'The Exodus to the Sun', *Social Science Teacher*, (The Journal of the ATSS), Autumn.

Wickens, E. and Harrison, A. (1996), 'Staging Modernity: The Consumption of Hybrid Playful Experiences in Chalkidiki, Northern Greece', in Robinson, M. et al. (eds.) *Tourism and Culture, Towards the 21st Century. Conference Proceedings: Culture as the Tourist Product,* Newcastle: University of Northumbria.

Wickens, E. (1997), 'Licensed for Thrills: Risk-taking and Tourism', in Clift, S. and Grabowski, P. (eds.) *Tourism and Health: Risks, Research and Responses*, London: Pinter.

Wickens, E. (1999), Tourists' Voices: A Sociological Analysis of Tourists' Experiences in Chalkidiki, Northern Greece, Oxford Brookes University, Unpublished Ph.D.

Wickens, E. (2000), 'The Sacred and the Profane: A Tourist Typology', forthcoming.

Managing customer retention: A case of tourist destinations, Turkey

Atila Yuksel

Sheffield Hallam University, UK

Abstract

In today's tourism and hospitality industry, marketing efforts have become increasingly focused on retaining the gained market and building customer loyalty (Oh and Mount, 1998). Interestingly, little research has been conducted on this issue. This research was an attempt to provide destination managers and marketers with an exploratory insight into how repeat and first-time visitors develop their satisfaction and return intention judgements. The results showed that the two types of customer groups develop their return intention and satisfaction based on slightly different aspects of holiday destination. While both type of tourists commonly regard food quality, accommodation, hospitality, and safety as a reason to come back, they consider different additional services to develop their return intentions. Another important contribution of this study is the finding that repeat customers promise more future business than new customers, suggesting that destination marketers should focus on repeat tourists. Marketing implications of the study are discussed.

Introduction

Customer satisfaction, coupled with customer retention, has been one of the most important concerns to hospitality and tourism marketers. It is generally emphasised that the generation of satisfaction, and hence customer loyalty and repeat business, is a cost-effective approach to maintaining a business (Murray, 1992). Recent studies have revealed that it is highly likely that a dissatisfied customer never returns (Dube, Reneghan and Miller, 1994), and repeated purchase is directly related to a company's cash flows (Oh and Mount, 1998), as getting a new customer costs more than keeping an existing one (Stevens, Knutson and Patton, 1995). For instance, while it costs about $10 in advertising, public relations, price incentives and other promotions to get a new customer, the cost to keep a satisfied customer is only about $1 (ibid.). Similarly, other studies suggest that it costs three to five times as much to attract a new customer as it does to retain an old customer (La Boeuf, 1987). Capturing new customers from competitors is costly because a greater degree of service improvement is needed to induce customers to switch from a competitor (Anderson and Sulvian, 1990). A study found that a 5% increase in customer retention resulted in a 25-125% increase in a number of service industry groups studied (Reichheld and Sasser, 1990).

The current consumer climate and the increasing number of competitive alternatives, and thus competition for market share, require destination managers to attend to customer retention and the hows or whys of a customer returning and continuing to repurchase (Pritchhard and Howard, 1997). However, despite the importance of the repeat-visitor segment and the heavy reliance of many attractions and tourist destinations on it, comparatively little research has been conducted on the retention of tourists (Gitelson and Crompton, 1984; Oppermann, 1998). In the hospitality area, Shoemaker and Lewis (1999: 345) note:

> *"For many years hospitality firms have believed that the goal of marketing is to create as many new customers as possible. While hoteliers believed it was important to satisfy the guests while they were on the property, the real goal was to find new customers. This constant search for new customers is called conquest marketing. In the future, conquest marketing will not be sufficient. Instead firms will need to practise loyalty marketing or retention marketing".*

Clearly, generating repeat business and building tourist destination loyalty is one of the most critical challenges facing destination marketers today. While the importance of understanding of repeat purchases and the returning traveller is acknowledged by researchers (Gitelson and Crompton, 1984), inadequate emphasis has been placed on the scrutiny of repeat and new visitors' satisfaction elements (Oh and Parks, 1997; Oh and Mount, 1998). It is highly likely that these two types of customer groups may base their satisfaction and return intention judgements on different aspects of the destination. Thus, an enhanced understanding of the nature and the relative importance of destination components to these two segments, for generating satisfaction and repeat business, is an essential prerequisite to the development and implementation of successful marketing efforts targeted at them. For instance, marketing efforts which are directed primarily at persuading new visitors to visit a destination, may be entirely inappropriate for encouraging previous visitors to return (Gitelson and Crompton, 1984). Thus, an understanding of what new and repeat customers are looking for and what they evaluate is warranted in order to manage and market programmes aiming to convert new visitors into repeat customers, to maintain existing repeat customer base, and consequently to enhance sales and profits.

The purpose of this paper was to investigate the relationship between destination service performances and tourist return intentions. Specifically, this study was interested in exploring what areas of service performance in destinations contributed to increasing tourists' return intention and whether first-time and repeat visitors develop their satisfaction, as well as return intention judgements, based on different components of the destination. From a destination management viewpoint, understanding the relative importance and contribution of destination components would be useful to developing effective management programmes as well as effective resource deployment strategies (Oh and Mount, 1998). To this end, the following section first presents a brief review of literature on tourist satisfaction, outlines the research method, and then discusses the research findings.

Background

It is important to note that the tourism product is an amalgam or package of tangible and intangible elements centred on activities at a destination (Medlik and Middleton, 1983). It is the "collection of physical and service features together with symbolic associations which are expected to fulfil the wants and needs of the buyer" (Jefferson and Lickorish, 1988: 211). It comprises the actual and perceived attractions of a destination, the activities, the facilities, and the destination's accessibility. The tourism product is the complete experience of the tourist from the time one leaves home to the time one returns. Thus, the nature and quality of the tourism product is the outcome of many individual activities with a range of people and organisations involved in the tourist experience (Hughes 1989; Hughes 1991; Krippendorf 1989; Laws 1995; Whipple and Thach 1988).

In a holiday experience, tourists encounter directly with not just one, but with several members of the production chain (Van-Rekom 1994), thus there is more than one tourist-provider encounter. For instance, the travel agent (when booking a trip) is the first member of the product chain with whom tourists meet. Then, a tour operator representative at the airport and airline personnel during the flight attend to tourists. Once in the country of the destination, a coach company (another member of the production chain), hired by the tour operator, transfers the tourists to their hotels. During the holiday, tourists meet different service providers, for example, restaurateurs, hoteliers, local people, etc. Many transient impressions and experiences occur during this total consumption, and it is this total experience that is consumed and evaluated (Teare 1998; Weiermair 1994). These experiences affect the consumer's state of mind at the end of the consumption, which forms the basis for subsequent travel decisions. Understanding which parts in this product chain matter and how they could be best combined to produce the desired experience is of significant importance to destination managers.

There is, however, a continuing debate with regard to potential dimensions affecting tourist satisfaction (or what the tourist evaluates). A number of tourist satisfaction studies indicate that destination related attributes (attractions, services, etc) account for tourist satisfaction, while others argue that consumer related factors such as personality, motivation, socio-economic status, demographics, and the familiarity with the destination play the most important role in tourist satisfaction. In their seminal study, Pizam, Neuman and Reichel (1978), for instance, analysed tourists' perceptions of a number of destination attributes and concluded that there were eight dimensions influencing holiday satisfaction. The dimensions that emerged, after a factor analysis of tourist perception mean scores, were; hospitality, beach opportunities, cost, eating and drinking facilities, accommodation facilities, environment, campground facilities and extent of commercialisation. In contrast, Lounsburry and Hoopes's (1985) examined vacation satisfaction in relation to demographic, work-related, and vacation-related variables. Their study revealed that there were five satisfaction dimensions; relaxation and leisure, natural environment, escape, marriage and family, and food and lodging. A correlation analysis, performed on demographics, work and vacation variables (21 variables) elicited that overall satisfaction was most strongly related to satisfaction with relaxation and leisure and also significantly related to satisfaction with escape opportunities, marriage and family satisfaction, satisfaction with food and lodging, and the level of education attainment. They found that vacationers with higher levels of formal educational attainment reported lower levels of vacation satisfaction and vice-versa. This could be because vacationers with higher levels of academic attainment may differ in terms of what they want out of a vacation; they may bring rather complex needs to vacation setting which are more difficult to satisfy in the setting.

Geva and Goldman (1989), in their study on satisfaction with organised tours, identified four factors contributing to overall satisfaction. These are: the *instrumental* aspects of the tour (hotels, meals and local services, which are perceived to be under the control of the tour operator); the *social activities* taking place during throughout the tour (mutual relationships among participants, and touring in an organised manner); the *performance of the tour guide* (his/her relationship with the participants, and the order and the organisation of the tour); and the *personal experiences* (the richness of the experience, entertainment on the tour, allocation of time, utilisation of free time and tour itinerary). Their study suggested that the nature and quality of the experience might be affected by different attributes at different points over the tour's duration.

Danaher and Arweiler (1996) surveyed tourists about their overall satisfaction with the tourism sector of New Zealand. These researchers attempted to determine the factors that influence overall tourist satisfaction and identify cross-cultural differences among tourists that might arise when evaluating satisfaction levels with their vacations. Using summary judgmental scales in their research (better than expected/worse than expected), the researchers investigated tourist satisfaction with transportation, accommodation, activities and attractions and their sub-components. Their regression analysis showed that activities accounted for one third of the explainable variation, with accommodation and attractions each accounting for over one fourth of the variation. However, the low R^2 (10%) value achieved in their regression analysis means that the researchers seem to have omitted some critical components, such as satisfaction with hospitality and foodservice experiences, in their variable list.

Chadee and Mattsson (1996) attempted to measure the quality of tourist experiences of students from different cultures and how different factors affect the global satisfaction of tourists. Using scenarios exhibited on a set of pictures for four different tourist encounters (eating out, hotel accommodation, renting a car and going on a sightseeing tour), they found that different variables impact on overall satisfaction with the specific encounter differently. For example, the impact of cleanliness on eating-out satisfaction was seven times higher than that of the prices of the meal. They also found that culture might play a role in the levels of satisfaction derived from the experience. Their results showed that compared to European students, Asians derived lower levels of overall satisfaction from the eating out experience, suggesting that culture plays a significant role in how individuals form their perceptions and satisfaction.

In their motivational investigation into the structure of service experience and satisfaction in tourism, Otto and Ritchie (1997) identified four dimensions. The first factor was hedonics, accounting for 33% variance, in which consumers stated the need to be doing what they loved, to have their imaginations stirred, and to be thrilled by the service activities. The second significant factor was peace of mind, in which consumers cited the need for both physical and psychological safety and comfort. The third factor, involvement, deals with the need for participation in activities and to be educated and informed. The final factor, the recognition, suggests that consumers want to derive a sense of personal recognition from their service providers, so that they can feel important and confident and that they are being taken seriously. These researchers suggested that satisfaction was a function of these dimensions only. While critical to the understanding of the concept, it seems that their research focused on the affective (emotional) side of the service experience only. These researchers overlooked the significance of so called technical aspects of a holiday (what is being delivered, for example, accommodation and meals) as well as functional aspects (how it is being delivered, service quality), in the formation of tourist satisfaction. As they have not included the technical and functional aspects of a holiday into their research instrument, it is not possible to assess whether these aspects affect the fulfilment of consumer motivations and satisfaction. As Noe and Uysal (1997) note, there might be a maintenance factor without which satisfaction would not be achieved. For instance, the need for relaxation and to participate in activities will never be attained when the tourist suffers from an upset stomach.

Others have suggested that overall tourist satisfaction may be evaluated along two broad dimensions (Reisinger and Turner, 1997). First, the instrumental dimension and second the expressive dimension. Instrumental dimension relates to the physical performance of the product, such as cleanliness. In contrast, the expressive dimension corresponds to the psychological level of performance (for example, comfort, hospitality, and relaxation). Some researchers argue that tourist satisfaction with the psychological performance of a product is extremely important. For instance, based on a study of tourism in India, Ohja (1982) reports that there were tourists who were satisfied despite some problems with the physical product offered, yet there were tourists who were dissatisfied with the best physical product. Drawing on this study, Ohja concludes that tourist satisfaction does not only come from good sights but from the behaviour one encounters, from the information one gets, and from the efficiency with which needs are served. Discussing the relative significance of these two dimensions, Reisinger and Turner (1997) remark that even the best physical product cannot compensate for psychological dissatisfaction. This suggests that when assessing tourist satisfaction with destinations, along with the instrumental dimension of satisfaction (satisfaction with physical performance), the expressive dimension of satisfaction (satisfaction with psychological performance) should also be assessed (Reisinger and Turner 1997). The relative significance attached to each of these two dimensions, however, may vary from individual to individual or from one situation to another.

In addition to the significance of the expressive dimension, several studies have shown that the instrumental dimension (practical aspects) of the holiday could contribute measurably to tourist satisfaction (Noe and Uysal 1997). For instance, Herzberg, Mausner, and Snyderman's (1959) research on work motivation suggests that hygiene factors (for example, cleanliness), if not satisfied, cannot be compensated for, which leads to dissatisfaction. Similarly, in Lounsburry and Hoopes's research (1985), although it explained only a small portion of the variance (6%), the "lodging and food" dimension emerged among vacationers' important satisfaction dimensions. In Whipple and Thach's (1989) research, along with the more expressive attributes of sightseeing, two instrumental service features, including a tour escort service and point of departure, were singled out as significantly contributing to satisfaction of the trip. In another study on organised tours, it was also evident that tourist satisfaction was influenced by factors unrelated to long term or planned motivational considerations (Geva and Goldman 1991). Such practical aspects of the pace of the tour, opportunities to use facilities, comfort, and cleanliness of the bus, figured noticeably among the satisfaction dimensions. This would suggest that motivations (such as knowledge seeking and escape, relaxation) may be more easily achieved if such practical aspects are taken into account and catered for on holidays. In other words, such instrumental aspects as the quality of accommodation and foodservice may have the potential to facilitate or inhibit the fulfilment of the holiday motivations. The practical implications of all this is that destination authorities should always try to satisfy the hygiene (or the basic) factors first, and then the motivational factors (Ross and Iso-Ahola 1991).

Clearly, the findings from these studies have added to the understanding of the multifaceted nature of tourist satisfaction, but managerial implications of some of these studies are rather limited for a number of reasons. First, the majority of past studies have not related the relative importance of destination service dimensions to certain key performance criterion variables such as tourist satisfaction or repurchase intentions. Thus, the relationship between individual factors and their extent of influence on repeat patronage/defection, remains equivocal. Obviously, destination management must know the elements of a satisfactory holiday experience in order to implement a program to attain and maintain a high level of quality and satisfactory service (Miner and Wain 1992). Destinations that are oblivious of their shortcoming stand to loose their market share.

Secondly, although the importance of generating repeat purchase is recognised by many of these authors, they have not provided guidelines on ways in which service elements can be managed to increase repeat business. Apparently, increasing the number of repeat visitors requires the development and implementation of appropriate marketing and management strategies. Moreover, some of these studies seem to assume that there is only one single homogeneous tourist market and thereby, have not taken into account the possible discrepancy that might exist between the satisfaction drivers (and their relative importance) of different sub-groups within the total tourist market.

The research method

The research questionnaire was developed to assess tourists' opinions about the prime components of their current vacations. As was noted, the tourism product comprises many individual products and services and it is highly likely that it is the combined effect of all services/products that determines the overall quality of holiday experience. Thus, based on the preliminary interview results and on the reviewed literature, main destination components such as accommodation, catering, hospitality, service quality, the environment, cost of vacationing and activities, were included in the questionnaire to understand how the individual destination components, each with varying effect, determines tourist satisfaction with the overall holiday experience.

As suggested by the reviewed literature, the location of the accommodation, cleanliness of the hotel and the room, the physical condition of the accommodation, the speed of check-in and check-out procedures, quietness, adequacy of water-electricity supply, room temperature, comfort, noise level, the quality of facilities offered at the accommodation, and the security were included in the list. The courtesy of service personnel (i.e. friendliness, politeness) was included; as the service experience is rendered in interaction with customers, it is an important factor in tourist service evaluations (Reisinger and Waryszack 1996). Furthermore, when tourists have specific problems with a hotel, such as an unclean room or poor temperature control, their problems should be resolved in a proper manner. Reviewed literature demonstrates that proper complaint handling would retain or even build customer loyalty (Bitner et al., 1990). Thus responsiveness of service personnel to tourist requests and complaints was included as an attribute. Note that responsiveness explained above has already been recognised by Parasuraman et al. (1988) as one of the most important service dimensions. The prices of services and price-value relationship were included because they were known to be among the important factors affecting tourist evaluation of a given service experience.

The inclusion of courtesy and attitudes of local people toward tourists in the survey as destination attributes is justified because, as Ohja (1982) and Reisinger and Turner (1997) have pointed out, holiday satisfaction does not only come from beautiful sights but also from the behaviour one encounters, from the information one gets, and from the efficiency with which needs are served. Satisfaction with tourist-host interaction is a vital component of tourist holiday satisfaction because hosts (or service providers) are the first contact point for tourists and remain in direct contact through an entire holiday (Krippendorf, 1989; Reisinger and Turner, 1997). Authentic interpersonal experience between hosts and guests leads to psychological comfort in satisfying tourists' needs. The extent of commercialisation in the area was included as an attribute because very commercial attitudes of local people toward tourists were said to cause poor satisfaction with the holiday experience (Pizam et al., 1978; Reisinger and Turner, 1997). Communication with local people and service providers was included because communication and understanding of tourists foster empathy and a feeling of safety (Reisinger and Waryszack, 1996).

The inclusion of the foodservice component is also justified, as it is among the destination components which, depending on its performance, has the potential to damage or promote a destination's image (Elmont, 1995). The unspoilt natural environment and scenery, the climate, the cleanliness of the beach and sea in the area, and the availability of tours, cruises, water sports, services, facilities and entertainment in the area were included as destination attributes because these were among the main pull factors used in destination attractiveness, image, satisfaction and choice studies. Feeling safe and comfortable in the area was included in the questionnaire because personal safety and security were stated to affect tourist enjoyment of the host environment and their future destination selection decisions (Pizam, Tarlow and Bloom, 1997). Public transport was included in the questionnaire because it is one of the main components of the tourist product which is extensively used by tourists during their holiday. Efficiency of services at the airport was included, as airport service encounter is the initial and the last experience the tourist has with the destination, which may affect tourist evaluation of holiday experiences (Laws, 1995).

The research instrument included 67 destination services. Based on its ease of application and potentially high construct validity (Yuksel and Rimmington, 1998), the performance only scale was adopted. To classify tourists into repeat and first-time visitors, participants were asked whether they had ever visited Turkey. The participants were required to assess the performance of facilities and services (67 items) on 7-point semantic differential scales. The items were derived from interviews and from previous tourist satisfaction studies, and their adequacy and appropriateness were verified through pilot tests. The study adopted the use of a single overall measure of tourist satisfaction. Although some researchers contend that satisfaction should be measured by a combination of attributes, the ease of use and empirical support for an overall measure of satisfaction led to its selection (Halstead, 1989). The study employed the "Delight-Terrible" scale for measuring overall dining satisfaction, as it has been reported to be the most reliable satisfaction scale (Maddox, 1985). A single "Definitely would-Definitely would not" scale was included, in order to assess the repeat and first-time visitors' return intention levels. The purpose of using overall satisfaction and return intentions as dependent variables in this study was, to identify the relative importance of determining holiday satisfaction and repurchase intentions of first-time and repeat visitors.

A pilot test was conducted prior to main research, and necessary amendments were made, and the main research was carried out with 400 randomly selected tourists departing from an international airport in Turkey. Given the flight time and language (English only), 35 tourists refused to participate, and 29 returned incomplete questionnaires. Of all the respondents, 55% were female, and 69% were first-time visitors. The majority of respondents were British, 80%, followed by Germans, Benelux, Scandinavian, Italian and others. The accuracy of the sample representation was assessed by comparing the list of departing tourists, acquired from the airport authority, with the actual sample profile. This comparison suggested that the departing tourists within this period of time were commensurably represented in the sample.

Analysis

Multivariate Analysis (factor and multiple regression) was conducted in order to find out the prime holiday dimensions and their extent of influence on total holiday satisfaction. The factor analysis was employed to create correlated variable composites from the original attributes' ratings. The second objective of the factor analysis was to obtain a relatively small number of variables, which explain most of the variance among the attributes from which to apply the derived factor scores in the subsequent multiple regression analyses. The purpose of regression analysis in this study was to explore how the holiday dimensions, which were derived from the factor analysis, related to the dependent variables of "total holiday satisfaction" and "future return intentions".

The Principal Components and Orthogonal (Varimax) rotation methods were employed in the factor analysis so as to summarise most of the original information, to a minimum number of factors for prediction reasons (Hair, Anderson, and Black, 1995). The criteria for the number of factors to be extracted were based on the Eigenvalue, the percentage of variance, the significance of factor loading, and the assessment of structure. Only the factors with Eigenvalue equal or greater than one were considered significant. The solution that accounted for at least 60% of the total variance was considered as a satisfactory solution. A variable was considered to be significant and was included in a factor, when its factor loading was greater or equal to 0.50 (Hair et al., 1995).

The regression analysis was then utilised to explore the relative importance of destination components (for example, hospitality, foodservice quality, etc.) within each of the repeat and first-time visitor groups, to provide destination managers with segment specific strategic insights. The first regression analysis was undertaken to explore how first-time and repeat visitors reached their satisfaction judgements. In order to understand how repeat and first-time visitors developed their intention to return to the destination, the measure of tourists' willingness to return was used, as the second dependent variable.

The scale was first subjected to a reliability analysis to assess the quality of the measure. Cronbach's alpha was used to assess the reliability of the measurement scale. The total scale reliability was high, 0.95, indicating that the sample of items performed well in capturing the measured construct (Nunnaly, 1967). Then, Varimax rotation was used to produce orthogonal factors, which provided simpler and theoretically meaningful solutions. From the Orthogonal (Varimax) rotated factor matrix, 16 factors with 58 variables were defined by the original 67 variables, that loaded most heavily on them (loading 0.50) (Table 1). The analysis produced a clean factor structure. The communality of each variable was relatively high, ranging from 0.54 to 0.83. This indicated that the variance of the original values was captured fairly well by the 16 factors (Hair et al., 1995).

Table 1   Composition of Factors and Mean Scores

Factor Name	Factor Loadings	First-time Tourists	Repeat Tourists	t Value	Eigenvalue	Variance (%)	x
Factor1: Food /Beverage Quality		5.35	5.74	-2.74**	18.130	27.06	.9011
Tastiness of food served in the area	.74243	5.63	5.88	-1.50			
Quality of food and beverage	.71911	5.43	5.83	-2.27*			
Temperature of food served	.63882	5.21	5.78	-2.81**			
Portions of food	.68601	5.17	5.69	-3.0**			
Presentation of dishes	.73088	5.51	5.71	-1.16			
Hygienic food preparation	.67355	5.07	5.50	-2.36*			
Variety of menu	.73581	5.42	5.61	-.89			
Availability of dishes liked	.79621	5.34	5.86	-2.65**			
Availability of traditional food	.52161	5.39	5.73	-.1.70			
Factor 2: Service Quality		5.69	5.97	-2.05*	4.532	6.76	.8730
Efficiency of check-in and check-out at the accommodation	.55674	5.96	6.37	-2.69**			
Friendliness of service at my accommodation	.76588	6.06	6.11	-.34			
Efficiency of service at accommodation	.72101	5.59	5.71	-1.03			
Responsiveness of staff to request	.67910	5.57	5.88	-1.61			
Responsiveness of staff to complaint	.69331	5.35	5.86	-2.28*			
Competency of staff	.79104	5.82	6.06	-1.48			
Factor 3: Accommodation		5.27	5.59	-2.17*	2.872	4.28	.8703
Cleanliness of the accommodation	.82772	5.80	6.0	-1.14			
Cleanliness of restaurant at accommodation	.60639	6.02	6.28	-1.97*			
Cleanliness of the room	.83935	5.32	5.74	-2.23*			
The physical condition of accommodation	.78732	5.32	5.65	-1.75			
Quality of facilities offered at accommodation	.62273	5.03	5.17	-.73			
Comfort of the room	.78631	5.15	5.54	-1.98*			
Adequacy of water and electricity supply	.55363	4.99	5.44	-2.07*			
Factor 4: Hospitality		5.81	6.16	-2.70**	2.766	4.12	.8780
Courtesy of residents	.72264	5.73	6.22	-2.83**			
Courtesy of employees	.62907	5.74	6.01	-1.53			
Willingness of employees to help	.71162	5.91	6.01	-.63			
Willingness of residents to help	.71420	5.53	5.91	-2.28*			
Friendliness of people	.76867	5.90	6. 38	-2.94**			
Feeling safe in the area	.59303	6.09	6.44	-2.43**			
Factor 5: Tourist facility services		5.46	5.73	-2.17*	2.303	3.43	.8683
Efficiency of services at tourist facilities	.76332	5.27	5.74	-2.97**			
Courtesy of services at tourist facilities	.65173	5.69	5.93	-1.59			
Waiting time for service at tourist facilities	.73237	4.99	5.46	-2.47**			
Quality of services at tourist facilities	.71473	5.26	5.68	-2.68**			
Convenience operating hours at tourist facilities	.54344	5.92	5.91	.11			
Accuracy of bill and tariffs at tourist facilities	.57806	5.57	5.78	-1.19			
Factor 6: Beach and environment		4.80	5.14	-2.23*	2.172	3.24	.7633
Cleanliness of the beach and sea in the area	.75691	5.01	5.33	-1.45			
Availability of facilities at the beach	.67954	5.10	5.34	-1.14			

Crowd level in the area	.52265	3.90	4.36	-2.00*			
The natural environment in the area	.59490	4.58	4.94	-1.65			
Comfort of sunbathing on the beach	.59056	5.48	5.69	-1.01			
Factor 7: Price and value		5.31	5.40	-.49	1.823	2.72	.7893
Prices of food and drink served at accommodation	.79515	5.06	5.18	-.55			
Value of the food services for price charges at accommodation	.75821	5.57	5.62	-.25			
Factor 8: Entertainment		5.66	5.87	-1.66	1.657	2.47	.6965
Quality and availability of entertainment	.55447	4.95	5.36	-2.01*			
Availability of tours and cruises	.66284	6.10	6.15	-.30			
Quality and availability of restaurants	.65914	5.87	6.11	-1.45			
Value of goods and services for the price charges	.50608	5.69	5.85	-1.00			
Factor 9: Quietness		4.36	4.95	-3.11**	1.524	2.27	.7498
Noise level at restaurant/bars of accommodation	.72149	4.30	4.80	-2.41**			
Noise level at accommodation	.72695	4.42	5.10	-3.15**			
Factor 10: Convenience		6.0	6.19	-1.60	1.445	2.15	.5343
Location of the restaurant/bars	.62217	6.04	6.41	-2.45**			
Location of the accommodation	.54051	5.75	5.99	-1.39			
Operating hours of the restaurant/bars	.71917	6.24	6.27	-.18			
Factor 11: Communication		5.28	5.19	.5	1.436	2.14	.7438
Ease of communication in your language with locals	.61139	5.27	5.16	.54			
Communication in your language with the staff	.68806	5.29	5.26	.15			
Factor 12. Safety		6.05	6.27	-1.74	1.276	1.90	.6991
Safety at hotel	.50385	6.33	6.56	-1.80			
Security of room	.50578	5.77	5.98	-1.25			
Factor 13: Water sports					1.165	1.73	-
Availability of water sports	.79969	5.86	5.58	1.44			
Factor 14: Transportation					1.122	1.67	-
Efficiency of public transport	.82193	6.02	6.20	-1.00			
Factor 15: Airport Services					1.074	1.60	-
Efficiency of check-in and check-out at the Airport	.74114	5.26	5.18	.34			
Factor 16: Weather					1.022	1.52	-
The weather conditions in the area	.72063	6.90	6.82	1.49			

[i]Entries are mean values
*$p < .05$.
**$p < .01$.

Each factor was named based on the common characteristics of the variables it included (Table 1). A composite reliability was calculated to measure the internal consistency of each factor. The results showed that the reliability coefficients for factors exceeded the recommended level of 0.50 (ranging from 0.53 to 0.90) (Nunnaly, 1967), and thus, all factors were retained in the subsequent multiple regression analysis (Table 1). It might be concluded that these 16 components were perceived as particularly important by the sample of tourist holiday-making in Turkey at that time.

A series of t-tests were undertaken to compare each item's mean level of perceptions, between repeat and first-time visitors. Table 1 summarises tourists' perceptions of the 16 unit performances at both individual item and component levels. The results indicated that two groups perceived the performances of some areas differently. 24 items showed perceptual differences between the two groups (Table 1). Repeat visitors perceived the food quality to be better than did first-time visitors (t = -2.74, p<.01). First-time visitors rated service quality component lower than did repeat visitors (t= -2.05, p<.05). Repeat visitors rated accommodation more highly than did first-time visitors (t = -2.17, p<.05). The hospitality component was perceived to be higher by the repeat visitor group than the first-time visitor group (t = -2.70, p<.01).

Additional t-test analyses were conducted to understand whether there was any statistically significant difference, between the ratings of first-time and repeat visitors, on overall satisfaction and repurchase intentions (Table 2). The results showed significant differences between the ratings; repeat visitors found their holiday more satisfactory than did first-time visitors (t= -2.04, p<.05). The results also indicated that repeat visitors indicated higher return intention than did first-time visitors (t= -4.12, p<.01). In order to understand whether this difference stems from any potential difference, between sample demographics and other holiday related elements such as length of holiday, accommodation type and resort area, a chi square analysis was undertaken. Results showed no statistical difference between repeat and first-time visitors on these variables (p>.05).

Table 2   Scores of First-time and Repeat Visitors on Overall Measures

	First-time/(FT) Repeat (R)	N	Mean	Std. Dev.	t	df	Sig.
Satisfaction	FT	234	5.9316	1.1097	-2.04	334	.042
	R	102	6.1961	1.0440			
Return	FT	228	5.3377	1.3651	-4.120	326	.000
	R	100	5.9900	1.2102			
Recommendation	FT	226	5.7212	1.3020	-3.595	325	.000
	R	101	6.2475	1.0238			

Determinants of satisfaction

In order to explore which of the factors had a significant effect on tourist satisfaction, the repeat and first-time visitor groups' ratings on overall satisfaction were regressed on their factor scores. The regression equation characteristics of overall holiday satisfaction, for first-time visitors, indicated an R^2 of 0.51, suggesting that 51% of the variation could be explained by this equation. The F-ratio of 19.862 was significant (p< .01). The relatively high measure of R^2 (0.51) indicates that the predictor variables perform well in explaining the variance in overall satisfaction. The highly significant F ratio indicates that the results of the equation could hardly have occurred by chance.

The t-statistic test was used for testing whether the 16 independent factors contributed information to the prediction of the dependent variable "overall holiday satisfaction". In this study, if the t-value of an independent variable was found to be significant at a 0.05 level, that variable was considered in the model. Ten factors emerged as significant independent variables in the regression analysis (p<.05) (Table 3). The results of regression analysis showed that each coefficient carried positive signs. This indicated that there was a positive relationship between those variables and the dependent variable "overall holiday satisfaction". It also suggested that the overall holiday satisfaction of first-time visitors, depended largely on these determinant factors.

Table 3   Satisfaction Drivers: First-time and Repeat Visitors

Group	Factors	Beta	t	F	R²
First Time Visitors	Service Quality	.373	6.539	19.862	.51
	Accommodation	.337	5.902		
	Convenience	.310	5.426		
	Hospitality	.274	4.788		
	Food Quality	.245	4.263		
	Beach and Environment	.223	3.858		
	Transportation	.132	2.299		
	Price and Value	.110	1.915		
	Constant		108.025		
Repeat Visitors	Hospitality	.444	6.010	18.775	.75
	Accommodation	.414	5.733		
	Service Quality	.334	4.552		
	Food Quality	.324	4.302		
	Transportation	.269	3.636		
	Tourist Facility Services	.209	2.808		
	Convenience	.156	2.082		
	Quietness	.150	1.956		
	Constant		64.687		

The relative importance of components was examined by comparing the magnitude of regression coefficients. The first component with the greatest effect on first-time visitors' overall satisfaction was service quality (Beta = .373) followed by accommodation (Beta = .337), convenience (Beta = .310), hospitality (Beta = .274), food quality (Beta = .245), transportation (Beta = .132) and price and value (Beta = .110). Given the relative factor weights (Beta²), it could be said that the service quality component (Beta² = 0.139) was almost eleven times as powerful in determining satisfaction of first-time visitors as the price and value component (Beta² = 0.012). The service quality component was almost eight times as powerful as transportation (Beta² = 0.017) in influencing satisfaction of first-time visitors. In addition, the service quality component was twice as influential in first-time visitors satisfaction judgements than hospitality (Beta² = .075). The accommodation component, had almost nine times as much impact, on determining satisfaction of first-time visitors, as did price and value of services (Beta² = 0.012).

A subsequent regression analysis was run to explore the relative importance of holiday dimensions on repeat visitors' holiday satisfaction. The results of the regression analysis showed that 75 percent of the variance, in repeat visitors' satisfaction, could be explained by this equation. The F ratio was 18.775. The results demonstrated that the set of components affecting repeat visitors satisfaction was somewhat different from that of first time visitors. The components affecting repeat visitors' satisfaction in order of significance were: the hospitality, the accommodation, the service quality, the food quality, the transportation, the tourist facility services, the convenience, and the quietness. An examination of $Beta^2$ values suggested that, the hospitality component ($Beta^2 = .197$) was almost nine times more influential, in affecting repeat visitors' satisfaction, than the quietness component ($Beta^2 = .022$).

Determinants of repurchase intention

As the second objective of this study was to ascertain how repeat and first-time visitors developed their intention to return to the destination, subsequent multiple regression analyses were employed. In this case, each groups' (first-time and repeat visitors) ratings, on their willingness to return, were regressed against their factor scores. Table 4 contains the results of the regression analyses. As can be seen, the set of components affecting first time and repeat visitors' return intentions to the destination was different. For the first-time visitors, the food quality, the service quality, the hospitality, the beach and environment, the convenience, the tourist facility, the water sports, the safety, and the accommodation appeared to be significant predictors of return intentions ($p < . 01$). A comparison of regression coefficients indicated that food quality was a stronger predictor of first-time visitors return intentions than was service quality (Table 4). Service performances by these nine dimensions could account for 39 percent of variance in first-time visitors' willingness to return.

Table 4   Repeat Visit Determinants: First-Time and Repeat Visitors

Group	Factors	Beta	t	F	R^2
First Time Visitors	Food Quality	.376	5.754	10.426	.39
	Service Quality	.271	4.092		
	Hospitality	.254	3.888		
	Beach Environment	.205	3.139		
	Convenience	.185	2.829		
	Tourist Facility	.165	2.511		
	Water Sports	.154	2.335		
	Safety	.151	2.302		
	Accommodation	.139	2.112		
	Constant		70.520		
Repeat Visitors	Hospitality	.437	4.143	8.274	.44
	Accommodation	.313	2.983		
	Quietness	.252	2.330		
	Safety	.227	2.120		
	Food Quality	.218	2.047		
	Constant		45.937		

The impressions of the repeat visitors of the hospitality, the accommodation, the quietness, the safety, and the food quality aspects were statistically significant in explaining this segment's return intentions (F= 8.274). Beach and environment, water sports, convenience, service quality and tourist facility services were not important in determining repeat visitors' return intentions when they were compared with the performances of other dimensions in the same model. Based on the size of the coefficients, it was found that the hospitality component contributed more than the food quality component in explaining repeat visitors' willingness to return to the destination. Combined, these five units could account for at least 44 percent of the repeat visitors' return intentions.

Discussion and conclusion

The results of this study provide destination managers and marketers with important information relating to destination components that matter most in satisfaction and return intention judgements and how these components can be combined to create a desired experience for different groups of tourists. First, the study results demonstrate that the perceived performance, satisfaction levels, and intention to return indicated by repeat and first-time customers are significantly different; repeat visitors rated a higher perceived performance, higher satisfaction and a stronger willingness to come back. Second, the results suggest that repeat and first-time visitors might develop their satisfaction and return intention judgements, based on different components of destination. Consistent with Oh and Mount's (1998) research findings in the hospitality industry, these findings support the reason why destination managers should focus on repeat business that leads to customer loyalty and need to undertake segment specific satisfaction analysis.

The study found that the service quality, the accommodation, the convenience, the hospitality, the food quality, the beach and environment, the transportation, and the price and value components were significant, in comparison to other components, in the formation of first-time visitors' holiday satisfaction. The hospitality, the accommodation, the service quality, the food quality, the transportation, the convenience, and the quietness were found to be significant in determining holiday satisfaction of repeat visitors. The beach and environment, and the price and value components did not emerge as important in the formation of repeat visitors' holiday satisfaction. Exclusion of these components does not necessarily mean that they are unimportant to repeat visitors' satisfaction. They are still important in an absolute sense, though they are not relative to the other components, in predicting tourists' satisfaction (Oh and Mount, 1998).

The study further found that the hospitality, the accommodation, the quietness, and the food quality components contributed significantly to repeat visitors' return intentions. Interestingly however, the components affecting first-time visitors intention to return to the destination in the future were slightly different. The food quality, the hospitality, the accommodation, the safety, the service quality, the beach and environment, the convenience, and the water sports components emerged to be the significant predictors of first-time visitors' willingness to come back. This difference might stem from how visitors form their first impressions (Oh and Mount, 1998). For instance, service quality, water sports, convenience, and beach and environment may be more influential in forming first-time visitors' initial impression. Then, tourists' impression with these components may get weaker, as tourists become more familiar with service quality, water sports, convenience, and beach and environment from their repeated visits; this could cause an insignificant contribution of these dimensions to explain repeat visitors' return intentions.

These results suggest that destination managers may need to highlight different aspects of their destination when they communicate with first-time and repeat customer groups. Marketing messages emphasising superior service quality, water sports, convenience, and beach and environment may be an effective strategy in developing new markets and, alternatively, emphasising hospitality, accommodation, quietness, safety, and food quality may appeal better to repeat visitors. Note that both tourist segments consider food quality, accommodation, hospitality, and safety most important to motivating their willingness to come back. Thus, these might be considered as essentials.

In today's tourism and hospitality industry, managers and researchers have long acknowledged the importance of retaining the gained market and building customer loyalty. Surprisingly, limited research has been conducted on this important issue (Oh and Mount, 1998). This research was an attempt to provide destination managers and marketers with an exploratory insight into how repeat and first-time visitors develop their satisfaction and return intention. The results showed that the two types of groups develop their return intention and satisfaction based on slightly different aspects of holiday destination. While both type of tourists commonly regard food quality, accommodation, hospitality, and safety as a reason to come back, they consider different additional services to develop their return intentions. Another important contribution of this study is the finding that repeat customers promise more future business than new customers, which clearly suggests that destination marketers should focus on repeat tourists. It is, however important to note that, unless managers strive to convert first-time visitors into repeat customers (Oppermann, 1998), the number of current repeat customers might shrink in the future, as a result of customer defection to rivals or other natural causes, which may drive the destination out of the business.

The findings in this study should be interpreted with caution, as a result of a number of limitations. The study should be regarded as preliminary due to the lack of accumulated research for comparison on related issues. In fact, the majority of the sample in this study comprised British tourists. Thus, this study should be replicated with different nationalities. The relative importance of destination components may be nationality-specific. The measurement items for each destination component should receive further refinement in future studies. The items used in this study were rather exploratory in that no previous study offered a representative set of reliable measurement items for the performance of destination components. In this study, the researcher used dichotomous categories to distinguish between repeat and first time visitors. While the category of first-time visitors is homogenous, repeat visitors category may not be, as there might be vast differences in what could constitute a repeat visitor (Oppermann, 1999). The study did not discriminate between repeat visitors who returns to the same destination year after year and who had visited the destination only once many years ago. There might be differences in repeat visitor categories in terms of destination components that they value most. Finally, this research was based on tourists' stated future behavioural intentions rather than their actual behaviour. Obviously, however, other variables, in addition to previous holiday satisfaction, may affect consumers' actual repurchase behaviour. Such factors as motives, accessibility, and other alternatives available at the time of purchase, or such constraints as time and money may condition repeat purchase.

References

Anderson, W. E., and Sullivan, W. M. (1993), The antecedents and consequences of Customer satisfaction for firms. *Marketing Science*, 12: 125-143.

Augustyn, M. and Ho, K. S. (1998), Service quality and tourism. *Journal of Travel Research*, 37, 71-75.

Bitner M. J., Booms, B. H., and Tetrault, M. S. (1990), The service encounter: diagnosing favourable and unfavourable incidents, *Journal of Marketing*, 54 (1): 71-84.

Chadee, D. D., and Mattsson, J. (1996), An empirical assessment of customer satisfaction in tourism. *The Services Industries Journal*, 16 (3): 305-320.

Danaher, P. J., and Arweiler, W. (1996), Customer satisfaction in the tourism industry, a case study of visitors to New Zealand, *Journal of Travel Research*: 89-93.

Danaher, P. J., and Haddrell, V. (1996), A comparison of question scales used for measuring customer satisfaction. *International Journal of Service Industry Management*, 17 (4): 4-26.

Dube, L., Renaghan, L. M., and Miller, J. M. (1994), Measuring customer satisfaction for strategic management. *The Cornell Hotel and Restaurant Administration Quarterly*, 35 (1): 39-47.

Elmont, S. (1995), Tourism and food Service- two sides of the same coin, *The Cornell Hotel and Restaurant Administration Quarterly*, February: 57-63.

Fick, G. R., and Ritchie, B. J. R. (1991, Fall), Measuring service quality in the travel and tourism industry. *Journal of Travel Research*, 2-9.

Geva, A., and Goldman, A. (1989), Changes in the perception of a service during its consumption; a case of organised tours, *European Journal of Marketing*, 23 (12): 44-52.

Geva, A., and Goldman, A. (1991), Satisfaction measurement in guided tours, *Annals of Tourism Research*, 18: 177-185.

Gitelson, R. J. and Crompton, J. L (1984). Insights into the repeat vacation phenomenon. Annals of Tourism Research. 11: 199-217.

Hair, J. F., Anderson, R., and Black, W. C. (1995), *Multivariate Data Analysis with Readings*, New Jersey, Prentice Hall Inc.

Halstead, D. (1989), Expectations and disconfirmation beliefs as predictors of CS, repurchase intentions, and complaining behaviour: An empirical study. *Journal of Consumer Satisfaction /Dissatisfaction and Complaining Behaviour*, 2, 17-21.

Herzberg, F., Mausner, B. and Snyderman, B. (1959), The Motivation to Work, Wiley, New York, NY.

Hughes, L. H. (1989), Resorts, a fragmented product in need of coalescence, *International Journal of Hospitality Management*, 8 (1): 15-17.

Hughes, K. (1991), Tourist satisfaction: A guided tour in North Queensland. *Australian Psychologist*, 26(3), 166-171.

Krippendorf, J. (1989), The holiday makers; understanding the impact of leisure and travel, Heinemann.

Laws, E. (1995), Tourist destination management issues, analysis and policies, Routhledge, London.

Lounsburry, L. W. and Hoopes, L. L. (1985), An Investigation of factors Associated with Vacation Satisfaction, *Journal of Leisure Research* 17: 1-13.

LeBoeuf, M (1987), How to win customers and keep them for life, New York, Berkley Books.

Jefferson, A., and Lickorish, L. (1988), Marketing Tourism, Harlow, Longman.

Maddox, N. R. (1985, Winter), Measuring satisfaction with tourism. *Journal of Travel Research*, 2-5.

Medlik, D. and Middleton, V. T. C. (1983), The tourist product and its marketing implications, *International Tourism Quarterly*, 28-35.

Miner, A. and Wain, O. (1992), Customer satisfaction. *The Dunvegan Quarterly*, 2:2.

Murray, I. P. (1992), Service Quality in Restaurant Operations, Unpublished PhD dissertation, Kansas State University, Manhattan, KS.

Noe, P. F. and Uysal, M. (1997), Evaluation of outdoor recreational settings, *Journal of Retailing and Consumer Services*, 4 (4): 223-30.

Nunnaly, J. C. (1967), *Psychometric Theory*, New York, McGraw-Hill Book Company.

Oh, M. and Jeong, M. (1996), Improving marketers' predictive power of customer satisfaction on expectation-based target market levels. *Hospitality Research Journal*, 19 (4): 65-85.

Oh, H., and Parks, C. S. (1997), Customer satisfaction and service quality: A critical review of the literature and research implications for the hospitality industry. *Hospitality Research Journal*, 20(3), 36-64.

Oh, M., and Mount, J. D. (1998), Assessments of lodging service unit performance for repeat busisness. *Journal of International Hospitality, Leisure and Tourism Management*, 1 (3): 37-54.

Ohja, J. M. (1982), Selling Benign Tourism: Case references from Indian scene, *Tourism Recreation Research*, June: 23-24.

Otto, E. J. and Ritchie, B. R. J. (1996), The service experience in tourism. *Tourism Management*, 17 (3): 165-174.

Oppermann, M. (1998), Destination threshold potential and the law of repeat visitation, *Journal of Travel Research*, 37: 131-137.

Oppermann, (1999), Predicting destination choice a discussion of destination loyalty, *Journal of Vacation Marketing*, 5 (1): 51-65.

Panton, R. D. (1999), A comparison of the effectiveness of two models in measuring customer satisfaction in the tourism industry, Unpublished MSc thesis, The University of Guelp, Canada.

Pizam, A., Neumann, Y, and Reichel, A. (1978), Dimensions of tourist satisfaction with a destination area, *Annals of Tourism Research*, July/September: 314-322.

Pizam, A., Neumann, Y, and Reichel, A. (1979), Tourist satisfaction: uses and misuses, *Annals of Tourism Research*, 195-197.

Pizam, A., and Milman, A. (1993), Predicting satisfaction among first time visitors to a destination by using the Expectancy Disconfirmation theory. *International Journal of Hospitality Management*, 12, 197-209.

Pizam, A., Tarlow, E. P., and Bloom, J. (1997), Making tourists feel safe whose responsibility is it? *Journal of Travel Research*, Summer, 23-28.

Pritchard, P. M. and Howard, R. D. (1997), The loyal traveller examining a typology of service patronage. *Journal of Travel Research*, Spring, 2-10.

Reisineger, Y., and Turner, L. (1997), Tourist satisfaction with hosts: A cultural approach comparing Thai tourists and Australian hosts, *Pacific Tourism Review*, 1: 147-159.

Reisinger, Y., and Waryszak, R. (1996), Catering to Japanese tourists: What service do they expect from food and drinking establishments in Australia?, *Journal of Restaurant and Foodservice Marketing*, 1 (3/4): 53-71.

Shoemaker, S and Lewis, C. R. (1999), Customer loyalty and future hospitality marketing, *International Journal of Hospitality Management*, 18: 345-370.

Stevens, P., Knutson, B., and Patton, M. (1995), Dineserv: A tool for measuring service quality in restaurants. *The Cornell Hotel and Restaurant Administration Quarterly*, April: 56-60.

Teare, E. R. (1998), Interpreting and responding to customer needs, *Journal of Workplace Learning*, 10 (2): 76-94.

Tribe, J. and Snaith, T. (1998), From Servqual to Holsat: holiday satisfaction in Varadero, Cuba. *Tourism Management*, 19, 125-34.

Van-Rekom, J. (1994), Adding psychological value to tourism products, *Journal of Travel and Tourism Marketing*, 3 (3): 21-36.

Weber, K. (1997), Assessment of tourist satisfaction, using the Expectancy disconfirmation theory, a study of German travel market in Australia. *Pacific Tourism Review*. 1, 35-45.

Weiermair, K. (1994), Quality Management In Tourism, Proceedings of the 44th AIEST Conference: 93-113.

Whipple, W. T., and Thach, V. S. (1988), Group tour management: Does good service produce satisfied customers, *Journal of Travel Research*, Fall: 16-21

World Tourism Organisation (1988), Quality control of tourism products and services, Madrid.

Yüksel, A. and Rimmington, M. (1998, December), Customer Satisfaction Measurement: Performance Counts, *The Cornell Hotel and Restaurant Administration Quarterly*, 60-70.

The dual effects of tourism on social economic development in China

Xiaoying Zheng

Peking University, China

Abstract

With social civilisation and economic development, the tourism industry has become a more and more prosperous business in China during the last two decades. Tourism's important role in international and national exchanges could easily be ignored. However, tourism development should be re-considered based on evaluating in the dual effect on social economic development. In this paper, there are several topics concerning the relationship between the tourism and social economic development addressed. Evidence shows that the tourism in China is increasing rapidly. For the past twenty years Chinese tourism, has been presented to different countries worldwide and different regions nationwide. However, there are a series of problems which influenced social and economic development to various degrees. In China, there are a lot of tourism sites most of which are located in large centres or in peripheral regions.

It is time to evaluate the role of tourism in China's development tourism and then to answer the question: what experiences and lessons have been learned in the tourism industry development? There is very few studies about tourism issues relating to China which makes it difficult to provide a definite answer to this question.

Development of tourism in China

China was not very open before 1970s. The international activities were mostly related political and foreign affairs. When the "Culture Revolution" ended, the economic reformation spread nationwide. People inside and outside China strongly felt that there was a failure to understand each other. The best way to understand both sides is to visit each other, so that more and more people become tourists except for political and foreign affairs travel. From 1978 the first year to really open the national gate and allow economic reformation, the number of international tourists received by only three major travel services increased dramatically (see Table 1).

Table 1   Number of International Tourists Received by Major Travel Services

Year	Total	China International Travel Service	China Travel Service	China youth Travel Service
		Unit: (10,000 person)		
1978	68.64	12.46	56.18	
1988	177.74	52.62	110.39	14.73
1998	167.00	77.45	53.79	35.76

Source: Chinese Statistics Yearbook, 1999

Over the past 20 years, the number of international tourists received by major travel services increased nearly 3 times. With international tourists increased, the civil tourism industry also reached a higher development (see Table 2).

Table 2   Conditions of Civil Tourism

Year	Total	Urban Residents	Rural Residents
		Unit: million person-times	
1994	524.00	204.55	319.45
1995	629.00	245.70	383.30
1996	639.50	256.20	383.30
1997	644.00	259.00	385.00
1998	695.00	250.00	445.00

Source: Chinese Statistics Yearbook, 1999

From the above data, we can determine that visits of rural residents relating to tourism activities are more frequent than urban residents'. Tourism has been increasing at the rate (including urban and rural residents) of 32.6%, rural residents at 39.3% and urban at only 22.2%. The reason may be the economic development in rural areas faster than urban areas and unemployment in cities becoming a serious problem. Urban residents would like to retain more money to spend on medical insurance, rent apartments, education, and so on. But for rural residents, actually they have not yet had access to these benefits as urban residents have with free-medical insurance, free-apartment, free-education and so on. When medical reformation and housing reformation came, urban residents faced bigger challenges and difficulties. However, total expenditure in tourism of urban residents was higher than rural residents in the same period. Total tourism expenditure of urban residents in 1998 was 155,113 million CY (Chinese Yuan), average per capita expenditure was 607.0 CY; but the rural residents only 87,605 million CY, per capita expenditure was 197.0 CY. We could think that quality of tourism (indicated by expenditure patterns) in urban residents was higher than that of rural residents.

Tourism and economic development

Undoubtedly tourism industry development will promote economic development (see Table 3). The composition of foreign exchange earnings was led by long distance transportation, this part already occupied one fourth in total earnings. The following categories were entertainment, accommodation and catering. This situation is similar international situation. Comparing the 1997 and 1998 situation, we find that the government began to develop commodity sales for continuing to develop long distance transportation, accommodation, catering and so on. In 1998, the composition of foreign exchange earnings in commodity sale reached 20.6, whilst ranking second to long distance transportation.

Table 3   Foreign Exchange Earnings and it's Composition

Item	1997		1998	
	Value	Percentage(%)	Value	Percentage(%)
Total	12,074	100.0	12,602	100.0
Long Distance Transportation	3030	25.1	3185	25.3
Air	2130	17.7	2237	17.8
Railway	304	2.5	333	2.6
Highway	270	2.2	327	2.6
Waterway	326	2.7	288	2.3
Visiting	665	5.5	548	4.3
Accommodation	1838	15.2	1737	13.8
Cater	1587	13.2	1548	12.3
Commodity Sale	705	5.8	2591	20.6
Entertainment	2438	20.2	810	6.4
Post and Communication	473	3.9	502	4.0
Local Transportation	446	3.7	442	3.5
Other Service	892	7.4	1239	9.8

Source: Chinese Statistics Yearbook,1998

However, the tourism not only has positive effects on economic development, but also can have negative effects on economic development and sustainable development. There are five main aspects of concern in economic relation tourism as following:

1. Environmental damage;

2. Health problem;

3. Economic development unbalance;

4. Tourism site development imbalance; and,

5.   Tourism management gap.

All the above concerns have not yet been fully researched in China, but we have found these problems are appearing. The government is planning to pay special attention to research into these concerns in order to address the problems.

The effect of tourism on social development in China

The positive effects of tourism have been stressed in the earlier tourism periods, in the middle of 1980s and the early of 1990s. With economic changes and the internationalisation of Chinese affairs being more active in the earlier of 1980s, people from various regions and countries could visit China, especially the famous tourism sites. Tourism brought new thoughts and technology as well as exchanged and shared the experiences. More people were involved in the tourism business, which improved family and community economic development. Meanwhile, the unemployment rate reduced with tourism industry development. But, tourism has not been organised very well. The tourism industry developed too fast because the industry could earn more quickly than with other industry development. The Chinese government understood the importance of tourism development several years ago. Tourism in China has a good basis for development particularly in big and middle sized cities.

In recent years, the Chinese government has co-operated with tourism organisations and initiated many well organised tourism activities. Chinese tourism is developing as expected. Briefly, tourism has provided more chances for tourists to understand each other, and also to promote social and economic development. Nevertheless, tourism has created some problems in China, such as in some aspects: floating population; communicating diseases; social security; heritage and treasures protection; legal and order economic development and so forth.

Comments and suggestions

Tourism industry development proceeded very quickly during the 1990s. It is an important part of social and economic development. In order to organise the tourism industry in China, we should re-consider, re-organise and re-order tourist activities specifically:

1.   Education on sustainable development should be provided to policy-makers, managers and tourists;

2.   Information should be provided on health promotion and disease prevention;

3.   The tourism industry should be organised on the basis of tourism site capacity. Development taking place too quickly will cause management and environment gaps, because facilities would fail to meet the tourist needs;

4.   Tourism should be administrated by the law;

5. The tourism industry in China could reach a more ideological level, if people and managers could understand more fully the principles of sustainable development.